Press On

Principles of interaction programming

Press On

Principles of interaction programming

Harold Thimbleby

The MIT Press
Cambridge, Massachusetts
London, England

MIT Press books may be purchased at special quantity discounts for business or sales promotional use. For information, please email special_sales@mitpress.mit.edu or write to Special Sales Department, The MIT Press, 55 Hayward Street, Cambridge, MA 02142.

This book was set in Palatino and Computer Modern Sans Serif by the author and was printed and bound in the United States of America.

Library of Congress Cataloging-in-Publication Data

Thimbleby, Harold.
    Press on : principles of interaction programming / Harold Thimbleby.
        p. cm.
    Includes index.
    ISBN 978-0-262-20170-4 (hardcover : alk. paper)
    1. Computer programming. 2. Human-computer interaction. I. Title.
QA76.6.T4493 2007
005.1—dc22

                                                        2007000519

Outline message

Part I ■ Context

■ Interactive systems and devices do not fulfill their potential for economic, social, psychological, and technical reasons.

Part II ■ Principles

■ Computer science provides many practical creative ideas and theories that can drive effective interaction programming—defined in box 0.1, "What is interaction programming?" (p. 4).

Part III ■ Press On

■ While knowing the science is fundamental, it is also essential to have the right attitudes and approaches to managing the complexity of designing systems for people to use. The interaction programmer must never say, "it's not my job to . . . "—interaction programming means understanding and weaving the science into the big picture.

Outline contents

Full contents

Part II   ■   Principles

Part III   ■   Press on

List of boxes

Acknowledgments

Writing a book is a mammoth task, and as I've been working on this book many, many people have made contributions—both encouraging and argumentative.

My wife, Prue, has supported me enthusiastically and has thought deeply and read and commented on everything, as have my children Jemima, Isaac, Sam, and Will. All my family proofread and gave fantastic comments on this book; I delight in them, and my thanks to them goes way beyond what they have done for this book.

Thanks to my colleagues from around the world who have gone over a great deal too, in writing and in conversation: including, especially, David Bainbridge, Tim Bell, George Buchanan, Richard Butterworth, Brock Craft, Ian Crew, Penny Duquenoy, David Harel, Michael Harrison, Lidia Oshlyansky, Jen Pearson, Simon Robinson, Yin Leng Theng, Chris Whyley, and Ian Witten.

Some people have worked directly with me on implementation and getting things to work, especially Paul Cairns, Paul Gillary, Jeremy Gow, Gary Marsden, Matt Jones, and Will Thimbleby. I'm very grateful to Matthew Abbate and Robert Prior of MIT Press who made this book finally happen. Sam Thimbleby drew the cartoons. Photographers are acknowledged on individual photographs, except Prue Thimbleby and myself who did all others.

My students over the years have suffered my teaching and greatly helped improve the content. I thank my students at UCLIC, University College London Interaction Centre, and my students at the Future Interaction Technology Laboratory in Swansea University, www.fitlab.eu, who have helped me work out and refine this material over the years.

The nature of the material of this book makes it ideal for giving interactive lectures. As Gresham Professor of Geometry, I was lucky to be able to give public lectures on some of the material at Gresham College (an independent London institution, founded in 1597). Almost all of this book has at one time or another, in one form or another, been presented to public and school audiences: it's young people who are going to change the world and make it a better place—it's also young people who are most likely to become fashion victims if they do not notice or think about bad design. Of course, audiences like the constructive ways you can identify and tackle bad design.

I have been supported in doing the underlying research by a Royal Society-Wolfson Research Merit Award and various grants from the UK Engineering and Physical Sciences Research Council, EPSRC. Gresham College kindly bought many gadgets to enhance my lectures. All other gadgets I've either personally owned or used extensively, like the railway ticket machine discussed in chapter 3, "Reality," and chapter 12, "Grand design."

This book was written in LATEX, first using TEXtures then TEXShop on the Apple Macintosh with Dot, JavaScript, Lineform, Mathematica, MetaPost, and Perl—though the only language *you* need to know is JavaScript (or C/C++/C#/Java). All the chapters discussing programs used those programs to generate the diagrams and output attributed to them.

Harold Thimbleby. Press on and coffee . . .

0

Introduction

Press On provides many ways of thinking clearly about the design of interactive devices and provides many ways of thinking about *interaction programming*. It covers the computer science fundamentals of the design of interactive devices, which are typically complex things with buttons, like mobile phones and photocopiers, but they range from the very simple—like torches and guns—to the very complex like word processors and the web browsers.

This book takes the view that we can build far better interactive devices than we do and that much of the initiative for better design can come from clear engineering creativity, knowledge, and perspectives based on sound computer science principles. Some things are possible or not possible, and competent computer scientists can work it out. Programmers can come up with solutions that would have escaped users or designers with limited technical knowledge; programmers can be more creative and more central in all areas of interaction design than anyone suspected.

0.1   The *Press On* sandwich

Press On is divided into three parts, like the layers of a sandwich. Programming concepts improve device design. That's the meat—or the salad if you are a vegetarian. But why do you want to improve design? Appreciating the complexity and impact of interactive devices is crucial to knowing what you want to improve. This context provides the two layers of bread to wrap the filling.

0.1.1   Is there really a problem?

Computers have become smaller and smaller and are buried inside all sorts of gadgets, from mobile phones to watches and ticket machines to completely novel gadgets that nobody knew were needed before they were invented. The first step in making these things better is to understand why we put up with them as they are. My emphasis throughout is on *making things better*. Problems are not the main thrust, but we do need to see them for what they are and why they are worth solving, because it's a big culture shift to be solution-oriented: *Press On* is a sandwich of motivation around a filling of real, working techniques.

I look at why we accept a system of poor design, upgrade, and obsolescence in computers, more than we would for any other type of product. I examine the psychology and logic of using various items of technology and why they are the way they are. It's a tangled story. If we can't even understand things as simple as a digital clock, then we are not going to understand more complex things. For that reason the book focuses on small-scale technologies.

Part I ends with chapter 4, "Transition to interaction programming," which puts the complaints of part I into perspective—reviewing the wider field of interaction programming—as well as introducing the role of programming in solving many problems. The programming language used in part II, JavaScript, is introduced and justified.

0.1.2   How can we design better?

I introduce state machines and discuss how they can be modeled to provide us with a simple and powerful way to analyze and design better user interfaces. State machines comprise perhaps 95% of interaction programming problems, and we understanding them—whether they are represented as statecharts, graphs, or matrices—lets us easily build and analyze better systems and generate accurate and up-to-date user manuals and interactive help.

State machines represent a fundamental idea, which will never be out of date. Any interactive system—past, present or future—can be understood from this perspective. State machines are sufficiently general to describe what a device does as well as what its user manual does. Getting them right is a major part of designing interactive systems.

Some people, however, say state machines aren't powerful enough for what they want to do. You probably wouldn't want to design a full office application with one, because it'd get too complicated to manage (that's why all office applications are hard to use). But for mobile phones, photocopiers, aircraft flight decks, robots, medical equipment, home entertainment stuff, and so on—all the gadgets we encounter in everyday life—state machines are ideal design tools. We will show how state machines are easy to work with, particularly when we use appropriate methods. We will analyze some specific designs and identify and solve design problems—some quite creatively.

If you are a programmer, you'll be pleased to see how relevant everything you already know is to interaction programming. It's time to use your computer science to make interactive devices easier to use for everyone.

0.1.3   How do we scale up to large design problems?

I discuss the ethics of design in technology, presenting a case for a rethink. Ethics is about how humans should interact. We have a lot to learn and put into practice about how interactive devices and humans should interact.

The design of interactive systems is complex, with people, technology and social systems all interacting, to say nothing of standards, obsolescence, market forces, and just our ability to keep up to date. Things get out of hand quickly, and what is surprising is not that things are awkward to use and can be improved, but that they work at all.

0.2 Principles

Various principles in *Press On* are summarized at the end of each chapter. The final chapter of the book summarizes the main themes of the book.

Good user interface design isn't a matter of following a recipe you can get from a cookbook: it's an attitude, along with a bunch of principles, skills, and provocative ideas.

Nothing can provide definitive solutions; ideas and theories have to be insightful and provocative. Given real-world complexity, then, this book cannot be a definitive solution to everything that can happen. No book could be. Instead, *Press On* is provocative; through many examples, stories, and simple ideas and theories, it tries to shift your values and create new vistas where your design problems become new opportunities to do better.

Interaction programming is an endless subject. Like a magazine, *Press On* has lots of asides and boxes to provide background and interesting ideas. There is a lot of cross-linkage between topics; this is a visible sign of the intrinsic variety and cross-disciplinary fertilization of design itself, but it also allows the book to be read in any order, for sections cross-reference themselves to different contexts, perspectives, and ideas in other parts of the book. For those who want background material to go deeper, this book includes suggestions for further reading at the end of each chapter. Like all good books, *Press On* has a web site,

mitpress.mit.edu/presson

▷ Linkage looks like this—brief paragraphs offset with a triangle marker. Linkage is a taken-for-granted part of the technology of books, along with tables of contents, footnotes, indexes, section and page numbering, even bookmarks. All these ideas make books easy to use and more useful. We'll mention the history of books and printing in section 4.2 (p. 96), because it is not only fascinating in its own right, it's a good example of using design to make things easier—it also suggests a range of effective aids we can put into documents, such as user help manuals, to make them more useful. Interaction programming is everywhere, even in things that aren't conventionally thought of as interactive.

▷ If all the linkage in this book were represented as buttons a user could press to jump around, the book itself would be interactive, much like a web site. Figure 8.8 (p. 246) provides a visualization of all the linkage in this book.

I hope you read *Press On* and are inspired that there are many ways to do a better job of design—indeed, any criticism of this book you have is your opportunity to do better. I want to give you an appreciation of how powerful simple computer science is and how it can influence, for the better, anybody doing anything.

Box 0.1 What is interaction programming?

■ Interaction programming is what is done by interaction programmers. Interaction programmers are computer scientists using their specialist skills to design, analyze and program interactive devices used by people.

■ Interaction programmers are people who think about new interactive devices, what they will be like, and how to make them better. They watch other people using interactive devices, try them out themselves, and think deeply about them and their internal structure. They see not just conventional users, but other designers, manual writers, trainers, and many others involved in using devices and needing programmed support.

■ Interaction programmers find opportunities for redesigning interactive devices to improve them, and they improve the tools and processes that support the design, programming and evaluation of devices, and all associated activities.

Press On is aimed at interaction programmers who like computers and programming, who want to know the principles of how to design, program, and understand interactive systems so they are easier and more satisfying to use.

0.3 How to teach interaction programming

The main way to teach any subject is to be enthusiastic about it and to encourage the students to teach themselves. Interaction programming is a naturally exciting subject, whether you are interested in fashionable devices like cameras and mobile phones, or are interested in making the world a better place by improving medical devices or the lives of elderly people coping with complex gadgets. Design issues abound on the web, in interactive exhibits in museums, in burglar alarms, in aircraft, in cars, in ticket machines, in games, and throughout computer applications.

I've found running the course in two sets of eight to ten lectures is ideal. First, I teach by giving ten lectures on the principles and background issues, simultaneously setting practical coursework and encouraging students to choose topics that engage them. When we have visitors to the department, I get them to give guest lectures.

Press On touches on a huge variety of material: human perception, environmental issues, programming, mathematics, design, economics. It is great fun to teach students by encouraging them to pursue their own interests more deeply than a single book can. If a student likes mathematics, there are plenty of mathematical ideas here that can be pursued further, even to postdoctoral research levels. The same goes for environmental issues: what *are* we going to do? Nobody knows.

Universities, departments, teachers, and students are all different, but if you want to teach interaction programming, I believe you *have* to build things and get students involved. Often those things won't work very well—and that's the first lesson! How can we build things, and what processes can we use, so that we can make them better? Indeed, how will we know they are not good enough, and that it is worth improving them? Thus coursework needs to get students engaged in these issues and experiencing them directly. Too much of the literature on interaction programming celebrates success; to be a successful interaction programmer you need to know how to survive failure. Coursework is a great teacher, especially when done in a supportive environment that pulls out the lessons from the experience.

> ▷ The culture of success, and the way it encourages us to ignore failure is developed in section 2.2 (p. 40).

Experience can be defined as what you get just after you need it. Students need experience, which means they have to be able to stretch themselves into building systems that will expose issues they don't know how to deal with. Much like real life, then, which a course on interaction programming should be training them for.

It is important to teach the material from *Press On* along with a course on research methods. It isn't easy for students to organize their coursework or projects; it isn't easy writing and doing research. What's the difference between the journalism of a product review and critical, insightful analysis of a design? Coursework is often seen as merely a way to get marks and to pass a course to go on to do the next course. But how do you recognize when your work is really worth pursuing and other people would be interested in it? When would it change the way the industry works? When would it be worth developing a piece of student's coursework to present at a conference on interactive systems design? These are really important research methods issues, and if *Press On* can be taught in an environment with a research methods course, the potential for improving the world—it surely needs improving—is unbounded. Alternatively, teach *Press On* with a business course so that the ideas students generate can be put into action in the business world as new products and ideas.

This is a big book, covering a fascinating and complex area. If you find any errors, or if your teaching or doing coursework uncovers improvements, please let me know by email. I'll look forward to hearing from you.

In some universities, if the course does not finish with an exam, student attendance will drop off. If exams are needed, they are hard to mark! How can the practical subject of interaction programming be assessed in a three-hour test? A good question would be to ask students to write about their heroes of interaction programming and what they achieved. This is motivating stuff; it requires the students to read around the subject and to understand the achievements of their heroes. People who come immediately to my mind include: Bill Buxton, Stu Card, Joelle Coutaz, Chris Evans, Richard Feynman, Brian Gaines, Alan Kay, Brenda Laurel, Alan Newell, William Newman, Don Norman, Seymour Papert, Jef Raskin, Brian Shackel, Harold Thimbleby (who naturally comes to my mind!), and Terry Winograd. This is by no means a complete list, and if you are worrying about important people I've missed, well, that shows just how important thinking about heroes is! What are the criteria for being a hero in interaction programming? Students should be asked to reflect on *why* they choose whom they do and asked why they *didn't* choose some other people ... learning is about joining the community and knowing who's who.

0.4   Devices, applications and product references

I refer to specific products in this book. Mostly, I have chosen relatively cheap and common consumer devices, as this makes it easier for you to get involved. Although the narrative of this book covers many simple examples, bigger issues are being addressed. My approach is to start with real interactive devices, and as they are real any reader can check that I have understood them, that I have represented them faithfully in the discussion, and that I have obtained nontrivial and interesting insights. I cover a range of devices providing many different perspectives, and some I have handle several times repeatedly in the book, but in different ways to illustrate the flexibility and generality of the approaches proposed.

Some of the devices may seem obsolete. For this book, though, there are advantages. Manufacturers need not worry about criticism. Earlier devices are simpler, so most readers will be familiar with all the features that they have—we don't want to spend time on introducing features but on the underlying interaction programming issues.

New devices grow out of earlier devices, so the design issues of the older stuff is still present in current and future devices. For instance, at the time of writing, one of the most recent gadgets is the Nokia N95, putting into a single device a phone, a media player, a radio, a navigation system, two cameras, a calculator, some games, a help system, as well as other applications. In one device it does things this book covers under separate topics, but this book also discusses important ideas like feature interaction and consistency, serious issues that combining separate applications in one device like the N95 raise with a vengeance. Our discussion of help systems are way ahead of it too.

If I had used trendy examples, they'd only be obsolete sooner! Today's CDs, which were originally promoted as lasting a lifetime, are already being replaced with ones that are designed to self-destruct, as this solves the copyright problems (for the suppliers, that is, not for the users nor even the environment)—the rules change. Already, CDs are physically larger than the personal music players that are replacing them. Although music players have pretty much the same user interface designs with or without CDs, in general the user interfaces of gadgets will certainly change as we think of more exciting things to do—but the design *principles* remain. This book is about the lasting design principles, not about today's time-limited fashions, however superficially tempting fashions may be.

> ▷ Find out more about obsolescence and its impact in section 1.9 (p. 27).

> ▷ Box 10.1, "Why personal video recorders?" (p. 331) discusses the choice of personal video recorders in more detail.

Getting a modern piece of technology to work at all, particularly in a commercial environment, is a miracle in itself; keeping an innovative stream of products rolling off the production line, and hence keeping the manufacturer in business to live another day, is more important than "perfection." On the other hand, I hope this book will help designers see how they can make products better, and by changing practices, make their products increasingly better over time.

A danger of referring to real products is that this book's accuracy relies on how good my understanding of the products is—how good is my reverse engineering? The manufacturers of these devices did not provide formal specifications—I had to reconstruct them. While this is a weakness, any reader can check my results against a real device, its user manual (if adequate), or by corresponding with the manufacturers themselves.

An alternative might have been for me to build new systems and discuss them and the design insights they inspired. Here, there would be no doubt that the systems were accurately specified—though the reader would not be able to obtain them as physical devices to play with. But the problem would be that I might not have implemented or thought about certain awkward features at all: I would be misleadingly talking about, say, "mobile phones" when in fact I was only talking about the simple mobile phone that I implemented for this book. It would be hard to tell the difference between what I had done and what I should have done.

Although they get occasional mention as needed, this book does not specifically cover safety-critical systems, the design of devices like medical equipment, aircraft systems, and nuclear plant control panels, nor does it cover mission-critical systems, ones that, for instance, directly keep a business working. To cover these, we would have to skirt the legal minefields, an unproductive diversion from our focus. Nevertheless even small contributions to user interface design significantly affect health and safety for many people—and some readers will take hold of the ideas in this book and use them for significant applications, like aircraft flight decks or nuclear power-station control panels.

What of the future of interactive technologies? The interaction programming issues and problems of future devices are going to be essentially the same as the interaction programming issues and problems for today's devices (to examine them in this book would take space to explain the unfamiliar domains). In the future, we will have implants, devices embedded inside our bodies: surely we will be able to control them, but we certainly do not want their design to drive us mad! We will want our exoskeletons—external robotic body enhancers—to be both natural to use *and* safe. When we release millions of nanotechnology gadgets, we will want to be sure they work as intended, especially when they interact with us and their environment. Why else have them?

0.4.1   Some *Press On* principles

- Nothing can provide definitive solutions; ideas and theories have to be insightful and provocative → section 0.2 (p. 3).

- To change the world, teach *Press On* along with a research methods course or a business course → section 0.3 (p. 5).

Any sufficiently advanced technology is
indistinguishable from magic.

— *Arthur C. Clarke*

Part I
Context

In part I, we review our culture and relationship with interactive devices: our love of interactive devices, and what they really do for us. This context for interaction programming forms the motivation for part II, when we will develop the tools to start fixing things.

1

Dodgy magic

Once upon a time, if doors opened as you walked toward them people would think you were a magician. Today we don't think twice about this magic, which happens all around us! We are surrounded by gadgets and devices that we interact with, from doorbells to mobile phones. Our houses are full of digital clocks—and it's a rare house that doesn't have some 12 o'clock flashing somewhere. My kitchen has complicated oven controls, washing machine controls, microwave controls, dishwasher controls, fridge controls, and a dead clock. Another room (whether we call it a living room, front room, lounge, drawing room, or bedroom, or even the West Wing) has a TV, a DVD player, and a sound system. The hall has a mobile phone left in it and some battery chargers. Then there is my car in the driveway, with all of its computers and gadgets.

That's today, in an ordinary modern, European household. Tomorrow we will be wearing clothes with embedded devices, which might show our moods or help us find our way when we are out driving.

When we meet one another, our clothes might shimmer and tell us whether we have common things to talk about. Or they might twitch when we walk past a music shop desperate to sell us something. Maybe our mobile phones won't work if they are stolen and taken too far away from our jackets—thieves won't be able to use them. Certainly our mobile phones and similar gadgets should behave differently inside cars, and perhaps have many or all features disabled so we drive more safely.

Maybe the government will require us to carry identification tags. Maybe these tags will be implanted into us, just as they are today into dogs and cats—and in cows, who have their feed automatically chosen for them. Maybe the tags we have will change the behavior of our gadgets; maybe our children can only play harmless games, whereas if the games console knows there is an adult in the room it could let adult games be played. The oven might forbid young children to switch on the grill unsupervised. If we are old and feeble, our medicines may be organized automatically.

Our homes and personal lives may become far more complicated than our work lives—at work at least somebody will have organized all the relevant interactive devices we encounter, whereas at home and in our clothes, there will be a hodge-podge of systems we bought and acquired over years.

We will interact with everything. What we choose to wear and own will, in turn, interact with us and with other people and their environment.

If we have problems with our television remote control or problems setting the timer on our oven *today*, just think what could go wrong in this future of more complex devices, that interact with one another in unpredictable ways! Today we worry that our pacemakers will be messed up by the airport security scanners, but that's just the beginning of the sorts of interaction problems we may face in the future.

The future might be exciting—that is the dream. The future might be out of control—that is the nightmare.

As we build this new world, we are going to create our interactive environment. We will create it by our choices as consumers. Some of us will create it as designers. Some of us will create it and transform it daily, as we modify the devices we use. We have preferences and loyalties, and our devices will learn from us, or we will teach them or replace them. As we configure them, and they configure themselves, we are designing an interactive world in which we are sorcerers and they are the sorcerers' apprentices.

1.1   The architecture analogy

Almost all of the features of a building are visible. If an architect adds another door or window, we can all see the new features. A big window will need cleaning. It might make the house hot in summer and cold in winter, and, while it might have a terrific view, the architect may not have thought about the privacy of the toilets. When the window opens, it might block something else or be a hazard to passers by. However, all these drawbacks of the design are obvious, at least in hindsight, though some design issues may be noticed more as people start to use the building. A light switch might have been wired wrongly, or a door not have a handle.

Even a really bad architect is unlikely to design a building with its doors wrong or unusable. Why would they make a room with no doors, and yet, over here, a room with fifteen? Or why would they put in eight staircases to a room on the same floor? These are such obvious errors that they would never happen.

Perhaps the key issue with computer systems is that as we can't easily see how they are built, they end up with doors in the wrong places, missing doors, and extra doors—and even curious one-way and revolving doors. How the doors and rooms relate isn't at all obvious. And still the designers add more doors, because they can't see the doors that are already there. The mess there is gets worse as more and more doors are added to make the place more "accessible." There may be a good reason to add *this* door, but whether it works well with the existing arrangement of doors is unknown. Worse, a new visitor to the building won't understand why it was a good idea to add that door, and for them it becomes just another opportunity to get lost.

The sorts of "buildings" we will consider in this book are a bit like that. They may be designed with the best of intentions, but they end up having a confusing complexity. Designers don't see the complexity in the same way as users.

Once a building is built, it will stay more-or-less the same forever unless someone deliberately rebuilds part of it—and the bigger the building, the more costly,

> **Box 1.1 The Code of Hammurabi** King Hammurabi was the sixth king of the first dynasty of Babylon. He lived around 1728–1686BC, and is remembered most for his famous code of ethics. The Code of Hammurabi was engraved on a large black stone, eight feet tall, so that all the people could see their rights. The usual "eye for an eye" codes are there as well as some interesting rules about buildings.
>
> There is an obvious analogy between building interactive devices and building houses, an analogy worked out in section 1.1 (facing page). Hammurabi's Law 229 warned that a builder who builds a house that collapses and kills the owner of the house will themselves be put to death.
>
> Although today's computer-based devices do almost as much for us as houses did in ancient Babylon, they are not taken as seriously. Who would put to death a designer who made a system that killed someone? Who would believe that deleting all the personal records of someone whose program deleted theirs was ethically justified as an "eye for an eye," as opposed to being mere retribution? Rather than encourage responsible design, society has done the opposite—most systems come with warranties that deny any responsibility for anything untoward at all.
>
> ▷ For further discussion of ethics, see section 13.4 (p. 467). Chapter 13, "Improving things," includes some historical discussion of codes of ethics, such as that of Hippocrates, in box 13.4, "Hippocrates" (p. 470). Section 2.6 (p. 48) discusses modern warranties.

generally, any substantial change would be. Computers couldn't be more different. Computers are flexible. They can be changed any time, and the bigger they are, the more things there are that seem to need changing. Computer-based things are *always* being upgraded.

Computer-based designers have a temptation. In the worst case, since many of their ideas are not fully visible to users, they are tempted never to finish—the design can always be fixed or updated later. More features can always be added to compensate for misconceptions. And users don't know how to recognize unfinished details, so they never complain.

Imagine starting to live in unfinished buildings. If they were like computers, when you saw the house you were buying, you would have no idea that the kitchen wasn't finished. When you start living in the house and some of its design limitations become obvious, stop complaining—buy an upgrade! That attitude wouldn't survive in the building trade; why does it survive in computers?

The final twist is that in some mad world where houses were designed like this, where architects and builders got away with complicated, unusable designs, we—the people who live in the houses—would *love* it. We'd *want* the flexibility! We'd want to move the living room upstairs and have the garage extended. If our neighbors got a jacuzzi, we'd want one too. We might change the garage into a storeroom and add another garage. If our buildings were like computers, we could extend them at will and do a lot of upgrading without moving. There'd be so much to upgrade that we would lose track of all our great ideas, and we'd end up with lots of unfinished projects around the house.

If house owners loved such flexibility—the flexibility made it easier to build houses and extensions—then more and more houses would be badly designed.

13

Problems would be dismissed: they can be fixed later—or why not move house if you don't like the one you have? There would be a whole industry of selling half-built houses pretending to be finished because we'd all come to expect that. Anyway we'd all want to play with the new rooms and revel in the *potential* flexibility. And the building trade would come to rely on the profits and continual upgrading we were forced into.

This comparison may seem forced. But consider my home entertainment's remote control—see figure 3.3 (p. 73)—which has 55 gray rubber rectangular buttons that all look and feel the same, especially in the dark when it is typically used. Frequently-used keys, like [Play] are almost impossible to find. The remote has two sets of volume controls, eight (!) separate sets of up/down arrows, two right arrows but one left arrow, and two setup buttons ... and this is just what it *looks* like; *using* it is so hard I can't explain it here. It's like a house that has been built by the worst sort of builders, who just added feature after feature without thinking about how it would be used when it was finished.

1.2 The conventional wisdom

Conventional wisdom holds that computers are impressive things, that sometimes don't work because the needs of their human users are ignored or muddled. Sometimes they don't work because their programmers over-stretched themselves but this is just bad engineering caused by bad management. Failures are attributed to the so-called human factor. It is easy to build computer systems forgetting that someone has to use them.

An organization decides to bring in computers to solve its problems. Computers are such fast, capable things that it comes as a surprise when the system does not work as expected. People do strange things, and somehow the computer does not allow for human nature. Sometimes the computer tries to force its users into unnatural activities that are difficult or impossible to follow and have nothing to do with what the users thought they wanted to do. The solution is simply to pay more attention to the real needs of the users and their tasks when working out what and how to computerize.

Since the time when those thoughts became the conventional wisdom, computers have become a lot smaller. They are now ubiquitous and buried inside all sorts of gadgets, from televisions to mobile phones, from personal organizers to photocopiers and fax machines. These small computers, so-called embedded computers, are so pervasive that it is hard to escape them. Some people have computers inside them (controlling drug delivery or pacemakers) and these people cannot walk away from them even if they wanted to. Yet we love them, as all the overflowing gadget shops show.

This book is about making these things better. The first step in making them better is to understand why we like them and put up with them as they are. This chapter and the next explore the culture that makes this so. Chapter 3, "Reality," then looks at the consequences.

1.3 Any sufficiently advanced technology is magic

Arthur C. Clarke is a great story teller: his fiction presents worlds almost like our own but with imaginative details that allow him to explore the boundaries of our experience. As a science fiction author, he envisages plausible ways of making things happen. In reality, Clarke is an accomplished scientist: he invented the communications satellite and is honored the world over for his scientific contributions.

One of the recurring ideas Clarke explores in his many stories is that sufficiently advanced technology, as might be needed for interstellar space travel, is indistinguishable from magic. Thus he writes about humans aboard alien spaceships unable to understand the technology. Their reaction to the alien spaceship is like some Stone Age human's response would be to twenty-first century technology. They understand it as magic.

Indeed, a lot of the technology we have around us is magic. The computer can do amazing things. It is complicated and powerful and solves all sorts of problems. A business that does not use computers is out of date. Computers are clearly what the next generation will be using, and if the rest of us do not keep up, we will be out of date, left behind on an illiterates' scrap heap.

If we believe that computers are magic, two things will happen. First, is that they will be used to try to solve every problem we can imagine. Is your business inefficient? Computerize! Do you have trouble with your taxes? Get a computer! Don't you know how to buy cheaper clothes? Get on the internet! Do you want to find a job? Surf the web! Are you lost? Get an in-car navigator! Second, we will start thinking irrationally, believing the magic.

1.4 We've been here before

At the beginning of the twentieth century, there were no computers and no bookshops filled with books on how to understand the internet. We like to think that the world was a simpler place—but it didn't seem simpler to the people then. They thought that their world was changing fast! The steam engine, for example, was making huge differences in many areas of life.

In his large two-volume *Modern Power Generators* (Gresham Publishing Company, 1908) the futurist of the day, James Weir French, stressed how important engines were going to be. Engines were everywhere and changing everything, and it was important, so French argued, that everybody understand them. There were steam engines, oil engines, petrol engines, and more.

French's assumption was that *we*, the people, should understand engines so our lives could be enhanced. When engines were as unreliable as they were in those Edwardian days, there was some sense in his urging. However, what French couldn't anticipate is that now, a century later, engines are *everywhere*, and they are so reliable we can ignore them. We don't need any of French's knowledge to use engines. I have a simple car; it has at least twenty motors in it, and I don't need to know anything about them apart from knowing where to fill up with fuel. My

15

Box 1.2 Cargo cult computers During World War II, the United States used the Melanesian islands in the Pacific Ocean for airbases. The airbases brought in huge volumes of supplies as cargo and apparently awed the islanders with the valuable goods.

When the war ended, the United States departed, leaving the islanders wanting to continue the benefits of cargo. So they built runways, lit fires, and even made airplanes out of bamboo and straw. They were doing everything they had seen done during the war—except that it didn't work. This was the essence of the cargo cult, practically a belief in a god of cargo.

Richard Feynman made good use of the confusion behind cargo cult when he defined what he called cargo cult science. Some scientists do what they think is science—they go through the ritual—but they are not being really honest with themselves or other scientists. They cut corners, not really caring how to be rigorous, and in a few cases being outright frauds: writing up their fake science as if it had been done properly.

Human nature likes cargo cults. We're all slightly superstitious. We want to be successful, and we want to imitate the things that seem to make us or other people successful. When we are lucky, we analyze what happened. Ah, we were wearing a bracelet. It must be a lucky bracelet! We think that because we put on the bracelet before we were lucky it must have caused the luck.

Computers are our modern cargo, and we have to be alert not to fall into the trap of worshipping computers in the same naive way. Just because we hear a lot of the successes of people and companies who use computers doesn't mean that just using or owning a computer will save us. We have to use it properly, and it has to be designed properly for what we want to use it for.

kitchen has at least nine engines, not counting the vacuum cleaner in the cupboard. Even my mobile phone has one in it. This is a world away from French's vision, of large engines that we needed to understand! We don't have to understand engines anymore—we just use them.

Instead of *us* having to understand engines, engines are now more reliable; *they* are better designed. Wouldn't it be nice if interactive devices changed like this? We wouldn't need to understand them because they were designed better.

A similar transition happened with cars. At first drivers had to know many technical details to drive them, then cars became easier to use. The story of cars is wrapped up with the birth of the consumer movement, triggered by Ralph Nader's agitation about car safety. Initially manufacturers argued that drivers were responsible for safety; then they changed their mind and started to make cars intrinsically safer.

▷   See box 2.3, "Ralph Nader" (p. 51) for the story of Ralph Nader.

Now we are at the point of another transition, this time from badly designed computer-based interactive devices that we, the users, are supposed to understand to better devices that are designed so that we can use and enjoy them.

1.5 Computers as consumer products

Computers are expensive, and once you have invested in a computer you need software to start doing useful things. Once you start using a spreadsheet, word processor, or whatever, you start noticing that the computer crashes—perhaps more than once a day. As you use it longer, you discover you need to upgrade your software, and then the computer crashes more often, or it becomes slower than it was. You then need to upgrade the hardware. The costs of owning a computer are considerable.

For some reason we put up with unreliable computers. If we compare the reliability of a computer with, say, a car: the conclusion is inevitable. If you bought a car and it would not turn left when it was doing thirty miles per hour, you'd get it fixed. In fact, the manufacturer would be so embarrassed by its flaw, they'd fix it for you. Or if you had a flat and took the car to a garage, you would think it outrageous if the garage said it would cost more to replace the tire than to buy a new car, which would come with new tires anyway. What if the garage said that it could replace the tire, but the car would not go as fast? it would be even more amazing if you just accepted this treatment and bought a new car. And next year you bought a new car again—and you had to send your old car into landfill because nobody would buy it from you.

The cost of progress is obsolescence. On the one hand we can emphasize the excitement and gains of keeping up to date with the latest technology. On the other hand, we can look behind us at the waste: every computer that is replaced or upgraded represents a computer that was a failure. Certainly, there is more money to be made in selling new products, and at least the stuff we are throwing away is getting smaller and not filling landfills as fast as it used to.

Because we are willing to buy replacements rather than take computers back and complain, manufacturers can put less effort into making them reliable. If a computer breaks after a couple of years, the manufacturer can safely bet that you would rather buy a faster computer than get the broken one fixed. After all, you will find that a new computer is cheaper than getting the older computer fixed, and is faster. If you are going to buy new computers, then there is no need for the manufacturer to worry about fixing the old computer: indeed, there is no need to waste design effort to make computers easy to fix. That makes the computers cheaper—essential in a competitive market. However, once they get as cheap as they have, the human cost of just unscrewing the lid to see what is wrong starts to make servicing too expensive in comparison.

Since computers are complicated, it takes a lot of skill to repair them. That skill is expensive, and the less effort manufacturers put into designing computers, the harder they are to service. Supply and demand in the market conspires to make buying a replacement a sensible decision. We can't fix them even if we want to.

The leading manufacturers have another idea. Intel and Microsoft are the obvious suppliers of most of the hardware and software that goes into desktop computers, but most handheld devices use different chips and less familiar operating systems. The Real-time Operating system Nucleus (TRON) is used on millions of

17

embedded computers—especially Japanese ones—and runs on NEC and Hitachi chips and many PDAs; and the ARM chip is the most widely used microprocessor in the world, accounting for about three-quarters of the embedded CPUs used. There are all sorts of complex licensing arrangements among the various manufacturers that enable, say, IBM to sell computers containing Intel processors. Intel knows that, although it dominates the desktop PC market, every time it brings out a new gadget other companies will try to build on its work. But it takes a lot of work to design computers and get them to work properly, so Intel's competitors usually only get around to competing directly with Intel months after Intel has brought about a new product. Thus a good business strategy for Intel is to continually bring out new products. The company then gets a higher proportion of the market, since its competitors haven't caught up. When it brings out new, improved products, and when there is no significant competition, Intel can charge higher prices to make a bigger profit; its better production methods allows it to sell in higher volume too. Intel can then feed that profit into developing further improvements.

Although I've illustrated the argument with specific companies, it makes business sense for any company. Once a company gets into a leadership position, it earns more and can invest more in research, so then it can bring out new products and make higher margins than its competitors. The more it does this, the more successful it will be. Even a second-rate company wants to be more efficient than its competitors. How it does this depends a lot on what it makes. If it can make cable more efficiently than its competitors, it will put pressure on its competitors to lower their prices. The competitors then have less income to invest in making their manufacturing more efficient, and the relative quality of their product will drop. Soon the first company gets more market share and more profit.

There are also psychological reasons to keep on bringing out new products. The new products will be more expensive, and because they are reviewed in the media as better, all their exposure pushes up market value. Inevitably, when any new product is announced it will initially be scarcer than the products it supersedes. It is well known to marketing people that scarcity in itself stimulates demand. Of course, the demand puts pressure on production, which in turn makes the product more scarce, which then makes consumers more desperate to be the first in the block to own one. It's one of many cycles of positive feedback.

One obvious way to become more efficient is to run your business using faster computers than your competitors. That makes every manufacturer eager consumers of the best computers: this then gives Intel (or whoever is running fastest) bigger markets and means they get even more money to invest in research.

> ▷   The big get bigger. This idea is picked up again in relation to interactive device design in section 8.9 (p. 264), where we introduce scale-free networks.

1.6 Externalizing use cost

An interesting way to be efficient is to make costs disappear. Computers are often used to convert a business's costs and overheads into other people's costs and overheads. A very simple example is the telephone menu (which of course is run by a computer). Suppose you want to get a visa to go to Australia. In the old days, you would go to the visa office at the Australian High Commission and sit on their chairs while you wait to talk to a member of their staff. You, as a customer, then pay for a visa to be stuck in your passport.

Now it's all changed: you telephone them and you get an automated voice menu system. "Press 2 for business visa information"—in a style we are all familiar with. Now you are waiting in your own home or office, providing you own chair. What used to be an internal cost for the business, you are now paying for yourself. They used to have to pay people to talk to you; now you are paying them to listen to the telephone. Finally you get an "electronic travel authority," which is a sort-of electronic visa.

We might argue that the system has become faster, more flexible, and more convenient. You can now get a visa by telephoning them from anywhere, without going to an office in a city far away. And your passport doesn't get cluttered up with visas and stamps, which might be handy if you don't want anyone else to know you have a visa to go to Australia.

A side effect of externalizing costs is that a business's priorities change. In the old days, *they* wanted to minimize overheads. So they would make their staff fast and friendly and efficient. They would probably want each staff member to be able to solve all problems, since the more staff a customer has to see, the more wasted staff time there is. They might have strategies to empower their staff to solve problems, because every customer problem ties up a staff member and costs them money in lost time. But now, when the process is automated and externalized, there is no staff time to save. In fact, the longer the business can keep customers on the telephone, the more money they can cream off the telephone service (unless they are using a free number). And while the customer is on the phone, why not play them some advertising? Thus the incentives change.

Externalizing appears in almost every sort of activity. Instead of going shopping, and spending time in shops, we are now encouraged to shop on the web. The shop no longer needs to have an expensive building and displays of products taking up shelf space, and it no longer needs to employ lots of shop assistants. A web site can control users much better than shop assistants. Shops are full of people browsing and asking shop assistants questions, which costs money to support. Few web sites allow users to engage in conversation—because conversation is a direct cost to the business. More enlightened ones may use forms or email for feedback so that suggestions and complaints can be sent in, but many web sites provide no details to contact the organization. Clearly the temptation, if not the business goal, is to use web sites to get lots of customers without getting into lots of costly conversations.

Externalizing costs can be achieved even where there are no products, visas, or food, to buy.

Organizations have lots of meetings. In the old days, meetings were held at the organization's premises. Now they can be done by tele-working, say, using email. Before, the organization met the direct costs of providing space, hospitality, and even the toilets; now the externalized members of meetings provide their own space and nourishment. Likewise, universities used to teach students in lecture halls: the lecture halls cost money to maintain, and they hold only so-many students—the direct costs are obvious. By promoting what's become called "distance learning," educators now get students to learn from material on the web. The universities have no space costs and have no physical limits on the numbers of students who can be taught.

Technology has always done this. Books, for example, are another technology. This book has saved me the effort of talking to you. If you are reading this on the web, it's even saved me (or my publishers) the effort of printing the book—you have taken on that cost.

Once an activity costs nothing to run, or, better, when it can get a payback from externalized costs (like getting a percentage of telephone costs, or charging students for time online), then the business can set its ambitions globally. Increased scale, especially on an international level, multiplies even small beneficial effects: before shops were on the web, everybody had to travel to them: now a single truck can deliver to many people. The supermarket has reduced its costs, expanded its market, *and* it has reduced environmental damage.

Many activities are computerized to make the workers' jobs easier. Typically a computer can speed up the work enormously, and the company can lay off people, do more work, or both. However, the customers now interface with a computer rather than a human, and the computer imposes a stricter and often more mysterious way of working—this is true of a system on the world wide web, an optical character recognition system, a telephone menu system, or whatever. Using it takes customers longer. If users need to have passwords, this is an extra hurdle: yet another password for them to remember and type in every time they want something done.

Our university library has decided to automate filling in book loan forms. In the good old days, I would go down to the library and fill in a little card when I wanted to ask the library to get a book it did not possess. For me, this was straightforward: I'm familiar with pen and paper. Now they have automated, which presumably makes their side of processing loan cards easier (the university has several libraries, and a computerized loan card makes centralizing the load processing much easier, as no cards have to be put in the mail). From the library's point of view, the computerization helps enormously.

Yet I now have a quirky new program to learn how to use, and I have to remember a special password. It takes me a little longer (and a lot longer if I forget the password). The library is deaf to my complaints, which really are quite trivial in the scale of things—don't you *always* have to learn programs and passwords? In any case, I'm probably the only user complaining, so my problems are easily dismissed as my problems, not representative of all users.

On the other hand, there are thousands of library users all on the university payroll: all the "trivial" problems they have collectively ought to be considered as an aggregate cost that the university is paying for. Since the library has externalized this cost—and made *their* processes efficient—they aren't interested.

Given the benefits to the librarians, the only people who can really influence things for the better are the programmers who design the systems. We must urge programmers to consider the *whole* process, not just the library's side of the job.

1.7 The productivity paradox

Computers are supposed to help productivity: they should make all sorts of things better and faster. Yet the productivity of industrialized nations is not growing as fast as one would expect. How can we explain this productivity paradox?

The conventional view is that computers are hard to use and that taking into account usability (or, rather, the time wasted through *un*usability) explains the productivity losses. According to this view, the solution is to make computers more usable. Every desktop computer installed in an organization requires technical support, and the user requires training to use it effectively. Users waste time because their tools are inefficient overall. A computer might make the Finance Department more efficient, but the gain can be lost overall because it encourages Finance to more easily manage a level of technical complexity that makes everybody *else* do more work.

Computers also change jobs in new ways. When in history would a company have bought its employees entertainment systems to do their work? Today every desktop computer has a CD drive and audio and video capabilities. It is no doubt good for staff morale and keeping the CD and DVD industries going, but it isn't directly increasing productivity where it is supposed to.

The productivity paradox goes way beyond desktop computers. For example, Sinfonia is a sophisticated music system that has been called a virtual orchestra, yet it needs an enormous setup effort from musicians to do a show. Productivity is redistributed around rather than average productivity increasing significantly.

Another aspect of the productivity paradox is that people don't understand computer economics very well. Productivity has to be based on revenue and expenditure. How should computers be costed? What sort of investment are they, and how should they be written off? Whatever accountants think, it's pretty clear that few understand the economics of computers, including training and software costs: for example, consider the huge investments in dot.com start up companies, investments that were made without the conventional requirements of business plans or experience. The result was part of the world's economic turndown. Although it was caused by financial dealings, not intrinsically by computers, that aspect of the productivity paradox was certainly stimulated by hyperbolic claims from the industry about the promise of computers to stimulate more or better business.

Computers encourage businesses to externalize costs. What used to be an internal cost (that accountants saw) now becomes an external cost. For example,

21

instead of employing and paying lots of employees' salaries, a company uses a telephone voice menu system. The costs to the company are reduced, but the costs are redistributed to customers. Costs are thus externalized. Therefore computers are attractive to individual businesses, but they don't help overall national productivity so much.

Computers are bought by businesses aiming to make them more efficient—but competitors also buy them for the same reason. Then companies find themselves *having* to use even more powerful computers just to stay ahead. In the end, companies are not relatively more productive. Having bought computers, everybody needs to upgrade their computers to stay sufficiently productive, and the productivity paradox continues.

1.8   Moore's Law

All ways of making business more effective cause positive feedback, and a cycle of improvement begins. When things get better, they leverage to get even better—or, rather, when things get more profitable, they can get even more profitable as profit is plowed back into development, quality, and so forth. It is rather like breeding rabbits: the more rabbits you have, the faster you can breed rabbits, and the faster your breed rabbits, the more you have. Provided you don't run out of food or space, the population grows exponentially.

Almost every aspect of computers has been growing exponentially. Every few years, you get twice as much. You get twice as much in the same space, you go twice as fast, or things cost half as much. Or you can squeeze twice as many transistors onto a chip. The industry has been improving performance exponentially for years, and the reliable doubling in performance is enshrined as Moore's Law, named after Gordon Moore, one of the founders of Intel, the chip manufacturer.

Moore's Law says that computers are getting better and better. My mobile phone has more computing power in it than NASA had when it launched space rockets for the Apollo space program. It might be tricky to use my mobile phone to get to the moon, but the advances in technology are indeed spectacular. You can buy 100 million transistors all wired up for less than the price of a single transistor a few years ago.

Moore's Law sounds impressive, but it isn't measuring anything relevant to most of us. Desktop computers have been the same size for years, and it takes just as long today to write a letter as it did twenty years ago. If Moore's Law meant anything significant for us computer users, the things *we* do would be getting easier or faster. But they aren't getting as easy as the raw technological progress suggests. We still take as much time word processing as we ever did, though we are slowing down because word processors bombard us with so many additional options and features—and we'd look uncool if we didn't show we could use them.

Moore's Law happens in part because of externalizing costs. Originally, chip manufacturers had to make many different sorts of chip, and they could not fully exploit the benefits of mass production because each chip took a lot of individual development. The invention of the microprocessor meant that manufacturers could make one chip that people could use in many different ways: instead of manufacturers working on designing many special purpose chips, the consumers of the chips had to learn how to program.

Chris Evans in his landmark book *The Mighty Micro* made the point that if cars had developed according to Moore's Law, then in 1979 when he was writing, already cars would have been small enough to put a dozen on a pinhead, have the power of the QEII (the large ocean liner), and would cost £1.35 (for a Rolls Royce). If cars were that small and that powerful, their impact would be inconceivable. Of course, cars that size would be difficult to use *as* cars—Moore's Law, even with the freedom of imagination, doesn't make things easy to use. Evans discussed the implications presciently: what will happen when computers are so small that when you drop them, they don't hurt your feet as they would have done in the 1970s, but instead stick to your shoe soles? We're answering those questions now.

Compare the improvements and speed-ups computers have undergone since they became consumer goods with the modest speed-ups that occurred in transport over the period of the Industrial Revolution. Before the Industrial Revolution the fastest way to travel was by horse. With staging posts properly organized up and down the country, somebody rich enough or with an important enough job would have been able to travel as fast as a horse for as long as necessary. The main difficulty in the system was that if you wanted to go fast you couldn't take much with you. If you wanted to carry goods for your business, it would require a wagon, which would go much slower.

After the Industrial Revolution you could get on a train. Not only could trains go faster, they could carry almost without limit, and at much the same speeds as the fastest passenger trains. Sea transport became much more reliable when steamers replaced sailing ships. The world became a smaller place. The British Empire expanded due to the efficiency advantages Britain had in being first into the Industrial Revolution. The world was transformed, by a speed-up factor of around a hundred. A hundred is a lot smaller than the speed-ups of computers, which already exceed millions over the few years we've had them. The difference is that people need to travel, whereas nobody needs to perform microprocessor instructions faster—what they want to do is get their *work* done faster. That everyone *thinks* they want faster computers—more megahertz—owes more to marketing than to effectiveness.

Of course a faster computer does things faster, but there are reasons why the speed-up in itself does not help most humans. First, computers already spend most of their time waiting for something to happen: however fast my computer is, I can't type much faster, and the computer might do everything it needs to faster, but that means it just spends longer waiting for the next keystroke from me. It is ironic that computers compete with one another on megahertz: and what is their CPU speed to us? Second, the way I interact with computers has not changed: since windows were invented, computers have not become much easier to use.

If you can get hold of one, a ten-year-old word processor or spreadsheet will work blindingly fast on a modern computer. Today's word processors, instead of getting faster, have added features. In 2000 you could put video clips and mul-

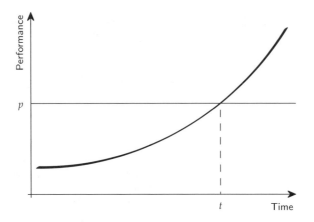

Figure 1.1: Performance of technology increases with time (curved line). As performance increases, it will exceed any given technical performance requirement, such as the line at height p. After the threshold time t, performance will exceed whatever is required to do the work; thereafter, all extra performance can be diverted into making the experience more pleasant, or the product more attractive in other ways. The diagram is based on Christensen—see the further reading (p. 35).

timedia into word processed documents, whereas in 1980 doing so would have been out of the question. All those features represent ideas that marketing people can use to catch our imagination: more magic! Moreover, we are willing to get the features even though this makes the programs we buy more complex and a bit slower. Next month, or maybe next year, we will be able to buy a faster computer and get back to speed again.

Certainly computers are getting better and have exponentially increasing performance over time. We can represent this by a graph, as in figure 1.1 (this page), using a curve of positive slope (it is not necessary to worry about the precise shape of the line or exactly what "performance" is measuring). For any particular task the user has, some minimal level of performance p will be required. There is a crossover time where the two lines in the graph intersect, with the performance equal to p and a point in time at t. Before the crossover time t, technology is delivering inadequate performance; after time t, technology delivers more than adequate performance.

Before the crossover time t, manufacturers need only promise technical capability (which is easy, since technology is getting better all the time). After time t, products get distinguished not by their performance, which is more than adequate, but by more subtle—and harder to supply—properties like usability. For technologies like wristwatches, we are long past the threshold, and they are now fashion items, chosen on criteria mainly other than technological. But for many everyday things, like word processors, we should also be well beyond the crossover. So why aren't word processors much better?

Manufacturers can increase consumers' expectation of p by providing or promising new "essential" features: it is in manufacturers' interest to increase p because this postpones the crossover. Thus many everyday things have numerous features, a factor influencing their usability.

"Software is a gas. It expands to fill its container," proposed as Nathan's First Law, after Nathan Myhrvold, a Microsoft vice president. "After all," he says, "if we hadn't brought your processor to its knees, why else would you get a new one?"*

Programs tend to get complex—a phenomenon called software bloat. Software bloat results partly from manufacturers squeezing in more features, because that helps sell products, and it is partly programmers taking advantage of the raw speed of computers to compensate for programming badly. Besides, the rate at which features change means that programs rarely need fixing: users prefer to buy new software with more features than get their current features working properly.

People who use computers don't work alone. They send each other email. If I send you an email with an attachment I wrote using my word processor, you might well find I used a feature you don't have. You either complain to me, or you go and buy a new version of your program. So when you reply, the chances are you have upgraded your software.

But of course, you bought your new software after I had got mine. So maybe I then get some email from you using another fancy feature that requires *me* to upgrade: after all, you have just bought a more recent version than I have. And I buy my upgrade after you bought yours, so I might buy a more recent version than yours. Then I email you later, and you have to upgrade.

▷ Figure 1.2 (next page) illustrates the arms race.

Maybe the continual upgrading won't happen with just two of us, but the world is a big place, and you can be certain that there are some people out there with obsolete versions of programs, and some people who've got newer versions than yours. You've only got to start communicating with the rest of the world—what else is the internet for?—for a few moments before the pressure to upgrade something influences you.

Perhaps if just the two of us were the only people in the world, we could come to some agreement not to enter an "arms race" in upgrading. If we both worked for the same company, it might impose some rules—for instance that email has to be plain text rather than word-processed, or when a file is emailed, it should first be saved in the format of an earlier version. But the world is a big place. There are lots of people running various versions of software, following various standards at varying degrees of obsolescence. Somewhere in the world someone is upgrading their computers and software right now, just to catch up. The world is also sensitive to prestige. If my boss decides to upgrade, who am I to put my career on the line to disagree? My boss gets the latest stuff, so I upgrade. When I next email others, in turn they have to decide what to do. Often they succumb to upgrade because they were secretly coveting the prestigious new software, and I gave them an excuse to upgrade without feeling guilty!

---

* Quoted in *Scientific American*, **277**(1), p69, July 1997.

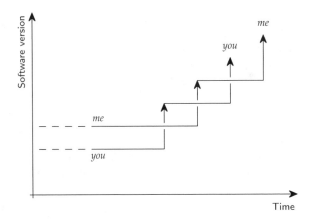

Figure 1.2: The arms race with just two people upgrading products. I start with a document written in version 1, which I email to you. To read my email you need to get the software, which is now at version 2. You email me a version 2 document, so I upgrade to the current version of software, which is now up to version 3. And so on.

The interaction among customers is crucial. When I drive my car, I don't get overwhelmed with a desire to buy a Rolls Royce when one overtakes me. I might imagine myself liking a Rolls Royce, but I generally think more rationally: they cost a lot, and their cost-benefit for my lifestyle would be negative. Even if I had the cash to buy one, I would prefer to have a cheap car that does all I need and to use the rest of the money more wisely. What is different is that cars do not interact with each other. What car I drive is hardly influenced by what car you drive. Granted, if everyone drove one sort of car, then owning a different make would inevitably be more expensive: it would be harder to find experienced garages, and so on. The car market in fact has a lot of diversity (although a lot of the apparent diversity is artificially inflated by a few manufacturers using a wide range of brand names), and for the time being, at least, we can and do choose cars for all sorts of personal reasons.

Why don't we do this with computers? I like vintage cars: even though they are slower and draftier, they have more character. But nobody I know runs a vintage computer. There's no point—you don't take computers out for a ride to show off their character. What matters is whether they are up to date: computers interact. Almost all computer use requires communication with other people: obviously email and the web are there for communication, but so are CDs, memory sticks and floppy disks. When you buy a computer, you are worried about compatibility, that is, how much you can work with other people.

If you go down to your local gadget shop to buy something like a home theater, it is bound to have several sockets on the back that need cables that are incompatible with what you already have. Already it's hard to buy video cassette players, and DVDs come in several formats. Should you get optical connections, to be "fu-

---

Box 1.3 An obituary for a fax My fax machine, model number DF200, died! It had a short life: bought new 1994, died 1999. Its cause of death was a power cut; it died when mains power was restored.

The postmortem revealed that the cause of death was multiple component failure on the main PCB (printed circuit board—the card that the electronic components are fixed to) due to the power surge. The separate power supply was still operational and would have been made available for organ donation had there been any way to make it available to power supply failure victims.

Funeral arrangements. The DF200 was buried at a community landfill site in the normal way. Will flowers grow on the landfill site? Donations can be made to Thames Water, the agency that will deal with the toxic leachate and other pollution from the fax machine.

---

ture proof" or should you have analog connections to be compatible with your old equipment? It is a nightmare to upgrade any part of your home electronics because of the continually shifting standards.

Bill Schilit, of Intel's Usability Laboratory, says that manufacturers are not to blame—consumers are. Consumers, he says, have unrealistic expectations. Schilit blames "ever-increasing improvements" for introducing incompatibilities as devices are upgraded.[*]

Hmm. Another reason for the incompatibilities is product differentiation. Manufacturers want to place their produces at different price points, and obviously they want the things that seem better to cost more, because consumers will be more willing to pay for the extra features. Thus product differentiation tends to encourage manufacturers to put different features on low-end and high-end devices, even if inside they are practically the same. The cheaper products probably have the same chip-set but don't have the sockets to access the up-market features.

▷ For more on home theater, see section 3.7 (p. 68).

1.9   Obsolescence

To take advantage of Moore's Law, we have to dispose of the old stuff to make way for the new. What happens to the old stuff?

The sad obituary in box 1.3, "An obituary for a fax" (this page) tells the final story of a fax machine that was just five years old when it stopped working and the light left its buttons. The obituary uses the demise of the DF200 fax as an example to raise and question wider issues about device design and marketing generally.

At the time of the fax machine's untimely death, BT (a UK telecom company, formerly called British Telecom) would repair the fax for a £100 engineer's callout, plus the cost of repair, which was estimated at £235. The fax was already running on its *third* main board, due to failures during its warranty period; these repairs had been free. However, the last repair wasn't too successful; for the last four

---

[*] Quoted in *New Scientist*, issue **2555**, p29, 14 June 2006.

years of its life the fax was wrapped in tape since the engineer broke some of the weak casing fixings.

Given that equivalent new faxes cost around £140 (or at least they did when the DF200 needed replacing) and come with one year's warranty, it made no financial sense to repair the DF200. The DF200 therefore joins the UK's electronics landfill.

The pricing of engineer service calls is probably designed to cover costs (or to dissuade calls being made in the first place) rather than to build customer relations, preserve the environment, or even to collect life-cycle feedback on products in use in the field.

Electric outages are not an unanticipated occurrence, so design should allow for them. When the (still functioning) switched mode power supply is switched on, it produces no significant surge over its operating voltage (I checked with a high-speed oscilloscope). The fax used to overheat and get uncomfortably hot probably indicating that the main board was under-rated. That the board was the third the DF200 needed in its short life appears to confirm the poor quality of design. Interestingly, the board was made by Sagem, who also make missiles (including the Exocet), so presumably they should know how to make reliable electronics. Thus one is led to conclude that the DF200 was *designed* for a short life.

Most obituaries recall the best memories of the dead, but in the case of the DF200, a typical representative of the electronics consumer marketplace, to go so quickly from desirable product to polluting debris is obscene. Its death, in such routine circumstances, was avoidable. But at least it was a broken, useless gadget: each year, UK consumers discard about 15 million *working* mobile phones as they upgrade to fancier models, contributing to the million tons of electronic waste disposed of annually in the UK alone. That is a huge hidden cost of chasing Moore's Law, to say nothing about the hidden human time costs of learning how to use all those new mobile phones.

Clearly designers make trade-offs, for example, balancing design time, product cost, reliability, servicing costs, and recall rates. But in these trade-offs, environmental costs have been discounted or ignored. The DF200 contains six wired-in NiCd batteries (NiCd, or nicad, batteries contain nickel and cadmium, which are toxic metals) and has no instructions for their safe disposal. Cadmium is toxic to humans, plants, crustaceans, and fish—pretty much everything. Long-term low-dose exposure to cadmium leads to malfunctions of the liver, kidneys, and lungs. Discarded NiCd batteries contribute about half of all the cadmium escaping into the environment from landfill sites.

Try to avoid buying products that use NiCd batteries; or if you have to, make sure the NiCds can be removed before you discard the device. NiCds are quite sensitive about how they are charged, and if they are treated well they will last longer. Charge them cold, and always fully charge them; never "top up" or partially recharge them, as this reduces their capacity. Lithium ion (LiON) and nickel metal hydride (NiMH) batteries are less polluting. Similar rules apply for using and charging NiMH and LiON batteries; you should read the instructions.

By 2005 there were 150 million PCs buried in landfill sites in the United States, and a similar number of the discarded PCs ended up as overseas waste—much of it in Africa, a region least able to cope with it. Those PCs will be buried somewhere (or partly reclaimed, burned or buried), complete with their NiCd batteries, lead screens, lead solder, flame retardants, and so on. Some people are keen on exporting old PCs to developing countries where they can be used—for a time. This is a short-term solution, merely using the rest of the world like a bigger landfill site, and probably a landfill site with fewer pollution checks and controls. Instead, we have to rethink how devices are designed.

▷   The DF200 fax will reappear in section 5.5.5 (p. 153), where we explore details of its interaction programming.

1.10   Reduce, reuse, recycle, rethink

Manufacturing systems developed since the Industrial Revolution are based on a one-way, cradle-to-grave stream of materials. It is a model that takes, makes, and wastes—and the waste is a cost to the environment. Economic incentives in manufacturing externalize costs: you can make a cheaper product if somebody else pays for some of its costs. It is cheaper to make devices with poor usability, because that is easier and the cost of doing so is borne by the user. It is cheaper to make devices that are thrown away as waste, because that is a cost borne by the environment rather than the manufacturers—externalizing use costs again. In the long run, cradle-to-grave design is not sustainable.

A good slogan is the standard three *R*s: Reduce, Reuse, Recycle. We can improve the environment and reduce pollution by reducing our consumption, reusing materials, and recycling. But these three guidelines, while helpful, do not radically change things—they just postpone the inevitable.

A better slogan is the *four R*s: Reduce, Reuse, Recycle, and *Rethink*. Can we design devices that are better for use and for the environment? Clearly we can. If designs are more usable, users will be more satisfied with them and less likely to discard them. If manufacturers had a take-back policy (when a user discards a device, the manufacturer takes it back), then they would have a vested interest in keeping customers satisfied with their products for longer. Regulations that promote take-back policies would therefore, as a side effect, improve usability. Manufacturers could promote their products as having longer useful lives; users would be more satisfied with their products for longer. From the consumer's point of view, the products would be better investments.

Here are some general principles that improve products:

■ Design for dismantling. Use snap fixings instead of screws, so that fewer materials are needed and dismantling is easier.

■ Design for recycling. Fewer materials mean greater purity and easier separation of materials.

■ Label components (or mold components so that labels don't come off). Identified chemicals can be recycled more easily and safely.

■ Design for upgrading. Use a modular construction, with simple casings.

■ Design for reconditioning. Parts that wear more quickly should be easily bought separately, and easily replaced.

■ Design for durability so parts that quickly wear are designed to last or become redundant.

■ Design for forward capability. Design to be upgradable, with easy access for extra ports, additional memory, newer components (like faster microprocessors). Other examples include washing machines and dishwashers with upgradable software that controls cycle times and energy use—new software might be required for handling new detergents or to handle degraded components (old motors might have slower spin cycles).

■ Design flexible user interfaces. The knobs and buttons on devices get a lot of wear, so expect them to break. Design the user interfaces so that the machines can continue to be used and to work well even when a knob or switch is broken. At least design so that controls can be reallocated—this makes products last longer and also helps users who have accessibility issues (somebody who has reduced mobility may like to swap around the locations of the device controls).

■ Eliminate or reduce use of hazardous materials (flame retardants, mercury connectors, cadmium and mercury-based batteries, lead-based solder). NiCd batteries are needed in most PCs to ensure the clock keeps running correctly even when the PC is not plugged into the mains. Why not use the internet to get the correct time? NiCds are also needed for basic memory backup, but this is only because it is easier to have battery backed up standard memory rather than a different sort of memory that needs no battery power—you could use flash memory, or a disk to store configuration information indefinitely and not need any batteries to do so. Note how rethinking design makes better products.

■ Consider whole-lifecycle energy costs—the energy things cost to make, use and dispose of. Consider also the energy costs of disposing of the devices the new ones replace.

> ▷ Box 1.4, "Energy consumption" (facing page) describes the surprising energy waste from DAB radios, because of a design decision to have external always-on power supplies.

By choosing to waste energy, manufacturers have saved costs in mains cabling, electrical safety, and in internationalization (the same radio works in any country, just with a different power supply—it doesn't need a new power cord and plug). In a different world, with different priorities, we could save megawatts and make a noticeable difference to our environmental impact. The future for DAB radios is supposed to be exciting, with new digital entertainment facilities being added all the time—put another way, the industry wants to keep selling DAB radios, even

> **Box 1.4 Energy consumption** I bought the UK's most popular digital audio broadcasting (DAB) radio, the latest bit of interactive technology. As of 2006, three million DAB radios had been sold in the UK (or about 500 million worldwide). I measured how many watts my radio consumed *when it was switched off*: it consumes 1.7 watts. Therefore, the 3 million sold up to 2006 in the UK collectively consume about 5 megawatts—though some use batteries, a different sort of energy consumption. The DAB radio could have been designed to consume a negligible amount of power when switched off; instead, it was convenient for its designers to use an external power supply that is always switched on. An external power supply makes it easier to make radios for different countries, it makes the electrical safety issues easier to manage, and it makes the wiring cheaper. Cynically, it makes the radio in the shop more appealing, lighter and smaller—unless you realize it needs another lump, which won't be on show.
>
> I measured how much my house consumes with only "switched off" devices, and in the summer it consumes 400 watts—from DVDs in standby, network hubs, burglar alarm, a fridge, and so on. Across the UK, that amounts to about 4,000 megawatts from domestic households (my sums allow for the various sizes of households)—the equivalent to the output of about four modern nuclear reactors. That's only domestic houses, not counting the standby waste of factories, shops, and offices. A 2006 UK Government Energy Review claimed 8% of the domestic electricity consumption is stuff in standby.
>
> In short, better design would reduce the need for energy considerably and have a dramatic effect on the world. The UK government is now considering a law to control energy-wasting standby features.
>
> Presumably all the old non-DAB radios are heading for landfill. According to the industry, DAB has many new exciting developments in store for consumers, thus ensuring that all those 500 million DAB radios bought up to 2006 will soon be obsolete—and also discarded.

to people who've bought them. This imperative will contribute to electrical waste problems, adding to the pile of pre-DAB radios already disposed of.

■ Finally, design systems *to* break. Things will break anyway, and if they are not designed to break, they will be impossible to mend—and they will ultimately end up in landfill because users don't know what else to do with them.

> ▷ Design to break is one of three prototyping principles presented in box 13.2, "Paper prototyping" (p. 455).

These principles should be seen not in isolation but in a framework of bigger incentives. Too little will happen without extending producer responsibility (EPR), for instance, in changing taxes and forcing improved product warranties, which requires legislation. Indeed, international legislation as it is an international problem. Ironically, enlightened countries that have laws controlling internal waste management may encourage greater pollution in developing countries that end up finally disposing of the materials. Yet we do not need to wait for legislation: if we, that is we as customers, are aware of environmental issues and the principles of externalizing costs to consumers, then our purchasing decisions will favor companies that try harder to make better products.

William McDonough and Michael Braungart (see www.mbdc.com) have started a challenging rethink of our whole approach to the environment. They call their approach "cradle-to-cradle^{SM} design." The whole manufacturing process is seen as a cycle—there is not a grave at the end of the product lifetime, but a new cradle, a rebirth into future products. Cradle-to-cradle works. Some companies, such as Fuji Xerox, have photocopier take-back policies, and they have modified their manufacturing processes to recycle—and even at this early stage, are saving about $50 million a year.

One of McDonough and Braungart's key ideas is that waste is food. In nature, of course, dead plants and animals become the nutrients for future generations. We need to rethink technology so that waste becomes the "nutrient" for future products. In their words, rather than being ecologically efficient (the three Rs) we should be ecologically *effective* (rethink!) and change the processes.

Even if these ideas sound idealistic, we as individuals can make contributions that are worthwhile. Discard of your electronics thoughtfully. If you (or your company) wants to donate an old computer to a charity so that it can be used a bit longer, don't delete the hard drive as it will zap the operating system. Buying an operating system and software probably makes a PC cost more to get working than it's worth. So don't forget to recycle your computer with its original software and passwords—remembering to make sure that your private information is deleted or (better practice) was properly encrypted in the first place.

> ▷ Chapter 13, "Improving things," from section 13.4 (p. 467) onwards, picks up the wider ethical design issues again.

1.11   Metcalfe's Law

In the early days of computer networking (before the internet had its name), Bob Metcalfe proposed Metcalfe's Law: the value of computers to a community increases straightforwardly with the number of computers.

While the cost of computers obviously goes up with the number of computers, the interactions possible among computers goes up faster as the number of computers increases.

If there are two computers, they can interact in one way, with each other. If there are only two faxes in the world, there is only one thing you can do with them—send faxes back and forth! If there are three computers, each can interact with two others, so there are six (three times two) ways of interacting. If there are four, each can interact with three others, so there are twelve ways. And so on. The number of ways to get computers to interact increases with the square of the number of computers. If the cost only goes up proportionately with the number of computers, as it does, but the benefit of having them goes up with the square, then at some "critical mass" point the benefits will outweigh the cost considerations and will continue to do so. Even if you don't interact with all other computers, once the numbers get large enough the power of squaring takes over.

Once you have enough computers (faxes, mobile phones, or whatever) the social benefits out-weigh the costs.

Putting this magic another way: once you can afford the entry cost to buy a computer or some other sort of device, and provided enough other people have them—and they are networked to you—then the computer is "worth it." People buy computers because other people buy computers ... positive feedback.

1.12 The tragedy of the commons

Magic and positive feedback are a powerful combination, and computers are in the middle of it. Computers are a magical solution to all problems. The magic is two-sided: we all believe it will work, and when it doesn't, we think it will work tomorrow (after we upgrade). We all run around behaving as if we had no choice. We have to upgrade to keep on running around. Yet somehow if we all agreed that this was a collective madness, because we thought the costs or the waste excessive, then we could all stop and get on and work with what we already had. This is called the tragedy of the commons. It is a problem that arises in many areas of life.

Imagine a village common ground where we all put our cows to graze. Perhaps there are too many cows or not enough grass, so everyone in the village should cut down on the number of cows. Doing this would benefit the whole community, but unfortunately everyone might think along the lines that they might as well try and keep as many cows as possible, because they have everything to gain by doing so. If someone else is cheating by keeping lots of cows, then obviously I'd miss out if I didn't have as many cows as they do. And if nobody is cheating, then the commons can easily support my few extra cows. Either way, it makes some sort of sense for me to keep as many cows as I can, regardless of the pressure on the commons.

When everyone reasons like this, the commons are overgrazed and everyone suffers in the end. Perhaps one of the most poignant examples in Britain is the dead or dying fishing village: fish stocks have been overfished, and now there are no fish left to support communities. As fish stocks became depleted, it was too difficult for the community as a whole to slow down enough. Danger signs were ignored for too long, and while there were any fish left, they might as well be fished for profit.

Here are some examples of the tragedy of the commons working in computer systems:

- In a company, individuals want a flexible work environment on their computer, customized for themselves. Thus their use of standard applications is configured to suit their work habits. But this decision, sensible for individual users, makes the supporting technician's much harder—everybody's computer configuration is different.

- It suits every user to work with a popular or common environment: more support is available (books, courses, technicians), and skills learned with the

33

common environment are more easily transferred to another job, and so on. The popularity of the system makes it a better target for viruses—the more common a product, the more it becomes a software "monoculture" that is easier for virus writers to target. Again, what suits an individual has undesirable consequences for the community.

■ Computers, and particularly the internet, allow people to work from home, to tele-work. As a personal choice, many people would rather work from home. If anybody decides to go into work, they may find the workplace practically deserted and no colleagues to make the day social. Although socializing at work is important for sharing news, the tragedy is that everybody would rather work at home. When everybody agrees to come in on a particular day, they are so busy that working at home seems even more preferable to the on-site workload!

■ It suits each individual and each company to ignore the environment. It suits me to have the fastest, best devices so that I am happier and more competitive. But to have the latest and fastest devices, I have to discard my older models—and so I contribute to the damage done to the commons, the environment.

1.13   Conclusions

Almost everyone makes a lot of money with computers, and interactive devices more generally, and nobody is clearly warning about the problems. We all seem to have a love affair with computers and don't want to hear about their problems! The market-driven solution is to spend more money getting replacements. For everything we replace, we end up with another computer to discard. It might end up in the attic. It will end up as waste—indeed as toxic waste. That's one danger sign. Another is how computers encourage us to make our society more and more complex—in fact, our laws (tax being a good example) are so complicated that it would be hard to stay in business without a computer to help. If the government assumes every business has a computer, then it can impose regulations that only a computer can cope with. Like the fishermen, we are totally entangled in the process. The point of this book is to help us step a bit outside of the cycle, so that we can think more rationally and make informed choices. As consumers, we should become more critical of computers and demand higher standards. This will put pressure on manufacturers to achieve higher quality. Gradually the world will become a better place—perhaps even a more magical place. (As interaction programmers, we should read on.)

Part of magic being successful is our manipulated perception, so we don't notice how the tricks work. The next chapter explores how technology and our perceptions interact.

1.13.1   Some *Press On* principles

■ Externalizing cost changes who benefits: improving a local problem may shift the usability burden to a bigger community of users → section 1.6 (p. 19).

■ Reduce, reuse, recycle, and above all rethink design → section 1.10 (p. 29).

■ Things break—if they are not *designed* to break they will be impossible to fix → section 1.10 (p. 31).

■ What individual users prefer is not necessarily best → section 1.12 (p. 33).

1.13.2   Further reading

■ Brown, J. S., and Duguid, P., *The Social Life of Information*, Harvard Business School Press, 2000. This book is full of insights and one of my sources for Moore's Law.

■ Christensen, C. M., *The Innovator's Dilemma*, Harvard Business School Press, 1997. The innovator's dilemma is that innovation breaks the mold and changes values. People who could benefit from innovation don't appreciate it; companies—and people—can get trapped in the old value systems that stifle innovation.

■ Davis, E., *TechGnosis: Myth, Magic + Mysticism in the Age of Information*, Harmony Books, 1998. This book goes into the deeper magic behind the surface this chapter skims; Davis's book is a fascinating review of human enchantment with technology, showing centuries of attempts to find deep meaning in technology.

■ Evans, C. R., *The Mighty Micro: The Impact of the Computer Revolution*, Gollancz, 1979. Chris Evans pioneered interactive computing after joining the UK National Physical Laboratory in the 1950s. His insightful book anticipates in detail what we now call ubiquitous computing.

■ Feynman, R. P., *Surely You're Joking, Mr. Feynman! (Adventures of a Curious Character)*, W. W. Norton & Company, 1997. The *New York Times* said this highly entertaining and stimulating autobiography shows that you can laugh out loud and scratch your head at the same time. Read it, especially for his essay on cargo cult science, "Cargo Cult Science: Some Remarks on Science, Pseudoscience, and Learning How Not to Fool Yourself" (which you can also find in many places on the internet)—and think about whether the interaction programming you are doing is cargo cult in any sense, and if so, how to do better.

■ Hardin, G., "The Tragedy of the Commons," *Science*, **162**(3859), pp1243–1248, 1968. Garrett Hardin wrote this readable article in *Science* popularizing the tragedy of the commons; he wrote widely on the subject, which is controversial—the original article at www.sciencemag.org has links to much further discussion. In particular, Hardin related the tragedy to ethics, a topic we will pick up again in part III, when we ourselves relate ethics to interaction programming explicitly.

■ Moore, G. E., "Cramming More Components onto Integrated Circuits," *Electronics*, **38**(8), pp82–85, 1965. Gordon Moore introduced what has become known as Moore's Law in this paper.

■ Norman, D. A., *The Invisible Computer: Why Good Products Can Fail, the Personal Computer Is So Complex, and Information Appliances Are the Solution*, MIT Press, 1999. Office desktop computers can do anything: they can be "information appliances" or interactive devices. If designed in an unthinking way, we end up with interactive devices that are as complex and awkward as PCs. Norman argues that we should make computers invisible. I disagree with his reasons (for example, his analogy of the PC as a Swiss Army knife, which does lots of things but none terribly well; there's no *fundamental* reason for PCs doing nothing well other than that they are badly programmed), but his conclusions are sound—unfortunately, lots of real devices are made like the worst sorts of Swiss Army knife.

■   ■   ■

Do an internet search for e-waste or for up-to-date WEEE (Waste Electrical and Electronic Equipment) advice on disposing of electronic devices, including PCs and monitors. The availability of recycling facilities will be different in different countries and locations.

2

Our perception

Almost everything we know comes through our eyes and our ears: perception is reality. It is easier for advertising agencies to modify our perception than to change reality. If something looks nice, it usually is nice; thus, advertisers create nice warm images to give us the perception that their products are nice. Since an entire industry is based on this premise, there must be something to it.

One example of our perception being used to mislead us is the promotion of lotteries. We all want to get lucky! Television and newspapers regularly report people who win big, and usually we see pictures of happy winners, complete with their grinning faces and an enormous check. Our *perception* of frequent winning fools people into thinking that *in reality* winning is probable.

If it wasn't for the media, our perception of frequency—how often something happens—would be a reasonable indicator of how probable that thing was.

Or, if in everyday life I see frequent murders and robberies outside my house, then it is very likely dangerous out there. But if I read in the newspapers about lots of murders and robberies, then I am perceiving lots of dangers, but it would be a mistake to conclude that everywhere was as dangerous as it seemed from my armchair reading—the newspapers have selected their stories from across the country. Unfortunately, most people do not work out what the statistics really are, and the pressure to "be safe rather than sorry," or to avoid litigation, leads schools, for example, to tighten their security because they perceive dangers to be far more likely than they really are.

Now let's return from the daily newspapers stories about everyday worries, back to considering interaction programming and computers.

2.1   Pyramids

We are bombarded by advertising and media reports of the success of gadgets and computers. For a while, we were told that dot.com businesses could not fail. Individuals like Bill Gates, who amassed a fortune, were held up as examples of the rewards available.

Pyramids have small tops and big bases. Bill Gates is at the top of one sort of pyramid, and most of us are consumers, pretty near the bottom of it. Because we each contribute a little, and the pyramid is so broad-based, a huge profit can be realized further up. The huge wealth and prominence at the top is a consequence of the base of the pyramid being so large (and, of course, that the business is basically making a profit; if its products were losing money, the losses would be huge too).

The bigger the pyramids, the greater the benefits for people at the top. Once the structure is in place, computers can provide a huge customer base. The organization benefits, and individuals at the bottom pay a small amount that *perhaps* they will put up with. If users complain, nobody is interested because the benefits of the pyramid eclipse the minor inconveniences.

When criminals use the same techniques, it is called "salami slicing": typically they find a way of taking a tiny amount of money from many transactions, and nobody notices the tiny amount going astray. With the help of computers, criminals manage to systematically collect the negligible amount of money but off millions of transactions. They end up with a huge income. When pyramid selling is done blatantly it is illegal, because our society recognizes that the "small" cost multiplied by large numbers of users creates an immoral *social* exploitation.

Of course, the more people at the bottom of the pyramid, the fewer at the top. Lots of people can own corner shops because the shops are small. Because they have a small customer base, the owners cannot make astronomical profits. When shops get bigger, merging into chains, they have more customers and proportionately fewer owner to rake in the profits. In other words, the more prominent and profitable someone or some company is, the fewer of them there must be. This is pretty obvious, but it is more than a tautology: as businesses become bigger, they have more resources, become more efficient, and can price their competitors out of the market.

What isn't so obvious is that once people get to the top of a pyramid and start to attract the attention of the media, they get lots more said and written about them. This influences our perception: because we know so much about them, because we know them so well, it's plausible that we could be like them. What's wrong with ambition? So just as it becomes harder and harder for anyone to succeed; the media, conversely, gives the *impression* that success is frequent.

Of course the media isn't going to go out of its way to report failures to put the successes into perspective; moreover, we are very bad at thinking through negative ideas. It's positive to win, but for every winner there are countless losers, and who wants to think about that? Hardly anyone buys lottery tickets *thinking* about losing.

2.2   The lottery effect

We hear a lot about the winners of lotteries, but next to nothing about the losers. When a business fails, it no longer exists, so what could the media report, unless it is an exceptional event, like Enron? When the business involves communication, it simply disappears. Companies that fail leave no trace on the web that they ever existed: there isn't even a boarded-up factory to see.

If we don't know about failure and hear only about success, then it is easy to conclude that success is practically automatic. The dot.coms rode on this positive feedback. If using computers makes you successful, then a dot-com can raise capital easily. Raising capital makes it easier to be successful, and it certainly makes it easier to get media coverage. Shareholders are bombarded with success stories, which in turn makes it easier to raise capital. The dot-com enthusiasm has burst, but it shows how easy it is to get carried away with lemming-like enthusiasm.

The lottery effect plays out in other ways too. If a web site asks for feedback from its users, for example, it will only get feedback from users who understand it well enough to get it to work. You won't get any feedback from users who are using incompatible browsers, because they won't even get far enough to find out how to send feedback. Worse, users who are in a hurry—which will include all the frustrated users trying hard to work the site—will have less time to provide feedback than the relaxed, successful users. The designers of the web site will hear lots from winners and virtually nothing from the losers.

For handheld gadgets, the same effect obtains. I've written to some companies about their designs because I feel strongly about either the designs or, when they aren't so good, about how to help the companies. But I've also had some disastrous gadgets, which were so nasty that I didn't use them long, and I certainly didn't waste my time working out exactly what was wrong with them. I would not have been able to write a useful complaint because I knew so little about the devices!

In everyday life there is a rather unsettling example of the lottery effect. We take risks when we cross the road. We base our behavior and risk taking on our perception of how safe it is to cross roads. But, in particular, we have never killed ourselves—so we think that we are going to be more successful than a full survey of the facts would support. Another example: we have all heard of dolphins pushing hapless swimmers back to the safety of the shore—but of course there are never any survivors to tell us about dolphins pushing swimmers *out* to sea to drown. We like to listen to the survivors' stories.

The lottery effect emphasizes success. We change our perceptions about our chances because we think success is more likely than it objectively is. The media enhance this effect, since journalists publish success more than failure, themselves biased by the lottery effect. Ironically, the media can reverse our assessment of reality. For example, you are more likely to die of a stroke than of a mugging, but because strokes are common they do not make good news. We believe what we read and are more worried about mugging than stroke.

As designers, we concentrate too much on success and on the positive outcomes (these, after all are the key selling points of our work). Particularly because of the lottery effect bias we should put more conscious design effort into avoiding problems and failure. We know we are bad at risk perception; the lottery effect shows that we are doubly bad at risk balancing—and design is very much about having a balanced view.

2.3   The media equation

The media equation is an intriguing idea from two sociologists, Clifford Nass and Byron Reeves, who argue that media equals reality. Millennia ago there was no media—newspapers, TV—what we saw and heard was reality. If you saw a tiger jumping at you, you either got out of the way or got eaten. People who got eaten tended to have fewer children than people who believed their eyes and ran for their lives. Thus evolution has favored people who believe what they see.

Recently (at least in evolutionary terms) we invented media, and as soon as we did, what we saw and what actually happened could easily be very different things. Yet our minds, the argument goes, are wired to react as if what we perceive is real. That's why when we watch a good film, which is only flickering lights, we become emotionally involved, and shed a tear or shriek.

I took one of my children into a virtual reality simulator, which was like a small cinema on hydraulics. We all sat in rows watching a film about a ski chase, and the box we were in bounced about as if we were skiing. The picture quality wasn't too good, and I looked around. Everyone seemed to be gripping the handles and enjoying themselves. But I knew it was all fake ... out of the corner of my eye I saw a tree coming right toward us. Aargh! Before I knew it I was screaming along with everyone else, and I was enjoying it. Somehow that bit of my brain that panics when it sees a tree rushing at it had taken over.

For most people, having a good time is more fun than analyzing the reasons for their enjoyment. We also try to make a clear distinction between work and fun so that it is quite clear when we can let our defenses down. You can enjoy yourself in a cinema, but few of us get the rush of adrenaline of real ski chases through woods.

There is reality, where things are serious and maybe a matter of life and death, and there is imagination, where we can do all sorts of things. The distinction is quite clear, and we tend to worry about anyone who isn't quite sure.

The media equation suggests that the boundaries are a lot weaker than we like to suppose. If something behaves like a human, we may well treat it as a human. We tend to treat many things as if they were human, and we respond to media (especially media that appears to have a personality) as if we were following human social interaction rules. We have a word for it: anthropomorphism, treating something as human—and we are very good at it. How it reaches into interaction programming will become obvious with some examples.

When we are with people, we are more polite than when we talk about them behind their backs. We do the same, it turns out, with computers. Reeves and Nass argue that you can take almost any psychosocial experiment between people, replace one or more of the people with computers, and you will get much the same results. In one test, for example, subjects were asked to play a computer game, and to rate it. Some subjects were asked to play the same game, but to then go into another room, where there was an identical computer, and rate the first computer. The computers being rated were the same, but the people were either in the same room or a different room when they rated it. The people rated the computer that "couldn't hear them" worse than the one in the same room.

People have different personalities, but we tend to fall somewhere between submissive and dominant and between friendly and unfriendly. People tend to prefer matching personalities, and when people of non-matching personality traits are mixed up, they do not get along as well.

Interactive devices, too, can appear to have different sorts of personality. "You *must* insert a disk," or "*Please* insert a disk." The phrases mean the same thing and could be said by the same part of the program, except one comes across as dominating and the other as submissive. You can guess that experiments show that people of the corresponding personality type prefer one sort over the other. What is more interesting is that a computer that mixes personality types—or, rather, mixes expressions of different personality types—will be disliked by almost everyone, because it feels inconsistent.

> ▷ Personality, particularly how it impacts design, is further discussed in
> chapter 13, "Improving things."

One of the classic, early examples of people imputing personality to computers was Jo Weizenbaum's program called Eliza, named after the very Cockney-cultured Eliza Doolittle in George Bernard Shaw's play *Pygmalion*.

In the play, Eliza is taught by Professor Henry Higgins to become refined. Eliza the program was a simple program that recognized a few word patterns in what you typed at it. So if you typed, "mumble mumble my dog mumble mumble," Eliza would respond by saying, "Tell me more about your dog," even though it (she?) hadn't the faintest idea what your mumblings meant. Of course, when I write "hadn't the faintest idea" what I really mean is that there was no matching pattern covering the rest of the string. Eliza can't have ideas, let alone "faint ideas," but it is so much easier to talk about computers *as if* they were human and have intentions, even when we want to say that they don't have any such abilities.

Weizenbaum's programming was quite clever. Suppose you typed "blah blah blah"—something that Eliza could certainly not recognize. Eliza would reply, "Earlier you said something about your dog. Can you tell me some more?"

Most of the time Eliza just recognized simple key words. If you said something with a "not" anywhere, Eliza might reply that you were being negative. To disguise Eliza's simplicity, each pattern (like "my" and "not") had several different responses that Eliza would cycle through to avoid obvious repetition.

There are now much more powerful ways of understanding human language than Eliza used, but in the 1960s Eliza was state-of-the-art research. What surprised Weizenbaum was how some people got carried away, as if Eliza was a genuine human confidant. Eliza's success inspired other programs. Parry the Paranoid tried to simulate a paranoid schizophrenic patient. Kenneth Colby, its designer, tested psychotherapists with it to see whether they could tell the difference between Parry and real human paranoids. The initial success of his work led to a heated debate about how soon computers would replace psychotherapists. It's perhaps ironic that these early experiments simulated—thoroughly enough to fool many people—what were thought to be deeply personal, and deeply human,

---

Box 2.1 Eliza meets Parry Eliza and Parry once met each other. Their conversation went like this:

⋮

PARRY	In my opinion, you have a one-track mind.
ELIZA	What makes you think I have a one-track mind?
PARRY	I used to go to the track every week.
ELIZA	What does that suggest to you?
PARRY	I avoid racetracks now because the races are fixed.
ELIZA	Is that the real reason?
PARRY	I'd rather not discuss it.
ELIZA	What else would you like to discuss?
PARRY	That's something I don't want to go into.

⋮

Certainly Parry comes across as the paranoid!

---

relationships with the most superficial of programming. Eliza is a persuasive example of how a simple text-based style of interaction can create and sustain deep emotional feelings.

Eliza's and Parry's believability is an example of the media equation. If something looks or talks like a human, we act and behave as if it is human. Weizenbaum's experience with Eliza was a turning point: he wrote a famous critique of artificial intelligence research, *Computer Power and Human Reason* (see further reading, p. 59).

Eliza-like behavior can be useful even with very simple gadgets. If you are unable to speak, a voice synthesizer attached to a device behaving much like Eliza would enable you to take part in conversations better than many other ways—you could interrupt and get attention using the same sounds and words as anyone else. If you stutter, an Eliza-like device could start speaking to get attention, so you can enter a conversation without losing other peoples' attention: you would just press some buttons, depending on how urgently you want to enter the conversation, and how much you agree or disagree with its current direction (so you can do something between saying, "Excuse me but . . . " and shouting "No!"). John Arnott and others at Dundee University have made such gadgets.

Of course, you'd expect an even greater impact if the conversation was held with a human rather than a scripted "fake," however compliant it was: and this is exactly what happens in role-playing games and in synthetic worlds, which allow people to engage in a rich fantasy, using only very basic language. Such worlds are further enriched by mixing human and artificial players—chatterbots, the descendants of Eliza. Interestingly, the objects one manipulates and plays with in these worlds (often things like wands, gold coins, and charms) behave much like interactive devices, in fact as finite state machines.

▷   Finite state machines are explored in chapter 6, "States and actions."

2.4 Drama

When we watch television, we know that what we are seeing is just flickering lights. But we soon forget this, and start enjoying it. Part of the enjoyment is not worrying about the TV's boundaries: we willfully suspend disbelief. When a character goes off the edge of the screen and comes back moments later, we would be wasting our time if we worried what they really did. That's not the point. It's theater; the point is to be stimulated by and to enjoy the program.

Now imagine we are not watching television but are watching something on a computer screen. The flickering lights are much the same, and we are entertained now not by some imaginary story, but by software.

Imagine you are in a shop deciding which computer and software to buy. You are looking longingly into a screen; the salesperson probably has some encouraging chatter about how sensible you are. It is hard not to suspend disbelief and be carried away with the demonstration. When you ask the salesperson a question, do you actually see the answer fully on screen, or do you have to imagine it—like imagining what a character does off the TV screen. You don't actually see what happens, but the salesperson won't let that spoil the effect. Obviously playing on our imagination is part of the power of sales: the salesperson wants to create an image of how successful your purchase will be, even if some of that success is imagination. You end up buying something that isn't what you want. This happens to everyone.

A programmer designs a system and shows it to the marketing manager. The marketing manager is now in the same position that you were in the shop; the demonstration is imagination, existing in the manager's head, not in reality. It looks good. The programmer might plead that it isn't finished, but the marketing department thinks it can be shipped already. When this happens, the products shipped to the shops you've just been in owe more to imagination than to reality. You are not in the shops long enough to find out: it's quite easy to make a program really so complex that you cannot begin to see how most of it works. You buy programs on faith.

When we watch a film, the film is exciting because of all the things that could happen. If we thought that the characters had no choices and had to behave as they do, the story would not be half so interesting—it's be without any dilemmas or surprising twists. Sometimes we know things that the characters do not yet know: they will open a door and be surprised, but we know what's there. Yet in reality they aren't surprised: they're actors; they've rehearsed! Of course, the film is just a reel of plastic, and there is only one story. Nobody has any choices. If you see the film twice, exactly the same things will happen again. To enjoy the film, we automatically imagine a whole lot more is going on, or could go on. Since we confuse media for reality, we confuse the narrow story-line for something with much more potential.

With films, this is the whole point, and a good director creates a bigger picture out of the narrative. With computers, it is a potential problem. If I show you something trivial on my computer, there is a good chance you will imagine some much

Box 2.2 Personas We can always think of more features, and if we are working in a design group everybody will have their own ideas. Soon the ideas get a life of their own—independent of reality.

A good design technique is to focus design questions on what particular users—personas—would make of them. Your design group (or you, if you are working alone) should decide on two or three—no more, otherwise it gets confusing and misses the point—"real" characters or personas. You should draw up their characteristics and make them as real and as personal as possible. Your personas should obviously be the sorts of people you expect to have using your design.

Once you have gone through this exercise, design questions can be focused. Would Jemima—use their name—like this? Would she need it?

Here's how we might draw up a persona called Jemima.

JEMIMA

Who she is:	Teenager
	Interested in horses, fashion, art
	Lives in London, big city
Her technology views:	Regular train user
	Good with a mobile phone
	Uses SMS a lot, but wobbly spelling
Her goals:	To get up early to see horses
	To get to school and back again safely

The photograph helps, as it makes the persona real. Was that last goal Jemima's or her parents'? What does she really want? What does the person who buys and uses the device want? We may need two personas to work this out.

After you've debated who you want your personas to be, they become the real people you are designing for. What might have been abstract design discussions can now be phrased in personal terms. Would Jemima like this? This person has a real need to get up early, but does she want to get up the same time every day of the week? Already you are asking interesting and focused design questions.

▷   See also box 13.7, "Scenarios" (p. 480).

richer tapestry. You will be most gullible if I take you through a demonstration sequence I have prepared beforehand: if I can show you something interesting where it doesn't crash, you likely go away thinking it can do all sorts of interesting things. Whether it can or not depends on how good a programmer I am and how much effort I put into it.

2.5   Selective perception of user surveys

Heathrow Airport is almost as complex as a computer program, and it is certainly as maze-like as many web sites! Here's a true story that illustrates the lottery effect in biasing Heathrow's idea of what a good airport it is.

▷ The lottery effect was introduced at the beginning of this chapter, in
section 2.2 (p. 40).

We were driving our car to Heathrow, which has four terminals. The road layout approaching Heathrow is very complicated. It's important you park your car
near the right terminal so that you can get to your plane on time. Imagine the
multilane roads driving up to the airport: over each lane is a sign, saying things
like "Departures: Terminal 3." Each departures sign has a picture of an airplane
taking off. We certainly want to take off and depart.

Eventually we find a place to park our car, and we walk down to departures in
our terminal. At this point we discover we do *not* want departures. Apparently,
what we want is check in.

Normally at an airport, you check in before you depart. All the signs along the
road to the airport primed us for departures, and now that we are here, we are
lost! Heathrow has no signs to tell you where check in is or how to get to it from
the departures area. So we make our way back to the car park, and then follow
signs from there to check in.

While we were walking back to find some signs, a woman walked up to me to
ask about my experience of Heathrow; she wanted to do a customer survey. At
that moment I was busy trying to find out how to get a plane. I had not time to
help her with her survey.

I then realized that those who would stop and help with her survey would be
relaxed people with time to spare. Frequent travelers, who are therefore familiar
with Heathrow, would tend to get asked more often than occasional travelers like
me who find the place a maze.

If Heathrow acts on the user feedback it gets, it will tend to optimize itself for
happy, frequent, familiar travelers, not for the one-off travelers who are hassled
and need all the help they can get.

The story illustrates two things about interaction programming:

■ First, when you get feedback on a design, don't just get feedback from
successful users. Hassled users can probably provide much richer information
and ideas for improvement. (It's surprising how many computer programs
and web sites do not even want feedback, let alone from successful users.)

■ Second, users are primed to behave in particular ways. Given that Heathrow
primes people that they are going to departures, it would make sense to
change the name check in to departures 1 and change the current departures to
departures 2.

People who themselves don't get lost (like the frequent travelers, the experts
who design airports, and even the airport staff doing surveys) don't understand
why anyone else would get lost. For them, it seems so easy. They tend to dismiss our problems as stupidity—which doesn't help them take our complaints
seriously. Not many disoriented users complain, let alone complain coherently—
if you are lost, it's hard to say clearly *why* you are lost; if you knew how you got
lost, you probably wouldn't have got lost in the first place. So useful complaints

47

are infrequent compared to the positive feedback Heathrow gets from regular passengers who don't have the problems.

For airport designers substitute interaction programmers. We tend to underestimate the difficulties of using our systems, and our evaluation of users tends to reinforce the wrong ideas. For many products, dissatisfied customers rarely bother to complain. (Worse, on web-based systems, dissatisfied customers typically can't complain, because the system is going so wrong for them.)

2.6   Software warranties

Standards have indeed been driven down to a parlous state. Read this software warranty, below, which I have slightly edited to make it more readable in the context of this book and to disguise the manufacturer.

It's a quite typical example, including the original block capitals (the italics are my contributions to it):

> You expressly acknowledge and agree that the use of the software and its documentation is at your sole risk. The software, documentation, and technical support are provided as is and without warranty of any kind.
>
> TO THE MAXIMUM EXTENT PERMITTED UNDER APPLICABLE LAWS, *the manufacturer* EXPRESSLY DISCLAIMS ALL WARRANTIES, EXPRESS OR IMPLIED, INCLUDING, BUT NOT LIMITED TO THE IMPLIED WARRANTIES OF MERCHANTABILITY, FITNESS FOR A PARTICULAR PURPOSE, AND NONINFRINGEMENT. *The manufacturer* DOES NOT WARRANT THAT THE FUNCTIONS CONTAINED IN THE SOFTWARE WILL MEET *your* REQUIREMENTS, OR THAT THE OPERATION OF THE SOFTWARE WILL BE UNINTERRUPTED OR ERROR-FREE, OR THAT DEFECTS IN THE SOFTWARE WILL BE CORRECTED.
>
> TO THE MAXIMUM EXTENT PERMITTED UNDER APPLICABLE LAWS, UNDER NO CIRCUMSTANCES, INCLUDING NEGLIGENCE, SHALL *the manufacturers*, OR ITS AGENTS BE LIABLE FOR ANY INCIDENTAL, SPECIAL OR CONSEQUENTIAL DAMAGES (INCLUDING LOSS OF BUSINESS INFORMATION AND THE LIKE) ARISING OUT OF THE USE OR INABILITY TO USE THE SOFTWARE OR ITS DOCUMENTATION ...

What does the word *warranty* mean?

If these manufacturers are so insulated and so well protected in law from their users' problems, they have little incentive to make good products. Worse, if they *really* think like this, then they evidently do not care much about their users' problems with the software.

The message of the warranty seems to be that the software and everything else is provided "as is," which could mean anything, and whatever anyone else might say, that's all you've got.

Ironically, some computer viruses come with warranties just like this. Obviously the people who write *deliberately* destructive programs want to evade any liability for their wanton destruction, and they take as their legal position the same wording as "respectable" software companies. They might be right.

I like to compare this standard computer warranty for a word processor with the warranty for my Cross pen. The Cross warranty is unconditional. Cross will repair or replace my pen if it goes wrong.

It's a different business model: Cross want to give the impression that they care about their product's quality. It's also a matter of customer expectations: a pen that came with a booklet of legalistic warranties, in lots of different languages just to make sure you understood, would give the impression that the pen, just perhaps, wasn't going to be reliable, or that perhaps you'd cut yourself on it or have some other accident that the manufactures have anticipated but daren't tell you.

Yet somehow we all happily buy word processors under these awful warranty conditions. They are supposed to be better than pens.

Actually, the legal story is far more complex than this neat irony makes out. The warnings—not warranties!—that come with medicines are even more worrying. With medicines, "side effects" are expected, and some medicines even warn of coma and death as possible side effects of the "cure."

So, compared with medicines, software warranties seem innocuous. Nevertheless, compared to warranties for complex devices, like cars or washing machines, which include complex software, the warranties for software seem a little feeble. Surely, we can design better stuff more responsibly. We should give ourselves better incentives to design better stuff.

▷ Compare these modern warranties with box 1.1, "The Code of Hammurabi" (p. 13).

2.7 Feature interaction and combinatorial explosion

It is very difficult to get design right, even if you *do* care. Suppose we've just built a word processor. This is easy to demonstrate, and it looks cool. Now someone thinks the word processor should handle tables. So program code is written and added to handle tables. It is almost certain that handling tables is easier to do by writing some special code that has nothing to do with, say, page numbering or running titles, since that is all handled in the original program. The little cells of the table can have text in them, but as they don't need page numbers or all the fully-fledged features of the word processor, they are easier to program separately.

Next someone suggests the word processor should handle color pictures. It should handle pictures in text and in tables. But we've just seen that these two contexts are two different bits of program, so we end up writing code to handle pictures in tables and code for pictures in text. Now we are doing twice as much work as we should: in an ideal world, there would be one bit of program to handle pictures, which would be shared everywhere it is needed.

It gets harder and harder to explain what goes wrong (which makes it harder and harder even to think through the consequences). When somebody thinks of the next feature, say colored backgrounds, then it takes four times as much work as it should. Then somebody will want to support Arabic, which is written right to left: so that requires a whole new text processing engine … before we know it, the program is enormous, and the various features combine in different ways in different places, which will cause feature interaction.

▷   Feature interaction is further discussed in section 3.8 (p. 74).

It may become obvious that a better approach is needed and that the program should be re-factored. But we've probably spent a lot of effort adding in all these features, and to start again means throwing away most of that effort. Besides, the delay to get all the features working together properly in a new design would be longer than the small delay to add just a teeny little new feature to the current mess. And so the arguments carry on: the program gets hideously complex, and it never seems worth starting over.

It ends up with lots of sensible features that occasionally interact with one another in peculiar ways. The number of ways in which features combine is explosive: this is combinatorial explosion.

Adding features, of course, helps sell products. The more features there are, the harder anyone finds it to decide which product suits them: this manufacturer's or that manufacturer's? If features were laid out and explained in an organized way, then customers could make rational choices. Just possibly, few people would want manufacturer X's word processor if they knew *exactly* what it did. But if they were confused a bit—but not so confused that they noticed—then X has as good a chance of selling its wares as any other. One of the simplest ways for manufacturers to use this confusion marketing to their advantage is to bombard the customers with half a dozen attractive features—without saying how the product deals with features that competitors are touting. Then the consumer has no easy way of comparing products, except on their brand or their pricing.

Combinatorial explosion is not just a problem for designers; it affects users too. Because of combinatorial problems, we often want to do things but it is not at all obvious how to start—how do I combine the many features the system provides to achieve what I want to do? I might want a picture in the top left of my page, but I can't get it to stay there. We know that the program underlying this feature is quirky, but that doesn't help! So we find an expert, who says we should use anchors—or something else. That's a really simple idea that has solved our problem, and in hindsight why didn't we know something so simple? In fact what the expert has done is to make us look like a fool. We didn't know something that only now is obvious. Conversely, the expert got some positive feedback about how helpful they were: they really like this software!

So the expert suggests that other people buy this software. And we will blame ourselves rather than the bad design that doesn't let us find out how to do things, let alone use our knowledge of other parts of it to bring to bear on new problems.

Box 2.3 Ralph Nader Ralph Nader was an investigative journalist who wrote the famous exposé *Unsafe at Any Speed*, which stirred up the 1960s car industry and was a keystone in founding the consumer movement. Cars in the 1960s were sold on style and appearance, and Nader found that many were unsafe and that, in some cases, the industry was covering up dangerous design.

Nader intercepted correspondence between insurers and a car company. Insurers were asking how to stem the increase in claims for accidents caused by parked cars rolling down hills. The memo said that bad parking was a driver problem, and that drivers should be trained to park more safely—for instance by turning the wheels so that if the car rolls, it rolls into the curb and stops. Another recommendation was for drivers to apply the foot brake before applying the parking brake: the hydraulics and servos of the foot brake add force to the hand-brake, making it grip better. Another view, of course, is that if the parking brake does not work very well, that's due to an engineering problem, not a driver problem. The problem could be solved either by training drivers better or by training engineers.

While the car industry hid behind the slogan "drivers have accidents," it was clear that blame would always be laid at the driver's door. Moreover, if drivers happened to kill themselves through "bad driving," they were an obvious scapegoat–who couldn't defend themselves. Some accidents are certainly caused by driver error (just as some aircraft accidents are caused by pilot error), but the driver and the car work *together*, and failure or bad engineering in the car can be just as effective a cause of accidents.

Unfortunately, if you identify car design as the cause of an accident, then all cars of the same make and model will have the same problems. Recall time! This is a very expensive business. In the long run, it's much easier to get everyone to believe that most accidents, if not all of them, are the driver's responsibility.

Ralph Nader's campaigning changed attitudes in the industry, and now thirty years later, car manufacturers are much more interested in safety. But compare historical car attitudes with today's computer attitudes. Today, it isn't drivers having accidents, but users having problems. The solution—we're being bred to believe—is that users should learn how to use computers better. "Life-long learning" is now everyone's right. Why? So that we can all learn how to use otherwise difficult to use gadgets! Wouldn't it be better if the engineers learned how to make things easier to use so the rest of us didn't have to learn how to cope with the complexity?

2.8 Demanding ease of use

Ralph Nader exposed a range of problems with 1960s car designs, from problems with brakes and sharp edges to steering instabilities. Although Nader's activities made him unpopular with the car manufacturers, he helped start the consumer movement. Now, as a result of consumer pressure, today's cars are much safer than they were in the 1960s: we have seat belts, air bags, side impact protection and more—because the car-buying culture has matured and seen cars not just as status symbols and as transport but as designed things with varying degrees of safety. When consumers demanded safety, manufacturers provided it. So why do so few computer users demand ease of use? It's as if we're still in the pre-consumer movement days of thinking problems are our own fault.

2.9   Cognitive dissonance

We may find an interactive device hard to use, or harder than we expect, but there are lots of careful messages in our culture and the media to reassure us that we have bought something substantial and easy to use.

Big adverts say that it's wonderful. The price is high, so it must be good. It came in a thick box. The box is covered with exciting pictures of features. (For a CD with no manual, why is the box it comes in two inches thick and full of air, if not to make it seem more impressive in the shop or in photographs?)

And of course everyone else is using the software, probably using more expensive "professional" versions than we are. If we read PC magazines, the reviews are always positive, though sometimes there are a few quibbles. All this positive marketing creates a tension with our private experience, or a cognitive dissonance, to use Leon Festinger's phrase—see further reading, p. 58. We don't like experiencing cognitive dissonance because it is not a comfortable feeling; we don't like being inconsistent. How, then, do we reduce cognitive dissonance?

You could stop worrying about something's lack of usability and *say* you like it. Concentrate on the two or three features that you do like. When you do have problems, blame yourself rather than the program. So, rather than think, "I have difficulty using the program, therefore I must be wasting money," think, "I spent a lot of good money; I don't waste money; so this is a good product. Indeed, I like this product that I so wisely chose. And therefore my problems can only be because I am a bad user or, more likely, I don't know enough about it yet."

In one step, as it were, we go from not admitting our complaints with the design of some product to blaming ourselves for our inability to use it. It seems it is easier to denigrate our skills with complex technology (after all, everybody has problems) than to let the thought creep in that we might have made a mistake buying it in the first place. If we don't blame the bad design of the device, when the manufacturer brings out an "improved" gadget, we'll buy it because we think it'll solve our problems. In reality, if we have problems with a device then the device wasn't designed very well, and certainly it wasn't designed for us, and if so then any of the the manufacturer's "improved" devices are unlikely to help us much more than the current one we have, which we are disappointed with.

If we thought clearly like that, manufacturers of hard-to-use devices would go out of business or at least they would soon stop wasting time making awkward things. Fortunately for them, cognitive dissonance means we are more likely to justify our wise choice of buying the device and spending time using it (or trying to use it!)—"that manufacturer makes great products"—than we are to admit we made a mistake because we were duped. We're not people who get duped are we?

> ▷ That children apparently find complex gadgets that mystify us easy to use is discussed in section 11.1.2 (p. 374), where we find out—not surprisingly—that this cognitive dissonance enhancer is a consequence of bad design, not our inabilities!

Professional organizations require their members to pass tests before they are admitted to membership. Often these tests check the members are skillful or

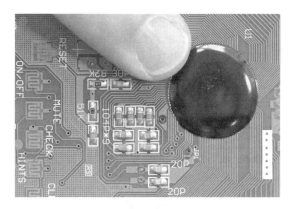

Figure 2.1: A finger points to the "chip" inside a typical interactive device. (The actual chip is hidden underneath the protective circle of resin.) The technology is amazing, it's so small, so fast and so powerful!! The gadget does so many useful things!!

Rather than being uncritically enthusiastic, one should also say that the device isn't easy to use. However, the technology itself is *not* the cause of the usability problems; for example, it would be trivial to make the device more powerful if doing so made it easier to use—there's plenty of space to make it more capable. In fact, devices are getting more powerful all the time but they aren't getting noticeably easier to use.

Ironically, the power of technology encourages devices to become over-complex, and too complex even for the designers themselves to understand fully. As technological power increases the design problems get worse, particularly as market competition on feature lists means "continual product development" is just piling on more features. By the time usability problems are identified, often the design has become so obscure that it is too hard to fix properly—and cognitive dissonance (see section 2.9: the design was a lot of work but usability studies suggest that it still isn't easy to use) leads programmers to deny the problems and blame users for their ignorance. In general, then, a root cause of usability problems and their persistence is designers' relatively limited ability or concern to manage the interaction programming well.

---

knowledgeable enough to work for their organizations. Midwifes, for example, have to pass stringent tests to practice.

Some organizations take membership tests to extremes: student societies, military and tribal customs often imposing gratuitously hard tests that may be physically challenging, even though physical fitness isn't necessarily relevant to the organization. When a navy ship crosses the equator, new seamen are often subjected to needlessly tough rituals—though the result is that the initiates are much more strongly bonded into the ship's crew, and in adversity they will all work much better together.

The point is that the harder the fazing (or hazing), as it's called, and the less useful it seems, the more cognitive dissonance rises in the new recruit to the society or tribe. The harder it is to join, the more worthwhile it is to be a member. If it isn't worthwhile to be a member, then you have the cognitive dissonance that you wasted your effort (possibly you risked or felt like you risked your life, too) by joining. So you decide it *is* worthwhile being a member—and in a society with fazing rituals, you then pass on your certainty in the form of devilish hardship tests for the next generation of recruits.

Perhaps fazing and cognitive dissonance explain why we are all so committed to bad design and hard-to-use systems. It is hard work learning how to use most things. The harder it is, the more time we waste, and often the more frustrations we have (such as losing all our work) and the more arbitrary things we have to learn to recover—much like fazing. Cognitive dissonance drives us into being committed users of the very systems that cause us anguish.

Large organizations often employ technical experts to give them technical advice. Who in an organization is likely to be the most committed to the hardest-to-use systems? The technicians—and these are the ones that managers ask for advice on what systems to impose on the rest of the workforce!

So, if you work in an organization planning to change systems, get managers to interview users, not experts (or perhaps do both at once, so users—who have to learn and live with the final system in any case—have its merits explained by technicians).

2.10   Persuasion and influence

Cognitive dissonance and fazing "just happen"—this is what people are like and how they behave. If you get somebody to persevere using a difficult product, quite likely they will cross the pain barrier and come out the other side a committed user of that product. From the manufacturer's point of view, product design should deliberately foster the user's final commitment to the product and other products from the same manufacturer. Manufacturers persuade users to be customers.

Throughout this book, we will see that design is difficult; design problems are in many cases simply unsolvable—designers have to take short-cuts and get good enough design solutions rather than "correct" ones. This is usually called satisficing. Finding the best solution would take so long (finding the perfect solution might be impossible) that we'd rather have an adequate solution now.

If it is hard for the designer, the user, with no special insight and no theories or tools, will find understanding a design even harder. The user, then, will also have to make decisions about design—do I like this product or that product?–by satisficing.

In fact, for life in general—not just for appreciating interaction programming—we often need to make decisions quickly rather than perfectly. It's better to buy some food and eat than go to a supermarket and spend the whole day deciding which of the various foodstuffs is best for you. If we are going to survive, we have to make decisions with imperfect information and before we've had time to fully reflect on all the issues. Evolution has set us up this way; if any of our ancestors

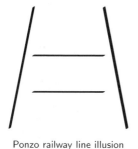

Ponzo railway line illusion

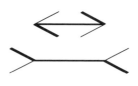

Müller-Lyer arrow illusion

Figure 2.2: Things are not always what they seem.

had spent a week deciding which antelope to kill, they wouldn't have lived long enough to have children and us their heirs.

So, like the media equation, satisficing is hard-wired into our approach to life, for very good reasons.

▷ People fall in love for the same reason. We'll make one more use of folk-evolutionary theories when we discuss beauty in section 12.3.1 (p. 416).

▷ The media equation was introduced in section 2.3 (p. 42).

As a special case, our visual system has heuristics to make decisions about things we see. The two optical illusions in figure 2.2 (this page), even if they are familiar to us, *still* make the horizontal lines look different lengths. Some people use these and similar illusions to choose clothes that flatter their looks; if visual systems can see lines as shorter or longer than they really are, the same illusion can make us look a better shape. Thus we suffer or benefit, as the case may be, from visual illusions (or enjoy them as party tricks), just as we also suffer or benefit from cognitive or mental illusions too.

We learn a lot of heuristics to help us satisfice more efficiently. (Heuristics are principles that aren't guaranteed to work.) Recall the heuristic of the media equation: if I see a lot of it, there's a lot of it about. This heuristic was good thousands of years ago but was undermined by the media, which can present our eyes with lots of cases that we don't experience directly, though we end up thinking we *will* experience something similar because the heuristic says it's likely.

In real life, cheap things are common; valuable things rare. It's easy to conclude that rare things are valuable. Indeed this heuristic is true a lot of the time; if there is only one nice painting, it's going to be more valuable than one of a million copies.

Another heuristic is called social proof. We think that doing something is correct if we can see lots of other people are doing it (that's the social proof); we don't need to check out the facts in detail for ourselves. Somebody will have thought it through, and we can just tag along. Social proof can get taken to extremes, alarmingly sucking us into what is called consensus trance.

Other reasonable-sounding heuristics are:

▷ If a group was hard to get into, it must be worth being a member
  → section 2.9 (p. 52).

▷ If schools teach people how to use difficult things, educated people should
  understand them; or, tools and devices schools teach must be well-designed
  → section 3.1 (p. 61).

▷ If a digital clock shows 24 hour times, it must be a 24-hour clock
  → section 11.1 (p. 368).

▷ If children can use something we can't, we must be ignorant → section 11.1.2
  (p. 374).

▷ If something looks symmetrical, it is symmetrical → section 12.3.1 (p. 417).

▷ If I find something easy to use, it is easy to use → section 13.1 (p. 446).

But, if you follow up the discussions in the indicated sections of this book, these
very reasonable-sounding heuristics are deeply flawed.

While using any heuristic makes us seem efficient and decisive, it also leaves
us open to mistakes and manipulation by others. In other words, we may make
quick rather than considered decisions.

Salespeople know how we think, and they often try to exploit our willingness to
rely on heuristics. Here I am looking at a car I am thinking of buying. Somebody
else comes over and says how much they like it and that they want to buy it—and
all of a sudden I *really* want to buy it. The other person looks fondly at the car
and mutters some sophisticated things about its emissions, its horsepower, and its
dynamic road handling. Wow! Now I have three heuristics triggered: social proof
(other people like this car); threat of scarcity (somebody else might buy it); and
authority (they know a lot, so they're right). So the car's value appears to shoot
up, and I am strongly tempted to buy.

If that other person appreciating the car was a random person, then my reasoning would be sound. But if that other person was a stooge deliberately placed there
by the salesperson, I am being manipulated. Being manipulated is not necessarily
a bad thing, though, I may end up making the decision I should made anyway,
but faster. I may really like the car, and it doesn't matter whether this feeling of
liking it is down to cognitive dissonance—I still like it. If I need a car and I like the
one I've got, then I'm happy and the salesperson has done their job.

In a different situation, a doctor might want to persuade a patient to change
their lifestyle to live longer; it seems right for the doctor to use any and all techniques of persuasion, however "manipulative," to intervene more successfully.
The doctor might give the patient a computer game or simulation, an interactive
device, to help see the consequences of their lifestyle. Or the doctor might give
the patient a heart monitor—a simple interactive device in many ways, but one
whose impact on the user can, and should, be designed to be effective. Among

other things, the heart monitor could use wireless communication to get the patient to make social contact with others who are using their devices successfully, thus using the heart monitor as a lever into social pressures and the deliberate triggering of heuristics.

Translate these ideas and issues fully into interaction programming, and the gates open to captology—a word grown from "computers as persuasive technologies." Just as visual illusions, triggering our perceptual heuristics, can make us look more flattering, captology seeks to make interaction more successful.

Interactive devices expand the opportunities for persuasion. They can be more persistent than human persuaders and they can be (or seem) anonymous, which is important for persuading people regarding private matters—ironically, anonymity can help overcome social forces. Interactive devices can also be everywhere and, like a mobile phone, accompany the user everywhere. They can hang around you much closer and more persistently than a salesperson!

The Baby Think It Over is an interactive device, a realistic baby doll, that interacts like a real baby would—see www.btio.com. It cries at random times, and it won't stop crying unless it gets attention, for varying lengths of time. It has to be carried everywhere. It is designed for teaching: a teenager might be lent the doll to look after over a weekend, and at the end of the weekend the teacher can get a summary from the doll's computer of how well the teenager cared for it. After using this device, over 95% of teenagers in one study decided they weren't ready for the responsibility of a real baby.

2.11   Conclusions

The Ponzo and Müller-Lyer illusions (p. 55) show us that things are not always what they seem to be. Similar, unavoidable, cognitive illusions conspire to make our perception of the world different from what it really is. To a great extent, this difference does not matter, but technology developments have put another layer between us and reality. Media, in particular, concentrates events and channels them into our eyes, giving us an experience we could only have had, until recently, if we had been there. Our perceptions are changed. Drama is the special use of media specifically to create the perception of a world, a story, that perhaps was never there in the first place.

How we respond to our perceptions determines how we feel and whether we like things. Whether we like interactive devices depends on how and to what extent they stimulate our perceptions. Some devices will be specifically designed to manipulate our feelings; sometimes, our feelings are an accidental consequence of design. The telephone started out as an aid for the deaf, but it is now marketed for the most part as a fashion accessory. A key part of successful interaction programming is to understand and either overcome or exploit perceptual factors.

A second thread in this chapter is that we, both of us, I and you the reader, are subject to the same forces. We live in a culture that has to balance the opposing messages that technology is wonderful, and makes lots of money, and that we are failures who at times don't quite understand how to use it.

Chapter 3, "Reality," next, explores examples of how bad current standards of interaction programming are—trying to take off our perceptual blinkers; it reviews a range of simple but familiar examples to bring us down to earth.

2.11.1   Some *Press On* principles

■ Lottery effect: we concentrate on success stories, and so we should consciously put more design effort into design for failure → section 2.2 (p. 40).

■ Drama: making something look good is quite different from making it work well when taken beyond the planned "demo" → section 2.4 (p. 45).

■ Don't just get feedback from successful users → section 2.5 (p. 46).

■ Software warranties reveal deep attitudes to usability → section 2.6 (p. 48).

■ Cognitive dissonance: the harder things are, the more users may justify wanting them → section 2.9 (p. 52).

■ In an organization, ask ordinary users not just experts what to design—experts typically know what *should* happen, not what really does happen → section 2.9 (p. 54).

2.11.2   Further reading

■ Cialdini, R. B., *Influence: Science and Practice*, Allyn & Bacon, fourth edition, 2001. The techniques of persuasion are discussed in a general way in this classic book, which is an excellent way to introduce our irrationality and how to exploit it. Cialdini also discusses Festinger and our need for consistency, the opposite of cognitive dissonance. See also Tavris and Aronson's book, discussed below.

■ Fogg, B. J., *Persuasive Technology*, Morgan Kaufmann, 2003. This is the book that started the captology perspective on interaction, applying the persuasion ideas discussed by Cialdini. *Persuasive Technology* is an easy read and well written—it has a lot of practical advice for good interaction programming.

■ Laurel, B., *Computers as Theatre*, Addison-Wesley, 1993. Complementing *The Media Equation*, Brenda Laurel's book examines the computer creating a dramatic experience for the user. There is a danger that by knowing how to make things more dramatic, exciting, or attractive you run the risk of ignoring underlying problems—though once the underlying issues are right (which is more the concern of *Press On*), it's very important to make devices attractive and enjoyable.

- McBride, L. H., *The Complete Idiot's Guide to Natural Disasters*, Alpha Books, 2000, is one of the many idiot's guides. The idea started life with computers, and now there's even a spoof, Dolt, T., and Dullard, I., *The Complete Idiot's Guide for Dumies*, Ten Speed Press, 2000. The success of the series says a lot about us as downtrodden consumers, feeling stupid when we can't use things.

- Piatelli-Pamarini, M., *Inevitable Illusions—How Mistakes of Reason Rule Our Minds*, John Wiley & Sons, 1994. The inevitable illusions of the title are the mental illusions that play tricks on our minds and are as unavoidable as optical illusions are that play tricks on our vision.

- Reeves, B., and Nass, C., *The Media Equation*, Cambridge University Press, 1996. The subtitle of this book, "how people treat computers, television and new media like real people and places," describes it well. Media equals reality: people respond (in interesting ways) to media like computers and television as if it were real. This fascinating observation provides ideas on how to make gadgets more attractive.

- Tavris, A., and Aronson, E., *Mistakes Were Made (but not by me)*, Harcourt Inc., 2007. This is an authoritative and very engaging book about cognitive dissonance, our need to justify ourselves and the consequences of doing so. It is an enormously useful book to read for its powerful insights about life generally but, instead, please read the book and when the book gives its examples—buying an expensive car, buying the wrong house, divorcing the person you married, the police arresting and interrogating an innocent person, terrorists attacking a country—imagine replacing those cases with the dissonant thoughts of being smart yet finding you've spent good money and wasted time on an interactive device that disappoints you. (Elliot Aronson was a graduate student of Festinger's.)

- Weizenbaum, J., *Computer Power and Human Reason*, Penguin, 1993. Jo Weizenbaum was surprised how people were fooled by his simple Eliza program, and the experience made him write this classic polemic against the excesses of artificial intelligence. This revised edition has a good foreword; it was originally published in 1977.

■　　　■　　　■

Read any software warranty and compare it with the warranty that comes with any other device, such as a washing machine or car. Your washing machine—and certainly your car—will have far more complex software inside, yet they work pretty well.

3

Reality

One of the most visible transformations computers have brought about is in calculators. The early calculators were enormous. Thomas Watson, the founder of IBM, supposedly said in 1943 that he couldn't imagine the world needing more than five computers, which in those days were hardly more powerful than today's cheap handheld calculators. Computers then needed air conditioning, special floors, and specially trained operators, and they cost a lot.

Today, calculators are small enough to be put into wrist watches; they are cheap enough to give away at gas stations. They are ubiquitous, and, it's tempting to think, if there are so many of them and even school children are taught how to use them, they *must* be good. How they work is magic, and this is where perception and reality part company.

3.1 Calculators

Casio is probably the market leader, in a market that includes Sharp, Hewlett Packard, Canon, and numerous other companies that make cheap calculators. So to be specific, let's look at two of Casio's models. Although I'm going to be critical of Casio's calculators, the same sorts of things could be said about the other makes. Casio's are easy to get hold of, and you can buy the calculators I am writing about to check the accuracy of my descriptions.

The calculator has a percent key, so let's use it to find 1 plus 100 percent. One hundred percent means, at least to my mind, "all of it," so 1 plus 100 percent should be one plus one—two.

Let's see what two similar-looking calculators do. Casio's calculator model number SL300LC gives 2 if we press the keys ① ⊕ ① ⓪ ⓪ ⍢ for calculating $1 + 100\%$. That is what we expected. Now imagine that we spill coffee over the SL300LC and need to buy a replacement. We might buy the Casio MC100, which looks pretty similar. Asking the MC100 to calculate $1 + 100\%$ *exactly the same way* gets a different result: E 0—there is an error, and presumably the displayed 0 is the wrong answer.

If we try another sum, say, $1 + 10\%$ the MC100 gives us 1.1111111, whereas the SL300LC gives us 1.1 for the same sum. You might think that this was rounding (1.1111111 rounds down to 1.1), but that isn't what it is doing if you try other sums.

Figure 3.1: The Casio SL-300LC. Note the highly visible self-advertising memory keys in the middle of the top row of buttons—imagine it being sold in a transparent bubble pack from a shop display.

Evidently these two calculators are quite different in their approach to percentage calculations.

I have used this example with audiences around the world. Well over a thousand people have been surprised, and nobody could explain why Casio should do this. And if there were good reasons to have different sorts of percentage features, why doesn't the calculator let you choose one?

Surprisingly few people actually use percentage, outside of shops, where they are always adding on tax. Almost everyone I've asked says that they don't understand percentage and they don't use it. In other words, most people think the problem is theirs, not the calculator's, and they rearrange their lives so that they need worry no more—they avoid using the quirky feature.

What is the percent key for, then? You can see on a calculator's packaging when you browse in a shop that there is a button there that does something. The $\boxed{\%}$ key makes the calculator look a bit more sophisticated and more useful. "With percent" can be emblazoned across the box to make it look better than the simpler calculators next to it in the shop's display. And we allow our perception of the calculator to overwhelm our assessment of its true utility.

Actually, anyone who doubted that a calculator did what it claimed could spend ages in the shop trying to assess it—you could test the problem I mentioned above, but if you are buying a different calculator, what should you look for? Moreover, if you are buying a calculator, chances are you are not very good at arithmetic, which is why you need one in the first place. That would make checking even harder!

Both of these calculators have a memory, which uses three buttons. The key $\boxed{\text{MRC}}$ recalls the memory, and if it is pressed twice it puts zero into the memory. The key $\boxed{\text{M+}}$ adds the displayed number to memory, and $\boxed{\text{M-}}$ subtracts the displayed number from memory.

The question is, how do you store a number you've just worked out in the memory? Pressing $\boxed{\text{M+}}$ sounds obvious, but that adds to the memory, so it will only do the intended thing if the memory already contains zero. To make the memory zero, you'd have to press $\boxed{\text{MRC}}$ twice, but the first time you pressed it you would lose the number you wanted to remember because $\boxed{\text{MRC}}$ recalls the memory number.

It is possible to store a number in memory. Here's one way: press $\boxed{\text{M-}}\boxed{-}\boxed{\text{MRC}}\boxed{=}$ $\boxed{\text{M+}}$, and finally press $\boxed{\text{MRC}}$ to get the display back to what it started with. That's six steps, and it's as fast as it can be done. (If you are cautious, you might worry that the memory might overflow, which is a problem that is not easily avoided.)

The upshot is that it is often easier to use a piece of paper than to use the memory. Yet surely the whole point of the calculator's memory feature is to make it easier to remember numbers?

Somehow the perception that the calculator has a memory and that it must be there to make the calculator more useful seems to overpower the reality. It is tricky to do these calculations, and it would be practically impossible to figure out in a shop, with pressure from the sales staff. You'd also give the impression that you couldn't even master a simple calculator!

Memory is intended to make the calculator easier and more reliable to use; if it is confusing, as it seems to be, then the calculator might be better off without the feature. Does the calculator need memory anyway? Consider working out a sum like $(4 + 5) \times (3 + 4)$—this is obviously $9 \times 7 = 63$ (we are using small numbers only so the example is quite clear):

1. Press $\boxed{4}\boxed{+}\boxed{5}$.

2. If we pressed $\boxed{\times}$ now, we would start working out 9×3, but we want $9 \times (3 + 4)$. We have to store the current number, 9 in this case, into memory because the calculator doesn't have brackets.

3. Now press $\boxed{3}\boxed{+}\boxed{4}\boxed{=}$, which works out the 7.

4. Now press $\boxed{\times}\boxed{\text{MRC}}\boxed{=}$ and we get the answer, 63.

So this calculation, or any like it, *requires* the memory features. If the calculator had brackets, we could have entered $\boxed{(}\boxed{4}\boxed{+}\boxed{5}\boxed{)}\boxed{\times}\boxed{(}\boxed{3}\boxed{+}\boxed{4}\boxed{)}\boxed{=}$ directly. Brackets, if it had them, would be easier and more useful than the memory feature.

▷ Section 12.6.4 (p. 432), shows better ways to design calculators to avoid problems like these.

3.2   Televisions

I have a Sony KV-M1421U type television together with a remote control, the RM-694. Sony is a leading manufacturer, and what I say about these devices is typical of any TVs and remote controls.

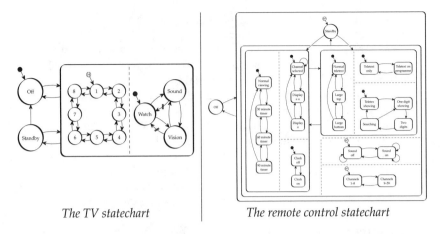

The TV statechart   *The remote control statechart*

Figure 3.2: Statecharts for a Sony TV and its remote control. Chapter 7, "Statecharts," explains them fully; for now it doesn't matter what a statechart is—just see how these two statecharts for controlling the same TV are very different, and that means they have to be used in very different ways.

The two diagrams in figure 3.2 (this page) show two statecharts specifying how the users interact with each device and the remote control. We don't need to understand statecharts to see that the devices are very different; even the corresponding buttons do different things. Some features can be done on the TV alone, some can be done on the remote control alone, some features available on both are done differently on each device.

▷   The television and the statechart diagrams will be fully covered later.
      Section 7.3 (p. 210) explains them fully and has full-size statecharts, which are more readable than the small ones shown in figure 3.2.

Although there is only one application, namely, the TV, you have two designs to understand, each with its own independent rules. If the television's user manual explained how to use the TV properly, then having two different interfaces for it would require a user manual of twice the thickness. Moreover if you become skilled with one interface, then your skill is of little use with the other: there is little scope for transfer of skills from one interface to the other. If you're accustomed to using the remote control, and then lose it, you will find the television hard to use.

One wonders if this is deliberate: people lose their remote controls, become irritated, and perhaps think it worthwhile buying replacements. Had the television and remote control been similar in their design, there would be less incentive to buy a new one. Remote controls are surprisingly costly: they are probably nice little earners for manufacturers.

3.3 Cameras

Cameras are different from calculators and televisions because using them be-comes a hobby and, for some people, a profession. It's hard to think of anyone (apart from me) playing with calculators as a hobby! Canon is a leading manufac-turer of cameras, and the Canon EOS500 was a popular automatic single lens reflex (SLR) film camera, that culminates decades of development from earlier models. Unlike the Casio calculators or the Sony TV, the EOS500 camera has a substantial user manual: not only does the camera manual explain how to use the camera, it also provided photographic hints and tips so you can get the best out of the camera.

The EOS500 user manual warns users that leaving the camera switched on is a problem. There is an explicit warning in the manual on page 10:

> When the camera is not in use, please set the command dial to 'L'. When the camera is placed in a bag, this prevents the possibility of objects hitting the shutter button, continually activating the shutter and draining the battery.

Canon evidently *knows* that the lack of an automatic switch-off is a problem. In short they ask the user to switch the camera off rather than designing it so that it switches itself off or has a more obvious way of switching on and off. The point is that two sentences have been put in the manual to warn the user, but we can read them as highlighting design problems for the designer: it's worth warning the user, of course, but it would have been far better to have avoided the problem in the first place.

Leaving the camera accidentally switched on is a recipe for wasting film. The next example from the manual is another example of potential film wastage built-in to the design:

> If you remove a film part-way, the next film loaded will continue to rewind.
> To prevent this press the shutter button before loading a new film.

Since this problem is documented in Canon's own literature, we can be sure that Canon was aware of the usability problem but somehow fails to fix it before the product was marketed.

Interestingly, three years later Canon released an updated version of the EOS500, the EOS500N. The user manual for this camera phrases the same problem thus:

> If the film is removed from the camera in mid-roll without being rewound and then a new roll of film is loaded, the new roll (film leader) will only be rewound into the cartridge. To prevent this, close the camera back and press the shutter button completely before loading a new roll of film.

It seems that the manual writers discovered that as well as pressing the shut-ter button the camera back must be shut too (it would probably be open if you were changing a film). It doesn't seem like the camera designers read the earlier EOS500's manual themselves; otherwise, they might have tried to fix the problems some people—at least the manual writers—at Canon knew about.

Canon now makes digital SLR cameras more popular than film SLRs. The digital SLR corresponding to the old manual EOS is the EOS300D (EOS350D, EOS400D ...), and Canon has changed its on/off switch design considerably. It is now a separate switch that cannot be moved accidentally, and the camera also has an adjustable timeout—if it is left on for a long time without the user taking any photographs, it switches itself off automatically (though it doesn't move the on/off switch into the off position as well).

3.4   Personal video recorders

The JVC HRD580EK personal video recorder (PVR) is old and simple, and it will be used as an example here and elsewhere in this book. The PVR's front panel has text two millimeters high, which is unreadable at arm's length, let alone from your armchair across the room. It has timeouts, so that in some circumstances if the user does nothing the video recorder resets itself. If you are reading the manual to try to understand it, there's a good chance that it will timeout before you finish reading the relevant bits of the user manual. Sometimes reading the manual makes a gadget *harder* to use!

> ▷ The PVR will be mentioned next in sections 5.4 (p. 145) and 10.3 (p. 330). See also box 10.1, "Why personal video recorders?" (p. 331), which raises the relevance of PVRs to this book's story.

This is a special (and rather perverse) case of what's called the system-manual synchronization problem. To be useful, the section of the user manual must be synchronized with the state of the interactive device, so that when you are trying to get the gadget to do something, you are reading the right part of the manual. If the section you are reading gets out of synchrony with the system, what you start reading will be counterproductive.

The Goodmans VN6000 is another typical midrange PVR. When it is playing or recording a tape and gets to the end of the tape, it simply stops. There is nothing the user can do in this state. Why doesn't the PVR rewind, or eject the tape? Since neither of these choices may be what a user wants, then why doesn't the PVR have a switch on it so that the user can make a "lifestyle" choice?

The remote control for the VN6000 has eight pairs of ⊞ and ⊟ buttons and arrow buttons on it. Although the pairs are visibly related (that is, one pair each of ⊞ and ⊟ buttons and arrows are on "rocker" buttons), few have simultaneously active meanings (they can be pressed with no effect), so at most four (up, down, left, right) would have been sufficient.

Despite having an on-screen help system, the remote control has a variety of functions (such as retracking the heads) that are infrequently used yet have dedicated buttons.

Box 3.1 **Turning the Pages** Housed in an impressive building in the heart of London, the new British Library must be one of the most civilized institutions in the world. It has the deepest basements in London, and over 300 kilometers of bookshelves on site.

Tucked away in a corner is a computer-based exhibit, Turning the Pages. Touch screens combined with photographic animations give people the sensation of touching and turning over the pages of books. The books are lovely works of art, and the touch screens give an impression much more real than using a mouse could: touch a page and drag it across the screen, and see it turn over under your fingers, just like a real page. The success of the system should not prevent us from being critical of its design. It is good but it could be *much* better.

Here are two simple things the designers of Turning the Pages got wrong:

■ The books *almost* work much like real books: you can turn over pages, and go forward or backward through the book. However, every so often you turn over more than one page—maybe some pages are blank or not very interesting. Yet when you turn over the last page, and you don't know which the last page is (because several pages may turn over at once), the book turns over and shuts. At this point you cannot turn back; instead, you have to start at the first page again! In an unpredictable situation, the user cannot undo the last action.

■ For some reason (perhaps the developers could not program mouse drivers) pages turn in a jittery way, and to be turned over successfully you have to move your fingers precisely. Some people don't and are mystified that the pages don't turn over—and once people have trouble, they start trying harder and are even less likely to move their fingers from the "right" positions at the "right" speeds.

▷ Both of these problems are breakdowns in affordance, a concept defined in section 12.3 (p. 415).

3.5 Microwave ovens

The Panasonic Genius microwave oven has a clock. The user interface allows the clock to be set to any number, from 0000 to 9999. Despite the impression that it may therefore be a 24 hour clock, it only runs when set to a valid 12 hour time, that is, when it is set to a number representing a time between 00:00 and 12:59. Nothing gives any indication why the clock will not run when it is set to a time such as 22:30.

▷ We'll consider the Genius in chapter 11, "More complex devices," where we will see how to correct its design problems.

3.6 Mobile phones

The Nokia 2110 mobile phone, like many others, has a menu-driven user interface, providing access to "all" the phone's functions. However, some functions, such as keypad lock, are not in the menu structure. Thus a user who does not know how to use the keypad lock (and without the phone's manual) will almost certainly be unable to discover how to do it. There is no reason why all functions should not be in the main menu, where a user could easily find them. If Nokia insists that it is a good idea to have a different way of accessing the keypad lock, it can still be done that way and be in the menu: there's no harm having a useful function in more than one place to make it easier to use. That's a design suggestion, but when you ask mobile phone users, you get the usual response. For users who know how to set the keypad lock, it's not a problem; for users who don't know how to set it, they've decided to change their lives—to reduce cognitive dissonance (p. 52)—so that they don't need the function or the embarrassment of not knowing how to use something they need. And then there are people who use a different make, and aren't interested in Nokia's problems.

We can criticize the Nokia's keypad lock design, but sometimes there is no satisfactory solution. In an emergency, you certainly want to be able to dial 999 (or whatever the national emergency code is—or if you are British you might want your mobile phone to treat 999 like the local national emergency number, wherever you are, so you don't need to know it), and fiddling with a keypad lock may be the last thing you are able to do under pressure. It may not even be your own mobile phone. Some mobiles therefore allow a user to dial 999 even when the keypad is locked. This makes the phone much easier to use in an emergency, which is a good idea—if you are in a panic, you don't want to have to work out how to unlock the keypad as well, especially if your phone is unfamiliar.

Unfortunately, if a mobile phone is in a handbag or pocket all day with the keypad locked, the buttons will be pressed randomly and eventually it will succeed in dialing 999, as the emergency services know to their cost. In fact, as I know to my cost, a phone with the keyboard locked will eventually unlock itself if it is banged around in a pocket for long enough—unlocking a keyboard usually is only two key presses, so it is easier to do by accident before calling 999 by accident. Once unlocked, your mobile phone can do anything, and probably does.

▷   For more on mobile phones see chapter 5, "Communication."

3.7   Home theater

Home theater uses a projector to give you a larger image and better sound than a TV. Although expensive, they can make pictures as big as your living room walls. You get a much more exciting, immersive experience than possible with a TV.

3.7.1   The projector

When you buy a projector you have to watch out for bad design. They may be noisy, which is hard to tell in a shop. Along with considering all the features and options available this makes choosing the right equipment a daunting process. I chose to buy the Toshiba TDP-T30, a pretty typical home projector. Most problems start when you get your projector home.

The user manual for my TDP-T30 projector runs to 32 pages, repeated four times in four different languages, but it does not seem to help with *any* of what follows. You have to figure things out for yourself.

You switch the TDP-T30 on, and it projects a startup image on your wall or screen. Probably, the start up image will be a trapezoid or other funny shape. Thus projectors have keystone correction, which can adjust the horizontal or vertical shape of the image to get a rectangular picture like ■■ from a keystone shape like ▲ (which happens to be the shape you'd get if the projector was higher than the center of the screen, as it would be if it was mounted on the ceiling). The projector has features to project its image any way up, or even backward, for rear projection.

The TDP-T30 has buttons on the projector itself and a separate remote control. None of the projector's buttons seem to access the keystone facility, so you try the remote control. None of these buttons help you either, though you notice that the buttons are quite different from those on the projector itself, and there is a hinged flap on the remote control hiding some of them. Some buttons have two labels, like [RETURN] and [ESC], and there are also two unlabeled buttons, one on the front and one on the back.

Trying to use the remote control, if you pause to think for a few moments, as you will, it reverts to being a computer mouse pointer. The 30 second timeout of the remote control is different from the projector's, which doesn't have one—so you are left looking at an on-screen menu but unable to control or dismiss it!

It's frustrating, because there is a substantial menu system. When search the menu system, though, you won't find keystoning. You quickly give up on the [Setup] button because it displays a big white X on a red background on the screen: presumably it does nothing.

It turns out that keystone correction can only be done when there is a video signal, say from your DVD player. *Now* the [Setup] button shows a menu and allows you to change horizontal keystoning. The [Menu] button still works and still gives you several menus—but it still does not mention keystoning. The setup menu shows both horizontal and vertical keystoning as options, but I still haven't worked out how to get vertical keystone correction to work (and I suspect it isn't possible on this model—providing it as a menu choice must be a mistake). There are several other features in various menus that do not seem to work at all, so it's not surprising to have some more inconsistencies.

Interestingly, as you correct keystoning when you have the video signal, the inverse keystoning starts to affect the menu shapes! In other words, although the technology can clearly adjust the menu shapes with keystoning, Toshiba chose to only allow correction when there was a video signal. That makes it harder to find out how to do it, since you might try (as I did) to correct the projection before switching your DVD player on—I mean, you don't want to watch your movie before the shape is corrected, do you?

Why, at least, wasn't that big but meaningless X explained in English, say, "Please switch on a video source to correct keystone easily?" (The word "easily" hints that you might even prefer to do it this way, rather than be irritated that there is no other way.) Almost all the other menus are shown in English, so it wouldn't have been difficult to do so. Why is a separate button needed for keystone correction when there is a general menu system that could do everything? Indeed, the range and variety of functions in the menu system fooled me into thinking that everything was in it. Why not redesign the device so the warning (here, about needing a video signal in order to correct the keystone shape) is not necessary?

So that's just setting up the projector. Now you want to use it. In my case, I screwed it to the ceiling, and that makes it just a bit too high to reach (which of course is why you want it fixed on the ceiling—to get it out of the way). I can switch the mains power on and off easily, but unfortunately this only switches the projector into standby—it does *not* switch on the light. The projector has a feature called "no signal power off" which I thought would mean that the projector could switch itself off when there is no video signal, that is, when you switch off your DVD player. But this feature is disabled: it's there in the list of on-screen menu options, but you can't use it. The projector also has a feature called auto power on, but even though the menu allows this to be switched on and off, I haven't found out what difference it makes—the menu seems to be misleading. The two features together, if they worked, could have been perfect: I'd keep the projector in standby, and it would switch on and off automatically with my use of the DVD player.

If your projector is on the ceiling or otherwise out of reach, you *have* to use the remote control—a design decision that, incidentally forces you to keep buying batteries (and disposing of the old ones) forever to keep it working. And given that the remote control is small, you are bound to lose it. And guess who benefits from you needing to buy a new one? Worse, I often find the projector still on after somebody else in my family has been unable to switch it off.

Guess what? Projector light-bulbs have limited lifespan (for this model, of only 3,000 hours). They are *very* expensive, about £170, which is nearly a quarter the cost of a new projector; and when they burn out they may explode, spraying environmentally harmful (that's the very words the owner's manual uses) mercury around your house—whatever happens, it's not just cost to the consumer, but pressure on the environment, whether it is sprayed round your house or buried in landfill which is where it will end up from most houses. Despite those problems, here we have a device clearly designed to burn out light bulbs as fast as it can, even though it has evidence of a lifespan-enhancing feature that has been deliberately disabled for some reason.

▷   See section 1.9 (p. 27) for more on waste and recycling issues.

I have no reason to think that Toshiba works like that, for if they knew what the wider consequences of their interaction programming was or if they had done any study of how home projectors are really used, surely they would know enough about the design to get the user manual right? The device itself isn't that complicated, so there's no plausible technical reason for the interaction programming to have become so unusable, as it seems to have done. So I read everything on the CD that comes with the projector, not just the printed owner's manual.

Reading the CD, I discovered that you *can* set auto power off, only you don't do it the same way as setting other menu options. Instead of selecting the choices by using left and right arrows, which I'd tried because that's how you select all other menu choices everywhere else, you are supposed to press [R-CLICK] on the remote control or [←]. For some reason, this is also called ENTER in the manual—probably a symptom of *their* having lost track of what it was called too, or that they were recycling another design.

On the CD, I read that auto power on feature means that switching the mains on switches the lamp on, not that a video signal wakes it from standby, which is what I'd wanted and assumed.

Why did I have to get to page 33 of the advanced manual that is only provided on the CD before I discovered all this? Would normal users persevere as I did?

It was only because I was writing this book and wanted it to be accurate and honest that I double-checked and rechecked the manual several times ... so I finally noticed that it said "For more details, please refer to the owner's manual of the CD-ROM version." Ah. Even now I'm still not sure that I've finished my discovery process.

So rather than having a projector that can switch from standby to on, or on to standby automatically with a video signal, we have one that can only switch off. To switch it on, we still need the remote control, or we have to use the mains power to restart it—but this risks shortening the bulb life, as it also switches off the fan. Furthermore, now we have set the projector to be as automatic as it can be, we need the remote control less than when it was manual, as it was configured out of the box. If we use the remote control less, we are more likely to lose it.

In summary, I suspect that this device has technical specifications sufficient to sell it—screen resolution, lightbulb brightness and so on—and that's all it needs to be a successful product. In the shop, I didn't notice the tedious user interface, nor did I realize how bad the user manuals were. I didn't notice the rainbow stripe effects of the projector technology either, but that's a different story.

The moral of the story is that bad design—which includes bad manual design and bad correspondence between device and manual—happens because there is no incentive to do any better. But the manufacturers could tell users (and shops or web sites) more about their products, which would allow users to make better-informed choices, and even to try out simulations of the products on the web—though of course to do this, the manufacturer would have to use a design method that allows them to build accurate simulations and web sites for their products.

▷ This book introduces a simple programming framework (not the only possible one, but an example of one) that solves these problems. The framework is discussed from chapter 9, "A framework for design," onwards.

Getting users to make better choices would put market pressure on the manufacturers to do better and to be clearer to customers (and indeed to manual writers) about what things really do. Well, maybe the fear of consumers knowing what they are buying keeps manufacturers from being clear about products before they're sold.

■   ■   ■

As with all critiques here, I don't write like that without giving the manufacturer a chance to respond. I found their contact email on their web site, and sent off a pretty clear email to them. I got a reply a few days later, asking me to phone their Projector Helpline on 0870 444 0021—so a human had read the email, I think. The phone number is an expensive UK pay number, costing *me* to call them. I did call them, and the phone was answered *immediately* by the words, "We're sorry to keep you waiting." Twenty five minutes later I gave up waiting to talk to a human. Thus Toshiba makes money from their customers' problems; perhaps it isn't such a bad approach to design after all.

▷ For issues relating to call waiting and externalizing costs, see section 1.6 (p. 19).

3.7.2   The sound system

The proper home theater experience needs a decent sound system, not just a projector. We bought the Sharp SD-AT50H, mainly because it's a small unit that fits nicely into a space in the room where we wanted it. Despite my being an expert in interaction programming, it was only when we got it home that we discovered that it's remote control was almost impossible to use.

The shop that sells gadgets doesn't want to lose remote controls, so they are not on display with the gadgets themselves. The gadgets are sold on eye-level shelves, so you don't need a remote control to try them out—they are right in front of you. The manufacturers know this, so little effort is put into designing the remote control since its design does not influence purchasing decisions.

But why does Sharp have a gray remote control, with gray buttons, with gray legends on the buttons, and tiny 1mm gray writing? There are two buttons with red legends, *both* labeled ON/STAND-BY. You might anticipate that a home theater is likely to be used in the dark, so what better choice of style than a color scheme, gray-on-gray that is unreadable in the dark? Why do some buttons have several meanings, yet there are four buttons for volume, and six buttons labeled ⩔ and ⩓, for tuning, tuner preset, and for channels. Why are there insufficient buttons on the device itself to control its features—so you *need* a remote control? Probably because a spartan device looks cool and simple in the shop, so you are more likely to buy it, not realizing that its simple-looking user interface is achieved by making many of its features inaccessible.

Worse, the meanings of the remote control's buttons depend on what mode the amplifier is in—and from a typical distance you might need to use a remote control as the amplifier's display panel is unreadable. As we've seen already—see section 3.2 (p. 63)—these problems are not unusual. Customer choice drives the manufacturers to sell on price-point, form factor, color, and a few sound-bite features. (They sold it to us on its small form factor.) The user interface doesn't count, and the user interface of the remote control is hidden from the customer until it is far too late for its terrible design to influence purchasing.

In fact, an after-market has developed that sells remote controls that are easier to use. "One For All" is one such remote control, which can be programmed to use

Figure 3.3: The Sharp (left) and One For All (right) remote controls, shown to scale—the originals are 17cm and 23cm (7 and 9 inches) long, respectively. The buttons on the Sharp always look the same regardless of the mode of the device; the One For All buttons have a back-lit screen that changes depending on what the remote control is doing.

the infrared codes for almost any remote-controlled gadget. Figure 3.3 (this page) shows the original Sharp and the One For All remote controls side-by-side. The One For All is a larger, more substantial remote control, with back lighting so you can see its buttons. Moreover, only relevant buttons are lit up in any mode—whereas the Sharp remote control provides buttons for your Sharp TV (I have no Sharp TV) that get in the way and make its interface more cluttered.

The One For All remote control is set up with a four-digit code so it can be told what device it is supposed to be controlling. It has a thick manual that includes a dictionary of companies and codes to try, as some companies (such as Sharp) have made devices that use different infrared control codes. Unfortunately I couldn't find a code for the Sharp SD-AT50H in the user manual. One For All has a web site, but you can't search for model codes like SD-AT50H. They have an email service, which provided me with more details, and—to cut the story short—I never found out how to get it to work, so I returned it to the shop and got my money back. I'm afraid that the process gives One For All no useful feedback, so the company will find it hard to improve the product; there isn't even a registration process with a comments box.

■   ■   ■

To conclude these two sections on home theater, it should be said that the Toshiba projector's picture is great and the surround sound from the Sharp amplifier is great; however, their *interactive* features are terrible. The remote controls are terrible, are physically awkward, and provide a different interaction logic than the main devices.

The designers seemingly didn't consider how their devices would be used, even though how they are supposed to be used is pretty obvious. The projector is on the ceiling, and the amplifier is across the room, both out of reach from where one sits. Yet neither device can be used fully using its remote control alone.

3.8   Feature interaction

When you telephone somebody, you pay for the call. That's the simple payment model. Then somebody introduced a new feature: conference calls. I ring you up, and there are two of us talking, with me paying. Then you ring up a friend, and we have a three-way conference call. Three of us can talk to one another, and I am paying for the call because I initiated it. I now hang up, and terminate my call, leaving you and your friend talking. Who is paying for this call?

3.8.1   Telephone conferencing

This is a simple example of feature interaction. One feature is the simple scheme for telephone call payment: the caller pays. The other feature is conference calling, which allows many people to share a phone conversation. The two features interact, and the possibility I've just outlined has to be worked out. It is likely that computer programs bill people for phone calls and the feature interaction described here was only discovered after a few problems! The problem with feature interaction is that each feature (here, caller pays and conference calls) makes sense in isolation, but they interact in unforeseen or unfortunate ways when they are combined.

3.8.2   Calculators

Sometimes features that ought to interact fail to do so. Many handheld calculators provide various features, such as, on the one hand, being able to handle fractions and, on the other hand, being able to do advanced maths such as square roots, sines, and cosines.

In fraction mode, you can add $1/9$ to $1/2$ and get the exact answer as a fraction (it's $11/18$), whereas in the normal mode $1/9$ ends up as a decimal and gets rounded. When it's added to 0.5 the final answer is only approximate, as there is no exact (finite) decimal number for eighteenths. In normal mode, you can find square roots of numbers. For example $\sqrt{16}$ is 4, and $\sqrt{.25}$ is .5. That feature works fine, then.

Very few calculators can cope with *both* features at once. Trying to find the square root of $1/9$ typically gets 0.3333333 rather than $1/3$, which is the correct answer. Worse, if you now square it you'd get 0.11111, which is not even $1/9$ to the original accuracy! (I'm assuming 8 figures; the calculator I tried this on rounded fractions to a lower precision.) Square root works fine, and fractions work fine; but somebody forgot to get them to work together. They forgot that the two features interact with each other.

A common feature interaction in so-called scientific calculators is that they provide complex numbers and all sorts of scientific features, such as trigonometry functions. But they don't work together. Indeed, few calculators that boast complex numbers can even do $\sqrt{-1}$, which must be *the* quintessential complex number.

3.8.3 Washing machines

Old washing machines used an electromechanical timer, a knob that could be set to the wash program the user wanted and turned as the machine washed, thus progressing through the washing cycles. A user could turn the knob to the program they wanted—delicates, wool, say—and once turned on, the machine would click around through the cycle and eventually go through the rinse and spin stages. Or the user could turn the dial to spin directly, and the machine would just do the spin part of the cycle. Unlike a set of buttons to press, the knob serves two purposes: it allows the user to set the state of the washing machine and it also lets the washing machine tell the user where it has got to. Since the knob rotates at a more-or-less constant speed, an experienced user can glance at the knob and estimate how long the machine will take before it finishes. An experienced user can also take control at any stage, say, to speed up the spin cycle if they would rather not wait for it to finish automatically.

When electromechanical timers were first replaced with fully electronic timers, the user interface was retained so that the new controls looked familiar. They had, however, a serious flaw: if there was a power cut, or possibly even if the user briefly switched the machine off, then they lost any idea of where they were in the cycle. The Indesit W123 washing machine solves this problem by keeping track of where in the program the machine is supposed to be, and it retains this information even if the machine is switched off or disconnected for any reason. This, then, seems like it is getting modern electronics back to the same user interface features the original electromechanical timers had.

Unfortunately, the W123 has a new feature, because it does not quite model the original idea. Suppose the user decides to take control and turns the knob to advance through the program settings—or turns the knob because they have just realized that the machine is set to a hot wash when they are trying to wash delicate clothes that should be done at a lower temperature. When the user has turned the knob, the washing machine notices that the internal state of the program and what the knob says are different—ah, there must have been a power cut, so the washing machine now automatically returns to where it was before the user touched it! So now the machine allows the user to think they have changed the program but undoes the changes the user tried to make. To make matters worse, the machine delays before it takes over resetting the cycle—so a user in a hurry may not notice. If you do want to change the settings, you have to switch the machine off and on again and wait until the "on" light flashes.

I'm never quite sure what to do because there is nothing on the machine to tell you what to do. You don't know whether the light flashing means reset or it's waiting for you to open the door. Here are Indesit's actual instructions:

> **Easy Operation** [...] instructions to perform a simple re-set [...] the programme will continue when the power supply is resumed or you switch the appliance back on.
>
> If you do not wish to continue the programme or you want to interrupt the cycle to set a new one, please re-set the appliance as follows:
>
> 1. Align the dial with one of the "●" positions, for at least 10 seconds with the appliance power on.
> 2. Simply press the ⸢Reset⸥ button for at least 3 seconds.
> 3. Set the appliance to any new programme you wish.
> 4. If in doubt always re-set the appliance as described above.

There are a lot of emphatic "easy" and "simple" words and a note that after you've finished, if you are *still* in doubt, you should start again! Notice that the user may want to do a reset frequently (in my household we do one every time we run the washing machine), yet there are timeout steps where *you* have to count up to ten or to three—and the machine itself gives no feedback to help. Why doesn't it just have a reset button and be done with it? Why does it need a reset anyway—surely it could tell the difference between a power cut and the user trying to do something?

▷ Box 6.2, "Timeouts" (p. 174) continues the discussion about timeouts.

In the good old electomechanical days, if there was a power cut, the timer would stay where it was. With an electronic timer, keeping track of where the machine is in the washing cycle is a problem, and Indesit's design solves this problem. Unfortunately, it solves the problem in a machine-oriented way and creates a completely new user interface problem: a feature interaction between the "power cut" *automatic* resetting and the "user resetting."

3.8.4   Mobile devices

Feature interaction gives designers and users more to think about. For physically small and mobile devices, the devices themselves may start to have problems. The most obvious example of unanticipated consequences is poor battery performance. The Nokia N95, mentioned in the introduction (p. 6), includes phone, cameras, radio, music player, navigation system and more, and has in a direct consequence of all its features such a short battery life that it's almost pointless being mobile—you don't want to go on a trip where you can't recharge the battery easily! It's surprising that the N95 and all feature-laden battery-operated devices don't pay more attention to the user's need to know about battery charge. How long have they got before the battery dies? How can they conserve battery power?

3.9 Ticket machines

Unlike most of the gadgets discussed in this chapter so far, a railway ticket machine *has* to be used: if you need to travel on a train, then you have to buy a ticket. The design is very important: the device is not a discretionary consumer product—there are no alternative manufacturers and devices for the user to choose. Users cannot take the ticket machine home and learn how to use it at their leisure—as they could with a camera, say—indeed, they typically use it when they are in a hurry to buy a ticket for a train that is already approaching.

Ticket machines are an example of the class of interactive devices called walk-up-and-use, a term that captures the idea that they must be easy enough to walk up to and be able to use straight away. This ticket machine, shown in figure 3.4 (next page), is an example of a device with soft buttons; unlike devices with physical buttons with permanent labels, this device has unlabeled buttons adjacent to a screen that can show different labels, depending on the context.

> ▷ A special case of a soft button is a physical button with two meanings: active and inactive. The state of the button may be indicated by a light.
> Section 11.3.1 (p. 383) shows some of the advantages for improving usability using such techniques.

Walk-up-and-use devices have a common problem: they are usually unaware of who is using them. If nothing happens for a moment, they need to reset to the starting state. Getting the reset timing right is tricky: if it is too long, a new user will be confused (because they are picking up where the last user left off); and if it is too short, a user struggling with the device (perhaps searching for the right coins to put in) is going to get frustrated because the device will timeout. Having sensors would be a better approach than using timeouts, but they cost more.

The ticket machine has a display rather like a bank's cash machine: a TV screen (of course it's a computer screen) surrounded by buttons that can be pressed to select choices. I have a "network card," a discount card, which allows me to travel on some routes and at some times at a discount, and today I want to travel to a station called New Southgate, taking advantage of the network card's discount.

New Southgate is not a major destination available on the first screen, so at the first screen I have to select the "other stations" option. A screen appears with each button taking a portion of the alphabet. For New Southgate, we need M–N–O (that is, a station name beginning with M, N, or O), and so a few presses later, as we go through the alphabetical list of station names we indeed find a screen listing New Southgate. We choose that and are given various options. Unfortunately the option we want (a discount with network cards) is not visible. One button is unused, but another gives further options, none of which have to do with network cards. Since one button is unused and further options do not cater for network cards, I conclude that the ticket machine does not handle network cards—so I join the line for the human in the ticket office.

I bought my ticket from the human and mentioned that the automatic ticket machine did not do network cards. I was told that it did! So I went back, and now that I was under no pressure to get a ticket quickly, I could experiment. I found

Figure 3.4: The West Anglia and Great Northern (WAGN) Rail ticket machine at Welwyn North railway station (just outside of London). There is a label "Easy to Use," the ten unlabeled buttons that do nothing, and payment slots that have pictures of the coins or credit cards underneath them. The paper money slot you *are* supposed to use is not marked.

that there is, indeed, a network card option available, but it is a choice given to you *after* you try to buy the ticket without a discount—whereas almost all of the other options are given to you before you buy a ticket. Moreover, the screen that lets you use the network card discount does not have a "go back" button, so you cannot change the type of ticket (you might want to do this after finding out how much it costs; say, you might decide to buy a one-way rather than a round trip ticket).

This experience highlights three design issues. First, the automatic ticket machine is inconsistent: sometimes there are "go back" options, and other times there are not—for no good reason. Second, some options are provided before you select to buy a ticket, and others are given after you try to buy; since you don't know where your options are before becoming experienced with the ticket machine, the interface can seem mysterious. Third, experts (such as the person in the ticket office) are oblivious to complaints about how difficult the machines is to use, since they already know how to use it.

The ticket machine does have a help button, labeled ⓘ, presumably meaning "information." This is not a soft button, so it is always visible. In any case, it provides misleading help. For example, the main top-level help, which is shown whenever the ⓘ button is pressed, is:

Using This Machine:

1. Select your destination.
2. Select the ticket type required.

3. Select the Railcard discount if applicable.
4. Pay by card or cash.

On the machine's help screen there is no full stop after the 2 on the "Select the ticket type required" line. I wonder why WAGN doesn't use automatic methods to help them—as I did using LaTeX for showing the example text above, which avoided this error. Every day lots of people use this machine, and a small effort to make the design better would have made a lot of people happier. Once you find a feature or detail that the tool can help with (like punctuation), it can automatically help *everywhere* with it, and therefore save a lot of design work, as well as improving quality throughout.

  ▷ Chapter 11, "More complex devices," gives many techniques for generating help text like this automatically. See section 11.6 (p. 396) for further ideas about building tools to help write user manuals.

Anyway, this help screen isn't helpful since some discounts must be selected before step 2 and some after step 2.

It's more fun to press the ⓘ key when you are wondering how to use a network card: this causes an error, as there is no help provided! The "help" says, "`Help not implemented for ContextID 0011.`" Yet if somebody wrote this help text into the program, they had *anticipated* this sort of error. If so, why didn't they check that it could never occur in the released product? There are only about one hundred destinations, so there are not even too many screens to check by hand, though a design tool would have helped enormously in the checking.

Since every destination has about ten variations of pricing, and we know that WAGN increases ticket prices regularly, surely there must be a computer database somewhere that organizes everything? If there isn't a database, there's going to be a big mess sooner or later. If there *is* a database, why wasn't it used to build a consistent user interface, and one where help was properly provided?

The ticket machine has another problem, which again shows how little effort its designers put into it. Suppose you are part of a family group: you want to buy a ticket for yourself and children. It takes about 13 key presses to buy your ticket, and then you want to go back a screen and buy tickets for your children. Your kids take 13 key presses each! You can't buy a ticket and then return to the previous screen to change the ticket type (from adult to child), let alone simply repeat the last purchase. Little wonder that the ticket machine is not used much, except when the ticket office is shut.

I chatted to the woman who'd bought a ticket just before me. She blamed herself for leaving her change behind. Her task was to buy a ticket. The ticket machine gave her a ticket (and a frustrating time), so she picked up the ticket and turned away. If the train she'd wanted had been already at the station, she'd immediately have been running toward it and not even had a chance to hear her change clunk into the slot. She had completed her task but the badly designed machine had not finished its part of the task. The ticket machine could have been designed to drop change before, or perhaps at the same time as, the ticket itself.

I then had a chat with a railway employee. He's not been trained to use the machine, let alone explain it to customers. There is an operator's manual, but he hasn't seen it. He has to empty the cash from the ticket machine from time to time, and the first time he did this he set off alarms, since he didn't know how to use the buttons *inside* the machine. The insight of his was that it was hard enough for him, but passengers have to learn how to use the ticket machine *while* they are trying desperately to get a ticket before the next train comes.

3.10   Car radios

Car radios are a familiar example of complex gadgets that may be unsafe to use in some situations. You are driving along and want to retune the radio, as might happen, for example, when you drive out of range of some station. This problem is recognized by designers, and car radios often use RDS, the radio data system, which transmits station information and allows the radio to retune itself automatically. So if you drive out of range of one transmitter in a radio network, the radio will automatically retune to another transmitter's frequency.

Usually the radio picks the strongest transmitter immediately, and you do not notice the change over from one to another. That part of RDS is good design: it's invisible yet does something useful—that used to be tedious when done by hand. RDS also addresses the problem of continuity. You may want to continue listening to jazz rather than a particular station, when that station changes, say, to broadcasting a news program. So RDS also transmits the program's topic. When you want to, you can use RDS to retune to another jazz broadcast.

Sophisticated car radios are harder to use than they sound. With my car stationary, using the Pioneer KEH-P7600R, it took me *twelve minutes* to find another channel transmitting the same RDS style of music. If I was driving, I'd have to spend twelve minutes not looking where I was going, though I'd parcel out the work into smaller bits over a much longer period. Needless to say, the radio has timeouts which make parcelling out tasks over a longer period almost impossible! If you start to do something on the radio and don't finish, the radio will timeout and go back to some previous state. You have to be aware of what the radio thinks it is doing, yet its display consists of tiny text that is very difficult to read.

My radio has a remote control about the size of a matchbox. Like the TV's (p. 63), the remote control works in a different way from the radio itself, but the real problem is finding it on the car floor. When you use the remote control, you have to point it at the radio. Unfortunately, I've lost the remote control, and there's not much more I can say about it! A remote control might be safer for rear seat passengers to retune the radio than for the driver, but if you are on the back seat, the radio display will be too far away to read.

Let's be specific and discuss some tasks that car drivers may reasonably want to do with their radios. For each task, we can make conclusions about the consequences of the design, and I suggest alternative design approaches that could have avoided the problems, which were *not* inevitable.

Figure 3.5: The Pioneer KEH-P7600R radio in a laboratory rig with its remote control and a loudspeaker. Usability experiments can be done without involving any car driving.

All discussion below relates specifically to my Pioneer KEH-P7600R radio and my old Peugeot 505 car. Experiments with the car radio were performed with the radio outside of the car, in a rig I made, that can be used in calm, "ideal" laboratory conditions, not under driving conditions with any of their attendant pressures. All measurements were taken with the car stationary. The rig is shown in figure 3.5 (this page).

If the driver wants to listen to music, here's what to do: Press the PT button (why is it called PT?). The radio then searches for an RDS channel, that is, a radio program that has the additional RDS information the radio understands (not all programs have RDS information). The RDS category the driver is searching for flashes on the front panel of the radio. It may be difficult to read unless the driver glances for several seconds at the radio—if the driver just glances down, the category may be flashed off, and the display will look as though there is nothing there. The driver needs to check the RDS category because the displayed category may be NEWS, say, not music. A category search for a suitable radio station, when stationary, typically takes up to 15 seconds.

To change the RDS category, the driver must press PT for 2 seconds, then press ⟩, then press ∧. This changes the category; then the driver must press PT, as before, to search for the newly selected category. This sequence of actions takes a stationary driver 10 seconds of full concentration on the radio.

There are now two choices open to the driver:

- The driver looks at the radio display to check which category is chosen (SOCIAL, RELIGION, whatever), and keeps on changing category until a music category is selected. The driver chooses music categories. This takes 15 seconds of full attention, plus the radio's 15 second search.

If the driver's search is unsuccessful (that is, because there is no JAZZ) then the driver must repeat the process. This may require up to 11 attempts, as there are that many different music categories. Total driver time is 165 seconds—assuming no errors and full attention to the radio. Total radio time is 165 seconds. Overall time is 330 seconds, or about 5 minutes.

■ To avoid looking at the radio, the driver can select each category in turn, then scan for that category until it finds some music. The radio will spend 15 seconds on each search—15 seconds for SOCIAL, 15 seconds for RELIGION, and so on. This requires less continual attention from the driver, but there are more RDS choices to work through. There are 30 categories, and in the worst case the one the driver wants will be the last one looked at. Although there are several music categories, there is no general music category; even OTH MUS means music not otherwise categorized (so, for example, it will not find JAZZ).

Total driver time is $30 \times 10 = 300$ seconds, and total radio time is $30 \times 15 = 450$ seconds. Total time is 750 seconds, over 12 minutes.

These times, five to twelve minutes, are surprisingly long, especially considering they are from ideal, stationary conditions without any of the demands of driving. If the driver makes mistakes using the radio, the times (to say nothing of the frustration) will increase, as will the amount of attention the driver needs to devote to the radio. If unable to concentrate on the radio, the driver will have to spend more time on the radio to recover, thus increasing the risk that the radio's timeouts will take over.

Having no timeouts would make it easier for the driver to pay attention to driving tasks without risk of losing their place in the interaction. Instead of timeouts, the radio could have a reset button: the driver should decide when to start again—not the radio.

To complete most tasks successfully with the radio requires looking at its display. Some indicators are merely informational (say, whether the subwoofer is on or off); others are relevant to how the user wants the device to perform (say, whether the radio broadcast may or may not be interrupted with traffic announcements). Some of the textual indicators are only 1.5mm high.

In my car, the radio-to-eye angle is 70 degrees (which makes text 1.5mm high as measured on the radio appear like 1.4mm), and my eyes are 80cm from the panel in a normal driving position. The UK traffic regulations, The Highway Code, require that a driver can, at a minimum, read a vehicle number plate at a distance of 20.5 meters in good daylight. Doing the sums, this translates to requiring 3.3mm for the height of text on the radio. In other words, even for drivers who pass the legal vision test, the radio displays are far too small to read.

Inevitably, to read the radio's status lights, the driver *has* to move their head closer and (in my car) lower: the driver would have to move their head at least 0.64 meters closer to the radio—very close. Doing so significantly reduces the driver's view. Special safe radios should have air bags in them: it's likely that the driver's head will be close to them when an accident occurs!

> **Box 3.2 Design blindness** There are all sorts of reason why interactive products fail to be as good as they should be. The simplest reason, and one this book tackles, is that nobody really knows what the products *actually are*.
>
> Sure it's a big program. And it's had features added to it so it does everything anybody can think of. But how do these features work? Can they be used together in all combinations? Is help provided for the user, and if it is, is it provided uniformly well? Who knows? Does the user manual describe the real system, or a figment of somebody's imagination that never got implemented? Is it even worth writing a user manual, because it probably won't be very accurate—and it will be extremely long to cover all the features it should.
>
> Sometimes it is too easy to worry more about the niche than the product is intended for rather than the design itself. We can spend endless time surveying the users, their tasks, their contexts, and how they run their lives with the devices we want to build. It is very important to do this, and there are various helpful techniques, like scenarios.
>
> ▷ Scenarios are discussed in box 13.7, "Scenarios" (p. 480).
>
> The people who like developing the human story of the design are rarely the people with the technical skills to build something well—somebody *also* has to specify the device so it can be built. That does not happen automatically just because a lot is known about the planned use of the system.
>
> If you build a system using finite state machines, as this book discusses (from chapter 6, "States and actions," onward), you will know *exactly* what you have built. It will then be easy to analyze, maintain, extend, and write manuals for it.

■   ■   ■

The examples of trying to use the radio, gone through in some detail above, do not exhaust the design problems. Here are some more:

■ The radio has some buttons that do nothing for several seconds when pressed. They have to be held continuously before they work, which is tricky when driving. It also means that a driver may hold the wrong button down for a few seconds before noticing they've made a mistake.

■ The radio has numerous features such as "FIE," an abbreviation whose meaning is lost on me.

■ The spacing of the radio's front panel buttons is about 8mm (and many of them are indistinguishable to the touch), spaced less than any other car controls.

■ Most cars are used by more than one driver, so the radio's programmable key with different meanings will cause problems.

■ Some cars are rentals, and the driver will not have time to sit down and read the manual before setting off. My radio has a 76 page user manual. It is not easy or even legal to read when driving.

In summary, this car radio may be technically brilliant, but it wasn't designed to be used while driving, and it wasn't designed to be easy to use. But it isn't much different from other car radios. The issue is why are car radios so bad? Like other gadgets, by the time you have a nice new radio installed in your car, and you discover how difficult it is to use, it's too late to do much about it, other than to resign yourself to coping with it.

3.11   And so on, and so on, and so on . . .

The list of interaction programming problems is as long as you like—you probably have your own examples to add, from bathroom facilities to web sites. It seems that every gadget suffers from avoidable problems, of varying degrees of stupidity, carelessness, and oversight—exacerbated by the inclusion of electronics and an apparently irresistible urge to make things over-complex. The tedium of reading about the use and design of gadgets is second only to the experience of trying to use them. Sometimes it is wonderful to get a device working its magic; other times, particularly early on, it is immensely frustrating. This frustration, if you eventually succeed, turns into commitment.

> ▷   Some of the reasons behind this powerful transition were reviewed in
> section 2.9 (p. 52), where we introduced the concept of cognitive dissonance.

Nobody complains enough about bad user interfaces, or if they do, they are made to feel inadequate by the young nimble-fingered sales consultant. Bad design is often far too difficult to explain to complain about! I have a camcorder that is so confusing that you would not have the patience to read about it, and no shop would understand why I couldn't figure it out. By saying that I fall into the trap of blaming myself: the camcorder is not so much a design that confuses *me* as a confused design that's confused *itself*.

Indeed, one of the problems in discussing design problems is that everything is idiosyncratic, and it is hard to describe what is wrong with anything concisely without getting deeply boring or sounding unnecessarily pedantic—unfortunately, it's easiest for most people not to worry. After all, these things are *magic*, aren't they?

One might argue that it does not really matter how difficult cameras, televisions, or mobile phones are to use: the fact that we buy plenty of them shows that they are good enough. We might worry a bit more about calculators, but then aren't children supposed to be *taught* how to use them properly? Same goes for any safety-critical systems. Pilots, nurses and other professionals should be taught to use them properly. So—if we wish to fool ourselves—we do not need to improve design.

3.12   Not just difficult, but different

Some design quirks we might put down to business strategy. If the Nokia mobile phone has a unique user interface that people get used to, then there is a good chance that when they buy a new mobile phone, they will prefer Nokia over some other company's design. No doubt users of Motorola, Siemens, and the others think the same way, and thus there is little incentive for standardization. Yet the lack of a decent user interface is bizarre when you compare it with the design of the radio part of the mobile phone. These phones can work all over the world in all sorts of conditions. If a phone did not work on a South African network, you'd want your money back, or the manufacturer would lose a country from its market.

Devices are not just difficult to use, they are *different* from one another, and the differences in themselves make them harder to use. At a hospital, there will be a range of devices for infusion pumps made by different manufacturers—and they all work in different ways. Even devices from the same manufacturer work in bewilderingly different ways. Nurses and doctors cannot be expected to understand the variety of user interfaces. A nurse might know how device *A* works, and next they are dealing with a patient using device *B*. That patient will be lucky if the nurse does the right things with the actual device delivering drugs to them—especially if there is an emergency and the nurse is under pressure.

The design differences have an interesting effect. The people who master a device form themselves into a community of like-minded people. Thus, I talk to people who use Macintoshes; other people stick to PCs. I talk to people who use Nokia phones, and I don't understand people who use Samsung—they do what I do, but they do it differently, so we talk different languages and form different communities. People rarely bridge communities and see things differently. Designers have to try harder.

Interactive devices clearly fall along a spectrum. A mobile phone may be a fashion accessory, and it doesn't matter that they are all different or "special." At the other end are safety-critical devices like medical equipment and interactive gadgets in aircraft cockpits. These have to be highly standardized for safety reasons. The problem is that the magical success of the fashion end of devices leaks into the other end; apparently successful design ideas we're all familiar with end up becoming the implicit standards at the safety-critical end. Indeed, any modern aircraft is full of user interfaces that would make our PVR or camcorder look easy.

3.13   User problems

Problems users have with gadgets and computers are naturally classified as *the user's problems*. Users believe that since they make mistakes (even though poor design encourages them to do so), they are responsible. They should buy upgrades, training, or perhaps get their children to use the systems for them. Seldom is the problem seen to lie with the design itself. Rather, it's something users can apparently buy themselves out of, thus giving more profit to the manufacturers. Ironically, manufacturers charge users for help-lines and bug fixes. Some manufacturers provide certification processes for experts to qualify themselves with, thus creating a hierarchy of skills, that consumers pay to climb! There is little incentive for design to improve when users are so keen to pay repeatedly for bad design. When we know that some users find things easy that we find hard, then that seems to confirm it's all our fault. Children are supposed to be very good at using modern interactive gadgets, so—the myth goes—we must be too old if we have problems.

    ▷   This myth is debunked in section 11.1.2 (p. 374).

3.14 Even "simple" design isn't

Perhaps all of this chapter has seemed to be liberally casting blame around. This final section shows that even very simple design raises deep questions; design is intrinsically difficult. What could be simpler than a light switch?

A typical toggle switch has a "toggle" that can be in one of two possible positions, up or down. The light a toggle switch controls can also be in one of two states, on or off, so there are two natural ways to connect the switch to the lights. One way is "toggle up/light on and toggle down/light off," which is what Americans like, and the other way is "toggle up/light off and toggle down/light on" which is what the British like. (There are more ways, but then the two states of the switch would not control the two states of the light: these ways would be considered a power failure, a faulty bulb, or a wiring fault if they occurred in practice.)

In Britain, the conventional choice is that down for a switch is on, and up is off. In the United States, the convention is reversed. If you know the convention, you can look at a toggle switch and decide what to do just by knowing whether you want the light on or off. You can also diagnose problems: thus if the toggle is down but the light is off, there is a fault, or you are in the wrong country—or possibly both.

In contrast, a push switch changes what it does each time it is pushed, and it never looks up or down. The switches in figure 3.6 (facing page) look identical to toggle switches, but they are in fact push switches.

For a single switch and single light, it isn't obvious which sort of switch is easier to use. If a user wishes to change the state of a light, using a push switch means they have only one action, namely, *push*. The user has half the number of actions to choose from to achieve any goal, whether to switch the light on or off. If the switch is a toggle switch, then the user decides whether to change the light to on or off, and flips the switch accordingly. Both choices have potential, but quite different, problems:

- A common problem with a push switch occurs when there is a delay in the light it controls (it might be a fluorescent light warming up): if the user is not sure that they have pushed, or pushed hard enough, then they may push again, and of course this action may return the light to its initial state, which the user wanted to change.

    ▷   This problem is an "overrun error"; see section 10.4.1 (p. 341).

- For a toggle switch, you need to know what your users will expect up and down to do.

Figure 3.6: Three push switches on a wall (which look like rocker switches). Each switch controls a different row of lights. How do they control the rows?

An unfamiliar switch is easier if it is a push switch, unless it controls a slow light, but a switch you are familiar with is easier as a toggle switch. We now understand *single* switches!

Sometimes a single light is wired to two or more switches that each separately control it. This is typical for stair lighting, where there are often separate switches at the top and bottom of stairs. How each switch works in a pair is changed when the other is used: if one toggle is changed, the other switch has essentially changed from a US to a UK orientation or vice versa. Now a user cannot look at either switch alone and know whether the light should be on or off. Thus, for stair lighting, using a push switch is preferable, since it removes this confusion. By the same argument stair lights should be of the sort that come on instantly, so that the user does not get confused and make overrun errors.

The three switches in the photograph are in my laboratory. They are push switches, mounted on the wall in a single bank. The lab has three rows of fluorescent lights on the ceiling, and each switch controls a different row of ceiling lights. Now we have a new problem: which switch controls which row of lights? There is nothing that says or suggests how they are related; in fact, they could be wired up in six different ways—and that's assuming we know that what orientation the rows of lights on the ceiling are in; there could be many ways if the room is wired up in an unconventional way, for instance, with spot lights.

Suppose your task is to switch on the front row of lights, but leave the rest of the lighting unchanged. You might start by pressing the leftmost switch. If a row of lights goes out, you should press the switch again to put that row of lights you accidentally switched off back on again. If nothing happens, you need to wait, because of the delays in lights changing. If the wrong bank of lights comes on after a delay (how long should you wait?), you must press it again. If so far you have not got the front row of lights on, you must try another push switch. If you are unlucky with the second, you will have to try the third switch too. If you are really unlucky and end up trying all of them but not finding out how to switch the row of lights on, perhaps you did not wait long enough when you pushed a switch a second time, and you will now have to start again, but wait longer after each push. Or, as often happens, you might change your mind and decide that you like the front row of lights off.

The order of the switches tells us nothing—the switch is vertical on a wall running east-west, and the rows of lights are horizontal on the ceiling running north-south. You can probably guess the middle switch controls the middle row of lights, but if you are not familiar with this room, you can't easily distinguish the middle row anyway.

In contrast, if the three switches had been toggle switches, we would know whether rows of lights were on or off. If our task was again to switch the front row of lights on, and two switches were in the on state and one off, it would be obvious what to do, namely, change the single off switch to its on position.

What have we learned? A single push switch and light combination is arguably easier to use than a toggle switch, and the advantages are more apparent when two (or more) switches control a single light. However, when several push switches control several lights, it inevitably becomes harder to use. On the other hand, toggle switches make most multiple switch banks easier to use.

Design does not stop there. We could have push switches with indicator lights on each switch. Now we have the advantage of a push switch ("just push") with the state-indicating clarity of a toggle switch, but now it is a light. An indicator light makes the switch safer, since then a user could reliably turn lights off as a precaution when replacing a faulty light bulb. Unfortunately, lights on switches can have other, conflicting, purposes: they are useful to help locate a switch in the dark, so they are usually on when the controlled light is off!

3.15   Conclusions

As this chapter shows, user interface design problems are everywhere. The stories may be so familiar that the reaction is to sigh. We've heard it all before—that's just how it is. We're in denial—several of the examples had "easy to use" labels on them or similar slogans in their user manuals. It will take effort, driven by consumer pressure, legislation, motivated designers, informed managers in the industry, and skilled designers, to make a difference.

The implicit theme of this chapter is that we must understand problems with user interfaces to be in a position to improve them.

Did you find this chapter interesting, or were the examples tedious and difficult to follow? Ironically, the more tedious the examples, the more important it is to fix the problems they describe. If it is hard to explain what is going wrong, even to a designer, it must be even harder to use. Quite often, one expects that conventional design processes never uncover problems that are too difficult to put into words—especially when a lot of conventional design processes rely on user involvement, and users have not been trained to explain complex design issues.

I'm sorry this chapter has been long and tedious. The point the tedium made is that we would be better off if we could avoid these sorts of problems, rather than live in a world where it is too late to avoid them. Instead of being negative and critical, we need to turn to positive ways to make systems better, which we do in part II, after the transitional chapter 4, next, which takes us from critique to framing a program of action.

3.15.1 Some *Press On* principles

- Convoluted user manuals are an indicator of bad design → section 3.3 (p. 65).

- Timeouts are often bad for users → section 3.4 (p. 66).

- Design for the user's task, activities, and context → section 3.10 (p. 83).

3.15.2 Further reading

- Harel, D., *Computers Ltd. What They Really Can't Do*, Oxford University Press, 2000. Most books on user interface design and interactive systems design concentrate on psychology and human factors. It's easy to forget what the computer can and can't do and how difficult computers find some things. David Harel's book is an excellent and definitive introduction to the limitations of computers.

- Jackson, T., *Inside Intel*, Harper Collins, 1998. If this is how the IT industry really works, then the moral issues that Ralph Nader exposed in his *Unsafe at Any Speed* are still around.

- Nader, R., *Unsafe at Any Speed: The Designed-in Dangers of the American Automobile*, revised ed., Bantam Books, 1973. This is the small book that made the car industry take safety seriously; for "car" read "interactive device" and shudder.

- Postman, N., *Technopoly*, Vintage, 1993. According to Postman, the uncontrolled growth of technology destroys the vital sources of our humanity. It creates a culture without moral foundation, with problems that create more problems. *Technopoly* is about the problems of this chapter writ on the large fabric of national culture, politics, and big systems.

- Weiner, L. R., *Digital Woes*, Perseus Publishing, 1994. If my one chapter on problems wasn't enough, this is an entire book—and quite scary at that.

4

Transition to interaction programming

Interaction programming is not just about identifying and understanding problems, which we belabored in the preceding chapters; it's about finding methods and processes to build good systems and to improve existing systems. As designers, we don't want to moan, but make the world a better place.

This chapter provides a brief overview of the wide field of human-computer interaction (also called interaction design and other names), preparing the ground for the next part of this book, part II, which concentrates on interaction programming and programming principles and what they can do.

Of course, better interaction programming is not the only way to help tackle the problems we've seen, so this chapter has a substantial further reading section to introduce the vast and diverse body of literature about interaction programming and related subjects.

4.1 What's in a field?

There are many ways to look at any issue. Take the question, why is my shirt red? To a physicist, it is red because it reflects red light of a certain wavelength. To a psychologist or neurologist, it is red because the retinas in your eyes respond to the red light, and you see a red shirt. A chemist might say the shirt is red because it is dyed with chemicals that absorb and reflect light so it appears red. A linguist would say it is red because you use the word red to denote a particular sort of visual perception. Maybe it isn't really red at all: it's possible that the shirt is in fact white but is bathed in red light so it only looks red. A quite different sort of reason—equally valid—is that my wife bought it for me and thought I would enjoy wearing a red shirt.

If people had not worked to manufacture it, transport it, market and sell it, then there would have been no red shirt to buy in the first place. My shirt is red because red shirts sell. However, the shirt I am actually wearing now is blue: the "red shirt" was a narrative fiction so that I could write the previous paragraphs and make a nice story.

Whichever one of these reasons you prefer—physical, chemical, philosophical, emotional, economic, or fiction—they certainly don't begin to exhaust the explanations for my shirt being red.

Even the simplest of questions have many answers. Instead of shirts, it could have been anything—this is the doctrine of multiple representations. Similarly, there are very many ways to look at interaction programming. We interact with devices. There are psychological stories about our experiences; there are choices made by designers; the devices themselves work because of electronics; and so on. The field of interaction programming allows and covers all of these explanations. All are valid, and emphasize different features of interaction. Are we interested in the user's experience? Are we interested in the technicalities of the microprocessor? Are we interested in the shape and physical features of the gadget? We relish this wide range of points of view in interaction programming because of the field's history and because each is important.

During World War II, people became acutely aware of the crucial role of interaction between people and complex machines. Decoding the Enigma, the German code machine, can claim the first explicit human factors insight: the Herival Tip, that operators would tend to make predictable slips that gave away clues on their secret codes—John Herival's insight revolutionized decryption in 1940. Aircraft pushed pilots to their limits, and it was obvious that some problems were caused by bad design, which had ignored the user, the human factors. Specialists soon tried to understand how people operate machines, and how to design machines to make them easier and more reliable. Ergonomics, or Human Factors in the United States, developed quickly.

During the 1950s it became increasingly obvious that the interaction of people and computers, which were then a new sort of machine, posed an important area for the very practical reasons that many problems and surprises again seemed to originate in engineering decisions. The field of man-machine interaction, or man-machine interface (MMI, conveniently, is the same abbreviation for both), grew up in the 1970s. Even today, particularly in industries such as car manufacturing, what we now call user interfaces are instead called the HMI, or the human-machine interface—at least HMI leaves behind the sexism of the term MMI. In any case, three scientific disciplines were involved: ergonomics (or human factors), computer science, and psychology.

> ▷   As an example of the interplay between different disciplines, chapter 5,
>   "Communication," discusses programming techniques to reduce key pressing.
>   This also helps avoid repetitive strain injuries, an important ergonomics issue.

There followed a period when the different disciplines staked out the area. Ergonomics moved into cognitive ergonomics, which concerned itself with cognitive issues of interaction, not just the physical issues that pertained to the conventional ergonomics of simpler interfaces. By the 1980s, however, the field had settled down, rebranded as human-computer interaction, abbreviated HCI in the

UK and CHI in North America—CHI puts the letters in a pronounceable order and also spells the Greek letter χ.

At first, the interest in computer systems revolved around the problems of large computer systems introduced into organizations: this is where the action was in those days of mainframe computers. There were management problems, because there was not enough participation of users with the designers of systems that were imposed on them: participative design became an important area. Now, rightly, HCI was expanding into sociology, anthropology and other human sciences. Computer supported cooperative work (CSCW), is the field that particularly looks at interhuman interaction, with computers fading into the background.

As interactive technology became more complex and reached into more of our lives, we realized that the field properly included *everything* that is relevant to humans. Exciting contributions were made from anthropology, design, philosophy, drama, and of course the many branches of psychology. As prices dropped, computers became consumer items—often dressed up as mobile phones, washing machines, TVs, cameras, and other products. The original concerns of usability began to take second place to marketing; certainly, if it doesn't sell, it won't be used. There has been much recent emphasis on enjoyment and emotion following the popularity of interaction as a driver for consumerism, and its "escape" from the world of work, particularly into the lives of children.

Within this enormous diversity of study, contrasting perspectives have crystalized:

■ Psychology has very strong experimental traditions, and HCI now emphasizes evaluation. Psychologists are interested in the way computers and complex systems push the boundaries of their understanding of *people*. For example, complex devices cause people to make all sorts of errors that have, or are believed to have, deep explanations—many of which are still open scientific questions.

■ Design has become very important. Products have to be packaged, designed for handling and use as physical objects—requiring industrial skills from concept to mass production. Interaction programming is the term for the specialized sort of design that envisages and develops interactive devices. Interaction design emphasizes the appearance and physical features (including the ergonomics) rather than the technical, how it works, details. "Interaction design" could have been a good title or subtitle for *Press On*, but as an unqualified term it is too closely associated with *industrial* design—what things look and feel like, rather than how they work inside. That's why we use the term "interaction *programming*."

■ A considerable range of social and human sciences became involved. How interaction makes people feel, how people respond to fashion, and how people collaborate—these are all social issues that concern anthropologists, social scientists, and ethnographers.

- "Usability" is the professional term for HCI. A usability professional is somebody who works in a team to ensure that "the HCI" is right, or at least gets that it gets better. Usability has taken as its cause user-centered design, UCD (sometimes human-centered design, HCD). Many failings of systems can be attributed to ignoring the user until it is too late. Conversely, user-centered design often turns up exciting design insights that professionals too closely involved with the design process would have overlooked. Somebody doing usability is typically trying to improve particular designs or devices; somebody doing HCI is typically trying to find ways to improve classes of system. There is a spectrum, at one end of which HCI is more theoretical and its experiments try to test principles; at the other end, usability is more practical and its evaluations are trials of specific devices rather than experiments that might give insight into general principles.

> ▷ UCD is discussed further in section 13.2 (p. 450).

From once being the innovator and creator of new things that worked, engineering has seemed to diminish in importance. Many HCI issues require experimental approaches, and neither engineering nor computer science have any tradition of experiments or any real view on experimental methods—particularly for experiments involving people. In contrast, the human sciences are very familiar with unreliable subjects (whether humans or mice) using statistics, experimental effects, as well as ethical issues. Any insight the human sciences have into design seem to apply to many designs, because humans are very similar, whereas any insights engineers have seem to apply to specific designs, because—for an engineer or programmer—each design is different.

In the broader domain of human-computer interaction, the human sciences have an edge: *any* device and its interaction can be analyzed and evaluated with the same techniques. In contrast, computer scientists have to use different approaches for different styles: how you program a voice-based device is different from how you program a graphical user interface and mouse. Thus any computing insight into interaction design does not seem to have the generalized leverage any human sciences insight has. Computing seems to be all detail and specifics, whereas the human sciences can claim wide-ranging theories and insights. It was not just the volume of issues; the type of issues and questions changed too. The sorts of design principles and rules that had dominated thinking to the 1980s, developed by a few insightful computer scientists, are now dismissed as untested private intuitions.

Computer science, then, diminished from its former role. Take the web as a more recent example. A few computer scientists developed it and created the tools that allow anyone to easily create web sites. The few original designers of the infrastructure are insignificant compared to the millions of web site designers. Almost all of the HCI issues—certainly, the *volume* of the issues—to do with the web seem to be to do with information architecture, web site content, and even areas such as economics (for e-commerce). The computer science issues now seem very remote to most people working in web usability.

Now interaction design is seen as rooted in the user, with the usability professional or human scientist best placed to interpret human-computer interaction. This current state of the field encourages a merely supporting role for programming and engineering, that of fulfilling requirements and correcting bugs that have been uncovered by people who understand users. "User-centered design" is the slogan. Center design on the user and then just tell the programmer what to do.

It's truth, but not the whole truth. Interaction design often, though understandably, overemphasizes the user-centered issues. The overemphasis leads to thinking such as: you should not design a staircase without knowing what users feel or how it will help them go to bed. Why, indeed, make a staircase that people don't like? Yet an engineer can build a staircase that is rigid or flexes; one that can hold elephants, or one that looks fine but is fragile. A good engineer knows what the staircase can do without any testing or human involvement. Sadly, too many interactive devices have been built like nice-looking but flimsy staircases, and we have all learned how to dance up the wonky steps.

This is an important point. Let's use another example to emphasize it differently. A physicist can say, purely based on theory and no experiments that a passenger in a car needs a safety belt to prevent being flung through the window if the car crashes. This follows from Newton's Laws of motion. We might engage psychologists in this scenario is find out why some people don't like wearing safety belts or how to make them more enjoyable to use. We might engage ergonomists to make car seats more comfortable and safer or the steering wheel less of an obstruction in crashes. No doubt, many experiments make sense. The mechanics of safety belts, however, *has* to be grounded in a quite different sort of science and theory.

Many things are hard to use because we do not understand how bad, or badly used, the engineering infrastructure is. We think computers and interactive devices are *like that*. But they are bad because they have been used in ways that their infrastructure does not support. It's as if we are worried about a staircase that wobbles and makes us sick, when the cause of our sickness is that it has been stretched to bridge a wide gap that really needed a balcony or an arch; the engineering is just wrong, and the result is something that is unusable and certainly not pleasurable to cross. The solution is not to wonder how it could be made a nicer experience for users crossing it; rather, the solution is to correct the engineering— or, better, to get the engineering right to start with.

As there is a lot of pressure to solve the problems of poor interaction design or interaction programming, most people look for the solutions outside of computer science, which appears to have let us down badly.

Two particularly eloquent books express the general feeling well: Tom Landauer's *The Trouble with Computers* and Alan Cooper's *The Inmates are Running the Asylum* (full references are given at the end of this chapter). Programmers don't know how to design, so human factors experts, usability experts, or psychologists must lead design. These conventional views miss a few points:

Box 4.1 Weapon salve In the sixteenth century, people injured by weapons got nasty, infected cuts. Weapon salve was an ointment of choice, you might say the cutting edge of medicine, and there was real evidence that it worked better than alternative ointments, which were often ineffective at best.

Curiously, weapon salve was spread on the weapon that made the wound, not on the injured person. Yet it worked! People recovered faster and wounds didn't fester as much.

In fact all ointments in those days were pretty nasty stuff and would probably make any wound worse through infection. Weapon salve was a technique to keep the germs away from the wound, except nobody knew about germs, so the explanation they had was something to do with the medicine working "through" the weapon. There was probably a lot of superstition too—it had to be the right weapon or else it wouldn't work. Whether an untreated wound would have healed was chancy anyway. In short, the reason for the strange power of weapon salve was that doctors had no theory to explain what was going on, so they relied too much on empirical evidence.

The warning of this story is that we may have techniques that make designs better, and they may seem to work. Almost all techniques for improving usability do not refer to the device itself; they have no theory of how interaction with the device works. They may really work just as weapon salve did, but in terms of really improving the "health" of the design they are very weak.

- Computers and interactive devices need engineering to work at all;

- While most programmers in business may find the job hard and be under considerable and generally unrealistic pressure to deliver products from marketing and management in particular, in principle this does not mean that computer science cannot contribute powerfully and imaginatively to interaction; and

- Basic computer science theory can quickly and reliably give insights into design *provided* it is used soon enough.

Landauer and Cooper represent the majority position well, but it's weapon salve—without the right theories, it is the wrong solution.

> ▷ The ancient idea of weapon salve is discussed in box 4.1, "Weapon salve" (this page).

4.2   From printed information to interaction

The history of interaction programming is still unfolding, and people are still taking sides. It's interesting to step back and look at what, at first, seems like a completely different thing: the history of the written word.

Poor user manuals are often blamed for the difficulty people have with gadgets. This may be true, but of course, good, clear manuals cannot be made for fundamentally flawed designs, even if there is considerable room for improvement in user manuals without solving the equipment's fundamental design problems.

Existing manuals are generally organized around the technical features provided by the technology rather than by the tasks the user is expected to perform. If a programmer was to design, say, a database for a computer, indexes would be provided to support the expected tasks of the computer. In fact, if a programmer wrote a program that did not explicitly address the tasks the computer was supposed to do, the computer simply would not do them. Why aren't manuals for humans—which indeed serve the same purpose for humans as programs do for computers—designed with the same forethought?

Tables of contents and indices for manuals provide users with access to the manual's contents "free of history." That is, without a table of contents or an index, users would have to read the manual as a narrative: they'd have to start at the beginning and read through it (they might skip and skim, but that's unreliable) until they found what they were after. But with an index or table of contents, the manual can be read in the order most appropriate to the users' specific needs. With an index you can go to what you want to read. You look up what you want to do and then turn to the appropriate page.

The index and table of contents are remarkable inventions. The printing press catalyzed the invention of many ideas that made reading books easier. Before the printing press, it was so tedious just to write a book (and much more tedious to copy one) that hardly anyone considered the needs of the book's readers. There is no point worrying about user interface design when getting the thing to work at all consumes all the author's energy!

Developing a table of contents is tedious, but developing a good index is a major piece of work. In the days before the printing press, hardly anything even had page numbers, so an index would have been quite useless. With numbered pages, an index makes sense, but without a reliable copying process—that is, a printing press—every copy of a book would have had different pagination because it was handwritten.

Clearly, aids that help the reader, the book user, like the index, become feasible once the technology for managing the written word becomes good enough. Once the same information in any copy of a book could be found in the same place on the same page, a teacher could say to their students, "look at page 42" and know everybody was looking at the same thing. In turn, the improved usability of the book changed the way teaching could be done. Tables of contents, indexes and so on became practical propositions because their cost/benefit had been transformed: the effort in working them out now only had to be done once, and the cost would be recovered from the profit of many copies sold.

Johann Gutenberg's printing press marked a turning point in civilization, during the period 1440–1450. Though the Chinese invented movable type much earlier, in 600, they were less successful mainly because of their enormous character set. In addition to page numbers and indexes, more major innovations occurred in just the next half century:

■ The author wrote not for a generous patron but for the wider public. Printing gave a single author many readers, and the author's income came from many readers unknown to himself. Latin books had an enormous international market.

- Diagrams became usable. Prior to printing, manual transcriptions of drawings made them unreliable. By the 1540s, Petrus Ramus (Pierre de la Ramée) was able to exploit the reliable duplication of diagrams to popularize his logic and analytical methods. His books were good enough to be suppressed.

- Aldus Manutius brought out a series of cheap "pocket" books (which were widely pirated). Books represented, for the first time, accessible, durable, portable and personal information.

Because information became cheap, knowledge could be questioned independently of the economic considerations of having the knowledge at all. In the early six-teenth century, the Aldine Academy started to *revise* standard books: a radical idea at the time. Finally, personal knowledge—"education"—became not a matter based on rote use of aural memory, but of flexible visual and spatial abilities.

The technology of book printing was so successful that William Caxton in England and his contemporaries on the continent published all they could of their national literature. In the process they helped define their own languages. Today, we're doing much the same with computers and the internet. Everything *must* be computerized!

The point is that the improvements that Aldus Manutius and the others brought about in book technology in the fifteenth century *were computational improvements* to the usability of books. What distinguishes a modern book from an ancient manuscript is that you can find your way around it: there are chapters, headings, tables of contents, and so forth.

> ▷ As well as chapters, headings, tables of contents, and an index, this book, *Press On*, also uses linkage. The abstract structure of the linkage used in this book is visualized in figure 8.8 (p. 246); it could easily form the basis of a web site that would present the book as an interactive (computer-based, rather than paper-based) experience.

We can easily overlook that turning to a page requires *pages*. The earliest books were scrolls, which could only be read sequentially, and when you had finished, you had to roll up the scroll to put it away. The codex, a sewn parchment book with separate pages, was popularized by the early Christians because all the Gospels could be easily fit into one codex—rather than taking up several scrolls. This technological breakthrough had numerous advantages over scrolls: a codex could be read in any order; it could be read faster (allowing skipping); there could be writing on both sides of the pages (so it had double the capacity); and it was small, flat, and robust.

In a book with pages, concepts may be arranged alphabetically, chronologically, or topically for greater ease of lookup; there may be cross-references. These features, tables of contents, and so forth, are really *computational devices*—ones that can be found as explicit algorithms in any computer science book, where they go under the names of look-up tables, indexes (of course!), hash codes, and so on. In other words, if you want to improve the medium—in this case, books—treat the user as a thinking being with things to do, and to do that you could do worse than to treat the user as a computer.

Printing itself was spread with missionary zeal—but as can be imagined from the enormous political impact (merely hinted at in the list above) many attempts were made to suppress and control the new technology. Such observations are reminiscent of the current assessment of computers and communications technologies, even down to the problems of copyright and piracy. Is the internet an information revolution rather than just another way of packaging information? Are we set to become mindless automatons?

■   ■   ■

We are now at a turning point in information provision. Computers will soon usurp books and bits of paper, not least because they can be far more interactive. Children, and many adults, use the web more than, if not instead of, reading ordinary paper. Getting news via the internet is as good as if not better than getting a paper copy. But so far, you can't safely "read" a computer in the bath, nor can you scribble notes in the margins. And there are various other cosmetic problems— for instance, computers look the same, whereas books mostly look different, since their covers are a function of their contents. But soon today's prototypes will be prevalent, in the same sort of way that personal stereos have let anyone carry around a complete orchestra (at least that's how our great grandparents would have thought of it).

4.3   Computers as sleight-of-hand

Conjurors do magic by sleight-of-hand, by distracting our perception from what they are really doing to what they want us to see. We don't see how they do their tricks. Likewise, a lot of computer "magic" is merely a result of people's ignorance of how they work. But, like conjuring, computer magic *intends* it this way. Surprisingly, good computer science deliberately *tries* to make computer working invisible, because the invisibility also helps the programmers.

Programmers are familiar with good programming practice, going under such names as abstraction, encapsulation, modularization, virtual machines, and avoidance of global variables. All these and many more ideas represent techniques to conceal and hide how things work.

Programmers hide details because they may want to change them later. If anybody else had relied on the details (or even if they had relied on the details somewhere else in the program), problems would arise when the details needed changing. Every operation that made assumptions about the details would need revising.

Let's recall the building analogy. From time to time, erecting a building may require some engineering innovation, but almost all of the time the construction can be safely left to workers following the grand plan of the architects, who follow the lead of the users. Few buildings are really innovative, few are innovative at the level of design detail and fewer still are innovative in a way that pushes the boundaries of tradespeople's skills.

Yet here this neat analogy is misleading, in two key ways. First, most interactive devices are innovative designs. You would not trust a novel building design to be built by a construction worker; you would use structural engineers to check and develop the design first. So because interactive devices innovate, we need more structural design skills. Second, just as you would not leave designing or building a large bridge to architects because the design and engineering problems are immense, most programming projects should not be left to users or human factors people alone. A bricklayer can build a bridge a few meters long without difficulty. Increase the span to a few tens of meters and serious engineering issues arise (for instance, the weight of the bridge is now a significant factor); increase the span to hundreds of meters and *really* difficult engineering problems need to be overcome.

Computer "buildings"—whether we software or hardware—are the largest intellectual creations of humankind, ever. These are not small bridges, but vast spans. Like vast bridges, they push science and engineering to the limits. Like bridges, once the engineering framework is right, the finishing off can be completed by tradespeople—the painting, the nut-tightening, and so on.

However, computer programs are very easy to "patch together," and it is surprisingly easy to build enormous programs that miraculously still work—a little like it is possible for bricklayers to build cities, however large, house by house, or how it is (sometimes) possible to build a long bridge from lots of small arches. The point is, it is possible to build *enormously* complex interactive devices using basic principles. Just keep fixing the bugs. This commonplace fact has led to the demise of computer science in the broader field of HCI, because all the interesting stuff left *seems* to be at the level of polishing.

On the other hand, many large computer programs fail, because "patching together" does not work reliably. Many large government IT projects fail because they are assembled as like bridges built by bolting girders together in the hope of making a span long enough to cross any river. Obviously bolting girders end-to-end will make something get longer and longer—just as obviously you can make a program have lots of features, eventually all the features you need. But if one girder can bridge ten meters, ten girders won't bridge a hundred meters. Likewise, the engineering needed to design a big program is not a matter of scaling up the skills needed for small programs.

> ▷ Government projects and procurement are further discussed in section 13.2.4
> (p. 456).

It is a rare skill to be able to build well. Equally, it is a real skill to be able to program on top of infrastructure; some, say, like CORBA, are very complex beasts in their own right. To use a framework, you need a lot of facts; to program without one, or to build a new infrastructure, you need analytic skills of a different type. I suspect the intrinsic skills are not rarer but simply needed seldom because of the way the industry works—just as there are more bricklayers than architects.

The engineering infrastructure of cities—sewage, water supplies, telephone networks, and so on—has to be worked out carefully, but once worked out it can be built on with ease; likewise, once the software frameworks are worked out, almost anyone can build on them. It took clever people to work out how to sort, but now a programmer just writes sort and the computer sorts anything, with pretty much nothing else said.

No practical programmers worry about sorting because the libraries and APIs do it better, just as a house builder does not worry about getting the gas boiler or telephone sockets to work; you just buy ones somebody else designed and built. No practical programmer worries about the hardware, because it just works—but *somebody* had to worry. In fact, hardware engineers have done a fantastic job of hiding their discipline from interaction more widely! Apart from on/off buttons and charging batteries, we hardly ever think about electricity at all, thanks to their success at hiding all the complex details of their work. The same sort of thing has happened with programming and computer science.

Sorting is just one example of the computer science infrastructure that is easy to take for granted. Window managers and user interface features, like mouse management and buttons, have generally been programmed already when people start programming interactive systems. Or web site design (information architecture) takes for granted that the infrastructure HTML, cascading style sheets, and so on works. Given that it works, there is quite enough for a designer to worry about at other levels. On the other hand, the infrastructure could have been different to take a tiny example, why don't domain names allow spaces? This was a technical decision but is now part of the unquestioned infrastructure.

If you use a web site design tool, it will be able to automatically check that any web site you design is connected, that there are no HTML links to pages that don't exist, and that there are no pages that have no links to them. Here, a sophisticated bit of programming and computer science design thinking has become concealed into a something as trivial as a menu item in the tool's user interface.

Once you can take infrastructure for granted, it is then easy to assume that all that matters is how people *behave* and *feel* about the buildings; the psychology is, after all, all that matters to people. There is a common assumption that the social, emotional, and other needs of users, not the technology, determine how people interact. Yet people can't interact without the technology—and the technology could be different, as you must know if you've ever been angry with a computer or other gadget because it was "designed the wrong way." How people interact with mobile phones is different from how they interact with land phones; technology and technological choices clearly make a huge difference.

Unfortunately, we don't know what the infrastructure corresponding to sorting is for interactive devices. We need good programmers to build good systems, but they are in short supply—and often concerned about more crucial issues (like battery management, communications protocols, graphics) than gilding features like usability. Most interactive systems, however interesting they may be to users, are largely made out of putting together computer science structures, like bonding courses of bricks in a building. The infrastructure and the science of its development have disappeared from sight.

Fortunately, for a very large class of interactive systems there is virtually no infrastructure. Push button gadgets are so "simple" that most developers, whether programmers or hardware engineers, build them from scratch. Here is a wonderful opportunity to rethink how we design interaction from first principles.

The theoretical underpinning of computer science that creates good interaction is known to relatively few—because few seem to need it, as I've explained. The theoretical principles underpinning interaction programming is known to fewer still! Because so few think about this sort of theory, most interaction programmers encounter interesting issues in computer science design very rarely. It is but a short step, but a mistaken step, to think that computer science has no theory or insight to contribute.

4.4   Programming background

As interaction programming is built on a foundation of programming, we are going to need to do some programming. If you are new to programming, don't worry: even the quite simple programming we need will give us a lot of leverage. Although many real systems are very complex systems, for a book it is sufficient to cover the important principles. We'll see that everything we need is simple and surprisingly easy to program: the main issue, which this book promotes, is the *attitude* to interactive system programming. It'll give you lots of ideas if you are an interactive product designer, a web developer, an embedded systems programmer, or any sort of professional programmer building interactive systems or documentation.

We will use JavaScript, as it is the main programming language used on the web and thus very widely available—it runs in any browser on just about any computer. In fact, if you only wanted to design web sites, it'd be worth learning JavaScript so that you could enhance the functionality of your web sites; you could use the ideas in this book to make your web sites more interactive. You can use JavaScript for extending and automating tasks in many programs, like Adobe Photoshop and Illustrator. There is a language standard, ECMAScript, and a Microsoft variant, JScript. JavaScript is a real programming language, despite having "script" in its name.

JavaScript is based on an international standard, which is also followed by ActionScript, the language of Macromedia's Flash. So if you learn JavaScript, then learning to script in Flash will be easy too, and you will be able to make very impressive interactive programs, both for interactive devices and for web sites— especially web sites that simulate interactive things (perhaps to help sell them or to provide customer support).

JavaScript is similar to the well-known programming languages C, C++, C#, and Java. JavaScript is thus a very good introduction to these languages, and it is much easier to make JavaScript run interactive programs, as you get the interactive web features for free. Documentation is widely available, and many examples and help for JavaScript are on the web.

JavaScript is practically the same as ActionScript, the proprietary programming language used in Flash, which is a very common way to provide high-quality interactivity on web sites, particularly with graphical animations. If you know ActionScript, you may prefer to mentally translate the JavaScript in this book and work in Flash instead. Or, you could use other languages—the program code in this book is deliberately straightforward so you can easily translate it into other languages. If you are more familiar with another language, think about how you could do everything I suggest in it—the point to remember is that it's the ideas and principles, not the choice of language that matter.

An alternative to using conventional languages such as C and JavaScript is to use languages that come with the features we already need. Examples are mathematical programming language such as Mathematica and MathCad—they are more costly, but if you have access to them, do explore what they offer. The main advantage of using a mathematical programming language is it will have a huge programming library that can do much of the work directly that we will instead have to build from scratch.

4.5   Introducing JavaScript

▷   Section 4.5.2 (p. 107) gives hints for reading JavaScript.

JavaScript is a very flexible and convenient programming language, which is usually written in HTML web pages so that web sites can take advantage of the flexibility of programming to do anything. In this chapter, we'll use JavaScript to add interaction to web pages, primarily so that we can simulate and explore the behavior of interactive devices with the familiarity and convenience of browsers and text editors.

Writing this HTML file to start experimenting with JavaScript. Use any convenient text editor and save the text to `file.html`.

```
<html>
 <head>
   <title>Experimenting in JavaScript</title>
 </head>
 <body>
   Any HTML works as usual, and JavaScript is written between tags:
   <script>
     document.write("<h1>Here is a header, generated from JavaScript</h1>");
   </script>
 </body>
</html>
```

It is just a typical HTML file, with some JavaScript embedded into it. Anything between the tags <script> and </script> is JavaScript, and will be run automatically just by loading the HTML file into your browser.

When you open `file.html` in a web browser, it will display a couple of lines of text: one of them was generated by you writing directly in HTML, and one was generated by your JavaScript program using the `document.write` function to generate HTML.

103

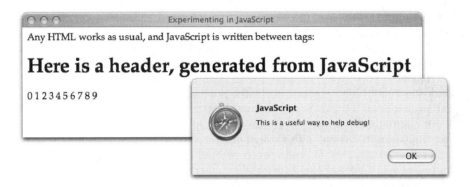

Figure 4.1: Checking out HTML and JavaScript in a browser—however, browsers will not render the page as shown until the alert box is dismissed.

Next we'll get a little more sophisticated:

```
<html>
 <head><title>Experimenting in JavaScript</title></head>
 <body>
   Any HTML works as usual, and JavaScript is written between tags:
   <script>
     document.write("<h1>Here is a header, generated from JavaScript</h1>");
     for( var i = 0; i < 10; i++ )
       document.write(i+" ");
     alert("This is a useful way to help debug!");
   </script>
 </body>
</html>
```

Try opening this in your browser; you should get something like figure 4.1 (this page). Then mess around and find out how to get more exciting things to happen.

Browsers differ a great deal. You will probably find yours doesn't quite handle JavaScript as we've used it here; it's best to find out details like this now, or to change your browser.

Even without browser problems, it is worth polishing your code. Suppose you have some pictures in JPEG files called pic1.jpg, pic2.jpg, and so on, then the following code will show you five of them:

```
<script>
  var pix = 5; // how many pictures we want to show
</script>
My first <script>document.write(pix);</script> pictures:<br>
<script>
  for( var i = 1; i <= pix; i++ )
    document.write("<img src=pic"+i+".jpg><br>");
</script>
```

You might prefer to write it as an uninterrupted stretch of JavaScript; it comes to the same thing:

```
<script>
  var pix = 5; // how many pictures we want to show
  document.write("My first "+pix+" pictures:<br>");
  for( var i = 1; i <= pix; i++ )
    document.write("<img src=pic"+i+".jpg><br>");
</script>
```

Since saying "My first 1 pictures:" when pix is 1 would be horrible English, I'd rather ensure we get the words picture or pictures appropriately by programming like this:

```
if( pix == 1 )
  document.write("My first picture:<br>");
else
  document.write("My first "+pix+" pictures:<br>");
```

We will want to use good English many times, so we should keep all the good English habits in one place. Then if we later decide to change our program to use French, the strange English plurals only happen in one place. To do this, we can use a JavaScript function:

```
<script>
function plural(n, word)
{ if( n == 1 ) return n+" "+word;
  return n+" "+word+"s";
}
</script>
```

The function plural(n, word) takes a number and a string, and it returns a string as follows:

n	*word*	plural(n, *word*)
0	picture	0 pictures
1	picture	1 picture
2	picture	2 pictures
3	picture	3 pictures
⋮	⋮	⋮

Now we've defined this function, the previous piece of JavaScript can be written neatly as

```
document.write("My first "+plural(pix, "picture")+":<br>");
```

... and we can use plural anywhere we want to take care of plural words. If you need the function plural a lot, you will want to make it more sophisticated. For example, the following definition gets plural(2, "press") correct:

```
<script>
function plural(n, word)
{ if( n == 1 ) return n+" "+word;
  if( word == "press" ) return n+" presses";
  return n+" "+word+"s";
}
</script>
```

Without that extra line in the function, it would have returned strings like, "2 presss" instead of "2 presses." It would come in handy when you want to tell the user things like "it takes 2 presses to get from Off to Reset," when you don't know in advance how many presses it will take.

■   ■   ■

From now on in this book, to save space, we won't keep showing the `<script>` ... `</script>` tags, which must be put around all JavaScript to get it to work.
A few more useful points:

■ If you prefer, you can keep all your JavaScript together in a file separate from the main HTML file. To do this, write `<script src="mycode.js"></script>` in the HTML file, and then you can keep all your JavaScript in the file `mycode.js`. You can of course have several files organized like this, for instance, the device specifications, your debugged framework code, and the particular experiments you are doing.

■ Browsers allow you to use other scripting languages than JavaScript. It's good practice to write `<script language="Javascript">` ... `</script>` just in case your browser defaults to running a different scripting language.

■ There are many commercial and shareware programs to help you develop web sites. Using these will make writing JavaScript and running it much easier.

■ Apart from `document.write`, and a brief mention of forms, I've deliberately avoided the document object model, so the code in this book is widely compatible across browsers.

4.5.1   Hints on debugging

JavaScript and HTML can be thoroughly, but straightforwardly, mixed together. It's handy to do this, since browsers are very bad at reporting errors in your JavaScript. Usually everything just silently stops working, and it is tricky to locate your errors.

To get a better idea of what is going on, every so often you can insert HTML like this:

```
</script> Got to here OK. <script>
```

which will reset the JavaScript parser and drop back into HTML to say where it's got to. If you never see "Got to here OK." that means something has gone wrong somewhere above where you put this HTML. This will help you narrow down where the problem is.

Another useful method to use within JavaScript is to place `alert("got here OK");` to see how the code is running. I find it useful to write calls to `alert` in functions to say what their parameters are, and when I'm happy the function is working well, I comment out the `alert` so it doesn't affect the program any more.

Debugging	*Debugged*

`function f(a)`
`{ alert("call f("+a+")");`
`  ...`
`}`
	`function f(a)`
	`{ // alert("call f("+a+")");`
	`  ...`
	`}`

Since you may well see this `alert` message come up lots of time, it pays to make it as clear and neat as possible. You may well need to debug the function next week when you have forgotten what it does, so it helps to say something more useful than just the parameter values. That's one reason why it helps to leave the `alert` in your code, but commented out.

Often it's better to introduce a global variable, say, debug, and to use this to control debugging. Instead of commenting out `alert`s that you think work, you make them conditional:

```
var debug = false;
...
function f(a)
{ if( debug )
    alert("call f("+a+")");
  ...
}
```

Now you can switch debugging on and off, so that only the parts of your program that need debugging generate any output. If you want debugging, say `debug = true;` and when you want it off say `debug = false;` This is of course very useful if your function (here, one called f) is used in parts of your program that work and parts that don't. You can also use `document.write(...)` instead of `alert(...)`—and it's usually more convenient unless you are trying to debug generating HTML, in which case it will further mess up the problems that are already worrying you.

Don't forget that browsers are different, and some provide very nice debugging facilities that you should explore.

4.5.2 A JavaScript quick reference

We'll describe enough of JavaScript's features to serve as a quick reference to read the code in this book. The further reading at the end of the chapter, p. 111, gives some book references that have full details.

Comments Any text from // to the end of a line is ignored. (JavaScript also has other sorts of comment we don't need for this book.)

Declarations A new variable is introduced by saying var *name*; or var *name* = *value*, if you want to initialize it. In JavaScript you can often get away without using declarations, but it's a bad habit and can cause hard-to-solve problems.

Assignments To update the value of a variable x, say, write x = x+1; What looks like an equals sign is the assignment sign.

Operators The operators of JavaScript are standard, with the exception of +, which can either mean add numbers or concatenate strings. So 1+2 is 3, but "1"+"2" is "12". Since = means assignment, equals itself is written ==, and not equals is !=. Logical *and* is written && and logical *or* is written ||. The logical operators are "short cut operators," in that false && *anything* or true || *anything* won't bother to evaluate any further, as the outcome is already known.

The increment operator ++ means "add 1 to." Increment can be used before or after a name. In this book, I haven't used it in any place where it would matter, but the difference is that x++ gives you the value of x then increments x by one, whereas ++x increments x by one and gives you the increased value.

Arrays Unlike conventional languages that have declared variable types, in JavaScript any variable can be assigned an array at any time. The expression new Array(*size*) creates an array with that number of elements, but they are all undefined until they are initialized, for instance, with a for loop. Typically, you will write something like var a = new Array(10) to create an array (here, called a, and initially with ten elements).

Array constants are written between square brackets, so [1,2,3] is an array initialized with three numbers, and [[1,2,3],[4,5,6]] is a two-dimensional table—this example is an array of two elements, each an array consisting of three elements.

Subscripts Array elements are accessed using subscripts written between square brackets; so a[i] is element i of the array a, and a[i][j] is element j of array a[i]—so effectively a[i][j] is the element at the jth column of the ith row of a.

Subscripts start at 0, and the length of an array a is a.length.

Types JavaScript has a type operator, typeof, which gives a string indicating what type an expression has. For example, typeof "woof" is "string".

Conditional statements are written in the form if(*test*) *truestuff*; or with an else part: if(*test*) *truestuff*; else *falsestuff*;

Blocks are written between curly brackets.

While loops are written in the form `while( test ) repeatthis;` The code is executed if the test evaluates to true, and then it is repeatedly executed while the test remains true.

There is a second form of `while` loop: the code is executed once, regardless of the test, and is then repeated while the test is true. This form looks like `do repeatthis while( test );` Warning: studies have shown this sort of loop often causes more conceptual problems that it helps solve elegantly.

For loops have the form `for( var i = value; test; increment ) stuff;` meaning that the code `stuff` is repeated with i starting with `value`, while `test` is true, and after each `stuff` is done, `increment` is done—almost always it will be something like `i++`, to increase i by 1 (which means the same as `i = i+1`).

It is perhaps helpful to remember that `for` loops are just a special case of `while` loops; the following two ways of saying the same thing are exactly equivalent:

For loop	*While loop*

`for( i = 0; i < 10; i++ )`
  `alert(i);`
	`i = 0;`
	`while( i < 10 )`
	`{ alert(i);`
	  `i++;`
	`}`

Often we write `for( var i = 0; i < 10; i++ )`, declaring the controlled variable i in the `for` loop. In JavaScript, this is pedantry, but it is good practice in languages (like Java) that take declarations more seriously. It helps avoid problems where the same name, here i, is used elsewhere in the program and might otherwise be messed up by the `for` loop.

Functions are defined by writing `function f(arguments) stuff` and called by writing `f(values)`, which then runs `stuff` using the values.

Output The main form of JavaScript output we use in this book is writing HTML straight into the web page that is being loaded by your browser. The function `document.write(string)` writes `string` as HTML as soon as it is run. HTML tags like `<br>` can also be written by `document.write`; it can even build them up, as in `document.write("<a href="+t+">")`—recall that + means string concatenation, not addition.

Objects If a variable is an object, it can contain different values in named fields, so `x.fred` is the `fred` field of x; it can be used just like a variable in its own right. Objects are initialized by writing, for instance, `var x = {fred: 2};` which would make `x.fred` equal to 2.

Experimenting If you don't understand something, don't hesitate to use `alert`. For example, try `alert("Test: "+typeof 1);` to see what happens.

4.6   Conclusions

This chapter moved us away from exploring the problems, to starting to see the importance and central role of computer science: the foundations of building interactive systems lie in computer science and in programming.

As well as introducing JavaScript as the programming language we shall use, we explored the history of interaction programming and HCI, one of its aliases. HCI brings together many disciplines to understand how to build better systems for users.

Indeed, conventional building makes a good analogy for us. Most building work is great fun; we can redecorate and replace kitchens with ease, and we all have opinions about what suits us. Building work that involves the infrastructure, the wiring, or the trusses—all of the preparation of a new building—requires great expertise. The point of this book is to remind us that quite a lot of building work requires good engineering; but once you have got the framework right, as we'll see, you can change other things pretty much at will—and you end up, because of the sound engineering, with a much greater freedom to be creative than you could ever have had in a rickety, even dangerous, building.

Badly engineered buildings fall down; well designed buildings are there to enjoy, to customize and to live in.

4.6.1   Some *Press On* principles

- User-centered design is the truth, but not the whole truth → section 4.1 (p. 94).

- Weapon salve: without good theories you can do wrong things even when justified with the support of empirical evidence → section 4.1 (p. 96).

- Treat the user at least as well as a computer → section 4.2 (p. 98).

4.7   Further reading

As a transitional chapter, we give a few references on programming and then cover the "whole field" of interaction programming.

This list is just a starter. There are some fantastic books and resources that we don't have space to cover and new ones are appearing all the time.

4.7.1   Programming

It's impossible to give a review of the vast range of computer science resources—though you can safely disregard almost everything, particularly anything you see in an ordinary bookshop. There is an overwhelming amount of elementary hand-holding material that at best only gives you recipes to follow and at worst locks you into a cut-and-paste mentality. You can recognize such books by the frequent screen shots and long stretches of program code.

Assuming you are new to computer science, I recommend the following books:

■ Aho, A. V., and Ullman, J. D., *Foundations of Computer Science*, W. H. Freeman and Company, 1995. Available in various language editions, this is an excellent all-round introduction to computer science, going to first-year university level.

■ Flanagan, D., *JavaScript: The Definitive Guide*, O'Reilly, 1996. While there are plenty of introductory books on JavaScript to choose from (browse in any bookstore or on-line), this book is a programmer's guide to JavaScript and is ideal for programmers who want to know the details of the language. There are, of course, very many examples of JavaScript on the web that you can work from or exploit as well.

JavaScript is only one of many web technologies; others are cascading style sheets (CSS), XML, DOM, ... and many other abbreviations! If you learn JavaScript, as well as being able to implement everything in this book, you are well on the way to being able to design and write far more interactive web sites (while keeping them well-written and dependable)—this will take you far beyond just programming interactive devices. If you want to follow a web development route, the best way to proceed is to learn Ajax, a very powerful JavaScript framework for web development.

■ Crane, D., Pascarello, E., with James, D., *Ajax in Action*, Manning, 2006. This is probably the best place to start on Ajax, its programming, patterns, and philosophy.

▷ More ideas on programming, including further reading, can be found in chapter 9, "A framework for design."

4.7.2 General resources on interaction programming

■ Degani, A., *Taming HAL*, Palgrave, 2003. The title is an allusion to the HAL computer in Arthur C. Clarke's 2001: A Space Odyssey. Asaf Degani's book is an excellent introduction of the issues discussed throughout *Press On. Taming HAL* goes from the design of handheld devices to aircraft cockpits and shows how bad design causes human error. His book uses statecharts, a clear graphical technique for representing designs, which we will cover in chapter 7, "Statecharts."

■ Jensen, S., *The Simplicity Shift*, Cambridge University Press, 2002. This is the shortest book I've listed here and the most practical. If you work in a company, how are you going to get these great ideas to work? Jensen's book makes the ideas in other books work in real companies that build interactive products. Various teams, marketing, designers, and developers work independently, and any great ideas for a new and better product get ruined by various sorts of blindness to what you are trying to achieve.

Most products get more and more complicated as designers think of new features. Simplicity is the antidote; Jensen explains how to get a design group thinking along the lines of simplicity—and he has some really good ideas. This book which provides some technical tools to build simple systems. If you can't build your systems with the ideas in this book, you aren't going for simplicity.

■ Jones, M., and Marsden, G., *Mobile Interaction Design*, John Wiley and Sons Ltd., 2005. If you think that small mobile devices are *the* exciting, key future technology, this book shows how to channel your enthusiasm in a human-centred way: it concentrates on use, usability and the complete user-experience. In particular it raises the issues and needs of the billions of future users in developing regions such as Africa. If you read *Press On* and the Jones and Marsden book, you'd have covered everything you need to know for the design, programming and evaluation of interactive devices worldwide.

■ Norman, D. A., *The Psychology of Everyday Things*, Basic Books 1988, also published as *The Design of Everyday Things* in paperback, Penguin, 1990. This book is *the* book of the field, and every interaction programmer should read it. Don Norman has the same problems with everyday things that I do, only he's a psychologist rather than a computer scientist; the advantage is that he has insights that you won't automatically dismiss by thinking, "I know a device that doesn't have that problem, so it's not an issue."

Norman has written many stimulating books. *The Invisible Computer*, MIT Press, 1998, in contrast to *The Psychology of Everyday Things*, *The Invisible Computer* expresses a vision about good design: that computers should be invisible (see p. 441). There's a lot to agree with here—and a lot to disagree with! For more, see his essays at www.jnd.org/dn.pubs.html.

There are many books that take a more computer science view of interaction:

■ Dix, A. J., *Formal Methods for Interactive Systems*, Academic Press, 1991. Alan Dix's book is over a decade old, but it is still a provocative and excellent place to start a PhD.

■ Raskin, J., *The Humane Interface*, Addison-Wesley, 2000. Jef Raskin worked on the design of the Apple Macintosh user interface and this book has a great deal to say about good design.

■ Thimbleby, H. W., *User Interface Design*, Addison-Welsey, 1990. I tried to get down to the key issues and design principles in this book rather than get bogged down in the technology (which goes out of date very fast). The book came out just as everyone was moving away from desktop computers to personal devices, like video recorders. All the work we had put into understanding how to design for graphical user interfaces and so on were lost on the new generation of interactive devices.

4.7.3 Other perspectives

There is no right way to design, and there are lots of other perspectives than mine. Notable among the alternatives are the following lucid books:

- Cooper, A., *The Inmates are Running the Asylum*, SAMS, Macmillan Computing Publishing, 1989. Wonderful polemic against software engineers and programmers being led purely by technical concerns—and making a mess of interaction.

- Landauer, T. K., *The Trouble with Computers*, MIT Press, 1995. This book deservedly became a classic argument for user-centered design: Tom Landauer catalogued the many failures of computer systems and laid the blame at the door of designers and programmers who had ignored the user. The book gives a good discussion of the productivity paradox, which was discussed in section 1.7 (p. 21).

- McCarthy, J., and Wright, P., *Technology as Experience*, MIT Press, 2004. To design, we must take account of the user's feelings and emotions—one of many complementary perspectives on the present book's approach.

- Moggridge, B., *Designing Interactions*, MIT Press, 2007. This mammoth book interviews nearly 50 key people in the development of interaction design; it is a direct resource from people who are leaders of the field. It's essential reading.

The study of human error is fascinating, and all designers should have some insight into how things go wrong. If we don't design for errors, errors will nevertheless surely happen, and then we—and our users—are certainly heading for disaster. At least read this classic:

- Reason, J., *Human Error*, Cambridge University Press, 1990.

  ▷ Human error pervades this book; box 11.3, "Generating manuals automatically" (p. 397) to take just one example, is a short summary of a railway accident that could have been avoided by better design.

There is a danger in thinking that users are the same as we are. All the books listed above treat the users as pretty ordinary—people, just like most of us designers. There are many books that cover different aspects of users, whether international and cultural, age related, or disabled. A good place to start is to read about children; we were all children once, and we still have some sort of resonance to that different world of users.

- Druin, A., ed., *The Design of Children's Technology*, Morgan Kaufmann Publishers, 1999. Allison Druin's book collects a wide variety of interesting and stimulating topics into one book.

4.7.4   Undergraduate resources

There are also many good general textbooks in interaction, some of the main being:

- Benyon, D., Turner, P., and Turner, S., *Designing Interactive Systems*, Addison-Wesley, 2005.

- Dix, A. J., Finlay, J., Abowd, G., and Beale, R., *Human-Computer Interaction*, Prentice Hall, 2003.

- Shneiderman, B., *Designing the User Interface*, Addison-Wesley, 2004.

These introductory textbooks cover so much material that very little is covered in great depth—but an interaction programmer should know everything in them! In particular, these books discuss more computer-oriented interaction techniques, such as number pads, menus and pointing devices, which *Press On* does not cover in any detail, even though many interactive devices need them. If you get hold of these books, make sure you get the most recent editions, since they are being revised continuously.

Design also requires us to be able to get things to work. We'll have more to say about programming later in this book, but you would do well to get some good programming and algorithm books.

Most books on software engineering give far too little emphasis to user interface design and programming interactive systems. The following book, however, is an excellent overview of the technical issues in designing interactive systems—in covering UML and other core topics:

- Wieringa, R. J., *Design Methods for Reactive Systems*, Morgan Kauffman, 2003.

4.7.5   Research resources

If you want to pursue a research career, there are several excellent reviews:

- Baecker, R. M., Grudin, J., Buxton, W. A. S., and Greenberg, S., *Readings in Human-Computer Interaction: Toward the Year 2000*, 2nd ed., Morgan Kaufmann, 1995. Almost a thousand pages of collected classic papers in HCI.

- Carroll, J. M., editor, *Human-Computer Interaction in the New Millennium*, Addison-Wesley, 2002. Here, Jack Carroll commissioned chapters from leading researchers reviewing and previewing HCI at the turn of the century.

- Carroll, J. M., editor, *HCI Models, Theories and Frameworks*, Morgan Kaufmann, 2003. This is a more recent, focused, summary of most of HCI.

- Perlman, G. maintains a very useful web site at hcibib.org, which includes www.hcibib.org/readings.html, covering readings in human-computer interaction, user interface development, and human factors.

4.7.6 Journals, conferences, digital libraries, associations

Journals and conferences will help you keep abreast of the subject. *Personal and Ubiquitous Computing* (Springer) is perhaps the closest journal to *Press On's* interests: the design, evaluation, and innovation for ubiquitous, handheld, and mobile devices and applications.

Better than going to your local library or surfing the web, join a society of like-minded people. Start with the ACM Special Interest Group in Computer-Human Interaction (*ACM SIGCHI*)—see www.acm.org/sigchi—and the British Computer Society group, the BCS HCI Group—see www.bcs-hci.org.uk, or join the The Usability Professionals' Association—see www.upassoc.org. These professional groups run conferences and have good journals; their web sites also link to many useful resources. Although ACM SIGCHI is international, if you do not live in either the United States or the UK, your own country will probably have a good national group to join. Join it.

The International Federation for Information Processing (IFIP, see www.ifip.org) is the umbrella organization for all national computing societies, such as the ACM and BCS. Its Technical Committee 13 (TC13) specializes in Human Computer Interaction and has numerous working groups—such as WG13.4, User Interface Engineering (see www.se-hci.org). You can join IFIP working groups and take part in their conferences and other activities.

■   ■   ■

The best resource by far is *you*. Don't take my short reading list as definitive; at least go to Amazon.com or some other good web bookshop and see what else the authors write, or explore what other books the people who buy them buy: follow the trails into new areas.

Don't just read stuff or join groups; start research by *doing* design, start doing experiments, write programs, get involved, build things, and make things happen (you'll find lots of ideas in this book). Find facts and principles to criticize other people's work—and find out how to do better. Then, of course, you talk about and write up what you have done and throw it into the pit with all the other contributions at conferences, and the community will help you improve, and you will help the community improve.

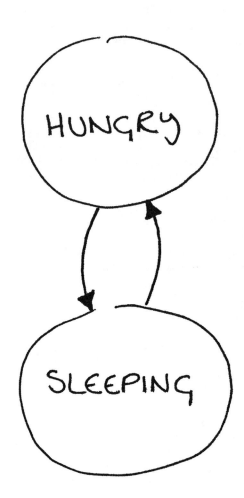

I wouldn't give a fig for the simplicity on the near side of complexity; but I would give my right arm for the simplicity on the far side of complexity.

— *Oliver Wendell Holmes*

Part II
Principles

It's hard to understand even simple interactive devices. In part II, we introduce and develop the principles behind interaction programming: how devices work and how they really should work.

5

Communication

As long ago as 1084BC people wanted to communicate over long distances. A series of beacon fires lit on hills enabled Queen Clytemnestra to learn of the fall of Troy when she was five hundred miles away. According to the Greek historian Polybius, by 300BC, a more sophisticated method of signaling using a code was in use. In this case, each letter of the Greek alphabet was written in a 5-by-5 grid, and the code for each letter was its row number then its column number. This code could be tapped out. Similar versions of the code have been reinvented and used by prisoners to tap to each other through cell walls, certainly since medieval times. In 1551 the mathematician Girolamo Cardano suggested using five torches in five towers, an innovation that would mean the code could be used over greater distances. From the early eighteenth century, people were starting to propose using electricity for long-distance communication, but the only methods known that would work at all were based on static electricity. Static electricity is prone to leakage and isn't reliable over any distance; it is useless outdoors, where wires can get wet. An anonymous letter written in 1753 proposed using separate wires for communication, one for each letter of the alphabet, and proposed watching swinging pith balls attracted by static electricity to read the message.

To cut a long story short, by the mid-1800s all the technological and scientific developments were in place to communicate over long distances—waiting only for a practical user interface—and a means to stay in business. In fact, they had much the same problems as any modern user interface designer.

The story of communication and how it developed over this lively period raises almost all of the issues of modern user interface design, but without the complications. And it's interesting.

5.1 The beginnings of modern communication

Depending on which side of the Atlantic your sympathies lie on, attention now turns to either Samuel Morse in North America or to Sir Charles Wheatstone in the United Kingdom. Almost simultaneously these two—and many others— were working on the telegraph. Both characters were highly creative. Morse was an accomplished painter who exhibited in the London Royal Academy and was founder of the US National Academy of Design; Wheatstone invented a wide variety of gadgets, including a pipe organ, the concertina, and the stereoscope. He

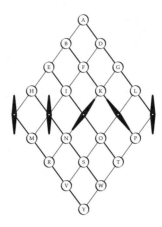

Figure 5.1: Schematic of the display of an original 1837 Cooke and Wheatstone tele-graph design. The five needles had brass stops, so that the operator could hear them clicking as they swung into position. Here, the display is indicating the letter K.

didn't invent the Wheatstone bridge, which was named after him, but he did in-vent the Playfair cipher, which was named after somebody else. Wheatstone and Morse's approaches to communication were very different, and their story high-lights ideas that are true for *any* sort of communication.

Wheatstone, and his colleague William Cooke, were first to develop a viable communication system that was made available to the public. The system was first demonstrated in July 1837 using wires strung along the railway track from Euston to Camden Town (railway stations in north London), covering a distance of about 1.5 miles. They successfully transmitted and received a message. The impact of this must have been enormous; bear in mind that the Penny Post—snail mail—was introduced three years later. A decent electric light bulb had to wait until the 1870s with Sir Joseph Wilson Swan's patent (granted before Edison's, by the way, and which explains the brand name Ediswan).

Not only were Wheatstone and Cooke working decades before the light bulb had been invented, they had to invent the entire user interface themselves. They had to invent keys and displays as well as a coding system that would work for sending messages.

How did Wheatstone's telegraph system work? The users of Wheatstone's tele-graph used (what we would now call) desktop-sized displays, which had five nee-dles. Each needle could be swung to the left or the right by electromagnets, so it would then point along a diagonal line of letters arranged in two triangular grids. When not energized, the needles rested in a vertical position.

To transmit a letter, the user pressed two keyswitches, which caused the cor-responding needles at the other end of the telegraph wire to move and together point along two lines in the grid. The letter at their intersection was the chosen letter. The Wheatstone grid allowed 20 letters: the letters C, J, Q, U, X, and Z had to be omitted. If only one needle moved, it was taken to point at a digit, so numbers could also be sent easily. By 1838, Cooke had patents for *mobile* devices, a premonition of today's mobile communications technology?

Despite its shortcomings, the Wheatstone telegraph could be used by relatively unskilled operators: using the grid was pretty self-explanatory and easily learned. Of course Wheatstone had to overcome ignorance and attachment to traditional methods—nobody knew what a telegraph was, or what advantages it would offer. So it was a big advantage minimal training was required.

One of Wheatstone's early telegraphs helped catch a murderer, John Tawell, on New Year's Day 1845. The message read:

> A MURDER HAS JUST BEEN COMMITTED AT SALT HILL AND THE
> SUSPECTED MURDERER WAS SEEN TO TAKE A FIRST CLASS TICKET
> FOR LONDON BY THE TRAIN WHICH LEFT SLOUGH AT 7H 42M PM HE
> IS IN THE GARB OF A KWAKER WITH A GREAT COAT ON WHICH
> REACHES NEARLY DOWN TO HIS FEET HE IS IN THE LAST
> COMPARTMENT OF THE SECOND FIRST CLASS CARRIAGE

Crucially, the telegraph message travelled faster than the train Tawell was on. Tawell was apprehended near Paddington railway station; he was later hanged for his crime.

The five-needle telegraph required five wires (Wheatstone had an ingenious way of avoiding a sixth wire for the common return that would normally have been needed). Over miles, the cost of wire (and keeping it working) was not insignificant. The original design of telegraph was soon replaced by a single-needle instrument, to cut down on the number of wires required. Each letter of the alphabet was then given a code of several right and left needle movements, but this now required skilled operators—they had to know what the code was, as it could not be read off the front of the telegraph "display" as before. One operator was needed to send the message, and *two* skilled operators were needed to receive it: one to read the needle movements and one to write the message down. As events proved, Wheatstone's modified scheme, though cheaper, was still harder to use than Morse code, which became dominant worldwide.

At almost the same time that Samuel Morse, working in the United States, was developing his code, he was developing his own telegraph to use with it. His first design was a machine that recorded the message on a moving paper tape, which he felt important for record-keeping purposes. Recording made Morse's telegraph uniquely different from all previous distance-communication approaches, such as smoke signals and semaphore, which leave no record of the message. Wheatstone's system too made no records—any message had to be written down by hand.

Morse was aware of the advantages of automatic recording, and thought it had potential. He soon found, however, that it was easier and faster for operators to listen to a buzzing sound rather than read the dots and dashes and transcribe them—you can listen and write easily, but you can't watch and write easily, as Wheatstone had found out. After several false starts, Morse devised his eponymous code.

Morse code was not at all like what we recognize today. In fact, it isn't totally obvious that Morse himself invented it. There is a lively dispute about the contribution of his assistant, Vail, and whether others helped. Regardless, Morse was a great promoter of the code.

Originally, Morse had each letter or digit coded on a metal ruler—so the user sending a message needed to find the ruler (but did not need to know the code on it), and then put it through the transmitting device. This idea made sending a message easy to learn, but slow.

One of Vail's innovations was to use a tapping key, so operators could tap out *any* code, an innovation with both advantages and drawbacks. The operators no longer needed to hunt and find the right ruler, so they were faster, but they now needed to learn the codes. Unlike the Wheatstone system, operators of the modified Morse system needed training to use it effectively. Even so, speeds of ten or more words per minute were easily achieved.

The first US telegraph message sent over a decent distance, from the Supreme Court room in the Capitol to Baltimore, was transmitted by Morse and recorded on his paper tape. Morse gave credit to Annie Ellsworth, the daughter of a friend, for suggesting the now famous message, "What hath God wrought?" from Numbers, chapter 23, verse 23. It seems Morse was acutely aware of the potential for abuse or misuse of the telegraph: "Be especially careful not to give a partisan character to any information you may transmit," he wrote to Vail. We could heed his advice today.

Morse had some problems getting his ideas accepted in Europe, not only because of patent problems (Morse code was patented in 1840) but also because of the continental European habit of using accents in their writing.

In the modern international Morse code, each letter and digit (and a few other signs) are represented by dots and dashes. For example Q is ▬ ▬ • ▬ which is spoken as "dash dash dot dash." Note that the dots and dashes must be separated by short silences; otherwise, we'd just hear a continuous buzz. The usual convention is that a dash is worth 3 dots, the gap between dots and dashes is 1 (silent) dot unit, and individual letters are separated by 3 (silent) dot units. To send Q therefore takes a total time of 16 dots. Words are separated by 6 silent dot-length units. If all letters were coded like Q, every letter would take 16 dot units to transmit.

But it was Vail, apparently, who realized that if the more common letters are given shorter codes, even at the expense of making other letters longer, the average length of a message could be shortened. The story is that Vail went to a newspaper printers and saw that they had more letter Es in lead type than other letters, because any page printed needed more Es than other letters to be in stock. Thus E, the most common English letter, is represented in Morse code by a single dot.

Roughly, the Morse code length of each letter is inversely proportional to the amount of lead needed for it at the printers. If this story is correct, then as the bar chart in figure 5.2 (facing page) suggests, the printers must have had most Es, then T, I, S, N, A, U, R, and so on, down to Y, Q and J being least used.

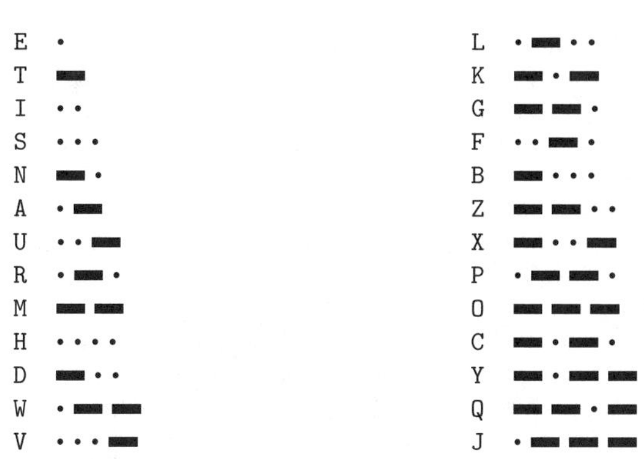

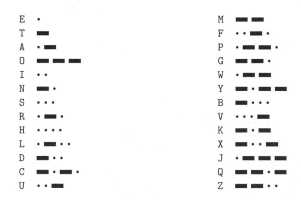

Figure 5.2: Morse code, drawn like a bar chart sorted by increasing length of the codes for each letter: E is the shortest code, just a dot, and Y, Q, G are the equal longest. Read the codes from left to right (for example, N is a dash followed by a dot).

Figure 5.3: Morse code, now drawn with each letter in frequency order, E being the most commonly used letter in English (at the beginning of the table), and Z the least commonly used (at the end of the table). The length of the codes does not correspond well to frequency of use.

In fact, using computer analysis, the letters in English ordered by decreasing frequency is more like ETAOIN ... (taken from the British National Corpus of 90 million words) not Morse's order, which starts ETISNA ... The graph plotted but with the letters in their actual frequency order looks like the graph in figure 5.3 (this page). Clearly, Morse is not optimal for English.

As it happens, the Brown Corpus, an American collection, has the same letter order as the British Corpus, so Morse isn't ideal for US English either. Morse would be bad for Welsh, which has Y as its second most common letter, yet in Morse, Y is one of the longest letters.

123

Box 5.1 Small screen interaction User interfaces come in four main screen sizes: TV sized—as on a typical computer; small—as on a mobile phone; tiny—as in 10 character LCD displays; and none at all—just lights and fixed text printed on the box.

Obviously the bigger the display, the more that can be done with it, but at the cost of greater size and expense. In the case of mobile devices, there is an issue of resolution: what might be good enough for watching television may not be good enough for reading text. But there is a surprising difference between TV and mobile-sized displays. The human visual system is very good at working out certain sorts of visual relationships: for example, we can see this object is in front of another one, because it partly occludes the other. These automatic features of our vision are one of the important perceptual supports on which windowing systems rely. We see windows as if they are real objects, and we can see quite easily (although not always) which window is in front, which is behind, and so on.

On a small screen, these visual cues may not be available. Even if little display markers are used to indicate in a theoretically clear way, our automatic visual processing skills won't be used.

This explains why WAP phones, which tried to duplicate the success of web browsers on PCs, failed miserably.

Morse code can easily be improved. The techniques we will discuss in this historical setting work for modern interaction programming.

5.1.1 Costs of improving designs

Morse could have got two more codes taking the same duration as Z, X, P, O, or C, using • • ▬ ▬ and • ▬ • ▬. These two codes aren't used anywhere else: so with this insight he could have made the codes for two of Y, Q, or J a bit shorter. Whether Morse wanted a six dot code, which would be the same duration, but harder to send, is another matter; perhaps it would be confused with digit codes? Morse might have thought about digits and other symbols: it is possible that he wanted to have punctuation, and he might have designed his code to send frequent punctuation efficiently—even if this is true, the rank ordering of letters should have been unchanged, and the bar chart in figure 5.3 (previous page) should have shown the lengths of codes increasing through the chart. They don't, so his code isn't very good for English.

It is also possible that Morse wanted his code to have properties other than speed. Perhaps he expected that users would confuse some short codes? By making the codes longer than strictly necessary, he introduced redundancy—perhaps a user could work out what a letter was if they missed a single dot or dash? Certainly, if a user ever heard the code • • ▬ ▬, they would know a mistake had been made. If our more efficient code had been used, then this might have been mistaken as a Y or Q even if it was a mistake. In other words, and as a general principle, the more compact a code, the worse it gets at handling errors.

Although we can improve Morse code to make it more efficient, technical improvements are different from *real* improvements. When lots of people use Morse

Box 5.2 The QWERTY effect The letters QWERTY are the first few from the first row of letters on a typical keyboard. There are millions of QWERTY-style keyboards; and "the QWERTY effect" is the belief that if there are so many of them, then they *must* be efficient.

History of course is a lot more complex. There were many styles of keyboards as the earliest typewriters were being developed, with all sorts of keyboard arrangements. One of the successful typewriters, made by Christopher Sholes and patented in 1868, happened to set the pattern for the future. It's important to note that the typewriter as a whole was a successful commercial product, not necessarily the keyboard design considered alone.

The prototype designs used by Sholes often locked up as the keys jammed; he avoided this problem by—depending on whom you believe—either arranging the keys to slow people down, or arranging them so that common digrams were typed by alternating hands. One complication to this story is that in those days, it was envisaged that people would type with their index fingers, and not touchtype using all their fingers and thumbs. Another complication to the story is that to start with there were very many typewriters and alternative keyboard layouts literally fighting it out—by typing competitions and by all the usual fair and foul means—and QWERTY was the winner.

It was late in the day, the 1930s, by the time August Dvorak did his experiments on keyboard layout and patented his Dvorak Simplified Keyboard. The improvements in typing speed are marginal, but for this new design to take over the world it would have to show a better whole-life efficiency in a world where most typists are trained on QWERTY layouts— and when small improvements in reducing carpal tunnel syndrome are discounted. Dvorak isn't *that* much better (evidently).

code, as they did, "improving" it is not just a technical game we can play in isolation to how people use it. We would have to retrain everyone who already uses Morse code. That human cost in something as widely used as Morse code overwhelms almost any other considerations.

There's also a nice twist: because a scheme is dominant means it does not get changed much, because the social costs of changing dominant systems are overwhelming. The denial of the need to change, together with the daunting thought of the cost of change, is an obvious design paradox.

▷ Some people think that if a design doesn't get changed much, it must be the best there is: see box 5.2, "The QWERTY effect" (this page).

■   ■   ■

Today Morse code is consigned to the pages of history, but the design lesson is still pertinent: get the user interface as well designed as you possibly can *before* you release your product—once it is released its very success in the market will squeeze out competitors, including its own future usability improvements.

The history of the telegraph is far more complex than we can cover in this book, but there is one final lesson. Weber and Gauss (the famous mathematician) invented and demonstrated an earlier telegraph in Germany in 1833, still not the first, but certainly predating both Morse and Wheatstone. Their telegraph failed because the German post office had a monopoly on long-distance communication: to go into business with a successful device, you need a commercial proposition, and you can't do that in a restrictive regulatory environment.

5.1.2 From Morse code to Huffman codes

On December 12, 1901, Marconi used radio to communicate across the Atlantic Ocean, and Morse code became widely used, particularly for shipping—it was used famously to signal the sinking of the luxury Royal Mail Steamer *Titanic* on its maiden voyage for the White Star Line in 1912 when it hit an iceberg. Morse code faded out in 1999 when, by international agreement, it was superseded by modern digital methods: today if you have the necessary digital equipment to transmit messages, you aren't going to need Morse code. Your mobile phone, for example, is far too sophisticated.

Jumping past the development of codes in World War II, for our story on interface design the crucial development was Claude Shannon's mathematical theory of information and communication. Shannon's theory suggested that codes could be designed that were much more efficient and also that there were fundamental limits to the efficiencies that could be achieved.

Shannon, and independently Robert Fano, found ways of creating such efficient fully compressed codes, but their methods were not practical. The quest was on for a practical way to generate efficient codes.

There is a story about the breakthrough that was achieved by an MIT student, David Huffman, who was in Fano's class. The story goes that Fano gave his class a choice: either they could solve the coding problem or they would have to pass the exams the usual way. Huffman hadn't done any revision, and at the "point of no return" he realized that he'd fail his exams or he'd have to solve the problem. Literally, as he threw his study notes into his rubbish bin, he had the insight that is now called Huffman coding—and Fano passed him.

5.1.3 The structure of codes

Although Morse code has dots and dashes, it is not strictly a two-symbol or binary code because it has conventions for gaps—gaps between letters and gaps between words—making a total of four symbols in all. Rather than stay with Morse code, then, we'll now describe how to construct a binary Huffman code.

In binary we have two symbols, 0 and 1, that are transmitted. Imagine a stream of 0s and 1s: those are the only symbols we have—there is no third symbol for gaps between them.

Suppose, as in figure 5.4 (p. 128), that we have coded E as 011. That means that no other code can be allowed to start 011. For example if T was 0110, we could not tell whether this was E followed by a 0 (perhaps starting something following) or a T (with nothing following it). If we decide that E is 011, then there must be no other codes starting with the sequence 011. We can use 00..., 1... and 010... for starting other codes, but we cannot use any code starting 011 other than E. This

---

Box 5.3 Information theory When we tell somebody or something a message, we transmit information. Information can be measured, and since Shannon's work, it is customary to measure information in units of bits. A binary digit is a bit too, and the information a binary digit can hold is exactly one bit.

Once you know how much information a message has, you know how many bits it would take to send it. It is not possible to do any better. More generally, once we know how much information a device takes to use (or a problem takes to solve), then the number of bits gives us a lower bound that no design can better. This is a very general result with wide implications. For example, although there are many programs that claim to do it, it is not possible to compress *all* files—because that would mean losing information. Instead, you can try hard to compress *likely* files, and many programs (such as zip, and the GIF and PNG graphics standards) are very good at compressing common sorts of files. Translated back into user interface design, we can make some things the user does easier, but we cannot in principle make everything easier. The trick is to find what is worth doing.

Usually nothing is perfect. In user interface design, we have to worry about users making errors. In information theory, errors are called noise. You want messages to be resistant to noise, just as you want user interfaces to devices to be usable despite the user making errors. One of Shannon's remarkable results (Shannon's noisy-channel coding theorem) was to show that you can work with noise and get arbitrarily low error rates; it's not that more noise (or more errors) decreases what you can do; rather, with judicious choice of codes (or user interface design) you can still make the final effect as reliable as you like, with the proviso that it may take longer to achieve.

The idea that you don't want to destroy a day's good work with a single slip is a special case of the principle of commensurate effort. When users work, they create information; the principle of commensurate effort says that the effort of deleting information should be comparable—little things should be easy, hard things harder—with the effort of creating it.

---

property of a code is called being prefix-free: it means that no letter codes share the same prefix.

The alternative to being prefix-free is to block the symbols, for instance, so that every 8 symbols code for a letter. ASCII code, for example, does just this. The disadvantage is that we make the code much longer; ASCII may be fine for computers with lots of memory, but if you were tapping out ASCII using a tapping key, avoiding repetitive strain injury and increasing the speed you can send a message would be more important.

How is a Huffman code constructed? Consider the two least probable letters in English, Q and Z. Because they are least probable, then they must have the longest Huffman codes, but whatever their codes are, they must certainly be different.

Suppose the longest Huffman code we need is XXXXX; if we could tell whether this was a Q or Z before we read to the end of it, the code could be shorter. Thus Q and Z must differ in their last digit. They will have codes such as $XXXX0$ and $XXXX1$, which differ in their last digit so that they can be distinguished.

In figure 5.4 (next page), we have chosen 000011001 and 000011000 for Q and Z. All other codes must differ from Q and Z *earlier* than the last digit—they can't differ later, because all longer codes starting like Q or Z obviously share the same

E	011	L	11111	Y	101001
T	001	D	11110	B	101000
A	1110	C	01011	V	000010
O	1101	U	01010	K	0000111
I	1100	M	00011	X	000011011
N	1011	F	00010	J	000011010
S	1001	P	00000	Q	000011001
R	1000	G	101011	Z	000011000
H	0100	W	101010		

Figure 5.4: A binary Huffman code for English, based on the letter frequencies in the Brown Corpus. Thus E, being the most common letter, has the shortest Huffman code. The letters are shown in decreasing frequency order, so the increasing length of their Huffman codes can be seen easily.

prefix as Q or Z. So, for example, 00001101 is the next shortest different prefix; we can either allocate this to a more frequent letter (say, S) or we can distinguish at least two further codes after it, namely 000011010 and 000011011. In fact, this is what we do for X and J.

We then allocate the next shortest code, 0000111, to K, and this differs from X, J, Q, and Z in K's last digit, which is a 1, whereas this digit is a 0 for all of X, J, Q, and Z.

There are clearly lots of decisions to be made; Huffman worked out how to make these choices optimally. There are many equivalent Huffman codes; for example, if we simply swapped 0 and 1 in the table shown in figure 5.4 (this page) we would get a different code, or we could just swap 0 and 1 in the third position ... but these changes just make new codes that are essentially the same as the one here.

As with the Morse code tables, the Huffman code is shown a bit like a barchart; the letters (E, T, A ...) are arranged in decreasing frequency order, and each code is a "bar" the length of which shows how long it takes to transmit. It is easy to see that frequent letters, like E and T, have short codes, and the lengths increase continuously up to the least frequent letters (X, J, Q, Z), which have the longest codes.

This binary code *looks* longer than Morse code, but Morse code has more symbols to play with than our Huffman code's 0 and 1—Morse has dot and dash *and* the gaps between letters and words. In fact Morse has six symbols: dot, dash, and four sorts of gap—between dots and dashes, between letters, between words and between sentences. The main reason Morse looks much shorter is because it uses more than two symbols; the Huffman table above isn't hiding any secret symbols.

The codes for the letters E and T are dot and dash, so every Morse code letter looks like it must start with either the code for an E or the code for a T. Nevertheless, Morse is prefix-free, even though it doesn't look prefix-free, because we have been ignoring the end-of-letter pauses—no letter other than E starts with dot immediately followed by the end-of-letter pause. Because of the end-of-letter pauses, Morse code has the advantage over a Huffman code that losing a letter

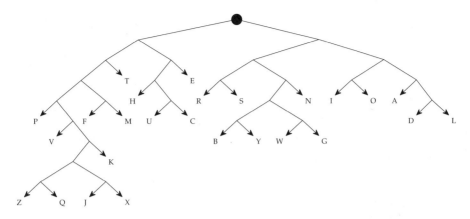

Figure 5.5: A Huffman tree for the alphabet, based on the Brown Corpus frequencies. Frequent letters are near the top of the tree (like T and E) and infrequent letters, with longer paths, near the bottom. Using this tree, the Huffman code for a letter is the sequence of left/right turns in the path from the root down to the letter—take left as 0, right as 1, and you should get the table in figure 5.4.

or two (as could happen with a dodgy communication line) does not matter too much; whereas, in the Huffman code above, if even just one digit is lost, the rest of the message will be garbled because we have no idea where to get back in step with the code.

As before, making a code more reliable makes it longer to send—unless we take into account the time it takes to recover from errors. In Shannon's theory, the error rate is crucial. The speed/reliability tradeoff cannot be avoided and applies to user interface design too.

I've drawn the table of Huffman codes above in what amounts to a user manual for them:

- If your task was to code N, say, then look N up in the table and find the instructions for "doing" N, namely to press 1011, or to press the keys ⓵ⓞ⓵⓵. (If it was a user manual, it'd be easier to use if it was in alphabetical order.)

- The converse task is to decode something, such as 1011, and find out what it means. It's easier to visualize the necessary decisions when the code is set out as a tree: start at the top of the tree and go down branches, going left or right, as you press ⓵ or ⓞ you will eventually end up at goals, like N.

It is much easier to follow the same rules in a diagram, such as those illustrated in figure 5.5 (this page), which represents the same information as the table. For example, if you were decoding 10011, start at the top of the tree, working your way down and turning left or right as you read digits 0 or 1 in the code.

▷   If you are good at programming, you can take it from here with no more help from me; if not, the next section gives you some code you can try out. Section 5.2 (p. 134) discusses applying the key principles in user interface design.

5.1.4   Implementing Huffman codes

Binary Huffman codes are straightforward to work out. This section shows how to get a Huffman code for English letters, assuming (for instance) the probabilities from the Brown Corpus.

First, we need a data structure to represent the probabilities:

```
var huffmanData = [
   {prob: 0.125067,    data: "E"}, {prob: 0.0926049,   data: "T"},
   {prob: 0.0804679,   data: "A"}, {prob: 0.0759412,   data: "O"},
   {prob: 0.0728741,   data: "I"}, {prob: 0.0709648,   data: "N"},
   {prob: 0.0654409,   data: "S"}, {prob: 0.0612792,   data: "R"},
   {prob: 0.0543712,   data: "H"}, {prob: 0.0413553,   data: "L"},
   {prob: 0.0397136,   data: "D"}, {prob: 0.0309693,   data: "C"},
   {prob: 0.027136,    data: "U"}, {prob: 0.0254125,   data: "M"},
   {prob: 0.0231277,   data: "F"}, {prob: 0.0201759,   data: "P"},
   {prob: 0.0194877,   data: "G"}, {prob: 0.0188393,   data: "W"},
   {prob: 0.0172529,   data: "Y"}, {prob: 0.0153575,   data: "B"},
   {prob: 0.0099783,   data: "V"}, {prob: 0.00657725,  data: "K"},
   {prob: 0.00198087,  data: "X"}, {prob: 0.00160446,  data: "J"},
   {prob: 0.00107099,  data: "Q"}, {prob: 0.000949201, data: "Z"}];
```

You can change the probabilities if you want to see how the Huffman code changes with different distributions of probabilities. If you do this, it's worth having some code to check that the probabilities add to 1 (a pedant would also check that each probability was a number between 0 and 1 too; you might have accidentally got a minus sign in the data):

```
var sum = 0;
for( var i = 0; i < huffmanData.length; i++ )
   sum = sum+huffmanData[i].prob;
document.write("Total is "+sum
   +" (which should be, or should be very close to, 1.0)<br>");
```

The numbers above add up to 0.999999971 (though JavaScript doesn't represent numbers accurately enough to do the addition correctly)—but it's close enough to 1 for our purposes.

The Huffman algorithm repeatedly finds the two lowest probability entries and merges them into a pair. In JavaScript, we will replace the `huffmanData` entry of the merged pair with an array of two elements, namely, the two items that have been combined; and we replace the old `prob` entry with the total probability of the two combined elements.

The first iteration of the algorithm finds Z, with probability 0.000949201, and Q, with probability 0.00107099: these are the two lowest probability entries in the original `huffmanData` table. These two entries are merged to make a new single entry, which (since we no longer need it) will overwrite the old entry for Z by

```
{ prob: 0.002020191, data: [data[Z], data[Q]] }
```

The line of code above uses the specific letters Z and Q, but in general, any two entries may be being combined. The code in the JavaScript program therefore uses apos and bpos for the two locations in the `huffmanData` array. For the first iteration with this data they will happen to be Z and Q (or, rather, they will be 25 and 24, respectively, which are the indexes of Z and Q in the `huffmanData` array). Thus on the first iteration in the program, `huffmanData[Z]` will be `huffmanData[apos]` and `huffmanData[Q]` will be `huffmanData[bpos]`.

Merging two elements reduces the number of items in the array by one. The easiest way to handle this is to move the last element of the array down to overwrite the other element; that's done by the last line in the for-loop, `huffmanData[bpos] = huffmanData[n-1]`.

```
for( var n = huffmanData.length; n > 1; n-- )
{ var a = 1, b = 1, apos, bpos;
  // find smallest two items
  for( var i = 0; i < n; i++ )
  { if( huffmanData[i].prob < a )
    { b = a;
      bpos = apos;
      a = huffmanData[apos = i].prob;
    }
    else if( huffmanData[i].prob < b )
      b = huffmanData[bpos = i].prob;
  }
  // merge apos and bpos into apos
  huffmanData[apos] = {prob:   a+b,
                       data:   [huffmanData[apos], huffmanData[bpos]]};
  // move last element of array down to overwrite bpos
  huffmanData[bpos] = huffmanData[n-1];
}
```

The process stops when there is just one entry left, which will be a Huffman tree (with its root at the final merged entry, which is entry 0). Note that the algorithm is destructive: we will have lost the original data in `huffmanData`.

Finally, we define a recursive algorithm to walk the Huffman tree and allocate binary codes to each letter:

```
function walk(tree, string)
{ if( typeof tree.data == "string" )
    document.write(tree.data+" "+string+"<br>");
  else
  { walk(tree.data[0], string+"0");
    walk(tree.data[1], string+"1");
  }
}
```

Using it just means walking starting from the root:

```
document.write("Data in Huffman code order:<br>");
walk(huffmanData[0], ""); // generate the entire Huffman code
```

This will generate a table of the letters and their corresponding Huffman codes, starting from P, whose code is 00000, to L, whose code is 11111 (unless you fiddled with the probabilities). Codes like E = 011 come near the middle of the table in this ordering.

Remember that all the JavaScript code above will work perfectly in an HTML web page if you place it between <script> tags:

```
<html> ... <body>
<h1>A Huffman code for the Brown Corpus</h1>
<script>
... JavaScript code ...
</script></body></html>
```

The key point is that you can replace the letters (A, B, ...) in the data structure with anything, such as function names for interactive devices, and the code will work just as well. Instead of making Huffman codes for efficiently transmitting letters, you'd be making Huffman codes for efficiently using devices.

Unfortunately, Huffman codes using more than two symbols (here, 0 and 1) are a little trickier to work out. Every step of a binary Huffman code construction combines two items into one; this reduces the number of remaining items by 1, and the final step necessarily has exactly two items to combine. If we have an N symbol code and S symbols to Huffman code, naively starting by combining the N lowest probability symbols has a couple of problems: there may not be that many symbols to start with (if $S < N$), and at the final step there usually won't be exactly N subtrees to combine, so the top level of the tree won't be full. That certainly would not make an optimal code.

The easiest way to solve this problem is to add enough dummy nodes with zero probability to ensure the tree will be optimal. Once the tree is constructed, the zero probability nodes can be ignored (because they occur with zero probability). You will need to add enough zero nodes so that $S \bmod (N-1) = 1$.

It is even harder to generate a Huffman code when symbols can have different lengths, as they do in Morse code (where dashes take longer to send than dots). Fortunately for us, Morse code is officially obsolete, and all of the user interface design we will do in the rest of this chapter with Huffman codes will use constant length symbols—they'll just be button presses.

5.1.5   Technical details

Huffman codes are widely thought to be optimal in terms of producing the shortest coded messages. There are several reasons why Huffman is *not* optimal. One is that there is no reason to suppose a *particular* message I send, like "What has God wrought?" should comply with the overall letter frequencies of a large selection of text, like the Brown Corpus we designed our code for; it doesn't even have an E.

A Huffman scheme that adapts to the particular message's specific letter frequencies would be better for that message: this is *adaptive coding*. Furthermore, as a message proceeds, the relative frequency of letters changes: in some parts of a message E may be rare and in other parts common. An adaptive scheme changes the code as it proceeds.

Morse's original message contains only 10 different letters, and we could design a special code for them rather than for the whole alphabet—and do it more efficiently, too, since we wouldn't waste code space for letters that are never going to be sent.

Huffman is a so-called symbol code; each symbol it codes, it codes as another whole symbol. Each letter becomes a distinct symbol in the Huffman code of so-many bits. If a letter has a theoretical minimum code length that is a fractional number of bits, like 2.3, Huffman has to round this up to a whole number of bits in the code: it cannot do better than 3 in this case. This inefficiency is pretty much inevitable, as there is no reason why the letter frequencies should come out at whole numbers of bits for the optimal code.

If we code more than one letter at a time, the fractional bits can be "shared" between the Huffman codes. As it were, if we needed 2.3 bits followed by 2.4 bits, we could combine them to 4.7 and hence use only 5 bits; whereas, sent separately, they'd need $3 + 3 = 6$ bits.

If we coded pairs of letters (digrams) rather than individual letters, in most messages many pairs don't occur at all (such as QX, QY, QZ, ...) and we don't need to code them. In Morse's message, we effectively reduce the alphabet to one about 1.5% the original size of $26 \times 26 = 676$ pairs, an even better saving than getting to 10 from 26 for the message-specific single-letter code. We can code letters with fractional numbers of bits too; and the more letters we combine into symbols, the more efficient it will be.

There is a trade-off, of course. If you want to send a message, the message is certainly going to be shorter, but you need to know more of the message before you start; and if you make mistakes, you are going to make bigger errors, affecting more of the message. Message sending will become less interactive.

■ ■ ■

We've covered all this ground to review efficient communication methods, and to look at some of the design trade-offs, with the added interest of a historical setting. Obviously efficient communication is important in many contexts, not just for the special case of sending messages between humans.

So far this chapter has discussed communication as a technical process that connects humans, from beacon fires to radio communications. But communication need not be human-to-human, it can also be between humans and interactive devices. In one case, your brain wants to get a message to somebody else's brain: you might use Morse code or a Huffman code to send the message to the other *person* efficiently. In the other case, your brain wants to get a message to a *device* you are trying to use.

> **Box 5.4 Video plus** To record a program on a DVD or PVR, the user must specify the date, the start and end time of the program and the channel it will be broadcast on. This is quite a lot of information, about 12 digits, and it is easy to make a mistake—and if you do make a mistake, you probably won't discover it until after you find out you failed to record the program, when it's far too late to do anything about it.
>
> Timing information is a good candidate for compression, to make it easier to enter correctly. The simplest approach is to have the user interface to remember the last details: typically, you won't change all of them, so to enter a new program time you only enter the changes needed. For example, for a whole year, you could get away with not reentering the four digits needed to specify the year. If you always record the same program every week, then usually the only detail that needs changing is the day of the month—only two digits.
>
> Gemstar's Video*plus+* is another scheme some DVD and video recorders support for making recording programs easier. With Video*plus+*, TV listings in newspapers and magazines additionally show a number, ranging from 1 to 8 digits, as well as the conventional channel and timing information.
>
> If you have a basic recorder, you'd have to enter the full details. If you have a Video*plus+* enabled recorder, you would enter the Video*plus+* number. This number is a compressed code for program times, so it is much faster to enter—and it uses Huffman coding to generate the code.
>
> The disadvantage of Video*plus+* codes is that they are meaningless, and the same code will record different things if used at different times—for example, on any given date, all Video*plus+* codes for earlier dates are be recycled to be used again for the future.
>
> ▷   Huffman codes are discussed in section 5.1.3 (p. 126).

How can we use the historical ideas of communication to improve interactive device design? We want to communicate our ideas not to other people at the end of a telegraph or radio, but to devices we are trying to use.

5.2   Redesigning a mobile phone handset

So far we have considered using coded messages for people to communicate with one another, when that communication is mediated by a telegraph or radio link that can only handle certain symbols, such as dots and dashes (and spaces) or 0s and 1s. We saw that compression techniques allowed us to reduce the number of wires needed from 26 to 1 (or 27 to 2 if we count the common return), and we saw that the ideas of Morse and Huffman allowed the codes to be chosen to reduce the time taken to send a message—Huffman's being a more systematic approach than Morse's.

The ideas for communication between people work equally well when we are sending a message from one thing to another thing: the "things" needn't be people and the messages needn't be human language.

Wires become buttons (or, more generally, actions a user can do), and the codes then become the rules the user follows to achieve things, which will be activating functionality in the devices rather than transmitting letters.

Now consider the following problem. I have two hands and ten fingers and I want them to send "messages" to my mobile phone. The messages are going to be coded instructions to get the phone to do useful things for me. For practical reasons, namely, that I need one hand to hold the mobile phone, I am only going to be able to use one hand for typing my message. Furthermore, the phone, being a phone, already has 10 digit buttons on it. To ask for many more buttons would make the phone bigger and heavier, which I don't want.

As before, we will need a prefix-free code, for the obvious reason that if 123 is the code for redialing, we don't want to have to have any confusion with another code such as 1234 that does something else: we want the code to specify dialing unambiguously when we've finished saying do it. Of course, we might want to allocate redialing a different code than 123, for instance because it is frequently used, a shorter code; but that is a different problem from being prefix-free—in fact, this choice of code is exactly like wishing to allocate E a shorter code in Morse because it is used more often than other letters.

The best way (under broad assumptions) to allocate efficient codes is to use a Huffman code. If I want to select functions on my phone quickly, I should be able to use a Huffman code that uses ten digits (rather than two binary digits we used in our comparison with Morse code) to select from the phone's functions.

For concreteness, let's take the Nokia 5110 mobile phone. We will be concerned with the Nokia 5110 mobile handset's menu functions, though there are a number of essential functions that are not in this menu (such as its quick alert settings and keypad lock), which we won't deal with here.

It probably would have been better had Nokia included these few functions, like quick alert, in the main menu, then users would be able to find them by searching the menu system. As it is, a user has to know these functions by heart, or else they cannot be used. There would be no harm in having them in both the menu (so they are easy to find) and as quick functions that can be used faster than going through the menu to find them. We will see later that the Nokia provides shortcuts for all menu functions anyway; again, the handling of keypad lock (and the few other functions) is inconsistent.

The general design principle that a function can be accessed in more than one way is called permissiveness. The argument for permissiveness is that it allows the same function to be accessed in several ways, so the user does not have to know the "right way" to use it, as there are alternatives.

In total, there are 84 features or functions accessible through the main menu. Menu systems on phones are all fairly similar. For the Nokia, a soft key, ⊟ (called the navi key by Nokia) selects menu items (whether or not they are functions; some menu items select submenus); the keys ⋀ and ⋁ move up and down within menus. The correction key ⊂ takes the user up one level in the menu hierarchy.

The structure of the Nokia menu is illustrated in the summary table in figure 5.6 (p. 137). So, with reference to the figure, the function "Service Nos" can be accessed from standby by pressing ⊟ (the phone now shows "Phone book"), then pressing ⊟ (phone now shows "Search"), then pressing ⋁ (now shows "Service Nos") followed by a final press of ⊟ to get the desired function to work.

135

> **Box 5.5 Permissiveness** As designers, we decide how a device should support some behavior or user task. For example, a phone should be able to send text messages. A user might want to keep an address book, so it should be possible to write a message and send it to a named person—so the mobile phone will use the address book to supply the actual number needed to send the text message. This is routine. Also routine is merely implementing this idea in the device.
>
> The device can now do what users say they want. Unfortunately, this design is impermissive. What about the user who thinks first that they want to send a message to George. If they select George from the address book, can they send him a message? On my Nokia 8310 the answer is yes, and it can be done the other way around: the user can write a message first, then decide whom to send it to. Fine. Except that Nokia decided to allow messages to be saved, so that they can be reused. Now, if I want to send a saved message to somebody, I must first select the saved message then decide who to send it to.
>
> Impermissvely, I cannot decide whom I want to send a message to, *then* decide whether to write a new one or use a previously saved message. In short, this design supports a task, but only if it is done in the "right" order. Yet I am free—that is, permitted—to do it either way if I want to write a new message.
>
> Had the designers made a list of tasks the device supports (which can be done automatically from its specification or program), then they could have listed the various ways each task could be accomplished. There would need to be good reasons why some tasks could be done only in one way. Each rule about how a device has to be used (you must do it in *this* order) is a burden for the user to remember and a potential error for the future. Permissiveness makes devices easier to use.
>
> Permissiveness is not always a good thing, however. Sometimes permissiveness encourages errors you would prefer to design out. Permissiveness is obviously bad when security is an issue: you generally should not permit a user to do something before or after they have entered their password—although you could work through the interesting design questions for the unconventional choice of entering a password afterward.
>
> ▷   See also sections 5.2 (p. 134), 8.7.2 (p. 253) and 12.3.1 (p. 417). For a "converse" example, see section 11.4 (p. 387)—you usually don't want a gun to be easy to use: you want to be certain it will only work (that is, impermissively) when it is used correctly, and by the right person.

All menu items have a numeric code (displayed on the Nokia's LCD panel as the user navigates the menu). For example, "Service Nos" can also be accessed by pressing ⊟①② (no final press of ⊟ is required). The shortcut is an example of permissiveness (shortcuts provide alternatives, so the value of shortcuts is another indication that permissiveness is a good design principle).

There are some little complications in the shortcuts I shall ignore in our thinking about redesigning the Nokia: except to say that ⓒ does not work with shortcuts (e.g., ⊟②ⓒ① is equivalent to ⊟②①, as if ⓒ was not pressed). It is important to note that there is no fixed relation between shortcuts and a function's position in the menu, since some functions may not be supported (e.g., by particular phone operators): if "Service Nos" is not available, pressing ⌵ would move from "Search" directly to "Add entry," but the shortcut for "Add entry" would still be ⊟①③ and trying ⊟①② would get an error. Taking these provisos into consider-

Phone book   [−] [1]
   ⟶   Search   [−] [1] [1]
           Service nos   [−] [1] [2]
           Add entry   [−] [1] [3]
           Erase   [−] [1] [4]
           Edit   [−] [1] [5]
           Send entry   [−] [1] [6]
           Options   [−] [1] [7]
           ⟶   Type of view   [−] [1] [7] [1]
                      Memory status   [−] [1] [7] [2]
           Speed dials   [−] [1] [8]

Messages   [−] [2]
   ⟶   Inbox   [−] [2] [1]
           Outbox   [−] [2] [2]
           Write messages   [−] [2] [3]
           Message settings   [−] [2] [4]
           ⟶   Set 1   [−] [2] [4] [1]
                      etc
                      . . .

Figure 5.6: Extract from the Nokia mobile phone menu, showing the menu items and their shortcut codes.

ation, our model of the Nokia 5110 is still substantial: it has 188 menu items and 84 user-selectable functions.

The table in figure 5.6 (this page) is a bit like the Huffman codes table. Apart from the indentation, down the left we have what the user wants to do, but now it is phone functions like "Inbox" rather than sending letters like N or Q. Down the right, we have what the user needs to do, pressing buttons, where in the Huffman table we had binary codes for letters. For the phone we can use more keys the Huffman binary code had, which used only two "keys," [0] and [1].

As with the Huffman tree, shown in figure 5.5 (p. 129), here we can visualize how a user chooses functions by tracing routes through a diagram, which is shown in figure 5.7 (next page). The Nokia tree is much bigger, and I have therefore not cluttered it up with the names of menus and functions; the tree therefore gives an accurate impression of the complexity of the user interface without, in fact, helping anybody use it because there are no details shown to do so.

The black dots in the figure 5.7 represent menu functions. "Standby" is at the top of the diagram and each press of a button ([∧], [∨], or [−]) moves downward (or diagonally downward)—if you make a mistake, not taking an optimal route to a black dot, you go upward. The diagram has been carefully drawn so that this is so. When you move through the diagram and land on a black dot, this is a menu function.

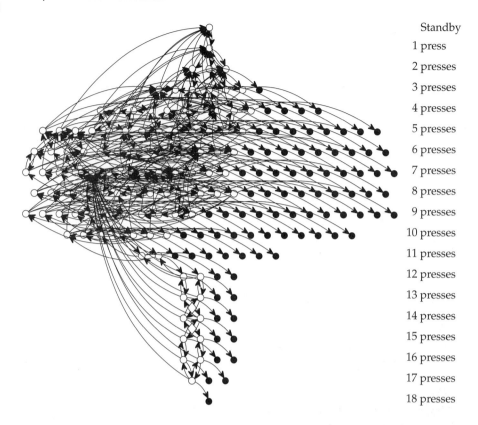

	Standby
	1 press
	2 presses
	3 presses
	4 presses
	5 presses
	6 presses
	7 presses
	8 presses
	9 presses
	10 presses
	11 presses
	12 presses
	13 presses
	14 presses
	15 presses
	16 presses
	17 presses
	18 presses

Figure 5.7: The menu tree for the Nokia 5110 mobile phone. Phone functions are represented by black dots, and all the white dots are intermediate menus. For clarity, arrows going out of phone functions (e.g., many go back to "Standby") have not been shown. The diagram is a ranked embedding: drawn so that each row is the same minimum number of presses from "Standby." To use the device, start at the top, and each *correct* key press will move you down a row toward the function you want—assuming you know the optimal route and you make no errors.

As the diagram makes clear, some functions are easy to activate (they are near the top), and some require quite a lot of pressing—these are the ones lower down in the diagram. For clarity, I've deleted all arrows going out of black dots: they all go back to "Standby" via the phone functions the black dots represent.

5.2.1   Estimating probabilities from a design

In order to use an efficient coding scheme like Huffman's, we need to know or estimate the probability that users do each function on the phone.

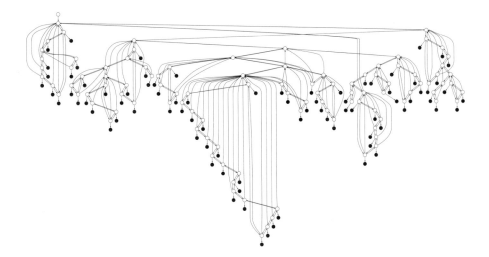

Figure 5.8: This is exactly the same menu structure as shown in figure 5.7 (facing page), but shown here with a different layout. As before, standby is at the top, and each black circle is a phone function; everything else is a menu item. Each wiggly column is an individual layer of the menu structure—in this diagram (in principle) it's easier to see that a user can go backward and forward within a layer of the menu. As in figure 5.7, the back arrows to standby are not shown, as they merely add a lot of clutter. The arrowheads on the lines are too small to see at this scale, but graphs as complex as this would normally be viewed with suitable visualization tools that can pan and zoom.

▷ This diagram was drawn by Dot, the graph-drawing tool discussed in section 9.5.1 (p. 291).

We could do some experiments, but let's suppose Nokia has done them already, and they chose the original menu structure accordingly to make it as easy to use as possible. If so, then Nokia considers the function that takes 18 presses to get to be the least likely to be used (how often do you change your phone to use Suomi, which is what this function is?), and Suomi is less likely to be used than either of the two functions taking 17 presses.

For the sake of argument I will take the probabilities of functions to be proportional to the reciprocal of the number of button presses the Nokia takes to achieve them. So if a function takes 17 presses, then its probability is 1 in 17 compared to the others. In particular, this means that the second most frequently used functions are assumed to have a probability of half the most frequent. Obviously all the probabilities should add up to 1.0, since the user is certain to do one of the possibilities. Looking at the numbers in the table in figure 5.9 (next page), the relative probabilities for the Nokia are $1/_1$ ("Search" is the most popular function), $1/_2$, $1/_2$, $1/_2$ (several functions come equal second) ... $1/_{15}$, $1/_{16}$ (the hardest thing to do is

Function	Presses	Rank	Assumed probability
Search	3	1	0.0613
Incoming call	4	2=	0.0306
Inbox	4	2=	0.0306
Speed dials	4	2=	0.0306
Service nos	4	2=	0.0306
...	...	...	...
Português	16	14=	0.00438
Svenska	16	14=	0.00438
Español	17	15=	0.00408
Norsk	17	15=	0.00408
Suomi	18	16	0.00383

Figure 5.9: The functions of the Nokia phone and the least number button presses required to get to them from "Standby." The table is ordered starting with the easiest function first. The probabilities are proportional to the reciprocal of the function rank: so, for example, we assume the user wants to do "Inbox" half as often as they want to do a search.

ranked sixteenth). These fractions add up to 16.325, so to get probabilities, which must add to 1, we divide through everything by 16.325; the probabilities are then 0.0613, 0.0306, 0.0306, and so on.

Working out the details, we get the table shown in figure 5.9. On the Nokia, we have 4 keys ($\boxed{\wedge}$, $\boxed{\vee}$, $\boxed{-}$, and $\boxed{C}$) to select from 84 functions. According to our table in figure 5.9 (this page), getting to a function takes the user from 3 to 18 presses; in fact, the average is 8.83, or if we weight by the Zipf probabilities, the average is 7.15 key presses. The weighted average is better because we don't often want to do hard things.

In fact, we are using what's called a Zipf distribution of probabilities. Originally, George Zipf noticed that in natural language we don't use long words often, and words we use often are short words, like "be," "the," and "do." If a common word like "the" had once been a long word, over time it would have shortened or abbreviated to save people the effort of saying it so often. In English "the" is a shorter word than "apostrophe," as you want to say it far more often; phrases like "intellectual property" are shortened by people who use them a lot to abbreviations like "IP." Eventually, a language follows a Zipf distribution—which is not just that frequent things are shorter, but in particular, that the second shortest words occur half as often as the shortest, the third shortest words occur a third as often, and so on.

Zipf himself elevated his ideas to a principle: the Zipf principle of least effort. That is, he found empirical data about word lengths, and to explain this he supposed that in principle people want to communicate with least effort. If people want to send messages efficiently, whether in English or to talk to their phones using menu selection codes, they will end up with word lengths or phone menu selection key counts following a Zipf distribution. English can be changed by its

---

Box 5.6 Card sorting For the mobile phone example, Huffman creates an efficient menu tree grouped one way, and Nokia has a menu tree grouped another way. The text shows that there is a way to combine the advantages of both, but if there are two different ways to do something, why not consider more? There may be ways that are more appropriate to what either the designers think or what the users think about the structure of the menu tree.

Card sorting is an easy technique that can be used to find tree structures that people prefer for any set of concepts, such as menu items. Card sorting can also be used to help design web sites—the items are then web pages.

First, write the names of the items on cards. Use a large font size so that the descriptions can be read easily by participants in the card sorting when the cards are spread out on a table.

Next get some participants, around six to fifteen people. It is advisable to use card sorting with designers and users: you then know both what the structure ought to be, and what the intended users think. Card sorting can be used for helping design a company's web site—a classic mistake is to think that the users are people *in* the company—the people who know it best—when in fact, the users are people *outside* the company.

Shuffle the cards, then simply ask the participants to group the cards in any way that makes sense to them. If you get the participants to name groups of cards, you can then replace those groups with new cards and thus create a tree hierarchy of the concepts.

If a group of people are card sorting, it's likely that there will be disagreements on how to sort the cards into groups. Usually renaming some of the items will help—card sorting thus not only provides a structure but also better names for the items.

Behind the simplicity of card sorting lies the statistical method of cluster analysis, which can be used when you have a big sorting problem or wish to combine data from many people. There are many programs available, such as IBM's EZSort, that can help in card sorting, and do the cluster analysis for you.

With a well-designed device, there is no need for the structure to be fixed; for instance, it could be redefined, either by the individual user's preferences or by uploading different firmware.

▷ For a warning to designers not to be oversimplistic when card sorting, see the discussion on cities and trees in section 8.7.2 (p. 253).

---

speakers to do just this but mobile phone users have to use what they are given. Thus it would be sensible for Nokia to have arranged the phone so that common things are easy to do, so the design should follow a Zipf distribution. We are now taking Zipf's principle of least effort the other way around: assuming the phone is efficient, then Zipf's principle implies using the probabilities we have chosen.

When we design what we hope will be a better menu organization in the next section, we will be comparing designs using Zipf distributions. However, we could redesign the menu structure using *any* distribution we pleased; Zipf is just one plausible choice. If we had better data, or a better theory of phone use, we would be able to design even better systems—maybe even ending up with Nokia's own design, if they happened to use the same theory. Our approach to design does not depend on the right theory; in order to be used it just needs some probabilities.

Code	Function
⊟ 1 1	search
⊟ 1 2	service nos
⊟ 1 3	add entry
⊟ 1 4	erase
⊟ 1 5	edit
⊟ 1 6	send entry
⊟ 1 7	*not allocated*
⊟ 1 7 1	type of view
⊟ 1 7 2	memory status
⊟ 1 8	speed dials
⊟ 1 9	*not allocated*
⊟ 2 1	inbox
...	...

Figure 5.10: Examples of numeric shortcuts for accessing menu items. From "Standby," if you press ⊟ 1 6, for instance, the phone would get to the menu item "send entry," which is faster than pressing ⊟ and then using the ⋀/⋁ buttons to go six entries then pressing ⊟ again to get to the desired state.

5.2.2   Creating a Huffman code for the phone

Now that we have some probabilities, we can create a Huffman code. We will retain the Ⓒ key for corrections, so we can only use the three remaining keys (⋀, ⋁, and ⊟) for the actual code. A Huffman code designed for these keys then takes an average cost of 4.14 presses to access any function, or 4.04 weighted with the probabilities. This is a considerable improvement, almost twice as good in terms of speed.

Nokia may not have designed the menu structure purely for speed, but it ought to make some sense to users (so, for example, all the messaging functions are grouped together under a single "Messages" menu). However, being slower by a factor of about two seems like quite a conflict.

Perhaps realizing the menu structure was not fast, Nokia has also provided shortcuts. The shortcuts use all ten digits; see figure 5.10 (this page). With the shortcuts, a user can either use ⋀, ⋁, ⊟, and Ⓒ to search the list of functions, as before, or, provided they know the shortcut number, they can press ⊟ then enter the shortcut code.

The average cost of a Nokia shortcut is 3.39 key presses. This is better than our Huffman code because Nokia's code is using ten digits, rather than three menu selection buttons the Huffman code uses, and so it can be coded more efficiently. But if we use a ten-digit Huffman code ourselves, the average cost can be better still, down to 2.98.

It's possible that Nokia chose their shortcuts carefully for some special reason. For example, if they bring out a new phone, perhaps they want ⊟②⑤ to do the same thing on the new phone as on the old phone. If so, they can't just use a Huffman code to allocate the codes; there are constraints. My guess is that an overriding constraint is that it is easier to program the shortcut codes the way Nokia did; I can't think of any usability reason for them to be as they are.

Perhaps the Nokia shortcut codes are important—say, so that new phones are as easy to use for users who have already learned the codes from older phones. If we don't want to lose the existing codes, we can exploit the fact that the Nokia short-cut codes don't use all the codes that are available: we can squeeze a Huffman code into the remaining shortcuts that haven't been used by Nokia. Not surprisingly, a squeezed Huffman code does worse than an unrestricted Huffman code using ten digits freely, but surprisingly at an average of 3.09 keystrokes to do anything it does *better* than Nokia's original shortcut codes.

We can now have a phone with Nokia's original shortcuts, to preserve whatever benefits they have, *and* we can have a faster Huffman code. The two codes can permissively coexist. Users can use the Huffman code whenever they want to be faster—which is presumably the point of shortcuts.

For some functions the original Nokia codes will be better than the squeezed-in Huffman codes, and if a sensible user uses the shorter of the two (if the new Huffman codes are worse, we don't need to say what they are: just provide one shortcut code for the function if the Nokia shortcut is the better), the average drops to a mere 2.69. In other words, if we want to design a well-structured menu system (following Nokia's original hierarchy), also retaining Nokia's original shortcuts codes, we can still make improvements to the user interface for experienced users. Furthermore, the design improvements can be determined automatically, merely by providing the usage data.

Design	Best case	Worst case	Average
Original Nokia	3	18	7.15
Huffman, 3 key	3	5	4.04
Nokia shortcuts	2	5	3.39
Unallocated Huffman	2	4	3.09
10 digit Huffman	2	4	2.98
Shortest	2	3	2.69

We've got an improved user interface design for the Nokia mobile phone without losing any of the (real or purported) advantages or features of the existing design.

There remain two intrigues. First, why do the shortest codes have a worst case (longest, hardest-to-do function) of 3 key presses, compared to 5 (for Nokia) or 4 (for Huffman)? Fortunately the hardest functions to do are different for the two-code systems; as it happens, the hardest functions to activate using Nokia's own shortcuts can be done more efficiently by the Huffman codes.

The second intrigue is more subtle. The combined shortest code, which is based on Nokia and Huffman, does better than the unrestricted 10-key Huffman code. The combined code has an average of 2.69, but Huffman got 3.09. How can a combined code be better than the theoretically best code? The answer lies in the fact that Nokia's shortcuts aren't prefix-free—they rely on the user pausing between

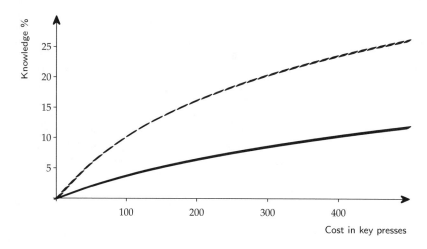

Figure 5.11: A cost-of-knowledge graph for the Nokia 5110 function menu. The dashed line is based on Zipf weights; the solid line is based on uniform weights—thus the graph shows that a user takes longer to learn this device if they press buttons equally often, rather than following Zipf probabilities.

codes. The pause amounts to using an extra PAUSE key, as it were—so the Nokia shortcuts are really using 11 keys. It is not surprising they can be a bit more efficient. A Huffman code with an extra key could do even better too.

▷ Further tree comparisons are made in section 8.7.4 (p. 256), which compares balanced and unbalanced trees.

5.3   Visualizing design improvements

The table above gives a dense and hard-to-follow comparison of several different designs. Fortunately, we can visualize the design options and benefits better than by using a table of numbers for each design. As a general rule, try to visualize design choices and decisions—seeing things in different ways gives the designer more insights and many issues can be represented visually rather than as text.

There are many ways to analyze and understand a user interface from its specification, and some lend themselves to visualization. The cost-of-knowledge graph is one visual representation that helps show how easily a user can access the features of a system. The cost-of-knowledge graph shows the number of goals a user can access (that is, functions they might want to do) against the number of user actions it takes to get to those functions. The graph shows the knowledge of discovering, learning, or using device features against the cost of doing so.

The cost-of-knowledge graph can be constructed from empirical data (from knowing what real users actually do), from cognitive analysis (psychological rules about behavior), or purely analytically, as we now do. The graph can be drawn from any data; a designer would use the best available. The more realistic the probabilities used, the more realistic the evaluations and new design insights that can be drawn from them.

A cost-of-knowledge graph for the original Nokia menu system is shown in figure 5.11 (facing page). The solid line shows an unweighted cost of knowledge graph, taking every user action as equally likely. Weighting (by the Zipf probabilities) gives a more realistic measure of knowledge, which is shown by the higher dashed line.

We can see that in "average" use to achieve a coverage of 25% of the device's features takes 455 button presses. (This figure does not translate nicely into a time, since the cost-of-knowledge assumes the user acquires knowledge and thus pauses in each new state.)

The dashed Zipf line is higher because it discounts features Nokia has made hard to use. Since the user is presumably less interested in some functions than others, the Zipf probabilities reflect this well. The differences between the two lines make a case for getting good data from experiments; nevertheless, it is worth noting that the *shape* of the two lines is similar, and a designer may want to gain insights from the shape rather than the absolute values.

Just as the functions can be weighted by how likely it is that the user wants them, the keys too can be weighted by how often they are used. For example, we took the probability of pressing the keys to be equal; the probability of pressing the $\boxed{\text{c}}$ key is 0.25, which is possibly too high, since a user would only use it for corrections. If we make using the $\boxed{\text{c}}$ less likely, then the graphs would show the devices to be easier to use, because the less often users correct errors, the sooner they can find out how it works. On the other hand, if we took the probability of pressing $\boxed{\text{c}}$ to be zero, then the device would become impossible, for once users have got to a function, they wouldn't be able to back out of it and find another.

Figure 5.12 (next page) shows that the cost-of-knowledge graph for the Huffman tree interface is considerably better (in terms of speed of access to the device's functions) than the original design; for example, it achieves 25% coverage after only 168 presses (compared to 455 presses for the original Nokia). Even so, the model still overestimates the costs because of the assumption of pressing the $\boxed{\text{c}}$ key with probability 0.25.

5.4   Make frequent things easy, unlikely things hard

Zipf's principle and Huffman codes are different ways of expressing the design principle, make frequent things easy, unlikely things hard. The principle both describes what people do naturally, and describes how a system should be designed to be natural to use. The ideas are all very well in theory, but using an interactive device is not theory. For example, we humans make errors, and we can learn to do some things (things we practice a lot) quickly regardless of their raw efficiency. All the advantages of a theoretically efficient code would be lost if we had to keep

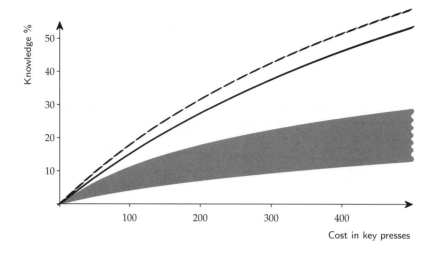

Figure 5.12: Cost-of-knowledge graph for the redesigned Huffman tree interface—as in figure 5.11 (p. 144), the dashed line is Zipf weights; the solid line is uniform weights. For comparison, the lower gray region represents the range of data from the original Nokia as shown in figure 5.11. Evidently, for any number of button presses, the user learns about twice as much as they could about the original design; also, the difference between random pressing and efficient Zipf pressing has been reduced—the new design is easier to learn even when you don't know how to use it efficiently.

looking it up in a user manual. Instead, then, we might make some codes longer to make them more memorable or to make it harder to activate some things by, for instance, a single accidental key press.

The designers of the JVC HRD580EK PVR made an infrequent and hard operation too easy to do. The remote control has a single button that advances the clock by one hour—in many countries the time changes by one hour for summer saving. This makes a normally hard job very easy to do. Conversely, press the button for two seconds and the device's clock goes *back* an hour, for winter saving. These operations need only be used once a year each, which is why they are worth simplifying because most users won't remember how to adjust the clock if they only do it once every six months. But the operations are *too* easy. The device is often running several hours fast because the button can be tapped by accident. (Also, for no reason I can understand, the clock advance function is the same button as the transmit button, which is used frequently for other purposes, so if you press [Transmit] when the remote control is not in the right mode, you adjust the time instead.) On the other hand, some facilities that are used far more often than once a year are designed to be much harder, and involve complex button sequences. These functions are hard to do by accident, but they are unnecessarily hard to do deliberately!

Box 5.7 The principle of least effort The least effort principle automatically solves a problem of closure. Closure is the sense of finishing a task; typically someone persists in doing something until they get closure. Problems arise when they get closure *before* they have finished—these problems are often called post-completion errors, because the error is caused after the person thinks they have completed their task.

If a user sets up a PVR to record a program at a later time, it is necessary to press the [Timer] button to tell the PVR to enter timer mode; otherwise, the PVR remains under direct control and will not record the program at the set time. This is a closure problem, since the user thinks they have completed the task of programming on transmitting the time details to the PVR (they have reached psychological closure). Thus, they may not think to press the [Timer] button, and there is no cue to prompt them to do so. In least effort terms, the user is more likely to want the PVR in timer mode after entering program recording times than not. Thus the code for entering program times and timer mode should be shorter than for entering program times and not entering timer mode. This directly leads to a design where there is a button to be pressed to exit timer mode after transmitting timer instructions.

 ▷   Post-completion errors are also discussed in section 11.4 (p. 387). Another example is given in box 6.1, "Syringe pumps" (p. 168).

Summer saving isn't the only problem. Every remote control has an [Off] button, which the designers *know* won't be needed as much as any other button (after all, you only need to press it at most twice for anything you want to do), yet it is as easy to press as anything else. Once you switch the device off, on the badly designed devices, you've lost part of the setup and have to start again. To make things worse, the [On] button is often made easy to find, which makes sense, but most remote controls make on and off the same button—so the [Off] button ends up being too easy to use.

On a mobile phone, at least in the UK, every number dialed is short (such as 999 or 111) or begins with a zero or plus sign (an abbreviation for the international prefix). Why doesn't the phone automatically insert a 0 before any long-enough number that the user hasn't already started with a 0 or + and make it easier for them? This idea is another example of making frequent things easy. It's ironic how easy it is to overlook ways of making things easier.

 ▷   This PVR is also discussed in sections 3.4 (p. 66) and 10.3 (p. 330).

5.5   Efficient but more usable techniques

Huffman codes aren't memorable, but if you want to be quick they are ideal. (You can also use Huffman codes to find out fast design, to compare with an actual design to see if it can be improved in theory.) Given that Huffman codes show it is generally possible to do much better, can we find ways that are faster *and* easier?

We'll now try hashing, a technique familiar from programming, that is an efficient way of searching. Users, too, want to search interactive devices, to find the commands or functions they want efficiently.

The digits on a mobile phone can be used for writing text messages. So, for instance, the digit ②has letters A, B, and C on it; the digit ③has D, E, and F on it, and so on. Text messages are sent by pressing digits the appropriate number of times to choose letters. You could send the message ACE by pressing ②once, pausing, pressing ②three times, then pressing ③twice—a total of 6 presses and a pause. This is an unambiguous but slow way of typing. (Note that this technique is not prefix-free—you would not get ACE if you pressed ②four times then ③twice.)

There is a way to do better. The sequence of key presses ②②③can only spell out one of the following 27 three-letter sequences: AAD, AAE, AAF, ABD, ABE, ABF, ACD, <u>ACE</u>, ACF, <u>BAD</u>, BAE, BAF, BBD, BBE, BBF, BCD, BCE, BCF, <u>CAD</u>, CAE, CAF, CBD, CBE, CBF, CCD, CCE or CCF. Only three of these 27 sequences are real English words, which are those that I've underlined.

If we are sending English messages, then ②②③can only mean one of three words: ACE, BAD, or CAD.

It should be easier to choose from three things than from 27. We saw above that the obvious way to use the keys ②②③to send ACE requires 6 presses. Instead, we can press ②②③then take *at most* two more presses of another button to choose ACE from the choice of the three properly-spelled alternatives. If the choices were in alphabetical order, this example would fortuitously work with no extra presses; ACE is the first word to match ②②③. In general we may not be so lucky, and it would make more sense to order the words in terms of likelihood—again using the principle of making the most frequent things easier to do.

Three versus six presses (and some pauses) is a small saving, but if we were trying to type a longer word, the saving gets better. The longer the words, the fewer properly spelled plausible words there are to choose from—and if there is only one properly spelled match, then the user does not have to press anything. That's a nice saving.

There are various schemes for typing on mobile phones like this. Tegic's T9 system is probably most familiar (www.tegic.com). Seasoned text users devise their own codes that are even more efficient than using conventional English. Words like CUL8R ("see you later") and abbreviations like IMHO ("in my humble opinion") and :-), a smiley face, convey large concepts in few keystrokes. A sensible text system would allow users to add their own words (including names) to the dictionary of possible matches.

Tegic's T9 is used to speed up writing text messages, and we can use the same idea to type not English words, but words from the list of functions the phone supports. Instead of English, then, our dictionary will have words like "search," "incoming call," "inbox," and so on. Instead of typing words, we'll be controlling the phone.

Imagine we are using the Nokia 5510 again. We press ⊡first—just as we would to start a standard Nokia shortcut. Now, however, we spell out the function we want using the letters on the digit keys. So if we want the inbox function, we type ④⑥②⑥⑨; in fact, inbox is found as the unique match well before we've needed to type all these digits.

We can do even better by being permissive. Suppose we cannot remember whether the Nokia function is called "speed dials," or called "dial speed." Our dictionary can have two (or more) entries for each function: in this case, one for "speed" and one for "dials." So long as users can remember at least one word of the function they want, they will be able to find it.

Gary Marsden and I built a phone using a variation of this idea, and we evaluated it comparing it with Nokia's original design. It did better. In one of our experiments, the Nokia design took users 16.52 presses against the improved redesign taking only 9.54 (a statistically strongly significant result). Better still, almost every user preferred our new design.

The new design excels when users do not know where the function they want is or even what it is called.

■ In the original Nokia, if you have to search for a function (you know it's there, but you can't remember its name or what submenu it is in), you are setting out on an exploration that will take over 100 presses—if you don't make a mistake (it's easily possible to cycle around submenus endlessly unless you recognize when you are going around in circles). As it is hard to count the number of presses required for a full search, I wrote a program to do it.

■ In contrast, at any stage of entering a function name, the new design presents all function names that have not yet been resolved but that match what you've pressed. In particular, when the user has only pressed ⊟, the device will present the user a list of every function to choose from—because every function name matches the nothing the user has so-far selected. (If the user pressed, say, ② next, you'd get a much shorter list, every function starting with A, B, or C only.) This means that users can press ⊟ and then scroll down the list till they recognize the function they want. There is no chance of going around in circles, and users don't have to do special things to enter submenus and get out of them when they've finished exploring them.

So the new design has a systematic way of searching through all function names, and it provides this feature "for free" as part of the improved approach to selecting specific functions.

5.5.1 Modelessness

When new features are added to a design, they often either introduce the need for more buttons (which will cost money and take up space), or they make the device more complex, by introducing more modes. In one mode, the device works as before, and it the other mode, the new feature is available. Since there are fewer buttons, the device is cheaper to make and looks simpler. On the other hand, a user may try to use the device when it is in the wrong mode for what they want to do: modes make errors more likely—worse, what might have been a harmless slip in the right mode, may do something unwanted and unexpected in the wrong mode.

Box 5.8 Dictionaries Samuel Johnson's invention of the dictionary was a major design feat: he had to invent alphabetical ordering, and use it consistently for every word in the dictionary. The first edition was printed in 1755, following about ten years of work. Dictionaries are a very good example of the need for appropriate structure in user interfaces.

How often have users complained that there are too many features in their mobile phone, office photocopier, or other device? "If only it did what I wanted and no more, I wouldn't get confused! I'd be able to find what I want!"

A dictionary would be almost useless if it only had the words in it you wanted today. Instead, dictionaries have millions of words in them—and, generally speaking, the more the better—within limits of size, weight and cost. Since words in a dictionary are in alphabetical order, you can find (mostly) what you want and not accidentally look up the wrong word. In contrast the more "words" or features your photocopier has the harder anything is to find. What gadgets need, then, is *structure*, like alphabetical order.

Johnson's dictionary would still have been useless if its users didn't understand alphabetical order, and of course, it would have been useless if he, its designer, didn't understand order either. We need design structures *users* must be able to understand too.

And there's another twist: there are some design structures that are easy to design with, and easy to understand—trees being a good example—but they compartmentalize features in ways that may not be what the user expects, so they are surprisingly hard to use. The designer might think the interface is well-organized, which it is, except the user doesn't know what that organization is.

▷   See the discussion on trees in section 8.7.2 (p. 253).

Sometimes modes are unavoidable, but sometimes we can develop a modeless or less modey design by careful thought.

How can we make the shortcut feature "modeless"? In a normal, basic, phone there are two modes: the user is either dialing or doing menu selection (or whatever they want to do after getting to a phone function)—and they have to decide which, before they can do it.

In the modified design, the phone can be doing either as the user enters numbers. The device does not care whether ④⑥② is about to call the number 462 or is about to select the "inbox" function. Users can decide what they are going to do after they have finished entering the numbers, rather than before. As they enter a number, the phone finds the all matching commands from the number, as described above. If they press ⊡ (or whatever ⌷Doit⌷ is called on the phone) the phone will do the corresponding function; if they press ⌷Dial⌷ the phone will call the number they have just entered, as usual.

This flexible rearrangement in order avoids a classic, and common, user error caused by modes. On the modified phone, you can't make the mistake of typing in what you think is a shortcut only to notice you forgot to press ⊡ first, and you are dialing a number instead.

▷   This sort of error is a completion error; see section 11.4 (p. 387) for more detailed discussion.

5.5.2 Adapting to the particular user

In our improved Nokia mobile phone design, the list of possible functions that match what the user has typed so far is given in alphabetical order. Alphabetical order is familiar and allows users to search methodically.

As users work with a phone, they will use features different amounts of times. If a function is very popular for a user, why not move it to the beginning of the list of matches, so it is easier to choose than scrolling through to it?

The phone could count which functions users access. The lists of choices are then displayed in a most-frequent-first order. Now the most frequently chosen function, whatever it is, can be accessed by the user in just two keystrokes: namely, first press ⊟ so the function is shown at the top of the list, then press ⊟ a second time to select it. Most of the next 8 most popular functions can be selected in 3 presses, namely, ⊟ then the digit corresponding to their first letter, then ⊟ to select them from the list. The functions the user never accesses, and therefore is unfamiliar with, would remain in alphabetical order for easier searching.

Although adaptiveness means that a phone becomes increasingly easier to use for particular users, it does have the drawback that the structure of the user interface keeps changing as the phone tries to be helpful. If the device can have the user's full attention, this may be fine, but if the device is, say, a car radio (see below) the user has better things to do—namely, driving safely—than to keep reading the device's screen to see what function to choose.

A compromise design, which reduces the possibly of surprising adaptiveness, is to display the first 4 (or so) matching functions in frequency order, then *all* matching functions in alphabetical order regardless of frequency. Now the user can get the most popular functions easily, and everything else stays fixed; moreover, the four most popular functions won't change order often, whereas if the entire list was frequency-ordered, the bottom of the list would change often.

I haven't done the experiments that might help us decide whether the number 4 ought to be 5 or 3 or something else. If I was rushing a new phone to market, I would make the number user-selectable—users could then choose to set it to 0 and effectively disable the adaptivity. Some users probably want 3 choices, some want more, and preferences would let them be in charge of their own user interface.

5.5.3 Context of use

This chapter has not considered where users work with their mobile phone; it's been taken for granted that making the device take fewer button presses would make it "better." It'll certainly make it faster to use, but it may not make it better, depending on what the user is trying to do. If we want the user to pay for using the phone, or play, or buy advertised products, then taking *more* time might be better than taking less time.

A cynic would also add that most users won't notice small improvements in efficiency; instead, a manufacturer putting effort into making a device more attractive would make the product more successful. Efficiency, ease of use, and reliability cannot be seen and therefore are easy to ignore.

▷ Making quality visible to consumers is a good reason for visualizing design properties—a topic we cover in many places in this book, including section 5.3 (p. 144) in this chapter, and section 9.5.1 (p. 291) later.

What the user is doing could cover a wide range of situations. For concreteness, we'll consider driving a car—an activity that demands almost all of the user's attention most of the time and on occasion demands all of it when hazards are encountered.

All of the mobile phone schemes considered thus far require the user to look at the phone's screen to see what is happening, or the user has to be skilled to know all the (possibly arcane) key sequences that activate desired functions.

Older people have reduced accommodation (they find it hard to change the distance they focus their eyes at). If they are driving a car, they will find focusing on a device's close-up screen difficult when most of the time they are looking into the distance to drive along the road safely. Older users are also likely to have many other impairments: their fingers may be stiffer, and small keys may be harder to use. Given that (with luck) we are all going to get older, we had better design with these needs in mind.

A head-up display could be used (the images they project onto the car windscreen can appear to be in the distance, which avoids the eyesight accommodation problems), and they have the advantage, for all drivers, of making them at least look in the right direction without being distracted from the road to look at the device screen.

Or we could use speech.

None of these techniques change the effort to use the device: the number of keystrokes or voice commands is the same. The driver has more important things to do than select one out of many functions on a mobile phone. A safe solution is for the phone to disable menu selection (and text messaging) when the car has the ignition switched on.

If it seems too radical to lock out all menu functions from the driver, a weaker but important improvement would be to disable all timeouts in the phone. On my mobile phone, and most others, if the user does nothing for 10 seconds, the phone changes mode to explain what the current function does. Now the user interface is subtly different—to continue searching for the function, the user has to either wait about 30 more seconds (to let the phone get to the end of its help), or press buttons to get out of the help. This is exactly the sort of unpredictable user interface drivers do not need—whether or not their phones are hands-free, they won't be brain-free.

5.5.4   Devices don't always need to be easier to use

This chapter has given various ways to make devices easier to use, but maybe that isn't what's needed.

Mobile phones reduce smoking amongst teenagers, probably because it is too tedious to hold a phone, dial, speak (or use texting) and smoke all at the same time. If we made mobile phones easier to use, it would make it easier to smoke. There are good reasons not to make using mobile phones easier!

Mobile phones are often stolen. Why aren't they sold in pairs with radio tags so that they won't work when they are more than a few meters away from their owner—or so that they squeal loudly when they are stolen or left behind by accident? Apart from issues of theft, many devices need to be differentially easy: authorized people should find them trivial, unauthorized people should find them impossible.

Games would be boring if they were too easy: their difficulty has to closely match the user's competence. Finally, some devices are intrinsically dangerous, or have features that are safety related and should not be used by accident—which means they must not be too easy to use.

▷ See section 6.2.1 (p. 176) for a case study of a gun.

5.5.5 Different techniques for different tasks

We have tried to make a mobile phone easier to use, but users have different tasks, and making some things easier doesn't always improve the overall experience. A user has at least two tasks—*accessing* a function they want, or *searching* for a function when they don't know where it is. Mostly differrent tasks cannot be optimized in the design in the same way—though texting to access phone functions automatically gave a simple search for the user.

For a change, we will now look at the design of a fax machine. The DF200 is a BT fax, with commands structured in a tree, much like the Nokia phone's menu. The DF200 has only 49 functions (compared to the Nokia's 84), so it is in principle easier to use and learn.

▷ See also box 1.3, "An obituary for a fax" (p. 27) and section 1.9 (p. 27) for more on the DF200 fax.

Most of this chapter, we've been quite slow describing interaction designs; now we'll speed up and compare several at once. The table below shows costs of accessing and searching for functions on the actual DF200 and on various alternative user interfaces that we could design.

Design	Average access cost	Worst case access cost	Complete search cost
Actual DF200	5.86	13	117
Linear search	24.5	49	49
Texting	9.29	17	49
Binary search	5.69	6	53
Direct access	1.9	2	1.9

We have taken the original design and worked out numbers for button presses to access or find a function in each of the ways; the table shows the average case, the worst case, and how many key presses it takes to search every function the device supports. Although the data for the figures is unweighted (and therefore makes no assumptions about the kind or frequency of user's tasks), it is clear that certain sorts of task are better served by different sorts of user interface design. The actual DF200 design is sub-optimal for almost any task.

■ The average cost is the cost to access any function averaged over all functions, assuming the user makes no mistakes and knows the most efficient way of doing everything.

■ The maximum cost is the worst key press cost (assuming the user knows the most efficient way to do anything and makes no mistakes).

■ The complete search cost is the cost to look for a function that the user knows is present but does not know how to access except by searching for it. Again, this is assuming the user knows how to use the device and makes no mistakes—they never get lost or go round in circles.

To know the complete search cost requires solving the Traveling Salesman Problem for the device, which is not easy to work out.

▷   The traveling salesman problem is discussed in section 8.1.2 (p. 231); it is also compared to the Chinese postman tour, its dual. Chapter 9, "A framework for design," explains in detail how to work out most of these numbers from a specification of the device design.

If a measure like the cost of a traveling salesman problem is difficult to work out in theory, it *must* be very difficult for a user to work out—users are unlikely to know or be able to keep track of optimal algorithms. In fact, there is no reasonable way users can solve the complete search problem without making mistakes on the DF200, and hence real users would do much worse than the table suggests. Put another way, if "complete search" is a likely task, then the user interface should be structured in such a way that a solution—or good enough solution—is easy to find. Unfortunately, this is certainly not the case with the DF200.

The different designs compared in the table are:

Linear search Linear search requires only a very simple three-button user interface, $\wedge$, $\vee$, and $\boxed{\text{Doit}}$. Pressing one button takes the user through all the functions, one by one; the other direction command is needed in case the user overshoots what they want; and of course $\boxed{\text{Doit}}$ does the selected command for the user. On average, finding a command the user knows about, such a simple design like this is harder to use than the original DF200, because there is no particularly fast way to find any command. On the other hand, if the user needs to search through all commands, it is much easier (49 presses against the original DF200's of 117), because all the user has to do is press $\wedge$ (or $\vee$) until they find what they are after. On average, a user would find a command half way, so on average they'd take 24 presses.

Texting the function Using the scheme introduced for the alternative Nokia design, in section 5.5 (p. 147), the more keys the user has the faster they can home in on their chosen function. The average cost is higher because the user has to spell the function name, and the function names were not chosen to be brief.

Binary search One way to search efficiently is binary search. With a binary search, the DF200 would show the user a command in the middle of the list in its display panel, the user would indicate whether the command they are after is alphabetically before or after this command. It is possible to do away with a (Doit) key, but having one allows the user to correct mistakes before selecting a function to do. The user would carry on until getting to the desired command. This is faster than linear search: in general, if there are n commands, a binary search will reduce the search time from n steps of a linear search down to $\log_2 n$ steps.

▷ There are good and bad binary searches; see section 8.7.4 (p. 256), which introduces balanced trees—as opposed to the unbalanced, bad trees.

Direct access The DF200 is a desktop-sized device, and it could have a list of functions printed on it, each one numbered. The user could read this list then enter the corresponding number. As there are almost 50 functions, functions can be accessed directly by pressing at most two digits. For this design, the table's figure for the complete search cost is a bit of a cheat, because the user has to search by eye through the printed list—the number of key presses (rather than the total time taken by the user) is still the same, 1.9, however. As before, a (Doit) key would allow users to confirm choices or if necessary correct mistakes, which for this design would be a good idea as the fax responds to commands so fast (under 2 keystrokes on average) that it may already be doing things before the user notices.

▷ What we've called direct access here is the same as using shortcuts, a feature the Nokia mobile phone uses, as discussed in section 5.2 (p. 134) earlier in this chapter; shortcuts give direct access to the corresponding functions.

From these five different user interface designs, we can say that direct access seems best, though it requires a help sheet or a very skilled user who has memorized the codes. Binary search seems next fastest, but it's user interface is not very intuitive. Linear search is very simple to use, but slow. Some of the approaches, such as linear search, are so simple and use so few keys they can be combined with other approaches, and thus achieve the advantages of both. Once you start thinking about ways to design a user interface, there are lots of possibilities—Huffman codes, for instance—and it isn't difficult to compare them and see what tasks they are better at for the user. Our quick survey of different approaches forces two questions: where do new design ideas come from, and why didn't the DF200 designers use a better approach?

5.6   Faxes and Huffman codes

Fax machines do use Huffman coding—but not to improve their user interface. A fax is a black and white picture, transmitted as a phone message. It's important to make the message—here, a digital binary encoding of a picture—as brief as possible, so it can be transmitted quickly and cheaply.

A fax image is transmitted line by line. Run length encoding is used to compress long runs of the same color on a line—this is a good method because most fax images are just the white background to the image being transmitted. Rather than transmitting each pixel in the white background separately, the lengths of the white stretches are transmitted as numbers. Each line of the picture will be alternating runs of black and white, so a line is transmitted as a sequence of numbers representing the length of runs of alternating color.

Different run lengths have different probabilities. Typically, runs of 2–7 white pixels all the same color happen more often than runs of 1 or 8–11 white pixels, whereas runs of 2–3 black pixels are more likely than either. With this information, Huffman coding is ideal.

Fax machines use a modified version of Huffman coding: runs of up to 63 are sent using a standard Huffman code, but runs of 64 or more of the same color are sent in two steps: first, the fax transmits the multiple of 64 (using a different Huffman code, for 64, 128, 192 ... runs of white or black), followed by the remainder, 0–63, coded as before. Such an approach cannot do better than pure Huffman coding on average, but as Huffman coding doesn't adapt to each individual fax sent, an almost-optimal algorithm is fine most of the time. In any case, simplicity was a sensible compromise when the code was designed in 1980, as the design reduces the size of the code tables needed in a fax machine: it reduces the hardware requirements (once), at the expense of a small increase in transmission costs (every time a fax is sent). Freedom from patent restrictions when the international standard was developed was another issue.

What's interesting for us is that if faxes use Huffman coding, with a thought-out modification, the designers *must* have been well aware of the importance of compressing information to make devices more efficient. They'd worked hard on the fax-fax interaction and chosen a good approach, but apparently they did not stop to think so hard on the human-fax interaction issues. It's a pity they didn't use exactly the same insights to make the user interface more efficient too.

The designers were well aware that faxes need to use the same coding standards, or else they wouldn't be able to talk to one another. Again, it's interesting that the designers didn't think that *people* might like to be able to use any fax too. Why aren't the user interfaces to faxes standardized? In fact, they are all different—and sufficiently different to make unfamiliar faxes extremely hard to use. Users often have to resort to work-arounds. Sometimes I've sent both sides of the piece of paper I'm trying to fax, because I can't work out which side is really being sent: a simple work-around that wastes time, wastes paper, but guarantees success.

If we added up all the time people waste on messing around with faxes, a few moments thought spent on the user interfaces would reap rich rewards for humanity.

5.7   A computer science of interaction

This chapter has explored many ways to improve and compare user interface designs, based throughout on the assumption that users have tasks they wish to achieve with the device, and that they want to optimize some performance criterion—typically reducing the number of keystrokes to activate functions.

The design problem is often thought to involve a lot of psychology and contextual study of users. What are they trying to do? How do they work? An alternative view is that the design problem is core computer science.

When we design computer programs, we want to get computers to do things efficiently and effectively. Standard algorithms have been developed to do sorting, searching, and so on, and to do these things well under a wide variety of assumptions. In this chapter, almost all of the user's tasks we considered corresponded exactly to search problems. Therefore there are algorithms available that a designer should draw on to see what benefits there are to be achieved by systematic design.

This chapter started with an outline study of compression—making shorter codes. Linear search and binary search, for instance are standard algorithms. Hashing is another efficient search technique—and the "text a function" technique explored with the Nokia functionality is merely a way of realizing hash functions for a user to run.

We do not have to think of computers running algorithms; users can. We can then design data structures—the namely the user interface—so that users can employ efficient and easy-to-run algorithms for their problem solving. Making things easier to use is an interaction programming problem.

> ▷ Section 4.2 (p. 96) reviewed the history of books, and argues that many improvements to book technology, to make them easier and more useful to read, like the invention of tables of contents, were fundamental *computational* or interaction programming improvements to their design.

It's a fundamental analogy, and it immediately opens up all of the algorithms and programming literature as a huge resource for user interface design. This book uses well-known algorithms like searching, shortest paths, traveling salesman, Chinese postman, graph coloring, compression, and many more to help design better.

The analogy is not just algorithms equals tasks. A central interest in computer science is not just algorithms but their complexity: how hard they are to use and how long they take. Complexity is a theoretical area, but it is addressing exactly the same issues as usability.

In user interface design we want low complexity (however exactly we define it)—we want user interfaces to allow users to be able to run efficient algorithms on their problems. Designing user interfaces can also be seen as designing computer hardware: what are the basic operations a user (or a computer) needs to run good algorithms? And information theory (particularly Shannon's information theory) underlies everything.

> ▷ Shannon's information theory was briefly reviewed in box 5.3, "Information theory" (p. 127). From chapter 6, "States and actions," onwards we'll start to explore exactly what the user interface "structure" is, and how we can think about it clearly to help make better designs.

5.8   Conclusions

Mobile phones bridge to the past when they ring with their distinctive • • • ▬ ▬ • • • sound, announcing the arrival of a Short Messaging System text message, using Morse code to say SMS. This chapter, too, linked to the past with a brief history of communication from the earliest times. We covered the history of long distance communication, covering a period of three millennia, from hilltop fires to digital mobile phones. The earliest example covered 500 miles; the last example covered the inches between your hand and your mobile phone. The insight is that the general theories of communication, which we illustrated with Morse and Huffman codes, apply equally to conventional communication problems as well as to modern user interface design problems. We saw that the theoretically-motivated design ideas did better than established market-leading commercial designs.

To conclude it's worth underscoring two points:

■ User interface design can always be much improved by a little programming, abstract, thinking

■ Success in design depends on usability—from issues of the balance of training versus usability we saw in the earliest telegraphs, to present-day mobile phones, where the right design balance depends on the task the user is doing.

When users want to use a device, they need to find the device's functions and access them. From an interaction programming point of view, this is a search problem: the user interface has to be searched until the user has found what they want. We know from programming that there are many ways of searching—linear search, hash codes, binary search, to name but a few. Many of these techniques can be taken over into the user interface and assessed for their effectiveness for a user and real tasks. We found, for instance, that a technique based on hashing made a mobile phone's user interface much easier to use.

5.8.1   Some *Press On* principles

■ Technical improvements must be balanced against human costs, such as retraining → section 5.1 (p. 124).

■ Design popular devices especially carefully; they are costly to fix because so many are made → section 5.1 (p. 125).

■ Efficient communication is important for interaction—use the techniques and theories that are available → section 5.1 (p. 133).

■ Make devices permissive → section 5.2 (p. 135).

■ The principle of least effort: make frequent things easy, unlikely things harder → section 5.2 (p. 140).

■ Dictionaries have a huge number of "functions" but are structured to be easy to use → box 5.8 (p. 150).

■ The computer science analogy: users run algorithms to achieve their goals, and computer science knows a lot about algorithms—therefore design by choosing appropriate algorithms for the user → section 5.7 (p. 157).

5.8.2 Further reading

■ Card, S. K., Pirolli, P., and Mackinlay, J. D., "The Cost-of Knowledge Characteristic Function: Display Evaluation for Direct-Walk Dynamic Information Visualizations," Proceedings of ACM CHI'94, pp238–244, 1994.

■ Marsden, G., Thimbleby, H. W., Jones, M., and Gillary, P., "Data Structures in the Design of Interfaces," *Personal and Ubiquitous Computing*, **6**(2), pp132–140, 2002. Introduces the novel mobile phone user interface and our usability evaluations of it.

■ Thimbleby, H. W., "Analysis and Simulation of User Interfaces," *Proceedings BCS Conference on Human-Computer Interaction*, **XIV**, pp221–237, 2000, provides full details of the Huffman code applied to Nokia mobile phones. Details of Huffman codes and fax machine standards are in Hunter, R., and Robinson, A. H., "International Digital Facsimile Coding Standards," *Proceedings of the IEEE*, **68**(7), pp854–867, 1980.

■ Zipf, G. K., *Human Behaviour and the Principle of Least Effort*, Addison-Wesley, 1949. This is the original and classic reference.

Two references of historical interest are:

■ Hubbard, G., *Cooke and Wheatstone*, Routledge & Kegan Paul, 1965. My discussion about Charles Wheatstone draws on this book.

■ Liebowitz, S. J., and Margolis, S.E., "The Fable of Keys," *Journal of Law and Economics*, **33**, pp1–25, 1990, provides more on typewriter keyboard layouts, like QWERTY.

There are very many books on algorithms, almost all of which include chapters on searching.

■ Cormen, T. H., Leiserson, C. E., Rivest, R. L., and Stein, C. *Introduction to Algorithms*, MIT Press, 2nd ed, 2001, is an excellent undergraduate reference covering almost every relevant topic.

■ Knuth, D. E., *Sorting and Searching*, Addison-Wesley, 2nd ed, 1998—which is volume 3 of Knuth's massive *The Art of Computer Programming*. Volume 1 of *The Art of Computer Programming* gives excellent details of Huffman coding. Knuth's *The Art of Computer Programming* is the most detailed and encyclopedic reference book in computer science.

■ MacKay, D. J. C., *Information Theory, Inference, and Learning Algorithms*, Cambridge University Press, 2003, is one of the best and most wide-ranging books on information theory I know.

■ Shannon, C. E., and Weaver, W., *The Mathematical Theory of Communication*, University of Illinois Press, 1998. Claude Shannon's epochal work is still in print.

■ Skiena, S. S., *The Algorithm Design Manual*, Springer, 1998, is an excellent resource giving details of a huge variety of algorithms, as well as their implementation on a CD and on the web.

6

States and actions

Interactive devices and systems range from implants to wearable computers and from clocks in our central heating systems to flight management systems in aircraft. Behind all interaction programming is a simple, core idea struggling to get out. Behind all unnecessarily complex interaction programming is a simpler idea struggling to be heard.

This chapter introduces and explores the key concepts behind interaction programming, which hinge on finite state machines. It turns out that finite state machines are easy to draw, and drawing them gives us more insight into design—finite state machines are pretty good at showing what users do too, that is, they can be used for more than design—they can be used for *understanding*.

6.1 Key concepts

There are four key concepts in interaction: actions, states, indicators, and modes. Put very briefly: the user performs actions, which change the device state, which in turn control indicators. But users may not know exactly which state a system is in; they only know (if at all) which mode it is in.

What are actions? Users can do anything, and one could define actions in many different ways. For our purposes, we are specifically concerned with discrete, atomic actions. *Discrete* means you either have an action or you don't; there are no half-hearted actions, no double-effect actions, no long and short actions. If you want to have a button half-pressed or lightly touched (as on the focus lock on a camera), then you have to think of these as separate actions. In contrast, *atomic* means that there is nothing simpler to consider in a user's actions. User's actions may be quite sophisticated and different people, perhaps people with microscopes, might be able to unravel smaller things inside actions, but we aren't interested in those. If we decide that "changing a CD" is the action, then we are not interested (or we pretend we're not interested) in the fact that this action could be broken down into smaller steps: press the [Open] button, remove old CD, place new CD, press drawer shut. A neurologist might notice even smaller steps going on inside the user's fingers, nerve impulses, even things inside their head, and whatnot; real as they may be, these are not actions that concern us.

Of course, there is a wide range of discretion. We might be interested in brain computer interaction, then rather complex signals from the brain are the actions that concern us. We might want implants in our arms to respond to some other muscle twitching—perhaps to gain more hand movement—then we would consider twitching actions we previously overlooked.

Having said all that, it is easy to overlook important actions. Removing a battery from a mobile phone is an action, very similar to switching the device off—but not quite. On mine, if I receive a phone call but miss it for some reason, the number calling me is stored in a list of missed calls. When the phone is ringing, if I press the (Cancel) button the call is terminated but the number is not stored in the calls list. As a work-around, if the phone rings but I don't want to answer it, the best thing seems to be to remove the battery, as this stops it ringing *and* stores the number as a missed call, so I can ring back later. If we notice, then, that removing battery is an action, later when the device design is analyzed we should notice that it does something useful as a side-effect, which ought to be allocated to an explicit action, perhaps a button.

However, once we have decided on our set of actions, they are atomic and we do not explore within them.

We usually give actions names, and as a typographical convention in this book, I usually write actions as if they were buttons on a device. So I write (On) to indicate the *on* action. This looks like a button you can press, and although it often is, it needn't be. It could be a puff switch you blow into; it could even be the word "on" spoken into a microphone. There might be no name at all; for instance in the United States, flicking a switch up means (On), even though in the United Kingdom that action means (Off)!

Now, what do actions do? Actions change the state of the system, although sometimes the "change" might be to leave the system in the same state.

Unlike actions, which you could imagine watching happen, states are very abstract concepts. They do not exist, or at least there need be nothing identifiable anywhere that you could call a state. Instead, states make their presence felt through indicators.

Indicators might be lights that can be on or off, words, or sounds. Indicators show the user something has happened. Like actions, we consider indicators to be discrete and atomic. Except informally, the volume of a sound is not *an* indicator; level 0, level 1, level 2, or level 3 are different (closely related) indicators. A user may not be able to tell the difference between some indicators; level 3 sound might seem like level 0 sound in a quiet moment.

Indicators can be complex things if we wish. If you press the (Play) button on a DVD, you watch a video. The *entire* hour-long video is an indicator that pressing (Play) had the desired effect. As with actions, we may wish to split indicators up into constituent parts to understand them better. For example, you might prefer to have indicators for each of the scenes in a DVD video, rather than having a single play indicator—indeed some DVD players can display the scene number, and if so, these numbers are indicators.

In very simple devices, there is a straightforward relation between actions, states, and indicators. A light switch controlling a light is an example. The actions are to switch on or switch off; the states are on and off; and the *two* indicators are the light bulb being on or off. Unfortunately life is rarely so simple. In reality, the light bulb may be a dud and not work. Now the device always indicates off!

A mode is a set of states that behave in the same way. It is sometimes useful to distinguish between different sorts of modes, such as action modes or indicator modes, but usually the context makes it quite clear. For example, the mode "dud light bulb" is a set of states (two, at the present count) that happen to behave in a simple way: namely, whatever action the user does in this mode results in the indicator being off. We could consider this case an indicator mode: whatever happens, the indicator is off. Or we could consider it an action mode: whatever we do, actions do, as it happens, nothing.

States are abstract things. It is usual to give them names, or when we can't conveniently think of names, we give them numbers: 0, 1, 2, and so on—programmers like to count from zero. If we understand a device and we know what state it is in (17, for example), then we know what *any* sequence of actions will do to that device henceforth.

Of course, the device got itself into state 17 by some earlier sequence of actions. In an important sense, all of the sequences of actions that result, or could have resulted, in the device being in state 17 are equivalent. In fact, this is how we can define states mathematically: states are the equivalence classes of behavior.

▷ Graphs are the mathematical way to model states and actions. Graph theory will be covered in chapter 8, "Graphs." Simply put, states are vertices in a graph, and the arcs of the graph are the actions. Arcs go from a vertex to a vertex, just as an action goes from a state to a state.

6.1.1 States versus modes

While they are central concepts, modes and states often get confused—not least because people do not agree on exactly how the words should be defined, and they may not even notice they are using the words in different ways. I defined modes as certain sets of states; obviously if all modes are sets of single states, then modes and states may as well be the same concept—and indeed for some device designs modes and states *will* be the same.

It is worthwhile to take a moment to explore the distinctions in more detail.

Mode In a given mode, a *specific* action has a consistent effect (including, possibly, nothing). For example, if the (Off) button always switches a gadget off, then there is a mode "on" where the button behaves that way; the mode "off" probably behaves differently, certainly the (Off) button won't be able to turn the device off if it is already off! There are two modes in this case.

A common design slogan is, "Don't mode me out!"—meaning avoid modes that stop many actions having effects. Computers mode out users frequently,

165

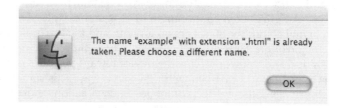

Figure 6.1: A familiar example of being moded out by a dialog box, here on an Apple Macintosh computer. To continue, the user *has* to choose OK. The program displaying this dialog box will allow the user to do nothing else; the user has been moded out. Here the user tried to change the name of a file, but they chose a name that was already taken. The dialog box tells them so, but the user is unable to look at file names to find out what the problem is; nor can the user try any other solutions, such as deleting or renaming the other file.

typically offering them a simple choice (the clearest example is the intrusive dialog box that says something ...OK? and that's the *only* choice, to click on OK). When this happens, all other actions are inaccessible! Figure 6.1 (this page) gives an example. Fortunately this is becoming less of a problem on computers, but it is still a real issue for interactive devices, like DVD players and ticket machines.

Moding out is not always a problem. On a gun, to give a stark example, you might want a safety catch, which modes you out of the possibilities of unsafe or accidental use.

State In a given state, every action *always* works in *exactly* the same way (though perhaps doing nothing). In contrast, modes need not be very specific. For example, the "on mode" of a device only tells you what the Off key does—it doesn't tell you exactly what anything else will do, which knowing the state does.

Thus a mode tells you what one or perhaps *some* user actions will do, whereas a state tells you *everything* and *exactly* what the device will do. A state tells you what any button will do.

For example, all televisions have two very important modes: on and off. A TV can be in the on mode or in the off mode, and the TV modes broadly define what user actions will do. When a television is off, the only button that will work is generally the On/off button, which should switch it back on. If the TV is off, most buttons will do nothing, but when it is off, it can be switched on. When a TV is on, the On/off button will switch it off, but that's just about all we know about it. To know what all the other buttons do when the TV is on, you need to know more— you need to know more about the states or other modes within the on mode. The on mode only tells us what On/off will do; it doesn't tell us what any other buttons will do.

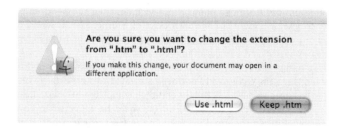

Figure 6.2: As well as being modey, the dialog box in figure 6.1 is rude—rude in the sense of section 6.3.4 (p. 185). This dialog box shown here precedes it, giving you a choice that the computer will *immediately* forbid: if you choose "Use .html" it will tell you that you must choose another name, using the dialog box of figure 6.1. This dialog box is giving you a choice that it won't let you take.

If modes describe so much, how do states help?

Suppose you switch the television off. In this mode, all buttons probably do nothing apart from the [On/off] button. Yet when you switch the television on, it will (probably) go back to whatever channel you were watching when you switched it off; it might also know what the sound and brightness settings were before you switched off. Somehow the off mode "knows" what channel—and what sound level, what color and contrast settings, and so on—you had the television in before you switched it off. The off mode must remember these details somehow, and it does so by keeping track of the state before the TV was switched off. Yet whatever stuff the TV was keeping track of did not affect what [On/off] does; that's all the same mode.

If modes contain states, how many different individual states are there when everything is unraveled? *A lot.* There are all the off states, and all the on states. In *all* of those states the television has to keep track of its channel, so (for a simple 9-channel TV) there are 9 off states and 9 on states. That's 18 sorts of state already. Suppose there are 64 sound levels. Each of those 18 sorts of states has 64 individual variants to keep track of sound level. There's off in channel 1, and sound level 0; there's off in channel 1, and sound level 1; there's off in channel 1, and sound level 2 ... so far, there are $18 \times 64 = 1,152$ states *just for these features*. We've got over a thousand states before we've even got a fully featured television!

Clearly when we design a device, we don't want to think about *all* the states all the time as there are just too many of them. Instead, we tend to think about modes as we concentrate on individual actions, button presses or whatever, that the user can do.

Very often, using a gadget is so straightforward that it is hard to keep the state and mode concepts clearly in focus as two different things. In particular, humans are very good at chunking ideas together to make more powerful ideas, and this happens with actions, modes, and states. If a pair of actions, say, are done often enough, the user behaves as if they were a single action, chunked together. Often

---

Box 6.1 Syringe pumps A syringe pump is a device designed to operate a medical syringe automatically, to give a patient a controlled dose of a drug over a period of time. They are often used in pain control, where regular doses of painkiller is needed. Some pumps are portable and can be used and carried around by a patient.

In one case, a pump was set to deliver 0.1ml/hr (a tenth of a milliliter of drug per hour) to a baby. However, the syringe pump had not been activated to start delivery of the drug. The nurse had told the pump to deliver 0.1ml/hr and then completed her task. If you (pretending to be a pump) had been told to deliver 0.1ml/hr, you'd be expected to do it. The pump didn't, and wanted further confirmation from the user—causing a post-completion error. After two minutes, the pump starts beeping, to warn the user that it has been told to do something that hasn't been confirmed. To stop the noise, the nurse reached over and pressed a button to cancel the beeping. Unfortunately, the baby died shortly afterward.

The nurse had pressed not [Cancel] but [10], which canceled the beeping, but unfortunately also started the pump delivering at 10.1ml/hr—a hundred times faster. This was clearly a design error, particularly as post-completion errors are well understood.

▷   Post-completion errors are discussed in section 11.4 (p. 387). Another example is discussed in box 5.7, "The principle of least effort" (p. 147).

Other errors with syringe pumps have included the following, all avoidable by better interaction programming:

■ 7ml/hr entered as 77ml/hr, by pressing [7] twice by mistake.

■ 0.5ml/hr entered as 5ml/hr. The nurse here didn't press [.] hard enough, and didn't realize the mistake.

■ 10ml/hr entered as 200ml/hr. Here the cause was a partly-obscured display. Displays should be legible, and sound feedback should be provided—using a synthesized voice would be easy.

■ A pump defaults to 0.1mg/ml, but the syringe was filled with a concentration of 1mg/ml, so the patient got a dose ten times too high.

---

since no interesting effect happens until several actions have happened, the entire sequence of actions seems a single event so far as the user is concerned. Whether this matters or not is a question for the user, designer, and application. In the long run, a user might be confused and then make innocent mistakes. Chunking is also an issue for us, as interaction designers. Do we want to treat every state as different, or do we want to gloss some differences? We might treat playing all the tracks on a CD as different states, but do we also want to treat all the positions within the tracks as different? Are we even worried about different tracks? On the one hand, we don't want to be overwhelmed by detail, on the other hand, we want to be precise and design good systems.

6.1.2 Examples of state machines

If we make the further proviso, along with being atomic and discrete, that the devices we are concerned with are finite, then we have defined ourselves a particularly useful form of finite state machine, or FSM. Finite state machines turn out to be very useful.

Many things can be described using states and actions.

- A web site has HTML pages (states) and links to other pages. Links are the actions to go to other pages.

- A flashlight has states, such as ON and OFF. It has actions, such as SWITCH ON and SWITCH OFF.

- An aircraft landing system has numerous states, including ON GROUND and IN AIR. Its actions will include LAND and TAKE OFF.

- A television set has states such as OFF, WATCHING CHANNEL 1, WATCHING CHANNEL 5, and it has actions such as ON/OFF (a combined switch on and switch off) and NEXT CHANNEL.

- A dog has states such as sitting, walking to heal, lying down. It has actions, usually voice commands, "sit!" "heal!" and so on. Many dogs have modes, such as "obedient," and "deaf."

- A computer has lots of states, and the actions on it include mouse clicking as well as switching it on and off.

- Many systems, from mobile phones and televisions to car radios, and desktop computers have menus. Each menu item is a state: the state where that menu item is displayed (or said) to the user; each action is either selecting another menu item, or activating the current selection.

Three points follow from this list.

First, the number of states and actions we consider depends on what we (as interaction programmers) are trying to achieve. For example, a basic understanding of a flashlight is possible with just two states (on and off), but we get a more detailed understanding by considering more states. We need enough states to be realistic, but there are, in the limit, an arbitrary number of states: thus, BROKEN might represent countless specific ways in which a flashlight can be broken. In principle, these sorts of state cannot be counted: there is no end to them and no systematic way of deciding what they are.

Second, some states are irrelevant to user needs (users don't much care what states are—they are details inside the device). For example, a flashlight behaves much the same whether it is on a table or in a car, whether it is in the dark or in the sunshine. For most purposes, there is no need to distinguish these different physical states. Many times, we do not bother about sometimes relevant possibilities, like "battery nearly dead," which is an intermediate state between battery OK and battery dead.

Finally, a computer, at least when considered as a whole, has far too many states to deal with, even though in principle they can be counted off. Instead, we take large clumps of states and treat them together—just as a user would ignore all the

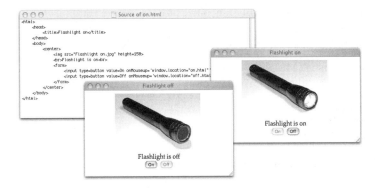

Figure 6.3: Interactive devices and web sites are both finite state machines and are thus essentially the same thing. Here, a trivial two-page web site behaves exactly like a simple flashlight. The web site has a page for the flashlight being on, and a page for the flashlight being off. The two pages are linked together by the form buttons, which are behaving like the flashlight's switch.

activities the computer is up to that have nothing directly to do with the present task.

A gadget can be understood using states and actions, and so can a web site. Can we get any mileage out of this similarity? Yes, we can. You could build a web site that behaved exactly like a gadget: when you click on the web site (using a browser) you would be taken to new pages that show you what would have happened if you'd pressed the corresponding button on the gadget. The web site might be just descriptive text, but it could be made up from lots of pictures (perhaps image maps), and if you did it really well, the web site would look and behave *exactly* like the device it described.

▷   We will build web sites from devices in chapter 9, "A framework for design."

You could imagine having a web site that *looked* like the gadget and a corresponding web site that told you what the gadget was supposed to do in each state. In fact there could be the obvious links between the two sites, and from any picture of the user interface you could immediately get the descriptive help for that state. For any bit of the help text, you could immediately transfer over to the simulation of the gadget, and it would be in the right state.

Of course it's quite irrelevant really that these things are web sites. We could have a *real* gadget that does exactly what it is supposed to do, and it could have a help button on it that displayed the "web help" on the gadget's own screen. If it was something like a DVD player or video recorder, it could use the TV screen that's already there.

This easy way to slide between different representations is the power of finite state machines. It doesn't matter whether they are DVD players, TVs, web sites, computers, or bits of string.

There remain three more interesting points:

- Because finite state machines are finite, they turn out to be easy to analyze thoroughly.

- Finite state machines cover an enormous range of interactive devices. The design, implementation, and usability of such devices can be supported and analyzed very well by finite state machine models.

- Many people dismiss finite state machines as being rather too simple-minded.

The first two points are advantages; the third is a misunderstanding that needs correcting. Most people who already know about finite state machines came across them in text books on theoretical computer science. Finite state machines are discussed (along with regular expressions) and then you turn over the page to the next chapter on Turing Machines. Turing Machines are infinite machines, and they are a good theoretical model of computers. In comparison, finite state machines seem pretty tame. You can prove finite state machines cannot do all sorts of things that Turing Machines find easy. Therefore, one might dismiss finite state machines as merely a conceptual stepping stone to interesting things.

This is a misconception. Finite state machines can have any number of states, and they can have more states than any real computer can; they are as powerful as any computer you can build. Turing Machines are, in fact, unrealistically powerful—they correspond to nothing that can be built in a physical universe. However, from a mathematical point of view, when you have huge numbers of states it becomes easier to think and prove things if you take the number of states to be infinite—you don't need to worry about the exact number of states. For example, if you prove a Turing Machine cannot do something then you can be certain no computer could do it either. On the other hand, if you proved a finite state machine couldn't do something, could one with more states do it?

If we allow our finite state machines to have billions and billions of states, in a purist sense we would be cheating. With *that* many states, it would be far easier not to count and to pretend that we could have any number of states—we'd be treating them as infinite machines for all practical purposes. If we are not going to cheat, then, we have to make some compromises so that our very definite idea of finiteness does not run away.

This book is about interactive systems, and we need finite state machines to talk about user interfaces, to describe what the user thinks the devices are doing—in a way that also makes sense to interaction programmers. Viewed like this, a very good argument for finite state machines (for our purposes) is that users don't understand bigger or more general things—and even fifty or a hundred states are problematic. There are plenty of devices with ten to twenty states that are very difficult to use. Turing Machines and other sophisticated models of computing don't describe what users think about.

> ▷ Box 12.3, "Defending finite state machines" (p. 430) reviews more defenses for finite state machines; the main one is that they encourage simplicity—which is the topic of the next section here.

Turing Machines are not the only possibility. There are very many alternatives to finite state machines and although they are important topics in their own right, this book doesn't cover pushdown automata (PDAs), Petri nets, and a variety of other viable alternatives, such as using programming languages (including modeling languages like CSP, Spin, SMV, and even regular expressions) that compile to finite state machines.

6.1.3   Ensuring simplicity

Discrete means you either have it or you don't—in contrast to *discreet*, which means unobtrusive. We have been talking finite discrete systems, indeed, all our examples have had a relatively few number of states. Discrete mathematics is the mathematics of things that you either have or don't have: an orange is either in a set of fruit or it isn't, so sets are part of discrete maths. In contrast, the weight of an orange is a real number, like 0.23, and that wouldn't be very interesting to a discrete mathematician.

Our discrete approach therefore in principle excludes continuous systems, such as virtual reality, gestures, speech, and even time delays from consideration. Such systems are not accurately understood by being in either one state or another, because their "states" merge with one another. Rather than using whole numbers, we'd more realistically describe these systems using real numbers.

It might seem that this book excludes a rather large (and interesting) area from our coverage of interaction programming! Philosophically, there are always going to be things you can't do with any approach, so we needn't worry *in principle* too much. More pragmatically, though, we can do a great deal with discrete systems—and fortunately when we need to, we can approximate continuous systems as accurately as we like by remaining discrete. Certainly as designers we can approximate continuous systems better than users can, which is perhaps all that matters.

Many gadgets, like video or DVD recorders, are both discrete and continuous. As well as their buttons, which are either pressed or not pressed, they have rotating dials and complex timing features needed, for example to set program schedules. The position of a CD or a tape is essentially a continuous variable. If we are going to design devices like this, we *have* to handle continuity somehow. If we are going to ignore it, we have to be certain that we are not glossing over important design issues.

We have four main choices:

Limit   We can treat continuous systems as the limit of discrete systems. Rather than having to deal with a continuous system, we can treat it as if it has a million states, say. The user won't be able to tell the difference. Actually, if we wrote a computer program to handle a continuous variable (such as the sound level), it would still have discrete levels, though probably under anybody's threshold to notice.

Mode   We can treat the continuous bits of a system as a mode that we won't explore in detail. We can just consider the mode to somehow include continuous states without going into detail. For example, we can consider the volume on a TV as either off or on, even though in the on mode there might really be a continuum of volume levels. For the purposes of design (and use), all those levels should work the same way—they are just one mode. In fact, it would be a pretty peculiar design that had a continuous feature that somehow behaved in a wide variety of ways and therefore needed lots of modes to describe it.

Forbid If a device requires more than a dozen or so states, then it is going to be a complicated device; if it needs thousands of states, then it is a very complicated device. As designers, we can *decide* that we are not going to countenance building overly complex devices. It is always best to begin with a device that is a small simple discrete system, *then* expand it with features if necessary.

Strategize ...

▷ The fourth choice is to think at a strategic level—see part III and particularly chapter 12, "Grand design."

One of the main continuous issues we cannot avoid handling is time. On many devices, how long a user presses a button or how long a user waits before doing something is a key part of the design. How then can we handle time?

One approach is to say "time is bad" and refuse to design with any timing constraints. In fact, this is such a popular approach that systems like this have a special name: a system that essentially takes no time at all to respond to actions applied to it is called a reactive system, because it can be thought of providing instant reactions to the user.

Generally, pure reactive systems are easy to use because the user doesn't have to understand or worry about any timing issues. If a button is pressed, it does one thing. It doesn't matter how long or briefly the user presses. If you leave a reactive device alone, it won't forget what it was doing; the user can have a break and return to exactly where they were.

Reactive systems are much easier to use because things mean the same however slow (or distracted) or however fast the user is.

The problem is that reactive systems are an idealization; many common systems—like the mobile phones—*do* have delays and timing issues, and we must know how to proceed. People don't answer their phones immediately, so there is a delay between calling somebody and their answering (if they do). Or, when you switch a mobile phone on, it takes a moment to get working fully. If a user asks a DVD player to rewind its tape it can't happen *instantly*. In particular, with a DVD player if a user does [Rewind][Stop] they can expect something quite different to happen than if they do [Rewind] *wait* [Stop]. In short, most things are not perfect reactive systems.

▷ Timeouts are discussed in box 6.2, "Timeouts" (next page).

We can make time itself into an action. A clock can tick, and ticks can be actions—the user doesn't have to do all actions on a device. The device can be acted on by its environment, and time is one of the things that can act independently. If we wanted to be imaginative, we could have a button on a device called

---

Box 6.2 Timeouts Many systems use timeouts: when the user does nothing for a second or two, or takes several seconds pressing a single button, different things happen.

   The main case where timeouts are useful—but often misused—occurs in walk-up-and-use devices that are intended to be used by a queue of people. The second person does not want to start with the mess left by their predecessor, so a timeout is used to reset the system for the next person. Actually this would be far better done by a heat or other sort of body sensor than a time out: what happens if the first person is too slow or the second too fast?

   When trivial things like airport toilets use proximity detectors to flush themselves when you move away from them, why can't more sophisticated gadgets? Why can't ticket machines detect people who are present and using them, or when they walk away and stop using them? Why guess with timeouts when you can do better?

   My favorite example is my old JVC video recorder, which had a timeout that would reset the device when you were setting up UHF channels. In the couple of minutes you took to follow the manual, which you need to do something complex like setting up UHF channels, the video recorder would have timed out—guaranteeing you couldn't follow the manual's instructions!

   ▷   Section 3.8.3 (p. 75) described timeouts for a washing machine, and box 6.4, "Bad
        user interfaces earn money" (p. 191) shows the problem with burglar alarms.
        Ironically, the burglar alarm problem arises with a device that *does* have a sensor
        that "knows" when the user is around!

Tick and we'd employ a little gnome to press this button every second (or every millisecond, or whatever was necessary).

   This hidden action idea is sufficient to treat timeouts in principle, but it is rather messy because it creates an enormous number of states to keep track of how many times the Tick action has occurred.

   Another sensible approach, the one we'll use, is to imagine clever gnomes inside the device. These gnomes have a stopwatch, and decide, using their detailed and intimate knowledge of the device design, what actions the user is really doing. If the user presses the Off button, and the gnomes start counting. If the user holds the Off for three seconds, the gnomes say, "OK, that wasn't and off action, it was a really-off action!" If the user presses Off Off in quick succession, the gnomes say, "OK, that *was* a double-off action, not two separate off actions." Now the finite state machine (there aren't really any gnomes) has actions like one-off, really-off and double-off. Instead, the user's complicated, time-dependent actions are translated into the device's internal actions.

   Henceforth, we will only talk about internal actions. We want to gloss over gnomes; we will talk about internal actions *as if* they are user actions. It is much easier, at least for most of our exposition in this book, to say things like the user presses a button Off, and the action off occurs, or presses a button Double-Off, and the action double-off occurs.

6.1.4   When is an action not an action?

Most actions change the state of the system in a straightforward way, but this is not always the case. A hotel keycard seems to unlock your room door, but it isn't as simple as that. When you first use your keycard after registering at the hotel desk, your card reprograms the room lock, so that the previous guest can no longer unlock the door (and of course your keycard won't reprogram any room other than the one you've been allocated). Now that the lock is reprogrammed, you can get in and out freely until the next guest registers and inserts their keycard on the lock. The previous guest can never reprogram the lock once you've started using the room; the lock only reprograms when a keycard is entered with a new code *and* the previous code. When your card is programmed by reception, they can program it with the previous guest's code; of course, the previous guest doesn't know your card's code, so they can't get back in or reprogram the lock. This cunning approach to hotel locks means that the reception desk doesn't have to keep reprogramming locks when somebody walks off with a keycard by mistake: in fact, you the guest do the reprogramming for them, with no conscious effort.

An abstract view of the lock is that it has two states, locked and unlocked, and inserting a keycard is a simple action that unlocks the door. This abstract view doesn't fully describe what goes on the first time a guest uses the lock—however, for designing the user interface it's probably sufficient only to model what the user *thinks* they are doing. Users don't think they are reprogramming the door, and there is no need for us to worry about that.

Incidental interaction is when an action, like this, occurs as a side-effect of the user interacting, and therefore with no additional effort from what the user was doing. Normally, incidental interaction achieves something the user wants—it does here, though most users won't have thought out the details of the room security that they need.

▷   See section 12.2 (p. 410) for further discussion of incidental interaction.

Nevertheless, knowing how the door lock works is crucial to how the hotel staff use the door. For example, if a porter carries your luggage to your room when you first register at the hotel, it's possible that the porter will use their masterkey to let you in. If so, the door lock will not have been reprogrammed to your card— there is a window of opportunity for the previous guest to return and steal your baggage. As usual, the simplest way around this flaw in the design is to train the user, in this case the porter, to ask you for your key to open the door. This not only tests your keycard works, but (if it does) it reprograms the lock for you.

6.2   Drawing state machines

Finite state machines have the terrific advantage of being very easy to draw and understand. They are therefore an excellent way to help support the interaction programming process: draw diagrams and think about them.

Actually, as we shall see, there is a caveat. Simple finite state machines are very easy to draw, but most finite state machines we want to use are not simple. They are huge and practically impossible to draw (unless you use a computer), and certainly impossible to understand and follow. Fortunately this is a problem we can leave for later. For the time being, we want to draw and learn how to understand simple devices. Later we can worry about how to handle more complex devices, which we may not want to draw at all.

> ▷ Chapter 7, "Statecharts," describes a better way of drawing devices, that
> handles more complex designs; chapter 8, "Graphs," describes the generic
> theory that can handle anything; finally, several chapters—particularly
> chapter 9, "A framework for design"—show how to write programs that can
> explore and answer design questions.

6.2.1   A bright example

A flashlight is either off or on. We represent these two simple states as two circles:

To understand a finite state machine diagram, imagine a counter or bead. You are allowed exactly one counter, and it must be in the circle representing one state; the device is then in that state. When an action occurs, you move the state along the corresponding arrow reaching from the state it is in to the new state.

To move the counter, we need to introduce arrows. The actions the flashlight allows are coincidentally called on and off, and we represent these actions with two labeled arrows:

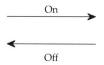

We can put the states and actions together to make a complete state machine diagram. We've bent the arrows to make a more pleasing diagram—the shape of the arrows doesn't matter, though.

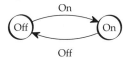

The flashlight can be in two states, but which state is it in when you get it? In general, we need to indicate the starting, or default state a device is in when we get it. By convention, we indicate the default state with a special sort of blobbed arrow, or default arrow thus:

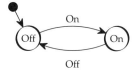

In other words, this flashlight will start its life in the off state. The meaning of this complete diagram can be spelled out:

- When we get the machine (the flashlight), it will be in the off state. We show the default state by the blobbed arrow.

- If the machine is in the off state (left hand circle), then doing ⬚On will take it to the on state.

- If the machine is in the on state (right hand state circle), then doing ⬚Off will take it to the off state.

- The diagram doesn't show what happens when we do ⬚On in the On state, or ⬚Off in the Off state. By convention, if there isn't an appropriate arrow for an action, the device does nothing—but this is a convention to stop diagrams from getting visually cluttered, not a conceptual convention.

Often in this book, to avoid visual clutter, we won't write down the labels on all arrows.

6.2.2 A darker example

The gun makes a very good example of an interactive device where clear, if not stark, usability and safety issues arise in simple machines.

In 1994, a seven year old, Brandon Maxfield, was shot in the face, leaving him a quadriplegic. He was shot accidentally with a Bryco Arms Model 38 semiautomatic pistol.

Pistols should have safety catches to stop them firing. When the safety catch is on, that is in the "safe" position, any action on the gun does nothing. The diagram below shows that if a gun is safe, *any* action keeps it safe.

From the diagram, it's clear that every action anybody can do in the safe state takes us along the arrow and back to the safe state—nothing ever happens. This isn't quite what we had in mind, since it isn't possible, as it's drawn, to get out of the safe state and do anything else. Even releasing the safety catch, as drawn, takes us back to the safe state.

Clearly the safe state needs an arrow coming out of it for when the user releases the safety catch, putting the gun in the fire mode. When the safety catch is off, the gun can shoot. The arrow coming out of it for the safety catch release action will go to an unlocked state, where the gun can do more things.

In the next, more accurate, diagram the safe state has *two* arrows leaving it: one for the safety release action, the other for every other action (which still do nothing).

177

In the case of this shooting, somebody was trying to remove the gun's ammunition clip, or magazine, so that the gun would have no bullets in it. Unfortunately, the design of the Bryco requires that the safety catch must be off in order to remove the magazine. So to empty the gun, you first have to release the safety catch; by design you *must* get the gun into the unlocked state to do this—and in the unlocked state you can, perhaps by accident, pull the trigger and go to the shoot state. From the shoot state, the gun fires and returns itself to the unlocked state when you release the trigger. So, the arrow from shoot to unlocked is done by the gun, rather than by the user, as all the other arrows are.

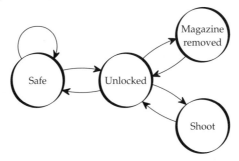

For most guns, there may still be a bullet left in the gun chamber when the magazine is removed. This is an intentional feature, so the gun can still shoot while the magazine is out and replaced or reloaded.

Here is a more accurate diagram, then, representing this possibility:

There's still an error in this diagram, as it incorrectly gives the impression that you can *continue* shooting with the magazine removed. The shoot once state returns to the magazine removed state, and the state diagram strictly does not say you can't go back to it and shoot again—it's only the name that says it can only shoot once in this state. In fact, even with the magazine in, you cannot shoot indefinitely—the gun runs out of bullets. The diagrams are not drawn with sufficient detail to count bullets; instead, they just show the "ability to shoot."

A basic rule of gun safety is that you should always assume a gun has a bullet in it, and that's the behavior the diagrams show too. In practice, you should also assume the safety is off too, but here the diagrams do not assume that, since they show the safe state.

The gun would have been safer if the magazine could have been removed with the safety catch engaged; arguably, it was a design flaw that the safety had to be released. The gun would have been even safer if the magazine could *only* have been removed with the safety catch engaged. However, for a gun that might be used in fighting, it is useful to be able to remove the magazine with the safety off, so you can shoot the remaining bullet in the chamber while you are reloading.

The designers had to decide whether the value of being able to shoot once in such circumstances outweighs the value of the gun never shooting accidentally when the magazine is removed; or they could have considered the cost and benefits of another safety mechanism (which might have given the user the choice between "cannot shoot with magazine removed" or perhaps "cannot shoot at all" and "can shoot with magazine removed").

> ▷ Making a device safer may make it more complicated, which in turn may make it harder to use and hence, ironically, less safe. Chapter 12, "Grand design," discusses how we can make more sophisticated devices without making the design more complex.

For guns, which are mechanical, every feature has a direct cost, both in manufacturing costs and in the risk that the mechanism may wear and become faulty. In contrast, adding features for electronic devices has essentially no cost except that the user interface becomes more complex—especially if a feature is added without adding further controls, because then existing buttons have to have more meanings to cope with the new feature. So, the design tradeoffs are very different, but the underlying theory is the same.

■　　　■　　　■

Some people argue that the best safety device for a gun is the user—that is, a sensible user would never aim a gun at somebody (unless they *wanted* to shoot them), so the child would not have been shot accidentally. This is the "guns don't kill, people do" argument. It is an argument that encourages gun manufacturers to blame the users and avoid improving their products; obviously to admit otherwise would be to expose themselves to all sorts of liabilities. If the same argument were applied to user interfaces more generally, then the user would be to blame for all problems, and this would similarly create a culture where nobody wanted to improve design for the sake of users. Of course, this is a politically charged argument; but so is usability.

> ▷ Car manufacturers took a similar position ("cars don't kill, drivers do"), until the exposé by Ralph Nader in the 1960s; see box 2.3, "Ralph Nader" (p. 51).

6.2.3　Basic rules for drawing state diagrams

Diagrams only make sense if they are drawn to adhere to certain conventions. State diagrams follow the following conventions—though as we shall soon see

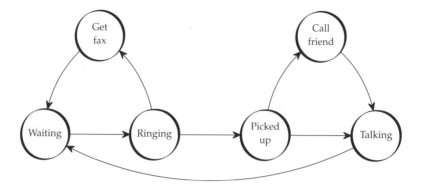

Figure 6.4: State diagrams do not have to describe devices and machines; they can describe what people do too. Here is a state diagram that says what you *and* a phone can do.

there are other ways of drawing state diagrams that will allow us to relax some of the rules when drawing. Behind our casual drawings there is always in principle a rigorous diagram drawn strictly according to these rules the system—if not the actual diagram—*must* obey the rules.

There are nearly twenty rules. The rules are all pretty obvious once you think about them. It is surprising how easy it is to build a device and accidentally forget some detail that these rules would have caught. The rules make sense for drawing *and* for using a device, but the rules are not visible in ordinary programs. It is possible to write a program that makes a device work, but for it to have elementary mistakes that go undetected.

1. Circles represent states. Sometimes rectangles are also used in this book.

2. States are never drawn as overlapping or intersecting.

3. Arrows represent actions. Arrows do not need to be straight.

4. Although it is sometimes unavoidable, arrows shouldn't normally cross.

5. States and actions are labeled, but if we are worried about the visual clutter in the diagrams, we may omit some or all of the labels.

6. Every arrow starts and finishes at the circumference of a state circle.

7. *Every* state has exactly as many arrows pointing from it as there are possible actions, one arrow for each action. For example, if a device has *b* buttons, every state will have *b* arrows pointing away from it. Arrows coming out of a state have different labels.

8. Arrows can start and finish at the same state; these are called self-arrows. For clarity, self-arrows are often omitted from a diagram, because they are implied by the previous rule.

9. A state with all arrows from it returning to the same state are called terminal states; they are states where the system jams—which is undesirable for interactive systems. They are (almost always) an error, for they represent a state where no action can do anything and nothing further can be achieved. Explosive devices, fire extinguishers, and a few other single-use devices, typically which destroy themselves, have terminal states by design.

10. If we are trying to avoid visual clutter by not showing action labels, we may merge arrows going between the same states.

11. If two or more arrows go to the same state, it is occasionally convenient to join them together before they reach the state, to reduce the visual clutter. Otherwise, arrows are never coincident over any part of their length.

12. The initial or default starting state (if we want to indicate it as such) is pointed to with an arrow coming from a small black circle. Only one state is indicated as the initial state.

13. States with no arrows or default arrow going toward them represent states that can never be reached. They *always* represent an error (or possibly that the designer has not yet finished the device).

14. Finally, with the exception of single-use and similar devices (see rule 9 above), it must be possible to follow a sequence of arrows from any state to every other state. This important requirement is called strong connectivity. If a state machine is not properly connected in this way, either there are some states that cannot be reached by any sequence of actions, or there are some states (more generally, sets of states) that a user cannot escape from back to the rest of the device.

▷ Strong connectivity will be defined properly in chapter 8, "Graphs." Strong connectivity is not easily checked visually but we'll see how to check for it using a program automatically in chapter 9, "A framework for design."

Some of these rules are aesthetic, but the most interesting rules are, like the last, ones that we can check by program.

6.3   From drawing rules to interaction laws

Our rules seem to be about *drawing* diagrams, but the rules also have an effect on the *behavior* of interactive devices. For example, if several arrows could come out of a state all with the same label (which we don't allow when we are drawing a diagram), this would mean that when the user does the action associated with that label anything could happen—we don't know which arrow the device would follow. This would mean that the device is nondeterministic: a user could not predict what would happen with a certain action. It's easy enough to detect when this problem arises by writing a program that examines the arrows (as we'll see in later chapters), but designers have to decide what to do. Is it merely a design error or oversight? More likely, *we* have not decided what to do, and the nondeterminism indicates that we haven't thought enough about the design.

The next diagram shows a flashlight with a removable lightbulb.

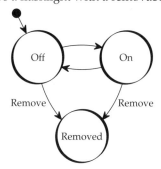

We can now remove the lightbulb, but as drawn above, we would get stuck with the lightbulb removed and be unable to do anything else: there is no way out of the removed state as the diagram is drawn. Let's add replace arrows, as in the diagram below. (I've removed the other arrow labels, as they'd make the diagram too cluttered.)

Box 6.3 Mealy and Moore machines There are many variations of finite state machine. The simplest kind merely recognize a sequence of actions, and are sometimes called finite state acceptors (FSAs). Finite state acceptors are familiar to programmers in the form of regular expressions, which are a concise and common way of specifying string patterns: regular expressions are compiled into finite state acceptors that then "accept" when the regular expression has been matched.

▷ Regular expressions are used in section 12.6.4 (p. 432).

Unless we are modeling a single-use device that does only one thing, like matching strings, these acceptors are not very useful for us. In this book, we are concerned with finite state *machines* (FSMs) that can provide output as a user interacts with them—an interactive device is only useful if it does something. For example a microwave oven must be able to cook, and a mobile phone must be able to allow the user to manage a call.

The two main sorts of FSMs are Mealy machines and Moore machines, named after their inventors. They differ in when they handle actions. In a Moore machine, the device does things *in* states, so a Moore machine may have a cook state or a call state. In contrast, a Mealy machine does things *between* states, on its transitions. When the user presses a button a Mealy machine does its action *as* it goes to the next state. The action of a Moore machine depends only on the current state, whereas the action of a Mealy machine depends on the current state *and* the user's action, because the effects happen on the transition.

Although the two approaches are equivalent, a Moore machine requires more states (that's how to remember which is which) because a Mealy machine can use different transitions—even to and from the same states—to do different things, whereas a Moore machine must have different states to do different things. This book uses Moore machines.

If we allow the number of states to be unlimited, then we have a labeled transition system (LTS). Of course, FSMs are finite cases of LTS, and some people use the terms almost interchangeably. Another variation is to make FSMs nondeterministic, so that they can effectively be in more than one state at a time; this makes them more concise, and you would think, more powerful. However, nondeterministic FSMs (NDFSMs) are mathematically equivalent to ordinary deterministic FSMs, because the states of an deterministic FSM can represent the possible sets of states of a nondeterministic FSM.

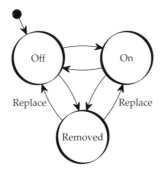

We're breaking our rules: we need to say which state the flashlight will be in when the bulb was removed when it was off, and one to say which state it will be in when the bulb was removed when it was on. In short, when we replace the bulb, the flashlight might be on or off. We have the problem! When the user does the action "replace," the bulb might end up being be on or off, *and we do not know which*, that is, this device design is nondeterministic.

Once the problem is detected, we then have to decide what to do. Perhaps we could make the state machine more realistic: actually, the bulb can be removed when it is on or off, so the single state is actually two states—this might be fine for a low-voltage device. Or perhaps we should modify the design, so that when a bulb is removed the state of the device changes to off, even if it was on. This is a nice solution: it removes the nondeterminism and makes the device safer as well, particularly if the device uses high voltages (like an ordinary domestic light, which of course has the same transition diagram). Or we could make the device have "no user serviceable parts" and simply make it impossible to remove or replace the bulb—this might be a good solution if the light bulb was a LED, which have very long lifetimes and are usually fixed in place, since having no socket makes the device even cheaper.

This is an example of a drawing law is a law about interaction programming. Indeed, once we start thinking of laws for drawing or designing interactive devices, it becomes obvious that there are many more that can be checked.

6.3.1   Avoid the reset escape

On some badly designed systems, the only arrow coming out of some states is called reset. A big button called [RESET] would be far too easy to press by accident, so the reset button is usually a little hole around the back of the gadget, which may well require a paper clip or pin poked in it to operate it.

I think the reset button is an admission of failure by the designer: "this machine may jam and we want the user to be able to reset it." The reset button makes it easier to make shoddy products—why bother to check the system design thoroughly if the user can *always* press reset and recover from anything that has gone wrong? On the other hand, a reset button is a better option than occasionally having to remove the batteries to do the reset.

6.3.2   Have consistent action names

Suppose we have an action called [Off]. Clearly, this should be represented as an arrow that points to (possibly more than one) state called off. If we checked that, we would know that the thing we were building had a reliable [Off] button.

6.3.3   Avoid pointless states

If a state has only one arrow coming out of it (all the other arrows looping back to the same state), the user has only one possible action. If there is no change in indicators, then the user sees no change out of being in this state. In which case, what is the point of the state? The next thing must eventually happen, and all the user can do is say when. The only way they can stop the next state happening is by walking away—and then someone else might do it.

Almost certainly a state with a single arrow coming out of it is a design mistake: it gives the user no choice (other than to delay). If we wanted the user to confirm a choice, then there would need to be at least two arrows: one for yes and one for no (perhaps more). Certainly any state with a single arrow coming out of it can be found automatically in the design process, and questions can be asked about what it is doing: if there is no time delay issue, then the state should be removed.

Note that during use, arrows can disappear if states or actions become impossible of forbidden. In other words, a check like whether the number of arrows leaving a state is one (or less!) is a check that may need to be done dynamically, while the device is in use.

All laws have exceptions. Although a state may allow the user only one choice—apparently no choice at all—and therefore be unnecessary from a choice point of view, there might be an opportunity to tell the user something, to help them understand what is about to happen, or there might be legal warnings.

An email program, to take one example, might want to pop up a dialog box that tells the user that new mail has arrived; this might be a case where the only response is OK—but why not OK *and* read it? It's a design choice that we could easily uncover automatically by checking the state machine design.

If there is only one exit from the help or legal state, the user cannot then change their mind. So in what sense is the help helping? Surely, if a user knows or understands something better, they might realize their choice was a mistake. So the state should not be removed so much as provided with an alternative exit: say, cancel.

6.3.4 Don't be rude

An obvious rule of good human behavior is this: don't be rude. Imagine asking the waiter at a restaurant if they have coffee. "Yes, what would you like?" You have a discussion about what they can do: latte, capuccino, americano . . . and you ask for a filter coffee. "With milk?" Yes, you'd like to have milk, you say. Then the waiter says, "We don't have any coffee!"

This human dialogue is rude and disappointing: the waiter must have known all along that they couldn't serve you coffee, however you liked it. But they kept on asking questions until you had made your mind up, and then they told you it was all impossible! Whereas this behavior would be exceptional between two humans, regretfully it's routine in interactive devices. Very often the device provides options that the designers hoped or expected would be available, but for some reason do not work fully when the device is being used.

Devices should always check that the "destination" state can always be reached with the choices being offered to the user—this is a dynamic check, since some resources (such as coffee) can disappear while a device is in use.

The Sony Ericsson T610 mobile phone, for example, tells you when you have missed an incoming call. It lists all your missed calls—there may be more than one—and has two responses indicated: Call and More. Unfortunately, More may not do anything. Many systems provide menus of features, with some features available on the device, and some on the internet. Mobile phones (like the Sony Ericsson) have a menu hierarchy that is partly on the phone, partly on WAP ("wireless application protocol"—a sort-of simplified web service). Users cannot tell which is which until they select an offered option and the phone then tries to connect. The phone may be useless while it is connecting. The phone might not have WAP enabled (because the user has decided not to pay for WAP services), so it is never possible to get any WAP feature. Yet the phone will still try to connect.

There are two solutions. The simplest solution to all of these problems is for the device to check that a user can complete all parts of a transaction before allowing it to start. Perhaps the unavailable options should be grayed out; trying to select them would bring up an explanation. Perhaps they would not be shown at all (depending on whether this is a permanent or temporary state of affairs). Alternatively, users could be warned that they won't be able to complete the activity but the device can "take notes" so that when the service becomes available it can be done automatically from the notes. This is like a more helpful waiter saying, "Thanks for your order. We're out of coffee right now, but I will go and get some from a shop myself for you and be back as soon as possible." Polite restaurants like that become famous.

The "don't be rude" rule is really a generalization of the drawing rule that every arrow must start and finish at a state circle. A device should never trap the user in a sequence of arrows they cannot get to the end of. Indeed, many useful interaction programming laws come from checking routes through the system design, rather than just checking states and arrows alone.

The "don't be rude" (or "do be polite") rule is bigger than just button-operated devices running simple state machines. Figure 6.5 (facing page) shows how well-designed menus in computer desktop applications are polite by using visual and typographic conventions: they show what is possible before the user even starts to try. Whether a menu item is active or grayed-out is worked out dynamically, depending on the current state and what is reachable from it, just as it should be in pushbutton-controlled devices like mobile phones.

▷ Section 11.3.1 (p. 383) introduces some polite pusbutton-type device techniques.

6.3.5 Don't be misleading

Being rude is a property of a device that is being rude. The device, or the designer analyzing the device, ought to know whether it is rude or not. On the other hand, whether a device is misleading or not, another unwelcome feature, really depends on where the user feels led in the first place. It's an example of an important usability property that isn't just a property of the device itself, but depends on the user too. Here's a story that makes the point.

I go to a public washstand to wash my hands. I put soap on my hands, and try to turn the water on. Of course, now I have all this soap on my hands, I *have* to

Figure 6.5: A desktop application menu (taken from running on Apple's OSX; in fact, Grab is the program that makes screen shots, like this one). Choosing a menu item is like pressing a button: it will usually make the application do something. Notice how good practice is to use visual conventions so that the user can see easily whether: (*i*) a menu item will work immediately, such as "About Grab" and "Hide Grab"—the latter has a keyboard shortcut as well; (*ii*) a menu item will bring up further menus to select actions from, as in "Services," because of the triangle symbol; (*iii*) the menu will bring up a dialog before it does something, as in "Preferences..."; and (*iv*) the menu item currently does nothing, as in "Show All," which is grayed out.

wash them. Although there is a knob, it doesn't turn on the water; no water comes out whatever I do. In fact, the whole thing is loose—indicating that people before me have forced it one way or the other. I try the next knob, as there are five of them in a row. Same problem on all of them. Somebody else now tries to get one to work too, and they are have the same problem as I do. So, I'm not stupid, at least. Perhaps there is no water at all?

And then we notice a paper notice; hand-washing is automatic. If you put your hand under the outlet in *just the right place* the water flows automatically. The knob is not one of the places that makes the taps come on. Now there's water, we soon find out that the knob controls the temperature of the water, not whether it is flowing or not.

Enough people have been misled by this design that there needs to be a notice, and indeed there is a sign above each knob. But who thinks of reading a sign, that isn't even where you are looking, to tell them how to use an everyday object?

The misleading here is that the knob allows the user to do an action, and a conventional action that would normally get water. It has the affordance of getting water, in fact. But we are wrong, misled. Once misled, we form a different model of what is going on: the device is broken and/or there can't be any water.

▷   There's more on affordance in section 12.3 (p. 415).

It's clearly a bad design, because the owner of the place found it necessary to put up a sign to help users who were misled. We do want to design interactive devices that mislead; at best, it wastes a lot of time. But whether a user is misled

187

depends a lot on the user's expectations, prior knowledge and so on. Generally, you have to do experiments with real users to find out what they expect before you can be sure a design is alright.

6.3.6   Don't be secretive

Another rule of good behavior is not to be secretive; being secretive frustrates people. Similarly, a device can be secretive and frustrate its user, particularly if there is only one way to do something, and that way is not very obvious.

The Alba TVD3406 is a television with a remote control with the usual range of buttons and an on-screen menu. Neither the remote control nor the on-screen menu seems to provide any way to tune in the TV. In fact, you need to press ⟨TV Menu⟩ *twice in quick succession* to be able to start tuning the TV. The on-screen menu provides help, but it doesn't say, "If you can't see what you want, try pressing the button twice quickly." In short, you can't tune in the TV without reading the user manual—despite having an otherwise nice on-screen menu system; the TVD3406 is unnecessarily secretive.

6.3.7   Check designs automatically

It is unreasonable to expect users to sort out design problems themselves—forcing the user to recover from the errors themselves, that is, if they notice them. Even in experimental situations where they are paid to help the designers, users may find it hard to describe what problems; far better to use an automatic tool and eliminate as many errors as possible before humans start working on it. Fortunately, checking almost all laws can be automated.

Once automatic design tools have been built, they can be used again and again with no further effort. If we rely on human user testing, every time the design is modified, we'd need to spend another few hours testing with people to see whether we've still got a decent design. It is far better to eliminate obvious errors automatically and speedily, and to save the users for more insightful things.

Imagine building a system with b buttons: it would be a good idea to check automatically, of every state, that there are b arrows coming out of it. If not, some buttons won't work in some states. This is next to impossible for a human to do, but it is trivial to do automatically, and of course, checking automatically (and hence rigorously) increases the quality of any device we build.

If we have such a design tool, when we think of a new design property, whether important or just interesting, we can add checking it to the design tool's repertoire. Immediately, this check becomes available for every design the tool is applied to.

> ▷ Section 10.7.4 (p. 356) suggests checking for error messages in source code. From chapter 9, "A framework for design," on we'll introduce more ideas for design tools.

6.3.8   Provide uniform help

If a device provides help, is help available in *every* state? We could imagine an automatic tool that reports the states where help is (or isn't) available. If the device says there is no help when it is off, perhaps the designer would tick a check box on the design tool, as it were, to say *this* problem is OK; this state is an exception where the rule does not need to be enforced. If we check this law, we then won't need to draw the "parallel universe" of the help states, because we know that every state has its own parallel with help.

6.3.9   Dynamic laws

There is not just an obligation for you, as a designer, to check your new designs *before* they are used—but also for the devices to recheck themselves *while* they are in use. Some features or services may unpredictably become unavailable (say, if the network goes down, or the user's credit runs out, or just when the CD music track finishes); if so, the user interface needs to change dynamically; it must not rudely provide the user with apparent options that will fail. Indeed, the restaurant that suddenly runs out of coffee has got to change how it interacts with customers; otherwise it will unexpectedly become rude.

6.3.10   Make generic devices

A device might be designed to be used in two or more countries that use different languages. Are these devices exactly the same, despite the different names and texts associated with all their states and actions?

Device equivalence can be achieved in two different ways.

■ Build two or more devices, then compare them.

■ Build a generic device, and then make different versions of it.

It is perhaps slightly harder to make a generic device, but once it is done, it can be extended to new languages or applications very easily. An automatic tool should be used to check that the generic bit of the device applies in all states, just as we might check help is available in all states.

6.3.11   Define your own laws

If you are designing a device, what laws should it obey? What laws would help a user? What laws would avoid bad outcomes—irritated users, dead users, lost work? As the examples of rudeness and secrecy show, it is not hard to think of sensible laws of interaction that make a design better and that are fairly easy to understand in terms of interaction programming.

It's not difficult to think of your own laws. Here are some more examples, which need working out a bit more, depending on what your users and device are trying to do. Don't make things too hard—which begs the question of how hard things are to do with the device being designed. Provide undo, so users can recover from mistakes—it's surprising how many devices have no undo at all. Make it compatible with a previous device—so if a user doesn't know about new features, it doesn't matter.

▷   We'll give lots of examples of measuring how hard things are to do in later chapters, particularly chapter 9, "A framework for design." Chapter 5, "Communication," gave examples of automatic ways of making design tradeoffs over how hard things are to do.

6.4   A four-state worked example

A flashlight (torch) can be off in lots of different ways. Let's consider a dud bulb and an OK bulb. There are many ways of drawing the device, but first we use a table to define all the states and actions—bearing in mind that some things are not possible, for example, you can't switch it on if it is *already* on, though you can replace a bulb even if the bulb is OK.

	—*Actions*—			
	Switch on	**Switch off**	**Bulb dies**	**Replace bulb**
on & OK	⟨*not possible*⟩	off & OK	on & dud	on & OK
on & dud	⟨*not possible*⟩	off & dud	⟨*not possible*⟩	on & OK
off & OK	on & OK	⟨*not possible*⟩	off & dud	off & OK
off & dud	on & dud	⟨*not possible*⟩	⟨*not possible*⟩	off & OK

(States)

Here it is, drawn as a diagram. In all we need four states, and lots of arrows:

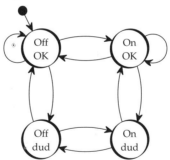

When I first looked at this diagram I wondered why it wasn't symmetrical. In fact, it could be: there is no reason in principle why a user can't replace a dud bulb with a dud bulb! If this action is allowed, then the diagram would have four loops rather than two.

A flashlight is very familiar and pretty trivial as things go. There aren't many ways to design them badly given that most of what they have to do is dictated by just linking up the basic states they require to work as a complete device.

Box 6.4 **Bad user interfaces earn money** When you leave a house with a burglar alarm, you enter your secret code and the alarm gives you a minute or so to get out of the building before the alarm is activated. The delay is a time out and can cause problems.

Georgia Institute of Technology has an "aware house" (www.cc.gatech.edu/fce/ahri) full of exciting gadgets—and it has a conventional burglar alarm, made by Brinks Home Security, the sort that could be used in any domestic house. What's unusual about this system is that lots of people use the house.

Here's the problem. When you arm the burglar alarm just before leaving the house, the alarm warbles for ten seconds to tell you what you have done, then it gives you a minute's grace—the timeout—to get out before the alarm is armed. So you leave. But this is a busy house, and someone else enters within that minute's grace, without the alarm making any noise—just as if the alarm wasn't set. Maybe they settle down to read a magazine in the living room ... Meanwhile, the alarm gets itself fully activated. It makes no noise that it has changed state.

Time for a cup of coffee? Oops, when they get up to walk to the kitchen the alarm goes off. They have to rush to the control box to key in the secret code. Hopefully they can remember the code in their panic! If not, the security people who rush to the scene to "catch the burglar" charge for their services.

Thus the company that supplies or supports the burglar alarm makes a profit out the bad user interface design. There is no incentive to improve a design when you can blame the users for the problems *and* make money out of it!

▷   See box 6.2, "Timeouts" (p. 174) and the discussion at the beginning of this chapter for more on how to avoid timeouts.

6.5   A larger worked example: an alarm clock

Let's try something more complex than a flashlight. A digital clock has states for each time it can display (60 minutes times 24 hours means 1,440 states). The number would be 60 times bigger if we (or the alarm clock) worried about keeping track of seconds.

The basic action of the clock is to tick. Each tick takes the clock from one state to another, and the time shown on the display shows which state it is in. There is nothing wrong with a device doing actions to itself.

We could imagine a gnome (small enough to fit inside the device) doing the tick action if we really want "users" to do all the actions and for the gadget to be a "pure" state machine. The gnome would have to do the tick action reliably every minute, day and night, and it would be such a boring job that it would soon be automated. The gnome could be replaced by investing in a metrognome as a matter of sound ecognomics (at least if you pay gnomes an hourly rate) as well as of sound ergognomics—as we wouldn't want our gnome getting repetitive strain injuries from all its button pressing.

An alarm clock, further, has to "know": whether the alarm has been set and what time the alarm should go off.

In principle, an alarm clock does not need to know whether the alarm is ringing, since this can be worked out from the time it is showing, the time the alarm is set

191

for (if it is set), and how long the alarm is supposed to ring for. Ringing is an effect, not a state.

Next, the alarm clock could have a button so the user can switch the alarm off earlier. Hence there is another factor to add to the list above: whether the key (Snooze) has been pressed.

We could carry on adding features to our clock; instead, we'll start to analyze what we have designed so far. Rather than analyze the full device, let's first imagine a "broken" alarm clock with a *fixed* alarm time, say 08:30. (Eventually we will need lots of these clocks, all "broken" at different times, so we can eventually change the alarm time by choosing the right clock!) This alarm clock must be able to display all 1,440 times, from 00:00 to 23:59, so it needs 1,440 states:

Here we've shown a state diagram but only drawn four of the 1,440 states explicitly; the dashed line is supposed to indicate all the missing detail.

Each tick of the clock takes the clock to the next state, going around the circle, and the display changes the time shown, say from 12:39 to 12:40, then to 12:41, 12:42, and so on.

When this alarm clock gets to the state corresponding to 08:30, the alarm is supposed to ring for that and the next three ticks: so there are four states (08:30 to 08:33) where the alarm rings. However, in each of these four states, the user might press the (Snooze) button and silence the alarm. So we need to add some more states, getting 1,440 + 4 = 1,444 states so far.

In the diagram, we've drawn the four snooze states outside the main circle. The idea is that the gnome's ticks on their own take the alarm clock around the inner circle. At 08:30 we're at the first state explicitly shown on the inner circle, and the alarm starts ringing. If the user does nothing, the next action will be a tick, and we go one state further around the inner circle—and the alarm continues to ring. If the user presses (Snooze), we would follow an arrow to the outer arc of states. In these states, the alarm does not ring, but as each tick occurs we stay moving along the outer arc, and thus avoid going to any state where the alarm rings. Eventually, after 4 ticks in the snoozing states, the clock goes back into a state on the main circle. Until we get back to 08:30 again the alarm will be silent.

Let's add another feature and so we can lock the alarm off, so it never makes a noise. Thus the 08:30 alarm clock needs another 1,440 states to show all the times when the alarm will never ring because it is off in addition to the original 1,440 states when it can ring.

Why can't it have on/off with just one or two more states? If the alarm clock had a single state for when the alarm is off, then it could not keep track of the time when the alarm was off. Remember, by our rules, we could only have one arrow coming out of this single state labeled (ON), and it could only go to one time with the alarm on. So we need 1,440 states, all for alarm off in each of the 1,440 different times.

These 1,440 states are shown on the right of the diagram below. (As before, I have only shown a few of the 1,440 states explicitly.)

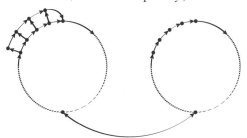

When the alarm is switched on, the clock goes from showing the time (perhaps 11:40) to showing the same time and the alarm being set. The double-headed arrow at the bottom shows what the alarm on/off button does.

If we have been pedantic, there would have to be 1,440 such arrows, to allow the alarm to be switched on and off in each of the 1,440 pairs of states. Really, there are 2,884 arrows, since there is one facing each way plus 4 one-way arrows from the snooze states—these 4 arrows are one way, because when the alarm is off it can't get back into snoozing, so the righthand circle has 4 fewer states than the lefthand circle.

Below, we've added in *just* the arrows to and from the alarm ringing and snoozing states to the alarm off states:

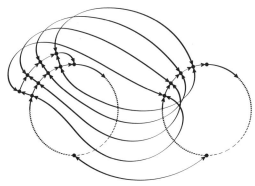

This last diagram shows the following:

■ If the alarm is ringing, we can press [Snooze] to switch it off. Alternatively, we can switch the alarm off and we go to the corresponding state on the right hand side circle of states, where the alarm does not ring. And ...

■ If the alarm is not ringing, there are two possibilities:

(*i*) If the alarm *is* set (we are somewhere on the left, except for the four inner states where the alarm rings), switching the alarm off takes us to the corresponding state on the righthand side.

(*ii*) If the alarm *is not* set (we are somewhere on the right), switching the alarm on goes from the righthand side to the corresponding state on the lefthand side. But note that if the time is currently 08:30, 08:31, 08:32 or 08:33, then putting the alarm on takes us to the inner circle of states, where the alarm rings.

■ The diagram omits showing 1, 435 arrows in each direction. It also does not show 2, 870 states.

So an 08:30 alarm clock, with the possibility of switching the alarm off, and of having a snooze button that immediately silences the alarm requires 2, 884 states. We've only sketched what it would look like.

In reality we need an alarm clock that lets us change the alarm time. In fact, we need an 00:00 alarm clock, an 00:01 alarm clock, and so on. That comes to 1, 440 alarm clocks, all much like the 08:30 clock but different.

There will be lots more arrows. Imagine we are running the 08:30 alarm clock and we want to increase the alarm time to 08:31. That means we must have arrows for the "increase alarm time by one minute" action from each of the 2, 884 states in the 08:30 alarm clock to corresponding states in the 08:31 alarm clock. In fact we need 2, 884 arrows to do this.

It is likely that a real alarm clock would have more buttons to adjust the alarm time, for example, in steps of 10 minutes and 1 hour, as well as just 1 minute. The extra buttons do not require any more states, but each button requires many more arrows of its own—each new button we add to the clock's design in principle requires one arrow from *every* state since the user can press the button whatever state the alarm clock is in. That's one of our original rules for drawing diagrams.

Finally, putting all these alarm clocks together into one box makes a giant machine with $1, 440 \times 2, 884 = 4, 152, 960$ states. This is a huge number, and clearly if we designed an alarm clock by *drawing* the states and actions, we'd get into a mess.

6.6   Doing your own drawings

Understanding state diagrams really requires playing with them: try doing some of your own drawings. Find one of your own flashlights, and work out its diagram. You could add an action to account for bulbs blowing (burning out)—then you would also need actions to replace dud bulbs with new, working bulbs. Draw in the extra arrows needed. How about doing a drawing for your car headlights, including full beam and dipped states? How do your fog lights work? (In Europe, you can have front and rear fog lights, separately controlled, but they can only be switched on when the main lights are on.)

6.7   The public image problem

Although we can't draw very big state machines, all the ideas are relevant to designing and understanding large systems. Indeed, because of the widespread confusion between drawings of state machines and machines themselves, the "public relations" problems with state machines have become dire.

- Any state machine you can draw is going to be small-scale and simple. So people mistakenly think state machines *are* simple.

- Almost any state machine that is interesting is too complex to draw. So people rarely think of interesting designs as state machines.

Regardless of their poor reputation, by drawing state machines, we'll get to understand them well, and we've seen how many problems about interaction programming can be understood and handled by treating devices as finite state machines. There are many good design ideas that become obvious when we exploit the clarity of state machines.

In short, if you don't understand state machines, you don't understand interaction. Once you understand state machines, you are welcome to program more interesting user interfaces: but don't lose track of the issues that matter.

6.8   The key design problem

If a user does not know what state a device is in, the device will be unpredictable; if the user doesn't know what mode a device is in, every action will have unpredictable effects. Unfortunately there are usually far too many states and modes to make it practical to tell the user which state or mode a device is in, or for the user to understand the difference between this mode or state and some fifteen others.

Much of user interface design boils down to balancing the device's need for many states and modes so that it can do a wide range of useful things for the user against the opposite constraint of making the modes clearly known or understood to the user, who should be in control—and with the constraint of the designer knowing what is going on too.

The key problem in interaction programming is that neither users nor designers can see states, modes, or actions (except in special, very simple cases).

With electronic gadgets, there are no visible features necessarily to be seen connecting actions to effects. In fact, inside gadgets there are, as it were, numerous features haphazardly crisscrossing. Because you can't *see* the mess of states, modes, and actions inside, nobody bothers to make them straightforward. Adding a random action seems as good as any other action. With a large device, a missing action or an action doing the wrong thing is not noticed—until somebody needs it.

Although a designer might satisfactorily conceptualize a simple system reliably, devices can get big and there are no *general* answers to the problem. People are still out researching how to represent what's "important" in design and use.

A confounding problem is that most devices are programmed in ways that obscure things even further. In a typical programming language—like Java, C, C++, or even Prolog—what the program says as a piece of text and what that program does, how it interacts with the user, are very different things.

You cannot read a program and *see* how it will interact; instead, you have to work out what it will do when it is interacting with a user. You have to simulate how it will work, going through it step by step.

In fact, interaction is a side effect of all conventional programming. Just as global variables and goto statements are generally frowned on because what they do isn't clear, interaction is never clear from a program.

Functional programming, which tries very hard to be clear, *avoids* doing anything with side-effects, such as interaction, on principle because it makes programs too messy to understand! Being event-driven or object-oriented does not change the basic problem.

When a programmer changes a program, the effect on the user interface can be arbitrary. In particular, improving a program (making it shorter or neater, say) has an unrelated effect on its user interface. Conversely, improving a user interface can have an arbitrary effect on the program code; worse, what might seem like a little improvement to the user interface can turn into an insurmountable modification of the program—so no programmer will want to do it.

Designers and users cannot see what they are interacting with: they just see the changes. There is no "big picture." Nor can programmers see what users are interacting with, even looking at the program code—and they are in a slightly worse position because they may *think* they can see everything as plain as the program code before them. But the code is not the interaction programming.

If we insist on a simple representation for interactive systems, namely, one based explicitly on states and actions, we can pretty much eliminate the problems.

Because the theory of finite state machines is simple, we can build all sorts of things *reliably* on top of them—and we can confirm, in many ways, that we are designing what we intend to design.

Interactive devices themselves are of course one of the main things we can build, but we can also make user manuals and many other things, such as transition diagrams, that will either help users or designers better understand and gain insights into the design of the device.

The more views of a device we have, the more able we are to get a good grip on its workings—and the more people who can be involved productively in the design process. Phrased more carefully, the more *reliable* views of a device we have, the more able we are to understand it—since devices are complex we *must* generate views and alternative representations automatically. As we will see, we can automatically generate working prototypes cheaply, so we can get users involved immediately, and we can generate draft user manuals quickly so we can get technical authors involved immediately.

In contrast, in a conventional approach to programming interactive devices, all of these things are very hard. To work out any sort of user manual requires a lot of careful—and error prone—thinking. Often, writing a user manual is therefore left until the program is "finished," since trying to write it any earlier only means that it will need expensive revisions as well. Ideas a technical author gets while reading or writing the manual—especially ways to simplify the design—are almost impossible to implement at this late stage.

> ▷ Well-written programs often simulate other styles of programming by building virtual machines. Chapter 9, "A framework for design," shows how conventional programming can simulate clearer models of interactive programs. Clearer models can then be used to create multiple views of interactive systems, for interaction, analysis, manual writing, and so on.

With a little care, then, we can arrange for insights from users or technical authors or other people to feed back into design. Since the state approach is simple to program, changes that are needed, say, in the user manual are *easy* to feed back into the core design. Thus we can have a *single* design, namely, a finite state machine, and all aspects of design work can follow from it.

There is only one thing to keep up to date, only one core thing to modify, rather than many independent versions—prototypes, scenarios, manuals, actual devices, and so on. We therefore end up with a more consistent, higher-quality design. This is concurrent design: when properly organized, many parts of the design process can proceed concurrently.

In contrast, in a normal sequential design process, you daren't make contributions to the design at the wrong time because your effort may be wasted; it may be calling for a revision to some earlier part of the process. In a sequential approach, there is no point working on the user manual too soon, because the device design might change. So, write the user manual *after* the device design is finalized. But then, if you have (or anyone else has) any design insights from reading the draft manual, you *cannot* afford to go back and revise the device design to help fix the manual.

Typically, a sequential design process has to keep users out of all technical parts of the design until practically the last moment, and then so much work has been done on the design that nobody is prepared to make many changes. Concurrent design is better, but it requires approaching design from a whole different set of assumptions.

6.9 Conclusions

What have we learned? We've defined states, modes, indicators, and actions, shown how to draw systems clearly, and how to get things done. Implicitly we have learned something very important: the user of a device, even as simple as an alarm clock, hasn't a hope of being able to check it out—these things are surprisingly big when all interaction details are considered. When people buy a clock, they will have to take it on faith that it works sensibly—there is no way a user can explore and understand the thousands of state transitions. Even a paid user that we might employ as a tester of alarm clock designs *cannot* work hard or long enough to check a device reasonably well. Most gadgets are more complex than alarm clocks, so the user's problems are usually worse. Most device designs are not thoroughly checked.

If users can't understand devices in principle, then designers are obliged to be all the more careful and honest in the design process. The only way to do that is to use automatic design tools.

The cost of all these advantages is that state machines are simple, and some interactive devices would be very hard to represent as state machines. The counterargument to that is that anything that is too hard to represent in this way is almost certainly too hard to use (it would certainly be too hard to write about in this book)—that's because we've made a very good stab at solving the key design problem.

Finally, if we draw state machines, we won't want to draw all of the states and actions explicitly, and we could be tempted to take shortcuts (as we did throughout this chapter) to make the diagrams possible to draw without being cluttered with massive detail. We therefore need tools to support the design process; we aren't going to do it well enough by hand.

6.9.1 Some *Press On* principles

- "Don't mode me out!" Avoid modes that stop actions having effects → section 6.1 (p. 165).

- We can *decide* that we are not going to build over-complex devices → section 6.1 (p. 173).

- Don't be rude: check a device is strongly connected—and dynamically recheck strong connectivity if there is any chance services or states might become unavailable → section 6.3 (p. 186).

- Design is not just designing a device—you have to think about the user's world → section 6.3 (p. 188).

- Design tools can be extended easily to add new checks, and the checks then become available at no extra cost for all design work → section 6.3 (p. 188).

- Make device laws hold dynamically while devices are being used → section 6.3 (p. 189).

- Users cannot see states unless a device makes them explicit in some way → section 6.8 (p. 195).

■ Conventional programming separates interaction from program code → section 6.8 (p. 196).

■ Concurrent design improves all aspects of interaction programming → section 6.8 (p. 197).

6.9.2 Further reading

■ Feynman, R. P., *Feynman Lectures on Computation*, Addison-Wesley, 1996. This book has an excellent introduction to finite state machines. The book is well worth reading as a clear, general introduction to computer science too—even if you are an expert computer scientist, Feynman's exposition is very lucid and insightful.

One of the nice things about state machines is that the ideas were introduced so long ago that the research papers about them are now easy to read. These are some classics I recommend:

■ Parnas, D. L., "On the Use of Transition Diagrams in the Design of a User Interface for an Interactive Computer System," in *Proceedings of the 24th. ACM National Conference*, pp379–385, 1964. Dave Parnas, now famous for his software engineering, introduced state machines for designing interactive computer systems.

■ Newman, W. M., "A System for Interactive Graphical Programming," in *Proceedings of the 1968 Spring Joint Computer Conference*, American Federation of Information Processing Societies, pp47–54, 1969. William Newman went on to coauthor one of the classic graphics textbooks, commonly called "Newman and Sproull": Newman, W. M., and Sproull, R. F., *Principles of Interactive Computer Graphics*, 2nd ed., McGraw-Hill, 1979.

■ Wasserman, A. I., "Extending State Transition Diagrams for the Specification of Human Computer Interaction," *IEEE Transactions on Software Engineering*, **SE-11**(8), pp699–713, 1985. Tony Wasserman extended state transition diagrams to make them more useful for specifying interactive systems; he built many UIMS—user interface management systems, which took state machines as their working specifications. (There are lots of other extensions to finite state machines.)

▷ We'll develop a framework—our name for a "skeleton" UIMS—in chapter 9, "A framework for design," onward.

7

Statecharts

The last chapter drew diagrams for state machines, but as they got bigger they quickly got messy. The more states and arrows there are, the worse it gets. A better method, using statecharts, helps draw complicated state machines more easily and more clearly.

A typical device will have an (Off) button and every state will need a transition for that button to go to the off state. That requires as many arrows as there are states, including the arrow to go from the off state to itself, as the off button usually keeps a device off when it is already off. Yet (Off) is a simple enough idea. Can't we avoid all the visual clutter?

In contrast to a transition diagram, which shows every transition as an arrow, a statechart is much easier to draw and visually much less cluttered. An (Off) button would only need one or two arrows, depending on how the statechart is drawn, regardless of how many states the device has. That's a huge saving.

Statecharts have many other useful features too. Typical interactive devices become much easier to draw and to understand—as the diagrams are much simpler, and they show many important properties of a design much more clearly.

Statecharts are quite complicated things in their full glory, so we shall only introduce the basic ideas here. Statecharts are a part of the Unified Modeling Language (UML) which is widely used for program development.

7.1 Modes and state clusters

Our basic flashlight example has ways to be off—it might be switched off, it might be missing its battery, or it might be missing its bulb—and lots of ways to be on but not necessarily alight. We often want to collect a lot of states together and ignore the details, like exactly how something can be on or off. Clusters do this simply by drawing a single "state," or cluster of states, as a rectangle.

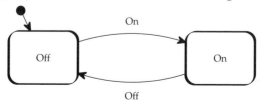

In this book, I've drawn most rectangles with rounded corners, because I think they look nicer—though some people use square and rounded corners to mean different things.

We can define modes in terms of statecharts. If we can (correctly!) draw an arrow for an action from a cluster of states, then those states represent a single mode for that action. In the diagram above, whatever happens inside the state cluster called "on" represents a single mode for the [Off] action, because the statechart is saying that whatever state inside On the device is in, [Off] *always* does the same thing—in this case, it takes the device to the Off state from *any* state inside the cluster called On.

This is why modes are a useful concept: they allow us to talk about a cluster of states—possibly a huge cluster of states—ignoring every detail of what goes on inside that cluster. What's important for a mode is that an action (here, "off") has a consistent effect for all the states.

7.2   Statechart features

Statecharts use drawing conventions like clusters and are a very powerful way to represent real interactive devices. Since statecharts are "just a drawing notation" many versions of statecharts have evolved, not all compatible—and you need to be careful if you are doing a rigorous design in case the statechart notation you are using has conventions that are not made clear. We'll only use the most basic, core features of statecharts, which are universally recognized.

7.2.1   Clusters

Let's consider details in the flashlight's On state cluster. Inside this rectangle we probably want to show how the bulb can go dud and how we are able to replace the bulb:

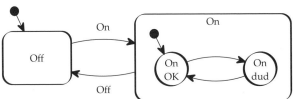

But this diagram breaks one of our original diagramming rules: the inside of the cluster is a state machine diagram, but we have not marked the default state. So, from this diagram we do not know what happens when we try the action [On] when the flashlight is off. It could go to On/OK or to On/dud, but we have not shown which.

There are two ways to solve the problem. We either make the [On] arrow point directly to the On/OK state, or we use a default arrow inside the cluster.

Next, we can use clustering to provide further information, making a multilevel statechart. Here we provide the default arrow and we indicate that the flashlight can be on or with a nonworking bulb in several different ways. For example, the bulb may be a dud or it may be missing.

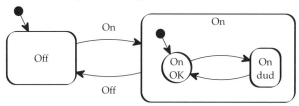

7.2.2 And-states

Actually, for our flashlight, the inside of the Off cluster is going to be exactly the same as the inside of the On cluster. The bulb can be OK or dud, whether the flashlight is switched on or off, and we can replace the bulb regardless of whether it's on or off. In fact, we can try to switch it on or off regardless of the state of the bulb. Statecharts can represent this "repetition" much better by using and-states.

In all the state diagrams we have drawn so far, the machine (like the flashlight) is in exactly one state on the diagram, and this is represented by it being in exactly one circle (or cluster). This is rather like having a *single* coin that follows arrows around the diagram—as the user performs actions. Where the coin is at any moment indicates what state (or state cluster) the device is in.

A state cluster divided by a dotted line means that the actions on both sides of the line can happen independently. It is in the states on one side of the line *and* in the states on the other side; hence the name.

We can now use more than one coin, and each coin will be in different states on different sides of the line. In theory, the machine will only be in one state since we are just using the two or more coins as a convenient way to keep track of the "real" single coin that we would have used if we had drawn all the states explicitly without and-states. In reality, it will be easier to program the device with as many "coins" as are necessary, and the program will be closer to a statechart than to a conventional state diagram.

The flashlight can be switched on and be OK, on with a dud bulb, off and OK, or off with a dud. That's why we need *and*-states. If we kept track of each combination in the usual way, we would need four states and one coin to be in any one of them. Using and-states, we represent the components separately, each as independent state machines. One state diagram therefore represents on or off; the other, dud or OK. If we keep track of the overall state using coins in states, now we would need two coins, one for each statechart on each side of the dashed line.

The statechart in figure 7.1 (next page) doesn't really need the default arrow at the top: there is, after all, only one cluster of states the device could possibly start in, namely, the one the default arrow points to. I put the default arrow in just to make the point that if there is only one default state, it does not need pointing out: the point of statechart conventions is to represent state machines as simply and clearly as possible without loss of meaning. Even so, the diagram is still simplified:

203

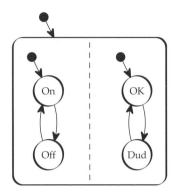

Figure 7.1: And-states for a flashlight. The flashlight can be in *four* states: on and OK, off and OK, on and dud, and off and dud. Its initial state is on and OK.

self-arrows are missing, the arrows that go from a state to itself, representing user actions that don't change the state.

Notice that we eliminated four arrows (although we've drawn two default arrows). Unfortunately, for persuading how effective and-states are in simplifying statechart diagrams, we don't seem to have achieved much: there are still four states, and now there is a dashed line. It hasn't achieved much is because, coincidentally, $2 \times 2 = 4$ and $2 + 2 = 4$.

Represented normally, as an ordinary state transition diagram, we need another circle in the state diagram for every state. But when it is represented as and-states in a statechart, the drawing multiplies up to the required number of states, and we don't need to draw so much. As the number of states in the device goes up, the difference between sums and products gets more significant and statecharts become more and more convenient. For example, whereas $2 + 2 = 2 \times 2$, if we needed three pairs of and-states rather than two, then $2 + 2 + 2 = 6$, which is smaller than $2 \times 2 \times 2 = 8$. For three pairs, the statechart would be a clearer drawing.

Furthermore, and-states make sense and are easy to use. If we wanted to draw a diagram of a flashlight that could also buzz, we would need twice as many states (every original state becomes two states, what it used to do without buzzing, and what it used to do *and* buzzing); but with and-states, rather than doubling the size of the diagram to cope with this extra feature, we need only add two more states to the statechart drawing (to buzz or not to buzz).

Let's add another feature to see how things get better and better as the device gets more complex. What if the flashlight could be blinking or not? With and-states, we need only add two more circles to the statechart diagram: to represent blinking and not blinking. With a conventional approach, without and-states, we would need to double the size of the diagram again. The comparison now is between $2 + 2 + 2 + 2 = 8$ for statecharts versus $2 \times 2 \times 2 \times 2 = 16$ for conventional diagrams. The advantage is even better when there are more states in each of the and-states. In our example, we've only had two states in each component. If we'd had three states (say, for off/dim/on rather than off/on, and so on), then the sums would work out as $3 + 3 + 3 + 3 = 12$ versus $3 \times 3 \times 3 \times 3 = 81$.

In summary, and-states allow us to draw simpler diagrams, and the benefits of using and-states get better and better as the devices get more complex. The only problem is—for this book—that when we draw simple devices that we can easily understand, the advantages don't look very impressive.

7.2.3 History connectors

In the and-state diagram for the flashlight, we used default arrows to indicate which states the device starts off in. To be pedantic, the flashlight won't always start off with an OK bulb. For instance, if we blew the bulb last time we used it and it is now a dud, the next time we use the flashlight it should default to being dud, not being OK, as the last statechart diagram suggests it would do.

Often, then, we want to say "be in the same state as last time" rather than to identify some state as being always the default. To do this, we use history entrances:

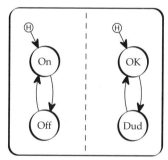

The history arrows, rather like the default arrows but with little H annotations, mean that next time the machine comes to these clusters of states (there are two clusters in this diagram, one on each side of the dotted line), go to the last state in each cluster the machine was in. In general, the history entrance is a very powerful and common feature of statecharts.

Playing with coins allows us to explain history entrances another way. When there is an action taking the machine out of a cluster of states, we might have to pick some coins up. If a cluster of states has a history entrance, we need to remember what state it was in when we came out of it. Simple: just leave the coins where they were, so that next time we know what state it was in. Somehow, though, we need to note that these coins are inactive: that is, they represent not the state *now* but the state the system will be in when it returns to this cluster. Perhaps we could indicate this by showing the coins as either heads or tails. The current state of the machine can be shown by a coin showing heads (more than one coin in and-states), and the historical states can be shown by coins showing tails.

Here is a statechart for simple TV with four channels and an operate button:

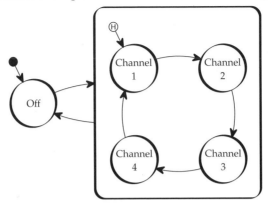

The statechart seems to show a TV with two buttons: one button switches it on and off, and the other button changes the channel. The history connector tells us that the TV will remember which channel it was on when it is switched off; when it is switched on again, it returns to the last channel the that was watched.

7.2.4   Deep history connectors

Sometimes we do not want to show all the details of a set of states, so we use a cluster. If we do this, then the history connector may not say the "right thing." Here's an example:

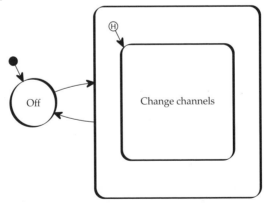

The problem is that although the history arrow correctly enters the cluster of states "change channels" it doesn't say which channel *inside* the cluster should be selected. The problem could be fixed by the change channels cluster having its own history arrow, but that would mean we end up saying history twice. What we want to do, rather, is say clearly that the history arrow reaches deeply into the nested cluster.

A history arrow is just an H, but a deep history arrow is an H with a star on it:

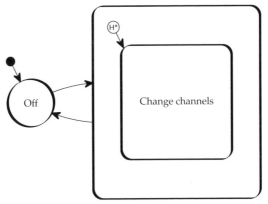

7.2.5 Leaving clusters

Whatever channel the TV is showing, we can always switch it off, for there is an arrow from the cluster to Off, which is a statechart shortcut to save us drawing individual arrows from all of the cluster's states.

Suppose we have an idiosyncratic TV that for some reason can only be switched off when we are watching Channel 4. This would be represented by an arrow directly from the relevant state inside the cluster. The statechart clearly shows the special treatment of the Channel 4 state.

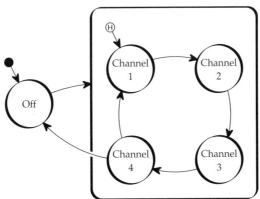

7.2.6 Delays and timeouts

Sometimes actions have no effect until after a delay, and sometimes actions can happen "all by themselves" after a delay. In a statechart, it is usually best to write out delays in full so there is no confusion.

Box 7.1 Computer demonstrations at exhibitions A common wooden printing press, several hundred years old, and a bookbinder's workshop are part of a permanent exhibition in the British Library. They are used for working demonstrations of the old arts of printing and book making. The working book press is of a type more-or-less unchanged since Gutenberg's time. In the corner of the room, for the last year or so, sit some sad large computer screens. A notice apologizes for the "temporary inconvenience" of the computers being out of order. I don't know what the computers would contribute to the exhibition, because I've never seen them working. Isn't this a good example of inappropriate technology, which is (particularly now that it has broken down in some way) completely beyond the abilities of its users to operate? Somebody installed the computers at great expense and forgot about their unreliability and the need for ongoing support, which the British Library is evidently unable or perhaps unwilling to provide.

When I checked up for writing this box, there were two notices: "This interactive [*sic*] is temporarily out of order," and "The printer is temporarily out of order." So things have become worse!

For example, if an action occurs after doing nothing inside a cluster for 10 seconds, we might write this:

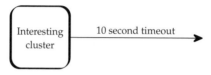

When space is at a premium, I sometimes use my own convention. A scribble on an arrow reminds me an arrow is special, rather than one representing an ordinary user action. It takes up less space:

Timeouts should be thought through carefully as they can be confusing for the user. You, as designer, may like a device to be "always" in a standby state ready for the user, even if the user was recently partway through some sequence before getting distracted from finishing. Timeouts are one way to do this: if a user does nothing, the system can reset itself somehow. Unfortunately, the user may be doing something—the device can't know.

Perhaps the user is reading the user manual, trying hard to understand what is going on. Now, after a timeout, the user is even worse off, as the device isn't even doing what they thought it was doing! Or if it is a walk-up-and-use ticket machine, maybe the user has selected their ticket, and is fumbling for suitable coins to pay. Perhaps they have dropped a coin on the ground. Returning to the ticket machine to buy the ticket, the user finds that it has reset—its designer has made it ready for the next customer—the machine has lost all knowledge of the ticket the user was about to buy. In most cases, a device ought to use a motion or proximity sensor, rather than a timeout.

7.2.7   Conditions

Sometimes actions can only occur when certain conditions hold true, for example, if our flashlight had two batteries, perhaps we can only remove the second after removing the first. As drawn below, the and-states give the impression that we can do actions on either side of the dotted line, but we've noticed that we cannot remove battery 2 unless battery 1 is already out.

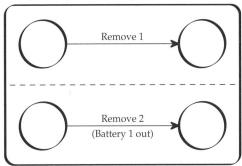

Of course, this particular state machine, with the battery removal order conditions, could also have been drawn more directly as follows:

In this last diagram, we don't need the condition to be explicit: the Remove 2 action is only possible if we have already reached the state after removing battery 1.

In fact we can always get rid of conditions by adding more states explicitly, as in this last diagram. Usually, conditions represent some far more complex arrangement of states and it is not so easy to do.

▷   A basic alarm clock was introduced in section 6.5 (p. 191), and we saw how messy its ordinary state transition diagram became.

Here is one way to represent some of the important states of an alarm clock without showing millions of states:

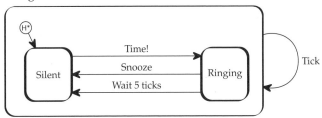

This deceptively simple statechart conceals a lot of sophistication—in fact, we'll shortly see that it isn't quite right.

Three user actions are shown in the middle of the statechart. If the alarm is set, and the time becomes equal to the alarm time, the clock changes to ringing. If the alarm is in any ringing state, the user can press the snooze button to silence it, or after five ticks the alarm silences itself.

The alarm clock has tick actions. The statechart does not say that the ticks occur every minute, but we can see that nothing inside the clock can ignore ticks: whatever the clock is doing, when a tick happens, the tick action occurs and we go back inside the cluster. Because we've used an H* arrow, this means that after every tick the alarm goes back to the *last* state. But we want ticks to take us to the *next* state—otherwise the clock won't work. Oops.

It would be clearer not to show the tick action at all. Given that the statechart represents millions of states and all their transitions hidden inside the two clusters, it is not surprising that it cannot describe the alarm clock's behavior completely accurately. Nevertheless, the simple statechart does show some important features of the alarm clock visually. It could be used as part of the design process of an alarm clock. Certainly the diagram allows us to talk about what we want more easily than almost any other visual representation. As we talk about the design, we see ways to improve the design—or we see ways to make the statechart diagram reflect more accurately what we thought we wanted.

7.2.8   Joining, merging, and splitting connectors

Joining and merging arrows is occasionally needed, generally with and-states. Joints and merges don't change the meaning of anything, as and-states and history connectors do, they just make statecharts look less cluttered.

It may be necessary to show that different and-states are entered after a single action. If so, the action arrow splits and goes to each state separately.

Arrows can merge as well. The main use of this feature is to get rid of clutter from statechart diagrams—sometimes a single state with lots of arrows going to it looks very messy.

7.3   A worked example: a Sony TV

A TV and its remote control are a good example of a device with two ways of controlling it. The buttons on a TV and the buttons on its remote control together form a single interactive device, even though they are physically independent. A statechart can represent such a combined system very easily using and-states.

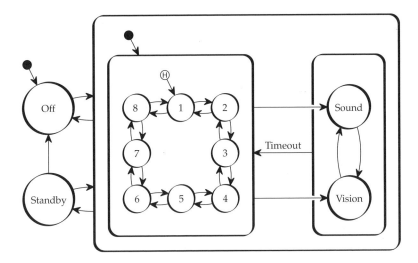

Figure 7.2: An outline statechart for the Sony KV-M1421U TV.

And-states directly represent the combined systems, TV and remote control, which the user can operate independently.

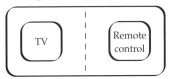

Strictly speaking, we should use some further features of statecharts to synchronize the two sides of this statechart, because states in different parts of the statechart are the same. Using the remote control affects the TV, just as using the TV affects the remote control: for example, changing the channel on either changes the exact meaning of "increase channel" on the other. In this book, we haven't worried about the advanced features of statecharts that can handle this interaction. Instead, if such a (simplified) statechart is drawn with the details of the two clusters filled in, the natural question to ask would be: "why aren't the two parts of the statechart the same?" They needn't be exactly the same—for instance, the remote won't be able to physically switch the device off—but major differences need careful justification.

We now return to the Sony television we first saw in figure 3.2 (p. 64). The Sony TV and remote control are different, and their two statecharts are very different, although the page size for this books makes them too awkward to draw as a single statechart. (Figure 3.2 was too small to see much detail.)

The television itself has very few buttons, and has a simple statechart, shown readably in figure 7.2 (this page). This statechart still does not show all the details; TVs, in any case, are familiar devices, and I don't need to clutter the diagram with

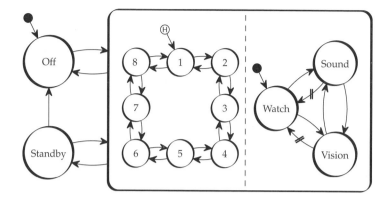

Figure 7.3: A more faithful statechart for the Sony KV-M1421U TV, using and-states.

obvious issues, like the button names, details of changing sound levels (which, at this level of detail, would just be self-arrows around the sound state), and so on.

The TV can be off, in standby, or switched on. There is a single button, ⓘ, that switches the TV on or off, depending on whether it is off or on; thus arrows that we might have been tempted to label simply On or Off, are more correctly labeled On/Off, since they are associated with a single button.

When the TV is on, you can watch a TV channel, adjust the volume, or adjust the vision properties (contrast, brightness, color). Although the TV can evidently be put in standby, it isn't possible to get it into this state without using the remote control. However, if the TV is in standby, pressing a channel-change button makes it on, whether you use the TV or remote control to change channel.

The numbers 1 to 8 in the statechart mean the TV channel selected. The TV shows the numbers on the screen for a few seconds: it would be distracting if 8, say, was shown indefinitely. We could add an and-state with a timeout to say when the TV channel number is actually showing.

An interesting user problem can be seen in the statechart: the TV has a class of states shown in the cluster at the right of the statechart that are exited by doing nothing until the timeout takes effect. If the user tries to get out—by pressing buttons—this would reset the timer. So if you think you must press a button to get back to the normal watching-TV mode, you will be stuck until you give up!

The statechart in figure 7.2 is not quite correct. When we use the TV, we find that we can still watch a program while adjusting either the sound or vision settings. In other words, watching a TV channel and adjusting are not mutually exclusive states, as the statechart indicates. In fact, we should be using and-states, because you can watch a channel *and* adjust settings, as shown more accurately in figure 7.3.

Notice the mixed use of default arrows and history arrows. When we switch the TV on or take it from standby, it will return to the last TV channel we were watching—that's the history arrow in the top part of the cluster doing its work; but

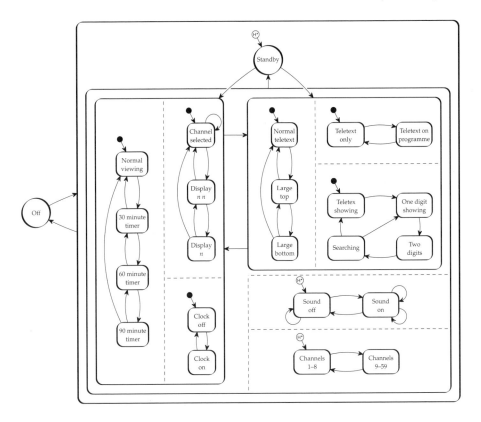

Figure 7.4: A statechart for the RM-694 control of the Sony KV-M1421U TV.

when we switch it on, it will always be in the watching mode, not adjusting sound or screen properties—that's the default arrow in the bottom part of the cluster doing its work.

The remote control for the Sony TV has a more complicated statechart, which is shown in figure 7.4 (this page). The statechart is *much* more complex than the TV itself—this was the main point made in section 3.2 (p. 63)—but let's now consider a few details from it.

From the statechart, we can see the TV as controlled by the remote can be off, in standby, watching a TV channel, or using teletext. Because of the deep history on the standby state, we can see that switching the TV on will take it to whichever was its last mode before it was switched off.

The clock is a simple subsystem we can look at first, with two state clusters, as shown in figure 7.5 (next page). The clock begins by being off, and the same [Clock] button is used to switch it on or off. We haven't shown the 1,440 states inside the clock needed when it is on!

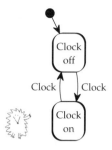

Figure 7.5: The simple clock subsystem, extracted from the remote control statechart.

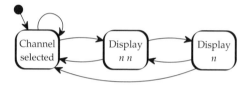

Figure 7.6: Selecting channels by pressing digits. Another extract from the remote control statechart, but rotated from figure 7.4 so that it takes up less space.

The details of the rest of the remote control statechart aren't too interesting, unless you like comparing details of TVs. I have to admit I've lost my remote control, but it allowed me to press digits to select a channel numerically—I wish I could double-check the details. This is represented in another part of the statechart, as redrawn in figure 7.6 (this page).

This is a different subsystem from the channels 1–8 and 9–59 cluster (shown in the bottom right): because that cluster uses ⊞ and ⊟ to change the range of channels, something that digits alone can't do.

7.4   Statecharts for discussion

It is great fun to retrospectively work out the statechart of a simple gadget you own, such as a table lamp or an electric kettle. When you've done one or two, try something more sophisticated, like a DVD player. It's *much* harder than you think, even if you work carefully from the user manual. The user manual and the gadget rarely correspond exactly! In fact one thing you learn is that criticizing user interfaces would be a lot easier if the manufacturers told us exactly what they had made. I guess they don't write accurate manuals because even they do not know—probably because they do not use statecharts or any other formalized design process.

It is interesting to work out a clear statechart for the remote control of a gadget and compare it with the gadget itself. Your car radio or sound system, especially if it has a remote control, would be a good case study. How are you supposed to use the remote control under pressure while driving?

7.5   There is no right statechart

There is no one right way to draw a statechart. The same functionality can be represented in many ways, and you may even want to have several different statecharts for the same device, each emphasizing a different aspect of the design. The best use of a statechart is to help you think about design, to help you develop the design that you, the users, or other people in the process really want. Sketch out a statechart that you know is not quite right, and people can easily contribute to improving it. Go to a design meeting with a "perfect" statechart, however, and you won't want to revise your hard work, and probably nobody will really understand what it already says in its refined, detailed way. They'll be less interested in talking about what it ought to say.

Here's a very simple system that has no correct statechart. Imagine a device with two buttons, one switches on and off a green light, the other switches on and off a red light. That's easy to represent as a statechart. Now consider that there is a third light, yellow, which comes on when both red and green are on. This is now a device that is hard to represent with a statechart, because the red, green, and yellow conditions overlap in ways that statecharts do not allow to be drawn. You have to decide which two colors to represent or not to use any statechart clustering to show all the colors clearly. If such a simple, albeit artificial, system has problems, imagine how bigger systems with more complexity become harder to represent faithfully.

To illustrate how effective "incorrect" statecharts can be, we'll discuss an erroneous statechart and see what sort of design questions get clarified. Let's imagine that we're starting a meeting and a complete statechart has been displayed, say by using a digital projector to show it on the wall. Everyone is sitting in the room, apart from you who is near the screen; and you are trying to explain the new operation of a planned small TV. Here's your first slide:

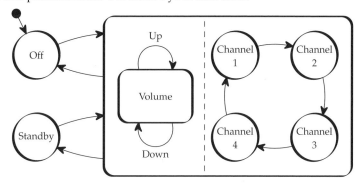

I'm sure somebody will comment positively that it is nice how all the arrows go round clockwise. In fact, the state names and arrows were *chosen* to go clockwise when they are increasing things—this is a nice consistency.

Since there isn't a history connection, we can't see from this statechart that when the TV is switched from standby or off back to being on (that is, in any state in the large cluster), that the TV remembers its last sound level setting. Likewise, we've forgotten to have an initial state for the channel—the statechart does not specify what channel the TV is going to be on *ever*.

Somebody will point out that surely if the TV is in standby, you ought to be able to switch it off directly. As it is drawn at the moment, if the TV is in standby, to turn it off, you would have to switch it on first! There is no arrow going from standby to off.

How many volume levels are there? The statechart doesn't tell us. Can we mute the sound? Well, not yet anyway. Surely we ought to be able to change from channel 2 to channel 1? As the statechart is now, we can only cycle through the TV channels, 1, 2, 3, 4 and back to 1. A user overshooting to 4 would have to go all the way around again, rather than going back directly from 4.

Here's an improved statechart. All the changes we've discussed can be drawn into the original statechart with minimal alterations.

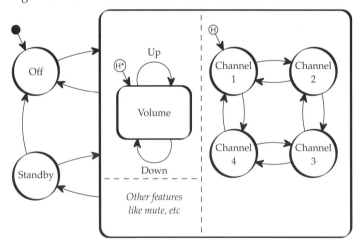

We've cheated a bit by not giving details of the mute feature, but at least the statechart now mentions it. We've fixed the default TV channel—now when the TV is switched on (whether from off or from standby), it will continue with the last channel used, thanks to the history arrow. We've added a new arrow from standby to off, so now that the TV can be switched off in one step—say by pressing the On/off button.

It's misleading that the off state has two arrows going to it when they are both the same user action. We should redraw the statechart so that only one arrow is required for each action. This will make the statechart clearer but won't alter its meaning. The default entry for the on cluster ensures switching the TV on from off still works the same way as before—when you switch the TV on it always comes on, rather than going into standby.

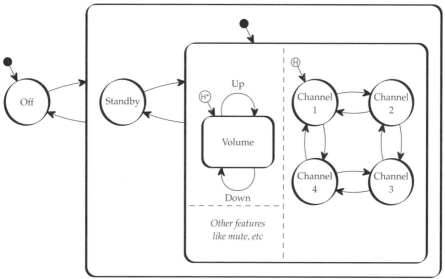

You can always make statecharts easier to read by removing detail from clusters. Of course, you can draw the detail of the clusters somewhere else, on another page, so the detail can still be seen, without the distraction of the rest of the diagram. In the last statechart, above, we're probably assuming that there is a separate statechart giving more details for features like mute.

7.6   Where did statecharts come from?

David Harel, who invented statecharts, wanted a better visual representation for reactive systems. Reactive systems are systems that react to their environment; finite state machines are one of the simplest sorts of reactive system. As we know, reactive systems often get so large that representing them in the obvious way as transition diagrams gets completely out of hand for all but the simplest cases.

Most interactive systems are therefore designed in ways that avoid the mess of transition diagrams by using general purpose programming languages such as Java. In safety-critical areas, just programming is too risky; instead, formal languages are used (such as CSP or SMV), and then the designers can prove that their programs, and ultimately the devices they build, perform as required.

Unfortunately, if you use programming languages of any sort, you lose the opportunity to visualize what the system is doing. Statecharts let designers visualize much more than the transition diagram can show, without getting unwieldy. They combine several visual formalizations into one effective whole:

■ Ordinary transition diagrams have arrows that connect single states; the states in a transition diagram have no other relation with one another than the arrows that connect them. Yet many states are conceptually related into sets, such as the set of "all states that are on." Statecharts add sets to the notation.

- Like hypergraphs, statecharts can have arrows between sets of states.

- Like Venn diagrams, statecharts allow drawing sets of states inside each other to show set inclusion. The set of all states that are on includes two sets: the set of states where the device is on and, say, the CD is in, and the set of states where the device is on and there is no CD in it. Venn diagrams allow these relationships to be drawn naturally. Statecharts are tree structured, so unlike full Venn diagrams, they do not allow overlapping sets of states—that's why the red/yellow/green light example given earlier was a problem.

- Many reactive systems have independent subsystems; if these are represented as finite state machines, you need a big machine that has as many states as the product of the two subsystems. (In fact, the system is the cross-product of the subsystems.) This can get out of hand very quickly! For example, three on/off light switches require a finite state machine of $2 \times 2 \times 2 = 8$ states. Statecharts use dashed lines to separate independent subsystems and thus avoid the multiplication of states. Three on/off light switches thus only take $2 + 2 + 2 = 6$ states to visualize.

- Statecharts have a variety of conventions to reduce the clutter of arrows. Default arrows, for instance, mean that you don't need long arrows reaching long distances inside sets of states.

In summary, graphs and hypergraphs show relations (visualized by arrows) among states and sets of states; Venn diagrams show structural relations between collections of sets (visualized by overlap and containment of shapes, usually circles, overlapping or inside other shapes); and statecharts combine both representations.

Full statecharts add a few more features that we have not used in this book, such as broadcast communication. In our use of statecharts, each action has been written on an arrow, and it causes a transition along that arrow. We didn't mention it, but if the same action is on several arrows, all of them work. This is obvious; for example the off transition might leave many sets of states in a cluster simultaneously. Generalizing this "broadcast" nature of actions, Harel allows any action to trigger more actions. In effect, arrows are labeled like $\xrightarrow{x/y}$, meaning to do this when x occurs and behave as if y occurs immediately afterward, that is, broadcast y to the rest of the statechart.

The actions in full statecharts can also have arbitrary conditions. For example, $y[\text{in } X]$ means only do transition y when some other part of the statechart is in the set of states X.

    ▷   It's interesting that statecharts combine graphs and Venn diagrams, for both of these ideas go back to one man, Leonhard Euler, the hero of the opening stories of chapter 8, "Graphs."

7.7 XML and the future of statecharts

This chapter has introduced statecharts as a visual notation, one that is better than transition diagrams alone. But statecharts are also a *conceptual* notation; they structure state machines in a way that makes them easier to conceptualize. There is no need for a statechart to be a drawing. Indeed the World Wide Web Consortium (W3C) is currently defining a statechart XML notation, which will be entirely textual.

HTML is perhaps more familiar than XML. HTML, hypertext markup language, is based on using matched pairs of tags to control formatting documents. For example, <b> to </b> will put the enclosed text into bold. XML works the same way, except that the tag names can be chosen freely and used for any purpose, not just for textual formatting. Thus XML has become a very popular form of data representation: it is flexible, easy to read, and has many tools that support its use (and it is cross-platform, and has lots of other benefits too, not least that it, despite all its shortcomings, is a very widely accepted standard).

An advantage of using XML is that there are many systems that can process it, and one can therefore define an interactive device and expect to be able to get it to work or be analyzed fairly easily.

VoiceXML and Voice Browser Call Control (CCXML) are variations on XML that allow voice-based interactive systems to be specified. You can thus define a statechart and get it to run a telephone voice menu system, for example.

SCXML is a statechart version of XML. In SCXML, state is defined using <state id=*name*> tags. For example,

```
<state id="1">
    <!-- this is a comment in XML -->
    <!-- state 1 has a transition to state 2, defined on the next line -->
    <transition next="2">
</state>
```

defines a state with a single transition to another state. Note how comments can be used to help you keep track of what you intend an XML specification to be doing.

A cluster of states can be defined naturally, simply by defining them inside a state:

```
<state id="1">
    <initial transition target="A"/>
    <state id="A"> ... </state>
    <state id="B"> ... </state>
</state>
```

makes state 1 a cluster containing two states, A and B, with A being the initial default state. And-states are defined by putting them between <parallel> and </parallel> tags in much the same way.

Obviously there are many more details to SCXML than we need to cover here. For instance, to get it to work, the SCXML needs wrapping up in the usual XML name spaces and other tags.

219

In the future, then, statecharts will be used for drawing and thinking about parts of interactive systems, but the full details probably won't be shown, or certainly they won't be shown all the time. Actually seeing all of a device's specification, even using statecharts, can be overwhelming: given a written statechart (probably in SCXML), we can extract simpler statecharts to visualize whatever bits of a design we are interested in and want to think about, but we won't have to see all of the design at once, unless we want to. We can still use statecharts for conceptualizing, building, and designing—but with XML and other tools, we will be able to build, analyze and run interactive devices, and document them, all from exactly the same XML text. Being able to do so much from one document will help improve quality—because different people will be able to work from exactly the same material. Any faults will be corrected—and will correct things for everybody. (In contrast, in a conventional design process, each aspect of design is independent and has its own life, so fixing problems, say in the user manual, rarely helps fix problems in the interactive device itself.)

▷ You can get more details of SCXML and other variants of XML from www.w3.org.

7.8 Conclusions

Most systems that we are interested in have *many* states. Unless we draw their diagrams carefully we get in a mess very quickly! Statecharts provide a clearer way to draw state transition diagrams. They are a widely recognized way of drawing interactive devices. For the most part, the ways statecharts simplify diagrams actually helps us do what we want—they bring out many interaction programming issues and make them easier to see. It would be unfortunate indeed if the gadget designs we wanted were still nasty to draw, but by-and-large statechart features correspond to useful features for designing interactive systems.

Statecharts are not perfect. For example, while they show states very well, they do not show actions very clearly. If a device has a button ⌧, a statechart gives no visual insight into how ⌧ is used, and whether, for instance, it has been used everywhere it should have been. For many properties, we will have to rely on automatic analysis to find out whether a design does the things we want it to, but statecharts are very good for starting a "bigger picture" discussion about design with designers.

▷ See chapter 9, "A framework for design," for many ideas of checks and properties about designs that can be worked out automatically—so we don't need to draw diagrams to see their properties.

Sadly, few systems are designed using statecharts, let alone state diagrams. Statecharts aren't used because not enough people know about them, and ordinary state diagrams aren't used because they get too complicated too quickly. So most devices are programmed without any careful analysis of the state and transitions, and all of the details that we took so much care to draw are never visualized by the designers. That's a shame, because then we end up with quirky designs. If we were designing for safety-critical applications, say, a gadget to monitor a hospital patient, then we *must* use a technique at least as good as statecharts to help make the design safe.

7.8.1 Some *Press On* principles

■ Think through the need for timeouts carefully → section 7.2 (p. 208).

■ Use statecharts for insight and discussion → section 7.4 (p. 214).

■ There is no one right way to draw statecharts → section 7.5 (p. 215).

7.8.2 Further reading

■ Degani, A., *Taming HAL: Designing Human Interfaces Beyond 2001*, Palgrave Macmillan, 2004. *Taming HAL* (an allusion to the HAL computer in Arthur C. Clarke's *2001: A Space Odyssey*), is an excellent introduction to the issues discussed throughout *Press On*—and it makes good use of statecharts. *Taming HAL* goes from the design of handheld devices to aircraft cockpits, and shows how bad design causes human error. *Taming HAL* covers much of the same ground, with the expertise of a NASA scientist. It discusses some nasty accidents and explores the design issues behind them, but it does not get into any programming behind the user interface.

■ Fowler, M. with Scott, K., *UML Distilled*, Addison-Wesley, 2003. UML, the popular unified modeling language, uses statecharts and several other notations to help in design. There are many books on UML; Fowler and Scott's has the advantage of being very clear and one of the shortest!

■ Harel, D. and Politi, M., *Modeling Reactive Systems with Statecharts*, McGraw-Hill Education, 1998. This is *the* book on statecharts, but David Harel has written several definitive papers: Harel, D., "Statecharts: A Visual Formalism for Complex Systems," *Science of Computer Programming*, **8** pp231–274, 1987, introduced statecharts; and Harel, D. and Gery, E. "Executable Object Modeling with Statecharts," *IEEE Computer*, **30**(7), pp31-42, 1997, also published in *Proceedings of the 18th. International Conference on Software Engineering*, IEEE Press, pp246–257, 1996.

■ Harel, D., "On Visual Formalisms," *Communications of the ACM*, **31**(5), pp514–530, 1988. A very clear and concise introduction to statecharts, as well as hypergraphs and Venn diagrams, written by their inventor.

■ Horrocks, I., *Constructing the User Interface with Statecharts*, Addison-Wesley, 1999. A much more practical, programming book on statecharts.

- Paternò, F., *Model-based design and evaluation of interactive applications*, Springer Verlag, 2000. Statecharts are not the only approach to designing interactive devices. A completely different approach uses Petri nets, invented by Carl Petri, which are basically transition diagrams with tokens that can be moved around. A Petri net can be in more than one state at a time, or put the other way around, a standard transition diagram has only one token to move around, to show the current state. This book discusses Petri nets from a user interface perspective.

- Samek, M., *Practical Statecharts in C/C++*, CMP Books, 2002. Although Samek is keen on his so-called quantum programming, don't let this put you off! His book is a very practical introduction to programming statecharts in conventional programming languages. This book should be read by anyone wanting to build interactive embedded systems.

- Wieringa, R. J., *Design Methods for Reactive Systems*, Morgan Kauffman, 2003. An excellent and easier to read text book than Harel and Politi's book and one that covers more than just statecharts.

8 | Graphs

All sorts of things can be represented by dots and arrows, from the world wide web down to how the neurons in our brains are connected. Interactive devices are finite state machines that can be represented by dots and arrows. Common to all is graph theory, the underlying mathematical theory. Graph theory gives us a powerful handle on what devices are doing, how easy users will find things—and it gives us lots of ideas for improving designs.

In the eighteenth century folk in the German town of Königsberg entertained themselves walking around the town and crossing the bridges over the River Pregel, which empties into the Baltic Sea. There were seven bridges over the Pregel, an island, and a fork in the river. Some wondered whether it was possible to walk around the city center crossing each bridge exactly once.

Here is a schematic representation of the city of Königsberg, its river and its bridges schematically:

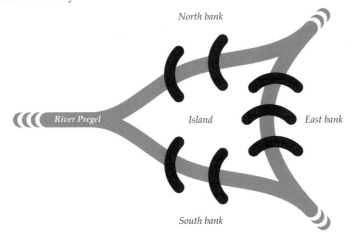

You can imagine that somebody walking around Königsberg is in different states depending on which bit of dry land they are on—north bank, island, south bank, and so on. Crossing a bridge changes state.

We can redraw Königsberg without the river and draw circles around the states, and we get something closer to a familiar state transition diagram:

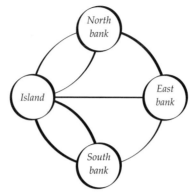

One frustrated person who tried walking across each Königsberg bridge exactly once, perhaps on some romantic evening stroll, wrote to the local mathematician Leonhard Euler about the problem. By 1736 Euler had published a paper that showed conclusively that there was no way to walk around the city crossing each bridge exactly once.

Euler's 1736 paper started the field of graph theory, which thinks abstractly about networks, like walks and bridges. In Euler's honour, a walk that crosses each bridge exactly once is called a Euler Tour, and any town with bridges that can be walked around in this way would be called Eulerian. Today, the Königsberg bridge problem makes a nice children's game—there are a few mathematical addicts who have built small-scale models of Königsberg for children to enjoy running around them—and maybe learning a bit of mathematics as well. Another bridge was built in Königsberg in 1875 and it then became possible to walk around the city center crossing each bridge exactly once: so post-1875 Königsberg is Eulerian.

The point for us is that graph theory analyses a network, here the bridges of Königsberg, and tells us what humans can do with it. In this chapter we will explore graph theory to see what it can say about interaction programming, and how design choices influence what a user can do and how easily they can do things.

■   ■   ■

Euler's name is pronounced "oiler," but Eulerian is pronounced "you-lair-ian." In graph theory "bridge" is a technical term that means something very different from a river bridge. To keep the confusion going, after World War II, Königsberg was renamed Kaliningrad.

8.1 Graphs and interaction

People in Königsberg had set themselves a certain sort of navigation task: to walk around a city under certain constraints—and some people got frustrated when it turned out to be too difficult to do. Today users navigate around interactive devices, pressing buttons and changing states, rather than crossing bridges and changing river banks. They set themselves tasks, to achieve things using the devices, or they just want to enjoy themselves as the people of Königsberg did. The underlying mathematical theory is the same.

A graph is a set of things, conventionally called vertices and a set of pairs of those things, usually drawn as lines between them, called edges. These are just alternative words for what we called states and actions in chapter 6 (p. 163). As far as graphs are concerned, states are vertices, and actions are edges.

In this book we are concerned with one-way actions, which are drawn as single-headed arrows: in this case the graphs are called directed graphs, and the directed edges are usually called arcs. Almost every diagram we've drawn in this book (apart from the two opening this chapter) is a directed graph.

Modern Königsberg has some one-way streets, and this makes it a mixed graph, as it has both directed and undirected transitions; however, none of the systems we look at in this book are mixed graphs.

Graphs get everywhere, and this chapter is where we pin down what can be done with them. If you thought that something as simple as graphs—dots and arrows—could not be useful for interaction programming, you'd be wrong! Even very simple graph properties have serious usability implications.

Graphs can describe many different things. They have many interesting properties and anything described by a graph, whether a garden maze or an interactive device, can be reasoned about as a graph and will enjoy the same sorts of general properties. It's rather like a pile of oranges and a pile of apples both enjoy the basic properties of numbers (if you add a piece of fruit, the pile goes from n to $n + 1$ pieces; of if there are n pieces of fruit, you can't take away more than n pieces; and so on)—anything that is a graph, or that can be understood as a graph, enjoys graph properties.

Humans made a giant leap forward when they realized that two apples and two hungry people both had the same property—two. When you know that you can use mathematical properties of numbers, for instance, to deduce that each of two people person can have one apple (from two) to stave off their hunger. Similarly, once we realize that lots of human experience is basically like finding your way around in graphs, we can apply more powerful reasoning—in the same way that numbers, once we get to grips with them, let us add 1 to $999, 983, 142$ as easily as to 2.

Let's begin with an example from a completely different area, well away from interactive systems—chemistry. A compound like paraffin can be represented as a graph, where vertices are atoms and edges are chemical bonds between the atoms.

One of the questions chemists are interested in is how many isomers a compound has: that is, how can the same numbers of hydrogen and carbon atoms be combined in different ways, perhaps each with different chemical characteristics? The graph theory here gets going when it starts counting off how many chemicals have particular properties; historically, graph theory got really going when it brought some clarity to chemical thinking.

Euler's original bridge-crossing problem corresponds to a modern problem, and one of concern for us. Suppose you give me a gadget and ask me to check to see whether it works properly—that it works correctly according to its user manual or specification. (Or you could give me a web site and ask me to check it; since both things are directed graphs, the problems are equivalent: both devices and web sites are graphs.) So I am supposed to press buttons and note what they do, and I must check that in every state every button behaves properly.

Of course, when I press a button on a gadget, my action changes the device's state. It's analogous to crossing a bridge in Königsberg—but instead of walking around the city, I am walking around the space of device states; instead of changing my location to different places in the city, I am pressing buttons that cause the state of the device to change. The only real difference is that in Königsberg, if I make a mistake I can turn round and go back over the bridge, but when testing a gadget there may be no way back—it's as if the bridges on the device are all one-way. In short, to test a device against a user manual efficiently, without recrossing "bridges," we would like to find an Euler tour of the device.

Unfortunately not all graphs have Euler tours. So we are being unreasonable to hope to be shown an Euler tour to follow to test the device.

8.1.1   The Chinese postman tour

The next best thing to an Euler tour is a Chinese postman tour, so called because it's named after its Chinese discoverer (Kwan or Quan), and it's called the postman tour because postmen walk down every street in a city to deliver letters. The postman wants to walk the shortest distance, not going down any streets more than strictly necessary. This simple generalization of the Euler tour was only discussed in the 1960s.

The Chinese postman tour turns out to be quite tricky to find by hand, but a computer can find the best Chinese postman tour of a graph easily. Once we have a Chinese postman tour, when you ask me to check a gadget I could follow the postman tour, though I might need a computer to help me work it out.

Left to my own devices, I would risk going around and around in the state space and most likely never managing to check all of the device thoroughly. If you want to check that a device does what you as its designer intended it to do, you should not just ask users to try it out; rather, you should work out a Chinese postman tour and check that—that will be a lot quicker and far more reliable. Of course the Chinese postman tour check would not confirm that users can do all the useful tasks they want to do, but it will make a basic (and necessary) check that the system is correctly designed. For example, a Chinese postman tour would check on a web site that every link was correctly named and went to the correct page.

Box 8.1 Chinese postman tools If we ask users to test a device, effectively to check "does this bit do what its manual says?" and "can you think of any improvements?" for every function available—without further help—they are *very* unlikely to follow an optimal way of testing the device. They are very unlikely to check every action (every button press in every state): they will miss some. In the very unlikely event that they do manage to check everything, they certainly won't do it very efficiently. They will use up a lot more time and effort than necessary. Trial users checking systems often have to use notebooks to keep track of which parts they have tested, and I doubt they can be sufficiently systematic even then not to waste time and miss testing some features.

In short, a program should be used to help users work through their evaluation work. This means finding a Chinese postman tour. Actually, rather than follow an accurate Chinese postman tour, it's more practical to follow a dynamically generated tour that suggests the best actions to get to the next unchecked part of the device. This is much easier! For the program, it only needs to keep track of which states have been visited and use shortest paths to find efficient sequences of actions for the users. For the users, it's much easier too: there is no problem if they make a mistake following the instructions, and they can easily spread the testing over as many days or weeks as necessary.

▷ Section 9.6 (p. 297) gives code to find shortest paths.

Since a device design may change as it is developed, the flags associated with states can be reset when the design changes if the change affects those states. Thus a designer can incrementally check a device, even while it changes, perhaps making errors or missing actions, and still know what needs evaluating and checking. Eventually the evaluation will cover the entire functionality of the device.

State flags can be used in two further ways. During design, documents may be produced, such as user manuals. A technical author may wish to flag that they have documented certain parts of the device and therefore that they want to be notified if those parts of the device ever change. This allows a technical author to start writing a user manual very early in the design process. State flags can also be used by an auditor, who checks whether an implementation conforms to its specification. The auditor can use the flags to assert that a vertex (or arc) has been checked out and must not be changed gratuitously.

The Nokia 5110 phone that was used in chapter 5, "Communication," has a Chinese postman tour of 3,914 button presses! And that's only considering the function menu hierarchy, not the whole device. In other words: to test whether every button works in every state on this device takes a minimum of 3,914 presses—and that's assuming error-free performance. If we made a slip, which we surely would, it would take longer. Obviously, human testing is not feasible.

Here is an extract from a Chinese postman tour of a medical device:

```
      :
478 Check ON from "Off" goes to "On"
479 Check DOWN from "On" goes to "Value locked for On"
    In state "Value locked for On", check unused these buttons do nothing:
    DOWN, OFF, PURGE, UP, STOP, KEY, ON
487 Check ENTER from "Value locked for On" goes to "Continuous"
      :
```

You can see how each check takes the user to a new state, and in that state only one check can be made there—you need a Chinese postman tour because each check necessarily takes you to a new state. In the example above, step 479 must be the first time the state Value locked for On has been reached in the tour, and the checking program is recommending that several buttons are checked in this state to confirm that they do nothing: these buttons can be checked easily since checking them shouldn't change the state.

▷ With the device framework we will develop in chapter 9, "A framework for design," it is easy to take the test user "by hand" through the best tour: the device itself can keep track of what the user has and has not tested. This idea is explained more fully in box 8.1, "Chinese postman tools" (previous page).

If the system can keep track of all this, why does a user have to work laboriously through the tour? The system can check that everything is connected, but no system can know deeper facts like what the [Pause] button is supposed to do when the device is recording. A user should get the device in the recording state and try out the [Pause] button, see what it does, then tick a box (or whatever) to "audit" the correct behavior of the device. Once a user has checked the Chinese postman tour (or any other properties), if the device is modified only the bits that have changed need to be rechecked—again, a good device framework can handle this and greatly help in the design and evaluation of a device.

The longer the Chinese postman tour, the harder a device is to check properly: it simply takes more work. A designer might therefore be interested not in the details of the Chinese postman tour (because the details are only needed for checking) but in how long it is, that is, how many button presses it will take to do, since that is a good measure of how hard the device is to understand. If a user was going to understand a device they would *have* to explore and learn at least as much of the device as a postman would have to, so the length of the postman tour provides a way to assess how hard a device is to understand or to learn. Even if this is not exactly correct (users may not have to know *everything*), the longer the tour the harder the device (or the web site, or whatever) will be to check. So, when a designer is contemplating adding a new feature or a new button, they might want to measure the lengths of the Chinese postman tours with and without the feature to see how the lengths change. Is the extra cost to the user in terms of complexity worth it in terms of the value of the new feature?

Some special graphs have simple Chinese postman tours: a so-called randomly Eulerian graph, for example, has a tour that can be found by pressing any button that has not yet been pressed in the current state. It's called randomly Eulerian because when you have a choice, you can behave randomly and still follow a Eulerian tour of the system. Such devices are very simple. If you had a design like this, its usability could be improved (if seeing all of it is the task—as it would be with a task like visiting an art gallery and wanting to walk down every passage to see everything) by having the system indicate which buttons have previously been pressed.

Art galleries might like to ask design questions like these. Presumably they want visitors to see many exhibits, even—and perhaps especially—when the visitors get lost. Equally, the designer of a walk-up-and-use exhibit at an exhibition might want to design their system's graph to be randomly Eulerian, guaranteeing that the user will be able to find more things on the console more easily.

8.1.2 The traveling salesman problem

More familiar to most people than the Chinese postman tour is the traveling salesman problem. We imagine that a salesman wants to travel to every city to sell their wares. Now the cities in the salesman problem are the vertices of the graph, and the roads between the cities are the edges (or if they are one-way roads, they are the arcs).

Unlike a postman, a salesman is not worried about traveling along every *road*—just about visiting every *city*. But like the postman, the salesman wants to travel the shortest possible distance.

If we think about web sites, the traveling salesman problem corresponds to checking each *page* of a web site rather than each *link*, which is what the postman tour checks. The traveling salesman tour of a general interactive device can check that each state of a gadget works as intended—for instance, that the various lights and displays come on properly in every state. In contrast, the Chinese postman tour checks whether the buttons (or other user actions) work correctly. Thus to check that a device works correctly, we need to check both its Chinese postman tour and its salesman tour.

As it happens, a Chinese postman tour must visit every vertex, so a user (or a designer) can check out every state by following the route of a postman: you don't need to do both. If we have a test rig for the device being checked, then it should be extended so that when a user visits a state for the first time, they are asked to check whether it is doing what it is supposed to do. When the test user checks the box, they need not be asked again even if they revisit the same state. Similarly, the first time they press a button in each state, they should be asked, but not subsequently.

The traveling salesman tour problem is not at all easy to solve, and computers get overwhelmed with relatively few vertices—the hundreds or more states of a typical interactive device would be way beyond finding an exact solution. In practice, the salesman therefore has to make do with an approximate solution, hopefully one that is good enough. But just like the Chinese postman case, if we are checking a gadget or a web site, *we* would take a very long time if we got lost without following the route instructions worked out by a program.

Compared with the traveling salesman, who visits everywhere, how well does someone using a device typically do? Or, put another way, if we ask users to try out a gadget so we can see how they do, so we can evaluate the device design, what proportion of the system will they explore? If users testing a system don't know where to go (if they are not following a recipe, such as a salesman tour), just as lost people in the real world, they will probably go around in circles and never get to explore the gadget at all thoroughly. This is a good reason not to rely exclusively on user tests for evaluating a device.

Euler tour To travel along each arc (in the right direction) exactly once, and get back to the starting vertex.	The graph must be Eulerian, and if so, checks every action is correct.
Chinese postman tour To perform a Euler Tour, or when an Euler tour is not possible, to travel along each arc at least once.	To check that every action (button press; link) is correct.
Hamiltonian tour To visit every vertex exactly once, and get back to the start.	The graph is Hamiltonian.
Traveling salesman tour To visit every vertex, using as few arcs as possible.	To check that every state (or web page) is correct.

Figure 8.1: Summary of four sorts of graph tours. The Chinese postman and traveling salesman tour have variants if arcs are weighted (have numbers associated with them): then they should minimize not the number of arcs used, but the total cost of the weights.

▷ The cost-of-knowledge graph plots how long a user takes against how much of a device they have explored. If the user follows a traveling salesman tour, they will do the best possible. Section 5.3 (p. 144), specifically, figure 5.11 (p. 144), draws some graphs, from random user behavior.

8.1.3   Coloring graphs

A long time ago, map makers noticed that only four colors are required to make a map with no adjacent countries or regions the same color. The only map we've drawn in this chapter, of the town of Königsberg, with four regions of land, would only take three colors: if somebody had painted the town, three colors are enough to ensure that the land color changes whenever you cross a bridge. The north bank has no bridge connecting it to the south bank, so these can be the same color. For more complex maps, you may need more colors. The four color theorem says, against expectations, that you never need more than four, provided the map is flat.

The four color property of maps can be expressed in graph theory: regions are vertices, and "being next to another region" is an edge between the regions or vertices. Although first proposed in 1852, it was over a century before it was proved. The proof of what seems like a trivial theorem turned out to be so complicated that it had to be done by computer—indeed, the computerized proof was quite controversial and called into question what mathematicians mean by proof: are proofs supposed to be clear arguments understood by humans, or can computers get away with vast so-called proofs that no human could verify?

Now exactly what has coloring got to do with interaction programming? Imagine, first, that you are back in Königsberg. (It's tempting to call the regions in this land "states" because that's what we will be calling them in a minute!) If the land had been colored by a painter who had arranged that no adjacent lands were the same color, you would always know when you crossed a bridge. If the painter hadn't used enough colors, sometimes you would cross a bridge and the country color would not change. You might not notice that you were in a different country, and perhaps wouldn't understand the local culture's colorful nature.

Back in the context of user interfaces, users would probably want to see confirmation every time they changed the state of the device. In some sense, the "color" of each state must be different from the "color" of adjacent states; if not, then some state changes cannot be noticed, because there is no change.

What corresponds to colors in an interactive device? Most devices have displays and indicator lights that help tell the user what state the device is in. For example, there may be a light that says the device is on. This is rather like saying that in the off state, the light is black, and in the on state (whichever state it is in when it is on) the light is red. A CD player might have an indicator to say whether a CD is in the device or not: another choice of two colors. The combinations of indicators correspond to colors: in the table below, each combination of the two indicators has been allocated a notional color.

State	Indicators	Color
Off	none	Red
On, CD out	on	Green
On, CD in	on, CD	Blue
Off, CD out	CD	Yellow

Every possible state change (like ejecting the CD) corresponds to a color change. In fact, for this simple abstract device, since every state is a different color, it's inevitable that any state changes the user can do results in color changes. In general, what a designer should check is that at least one indicator changes for all possible state changes; then the device is adequately colored, and in principle the user can tell whenever there is a state change.

▷ Section 10.3.2 (p. 334) shows how to work out tables like the one above, automatically so that they can be used to help design better systems.

The four color theorem only applies to flat, conventional, maps. For more complex graphs—such as those we encounter with interactive devices—almost any number of colors may be required. The worst case is a complete graph: a complete graph has every vertex connected to every other, so that all vertices must be different colors. If there are N states, N colors are required.

A graph's chromatic number is the minimum number of colors it needs. The chromatic number of any two-dimensional map is at most 4, unless it has tunnels or other ways of cheating. The chromatic number of any map drawn on a sphere is 4 too but the chromatic number of a map drawn on a torus (a shape like a sausage bent into a circle) is 7. An interactive device whose graph can be drawn on paper without any crossing lines will necessarily have a chromatic number at most 4, but usually the chromatic number will be higher—most device's graphs cannot be drawn without crossing lines.

For any specific graph, it is possible to work out the chromatic number—the programming is not too hard. If the chromatic number is c, then there must be enough indicators to count from 1 to c (or, equivalently, from 0 to $c - 1$) in binary. Imagine each state is given a color. The chromatic number tells us the least number of colors we need so that when we go from one state to another, the color changes.

If our device had a single colored light with c colors (or c different phrases), that would be sufficient to tell the user whenever they changed state. With fewer than c colors, some state transitions could be missed using the indicators alone: the light's color wouldn't change.

Now it is unusual to have a single indicator with lots of colors; instead, there are usually several indicators, red lights or whatever, that are either on or off, rather than showing different colors. In principle, the indicators can count as binary digits, bits. If you have n indicators, you effectively have n bits available, and you can count up to 2^n different things. This is how binary works. So you need 2^n to be at least as large as c to be able to distinguish all state changes. In other words, you need at least $\log_2 c$ on/off indicators to distinguish every state for a device with chromatic number c. Even then, the indicators may not be used properly (the device might have the right number of indicators but not use some of them or not use them very well), so that needs checking as well. That is, having enough indicators is necessary to distinguish all the states, but it is not a sufficient design criterion to ensure that the device is easy to use.

For a JVC video recorder I worked out the chromatic number, and it was higher than the number of indicators could handle. In fact, the video recorder did not say when it was in the states "preview" and "cue." That's a potential problem identified by graph theory—though whether a user would be worried about it is another matter. For a video recorder, a user would probably be looking at the TV, not the device itself, and it would be obvious whether it was playing or fast forwarding from the TV picture. Once or twice, though, I have found myself fast forwarding the tape when I wanted to rewind it and not noticing the difference.

▷ This JVC PVR is discussed in detail in section 10.3 (p. 330).

For a safety-critical device (say, a medical device to be used in an operating theater), knowing when or whether it changes state is likely to be very important. What happens if an anesthetist presses 8.0 to deliver 8.0ml of a drug but accidentally does not press the decimal point hard enough? The patient would get 80ml of the drug, which for many drugs would be quite enough to kill the patient. In such cases, the device should tell the user, the anesthetist, *every* time it changes state—so, in particular, not pressing the decimal point hard enough should be recognized by the user.

8.1.4 Coloring graphs to highlight interesting features

Any graph I draw in this book is going to be small, but I hope you agree, worth studying. If it's too big to draw, I won't include it in *Press On*; and if it's a boring graph, there's no point in drawing it.

Unfortunately, the real world has a lot of enormous and potentially boring graphs in it (the web may be a good example). Fortunately, we can use coloring as a way to transform the boring world into exciting and manageable small graphs.

Imagine a huge graph, for instance, one of the enormous state machines from the previous chapters. We color everything we are really interested in red, and

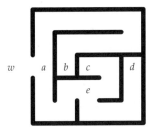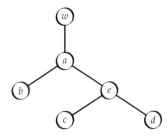

Figure 8.2: A very simple maze (left), with intersections and end points marked, and its corresponding graph (right). The state *w* represents being in the "rest of the world," and the states *a* to *e* are places to be inside the maze, where the explorer has to make a choice or has come to a dead end. The graph representation, being more abstract than the maze, does not distinguish between the inside and the outside of the maze—for instance, it could be redrawn with *c* or *b* at the top of the diagram.

leave everything else black. We now have a colored graph, that is a lot simpler than the original. Hopefully, we will have colored in something that has an interesting structure that we can critique, understand, and improve.

For example, later in this chapter we will talk a lot about a type of graph called a tree. Many interactive systems considered as state machines are *almost* trees, but they have details that make them more complex. So imagine that the tree part of the graph is colored red. What we want for good interaction programming is a *good* red tree. The other stuff, which we haven't colored red, can wait, or perhaps it can be handled automatically and generated by a computer—for instance, features for error correction. Then we look at the red tree, ignoring all the other detail, and try to improve the design of the red tree.

▷ Trees are discussed in section 8.7 (p. 249).

8.2 Mazes and getting lost in graphs

Graphs get much more interesting when they are too big to look at. Whether using devices or testing them, users can get hopelessly lost, even in quite small graphs, even comprising only a dozen states. You can write programs that manipulate graphs of millions of states, and typical interactive devices have thousands of states. Is there anything else from graph theory that can help?

When the Attic hero Theseus explored the Minotaur's labyrinth, he unwound a cotton thread so that when he wanted to get out, he could be guided out by following the thread back to the entrance. If he hadn't had the thread, he would have become lost—and he would have figured on the Minotaur's next menu.

When our contemporary hero explores an interactive device, say a ticket machine, what "threads" can prevent getting lost? What can they do if they take a wrong turning? What happens if they fall through a trap door that only lets them go one way and not back?

The answer is that an interactive device should provide something analogous to Theseus's thread. Following the thread back will always get the user out. It's easy enough to do this. The thread is usually called "undo." When users get lost, they press (Undo) and get pulled back by the thread to where they just were.

There are a few complications, most notably when the user undoes back to a state where they have been twice (or more times) before. It isn't then obvious what pressing (Undo) should do—it's a state where the thread crosses over—go to the previous state, or to go to the state that first got there. There's a sense in which, if the user is trying to recover from a mistake, simplifying the undo trail will help; on the other hand, any simplification is second-guessing the user and may contribute to further problems.

When Theseus got back to any doorway he'd been through twice before, he would see threads going in three directions, and he'd run a small risk of going around in a circle and taking longer to escape the maze. Even if he had been using Ariadne's special directional thread (so he knew which direction he was going in when he unwound it), he would have two choices—or more choices in a popular intersection. The moral for Theseus is that whenever he *first* gets to an intersection, he ought to leave a stone behind to mark the first entrance, where he entered, to the intersection—and then it will be easy to decide which way to get out when the Minotaur chases him and he hasn't time to think hard about it.

The great thing about graph theory is that we know these two problems—Theseus panicking about the Minotaur and a modern ticket machine user (with a train coming to pick them up *if* they have managed to get a ticket out of the machine)—even though one is the stuff of myths and the other the stuff of modern stories and HCI textbooks—are precisely analogous. Thus a good ticket machine design will give the user different choices in different states, depending on how to get out. A ticket machine has to make other decisions: as the user travels around its "maze" they will be picking stuff up at different "intersections," like going to states where they can tell the ticket machine where they are going, how many tickets they want, how many children are traveling with them, and so on. When a user wants to "get out" not all of these details should be lost. Escaping from the labyrinth is easier in comparison: Theseus merely wants to get out fast, not get out with a valid ticket!

Another solution is to have more than one action available to the user. A key (Previous screen) is potentially ambiguous, since there may be two or more previous screens for the user—like having two or more threads coming to an intersection. We could design the device to have (Previous screen) and (Original way here), which (easily if it was a soft key) would only appear when there was a difference. Really the only way to tell what approach would help is to do some experiments with real people, under the sorts of pressure they'll be under when they need to buy tickets before the train comes.

It is possible to escape from certain sorts of real mazes without needing a thread or without needing an exceedingly good memory for places. In some types of maze you can put your hand on the right hand wall or hedge, and keep on walking with your hand following the right hand wall. This will take you in and out of cul-de-sacs (dead ends), but eventually you will escape. If you happen to start trying to get out when you are in an island within the maze, all you would achieve then is to go around the island endlessly, never escaping. Hopefully, in real life, you'd notice this repetition and at some point change hands to touch a wall you'd never touched before. This would get you off that island, and perhaps closer to the exit.

In 1895 Gaston Tarry worked out a general technique for escaping from mazes. His assumption was that the passages in the maze were undirected, so you could walk along them in either direction. Of course, the actions in a state machine device are directed so Tarry's method does not work for a gadget, unless we design it so that actions are, like passages, undirected. This would mean that there needs to be an inverse for every action: if you can get to a state, you can always go back: to use Tarry's ideas, the device would need an [Undo] button.

Tarry had two ideas about goals. The simpler is that we want to find the center of the maze, and his systematic way to do this is to obey the following rule:

■ Do not return along a passage that you took to an intersection for the first time unless you have already returned along all the other paths.

This would be one way for a traveling salesman to work if they didn't have a map of the country (or a map of the maze): eventually they will get to every city. This method of Tarry's eventually visits everywhere, so it will certainly get to the center of the maze. In fact, for a device, it is a technique for a user to get the device to do (or be able to do) anything it can do—provided the device has a proper [Undo] button.

His more complex idea was that from the center you would want to get out efficiently. The first method, above, of finding the center takes you all over the place; because you don't know where the center is you need to try going everywhere. But to escape faster, rather than reexplore everywhere, carry a bag of stones and mark each passage you travel down—roughly speaking you use the stones as marking the "ends" of a thread. If you are Theseus, you need a big reel of thread, at least as long as the passages put end to end; if you are Tarry, you need a bag of stones, big enough to leave stones at each junction you visit. Tarry's stones are equivalent to Theseus's thread, except no trail is left down the passages only at their ends. If you are a modern interactive device user, you just need the device to be designed to keep track of the paths that would have been marked with threads and stones.

I haven't given quite enough details, but Tarry's approach is equivalent to the following more abstract description. He effectively replaces each edge in the original maze with a pair of directed, one-way edges going in each direction. He uses the stones to keep track of which way you've been down any edge. His procedure then efficiently finds an Eulerian tour around this directed graph (there always is one as he's added edges)—you walk down each maze passage twice, once in each direction—so effectively along each virtual directed edge once.

What use are these graph theory ideas for interactive systems? It's interesting that web browsers typically change the color of links (hot text) when they have been used. This is like putting stones down in passage entrances: the links are the ends of passages (to further pages on the web site) and the change in color marks the fact that the passage (or link) has been used before. Tarry himself suggested this is useful idea, and no doubt usefulness is what prompted the feature in browsers, though I don't think the designers of web browsers got the idea from systematically thinking through graph theory ideas.

Why don't interactive devices have lights on their buttons? Maybe the color of a button should change if it has been used before in this state? Maybe a button should flicker tantalizingly if the user has never tried pressing it in this state? Such a device would encourage and enable the user to explore it fully over a period of time. In fact, this idea is a bit like putting the user testing features of a framework (like the one we mentioned above for checking that the test user is following a Chinese postman tour) into the device itself. What's a good idea for the tester is probably good idea for the general user too.

It is important that there is an algorithm, Tarry's procedure, for getting around a maze. The algorithm does not rely on there being a map or bird's eye view or indeed having any prior knowledge about where the center of the maze is. This is rather like wanting to build a device that allows the user to succeed, but (even *with* a map of the gadget) not knowing what the user's tasks are. What state or states would the user consider the center of their maze of tasks? We don't know. What we do know, though, is that it is possible to help users to systematically explore a gadget so that eventually they can find anything they want in it (*provided* they can recognize it when they get there).

In complete contrast, recreational mazes are deliberately designed to be a challenge. Mostly when we design user interfaces we want to help users rather than challenge them, which suggests that rather than helping users cope with the current design, we could try redesigning to make finding our way around easier. Graph theory gives us several ideas to do so, from changing the structure of a device (so a particular way of navigating it will work), changing the actions or buttons available (so [Undo] works usefully), changing the indicators or lights at certain states (so users know they have been there), and so on.

8.3   Subgraphs

Most devices are more complicated than the conceptually simple sorts of graphs—complete graphs, cycles, or trees—yet these are clearly relevant and useful design concepts. How can we get the best of both worlds?

Inside a mobile phone, one would expect to find a cycle of menu items that the user can choose and a [Scroll] button or a pair of buttons [∧] and [∨] that cycle through them. Yet the device's graph as a whole is not a cycle: there is more to it.

A subgraph is part of a graph, obtained by taking some (possibly all) of the vertices from the original graph as well as some of (possibly all of) the arcs that connect them. Thus we expect a mobile phone, for example, to include a subgraph that *is* a cycle, namely, the cycle of menu items.

Subgraphs have other applications. From a usability point of view, if a user does not know everything about a device, but what is known is correct, then they know

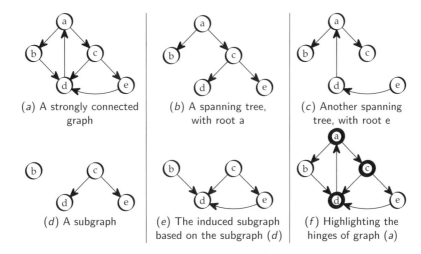

(a) A strongly connected graph

(b) A spanning tree, with root a

(c) Another spanning tree, with root e

(d) A subgraph

(e) The induced subgraph based on the subgraph (d)

(f) Highlighting the hinges of graph (a)

Figure 8.3: A graph (a) and various graphs derived from it. The subgraph (d) is just some of the arcs and some of the vertices and, as it happens, is not connected. In contrast, an induced subgraph (e) contains all relevant arcs. The spanning trees (b and c) are subgraphs of (a).

a subgraph of the device's full graph: in other words, the user knows some, but not all, of the states and actions.

Probably the most important two sorts of subgraphs for designers are so-called spanning subgraphs, which have all the original vertices but not all the arcs, and induced subgraphs, which retain all of the relevant arcs but not all the vertices.

Figure 8.3 (this page) shows a simple graph, some subgraphs, two different spanning trees, and an induced subgraph.

▷ Trees and spanning trees are discussed at length in section 8.7 (p. 249) onward later in this chapter.

The figure also shows the hinges (sometimes called articulation vertices) of the original graph. If you delete a hinge, the graph becomes disconnected. If a user does not know about a hinge, they cannot know about the component of the graph on the other side of the hinge. It's therefore crucial that users know about hinges— or that a graph does not contain them, or contains as few as possible.

We'll consider induced subgraphs first. If, from an entire graph for a mobile phone, we pulled out just the vertices corresponding to a submenu of the phone (say, all its language choices), we would expect to find that the induced subgraph was indeed a cycle. In other words, if a user gets down to this language submenu the graph of that menu should be a cycle; otherwise, the user would not be able to get around it easily. In fact, the induced graph of any menu should be a cycle for this sort of device.

8.3.1   Spanning subgraphs

Spanning subgraphs cover all of the original vertices and include enough arcs so that the subgraph is connected. Thus if a user knows a spanning graph of a device, they know everything it can do, but they may not know how to get it to do everything. In particular, if the known spanning graph is not strongly connected, the user will know some things the device can do, but they will sometimes be unable to do some of them—that is, when the device is in a state that is not connected to where they want to go.

What a user knows about a device is of course unlikely to be equivalent to the device: they won't know the device's graph in detail; they may have missed arcs (they don't know that a button does something in some state) or they may have misrouted arcs (they incorrectly think a button does something, when it does something else). However, they must know a subgraph of the device if they are going to be able to use it at all reliably (unless they are playing and don't care whether they remember how to use the device).

A user might rely on a user manual rather than their own understanding of the device in order to use it, in which case, as designers, we should check that or use an automatic (or partly automatic) process that ensures that the user manual represents a subgraph of the system.

> ▷ In chapter 9, "A framework for design," and chapter 10, "Using the framework," we will talk about generating user manuals further; as a general principle, you can generate smaller user manuals for subgraphs. The user manual may have interestingly different graph theory properties than the interactive device it documents.

8.4   User models

We have described graphs as if they define what a system does. The user's brain is also another system, so graphs define in some sense what the user thinks. In particular, if a device is a graph (it is!) then the user's mental model of how it behaves is also a graph.

As designers, we clearly want the user's model graph to correspond with the actual graph of the device. The user's model should be a subgraph: there may be bits of the device graph that the user does not know, but what they do know should be identical to those bits of the device. That requirement is the same as saying that the user's model is a subgraph.

In practice the user's model is likely to be *almost* a subgraph: the user won't know everything, much of what they know will be correct, but there will be some embellishments. See figure 8.4 (facing page) for a suggestive pair of user and device models.

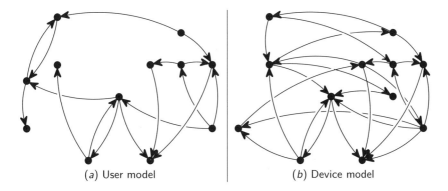

(a) User model　　　　　　　(b) Device model

Figure 8.4: An illustrative user model (a) is almost a subgraph of some device model (b), except that the user thinks there is another state that is connected to the rest of the state space of the device.

8.5 The web analogy

When you start a word processor, your computer shows a screen, which could be simulated by a web site, with the word processor's features shown as little pictures on the web page. When you click on word processor features, you could just as well be clicking on a web link. If you bring up the dialog box to save the file you are working on, the word processor's screen changes: equally, you could imagine clicking on a link and the web bringing you a page that *looked* the same.

Or suppose you were thinking about a mobile phone. A web page could show a picture of the phone, and the keys could be linked to further pages. When you click 1, you could be taken to a page that shows the mobile phone's display changed to show the 1 you've dialed.

▷　In chapter 9, "A framework for design," we show how to make state machines work on the web, and in particular in section 9.5.1 (p. 294) shows how to make a state machine diagram (in fact, an imagemap) work by clicking on its states.

In general, anything—computer program or simulation of a gadget—can be handled as a web site, perhaps an enormous web site. The point is we can talk about the way anything is designed just by considering one type of system and how it is designed. Rather than talk about each sort of interactive system as if it were different, we can see the key interaction issues are shared with everything.

In graph theory terms, a web page is a vertex, and the links written into HTML indicate where arcs go. The label of the arc is the hot text.

Actually, a web page (or a set of web pages) can be converted to a graph in a variety of ways, depending on which conventions we follow. The label could be the hot text, or it could be the name of the HTML link, which the user normally cannot see: `<a href=#linkname>hot text</a>` could be the start of an arc with either "linkname" or "hot text" as its label (or both). Is the HTML text `<a`

Graph theory	State machines	Web sites	Hypertext	Garden mazes
vertex	state	page or anchor	node	junction
edge or arc	transition	link	link	path
label	button name	hot text	link text	rarely labeled!

Figure 8.5: Equivalent terms from different fields. Is it ominous or obvious that the same theory works equally well with web sites and mazes?

---

href=#linkname>hot text</a> the initial vertex, then, or is the page containing this text? (It's more useful to make the whole HTML page the vertex; otherwise, the out degree of every vertex would be at most 1.) Similarly, the end vertex is either the text between the tags, <a name=linkname>target text</a> or is the page containing the tag.

▷   Section 9.4 (p. 280) shows how to convert a finite state machine into a set of web pages or into a single web page. Either choice can be a faithful representations of graphs.

■   ■   ■

Consider the following syllogism:

■ A (big enough) web site can simulate any interactive device or program;

■ A web site is a graph;

■ Therefore any interactive device is a graph.

There are other ways of putting this, but this way of putting it makes intuitive sense. In fact, as this chapter has made clear, "interactive device" can be much broader than a handheld electronic gadget. Even a maze is an interactive device, where the user's actions are not button pressing but walking.

8.6   Graph properties

When designing a device we will want to check that many things are right or as good as they possibly can be, particularly things having to do with its usability. In general, the questions we want to ask will depend on what we want the device to do and how we want the user to experience it, and how the user is supposed to be able to operate it. Importantly, many things we are concerned about in interaction programming (how fast, how easy to use, how reliable, and how safe) can be expressed in graph theory terms and then precisely checked.

Some people think that we are confused if we say that we can check usability from a graph. Usability depends, they say, on much more than technical properties of graphs! Does the device have the right feel? What do real users really think?

What happens when the device is used in its intended setting, rather than in a laboratory setting or in the designer's office? Usability, they say, is far more.

To avoid the confusion, it's important to distinguish between different sorts of properties and how we use them; no single property on its own can claim to characterize "usability" in its widest sense, but we can nevertheless make some very insightful, and often very clear, assertions.

- If a necessary property is absent, a device won't work correctly. Two very important necessary properties are liveness and safety.

- A safety property says that something (usually dangerous) cannot happen.

- A liveness property says that something (usually desirable) can happen.

We do not need to agree about specific properties. For example, if I am pointing a gun at an aggressor, to me it may be a liveness property that I *can* fire my gun, but to the other person, it may be a safety property that I *cannot*. Yet we'd both agree that the property was important!

- A metric, or measure, says in some sense how hard something is to do (of course, it could measure other factors).

- A metric may not be accurate; it may even be inaccurate in a systematic way. A low bound is a measure that lets us be certain that the correct value is larger; a high bound lets us be certain that the correct value is lower. Generally, our measurements will be off by an unknown factor, for instance, because we don't know whether the user is an athlete and how fast they perform—and then we can only compare measures made the same way relative to one another, rather than make absolute judgments.

Metrics and properties are often mixed up. How well can we achieve a property? Is it true in 65% or 95% of states, say? Or a property could be that a measure achieves or doesn't exceed a certain value. A cash machine might have a safety property that it will never dispense more than a certain amount of money.

In contrast to all these hedges, a property or metric worked out for a graph is quite precise. (Occasionally we deal with such large graphs that we can only guess on the property, but that's not a problem for any properties or graphs that we will consider here.)

We might work out that there are *exactly* 23 arcs between this and that vertex. Whether that 23 means that a user would take 23 seconds or 17 days to get from one to the other, we cannot say. We can guess that if the number was reduced, the user could be faster. We can guess that if the number was enormous, the user might never make it. We can be certain, however, that if we increase the number, even the fastest user would take longer.

All numbers, measures, and properties work like this; in graph theory terms we can be certain of what we mean; in interaction programming terms and usability terms, we need to interpret the properties carefully.

In design, we may find some properties are not as we wish; we then improve the design. For example, we may want to revise a device design so that some things

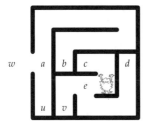 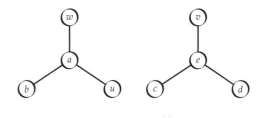

Figure 8.6: The simple maze of figure 8.2 (p. 235) redrawn with an extra wall, cutting off c, d, and e from the rest of the world, w. Building this wall in the maze creates two new vertices, u and v. Representing the new wall in the graph means deleting the old edge between a and e—the maze now has a disconnected graph.

we've noticed become impossible to do—this is an aspect of debugging, that is removing all actions that lead to device faults. Often, though, when we are debugging, we go about it in an informal way. Graph theory gives us an opportunity to catch at least some design bugs systematically.

Sometimes you may want a property but not want it in a particular design project. A manufacturer may want to sell two versions of a product, a basic one and a version with a value-added feature. The value-added feature should be checked as actually unavailable on the cheaper version of the device but available on the more expensive version. (You would certainly want to check that if a user of the cheaper device accidentally got the device into some "value-added" state that they could get it back again, without returning it to the manufacturer to fix under guarantee!)

How we use graph properties is a matter of judgment. Certainly they can protect us from many silly and some profound design mistakes, and they can help guide us in improving design.

Many of the properties we want a device (or a graph) to have depend on what sort of graph we have chosen to represent the design. Although I will give examples, there are always different contexts; in different contexts, with different assumptions, different properties would be better.

8.6.1   Connectivity

To be able to use a device freely, users must be able to get from any state to any other, and that means that there must be paths in the device's graph from every vertex to every other. Thus a simple usability question has been turned into a simple but equivalent graph theory question.

A graph that is connected has paths from everywhere to everywhere; a graph that is disconnected does not. Compare figure 8.2 (p. 235) with figure 8.6 (this page), which is a disconnected maze. For such a simple maze, it is pretty clear that it is impossible to do some tasks, like getting in from the outside world (represented by the vertex w) to the center (c).

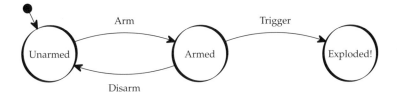

Figure 8.7: A graph that is connected but not strongly connected. A user can go between Unarmed and Armed states without restriction, and from Armed to Exploded, but not back again to Armed (or Unarmed) once the Exploded state has been visited. Compare this graph with figure 9.1 (p. 275), which is a similar, but has an extra arc and is strongly connected.

Most mazes allow you to walk in either direction down the passages; their graphs are undirected. Interactive devices are better represented as directed graphs, in which the notion of connectivity has to be stronger. States may be connected, but are they connected in the right direction? Figure 8.7 (this page) shows a directed graph that is connected, but not strongly connected. Every vertex in the graph is connected by a path through edges to every other vertex—but not if you try to follow the edges in the one-way directions indicated by the arrows.

This book is a graph, from which we can extract many interesting subgraphs. For example, figure 8.8 (next page) shows the subgraph defined by the explicit linkage between sections. For example, one arc in the figure represents the link from this paragraph to the figure itself. The graph is clearly not strongly connected. It is a set of components, each of which represents a related topic explored in the book. Unlike a maze, this graph is directed: if users (readers of this book) follow a link, they would have a hard time getting back—the links are one way. If the book was converted to a web site so that the links were active links that the readers could click on, the browser would rectify this directedness by making all links reversible. This is a good example of how an abstract structure (in this case, the book's explicit linkage) can be made consistent and easier to use by a program (in this case, a web browser).

It is easy to write a program to check whether a graph is strongly connected. Every interactive device should be strongly connected, unless the model of the device includes irreversible user actions—for example, a fire alarm has a piece of glass protecting its button: once the user has smashed the glass, there is no going back to the standby state. If the answer is that the graph is not strongly connected, you'd want to know where the graph fails to be strongly connected; for these indicate areas that may represent design faults or deliberate features you'd want to check.

▷ Section 9.6 (p. 297) gives one way to check strong connectivity.

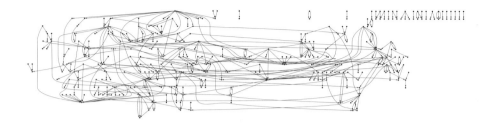

Figure 8.8: This is the graph of all the linkage cross-references in this book. Each section in the book is a vertex, and if a link refers to a section, we draw an arrow from one section to the other. For convenience, we do not show the section numbers (it would make the visualization too detailed) and we do not show isolated vertices. Connected components of this graph are clearly visible, and the small ones represent coherent sub-themes within the book. Of course, if we allowed that each section is connected to its successor, and added linkage like the table of contents and the index, the graph would be more realistic in terms of representing how the user can navigate the book—but harder to interpret! Put another way, if I make this book into a web site, the graph of the web site would contain this graph, shown above, as a subgraph.

8.6.2   Complete graphs and cycles

Graphs can be designed to *be* strongly connected. In particular, the complete graph is one in which there is an arc from every vertex to every other vertex—so it is strongly connected. This corresponds to a device with a button for every pair of states, and the user can get to any state from any other simply by pressing one button. The simple light bulb, with a push on and push off button, has a complete graph of two vertices and two arcs.

In a complete graph there is no requirement that the same button always takes the user to the same state: connectivity and completeness do not care what the arcs are called (that is. the names of the buttons the user has to press), merely that there *is* a connection from every state to every state. A stronger usability question is to ask whether all arcs have the same name as the state they go to: this would clearly make the device even easier to use.

Another strongly connected graph is the cycle or cyclic graph. In a cycle, each state is connected to one other state, and the states are connected in sequence, eventually returning to the first state. Thus you can get from any state to any other state by doing a sequence of actions. For many devices, the consistency would make them easier to use—just keep going and you are *guaranteed* to eventually get anywhere. There is a naming question again: whether all actions have the same name, [Next] (or [∧]), say. Repeatedly pressing [Next] should take the user through all states cyclicly.

It is an interesting contrast that for a complete graph we typically want to check that each button always goes to the same state, whereas for a cycle we want to check that the same button always goes to the *next* state. As we said, many of the properties we want a device (or a graph) to have depend on what sort of graph we have chosen to represent the design.

We could write a program to find all cycles in a device's graph: typically we would expect to find many cycles, for instance, because the device will have a correction action so the user can undo unwanted menu selections. Often we expect there to be many simple cycles such as menu↔submenu. If we are checking a device design, then, we might first delete all arcs corresponding to correction or undo actions and then check that the remaining cycles consistently use [Up] (or [∧]) and [Down] (or [∨]). The sorts of questions we can pose of a device are endless!

8.6.3 Cliques and independent sets

If each button or action available to the user does what it says, the device will be easy to use—though for some purposes it might be *too* easy to use. The [On] switch of a light bulb switches it on; the [Off] switch switches it off; that's the sort of sensible design we want for a light bulb.

In graph theory terms we can spell out this simple property for a device, as follows:

■ If a device has a complete graph, then the arc to each state (the button or action getting to that state) can be uniquely labeled with the name of the state. That is, each button does what it says.

To be complete requires exactly as many buttons as states. Unfortunately if you have a device with more states than buttons available, it cannot be as simple to use as this.

However, parts of the device may be complete. A part of a graph, considered on its own, that is complete is called a clique. Even if a graph has several cliques, it may not be possible to name the buttons consistently, since some button names may be used in more than one clique—they'd have to do different things for each clique. Instead, it may be more helpful for a designer to think about the parts of the graph that are *not* cliques. The graph theory concept of independent sets helps here.

An independent set of a graph is a set of vertices taken from the graph such that no pair of the vertices in the set is connected in the original graph. Another way of putting it is that in an independent set, the shortest path getting from anywhere to anywhere takes *at least* two steps.

Or we could say that if the user is "in" an independent set and wants to do anything else within the set they *must* have to do more than just choose the right button, because to do anything else in the set requires having to press at least two buttons. To get around within an independent set, the user has to plan and think beyond just what the next button press will do.

Given the graph of an interactive device, the sizes of the independent sets gives the designer a useful indicator of how hard the device is to use. Traditionally, graph theorists are interested in the maximal independent set (since there are generally lots of them), and the size of this set, which is called the independence number, is a useful metric.

If the independence number is zero, the graph is complete and in principle easy to use (if the buttons are labeled sensibly). The bigger the number, the more difficult the device. Since bigger graphs typically have bigger independence numbers, a more realistic measure for usability is based on the probability that the user has to think, rather than just read and interpret button labels. What we can call the independence probability is an estimate of the probability that the user has the device in an independent set and also wants to get the device to a state in the same set. We could write programs to work this out for any particular graph—it's only an estimate because we don't know precisely which states the user is likely to be in.

▷   Section 10.4.3 (p. 343) gives example program code to work out the independence probability. Chapter 10, "Using the framework," gives many other examples.

▷   Section 9.6.5 (p. 311) assesses how the user can solve the task/action mapping problem—the problem of getting from one state to another efficiently. We will be especially interested in the designer assessing how hard this is to do over all cases that interest the user. As we've seen, for any tasks that involve an independent set, this is a nontrivial problem for the user.

8.6.4   Bridges and hinges

I've emphasized that any normal interactive device must be strongly connected: it must be possible to get from anywhere to anywhere. It makes sense then to talk about how well a graph is connected. In an interactive device, some things are more important than others for the user to know about. In an extreme case, if we do not know what the (Off) button does, then lots of things may become impossible to do—once stuck, always stuck! In general, missing a little information will disconnect our whole model of the device.

■ If deleting a vertex disconnects a graph, the vertex is a hinge.

■ If deleting an arc in a graph disconnects the graph, the arc is a bridge. Note that these bridges have nothing to do with the real bridges over the River Pregel—which were (at least in graph theory terms) edges and *not* bridges.

Identifying bridges and hinge vertices in a graph is routine. Every bridge and hinge represents a piece of critical information: without it, the user cannot (or does not know how to) access any states on the other side of the bridge or hinge.

If the device is supposed to be easy to use, then it should have few hinges, or at least, few states hiding behind hinges. On the other hand, if the device is safety-critical—if it can do dangerous things—then it is probably best if these dangerous states are safely protected by bridges, perhaps even chains of bridges.

If a user does not know about a hinge, then it follows that they cannot get to some states (they might be able to proceed by accident). Having found a hinge, the graph can be separated into at least two component subgraphs. One of these components will include the standby or start state, which we'll assume the user knows about. The question is, what's in the other components that the user cannot get to except via the hinge? If these components contain states that are important, then the user *must* know about the hinge.

It may be appropriate to make the hinge (if the graph has one hinge) into the standby state (or the home page for a web site) or otherwise redesign the device so that hinges are close to standby and therefore easier to find and more familiar through use. Conversely, if a device has more than one hinge, as it can't have two standby states, this may well be a design problem the designer should know about.

▷ Section 10.1 (p. 325) introduces the farmer's problem and uses it to give further examples of strongly connected components and how they relate to design.

Some graphs have no hinges. The connectivity of a graph is defined as the smallest number of vertices you'd have to delete to disconnect the graph. In particular, if deleting just one vertex disconnects the graph, that vertex is a hinge. If you need to delete two vertices to disconnect a graph, then the user has two routes into the states on the other side of them.

If the connectivity of the graph is two, the user is safer, but if they do not know about at least one of the two vertices, so again part of the graph will be unreachable for them, except by accident. Can we design to ensure, as far as possible, that the user knows about at least one of these vertices? As the connectivity of a graph increases, it becomes less dependent on critical knowledge—the user has more ways of doing anything.

As a conscientious designer, you will want to (somehow) make sure the user understands the importance of every hinge in a graph when they are using the device. Perhaps the device should flash something, or beep. Or perhaps a button should flash when the device is in a state that makes buttons correspond to a bridge.

Graph theory gives us ways of evaluating interesting usability issues and giving them precise measures, which can then be used to guide modifying designs and try to improve them against the measures. Graph theory also suggests ways of finding things that can be improved without changing the structure of the device. We could either eliminate bridges from a design, or we could highlight them so a user is more aware of their importance. Or we could write more prominently about them in the user manual.

8.7 Trees

Graphs might seem pretty trivial things on the grand intellectual landscape—just arcs and edges—but trees, which are even simpler and therefore easier to dismiss, are in fact *very* useful.

Trees are of course familiar in the countryside, and sometimes help form the walls of mazes. Ordinary trees can also be represented as graphs; in fact, a treelike graph is so common that tree is the technical term in graph theory. A tree is a particular sort of graph that, well, looks like a tree.

For some reason, as shown in figure 8.9 (facing page), we usually draw trees upside down, rather looking like the underground roots of a tree without the tree itself. Indeed, we use the terms "above," "beneath," "top down," and "bottom up" assuming trees have their roots at the top.

A collection of trees is, unsurprisingly, called a forest. Some people call the arcs (or edges) in trees their branches, and the ends of branches (that don't go on to other branches) are called leaves. The ends of branches, whether they are leaves or not, are called nodes, just as an alternative to the word vertex.

The root of a tree is a special node with no arcs going to it. We can define leaves similarly: a leaf is a node with exactly one arc going to it and none from it.

A tree is connected, but as there is only one branch connecting any two adjacent nodes and there are no cycles (because a tree does not grow back on itself), a tree cannot be strongly connected. Trees have the property that there is *exactly* one path from the root to any other vertex; if the tree was undirected (so you could go back on the arcs) then there'd be exactly one path between *any* two nodes. Put another way, every vertex in a tree is a hinge and every arc a bridge.

Trees are very useful information structuring tools and have all sorts of uses. They are often used in family relationships and genealogy. Branches can represent the relation "child of," and inevitably leaves or nodes of a tree at the same level immediately below a node are then called siblings. This sort of tree shows the descendants of the person named at the root of the tree. Or a genealogical tree can be used the other way round, so the arrows represent "parent of." In this case, you would be at the root, and your parents would be one level *down* from you, and your oldest ancestors you know would be at the leaves of your tree.

Trees are very often used to represent web sites; the root is the home page and the leaves are pages where the user does things (like buy a book, if each leaf is a book description); all the other nodes are then basically navigational, but they might also have incidental information on them.

In this book, we need directed trees, where each branch points away from the root. Trees are ubiquitous in user interface design, because almost every device presents the user with choices—menus being the obvious example. For a user interface, the root of the tree would probably be "standby" or "off" and the other nodes might be functions the device can do or menus of further choices. Users might think that functions are "in" menus but in fact the *choices* are in the menus and the *functions* are leaves one arc below the menus.

A problem for a user interface designer is that it is tempting (and, indeed, often sensible) to draw a tree to guide the design of the system. Trees are simple and therefore good for conceptualizing a device. But because a tree is not strongly connected, designers may forget about the importance of strong connectivity. One may end up with a device that has a tree-like user interface that appears to be simple and elegant, but which has some weak spots that are not strongly connected.

More precisely, a designer trying to design a device as a tree should think of it as a subgraph. If this subgraph is a tree that includes every state of the device, they

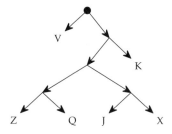

Figure 8.9: This is a subtree of figure 5.5 (p. 129), which was a Huffman code for the complete 26-letter alphabet. The root of the (directed) tree is shown as a black disk; the leaves are shown as letters; the branches are arrows. Either end of an arrow is a node; if no arrow points *to* a node, it is a root; if no arrow points *from* a node, it is a leaf. To be a tree, there is exactly one path from the root to any leaf.

are designing a spanning tree. A spanning tree guarantees exactly one route from its root to every other vertex. Users who know a spanning tree for the device, provided the device starts off at the root state, can do anything with the device even if they don't know any more about it. In general, the root will be some obvious state, like standby. Typically we would then require every state to have some obvious action that gets back to standby—this would not be part of the spanning tree, but it would ensure that users can always get back to the root easily and thence to any other state by following paths in the tree. In fact, in this case, users would need to know meaning of some key like [Reset], or else they would not be able to navigate the interface.

8.7.1 Trees are for nesting

Imagine you are using a gadget and it is in standby. You want to access one of the device's functions. If you know how to do it, you will press buttons and follow a short path through the graph that represents the gadget until you get to the state you want. If you worked out the shortest paths to get to every state from standby and drew them on your state diagram, you would have drawn a tree with its root at standby. If, further, we make the assumption that a path to a state never activates any other state we are interested in, then all the states we are interested in will be leaves of the tree.

Any device (precisely, the graph of its finite state machine) contains trees, which represent the best way of using the device starting from a key state, such as standby. In graph theory terms, any strongly connected graph has at least one subgraph that is a directed tree. To design a device, we first design a simple tree, then we can add more arcs to give the user more choices in how to achieve things with the device.

▷   Subgraphs are defined in section 8.3 (p. 238).

251

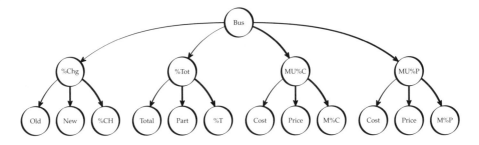

Figure 8.10: Part of the tree-based menu structure for the Hewlett-Packard 17BII handheld financial calculator. Cost and Price are both shared under two different headings, so it is not a proper tree (it would be a semi-lattice). The terms are HP's—they appear exactly the same, but in block capitals on the calculator display: "Bus" means business, "%Chg" means percent change, "MU%C" means markup as percentage of cost, and so on.

This book is a graph that contains lots of trees. For example, the book's index is the root of a tree of ideas and people's names; each page number in the index is a branch leading to a page, which is the leaf. Or the table of contents is a root of another tree, and each chapter the first node down from it, with sections being children of the chapter nodes ... down to paragraphs, words, and letters finally as the leaves.

All these trees structure the book in different ways, but none of them are any good for reading the book. For reading, there are two further sorts of arcs added: one, implicit, is that as you read you read on to the next leaf without thinking—you read the book linearly; the second sort of arc is the linkage and cross referencing that encourage you to read nonsequentially.

▷ For a brief history of the inventions that make reading easier, see section 4.2 (p. 96).

The ideal plan is not as easy as it seems. Figure 8.10 (this page) shows a subgraph of the structure of the Hewlett-Packard 17BII handheld financial business calculator. The structure shown is a tree, but some items are actually shared between branches. Thus the simple-looking tree structure in figure 8.10 is misleading, since it looks like a tree only because the repetition of COST and PRICE is not visually obvious. The design of the 17BII therefore makes the user's choices for COST and PRICE permissive.

▷ The advantages of permissiveness are discussed in section 5.2 (p. 134).

Drawing the structure pedantically, so that each item had exactly one box, would in general make lines cross, and the diagram would become cluttered and unhelpful. A designer would be unlikely to design it looking as bad as this, which would unfortunately encourage them to make it a strict tree.

Merely drawing trees as a visual aid in the design process tends to lead designers into making user interfaces that are too strict. You almost always need to add

---

Box 8.2 Trees versus DAGs You can't go round in loops in directed or undirected sorts of tree, so they are said to be *acyclic* graphs. Acyclic graphs are useful—they guarantee you can't get into loops. You may not get where you wanted to go, but you will eventually get somewhere! In contrast, a user (or a computer program) can get stuck going around a loop in a cyclic graph forever.

Directed trees are a sort of directed acyclic graphs or DAG. But DAGs allow more than one path between the vertices, so they are more general than trees. Many DAGs are trees, and all directed trees are DAGs, but not all DAGs are trees. A DAG might have several roots—vertices that have no others pointing to them—whereas a tree can only have one root.

While you might design a device as a DAG or tree, very few interactive devices would be satisfactory as DAGs, because they do never allow the user to go back to previous states. Typically, then, you may *design* a device as a DAG, but use a program to systematically add more arcs to it to make it easier to *use*.

---

further arcs (and that's best done systematically by program), and great care must be taken that repeated states are exactly the same state, rather than being duplicates that may not be exactly the same. For example, the state Cost in figure 8.10 may or may not be exactly the same state, though it has the same name, which suggests to the user it *is* the same state.

8.7.2   A city is not a tree

Although trees are clear and easy to draw and, as the last section emphasized, trees are subgraphs of any design, and they can be misleading design tools. Trees encourage designers to slide into bad design, an insight first spotted by Chris Alexander in the context of town planning.

Chris Alexander is an architect, famous among programmers for introducing pattern languages, but also widely known for his views in architecture. In his classic discussion of the design of towns and cities he argues that town planners too easily lay out a city as a tree.

In a tree-structured design, the industrial area is over here, the housing is over there, and the shopping is somewhere else. A tree-structured design makes it conceptually very easy for the designers. While the designer keeps the design concepts, "housing" and "shopping" and so on, separate in their minds, they have a lot less to worry about. Indeed, it's called "separation of concerns" and is a design principle that encourages you to avoid getting features mixed up.

Unfortunately if a town is designed as a tree, the shopping area is dead at night because nobody lives there, and the housing area is dead during the day, because everybody is at work or school. So Alexander argues that a well-designed place mixes the housing, shopping, and work regions. Mixing means that shops do not appear in one place, workplaces are not in one segregated area, and so on. A good city, then, is not a tree—most things (housing, shops, doctors) can be found in several places in several different ways. A good city is permissive.

253

Indeed, if we push Alexander's thought to the limit, even in a highly regimented tree-structured city it is hard to imagine that there would be only *one* place where a user could find a newspaper—people find duplication of resources (whether newspapers or user interface features) helpful. But trees do not allow for any duplication: everything has to be in its place as a single leaf.

Figure 8.11 (facing page) shows an alternative, but equivalent, view of the HP calculator tree drawn in figure 8.10 (p. 252). Figure 8.11 can be imagined as viewing a tree seeing the menu choices as enveloping circles: each menu encloses all of its submenus. More formally, this alternative view is a tree represented as a Venn diagram, as a collection of sets.

> ▷ Venn diagrams were developed by the British logician John Venn in 1880 from a simpler and much earlier visual formalism of Euler's, Euler circles (this is the same Euler who invented graphs). Statecharts combine the two techniques, and were reviewed in section 7.6 (p. 217).

Because the diagram represents an interactive device, each set (drawn here as a circle) appears to the user as a menu, and its elements are the submenus (or the functions) of the menu. In a tree the sets that define it do not overlap. In fact, *any* set of nonoverlapping sets defines a tree (or a forest of trees if there is no overall enclosing set to define a single root).

As we said above, the 17BII is not strictly structured as a tree: the MU%P and MU%C sets *should* be drawn with some overlap, with their intersection containing COST and PRICE. In short, drawing simple diagrams—here, trees and Venn diagrams corresponding to trees—tends to encourage design oversights.

Just as a city designer finds a tree convenient, a designer of interactive devices finds a tree easy as a structuring device because each function or purpose of a device goes in one sensible place. For a mobile phone, all the network settings would go under Network; for a city, all the houses would go in Living Quarters. Once you've decided to have an area called Language, the rest of the design fits into place.

But this means that to use a tree, the user must know the designer's classification. My mobile phone has menus called Extras, Settings, and Profiles. Where would I find the alarm clock feature? Is it an extra? Is it a setting? Or is it something to do with my profile? Just like a city, if functions, like alarm settings, appear more than once in different sections (particularly in different forms or aliases) they will be easier to find. I could find the alarm clock under Extras or Settings and not need to choose "the" right one. But if the mobile phone is of this easier-to-use structure, it will not be a tree.

8.7.3 Getting around trees

Trees provide a single, short path from the root to every leaf. Thus, as interactive devices, trees ensure that the user has a short route from standby to any function—provided they know the route.

However, if a user does not know the right route through the tree, they are likely to get lost and then they need to go back, probably all the way back to the root. But

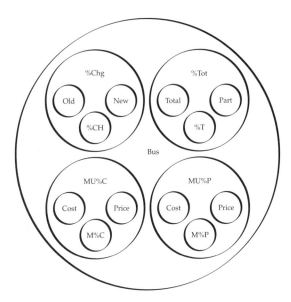

Figure 8.11: Venn diagrams are nested nonoverlapping circles that represent trees. A Venn diagram is used here to represent the command structure of the HP 17BII calculator, which was also shown in figure 8.10 (p. 252) as a tree. As the text explains, this drawing is subtly misleading—it looks simpler than the device really is.

directed trees are not designed for going back. Or if a user wants to explore a tree to see what it has in it, this again is not a simple get-from-root-to-leaf procedure.

In short, trees are not sufficient for all but the simplest user interfaces; even if functions (leaves) are repeated to make a tree more permissive and easier to use, a user will still sometimes want to navigate the structure in an essentially a non-treelike way.

Unfortunately, searching a tree efficiently is quite complex. The user has to go into each submenu, search it, then come out of the submenu and search the next submenu. It is very easy for a user to make mistakes, go around some submenus more than once, and (worse) come out of a submenu prematurely and miss out altogether a subsubmenu that might have what they are looking for somewhere in it. Once a user makes a mistake, they may "panic" and lose track of where they have got to, even if it wasn't too hard before getting lost in panic!

For a user who does not know how a device tree works, or what classification scheme a designer used for the tree, a linear list would be far better. In fact, a cycle (a list that joins up at the end to start again) would probably be better. You can start on a cycle anywhere and eventually get everywhere, whereas with a linear list, you have to know where the starting point is and you get stuck at the end. Whichever you have, there is no wasted time in learning how the list is organized; for users who learn how it is organized, they are guaranteed that a simple scroll

Figure 8.12: A linear list for seven commands. The user interface merely requires buttons equivalent to (Next), (Previous) and (Select).

(say, repeatedly pressing (∨)) will get through everything in the entire list. With a list, a user will inevitably find whatever they want (provided it is available).

In short, we often want to design a device that is both a tree *and* a cycle (or, more precisely, contains two subgraphs, a tree and a cycle, whose vertices are the device functions). It is not difficult to build a design tool that allows the designer to see the device as a tree but which systematically inserts all the cycle links in—to help users in a consistent way, without distracting the designer with the added complexity of extra permissiveness in the final design.

▷ Section 5.5.5 (p. 153) compares different structures (including the manufacturer's original tree) for searching and access times for a fax machine.

8.7.4   Balanced and unbalanced trees

Trees are very efficient for searching, *provided* they are organized appropriately. For simplicity, suppose the device has seven functions called A, B, C, D, E, F, G— instead of spelling out their full names, like "send text message" or "rewind" or whatever functions your favorite device does.

The user could have an (Up) and a (Down) button and simply scroll through the commands. Figure 8.12 (this page) shows the graph of this device. Here there are 7 commands, and on average the user would need to search half way, taking 4 button presses to find what they want.

The average is 4 because if we start at A, then selecting A (which is done 1/7 of the time) can be done in one press, (Select); selecting B would take 2 presses, namely, (Next), (Select); ... up to selecting G, which would take 7 presses. The average of $1, 2, \ldots, 7$ is 4. The cycle, figure 8.13 (facing page), does better with an average of 2.7. Depending on the usage we expect, a cycle may or may not be an improvement, however: (for a sufficiently large cycle) will some users go round and around endlessly and be stuck, or will knowledgeable users always be able to take advantage of the almost-halved average distances?

A binary tree, such as the one shown in figure 8.14 (facing page), can do better. Starting from the root (an action that might take a key press we are not counting here) it takes 1 step to activate the function D (which the user will do 1/7 of the time on average), by simply doing (Select), or 2 steps to select either B or F (by doing (Less), say, then (Select)), or 3 steps to select any one of A, C, E, or G. So the average is $1/7 + 2 \times 2/7 + 3 \times 4/7$, or 2.3.

Of course, to gain the benefit (which gets better the more commands there are in the tree) the user must use the right systematic way to find commands. That is,

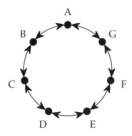

Figure 8.13: A cycle for seven commands. Whether this is better than a linear list depends on whether A and G are related or should be kept separate, and whether it matters that the user may not notice they are going round in circles indefinitely—particularly if the cycle is very big and the user doesn't remember where it starts. The buttons or commands for this user interface are the same as required for a linear list.

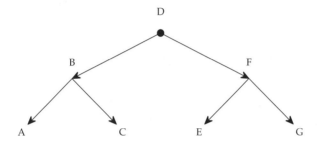

Figure 8.14: A balanced binary tree, with 7 nodes. Imagine the user wishes to select one of the 7 lettered commands, A–G, and starts from the root of the tree.

if the display shows a command X, and if this is what the user wants, they should stop. If not they should press (Before) (or whatever it is called) if what they are after is earlier in the alphabet than X; otherwise they should press (Later).

Unfortunately, there are trees that, though they follow the same rules, are much less efficient. One is shown in figure 8.15 (next page). Now the average cost to find a function is $(1 + 2 \times 2 + 3 \times 2 + 4 \times 2)/7 = 19/7 = 2.7$, which is a bit worse—but the more functions there are, the worse it gets. For instance, if we had 127 functions, it would be worse by 33 instead of 6. The interesting thing is that both trees work exactly the same way, and (apart from the time it takes) a user cannot tell between them.

Perhaps a designer can't either. That would be very worrying. There are an exponential number of trees, but there is only one balanced tree (if it's full). The chances that a designer hits on the best tree by chance is negligible. Unless the designer uses design aids or tools, they are very unlikely to make an efficient tree by designing it by hand—it is too much work.

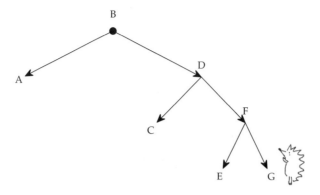

Figure 8.15: An unbalanced binary tree, with 7 nodes. The user's strategy for using this inefficient tree is the same as for using the efficient balanced tree of figure 8.14 (previous page).

In these two examples of balanced and unbalanced trees, I've assumed that the tree is a binary tree, with two choices at every node. If we increase the number of choices, the user can get to where they want faster. The "hidden" cost is that showing the user more choices requires a bigger screen, and as the screen gets bigger, the user will of course take longer to read it—and perhaps not read the occasional extra lines sometimes needed, but which don't fit in.

The moral is that when you use trees, balanced trees are much more efficient— and for some applications, such as alphabetic searching, it makes no difference to the user—other than being faster.

We worked out average costs assuming that everything (using any of the 7 commands or functions of the device) was equally likely. If functions are not equally likely for whatever the user is doing, then a Huffman tree will give better average performance than a balanced tree; in fact, if all the probabilities are the same, the optimal Huffman tree turns out to be a balanced tree. There is one proviso to this comparison: when I introduced Huffman trees, the functionality was at the leaves, and in our discussion here, we have functionality of the device both at leaves and at nodes interior to the tree.

▷   Huffman trees are discussed in section 5.1.3 (p. 126).

When we used Huffman trees for the functions of the Nokia handset, the functions of the handset device were at the leaves of the tree, but submenus (like "Messages") were at interior nodes. With this design, the user would never want to *use* the device's Messages function, because it isn't a function—it is merely a menu providing all the different sorts of message function.

8.8   User manuals

Books contain subgraphs that are trees. A book has chapters, and within chapters, sections, and within sections subsections. The book itself (or perhaps its cover) can be considered the root of a tree, with branches off to the chapters, then each chapter has branches to its sections. Some of those sections may be leaves, and some sections will have further branches off into subsections. If you want to pursue the structure, you can continue down into paragraphs, diagrams, tables, and so on. In fact, this is exactly what XML does: it provides a tree-nesting structure for documents.

User manuals are books of a sort, so they are trees in the same sense. Devices, or subgraphs of devices, are trees too. Both are trees from the vantage point of graph theory. Can we do anything useful with this correspondence?

Since interactive systems are graphs and web sites are graphs, we can easily build a simulation of a device by using a web site. As the user clicks links in the web site, they go to other pages. This is the same as if the user clicked buttons and went to other states of the device.

Web sites are conventionally used more to provide information than to simulate gadgets. The original term, before "web" was suggested, was hypertext, then thought of as a collection of mostly textual pages that were linked together in a more flexible way than bound in a book, which forces them to be ordered sequentially. It follows that the underlying graph idea can also be used to generate a user manual. To do this we first must represent the device as a web, and then we will see how to get the web or hypertext into a conventional written form.

▷   Programming manuals is covered in sections 9.4 (p. 280) and 11.5 (p. 392).

To generate a basic user manual as a web site is easy: instead of taking care to simulate the device and show pictures of what it looks like in each state, we show manual text describing each state. Instead of having hot text called [Operate] (or whatever) that links to other pages, we write text that says, "If you press [Operate] then such-and-such happens." If we think of the manual as an interactive web, then pressing [Operate] in this sentence can "do" whatever it says and take the user to another part of the manual. In a written, paper, version of the manual, the text that would have been shown on another web page can be written out in the following section.

How to do this well raises several interesting issues, not least because there is not a single, best way to represent devices as manuals. Conventional paper manuals are trees in more than one sense: they are made out of paper derived from trees of course, but they are also made up from sections, containing subsections, containing sub-subsections and paragraphs of text—they are trees in the graph theory sense of the word too. But the device we are trying to write the manual for is not usually *just* a tree; it will be an arbitrary graph, and any sensible interactive device will have loops in it (it will typically be strongly connected so it must have at least one loop). Since no tree has loops, we have to think about ways of getting the best trees out of graphs in order to start making manuals.

Or perhaps we might write user manuals on continuous loops of paper, which aren't trees, or only represent them as web sites, which, being arbitrary graphs, can directly represent devices.

8.8.1   Spanning trees

A spanning tree is a tree that uses a graph's original edges to include all its vertices (in contrast to a subtree, which is merely a tree including *some* of the vertices). To make a user manual, then, we could do worse than look for a spanning tree of the device and then format it as a readable manual, for instance with its root as the table of contents branching out into chapters.

Unfortunately there are lots and lots of spanning trees for most graphs, and the chances of finding a good one by chance is slim. We need to have an idea of which one is best. One way to do this is to score everything that could go in a manual with how interesting or insightful it is. For example, to repeatedly tell the user that pressing Off switches the device off is not very informative. So we could score any arc ending in Off low. Many music devices are intended to play music, so any arc that ends in playing music might be scored high.

We want to find the spanning tree with the maximum score, which we anticipate will be of most use or most interest to the user. Such a tree is a maximal spanning tree, and it has the highest cost or score of all spanning trees.

There are many ways to find spanning trees: the most intuitive is to start drawing a tree over the existing graph and make sure you never join up back to a vertex that is already part of the tree (otherwise you would create a cycle)—this is called Prim's algorithm. Another approach is to find any cycle in the graph and delete an arc, provided that deleting that arc does not split the graph into two isolated components—this is Kruskal's algorithm. Both of these approaches can easily be modified (and often are) to choose the highest scoring arcs as they build the trees; finally they result in maximal spanning trees.

Rather than maximizing scores, if we define the arc costs as, say, the length of English it would take us to explain something to a user, then we can set a program to look for a spanning tree that corresponds to the shortest user manual we can generate. Of course, our estimate of the length of English will be approximate, based on some rules of thumb; it'll probably be most easily measured by generating very bad machine-generated English, and simply counting the number of words needed.

> ▷ We discuss the importance of short, minimal manuals in many places in this book; see also section 11.6.1 (p. 397).

If we improve our English-generating programs, we would be able to get more informative scores than mere length measurements; we could also measure readability or count verbs or lengths of sentences. If sentence length, for example, is an important measure for our users or what they will be doing, we could design our English generators to produce short sentences, and we then choose spanning trees that reduce total sentence length, ending up with better manuals.

Box 8.3 Computers in 21 days Visit a book shop and you'll be spoiled for choice with all the books explaining computers for people like you. Isn't it reassuring to discover that you are not alone and have joined a great band of people who find computers fundamentally difficult?

Using computers requires lots of trivial knowledge, like when to press the F1 key. That's why those self-help books are so thick. Certainly, nothing works unless you know the right trick. When you do know something, it seems so simple. It is then easy to slip into thinking that you must have been stupid for not knowing in the first place.

What if all those people who wrote books on how to use computers talked to the manufacturers who made the difficulties? One of my hobbies is to go through manuals, to find instructions to tell us how to cope with quirks that need not have been there in the first place. When a manual says, "make sure such-and-such," I ask why wasn't the computer designed to make sure for you? Almost all problems with computers are easily avoided by proper design, by manufacturers doing a little thinking first. What are computers for if they can't do obvious things?

Take any other modern product. You can buy a car. You don't get thick manuals telling you how to stop the wheels from falling off. Wheels don't fall off on their own. In comparison, most computers are totally unsatisfactory: you get lots of "wheels" that fall off when you are not watching.

Computers are badly designed because manufacturers can make money without trying any harder. Yet most people say computers are truly wonderful! Before you know it, you too will be buying upgrades, more RAM, and some training books and when you've spent another thousand dollars you'll agree that they *are* wonderful. It's not you who benefits from this, but consumerism that likes to keep you dependent, believing that you are responsible for fixing the computer's problems with more of your money.

Since there are so many spanning trees you can get from even modest graphs, the designer and technical author need all the help they can get. If they choose a user manual structure on their own—any spanning tree—there's little chance that it will be optimal or even nearly optimal.

Even a simple design tool would be a great help. Prim's algorithm has the nice advantage that it can be used to extend an existing or draft manual. I envisage a designer writing a basic manual (which is of course a tree but may not be a spanning tree), then Prim's algorithm will provide suggestions for extending the tree to make it more like a spanning tree—but suggesting a good extension by however we are measuring "good."

A designer would like to be able to assess how easy a device is to use. But we can produce user manuals automatically (or semiautomatically), and there are now more usability measures we can get by measuring the manuals rather than the devices directly. The longer a user manual is, for instance, certainly the longer a user will take to read it. In fact, the longer a user manual has to be to correctly describe a gadget, the harder the device must be to learn to use. We could automatically generate a user manual, and measure its length. Then if we can modify the design and reduce the length of the manual, we have in principle an easier-to-learn device design. The depth of nesting in the user manual too is another useful measure of complexity. It corresponds to how hard a particular feature is to learn.

To take advantage of these ideas we have to have design tools that can generate user manuals from device specifications. Otherwise, we would make a small change and have to wait until the technical authors had rewritten the manual! A designer needs to be able to experiment with the specification of a device and see whether the manual gets longer or shorter. If this can be done fast enough, as it can be by drafting rough manuals using automatic design tools, then designers can very quickly optimize designs to make them easier to learn or use (depending on what measures they are using).

Generally, better manuals are indeed shorter, but of course there are exceptions. A manual for a gun would have a lot of safety instructions, and blindly removing the safety features so that a manual does not have to discuss them (and would therefore be shorter) would be counterproductive. Different sorts of features should be flagged as having different weights in the calculation of the "length" of the manual. Possibly the more safety discussion, the better—if so, for such a device, text on safety features would have a negative weight; thus the more safety-related text the shorter the manual appears to be. Imaginative designers will be able to come up with more sophisticated approaches that can be programmed into tools.

A technical author can tidy up the automatically generated English. Provided we have a way of keeping track of what the technical author has rewritten, text never need be rewritten unless the automatically generated text for the affected parts changes. Thus if we have automatic tools to help with manual generation from a device specification, we can do something very useful: when the device specification changes, (most) effort put into writing a clear manual need not be lost. Furthermore, we can *deliberately* change the device specification to get a better manual. If our user manual-generating program can quickly give an estimate of the complexity score of the user manual, then it would be worthwhile for the designer to experimentally mess around with various alternative designs to find the one with the clearest, briefest explanation.

8.8.2   Ordered trees

All the trees we have discussed to this point have been ordered trees. As well as being either directed or undirected, a tree can be ordered or unordered.

Just as adding arrows to an undirected tree involves a choice—you have to choose the root, then every arrow direction flows away from the root—ordering a tree involves choice. Every choice one makes in the structure of a system represents a design choice, and if it affects the user of the system then it is an important interaction programming issue. Tree ordering is one such issue.

As figure 8.8.2 (facing page) indicates, in drawing a tree, the designer must make choices to order the children of every node, placing them left-to-right or in some other order across the page.

The previous section discussed how to construct a user manual as a spanning tree. The spanning tree itself needs ordering before it can be printed—at least

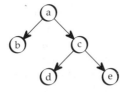 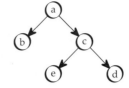

Figure 8.16: One or two directed trees? If these two trees are unordered trees, they are the same (rather, they are different representations of the same unordered tree); if they are ordered trees, they are two different trees. As ordered trees, the trees differ in the order of the two children d and e.

---

assuming it's not a degenerate spanning tree in which every node has exactly one child, stretched out as list, as in figure 8.12 (p. 256).

How do you order the tree in the order that suits the reader? The best orders depend heavily on the application, but these three ideas can be used separately or in combination:

- The user or a technical author—any expert in reading—gives hints on ordering the sections of the manual. This must be first; this must come before that; that must come after this.

- Flag every mention of a concept in the manual; flag *definitions* and *uses* of concepts. Then order the manual so that definitions precede uses. That way the user gets to read the section that defines what a dongle is before reading sections that say what to do with them.

- If, in addition to being a tree, the manual contains cross references (as this book does), we minimize the total length of cross reference links. If we strongly prefer cross references of length one, that is which go to the previous or next section, then we can remove them from the document since the reader can easily read the next section without being told to by a cross reference!

All of these rules (and no doubt others will occur to you) have corresponding algorithms for implementation.

The first two can be combined; they require topological sorting, which is a standard and straightforward algorithm. Topological sorting may, on occasion, fail to find an ordering that satisfies all the requirements.

For example, the standard dictionary joke that badminton is played with shuttlecocks and shuttlecocks are things used in the game of badminton is a case of two sections both defining words the other uses. There is no ordering that puts definitions before uses. Topological sort will point this out; the designer or technical author will then have to make a decision that one or other rule has to be relaxed— or perhaps the document rewritten so that the problem does not arise. To resolve the dictionary paradox, we need only rewrite the definition of badminton to include its own definition of shuttlecocks; we could then optionally simplify the definition of shuttlecock to the terse "see badminton."

Doubtless, dictionary writers either spend sleepless nights with worry, or they use computers to help them spot problems automatically.

The last of the three ideas for ordering trees is more obscure and requires the so-called jump minimization algorithm, because the problem is the same as reducing the length of jumps in a program with goto statements (which correspond, for the program, to our cross references). A variation of jump minimization is bandwidth minimization, which tries to minimize the maximum length of any cross reference, rather than the total length (which of course might mean that some cross references span great distances).

If the user manual was split into two volumes, an introductory overview leaflet and a detailed in-depth reference manual, it might be wise to minimize the number of cross references from the overview to the reference manual, or we might want to make the reference manual self-contained, with no references to the overview.

There are many choices in ordering a tree. The point is that we can be precise about the rules we wish to apply or enforce to make the user's use of the manual (or device) easier, and we can use algorithms to automatically generate the best results—or to point out to us any problems or inconsistencies in our requirements. There is a key advantage to doing this (which I repeat in many ways throughout this book): if we decide to modify the design in any way, we *automatically* generate new manuals without any further effort.

In contrast, if we worked conventionally, even a minor design change could do untold damage to a carefully written user manual (or any other product of the design process)—and that potential problem would mean we don't make improvements because of the knock-on costs, or that we don't have accurate manuals, or that we write the manuals at the last possible minute and don't thoroughly check them. Very likely, when the manuals are written late, we would not read them ourselves and get no further insights into how to improve the design (some design problems will stand out in awkwardly written sections of the manual).

8.9   Small worlds

I've described graphs and graph properties as if graphs are "just there," as if they are static structures that just happened to be so. A device has a particular design, represented by a graph, and that may be analyzed. Is it strongly connected or not? What is its Chinese postman tour? What user manual might we be able to generate for it?

We haven't yet thought about *how* to get the graphs in the first place. Most graphs in real life grow; they don't just appear out of nowhere. This year's device, and its underlying graph structure, is going to be based on last year's structure: so the device graph for this year will be last year's plus or minus a few more features—a few more states and a few more arcs, and some bug fixes. Device graphs thus have a history, and how they are designed depends a lot on that history.

Suppose the designer wants to introduce new features for next year's model. These additions will join to the old device graph, which probably won't be changed much, because it would be too much trouble to redesign what is already known to work.

Rather than being created out of nothing, a device graph grows over time. Iterative design occurs for new models based on previous years' models, but even new devices will have had some design iteration: when design started, there would have been some earlier sketch design, and that design then grew and was elaborated over a period of time, mostly by being extended with new features as the designers or users think of things to add.

When graphs grow, they tend to have special and very interesting properties. In technical terms, these graphs are called small world or scale-free, and the popular, well-connected vertices are called hubs. Here are two familiar examples:

The world wide web When I create a web page, I tend to link it up to sites I am interested in and that are popular. Of course, I'm unlikely to link to unpopular sites because I probably won't know about them. In turn, if my page is popular, lots of people will link to me. Again, as more people get to know about and link their pages to my page, then my site becomes even more popular, and even more people link to me. Popular web pages quickly become very popular. Hopefully, my page will end up being a hub.

The airport network There is already a network of airports and rules about where airplanes fly. If I want to build a new airport, I'm going want routes approved to somewhere like Los Angeles or Heathrow, because they are popular airports, and if I can connect to one, I'll make my airport far more popular. Heathrow and Los Angeles are a hubs in the airport network.

If a graph is a small world, the average distance between its vertices will be surprisingly low. In an ordinary random graph, most vertices have about the same number of edges, and there are no shortcuts from anywhere to anywhere. In contrast, in a small world graph, the hubs tend to connect seemingly "distant" vertices in at most two steps.

Of course, path lengths in a small world graph won't be as low as in a complete graph, because if a graph is complete, the user can get anywhere from anywhere in exactly one step: the characteristic path length (the average shortest distance between any two vertices) of a complete graph is exactly 1. At the other extreme, a cycle connects every vertex with the longest path possible: if a graph of N vertices is a cycle, its characteristic path length is $N/2$—on average a user has to go half way around the cycle to find what they are after. In general, the characteristic path length will fall somewhere between 1 and $N/2$, and the smaller it is, the faster the device will be to use, other things being equal. (If a user doesn't know how to find short paths, the fact that there are theoretically short paths may not help. However, the converse is always true: making paths longer makes a device harder to use.)

▷ On calculating the characteristic path length, see section 9.6.2 (p. 302). Other uses of the characteristic path length are discussed in section 10.3.1 (p. 333). The characteristic path length is not the only unexpectedly low measure of a

---

Box 8.4 Small world friendship graphs Consider a graph of people, where everybody is a vertex, and if two people are friends, then we say there is an edge between the corresponding vertices. This graph, the so-called friendship graph, forms a popular example of small worlds.

The graph isn't exactly random, because people tend to make friends depending on other people's popularity and the friends they know. That is, naturally, we tend to know people who are popular, and we make friends either with them or with people they are friends with. Although the graph is far from complete—nobody can possibly know everybody—it's a small world graph.

The graph is small world because friendly, popular people tend to be people other people become friends with. Popular people become, in small world terms, hubs: bigger and bigger friendship networks grow around them, reinforcing their hubness. If you know a hub, you know at one-step-removed very many friends through that hub. Hubs are worth knowing *because* they are well-connected.

It is said that everybody is separated by at most six people in this world-wide friendship graph. This sounds surprising at first, given how many people there are in the world, and how few of them each of us know. Indeed, it isn't quite true.

The psychologist Stanley Milgram wanted to know how well connected we are, though his definition of connectedness was more like "know of" rather than "friends with." In the 1960s he asked 160 people in Omaha, Nebraska, to write a letter to somebody as close as they knew to a target stockbroker Milgram had chosen in Sharon, Massachusetts. And when that intermediate person got a letter, they were to repeat the process and forward the letter to the next closest person they knew toward the target person.

You would expect the letters to go a long, round-about route—and you'd expect lots of steps to be needed to link Omaha to a nondescript person in Sharon. Milgram found that in fact only about 6 steps were needed, and about half of all letter chains passed through three key people. These key people were hubs of this network.

If it is true that 6 (or thereabouts) is the maximum path length of the friendship graph, then applying our shortest paths algorithm to it would create a matrix of numbers all (roughly) 6 or less.

▷   How to find and calculate shortest paths is discussed in section 9.6 (p. 297).

---

small world graph. The eccentricities and in particular the diameter are also smaller. These properties are defined in section 9.6.3 (p. 303).

In a complete graph, every vertex has $N - 1$ arcs coming from it, and in a cycle every vertex has one arc coming from it. These are the two extremes. As we add more arcs to an intermediate graph, the characteristic path length will get smaller, but generally we need to add a lot of arcs to get a low characteristic path length. Or we can add arcs preferentially to popular hubs. Then the graph becomes a small world, and the path length will be lower than we'd expect from its number of arcs, at least compared to a random graph. In practical terms, this means that each vertex has a low out-degree (a low number of out-going arcs) yet is closely connected to every vertex.

In interactive device terms, this means that each state needs few buttons (outgoing arcs), yet is not too far from any other state. Making a device a small world is a way to make every state easier to get to without greatly increasing the number

> **Box 8.5 Erdös numbers** Another human-grown network is the network of people who write articles together. Paul Erdös was a prolific mathematician who wrote a lot of articles about graph theory, and he coauthored many of his vast output of 1, 535 papers.
>
> Anyone who wrote with Erdös is said to have an Erdös number of 1, Erdös himself having an Erdös number of 0. Anyone who wrote an article with someone who has an Erdös number of 1 will have an Erdös number of 2, and so on. I have an Erdös number of 4, because I wrote a paper called "From Logic to Manuals," with Peter Ladkin (it appeared in the *Software Engineering Journal*, volume **11**(6), pp347–354, 1997), who wrote a paper with Roger Maddux, called "On Binary Constraint Problems," in the *Journal of the ACM*, **41**(3), pp435–469, 1994, who wrote a paper with Alfred Tarski (himself a prolific mathematician), who wrote several papers with Erdös, for instance in the *Notices of the American Mathematical Society*. Tarski has an Erdös number of 1; Maddux, 2; Ladkin, 3; and I, 4. That's a low number—but all of us tend to write papers with people who like writing papers with one another. We tend to write papers with authoring hubs, and hubs are well connected and reduce the distances enormously.
>
> Since "standby" is the main state of an interactive device, where every user action must eventually return, perhaps we should be interested in standby numbers—which are a measure of how hard a state is to reach from the standby state.

of buttons. For example, a complete graph of N states needs N buttons, which is impractical for large numbers of states. Moreover, the concept of hubs, which are important states, makes sense for the user. So we win both ways.

We expect to find that interactive devices, especially ones that have been built and revised over a period of years, to be small worlds. We also expect user models to be small worlds too: whatever the graph of the physical device a user is interacting with, they will tend to learn a subgraph of it, but of course as they learn more about the device, they can only add states and arcs to their model when they are actually in those states or traveling those arcs.

A user's mental graph, modeling a system, will grow preferentially as the user learns more, but it grows according to what the user does—users can't know what they don't explore on the device! Whatever states are most popular for the user will be best connected—they will become hubs in the user's model. It's nice that the user's model, being a small world, will give the user efficient ways (short paths) to get from any state to any other state. The user will understand devices faster by building a small world model—and that is exactly what happens!

■　　　■　　　■

That's a quick overview of small worlds. So what? All small world networks have two very interesting but contrasting properties that are relevant to interaction programming. Small world networks are robust, but they are susceptible to attack.

■ In an random, non-small world graph, if we delete a vertex, the average path length will increase. In a small world graph, if we delete a random vertex (or a random edge), average path lengths won't increase much—unless we remove

---

Box 8.6 LATEX I used LATEX to write this book instead of a conventional wordprocessing application like Microsoft Word—LATEX is a markup language, a little bit like HTML.

If I had used Word, when I wanted a special symbol, say the Greek letter α, I would have to have moved the mouse, clicked on a menu, then muddled around to find the right symbol, then clicked "insert." However, if Word's help system was complete, I could have typed "alpha" into its search box, and found the Greek letter α directly, and perhaps (if I was lucky) a button called [Do it now]—like my dialog box on p. 353.

In fact, LATEX *already* works like this: I just type \alpha, and I get what I want directly. Typing \ is faster than moving the mouse to some "insert symbol" menu—and I can do it by touchtyping without looking at the screen or menus.

In effect, the backslash character \ puts LATEX into a hub state. Although this makes LATEX sound better, its disadvantage is that LATEX itself doesn't provide the user with any help; in Microsoft Word, a user searching for symbols can see menus of the things, whereas in LATEX users have to know how to spell what they want.

Of course, there is no reason why the best of both worlds could not be combined, but that's a different story . . .

▷ Features like [Do it] are discussed in section 10.7.2 (p. 352).

---

a hub. But there aren't many hubs, so we are unlikely to pick a hub by chance. Thus if a random vertex "goes down" in a small world network, very little of the connectivity suffers. For example, if we pick a purely random airport, say, Luton, few people (outside of Luton!) would notice if it wasn't working.

■ However, if we deliberately kill off a hub, then the average path length will increase a lot. For example, if a terrorist destroys Heathrow, the airport hub, then very many routes would be disrupted. Hopefully, then, we work out where the hubs are and defend them better against failure or against deliberate attack.

For interactive devices, if what the user *doesn't* know is random, then they probably have a good model of the device. However, if the user is missing critical information, namely, information about the hubs, then their knowledge of the device will be very inefficient. So designers should work out where their device's hubs are and make sure that users are aware of them, through the user manual and by using screen design, layout, or other features to make hubs more salient to the user.

Fortunately, there is an easy way to create hubs. An interactive help system is a state cluster that could be connected to every significant state—if every entry in the help system has a [Do it] button. The theory suggests that a user would find the system easier to use because everything becomes easier to find. In fact, it would not be too surprising if users started describing what they wanted in the help systems search dialogue box as an easier way than using the normal menu structure.

8.10   Conclusions

Graph theory gives us a very clear way of thinking about interaction programming, and as the bulk of this chapter showed, almost any question about usability design can be rigorously interpreted as a question about graphs. In turn, any rigorous question about graphs can be answered by computer programs analyzing the design.

A graph is a way of representing an interactive device, and once you think of a device as a graph, you can ask all sorts of graph-type questions about its design and figure out how those questions (and their answers) relate to usability and what you want the device to do well.

Few interactive systems are really programmed as explicit graphs, and the programmers end up not having a clue what the interaction graph really is. They then cannot change it reliably, and they certainly cannot verify that it conforms to anything. The result is bad interactive systems, that cannot use computers to help with the design process, for instance, to draft user manuals for technical authors. Almost all graph theory questions are too hard for designers (or even users) to answer without a lot of help from a computer. Since we've shown that lots of graph theory questions are highly relevant to usability, then it follows that designers ought to be using computer-supported design tools that can answer various graph theory questions.

Sure, some graph theory questions take longer to answer, and a few questions take far too long to answer in practice, even on smallish graphs (the traveling salesman is a case in point). The chances are that any question that takes a computer a long time to answer is not going to be very relevant for making the user interface easier to use, since such questions won't have much meaning in the user's head—users aren't going have time to stay around and find out if they take too long to work out. Nevertheless, there's no reason not to use graph theory more.

8.10.1   Some *Press On* principles

■ Chinese postman tour: evaluate the cost of a user checking every action a device supports is correct → section 8.1 (p. 228).

■ The traveling salesman: evaluate the cost of a user checking every state a device supports is correct → section 8.1 (p. 231).

■ Generate draft user manuals or parts of them from subgraphs of the device → section 8.3 (p. 240).

■ User models are subgraphs (or not!) of the device → section 8.4 (p. 240).

■ A city is not a tree: although it is easy to design devices as trees, trees are typically harder to use than other structures → section 8.7 (p. 253).

■ Work out a device's hubs, and make them easy for the user to learn about and become familiar with → section 8.9 (p. 268).

8.10.2   Further reading

Graph theory is a very rich area, and well worth mining for ideas relevant to interaction programming. I've covered only a very few of the ideas in this chapter. There are many more types of graph (star, de Bruijn, bipartite …), many more types of graph properties (diameter, radius …), many more properties of vertices (eccentricity, centers …) and many more ways of manipulating and combining graphs (cross product, complement, transitive closure …)—a designer should explore these to see if some ideas match user needs for their devices.

> ▷ We'll cover a few more graph concepts later in this book as we need them. For example, eccentricity is defined and used in section 9.6.3 (p. 303); we need it because it measures the worst thing a user can try in a given state.

■ Bell, T., Witten, I. H., and Fellows, M., *Computer Science Unplugged*, 1999. This book is full of activities that can be done by individuals or groups of people, whether students or school children. This brilliant book is highly motivating and goes against the boring standard ways of teaching graph theory, which all too often make it look as if it is a complex and arcane subject. See unplugged.canterbury.ac.nz to get a downloadable version.

■ Biggs, N. L., Lloyd, E. K., and Wilson, R. J., *Graph Theory: 1736–1936*, Cambridge University Press, 1986. As its title suggests, this presents a historical perspective on the development of graph theory, complete with (translated) extracts from key papers. It is an easier read than most books on graph theory because, as it works through history, the earlier stuff is inevitably simpler. In contrast, ordinary books on graph theory plunge into definitions and give you everything (I think) too quickly.

■ Buckley, F., and Lewinter, M., *A Friendly Introduction to Graph Theory*, Prentice Hall, 2003. This really is a well-written, friendly book on graph theory, as its title suggests, at a level equivalent to this book's treatment, but obviously emphasizing the mathematics and going more deeply into graph theory than we could here.

■ Michalewicz, Z., and Fogel, D. B., *How to Solve It: Modern Heuristics*, Springer, 2000, is a wide-ranging discussion about problem-solving in programming, with the added benefit that it puts the traveling salesman problem in the context of other problems and techniques.

■ Milgram, S., "The Small World Problem," *Psychology Today*, **2**:60–67, 1967. The original paper that established the "six degrees connectivity" of the human race.

■ Watts, D., *Six Degrees*, Heinemann, 2003. This is a popular account of small world networks. Note that most discussions of small worlds, including this one, are not very interested in the names of edges—in device terms, the names of buttons. For a user of a device, the names (or appearance) of buttons are very important. For example, what might be a simple cyclic graph (considered as an unlabeled graph) might need different button presses for each edge: the apparent simplicity of the cycle would be lost on the bemused user.

■   ■   ■

Or see the ACM digital library at www.acm.org/dl; Google at www.google.com; or the online encyclopedia, www.wikipedia.com—all hubs of knowledge.

9

A framework for design

This chapter describes a basic programming framework that lets us build, test and analyze any interactive device. Once we have a framework for programming finite state machines, we can do all sorts of things efficiently. The design framework presented here is very simple, trimmed as it is for the purposes of the book. If you like programming, please be inspired to do better with your own design projects. If you don't like programming, it is still worth reading through this and the next few chapters, but be reassured that non-programming designers could use tools that hide the programming details. However, the insights a designer can achieve through this sort of programming are very important—so read the this and the next few chapters to see what can be achieved.

9.1 Future-proof frameworks

An important question to ask at the start is, "How extensible and future-proof is this approach?" A very cynical answer is that the framework holds together for the devices we want to cover in this book, and not much else, let alone the future. A more useful answer is that the framework is about *ideas*, which it illustrates perfectly clearly, and if you want to really use it, it will need developing and extending for whatever your particular application is. Most likely, you would build something like it into a design tool. Of course, if you are developing real production devices, you may not want to use JavaScript anyway—but the JavaScript ideas we describe will convert easily to any programming language.

A more realistic answer is that the framework is based on finite state machines. These are core technology for any pushbutton style user interface, though you may wish to make minor modifications to the framework to handle details of your specific applications.

> ▷ The framework is not restricted to "pushbuttons" as such, although they are practically ubiquitous ways of interacting with devices; for example, we'll have a look at a cordless drill—which has knobs and sliders—in section 9.8 (p. 316). We will discuss some variations on the framework, with ideas for programming in more professional ways, in section 9.7 (p. 312).

In the future, user interfaces will no doubt move beyond push buttons. Devices may be controlled by speech or even by direct thought, through some sort of brain implant. The framework will work just as well for such user interfaces, although we've only developed it here with button pressing in mind. In fact, a really important idea lies behind this: speech (or any other panacea) does not escape *any* of the interaction programming issues our framework makes clear and easy to explore.

9.2   A state machine framework

We first introduce our programming framework using a simple toy example—the framework is more important than the example, for the time being.

The first, and simplest, device we'll consider is a lightbulb, with three states: off, dim, and fully on. This can be drawn as a transition diagram with three circles, one for each of the states, and with arrows among them showing how one could change the state. As it happens, this lightbulb allows any state to go to any other state directly—but this is rarely the case with more complex devices. Figure 9.1 (facing page) is a state transition diagram showing how the lightbulb works.

The user interface is simple—buttons as well as states are called Off, On, Dim. For this device, regardless of what its called, a button *always* changes from any state to a state with that name. This makes the user interface very simple and consistent. There are only two disadvantages: if there are lots of states, there need to be lots of buttons, and—for the purposes of this book—there is a small risk that we may confuse the state names and the button names (in general, they need not be the same).

Most device descriptions are much bigger, but the lightbulb is simple and familiar enough to show it in its entirety.

There are many ways to program. For such a simple device, it would be tempting to go straight into programming: there are only three states and three buttons, and this is easily programmed. Indeed, we know that each button sets the state with the same name, so we may as well program as follows:

```
var state;
function action(button)
{ state = button;
}
```

However, if we wrote program code like that, we would have several problems. We would find it hard to modify the design (what happens when we change the name of a button, say to make a device for a foreign market?), and we would find analyzing the design hard (the code above is so terse that it isn't obvious what it does). We need to avoid both problems: we want a flexible framework that allows easy analysis to help the designer.

First, we will represent the device by a set of arrays. We have an array of button names, an array of state names, and a table (a two dimensional array) specifying how each button changes each state. The advantage of this approach is that it makes a working device, and it permits any analysis.

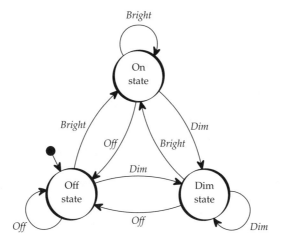

Figure 9.1: The transition diagram of a simple three-state lightbulb, which can be in any of three states: on, off, or dim. The initial state is Off, as shown by the default arrow. All actions are shown, even where they do not change states, so there are always three arrows out of all states.

Since every device has its own arrays, and we want to have a general approach for any device, it helps to group all of the device details together. JavaScript (and most other languages) allow data structures to be combined into single objects, and that is what we will do here.

The approach shown below is a pretty full description of how a device—in this case, our lightbulb—works.

```
var device = {
    notes:  "simple lightbulb, with dim mode",
    modelType:  "lightbulb",
    buttons:  ["Off", "On", "Dim"],
    stateNames:  ["dim", "off", "on"],
    fsm:  [[1, 2, 0], [1, 2, 0], [1, 2, 0]], // see Section 9.2.2 (p. 277)
    startState:  1,
    state:  0,
    manual:  ["dim", "dark", "bright"],
    action:  ["press", "pressed", "pressing"],
    errors:  "never",
    graphics:  "bulbpicture.gif"
};
```

Notice that we have allowed for quite a few more features: we've specified the initial state (the lightbulb will start at the state off); we've given the device a name and picture; and we've chosen simple words and phrases to describe what the device does. We can now concentrate on getting the simulation and analysis

275

to work, confident that we can easily change the device specification later if we want to.

9.2.1   How the specification works

The lightbulb definition creates a JavaScript object and assigns it to the variable `device`. The various fields of the object can be accessed by writing them after dots; for example, for this object the field `device.modelType` is the string `"lightbulb"`.

Some of the fields are arrays. For example `device.action` is an array with three strings: `["press", "pressed", "pressing"]`. The elements of arrays are accessed by using numbers written between square brackets. Given these values, `device.action[1]` will be the string `"pressed"`. Like Java and C, JavaScript counts array elements from 0, so `device.action[0]` is the first array element and `device.action[1]` the second.

Some devices won't have buttons to press; they might have pedals, levers, or knobs to turn. So the `device.action` field says how the user is supposed to do things: for this simple lightbulb, the basic action is to *press* a button. Since we might want to use the right word with different tenses, we've provided for present, past, and future forms of the word. The field `action` can be used to generate English explanations of how to use the device: we may want to generate text like, "If you are in the dark and want the lightbulb to be on, try **pressing** the On button," or, "To put the lightbulb off, **press** the Off button," or, "You **pressed** the On button, but the lightbulb is still on." You can see that the various English fields in the device specification will give us great scope for generating helpful text messages for users and indeed for our own analyses, making it easier for the designer to understand too.

The framework is simple but very flexible. If you want to change the names of the buttons, you could change the line that starts "`buttons:`" and give them different names. The advantage is that the complete definition of the lightbulb is kept in one place. It is quite separate from how we get the user interface to work and quite separate from how we make the device look.

An obvious limitation with the scheme is that I've only got one graphics image to cover all three states of the device. It might have been better to make `graphics` an array with, in this case, three images. With only three states and hence only three images, that seems to make sense, but in general we might have thousands of states and we would probably not want to end up having to organize thousands of pictures too. Instead, pictures would be better generated by a concise bit of program (which is how almost all graphical user interfaces work: all the images are drawn by program), and each state's specific drawing would be laid on top of a basic background image.

The lightbulb has three states, and as can be seen reading the `stateNames` field, they are called dim, off, and on; because of the way JavaScript array subscripts work, they are numbered 0, 1, and 2, respectively. The actual numbers are arbitrary (though they have to be used consistently throughout the definition). Note that I've chosen the numbers for buttons and states so that their names do not correspond, as in general there will be no clear-cut correspondence even though for this simple device there is one we could have exploited. But we're trying to build a general framework for any device, not just for special cases.

9.2.2 State transition tables

The key part of the device's definition is the bit fsm. The numbers here define the finite state machine (FSM) that implements the device, the three-state lightbulb in this case. The definition of fsm in JavaScript, [[1, 2, 0], [1, 2, 0], [1, 2, 0]], is equivalent to a simple matrix of numbers:

$$\begin{matrix} 1 & 2 & 0 \\ 1 & 2 & 0 \\ 1 & 2 & 0 \end{matrix}$$

These particular numbers are not very exciting, but in general the fsm matrix tells us how to go from one state when a button is pressed to the next state. Every row of this matrix of numbers is the same only because the lightbulb is so simple, and its buttons always do the same things; in general, though, each row would be different.

The matrix structure is easier to understand when it is drawn out more explicitly as a table:

When in this state	*Go to this state* *when this button is pressed*		
	Off	On	Dim
0: dim	1: off	2: on	0: dim
1: off	1: off	2: on	0: dim
2: on	1: off	2: on	0: dim

From this table we can read off what each button does in each state. This lightbulb isn't very interesting: the buttons always do the same things, whatever the states.

The same information can be presented in many other forms, and often one or another form will be much easier to read for a particular device. State transition tables (STTs) are a popular representation.

The full state transition table for the lightbulb is particularly simple:

Action	Current state	Next state
Press Off	on off dim	off
Press On	on off dim	on
Press Dim	on off dim	dim

Each row in the table specifies an action, a current state, and the next state the action would get to from the current state. Other features may be added in further columns, such as how the device responds to the actions, or the status of its indicator lights. (We would also need corresponding entries in the `device` specification.)

State transition tables can usually be made much shorter and clearer by simplifying special cases:

■ If an action takes all states to the same next state, only one row in the table for the action is required (cutting it down from as many rows as there are states).

■ If an action does not change the state, the row for that state is not required (with the proviso that if an action does nothing in any state, it needs one row to say so).

■ If an action has the same next state as the row above, it need not repeat it.

Here is a state transition table for a simple microwave oven, illustrating use of all these rules:

Action	Current state	Next state
Press [Clock]	*any*	Clock
Press [Quick defrost]	*any*	Quick defrost
Press [Time]	Clock	Timer 1
	Quick defrost	
	Timer 1	Timer 2
	Timer 2	Timer 1
	Power 1	Timer 2
	Power 2	Timer 1
Press [Clear]	*any*	Clock
Press [Power]	Timer 1	Power 1
	Timer 2	Power 2

This table was drawn automatically in JavaScript from the specification given in section 9.4.6 (p. 286)—it was typeset using LaTeX, though HTML would have done as well. Unfortunately, and ironically because of the simplifying rules, the JavaScript framework code to generate this table is longer than it's worth writing out. The full code to do it is on the book's web site, mitpress.mit.edu/presson.

Our simple framework is written in JavaScript, because it has lots of advantages for a book, but a proper development framework would be much more sophisticated. It would allow designers to write state transition tables (and other forms of device specification) directly—just as easily as if they were editing a table in a word processor. Behind the scenes, a proper design tool constructs the finite state machine data, which is then used to support all the features of the framework. Ideally, the finite state machine would be reconstructed instantly when even the smallest change was made to the table, and every feature the designer was using—simulations, user manuals, analysis, whatever—would update itself automatically.

To recapitulate, from the framework model we can generate representations of the device—such as STTs and, later, user manuals, analysis, diagrams and help—but we can also (with a little more effort) use those representations to either edit or generate what we started with. This creates a powerful two-way relationship, and it is *always* worth thinking about what opportunities there are to do this.

The general idea is called equal opportunity: everything has an equal opportunity to contribute to the process. When equal opportunity is used in a design process, there is no need to see one product—such as a user manual—as the output of the design (and therefore likely to come last) but as part of the design. If a technical author makes changes to the manual, those changes get carried back in the appropriate way to the original design, and the device would then behave differently—and no doubt have a better manual for it too.

9.3 Prototyping and concurrent design

Now that we have come this far, it's a simple matter to write a program that can run the device from the table. Since we are using JavaScript, we'll first build the device simulation as an interactive web page.

> ▷ Practical programming continues in section 9.4 (next page), but first, we want to philosophize about frameworks and design processes.

In conventional design, we distinguish between low-fidelity prototypes and high-fidelity prototypes. Typically, a low-fidelity prototype will be made out of paper drawings and will be used to help users and designers understand the major states of a system; high-fidelity prototypes are usually devices that look more realistic, typically being drawn using decent computer graphics.

The problem with this view of design is that in progressing from low to high-fidelity, you practically have to start again. You make paper models, throw them away, make more realistic models, throw them away, then start making a prototype on a computer—then you make the *real* device. You have to do several times as much work, and each stage loses whatever it learns: paper models for a low-fidelity prototype don't have any program code in them anyway; later prototypes are often written in Flash, Tcl/Tk or some other easy-to-use and flexible programming environment, but the final product has to be rebuilt as a standalone or embedded device using some completely different technology, such as programming in C or a burned in firmware on a chip.

Often the final implementation is such a technical process—it must deal with things like wireless communications protocols, battery management, screen updates including cool animations—that the programmers closely involved with the earlier design stages are now not involved at all.

Why be so inefficient? Why not have a design framework that covers a wide range of development needs? This chapter will get a design to a stage where it runs like an interactive web page; if you print off the web pages, you will have a low-fidelity paper prototype. If you get a user to interact with the web site (perhaps after putting in some nice images) you have a higher-fidelity prototype where you can start getting feedback from users. You'll also be able to generate user manuals and get lots of interesting design analysis to help you pinpoint design issues that need attention—or are opportunities for innovation. Crucially, as you discover ways of improving the design—say, when a user spots something—you can revise the design and redo everything very efficiently.

The framework is surprisingly simple. Obviously what we are sketching is more pedagogical than real, but the approach—the ideas and motivation behind the approach—has many benefits. It helps makes design concurrent: everything can be done more-or-less at once, and no information need be lost between successive phases of the design process.

When we use a design framework to design *concurrently*, the following advantages become apparent:

- Complex information is shared automatically among different parts of the design process and with different people (programmers, authors, users) engaged in the design process.

- Design ideas and requirements formulated in the framework can be debugged and quality-controlled *once*, yet used for many device designs.

- Work need not get lost. The same design representation pervades everything and does not need to be redone or "repurposed" for other aspects of the design.

- Many problems for any part of the design can be identified immediately. For example, technical authors can start to write user manuals immediately; problems they face (say in explaining difficult concepts or in using draft manuals in training sessions) are then known from the start, rather than when it is too late.

- Rather than waiting for later stages of a design process to confront problems, it is possible to test how the "later" stages work almost immediately. The entire design life cycle can start to be debugged from the earliest moment, and feedback from draft final stages is available to improve the earliest conceptual work.

- It is possible to improve the design framework itself. Insights to improve the framework that help particular design projects are programmed into the framework and then are freely available to other projects.

These are grand claims for something so simple, but this is a different philosophical approach to design: you start with a simple framework and embellish it, by extending the framework in different directions as need arises. Since the extensions are automated, if you make any changes, the products are regenerated. The alternative is to have a complex design environment, where each product—low-fidelity, high-fidelity, whatever—is done from scratch, and has to be done again if there are any changes. Put another way, since every interactive device is a state machine, we build a framework to run and analyze state machines.

9.4   Prototyping as a web device

There are three main ways to convert a device into an interactive web site, which we'll now explore in turn.

9.4.1   Using HTML links within a page

The simplest and most direct way to convert a device specification into an "interactive experience" is to translate it into a *single* HTML page.

First, check that your JavaScript device specification works—for if it has any errors in it (like a missing comma) nothing will work. It's good practice to start off with something simple, make sure it works, then get more sophisticated—but only once you that know the foundations are sound.

```
var device = ...; // insert your device specification here.
document.write("<h1>Summary of "+device.modelType+"</h1><br>");
document.write("This device has "+device.stateNames.length+" states and ");
document.write(device.buttons.length+" buttons.");
```

> ▷ As described in section 4.5 (p. 105), where we defined the function `plural`, this JavaScript would generate better English if we wrote ... `"This device has "+plural(device.stateNames.length, "state")+" and "+plural(device.buttons.length, "button")+"."` ...

You can either use + to join strings together (+ will also add numbers), or you can just as easily use several calls to `document.write` on the strings separately. It's a matter of personal style.

```
for( var s = 0; s < device.fsm.length; s++ )
{ document.write("<hr><a name="+s+">In state <b>"+device.stateNames[s]
    +"</b> you can press:</a><ul>");
  for( var b = 0; b < device.buttons.length; b++ )
    document.write("<li><a href=#"+device.fsm[s][b]+">"
      +device.buttons[b]+"</a></li>");
  document.write("</ul>");
}
```

This will generate a hugely insightful web page! It'll look like this:

In state **dim** you can press:
• Off
• On
• Dim
In state **off** you can press:
• Off
• On
• Dim
· · ·

If you click on one of the buttons, shown in your browser as underlined hot text, the web page will scroll up and down to get the current state at the top (depending on your browser: you may need to make the window smaller so you can see it scrolling—otherwise, your browser won't seem to do anything if the target state is already visible in the window without scrolling). In a sense, you've not so much got an interactive simulation of an interactive device as a rather banal interactive (hypertext) user manual for it.

It's easy to do much better. Here's one idea: give the user some hints about what pressing a button will do:

```
for( var s = 0; s < device.fsm.length; s++ )
{ document.write("<hr><a name=new"+s+">In state <b>"
    +device.stateNames[s]+"</b> you can press:</a><ul>");
  for( var b = 0; b < device.buttons.length; b++ )
    if( device.fsm[s][b] != s )
    {  document.write("<li><a href=#new"+device.fsm[s][b]+">"
          +device.buttons[b]+"</a>");
       document.write(" - goes to state <b>"
          +device.stateNames[device.fsm[s][b]]+"</b>");
       document.write("</li>");
    }
  document.write("</ul>");
}
```

In this example, I changed the HTML link names from simple numbers (in the first example) to new followed by the state number (in the second example)—to ensure that the examples can safely work together without their link names clashing. I've also removed all transitions that do nothing; this makes the manual a lot shorter for many devices.

9.4.2   Multiple HTML pages

Rather than use a single page and rely on scrolling, we can convert a device into a multipage web site with lots of HTML files. The easiest way to do this is to have each HTML file correspond to a single state, HTML links among the pages then correspond to transitions. With this approach, it is very obvious that clicking a button changes state, since the browser loads a new page.

Typically, each page would say which state it was, and every page would have named hot text representing the device's buttons, much as before. Each page can have a name like device1.html, device2.html and so on, corresponding to the HTML description for what state 1, state 2, and so on do.

If you represent a device like this as lots of linked web pages, try using a web-authoring tool, like Dreamweaver, which can run checks on web sites to check that all the links work—for exactly the same reasons an interactive device should be checked.

> ▷ Dreamweaver has built-in tools to find pages you never link to and to find links that don't work. These are issues we will deal with later, in section 9.5 (p. 288), when we will write JavaScript to do these and other checks.

Representing a device as lots of web pages requires some way of writing lots of files automatically, which, unfortunately, is beyond JavaScript's capability when it is running in a browser.

Using one file, many URLs

Instead, we can "cheat" to achieve the same effect. Rather than naming lots of files device1.html, device2.html, and so on, we use the URLs device.html?1, device.html?2, and so on. This is practically the same thing, except that everything can now be done with a *single* file, device.html, with the "search" part of the URL (what comes after the question mark character) selecting which state the device is in.

In the approach we used above, a for loop ran over all possible values of the state number. Now each page only has to deal with one state, but it gets the state number not from a for loop but from the search part of the URL, as follows:

```
var device = ...; // pick a device
var state = location.search.substr(1); // get the search string

if( state == "" || state < 0 ||  state >= device.fsm.length )
  state = device.startState; // use initial state if not given explicitly

document.write("<h1>"+device.modelType
   +" is "+device.stateNames[state]+"</h1>");

document.write("<ul>");
for( var b = 0; b < device.buttons.length; b++ )
  document.write("<li><a href=device.html?"
    +device.fsm[state][b]+">"+device.buttons[b]+"</a></li>");
document.write("</ul>");
```

Using URLs for states

An alternative to these simple (but systematic) methods of using the state number to directly select an HTML page is to use stateNames to apply URLs to states. Each state has a name that is the file you want the browser to show when the device is in that state (of course, if you want the names to be sensible, you could add an array url to the framework to serve the same purpose and keep stateNames with its original purpose).

Associating URLs with states reminds us that a state can be sophisticated, just as a URL could be a movie, an interactive form, or even a whole other web site, with *any* features within it. In other words, states in the framework are really clusters, in the sense of statecharts.

▷   For more on statecharts and clusters, see section 7.1 (p. 201).

9.4.3   Using forms

The third way of converting a device to an interactive web page can be done easily in JavaScript and is by far the best way for our purposes. It uses an HTML form to set up some buttons and a simple display, and the form text is updated with the state name (and anything else you want to say). This is an extremely easy and reliable way to get dynamic HTML working. Forms also give us buttons that look like buttons, so we can do better than using underlined hot text.

Loading up a web page in your browser with the code we will develop in this section will get a picture something like figure 9.2 (next page).

Figure 9.2: What the lightbulb device simulation looks like after you press the Dim button. The three buttons of the device are shown along the top row, and underneath is the text field that displays the current state name, all generated by the framework code.

First you need a basic form (written in standard HTML) for the buttons and a text field for the state name:

```
<form>
  <input type='button' value='Off' onMouseup='press(0)'>
  <input type='button' value='On'  onMouseup='press(1)'>
  <input type='button' value='Dim' onMouseup='press(2)'>
  <br>
  State = <input type='text' name='display' readonly><p>
</form>
```

Rather than calling specific button functions like `off` in the HTML code for the form, we've used a more general approach by having a single function `press` that can do *any* button; it just needs to be told which one. Thus `press(0)` means do whatever pressing Off should do, `press(1)` means do whatever pressing On should do, and so on.

The HTML form above can only handle a three-button device, and it is restricted to fixed button names (Off, On, Dim) at that. It is better to use JavaScript to generate a form for *any* device specification. We only need a JavaScript `for` loop to do it and to use `document.write` to generate the correct HTML. Here's how to do everything automatically:

```
function makeForm(d)
{ document.write("<form>");
  // generate one line for each button
  for( var s = 0; s < d.buttons.length; s++ )
  { document.write("<input type='button' ")
    document.write("value='"+d.buttons[s]+"' ")
    document.write("onMouseup='press("+s+")'>")
  }
  // plus some more HTML to get a working display ...
  document.write("<br>State = <input type='text' name='display' readonly>")
  // then finish the form
  document.write("</form>")
}
```

Now, if we write `<script>makeForm(device)</script>` anywhere, this will generate the HTML form code automatically. If the device is the lightbulb we defined earlier in this chapter, then this code will automatically generate the example form given above.

9.4.4 Look and feel

The last few sections developed very different appearances for the device, yet they all worked the same way. First, the device was presented as a single web page, then as many separate web pages of text, and finally we generated a form. The design and layout of the form was built into the code of makeForm()—the earlier two "look-and-feel" approaches were so banal we didn't even give the JavaScript that generated them a special name.

Every device we work with will now end up looking much like this. If we wrote a different makeForm() we could generate a form with a quite different layout, color scheme, or whatever. Then every device we worked with would look different, but consistently. So in particular, we can change how they look without changing how they work—a process sometimes called skinning.

Crucially, the look-and-feel of the interactive device is separated from its interaction rules. We can change one without affecting the other. In a professional design environment, we might have different people working on each aspect separately. If changes are made to the look and feel, say, changing the color scheme, the other people on the design project do not need to know; conversely, if the device specification is changed, the look and feel is automatically revised to work on the new device.

In an ideal world, we would invent a language (no doubt in XML, so that other programs could help us store and manipulate it) to describe the look and feel of a device, just as we invented a language (actually a JavaScript data structure) for specifying the state machine part of the device. Here we've simply written JavaScript code to specify the look and feel. Although JavaScript is very easy to fiddle with, it isn't a good language for a design tool to control.

Our makeForm() might be totally flexible, but our design framework has no insight into how it works. For example, if we accidentally made the background and the text colors the same, nothing in the form would be readable—and there is no general way that we can program in checks like this that would work with every device and every look and feel we used.

> ▷ Section 11.7.1 (p. 402) presents a case for adding look and feel information in the framework (rather than into program code).

In a way, then, the possibility of improving the approach to look and feel, and the advantages of doing so, is a small parable about the philosophy of the design framework. The design framework as we develop it in this book only works with interaction, not look and feel.

9.4.5 Initial checking

Creating the interactive form is only one part of initializing a device, and it is useful to have a single function to do all the necessary work:

```
function initialize(d)
{ d.state = d.startState; // start off the device in the initial state
  makeForm(d);
  ... other details to be added ...
}
```

It's convenient to have a function `displayState` to display the state name by writing the name of the state to the form field:

```
function displayState(d)
{ document.forms[0]["display"].value = d.stateNames[d.state];
}
```

The initialization function will call `displayState(d)` to make sure that the initial state is correctly displayed. A more exciting simulation of a device would show different images for each state, rather than just writing strings of text—the state description—to a field, as we've done here.

Now all that is needed is the next state function, which we've called `press`. Notice how `press` uses the `fsm` table to work out the next state from the current state and the number of the button the user has pressed. It then calls `displayState` to show the user the new state name.

```
function press(buttonNumber)
{ device.state = device.fsm[device.state][buttonNumber];
  displayState(device);
}
```

It takes a little bit more tinkering to get it all perfect, but when all the details are sorted out, we can run the lightbulb simulation as a self-contained web page.

9.4.6   Specifying a different device

Once we have a framework, changing or revising the device specification is easy. The *same* Javascript code will work for *any* device: we can easily change the definition of `device` to change its behavior. Here is the device specification for a microwave oven:

```
var device2 = {
  notes: "A basic microwave oven, based on a Hyundai model",
  modelType: "Microwave oven",
  buttons: ["[Clock]","[Quick defrost]","[Time]","[Clear]","[Power]"],
  stateNames: ["Clock","Quick defrost","Timer 1",
               "Timer 2","Power 1","Power 2"],
  fsm: [
        [0,1,2,0,0],
        [0,1,2,0,1],
        [0,1,3,0,4],
        [0,1,2,0,5],
        [0,1,3,0,4],
        [0,1,2,0,5]
       ],
```

```
    startState: 0,
    action: ["touch","touched","touching"],
    manual: ["has the clock running","doing quick defrost",
             "using Timer 1","using Timer 2",
             "on Power level 1","on Power level 2"
             ],
    errors: "never",
    graphics: ""
};
```

▷ We shall use this definition of a microwave oven as a frequent example. The oven was discussed at length in Jonathan Sharp's PhD thesis (see the further reading at the end of this chapter, p. 323); we use his *exact* definitions to emphasize the generality of the approach.

If we just do device = device2 the framework will obligingly change from simulating a lightbulb to simulating this microwave oven.

9.4.7 Using an image map

Our definition of the lightbulb included a picture file: instead of boring buttons, an image and image map could be used to make the interaction simulation far more realistic. If you want to use an image map so the user can click on regions within the large picture that correspond to buttons or knobs, then the device specification should include coordinates for its hot regions.

▷ An example of using an image map is given in section 9.5.1 (p. 291), though the image there is the device's state transition diagram, not its buttons and front panel.

9.4.8 Handling errors

Although the lightbulb has no scope for errors, the device specification had some information about errors, namely, a string device.errors. This field could be set to "beep" if we wanted the device to beep when there is an error, to "never" if we wanted to ignore errors, or perhaps to something more complicated, say, to identify some states with an error. For this book, I decided not to make error handling a big issue for the framework, because the way errors are handled affects almost all of the framework and makes it much more complicated than we need to bother about here.

In fact, error handling is always tricky, and most interactive systems do it very badly. If we put decent error handling into the framework, we'd only have to do it once (perhaps leaving some details to the requirements of specific devices), and then every device developed with it would "inherit" the careful error handling.

For some devices we might want to warn the user that pressing a button does nothing. We could use code like this:

```
if( state == device.fsm[device.state][buttonNumber]
    && device.errors != "never" )
  alert(device.action[2]+" "+device.buttons[buttonNumber]+
       " doesn't do anything in this state!");
```

Notice that we used the pressing device action from the `device.action` array. The program will test whether `device.errors != "never"` again and again, so better programming might call for writing:

```
var reportErrors = device.errors != "never";
...
if( reportErrors && state == device.fsm[device.state][buttonNumber] )
...
```

Remember that most errors we can report to users (while they are interacting with the simulation) could have been detected before running the device. For instance, if we think that buttons having no action is an error, then we can write program to find all such cases automatically and then modify the design to eliminate them before a user ever interacts with it.

9.4.9   Logging a commentary on user actions

The device specification includes a simple manual entry for each state as well as a choice of words for what users do when they press buttons. Here's one way to use the manual part of the specification to provide a running commentary on the user working the device:

```
function press(buttonNumber)
{ ...
  document.forms["info"].comment.value = "You "+device.action[1]+
        " "+device.buttons[buttonNumber]+
        ", and "+(same? "nothing happened.":
                        "it is "+device.manual[device.state]+" now.");
  ...
}
```

We could easily extend the framework to have a button (PROBLEM) that would let the user write a description of any problem they have found, and we could automatically annotate the user's comments with the state where it was found (and perhaps also the last few states so a designer looking at the report would know how the user got there and experienced the problem).

9.5   Basic checking and analysis

Any device may be specified with accidental errors the designer hasn't noticed. One job for a framework is to perform checks that basic design errors have not been made—this is an important part of design that is often forgotten in ordinary programming, where the designer just writes code to do things and then has no easy way to check what has been done.

If every program is written from scratch, the effort to do detailed checking will rarely seem worthwhile: most of the useful checks are not particularly easy to program (and it is always going to be easier to hope that the design is correct than do hard work). Instead, in a framework, we only have to write the checking program code *once*, and it is then *always* available for every device we want to use. That is a very useful gain and a good reason to use a framework.

The first and simplest thing to check is that we have a valid finite state machine with the right number of buttons. The properties to check are as follows:

- The basic fields are defined in the device specification. (In a strongly typed programming language like Java this step is not be required.)

- The number of buttons and the number of states conform to the size of the various fsm, indicators, manual, action fields. (This is a check that both Java and JavaScript cannot do without some explicit programming.)

- The startState and all entries in the fsm are valid state numbers. (Again, this is a check that Java and JavaScript cannot do without programming.)

- Report on whether any states have no actions in them. This is generally an error, except for special devices.

- Report on whether any states have only one action in them. This is an example property of a device that may or may not be a design error; it may be deliberate in some states for some devices, but generally it is worth highlighting for a designer to take note.

  ▷ Pointless states can be identified visually from transition diagrams; they raise a potential design issue discussed in section 6.3.3 (p. 184).

In JavaScript almost anything goes, so we have to check explicitly that strings are strings, numbers are numbers, and so on. It is easiest to define some handy functions to do this and to report errors as necessary:

```
function isString(s, name)
{ if( typeof s != "string" )
    alert(name + " should be defined as a string");
}

function isWholeNumber(n, name, lo, hi)
{ if( typeof n != "number" || Math.floor(n) != n || n < lo || n > hi )
    alert(name + " (which is "+n+
                  ") should be a number between "+lo+" and "+hi);
}
```

```
function isStringArray(a, name, size)
{ if( a == undefined )
    alert(name+" field of device not defined");
  if( a.length != size )
    alert(name + " should be a string array, size "+size);
  for( var i = 0; i < size; i++ )
    isString(a[i], name + "["+i+"]");
}
```

The curious bit of code in isWholeNumber, namely, Math.floor(n) != n, checks that n is a whole number in the appropriate range, lo $\leq$ n $\leq$ hi. The standard JavaScript Math.floor function removes any decimal part of a number, so 2.3 becomes 2; of course, 2.3 is not equal to 2, so the function determines that 2.3 (or any number with a fractional part) is not a whole number. We need to check whether the type of n is a number too since Math.floor would fail (returning NaN—not a number) if it wasn't.

In Java, or another statically typed language, we could check this much more easily by declaring things to be int—then the Java compiler would do the checks with no further effort on our part, but JavaScript does not check whether a number is an integer or a floating point number.

Next we want to report on any pointless states. This is just a simple matter of examining each state and counting the number of transitions from that state to other states. If a state has only one exit, then it possibly serves no purpose, unless that state does something useful for the user as a side effect. In any case, the designer should know the list of pointless states in order to review that they do indeed have some use; otherwise, they should be deleted.

```
function reportPointlessStates(d)
{ for( var i = 0; i < d.fsm.length; i++ )
  { var count = 0;
    for( var j = 0; j < d.fsm[i].length; j++ )
      if( d.fsm[i][j] != i )
        count++;
    if( count == 1 )
      alert("State "+d.stateNames[i]+" may be pointless.");
  }
}
```

In a perfect world (that is, one where the framework is developed to be more sophisticated and "industrial strength") designers could record their decisions: each state could have a flag to say that it is alright for it to be "pointless," and the check code would not report it again. Indeed, as soon as you write any program code like this, many other checks and features will occur to you. For example, why not check that the count of transitions from a state is at least 1, because surely 0 would be an error too? Checking that a single state has no exit is one problem, which we could report with a simple change to reportPointlessStates, but what if a set of several states have no common exit, but each state within the set does? That's harder to check.

▷   We will make more powerful checks like this later, in section 9.6 (p. 297).

With these functions, the checking is now straightforward:

```
function checkDevice(d)
{ // check strings
  isString(d.modelType, "modelType");
  isString(d.notes, "notes");
  isString(d.errors, "errors");
  isString(d.graphics, "graphics");
  // how many buttons?
  var b = d.buttons.length;
  // how many states?
  var s = d.stateNames.length;
  isWholeNumber(d.startState, "startState", 0, s-1);
  // check right number of things of right type
  isStringArray(d.buttons, "buttons", b);
  isStringArray(d.stateNames, "stateNames", s);
  isStringArray(d.action, "action", 3);
  isStringArray(d.manual, "manual", s);
  // check fsm
  if( d.fsm.length != s )
    alert("fsm does not have "+s+" rows");
  for( var i = 0; i < s; i++ )
  { if( d.fsm[i].length != b )
      alert("fsm row "+i+" does not have "+b+" columns");
    for( var j = 0; j < b; j++ )
      isWholeNumber(d.fsm[i][j], "fsm["+i+"]["+j+"]", 0, s-1);
  }
  reportPointlessStates(d);
}
```

Of course the checkDevice function can be applied to *any* device. This generality is one of the huge advantages of using a framework: once you notice that one device has potential problems you can identify (or even fix) automatically, modifying your framework will avoid those problems in every other device too. The same applies to all the analytical results. Good ideas can automatically be made available to every device we want to try out.

▷ Chapter 8, "Graphs," presents many ideas for measuring the effectiveness of interactive devices, in particular whether the device *structure* has any dead-ends and other traps for the user—issues that are not checked with the basic code here.

Finally, we must not forget to actually check the device, by calling the function checkDevice(device) on the device we intend to run.

9.5.1 Drawing transition diagrams

The easiest way to draw a transition diagram is to exploit an existing tool to do it for us. There are several graph-drawing standards, and we just need use one to generate a basic description of the finite state machine, and then run a program to do the work for us. When drawing is automated, if we change our device specification, the diagrams can be automatically updated—with speed and accuracy.

To draw diagrams, we will use Dot, an open source standard for drawing graphs. Dot specifications can be read into many programs, which then do the details of drawing, creating web pictures, PostScript, or whatever graphic formats we want.

If state *a* has a transition to state *b*, we write this in Dot by saying a -> b, and if we want to say that this transition is caused by some action, such as pressing a button [On], then we tell Dot the transition has a named label by writing a -> b [label="On"].

Here is a basic description of the microwave oven (generated automatically from the last example in our framework, on p. 286) in Dot:

```
digraph "Microwave oven" { /* basic Dot description */
    0->0 [label="[Clock]"];          0->1 [label="[Quick defrost]"];
    0->2 [label="[Time]"];           0->0 [label="[Clear]"];
    0->0 [label="[Power]"];          1->0 [label="[Clock]"];
    1->1 [label="[Quick defrost]"];  1->2 [label="[Time]"];
    1->0 [label="[Clear]"];          1->1 [label="[Power]"];
    2->0 [label="[Clock]"];          2->1 [label="[Quick defrost]"];
    2->3 [label="[Time]"];           2->0 [label="[Clear]"];
    2->4 [label="[Power]"];          3->0 [label="[Clock]"];
    3->1 [label="[Quick defrost]"];  3->2 [label="[Time]"];
    3->0 [label="[Clear]"];          3->5 [label="[Power]"];
    4->0 [label="[Clock]"];          4->1 [label="[Quick defrost]"];
    4->3 [label="[Time]"];           4->0 [label="[Clear]"];
    4->4 [label="[Power]"];          5->0 [label="[Clock]"];
    5->1 [label="[Quick defrost]"];  5->2 [label="[Time]"];
    5->0 [label="[Clear]"];          5->5 [label="[Power]"];
}
```

The JavaScript to generate this would be easy—just a couple of for loops to run around the definition of device.fsm. However, if you run this through Dot, it is immediately obvious that there are lots of ways to improve it; we'll make the following improvements in our JavaScript:

- The states need names, and we could identify the start state specially.

- If a state has a transition to itself (that is, the action does nothing)—for instance like 0->0 and 4->4 above—we needn't show the arrow for the transition. This simplification will remove a lot of clutter from the drawing.

- If the same action transitions between two states in both directions—for instance like the pair 2->3 [label="[Time]"] and 3->2 [label="[Time]"] above—then we can draw a single arrow but with arrowheads on both ends, rather than two separate arrows.

- If several actions do the same transition, we draw them as a single arrow but with a label made out of all the actions. Thus 1->1 [label="[Quick defrost]"] and 1->1 [label="[Power]"] do the same thing and should be combined to make a single transition 1->1 [label="[Quick defrost], [Power]"].

All sorts of ideas will occur to you on further ways to improve the diagram. Dot is a sophisticated language and can take lots of hints about what you want. You can change the color and shape of the states, the arrowhead styles, and so on. What is important for us is that Dot draws a good enough diagram with no effort on our part. If we modify the finite state machine definition, the diagram will be updated automatically. Designers need easy and efficient tools, and this is one of them.

Here's the JavaScript code to achieve the improvements mentioned above. I won't describe the workings of the code in detail; if you copy it out (or copy it from mitpress.mit.edu/presson), it will work and generate HTML, which you then cut-and-paste to a Dot program to draw the graph.

```
function drawDot(d) // generate Dot code for any device d
{ document.write("digraph \""+d.modelType+"\" {\n");
  document.write("size=\"4,4\";\n");
  document.write("node [shape=ellipse,fontname=Helvetica,fontsize=10];\n")
  document.write("edge [fontname=Helvetica,fontsize=10];\n");
  document.write("start->"+d.startState+";\n");
  document.write("start [label=\"\",style=filled,height=.1,");
  document.write("        shape=circle,color=black];\n");
  for( var s = 0; s < d.fsm.length; s++ ) // state names
     document.write(s + " [label=\"" + d.stateNames[s] + "\"];\n"); // *
  for( var s = 0; s < d.fsm.length; s++ ) // single arrows
     for( var t = 0; t < d.fsm.length; t++ )
       if( t != s ) // ignore self arrows
       { var u = true;
         for( var b = 0; b < d.buttons.length; b++ )
         if( d.fsm[s][b] == t && d.fsm[t][b] != s ) // single arrows only
         { document.write(u? s + "->" + t + " [label=\"": ",\\n");
           u = false;
           document.write(d.buttons[b]);
         }
         if( !u ) document.write("\"];\n");
       }
  for( var s = 0; s < d.fsm.length; s++ ) // double arrows
     for( var t = s+1; t < d.fsm.length; t++ )
     { var u = true;
       for( var b = 0; b < d.buttons.length; b++ )
       if( d.fsm[s][b] == t && d.fsm[t][b] == s )
       { document.write(u? s + "->" + t + " [dir=both,label=\"": ",\\n");
         u = false;
         document.write(d.buttons[b]);
       }
       if( !u ) document.write("\"];\n");
     }
  document.write("}");
}
```

After the definition of this function, call `drawDot(device)` in the JavaScript. Here's the diagram it draws for the microwave oven—with no further touching up:

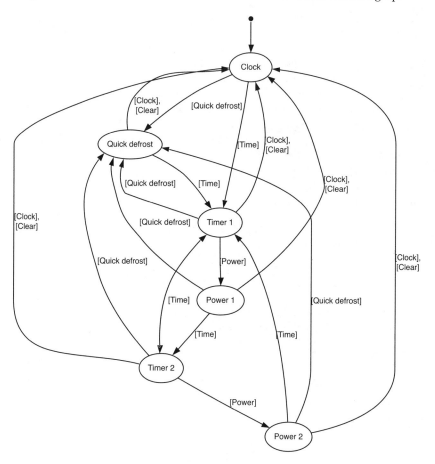

If you are keen, you can tell Dot to associate a URL with each state and then you can click on the transition diagram (in a web browser) and make the device work by going to the state you've clicked on. To do so, add the string

```
"URL=\"javascript:displayState(state = "+s+")\""
```

into the line marked ∗ above—the URL runs the JavaScript to simulate the device.

This transition diagram is a detailed technical diagram that might be of interest to the designer but is too detailed to be of much use to a user. Instead, we can generate code for Dot (or whichever drawing program we are using) to make things more helpful for users.

The following Dot code draws a four-state transition diagram but uses photographs of the device taken when it was in each of the states, using Dot's parameter `shapefile` to use a picture file rather than a geometric shape. Here the device is a Worcester Bosch Highflow-400 central heating system, and the transitions occur when the user presses the Select button. A diagram like figure 9.3 (next page) might be useful in a user manual.

Below, we've only shown the Dot code, not the JavaScript that could generate it. You would write some JavaScript that generated the Dot code for only part of the system (that is, a subgraph), rather than the whole system, for instance, based on lists of states that are needed to make each diagram to illustrate the user manual.

```
"Off" -> "Twice" -> "Once" -> "On" -> "Off";

"Off"   [shapefile="Off.jpg" label=""];
"Twice" [shapefile="Twice.jpg" label=""];
"Once"  [shapefile="Once.jpg" label=""];
"On"    [shapefile="On.jpg" label=""];
```

The easiest way to extend the framework is to add a line to the device specification like `stateNames: ["dim", "off", "on"]`, but giving the file names (or URLs) of images: `stateImages: ["dim.jpg", "off.jpg", "on.jpg"]`, for example.

Instead of photographs or pictures, you could generate text into a template representing the device's screen: you could have a function `generateScreen()` that puts together the appropriate string representing the screen for any state. The possibilities are endless!

It is worth emphasizing again (and again) that once you have set up your framework, you can draw, analyze, and animate interactive devices automatically with no further effort. And, the diagrams, analyses, or animations get modified automatically (and correctly) with no further effort when you revise the device specification.

▷ Instead of Dot, the JavaScript code can be modified to generate XML or specifications in other languages just as easily from our framework. See 7.7 (p. 219) for more on SCXML, the XML for statecharts.

9.5.2 Adding more features

You can keep on adding features to the framework indefinitely. However, the whole point of our approach is that the "way it works" features are clear and well defined, and any cosmetic ideas—like pictures—can be added in independently. Whatever fancy ideas we have to make the simulation more realistic, we should keep at its heart the nice, elegant finite state machine simulator we can understand, draw, and think about easily.

Very often we will want a state to encapsulate or do several things. Originally we had a single function, `press`, to do everything, which has the huge advantage of ensuring consistency, but now we want to be able to handle some states differently. We can either modify `press` so that it does different things in different states or add a field (like `stateNames`) to list functions for each state.

We may want it to draw a picture, or we might want it to handle something quite complex for the device like initiating a phone call.

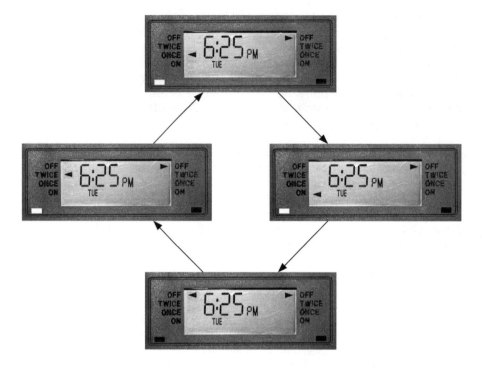

Figure 9.3: A state transition diagram, drawn automatically but using photographs of the device in each of the relevant states. This sort of diagram can be used directly in user manuals. The device here is a domestic central heating boiler, and the states are hot water off, on twice a day, on once a day, or on continuously. Note that the photographs show both the state indicator and the heater-on light.

One approach to handle state encapsulation is to arrange each state to call its own JavaScript function. The function can then do what it likes *in* that state. In many cases, simple modifications to press will seem easiest:

```
function press(buttonNumber)
{ state = device.fsm[device.state][buttonNumber];
  displayState(state);
  switch( state )
  { case 1:  dostate1(); break; // do something special in state 1
    case 5:  dostate5(); break; // do something special in state 5
    default: // in this design, no other states do anything special
             // but the default lets other states work consistently
             // if we added code here for them
             ...
  }
}
```

Before long, this approach of overriding the definition of each state will get too complex, especially if you are tempted to write all the code directly into press itself. Much better is to improve the way each state is defined centrally in the device definition. One way to do it is to have a (potentially) different press function for every state:

```
var device = {
  notes: "Simple lightbulb, with dim mode",
  ...
  stateNames: ["dim", "off", "on"],
  stateFunctions: [stateLit, stateOff, stateLit],
  ...
};
```

and press does it's basic work then dispatches to the appropriate state function, stateLit, stateOff, or whatever:

```
function press(buttonNumber)
{ device.state = device.fsm[device.state][buttonNumber];
  displayState(device);
  device.stateFunctions[device.state](); // do special action
}
```

It's important that everything can be done from the *same* core representation of devices. The JavaScript framework we've designed will work well even if we change, perhaps radically, the definition of the device we are simulating or analyzing. The interaction, as done here in Javascript, the drawings and all of the analysis and manual writing is done directly from the same definition. We can easily change the design (by editing the device specification) and then rerun the simulation or the analyses. If the ideas sketched out in this chapter were used in a real design process, it would permit concurrent engineering—doing lots of parts of the design at the same time. Some designers could work on getting the interaction right, some could work on the analysis, some could work on implementation (like writing better code than we did just now), and so on.

9.6   Finding shortest paths

Designers want to know whether users can do what they want to, and if they can, how hard it is. Let's use the framework to answer these design and usability questions.

The data structure device.fsm describes the complete graph of the user interface design. Here is the data for the microwave oven again:

	Buttons →				
States	0	1	2	0	0
↓	0	1	2	0	1
	0	1	3	0	4
	0	1	2	0	5
	0	1	3	0	4
	0	1	2	0	5

This table, which is stored in `device.fsm`, tells us the next state to go to. Given a button press (column) in any state (row), the entry tells us the next state to be in. For example, the last line (which is state number 5) tells us that button 0 (which is called ⌐Clock⌐ and is the first column) would take the device to state 0—this is the number in the first column of that row.

To work out how many button presses it takes to get from any state to any other state, we need a new table that has rows *and* columns for states; each entry will tell us how many presses it takes to get from one state to the other.

By reading the state-button table above, we can work out the beginning of this new table, which we will call `matrix`. If a button pressed in state *i* causes a transition to state *j*, then we want to have a 1 in entry `matrix[i][j]` to indicate that we know we can get from state *i* to state *j* in one step. Also, we know as a special case we can get from state *i* to state *i* in no steps at all; so every entry `matrix[i][i]` should be zero. Any other entry in the matrix we'll set to infinity because we think (so far) that there is no way to get between these states.

Note that `matrix` has less information in it than `device.fsm`, since we have lost track of buttons: the new matrix only says what next states are possible from a given state, whereas `device.fsm` *also* says which button should be pressed to do it.

All the code that follows is written inside a function, `shortestPaths(d)`, and then `shortestPaths(device)` will work out the shortest paths for that device. Throughout the following code, d will be the device we're working on.

Inside the function, we first need a few lines to create a blank matrix of the right size:

```
var fsm = d.fsm;     // convenient abbreviation
var n = fsm.length; // number of states

var matrix = new Array(n);
for( var i = 0; i < n; i++ ) // create the 2 dimensional table
  matrix[i] = new Array(n);
```

For a finite state machine of *n* states, if any shortest route takes more than *n* steps it must be impossible: $n - 1$ steps is always sufficient to visit every state in the machine (if it's possible, that is), so we can define "infinity" for our purposes to be any number *n* or larger. The value $n + 1$ will do nicely.

```
var b = fsm[0].length; // number of buttons
var infinity = n+1;     // no route can take this many steps!

for( var i = 0; i < n; i++ ) // build one-step matrix
{ for( var j = 0; j < n; j++ )
    matrix[i][j] = infinity;
  for( var j = 0; j < b; j++ )
    matrix[i][fsm[i][j]] = 1;
  matrix[i][i] = 0; // zero steps to get from state i to itself
}
```

The tricky line in the inner `for` loop, `matrix[i][fsm[i][j]] = 1`, says, "we're in state i, and we know button j gets us to state `fsm[i][j]`, and therefore the entry in the matrix for state i to state `fsm[i][j]` should be 1."

Here is what the cost matrix looks like after running that initialization code:

	To state ...					
From state ...	0	1	2	3	4	5
0: Clock	0	1	1	∞	∞	∞
1: Quick defrost	1	0	1	∞	∞	∞
2: Timer 1	1	1	0	1	1	∞
3: Timer 2	1	1	1	0	∞	1
4: Power 1	1	1	∞	1	0	∞
5: Power 2	1	1	1	∞	∞	0

I printed this table directly from the actual values in `matrix`, by using a couple of `for` loops:

```
for( var i = 0; i < n; i++ ) // display matrix
{ for( var j = 0; j < n; j++ )
   if( matrix[i][j] == infinity )
     document.write("&infin; ");
   else
     document.write(matrix[i][j]+" ");
  document.write("<br>");
}
```

It would not be hard to use an HTML `<table>` to lay the data out nicely.

The symbol ∞ in the table (`&infin;` in HTML) means for the time being we don't know a state transition is possible—that is, it might take an infinite number of steps—to get from one state to another. More precisely, the matrix entries mean: it can take 0 steps to get from one state to another (if they are the same state); it can take 1 step to get from one state to another (if there is a single button press that does it directly); or it can take more, which we've represented as ∞.

In short, for any pair of states, say i and j, the matrix tells us whether we can get from one to the other (in zero or more steps). We now use a standard algorithm, the Floyd-Warshall algorithm, that considers every state k and determines whether we can get from i to j via the state k more efficiently. If we can go $i \rightarrow k \rightarrow j$ more efficiently than going directly from $i \rightarrow j$, we record it in the matrix. Thus we expect those ∞ values to reduce down to smaller values. The direct cost is `matrix[i][j]` and the indirect cost, via k, is `matrix[i][k]+matrix[k][j]`. Whenever the indirect cost is better, we can improve the recorded cost. Here's how to do it:

```
for( var k = 0; k < n; k++ )
  for( var i = 0; i < n; i++ )
    for( var j = 0; j < n; j++ )
    // replace cost of ij with best of ij or ikj routes
    { var viak = matrix[i][k] + matrix[k][j];
      if( viak < matrix[i][j] )
        matrix[i][j] = viak;
    }
```

At the end of running these three nested for-loops, the program has tried every way of getting from anywhere to anywhere. The inner two loops find the best way of getting from state i to j via any intermediate state k, but the outer loop ensures that we have tried all intermediate routes via 1 to $k - 1$ first. Thus when the outer loop is finished, we know the best ways of getting between any two states via any state $1 \ldots k$, which covers all possible cases. This is sufficient to know all of the best routes through the finite state machine.

Here is the result of running this code on our cost matrix:

		To state ...					
		0	1	1	2	2	3
		1	0	1	2	2	3
From		1	1	0	1	1	2
state		1	1	1	0	2	1
		1	1	2	1	0	2
		1	1	1	2	2	0

We can write the same information as a mathematical matrix (just put it between round brackets), which is highly suggestive of things you might want to do if you know matrix algebra; however, to go there is beyond the scope and immediate interest of this book.

▷   For more on matrices, see box 11.1, "Matrices and Markov models" (p. 382).

Note that there are no ∞ (infinity) symbols in this shortest path table; this means that (for this device) it is possible to get from any state to any other in a finite number of steps—thus this device is strongly connected. In particular, each entry in the matrix gives the least number of steps it will take between two states (specifically, matrix[i][j] is the cheapest cost of getting from state i to state j by any means).

It goes without saying that our knowing the least number of steps to do anything does not stop a user from getting lost or perhaps deliberately taking a longer route. But we can be certain a user cannot do better than these figures.

In technical terms, the costs are a lower bound on the user interface complexity, as measured by counting button presses. That is one reason why the costs are so important; we have a conservative baseline to understand the user's performance— or lack of it—regardless of how good or sophisticated the user is they cannot do better than these figures. If the costs turned out to be bad (or, more likely, some of the costs were bad) there is nothing a user can do and nothing training can do; we either have to live with a difficult-to-use feature (some things we may *want* to be difficult), or we have to fix the design.

If we multiply the counts in the cost matrix by 0.1 second, we get an estimate of the minimum *time* a fast user would take—and of course we could do some experiments and get a more accurate figure than our guess of 0.1 second; then the timings become a much more useful design measure.

9.6.1   Using shortest paths

Once we have worked out the shortest paths matrix, we know the most efficient cost of getting from anywhere to anywhere. For instance, to get from Clock (state 0) to Power 2 (state 5) takes 3 button presses—that's the number 3 in the top right, at the end of the first line in the matrix above. Here's the best route between these two states:

1. Press $\boxed{\text{Time}}$ to get from Clock to Timer 1

2. Press $\boxed{\text{Time}}$ to get from Timer 1 to Timer 2

3. Press $\boxed{\text{Power}}$ to get from Timer 2 to Power 2

In fact, a designer might be interested in *all* the hardest operations for a device; for this device there are two, both taking at least 3 steps (the user will takes longer if they make a mistake; the analysis shows they cannot take *less* than 3 steps). The other worst case is getting from Quick defrost to Power 2. If the worst cases take ∞ steps, then very likely there is something wrong with the design: some things the device appears designed for are impossible to do.

Some devices—like fire extinguishers—may be designed to be used only once, and then the designer will expect an infinite cost for getting back from the state "extinguisher used" to "extinguisher not used." But even then, it would help the designer to have these states and problems pointed out automatically by the framework. For instance, why not make the fire extinguisher refillable?

To find the best route, the correct sequence of button presses, not just the total cost to the user of following the best route, requires a few extensions to the program.

We need to keep another table via[i][j] to record the first step along the best route $i \rightarrow j$. Every time we update the cost of the route, we've found a better step. Here are the details:

■ In the original initialization of matrix we add an initial value to via:

```
for( var j = 0; j < b; j++ )
{ matrix[i][fsm[i][j]] = 1;
  via[i][fsm[i][j]] = j; // to get from i to fsm[i][j], press button j
}
```

■ In the easy case of going from a state to itself, the first thing to do is to go there.

```
matrix[i][i] = 0;
via[i][i] = i;
```

■ In the code that updates matrix, if it is better to get from i to j via k, we replace the first step of $i \rightarrow j$ with the first step of $i \rightarrow k \rightarrow j$, which is already in via[i][k]:

```
var viak = matrix[i][k] + matrix[k][j];
if( viak < matrix[i][j] )
{ matrix[i][j] = viak;
  via[i][j] = via[i][k];
}
```

■ Finally, after finding all the shortest paths, to get the best route between any two states $i \rightarrow j$, the following code will print out the route:

```
var start = i;
var limit = 0;
while( start != j )
{ var nextState = device.fsm[start][via[start][j]];
  document.write("Press "+device.buttons[via[start][j]]
      +" to get to "+device.stateNames[nextState]+"<br>");
  start = nextState;
  if( limit++ > n ) { document.write("?"); break; }
}
```

This code uses the variable `limit` to ensure that we don't try to solve an impossible task—in case it is called when the route has the impossible length ∞. Recall that no route in a finite state machine need take longer than the number of states; otherwise, it is going around in circles (it must visit some state twice) and therefore can't be a shortest route to anywhere.

The code in the last step above prints out the sequence of user actions a user needs to do to get a device from state i to state j. If we put that code inside a couple of loops to try all values of i and j we can find out how often each button is used. We could then design the device so that the most popular button (or buttons) are large and in the middle. Or we might discover that the popularity of buttons is surprising (some buttons may never be used on shortest paths, for instance), and then we'd want to look closer at the device design. Here's one way to do it:

```
var bcount = new Array(b); // an array with one element per button
for( var i = 0; i < b; i++ )
  bcount[i] = 0;
for( var i = 0; i < n; i++ )
 for( var j = 0; j < n; j++ )
  { var limit = 0, start = i;
    while( start != j )
    { var nextState = device.fsm[start][via[start][j]];
      bcount[via[start][j]]++; // count how often buttons are used
      start = nextState;
      if( limit++ > n ) break;
    }
  }
for( var i = 0; i < b; i++ )
  document.write(device.buttons[i]+" rated "+bcount[i]+"<br>");
```

9.6.2   Characteristic path length

Now that we have worked out shortest paths, the characteristic path length is just a matter of finding their average. Here's how, printing the results in HTML:

```
var sum = 0, worst = 0;
for( var i = 0; i < n; i++ )
  for( var j = 0; j < n; j++ )
  { sum = sum+matrix[i][j];
    if( matrix[i][j] > worst )
      worst = matrix[i][j];
  }
document.write("Characteristic path length "+(sum/(n*n))+"<br>");
document.write("Worst case path length "+worst);
```

For our microwave oven example, the characteristic path length is 1.22, and the worst case is 3.

▷ The characteristic path length was introduced in section 8.9 (p. 264).

Since the microwave oven happens to have as many buttons as states, the characteristic path length could have been as low as 1, with a worst case of 1 too. Perhaps the designer should take a closer look to see whether the extra effort for the user is justified by greater clarity or other factors.

9.6.3 Eccentricity

The eccentricity of a state measures the cost of the *worst possible* thing you could try in that state, that is, getting to the most distant state you could get to from that state.

In graph theory terms, the eccentricity of a vertex is the maximum distance it has to any other vertex. The diameter and radius of a graph are then defined as the largest and smallest, respectively, of the vertex eccentricities. Here's how to find out all the information:

```
var radius = infinity, diameter = 0;
for( var i = 0; i < n; i++ )
{ var eccentricity = 0;
  for( var j = 0; j < n; j++ )
    if( matrix[i][j] > eccentricity )
      eccentricity = matrix[i][j];
  document.write("<b>"+d.stateNames[i]
      +"</b> eccentricity is "+eccentricity+"<br>");
  if( eccentricity > diameter )
    diameter = eccentricity;
  if( eccentricity < radius )
    radius = eccentricity;
}
document.write("Diameter (worst eccentricity) = "+diameter+"<br>");
document.write(" Radius (least eccentricity) = "+radius+"<br>");
```

The designer will be especially interested in any states that have a very high or a very low eccentricity; the extreme values might indicate an oversight, or, of course, they may be intentional—sometimes a designer *wants* to make certain things hard to do.

For the microwave oven, it turns out that the diameter is 3, and the most eccentric states are Clock and Quick defrost, and in both cases the worst thing to try to do is to change to the state Power 2.

Clock is a state used for setting the clock, so you'd expect to have to get out of clock setting, start power setting, then set Power 2, so a shortest path to Power 2 of 3 doesn't sound unreasonable. If a user is doing a Quick defrost, they are not very likely to want to ramp up the power to its highest—it's easy to burn stuff on the outside but leave the middle frozen. So we have a no reason to worry about the two largest eccentricities.

9.6.4   Alternative and more realistic costs

We've described shortest paths as a way of finding the most efficient route, or path, from any state to any other. By "efficient" we meant using the least number of button presses, or user actions of some sort if they aren't button presses. It's time to find out whether we can be more accurate—and whether being more accurate helps us design better systems.

If buttons are close to each other, a human can operate them with one hand. If the buttons are several meters apart, then they will be much harder to use; in fact, if they need pressing simultaneously, two users might be needed or a user might have to put their feet on a bar and touch two distant buttons to guarantee their limbs are kept out the way of the dangerous machinery.

To be more realistic, we should include more information in the design framework about the device, such as button and indicator sizes and positions. Secondly, we should get some data from real people about how they perform with different representations of devices.

Instead of measuring how long users take, which requires an experiment, it is possible to estimate how long they take from theory. For each action on a push-button device, the user has to do three things: decide which button to press, move their fingers to get to the button, and then press the button. The Hick-Hyman law says roughly how long a user will take to decide which button to press: the time is $a + b \log(N + 1)$, where N is the number of choices the user has to decide between—here, it will be the number of buttons. The Fitts law says how quickly the user can move to hit the button, depending on the distance to move and how large the target button is: the time for a movement is $c + d \log(D/W + 1)$, where D is the distance to move and W the width of the button measured in the direction the finger is moving. If the device has tiny buttons, then you must also take account of the size of the user's fingers.

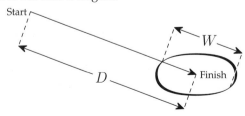

> **Box 9.1 Facilities layout** Most problems have appeared under different but more-or-less equivalent guises before. Improving the design of interactive devices by looking at shortest paths and user data is "the same" as the facilities layout problem. You have some facilities, like workstations in a factory, and you want to minimize the cost of people carrying stuff around the factory.
>
> How people can move stuff around the factory is a graph. You collect data on where people go and how often, you work out the shortest paths, and you then move the facilities around to reduce the overall costs of moving things. This problem is very well studied; it is estimated that about 10% of a nation's industrial effort goes not into just moving stuff around, but into rearranging facilities or building new ones to move stuff around!
>
> It's the same problem as deciding where to put interesting states in a state machine, or deciding where to put interesting pages in a web site, if you know shortest paths and have some usage data. It turns out that finding a solution to the problem is NP-hard, which is just a fancy way of saying nobody knows a good way of solving the problem.
>
> It's nice to know that re-designing an optimal web site, or re-designing an optimal device, based on user data is NP-hard, for this is effectively saying it's a very hard job, however you do it. On the other hand, since the problem is so hard, if you do not use a systematic way of re-design—using one of the standard algorithms for solving the problem—then it is very unlikely to be much of an improvement.

The constants a, b, c, d are usually found from experiment, and depend on the users, their age, fitness, posture, and so on.* The total time to do anything is the sum of these two laws for each user action required. Whatever the exact values, we can immediately see that there are some generic things that can be done to speed things up. We could:

- Make buttons larger, so W is larger.

- Make buttons closer, so D is smaller.

- Reorganize buttons into a better layout, to reduce average distances.

  ▷ See box 9.2 (p. 310) for an example of this idea.

- We could reduce N, for instance by illuminating only active buttons, or we could use a dynamic approach to showing buttons, say using a touch screen that reconfigures itself. However, if the screen changes, although N is reduced, we would find that the "constants" increase, as the user has a harder job to decide which button to press—they cannot learn a fixed layout.

  ▷ Illuminating active buttons is discussed in section 11.3.1 (p. 383).

- On devices with touch-sensitive screens that show buttons, we can change the size of buttons depending on what state the device is in. For example, making

---

* Often these laws are given differently, using logarithms to base 2. Since the constants are experimentally determined it does not matter what logs are used.

the buttons that are used at the beginning of any sequence of user actions larger will help the user notice them (as if they are lit up).

■ We could change the constants by "modifying" the user rather than the device: we could train the user to be faster, or we could select users who were good at our tasks.

■ We don't always design by minimizing costs; we could try to increase costs instead. If the user is using a gambling machine, we may want the users to spend as long as possible losing money. Or, although we know that hitting the big red [EMERGENCY OFF] button switches a device off immediately, it may not be the best way of switching it off normally; we should make its cost higher, for instance putting it under a protective cover.

Programming Fitts Law times

The design framework could be extended to allow designers to edit the look and feel of a device in a drawing program. As the graphic designer moves and changes the sizes of buttons, they would get continuous feedback from the design framework analyzing its performance. Such ideas would take us beyond the scope of this book, but we'll explain how to get the framework to use Fitts Law (or any other formula) to estimate how long a user takes to do tasks. To do this, we need to extend the framework with details about where buttons are and what sizes they are. For simplicity, we'll assume all buttons are circles of radius r and they are on a flat surface.

If `buttonLocation` is an array of (x, y) coordinates, the following function called `Fitts`, converts the distances between buttons into the time, in seconds, Fitts Law says it will take a user. Fitts Law doesn't need to know the units of measurement, but the radius and (x, y) coordinates must be given in the same units. (Which just shows Fitts Law is an approximation: if the distances are huge, then Fitts Law will underestimate the times.)

The following code uses constants typical of typewriter keyboard speeds:

```
function Fitts(b, c) // time taken moving between buttons
{ var dx = device.buttonLocation[b].x-device.buttonLocation[c].x;
  var dy = device.buttonLocation[b].y-device.buttonLocation[c].y;
  var d = Math.sqrt(dx*dx+dy*dy); // distance to move
  if( d < r || b == c ) return 0.14; // a double tap
  return 0.16+0.07*Math.log(d/device.r+1); // index finger
}
```

The code shows Fitts Law numbers estimated for index-finger movement; use `0.18+0.09*Math.log(d/device.r+1)` for slower thumb movement.

If we are not sure what constants to use the function `Fitts` can be modified to return `Math.log(d/device.r+1)/Math.log(2)`, and it will then be returning the index of difficulty (IOD), which is a number representing how hard something is to do, without regard for the exact timing.[*] Then the algorithm will then return not

---

[*] The index of difficulty is properly measured in bits, and hence needs $\log_2$.

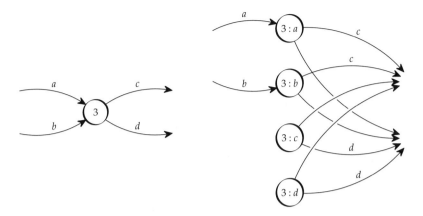

Figure 9.4: How a single-state (state 3, left) with two transitions to it (a and b) would be replaced with four states (right), each "remembering" the original state's different ways of getting to it. Now the transitions "know" how the user's finger has moved: for example, transition c from state $3 : a$ required the user to move their finger from button a to button c. In this example, two of the new states ($3 : b, 3 : c$) are unnecessary as there is no way to enter them. (For clarity, the righthand diagram does not show all transition labels, and states $3 : a$ and $3 : b$ will also have more transitions to them than are shown.)

best times, but best measurements of the index of difficulty, depending on button layout and the device interaction programming.

We can't reuse the shortest paths algorithm directly because the time it takes a user to get from one state to another depends on what the user was doing *before* they got to the first state. How long it takes to get from state to state depends on the distance the user's finger moves. Pressing button (A), say, got the device into state 2, then the user moved their finger from (A) to press (B) to get the device to the next state. The shortest path algorithm assumes each action (arc) has a fixed cost—but to use Fitts law we need to know which button the user pressed to get the device to the first state: for instance, the physical distance (A) to (B), if (A) got us to state 2, or the physical distance (C) to (B), if (C) got us to state 2. Somehow the states need to know which button the user pressed to get there.

Suppose the device has got B buttons and N states. We create a new "device" with B states for each of the original device's states. Give the new states names like $s : b$, so that in the new device the state $s : b_0$ represents entering the original device's state s by pressing button b_0—thus we have states that record how the user got to them. If on the old device pressing button b_1 went from state s to state t, then on the new device state $s : b_0$ will go to state $t : b_1$. This transition will take time according to the Fitts Law to move the finger from the location of b_0 to the location of b_1, and we now have enough details to work the timings out.

To program this in JavaScript, we give the state we've called $s : b$ the unique number $sB + b$. The code starts by creating a table of all weights for all the new state transitions, first initializing them to ∞:

```
var w = new Array(NB);
for( var i = 0; i < NB; i++ )
{ w[i] = new Array(NB);
  for( var j = 0; j < NB; j++ )
    w[i][j] = infinity; // default is no transition
}
```

Then we construct the new "device":

```
for( var i = 0; i < N; i++ )
  for( var b = 0; b < B; b++ )
  { var u = device.fsm[i][b]; // b takes us from i to u=fsm[i][b]
    for( var c = 0; c < B; c++ )
      // we've just pressed b, now we press c
      // pressing c takes us from u to fsm[u][c]
      w[u*B+b][device.fsm[u][c]*B+c] = Fitts(b, c);
  }
```

We can now use the familiar Floyd-Warshall algorithm to find fastest paths. This part of the code works exactly as before—though for simplicity here we are not recording the actual paths taken.

```
for( var k = 0; k < NB; k++ )
  for( var i = 0; i < NB; i++ )
    for( var j = 0; j < NB; j++ )
      if( w[i][k]+w[k][j] < w[i][j] )
        w[i][j] = w[i][k]+w[k][j];
```

▷   The Floyd-Warshall algorithm was introduced in section 9.6 (p. 299).

We've found fastest paths but paths in the *new* "device." We need to translate back to the original device: that is, all states $s : b$ need to be called s whatever button got there. We create a new table v for the results:

```
var v = new Array(N);
for( var i = 0; i < N; i++ )
{ v[i] = new Array(N);
  for( var j = 0; j < N; j++ )
    v[i][j] = infinity;
}
for( j = 0; j < NB; j++ )
  for( k = 0; k < NB; k++ )
    if( v[Math.floor(j/B)][Math.floor(k/B)] > w[j][k] )
      v[Math.floor(j/B)][Math.floor(k/B)] = w[j][k];
```

We now have a table with entries v[i][j] that gives the best time in seconds it takes a user to get from state i to state j. Note that the timing is only useful for pushbutton devices; common devices like cameras, with knobs and sliders, will require slightly different treatment than the "raw" Fitts Law. Devices like the

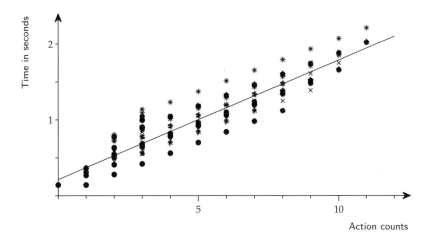

Figure 9.5: A plot of Fitts Law timings (vertically) against button press or action counts (horizontally) for all possible state changes on the PVR used in section 10.3. Button counts are closely proportional to user times.

Points close enough to overlap are rotated, like × ✳ ✹ ● ▪ ⋯ ● —the more points at the same coordinates, the darker the blob. The graph also shows a best-fit line 0.21+0.16x.

radio—section 3.10 (p. 80)—require the user to spend a significant time interpreting the display, and Fitts Law does not consider that either. If your device takes many button presses to change states, Fitts Law will become inaccurate as it increasingly under-estimates times, ignoring the user checking the device feedback and thinking.

In figure 9.5 (this page), I've used the program code and shown Fitts Law timings plotted against button counts to do the same tasks. As can be seen, the timings and counts are closely related (at least for this device), so button press counts—which the basic shortest paths algorithm gives directly—will be sufficiently accurate for most interaction programming design issues (in fact, as accurate as you could expect from either experiments or from Fitts Law alone). However, if you wish to design button layouts, the plot also shows us that user timings can vary by a factor of two or more simply because of the time taken for finger movement; for button layout, then, Fitts Law can be very helpful.

Familiarity

Another useful cost we can explore is familiarity. There are many ways to represent familiarity, but suppose we keep a matrix inside the interactive device, initially with the one-step costs: 1 if a transition is possible, 0 if it is not possible. Now, every time the user does something, the corresponding transition "cost" is

---

Box 9.2 Button usage Finding the absolutely best layout of buttons is hard, especially all possible button positions are considered in all possible layouts (rectangles, circles, hexagons ...). It may be just as useful to find out which are the most used buttons. A model of the JVC HRD580EK PVR suggests that buttons are used very differently:

Button press or action	Relative use on shortest paths		Button press or action	Relative use on shortest paths	
Record	67.36%	(1876)	Operate	2.87%	(80)
Stop/Eject	15.44%	(430)	Forward	1.94%	(54)
Pause	8.58%	(239)	Rewind	1.94%	(54)
Play	5.03%	(140)	insert tape	1.87%	(52)

The Record seems to be used excessively: it has too many uses in this design—surely, there aren't that many ways of recording? Thus, some of its uses might be reconsidered and handed over to another, possibly new, button. Or, if we do not change the meaning of the button (which would change the figures in the table), it should be physically positioned in the centre of the buttons, to reduce hand or finger movement times.

Inserting a tape is used 1.87% of the time, which also seems high—surely there is only one thing inserting a tape should do? As it happens, on the JVC PVR, inserting a tape *also* switches the PVR on if it is off, so inserting a tape is faster than switching on, then inserting a tape. Again, analysis questions a user action possibly having too many uses.

▷   The JVC HRD580EK PVR is used in section 10.3 (p. 330). The path length data is illustrated in a bar chart in figure 11.4 (p. 381).

---

incremented. The matrix counts how often a user does something; we can assume counts indicate how familiar the user is with each action. Now maximum cost paths indicate paths that the user would tend to take themselves. We can find solutions that are not fastest but—we hope—are most familiar. Alternatively, we might want to train the user to be proficient in all ways of using a device; then we would want to recommend they learn and do things they are *not* familiar with.

If the user was a pilot, nurse, or fireman, then they might be required to be familiar with *every* operation of the device; the ideas here then allow the framework to tell them what they have missed or not yet done enough of. Perhaps their professional license requires them to do a certain sort of procedure every year or so; if so, we can check, and tell them what they have missed.

These ideas give advice depending on what users do. Instead, we could fill the cost matrix with how experts think the device should be used. In this case, the shortest paths will automatically give expert advice.

▷   More uses of costs to use in products (rather than just for the designer to analyze) are discussed in section 10.7 (p. 351), particularly 10.7.5 (p. 358), and 11.5 (p. 392).

9.6.5 Task/action mapping

The shortest paths program finds paths between states. Unfortunately, the user is not interested in states as such; states are abstract things inside the device. The device can do what it likes, as it were, but the user is interested in achieving things in the world. More specifically, the user has goals, and they want to undertake tasks to achieve their goals.

Of course, this is a gross simplification; a user's goal might be to have fun and there may be no specific task associated with that experience. But for a great many cases, the user will have goals—such as getting a device they are using to do something important for them—and their task then amounts to doing the actions that get the device to actually be in the right state to have done whatever they wanted.

The general question is to find the best way of getting from the set of states the device may be in (they need not know specifically) to the set of states that achieve the goal the user wants to achieve (they may not know these specifically either). The user's goal may further require that certain intermediate states are visited. For example, a user might want to get a CD player from any state (however it was last left) to playing a track on a new CD. What should they do?

The standard term for doing this is called solving the task/action mapping problem. Given the task (or the goal that ends the task), how do we map that into the actions the user should do?

What the user should do is spelled out by the program; what the program should do and how it works is our present interest. Clearly, there are as many solutions to the programming problem as there are different sorts of user problems that we might want to handle. The best way of starting is to introduce indicators to the device framework, which indicate things the user is particularly interested in. Indicators, then, represent sets of states. For example, a device can be off in several ways—with a CD in it or no CD in it, say—but the user knows it is off. We can then have an indicator off, to represent the set of (in this case) two off states.

Users then specify their goals in terms of changes to indicator settings. The previous task we described is simply to go from (any state) indicating off to (any state, preferably the nearest) indicating play.

> ▷ Details of how to do this sort of thing are given in section 10.7 (p. 351), where we will examine how to solve problems for microwave oven tasks and video recorder tasks. Indicators are introduced in section 8.1.3 (p. 232); see also section 10.3.2 (p. 334).

Once we have some program code to solve user problems, it can be used in four quite different ways:

- For the user, as we already know, it can solve *particular* problems.

- For the designer, it can solve *every* user problem and then generate statistics, such as the average and worst-case costs for the user.

- For the technical author (or the designer), who writes user manuals and perhaps interactive help for users, it allows them to review all sensible solutions to problems so they can be written up accurately.

▷ User manuals can be generated with automatic help; see section 11.5 (p. 392).

■ The fourth point of view is the most interesting: how hard is it for us to work out how to write a program to solve the user's task/action mapping problems? The harder it is for us to solve the problem, then certainly the harder it will be for users (who know less about the device than we do). We may find that our programs need hints; if so, so will the users.

In some cases, we may find that the task/action mapping problem is very hard to solve (it might take exponential time to solve, or worse); then we really need to redesign the device—because if a problem is theoretically that hard, the user *must* find it hard too.

▷ The key importance of the designer getting insight into the difficulty (or ease) of the user solving problems is part of the computer science analogy, which we introduced in section 5.7 (p. 157).

9.7 Professional programming

Our style of defining a device is very simple, so there are inevitably more "professional" ways of doing it. This chapter is not about how to program. I want you to know, rather, what is possible and easy to do—and the automatic benefits of being simple and systematic. If we had used a more sophisticated way of programming in this book, we could certainly handle much larger device specifications more easily and more reliably, but then too much text would have been taken up with explaining sophisticated programming ideas; we would have lost the simplicity at the core of the approach.

Here are some suggestions for improving the framework, depending on what you want to do:

■ With lots of states, keeping track of the differences becomes impractical, but to fill in most array fields in `device` you have to be aware which state is which. Instead, a single state field should be an array of objects. Thus each state says what its name is, and what its user manual text is. Instead of writing,

```
var device = {
  ...
  stateNames: ["dim", "off", "on"],
  fsm: [[1, 2, 0], [1, 2, 0], [1, 2, 0]],
  ...
  manual: ["dim", "dark", "bright"],
  ...
};
```

you would write more like this (shown on the next page):

```
var device = {
  ...
  states:
  [{name: "dim", fsm: [1, 2, 0], manual: "dim"},
   {name: "off", fsm: [1, 2, 0], manual: "dark"},
   {name: "on",  fsm: [1, 2, 0], manual: "bright"}],
  ...
};
```

This way of coding brings everything in each state much close together and therefore helps you get the correspondences right. If you know JavaScript, you can use object constructors rather than repeatedly writing out name, fsm, and manual.

■ The finite state machine field, fsm, is defined using state numbers, and it is sometimes too easy to mix up state numbers. Instead, every reference to a state should be to its name. If you want to do this, you will probably want to preprocess the device to build an internal specification that uses numbers (because they are much more efficient when the device is running).

▷ Section 9.5 (p. 288) gives other ideas for preprocessing the device specification to improve its quality.

■ Strings are readable and make a device specification very clear, which is why we're using them a lot in this chapter. But, what happens if you mistype a string? The device would misbehave. If you are using a typed language like Java, there are many better approaches. You could have a state constructor, say,

```
State sOff = new state("off", "dark");
```

The advantage is that Java will only let you use sOff where you need a state, and you can only use states in those places. You could not get a button and a state confused. (Here you'd need to add actions to each state separately, say, sOff.addAction(button, nextstate).)

■ If you spend another half hour or so programming, you will be able to generate code to work on hardware (or Java, or whatever) from the JavaScript framework we're using, and you will then be able to get the real device to work straight from the framework.

■ It is easy to add special-purpose features to the framework, but we won't dwell on them in this book. For example, the framework can be extended to be a pushdown automaton in which each user action stores the last state in a stack (in JavaScript, it would be an array, using the methods push and pop). The [Undo] button is then programmed to pop the stack and restore the last state.

▷ Section 10.8 (p. 362) suggests how to implement consistent user interfaces by using program code to define interaction features.

313

■ Our framework has finite state machines as explicit data structures. It's tedious writing down finite state machines like this—every bit as tedious as drawing state transition diagrams. Just as statecharts improve the visualization of state machines, there are many programming language approaches (including SCXML, the XML statechart notation) that improve the clarity of finite state machine specifications.

▷ You can use JavaScript as a specification language to build the finite state machine directly; we show how in section 9.8 (p. 316). We discuss more general approaches to design tools in section 12.6 (p. 428). For other ideas extending the framework see section 9.5.2 (p. 295).

9.7.1   Going further: JSON

Our framework is written in JavaScript, which may give the impression that it is not as serious as, say, a framework written in Java or C++. In fact, our framework will work in many other languages *directly*, and therefore is as serious as any other approach. JavaScript has inspired the JavaScript object notation, JSON, which uses what is essentially JavaScript notation to define objects in a portable way that can be used in a very wide variety of languages, including ActionScript, C, C++, C#, Lisp, Haskell, Java, JavaScript (of course), Perl, PHP, Python, Ruby, and Tcl/Tk.

JSON is exactly our framework notation, except that JSON's field names have to be written in quote marks—although most JSON systems don't worry unless the field names need funny characters (and none of ours do). So when we wrote definitions of devices like {fsm: [[0,1],[1,1]] ...}, all we need to do is change them to {"fsm":   [[0,1],[1,1]] ...} and they are then proper, strict JSON.

If you want to program using our framework in Java, get hold of the Java-JSON package, use it to read in the JSON notation, then you have objects in Java that you can use exactly as we have been doing in this book.

▷ You can get more details from www.json.org

9.7.2   Going further: Phidgets

Our framework works nicely in web browsers on any platform, which is an advantage of using JavaScript, but you might want to build *real* systems, not on-screen devices restricted to a web browser style of interaction.

Phidgets are a very nice way to get into programming hardware. Phidgets are so-called because they are the physical equivalent of on-screen widgets—buttons, text fields and so on.

Phidgets allow you to build user interfaces using LCD displays, LED indicators, buttons, knobs, sliders, touch sensors, RFID tags, motors and so on—as well as relays, so you can control real systems. The touch sensors can be placed behind paper you have printed with button designs or controller layouts, so you can get realistic prototype designs to work very easily.

Figure 9.6: A Phidget, connected to a USB port on a PC, simulating a device display.

Phidgets use USB interfaces and are well supported. So, for example, you could use JSON to get our framework into ActionScript, C or Java, then use the Phidget libraries provided for these languages to run the hardware. Figure 9.6 (this page) shows a simple user interface built out of Phidgets, running a syringe pump user interface written using this book's framework.

▷ You can get more details from www.phidgets.com

9.7.3 Going further: web sites, XML and so on

In our framework, a state is "just" a name. We can add more attributes to states, such as manual sections, images, indicators, and so on indefinitely, but each extension makes the framework more complex. A neater and more general extension is to make states themselves HTML or XML pages (the state names could be URLs). Now a state can not only display different images and text, but a state can have internal programmed activities as well—anything an HTML page can do, even be another interaction framework. In fact, we have obtained a hierarchical FSM; where the states at one level are FSMs in their own right at the next lower level.

For example, one state might allow the user to enter numbers for, say, selecting a CD track or dialing a phone number, but at the higher level of the FSM, these are details that are abstracted away. Thus we get the advantages of a nice, clean FSM, as well as the advantages of arbitrary programming—or even nested FSMs—that can do anything in any state.

If you wish to build hierarchical FSMs like this in Java/C++/C#, there are many ways of rendering sub-FSMs; if you continue using JavaScript, you can most easily use HTML frames to maintain and carry the simulated device's state variables (like the selected CD track number) from one sub-page to another.

9.8   Generating device specifications

A problem with our framework is that device designs look like so-much JavaScript and numbers. To designers, interactive devices just don't *look* like that! We need more conceptual ways of representing devices that are easier to think about.

How can we go from conceptual designs to a table of numbers that represents a finite state machine? For very simple devices, such as this book has space to cover, we can construct the framework by hand, and then check it. But for large devices, we have a problem.

Either you need to use a design tool that generates framework specifications (and there aren't any yet) or you could use whatever approach you've always used but add program code that generates data that can input to our framework. For example, you might build a conventional device in Java or C++, and write in it calls to generate framework data, perhaps in JSON. This way, you get the benefits of your usual approach *plus* all the analysis and benefits our framework provides. You might consider translating the code in this book so that the framework's benefits can be obtained within the same program; there's no need to use JavaScript.

Another way is to write a program to construct the finite state machine. Now, you can use the high-level features of your programming language to specify the *structure* of the interaction programming.

Figure 9.7 (facing page) shows an electric drill, which is a very simple FSM, but with an interesting structure. The drill has 8 user actions, twisting knobs, pressing buttons—not counting "indirect" actions such as removing the battery or letting it go flat. The finger trigger controls the drill motor. On the assumption that we are interested in examining how the drill behaves at T different speeds, we need to model T different trigger positions. The drill then has $216T$ possible states—the 216 comes from the combinations of knobs and buttons. However, some states are disallowed by the physical construction of the drill: for instance, when it is locked off, the trigger must be out and the drill cannot be running. More accurately, then, there are $144T + 72$ possible states. In our program below, we will take $T = 2$, that is, we will only distinguish between the drill running or not running, not the exact speed it is running at.

With $T = 2$, the drill model has 360 states. In one state, for instance, it can be running clockwise in second gear in hammer mode. There are 8 different actions—increasing the clutch, decreasing the selected gear, and so on—so the drill could have $360 \times 8 = 2,880$ transitions. In fact it only has $1,746$ transitions. The "missing" transitions are impossible because of physical constraints in the design. For

Figure 9.7: An unusual device to consider as an interactive device, but a finite state machine nevertheless, with 360 states—more if we distinguish the motor running at various speeds. The device can be specified using a statechart or program—see figure 9.8 (p. 319) for the statechart and section 9.8 for the program.

example, you can only change direction from clockwise to anti-clockwise if the motor is not running.

The best way to define this device in the framework is to write a program that provides the details. It would be far too tedious and error-prone to write out everything by hand. Every physical constraint will appear in the program as an explicit test.

Interestingly, the user manual for the drill (a DeWalt DC925) only mentions one of the constraints—it says you must not change gear while the motor is running. Trying to specify this device as a FSM therefore highlights a possible design issue: should the gears be improved so that nothing need be said in the user manual? Would it be a better tool if the gears were modified? It would certainly be easier to use, and with a reduced risk to the user of wrecking the gearbox, which the manual currently warns about. So, even without doing any analysis with the framework, the *discipline* of being explicit about the interaction design of the device has raised a design issue.

What follows is one way to program it in JavaScript. First we need state numbers for every possible state the drill can be in. The drill allows the user to set the gear, the clutch, and so on, to various settings:

```
var clutchSteps = 24, directionSteps = 3,
    gearSteps = 3,    triggerSteps = 2;

// all values are numbered from zero
// e.g., the program uses 0,1,2 for the drill's gears 1,2,3
```

```
function conceptualState(trigger, clutch, gear, direction)
{ return trigger+triggerSteps*(clutch+clutchSteps*
                                (gear+gearSteps*direction));
}
```

Given some user settings, for example that the clutch is in position 3, we use `conceptualState` to generate the state number, which will be a number from 0 to 431. We allow for 432 states because, so far in the programming, we are not worrying about the physical constraints that disallow some user actions in certain states.

In our framework, each state needs a name and we can generate these automatically:

```
function stateName(t, c, g, d)
{ var n;
  n = t == 1? "running ": d == 1? "": "stopped ";
  n += d == 0? "reverse, ": d == 1? "locked ": "forwards, ";
  if( c == clutchSteps-1 ) n += "hammer mode";
  else if( c == clutchSteps-2 ) n += "drill mode";
  else n += "clutch set to "+(c+1);
  n += ", gears set to "+(g+1);
  return n;
}
```

This function converts the numbers that describe the state to a string. For example, c is the clutch position; the code treats the clutch as a number 0 to 23, modeling the position of the twist control on the drill, which has 24 positions (there are 22 different strengths of screwdriving, a drilling mode, and a hammer drilling mode). Calling `stateName(1, 4, 2, 2)` generates the string "running forwards, clutch set to 5, gears set to 3"—a good state to do some screwdriving. The function doesn't ever say "stopped locked" but just "locked" as it is obvious that when it's locked it's also stopped.

To test the code on *all* states, it can be put inside nested for loops to try it in all possible states. As we shall need nested for loops running over all the drill's states several times, we write a function to make them easier to manage:

```
function every(doThis)
{ for( var t = 0; t < triggerSteps; t++ )
    for( var c = 0; c < clutchSteps; c++ )
      for( var g = 0; g < gearSteps; g++ )
        for( var d = 0; d < directionSteps; d++ )
          doThis(t, c, g, d);
}
```

At this point, we can test the state names work by the following code, which defines a test function and calls it for all combinations of settings:

```
function test(t, c, g, d)
{ document.write(stateName(t, c, g, d)+"<br>");
}

every(test);
```

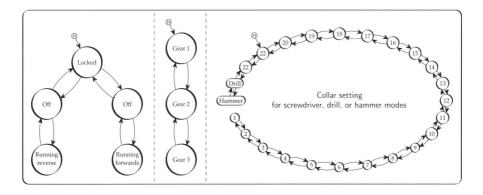

Figure 9.8: A statechart description of the DC925 drill shown in figure 9.7 (p. 317). Unusually, this device has no self-loops—if the user can physically do an action, the device changes state. In contrast, pushbuttons on most devices can be pressed even when they do nothing, which creates self-loops in their FSM model.

Amongst the mass of output this generates, it will print "running locked" a few times, which is a combination that ought to be impossible! You can't press the trigger in to get it to run when the direction slider is in the central, locked, position. We obviously still have more programming to do.

Next, for all possible user actions in any state, we need to work out what transitions are possible:

```
function action(t, c, g, d)
{ transition(t, c, g, d, "trigger in", t+1, c, g, d);
  transition(t, c, g, d, "trigger out", t-1, c, g, d);
  transition(t, c, g, d, "clutch increase", t, c+1, g, d);
  transition(t, c, g, d, "clutch decrease", t, c-1, g, d);
  transition(t, c, g, d, "gear up", t, c, g+1, d);
  transition(t, c, g, d, "gear down", t, c, g-1, d);
  transition(t, c, g, d, "direction +", t, c, g, d+1);
  transition(t, c, g, d, "direction -", t, c, g, d-1);
}
```

This function is saying, for all of the features on the drill, things like "if the current state is t, c, g, d then we could increase the clutch setting by 1, and if we did, it would be in state $t, c + 1, g, d$." If we wrote every(action) this would generate calls to the function transition for *every possible* thing that could be done in *every possible* state. Unfortunately, not all the states and not all actions are actually possible. For example, if the drill is locked, the trigger cannot be pressed in to make it run; and if the drill is set to gear 2, we can't increase the gear to 3, because there are only three gears (gears are numbered 0, 1, 2, even though the drill itself calls them 1, 2, 3). We need to program a check on the drill's constraints:

319

```
function allow(t, c, g, d)
{ if( t < 0 || t >= triggerSteps ) return false;
  if( c < 0 || c >= clutchSteps ) return false;
  if( g < 0 || g >= gearSteps ) return false;
  if( d < 0 || d >= directionSteps ) return false;
  if( d == 1 && t != 0 ) return false;
  return true;
}
```

The important point is that this function and `transition`, discussed below, capture *all* the device's constraints in one place. The complex constraints are captured in a clear programmatic way. For example, the last test in the code above, `if( d == 1 && t != 0 ) return false` effectively says, "if the drill is locked, then the trigger must be out and the motor off."

Writing the code prompted me to think more about the drill's constraints: have I written accurate code for this book? It turns out that you can stall the drill if you try hammer drilling with the motor in reverse and simultaneously apply some pressure. This could happen if you are drilling, for instance, reinforced concrete and wish to free a drill bit that has got stuck—if you reverse the drill but leave it in hammer mode, the drill itself may get jammed. It must be an oversight that this case is not mentioned in the user manual. The extra code needed to express this constraint in the function `allow` is `if( d == 0 && t == 1 && c == clutchSteps-1 ) return false`, or in words, "if in reverse, and the trigger is pushed in, and the clutch is set to hammer, then disallow this state."

Our framework requires consecutive state numbers $0, 1, 2, 3\ldots$ with no gaps, so if some states are not allowed we need a way of mapping conceptual state numbers to real state numbers, skipping the states that are not allowed. The easiest approach is to construct a map as a JavaScript array:

```
var map = new Array(triggerSteps*clutchSteps*gearSteps*directionSteps);
```

```
var n = 0;
function makeMap(t, c, g, d)
{ if( allow(t, c, g, d) )
    map[conceptualState(t, c, g, d)] = n++;
}
```

```
every(makeMap);
```

After running this code, `map[s]` gives us a number 0 to 359 of allowed state numbers, provided that s is an allowed state from the original 432 conceptual states; otherwise `map` is undefined.

Recall that the framework requires each state to be named. Here's how the map can be used to name the real states: if a conceptual state is allowed, map the state number to a real state number, then give it its state name. As before, we generate the state name from the combination of gears, clutch settings and so on, using the function `stateName` we've already defined. Notice we use `every` to conveniently run over all possible states.

```
drill.stateNames = new Array(n);
function nameEachState(t, c, g, d)
{ if( allow(t, c, g, d) )
    drill.stateNames[map[conceptualState(t, c, g, d)]] =
        stateName(t, c, g, d);
}
```

```
every(nameEachState);
```

To complete the framework FSM, we must make sure all the user's state transitions are allowed; that means both the state we are coming from t0... and the state we are going to t1... are allowed. For the drill, if both states are allowed, the transition between them is always allowed. More complex devices would need further programming to allow for more complex conditions on what transitions are allowed—for example, although the drill allows us to change gear when it is running, the manual warns this is a bad idea because the gears may grind, and this constraint could be handled by writing ... && (t0 == 0 || g0 == g1)—meaning "trigger out (motor not running) or the gears aren't changed."

```
function transition(t0, c0, g0, d0, button, t1, c1, g1, d1)
{ if( allow(t0, c0, g0, d0) && allow(t1, c1, g1, d1) )
    drill.fsm[map[conceptualState(t0, c0, g0, d0)]][lookup(button)] =
        map[conceptualState(t1, c1, g1, d1)];
}
```

The details we haven't yet provided are for initializing the FSM and defining the function button, needed as a way of getting a button number from the button name.

```
drill.fsm = new Array(n);
for( var i = 0; i < n; i++ )
{ drill.fsm[i] = new Array(drill.buttons.length);
  // if you try an action, by default stay in the same state
  for( b = 0; b < drill.buttons.length; b++ )
    drill.fsm[i][b] = i;
}
```

```
function lookup(button)
{ for( var b = 0; b < drill.buttons.length; b++ )
    if( button == drill.buttons[b] )
      return b;
  alert("Button "+button+" isn't recognized!");
}
```

The alert in the function lookup will happen if we misspell a button name anywhere; it's a useful check.

Now we've finished the programming, calling every(action) will create the FSM we wanted. The FSM will have hundreds of rows like [346, 195, 352, 340, 346, 344, 346, 346], *but we need never look at them.* We should use the framework to analyze the drill's properties rather than looking directly at the raw data.

Generating a FSM might take a long time—especially in a slow language like JavaScript—but it only needs to be done once. It doesn't matter how complicated the functions like `every` and `allow` are; write them clearly, without worrying how inefficient they seem. The point is to make the device's interaction structure clear.

> ▷ Physical constraints are closely related to *affordance*, a topic covered in section 12.3 (p. 415).

9.9   Conclusions

This chapter has introduced and explored the benefits of programming interaction frameworks: general purpose programs that can run, simulate, or analyze any device. The advantage of a framework is that it can check and measure all sorts of useful properties—and it becomes worth doing so because we can compare and contrast different designs very easily. Without a framework, each device is a completely different programming problem, and it probably won't seem worth going to the trouble of writing high-quality program code to evaluate it.

In particular, this chapter developed a framework in JavaScript that readily allows a device to be specified, simulated, and analyzed. Professional programmers will perhaps want to redesign the framework for their favorite languages, and there is much to be gained by doing so.

We could develop the simple framework here into a full-blown design tool. There are many possibilities ... it's astounding that the user interfaces of most devices are so routine—even a simple framework helps designers become more certain in their processes, and in turn become more confidently creative.

9.9.1   Some *Press On* principles

■ Once there is a prototyping framework, changing or revising a device specification is easy and reliable → section 9.4 (p. 286).

■ A framework can check for many basic design errors—something that cannot be done when a system is written in a standard programming language → section 9.5 (p. 288).

■ Find all least cost paths through a device; any impossible paths should be justified carefully or fixed → section 9.6 (p. 301).

■ By programming user problems, the designer can get useful statistics and measurements about a device's overall behavior → section 9.6 (p. 311).

■ Technical authors should use automatic tools working with device specifications so they have reliable advice for users → section 9.6 (p. 311).

■ The harder it is for a designer or a programmer to solve task/action mappings, the harder it will be for the user; find a way to make it easier → section 9.6 (p. 312).

9.9.2 Further reading

Before starting any project, do an internet search and see whether somebody has solved your problems for you, or defined standards that you can take advantage of. There are many programs and libraries on the web you can start from more easily than working on your own.

■ Dot is an open source research project at AT&T. Full details of Dot can be found at www.research.att.com/sw/tools/graphviz. I used Pixelglow's award winning OSX implementation, GraphViz, to draw the graph earlier in this chapter.

■ Kaye, J., and Castillo, D., *Flash MX for Interactive Simulation*, Thomson, 2003. The authors professionally develop medical devices and training systems, and their book is the best book for programming in Flash. It gives many examples of device simulators and has more material on statecharts. Their techniques for building interactive systems can be copied into other languages.

■ MacKenzie, I. S., Motor Behavior Models for Human-Computer Interaction, in Carroll, J. M., ed., *HCI Models, Theories and Frameworks*, pp27–54, Morgan Kaufmann, 2003. Scott MacKenzie provides a very good discussion of Fitts Law and other models.

■ Sharp, J., *Interaction Design for Electronic Products Using Virtual Simulations*, PhD thesis, Brunel University, 1997. This thesis gives the definition of the microwave oven we used.

■ There are many programming tools and standards out there, from JavaHelp to XML. In particular, SVG is a standard for vector graphics, effectively an open source version of *Flash*.

MILES J. HART

10

Using the framework

Although our main interest is designing good interactive devices, we don't have to work with conventional interactive gadgets; things can be very different—from lightbulbs and microwave ovens to guns and fire extinguishers. Our first example is an old puzzle—we hope that user interfaces to gadgets won't be puzzles, unless they are supposed to be!

10.1 The farmer's problem

The farmer's problem is an imaginary problem set in a far-off land, where goats eat cabbages, rivers flow, and farmers work hard. Somehow, this farmer has got a wolf, goat and cabbage stranded on one side of the river and wants to get them across using the only boat they have—a flimsy canoe. If the farmer leaves the goat and cabbage together unsupervised, the goat will eat the cabbage; if the farmer leaves the wolf with the goat, of course the wolf will eat the goat. And for some reason, the canoe is only big enough for the farmer and one other thing. Presumably, if the farmer is rowing the canoe, keeping a wolf or goat under control is hard enough to do without having to stop the cabbage rolling away.

A farmer trying to get a cabbage, goat, and wolf across a river is really far too silly a story to believe! Possibly the craziness helps people remember it, but the story has the same structure as many other stories that are more plausible. The *structure* is the same as the story of the farmer with a hen, bag of chicken feed, and a dog—and a car instead of a canoe. When we explore the problem using a computer we are only interested in its structure and what we can learn about the structure of the problem, not whether we are dealing with hens or goats. As we shall see, we aren't at all interested in farming problems as such except that their structure can be analyzed in exactly the same way as the structure of interactive devices.

Like any interactive device, this problem has states, which correspond to various combinations of wolf, goat, cabbage, and farmer being on one side of the river or the other, and it has actions, which correspond to the canoe carrying things across the river. You could imagine making an interactive game that simulated the farmer's problem, and then the farmer's problem *would be* an interactive device.

To solve the problem requires two things: that the goat is never left alone with the cabbage, and for the wolf never to be left alone with the goat—in either case, something will get eaten! If the farmer is silly enough to leave the goat, wolf and cabbage alone on the same side of the river, then the wolf will wait until the goat has eaten the cabbage, thus becoming a fat goat, before eating it.

We first show this problem as a finite state diagram, with the states in a circle in no particular order:

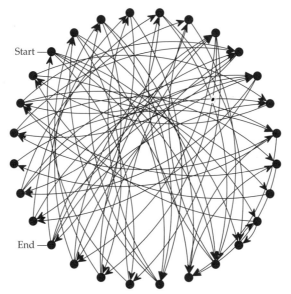

It's clearly got a lot more states than a lightbulb! In this diagram, the problem has effectively been changed into finding a route following arrows from one circle to another, starting at the circle labeled "Start" and going on to the finish of the puzzle at the state "End."

> ▷   I wrote a program to generate the farmer's graph, much like the program to
>   construct the drill in section 9.8 (p. 316). We don't need it here, but the
>   program is available on the book's web site, mitpress.mit.edu/presson.

Some, but not all, of the arrowed lines are one way: if you make a mistake, you cannot get back. This corresponds to something irreversible happening, like the wolf eating the goat if they are left alone with the farmer on the other bank of the river.

If the farmer canoes across the river (following an arrow in the diagram), that may create an opportunity for the goat to eat the cabbage or for the wolf to eat the goat. If so, it is a one-way trip. Although the farmer can canoe back to the other river bank, they can't get back to the state they left.

You could imagine a gadget with eight labeled lights on it, representing all combinations of the presence or absence of cabbage, goat, wolf, and farmer on either side of the river, and some buttons to choose what to take in the canoe. Thought of like this, the farmer's problem represents quite a hard-to-use interactive device. Thinking about the farmer's problem will help get us into useful ideas for interaction programming.

The farmer's problem is just like the problem users have with devices: users want to get devices into certain states that achieve their goals. The farmer wants to get their stuff to the other side of the river with nothing missing. For both users and farmers, the problem is to get from one state to another, usually in the fastest possible way. This is merely a matter of finding the right path through a finite state machine.

10.2 Strong connectivity

In a simple interactive device, a user can get from any state to any other state. Thus whatever state a lightbulb is in, we can always get to any other state. Whether it is off, on, or dim, we can always get it to be what we want without restriction. Once we know it is possible, we can then worry about whether it is easy enough to get from state to state; but first, designers should worry about whether it is possible to do anything in principle.

▷ A device that has the property that you can get anywhere from anywhere is called strongly connected. See section 8.6.1 (p. 244).

The farmer's problem makes an interesting problem primarily because it's *not* strongly connected. If the farmer makes a mistake solving the problem, you can't get back to a previous state (unless the farmer cheats). Some states cannot be reached from other states: for instance, once the wolf has eaten the goat, the farmer cannot go back to any states that represent the goat being alive. In particular, once any of these "error" states have been reached, the farmer cannot possibly reach the solution state, which requires both the cabbage and the goat to be available.

Even if a device is not strongly connected, there will usually be some states that, considered in isolation, are strongly connected. The simplest case is a state having an arrow to itself, in which case "getting anywhere from anywhere" is trivially true of that single state alone.

There may be two states that have arrows each way between them: these two states considered on their own would be strongly connected. Those two states may be connected to a third, which is connected back. In general, the largest such sets of states are called the strongly connected components. In a device that is strongly connected, there will be one strongly connected component, namely, the whole device.

▷ On strongly connected components and other sorts of graph components, see also section 8.6.4 (p. 249).

In an important sense, the strongly connected components are the "safe" parts of a device. As long as the user stays within a strongly connected component, they can do anything because they can always get back to whatever they were doing *within* that component.

It's possible that a device has no strongly connected components. A very simple example would be a sequence of states like $a \rightarrow b \rightarrow c \rightarrow d$. Here, we can get from a to b, and from b to c, and so on, but we can never get back to a, or indeed never back to any state once we've left it. This simple device is connected—if we start in the right places, we can get anywhere—but it isn't *strongly* connected—we can't get from anywhere to anywhere.

It would be very surprising if an interactive device was not connected—it would mean that the designer had thought of and specified states that the user could never get to—but there are times when it is useful for a device to be connected but not strongly connected (otherwise known as weakly connected), and this usually happens when the world in which the device operates can change. In the farmer's problem, cabbages can get eaten and that is one sort of change—because the farmer's problem is a game, the changes are merely "interesting," but we might want to study devices like a missile launching controller, or a burglar alarm (so far as a burglar is concerned, the device is connected—it can go from silent to alarmed—but it is not strongly connected—the burglar cannot get it back to silent once it has been triggered).

Now for some important points:

■ Strong connectivity and strongly connected components are important for usability.

■ There are standard algorithms to find connected components, though we won't use them in this book as it is unusual for an interactive device not to be strongly connected.

■ Neither users nor testing with users can establish such properties, because it is generally far too hard to do humanly.

   ▷   Other properties of interest to interaction programming are based on shortest paths, section 9.6 (p. 297); see also figure 8.1 (p. 232) in chapter 8, "Graphs," for a brief summary. Shortest paths efficiently determines whether a graph is strongly connected.

Given these points, designers have an obligation to do design analysis, and to use programs to do it for them—they can do it; users can't; and it's worth doing.

The farmer's problem (at least as we've represented it as a graph) has four strongly connected components—the strongly connected component with everything; one with just the cabbage eaten; one with the goat eaten; one with both cabbage and goat eaten. These are the components in the farmer's problem that you can get to, once there you can move around freely, but if you leave—something gets eaten—you can't get back. The trick to solve the problem is never to leave the original strongly connected component, which has everything in it and includes both the initial and the final states.

One strongly connected component is the cabbage and goat having both been eaten. This component contains everything that can be done by transporting the wolf with the farmer, or the farmer alone across the river, but from any of these states it isn't possible to go back to any state where the eaten cabbage or the eaten goat exists again. Below, we've summarized the four states of this strongly connected component, one state per line:

farmer	〰	wolf
	〰	farmer, wolf
wolf	〰	farmer
farmer, wolf	〰	

In this strongly connected component, two of the states are, in our technical terms, pointless since there is only one thing that can be done, just for the farmer to row across the river. When there is only one thing to do, we should consider designing pointless states out of the device—in fact, we could redesign this part of the device down to two states, depending on which side of the river we want the wolf. And then in each of those two states, there's now only one thing that can be done (in each state, we eliminated one of the two choices because it was pointless), so why do we still need them? And so on. In other words, identifying pointless states is an iterative process; the designer stops when a "pointless" state actually has some purpose for the user—or, as happens here, it becomes a terminal state.

In our usage, "pointless" is a technical term, which helps us critique design. But we should talk to the user—in this case the farmer—to see whether what we think is pointless is in fact so for them. Here, the farmer might like admiring the wolf from either side of the river, if so, we would need all the states and they wouldn't be pointless—that is, provided the farmer has some reason to need the states where there is only one choice. Indeed, once we start talking to the farmer, we might discover that *really* there are two choices in each state here: the farmer can stay or row across—we failed to consider the "choice" represented by the self-arrows.

▷ Pointless states are discussed in section 6.3.3 (p. 184).

10.2.1 Redesigning devices

The farmer's problem is tricky because sometimes cabbages or goats get eaten, and there is then no going back. In the transition diagram of the full problem, some paths are one way: if a canoe trip is taken that corresponds to one of these paths, it is a one-way trip in terms of the states that can be reached. If the cabbage gets eaten by the goat, states with cabbages are no longer accessible. If a PVR was often like this, it would be tedious to use! Of course, PVRs do this when you accidentally record over a favorite program.

We can write a program to automatically find the states that cannot be gotten out of, delete them, and hence make a simpler design where nothing can go wrong. The aim is to create "easy sets of states" that are all strongly connected, and allow the problem to be solved easily. This idea can be expressed in graph theory terms:

■ If the graph is strongly connected, we can stop—the graph does not have the problem we are trying to correct.

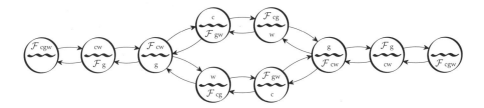

Figure 10.1: A subgraph of the farmer's problem, namely the strongly connected component containing the start and end states—all the possible states where nothing gets eaten. As usual, we have not shown the self-arrows.

■ Find the strongly connected components (preferably using some library routine).

■ If this strongly connected component does not include all states the user requires for their task, the graph has other flaws in it that need correcting.

Doing this will reduce interest in the farmer's problem as a puzzle, because it will make it trivial—but if the farmer's problem was an interactive device, we've turned it from a hard thing to something that is far easier to use.

The graph of the strongly connected component, shown in figure 10.1 (this page), for the farmer's problem has a pleasing, elegant structure, and we derived it from the full puzzle automatically. If we decide what criteria we want, we can redesign anything automatically.

▷   We will see this principle in action again, but with a PVR, in section 10.4.6 (p. 345).

The diagram in figure 10.1 (this page) was drawn automatically using the shortest path code developed in the framework: each state is drawn at a position corresponding to the length of its shortest path from the start state, and its vertical position is chosen simply to be different for all other positions in the same column. A little effort then centers the columns vertically along the row. The layout of the graph is called a ranked embedding, and it has the useful property that you can easily see how hard it is to get from the starting state to any other. Interestingly, for this puzzle, the ranked embedding directly shows that solving the problem, getting everything from one side of the river to the other, is in fact the hardest thing the user can possibly be asked to do.

▷   Programming shortest paths is discussed in section 9.6 (p. 297).

10.3   A recording device

After farming problems, let's return to conventional interactive devices. We will start with the JVC HR-D540EK. Video cassette recorders, VCRs, are (or almost are)

Box 10.1 Why personal video recorders? Why do I keep mentioning video recorders when everybody today uses DVDs or computers to watch and record their TV? I'm not just talking about video cassette recorders (VCRs), which were the original mass-market personal video recorders (PVRs). Or why does this book keep mentioning PVRs when the world is going to fill up with robots and implants?

Video recorders suddenly got more complicated in the late 1980s when their mechanical controls were replaced by embedded computer-based control. Suddenly the user interface became cheap, little rubber buttons, and the computers could "do anything." The designer lost all affordance that the mechanical constraints had imposed.

As anything could happen, anything did. The PVRs became more complex and more arbitrary from the user's point of view. The user population had a lot of conceptual catching up to do as the complexity initially overwhelmed them. Today not many people have problems (or at least problems they admit to) using video recorders: we are all using MP3 players, camera phones, PCs, and encounter complicated web sites everyday. That's how it is.

Even though my first personal video recorder (the JVC model discussed in several places in this book) has fewer than 30 main states, it still baffles me as a user. But more so it baffles me why its designers hadn't been able to structure its few states in a way that made it easier to use.

Today I don't think there is any immediate panacea: "this is how all PVRs (or whatever) should be designed." I think that analyzing their designs in the way this book promotes will give designers the tools to build what they really want to build; they'll be able to see how to optimize and modify their designs to better support users' tasks. And insights here are going to help design all those robots and implants—they'll still have states their users are baffled by, and probably far more than 30.

---

obsolete, but I've used this example for very good reasons: see box 10.1, "Why personal video recorders?" (this page). A VCR is just a gadget that can record and playback media; it could be an MP3 player, a DVD recorder, a computer, or anything yet to be invented—we are interested in the principles, not the specific product (but it helps to have a specific product in mind). The preferred term is PVR, short for personal video recorder—since we need an abbreviation that does not commit us to a particular technology.

▷ We mentioned this PVR in section 3.4 (p. 66), and section 5.4 (p. 145).

We first show this PVR state machine drawn as a circular graph. The advantage of using a circular drawing is that no two lines between different states can ever be drawn on top of each other (all lines must be at different angles), so we can be certain that we are looking at everything (unless in some states more than one button does the same thing, then their lines would be coincident). It helps to write the names of the states too, but there are so many that the drawing gets quite messy!

Even though the circular diagram in figure 10.2 (next page) is messy—and we haven't put the states in a useful order around the perimeter of the circle—you can see little design facts like the two states "on with tape in" and "off with tape in" seem very easy to get to from almost anywhere—you can clearly see the cluster of arrow heads hitting each of these states from almost every other state.

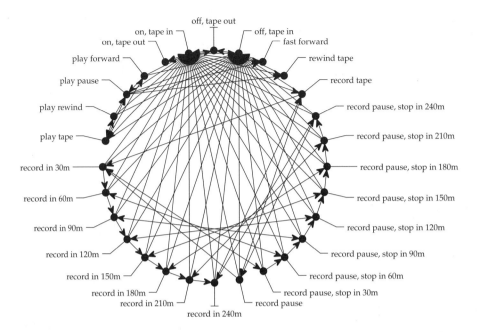

Figure 10.2: Transition diagram for the JVC PVR drawn as a circle. Circular embeddings have the advantage that no lines coincide—they are unambiguous unless there are several lines between the same pairs of states. Tools like Dot can be asked to try to minimize line crossings, to draw neater diagrams.

An alternative way of drawing the same graph is to rank the states, using the technique used in figure 10.1 (p. 330) for the farmer's problem. Figure 10.3 (facing page) shows a ranked transition diagram for the JVC PVR. To draw it, we chose the initial state for the machine, which for this machine is off with the tape out, and drew that state at the far left. Then each column of states drawn is the same distance, that is, the same minimum number of button presses, from the initial state. Thus the further right you go in this diagram, the harder things are to do starting from the initial state. One could draw the ranked graph taking any state as the initial state; it would then show the user effort getting to any state from that chosen state. Indeed, we could use the shortest paths matrix to find the most eccentric state, and hence draw (what for most users would be) the worst-ranked graph.

The long tail of states, each increasingly hard to get to, makes this JVC device hard to use—or, rather, it makes doing *some* things hard to do. The very long tail out to the right means that these states are unusually hard to get to.

This "stretching" of the device design may or may not make sense for a PVR, depending on what those tail states are and how they relate to one another. Cer-

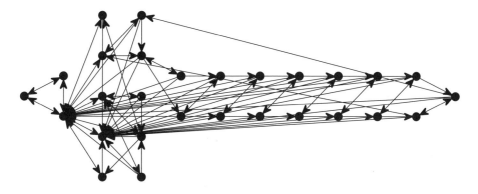

Figure 10.3: A ranked embedding for the JVC PVR. Off with the tape out is at the far left. State names and button names are not shown to avoid visual clutter. If you want to avoid visual clutter and be more informative, make the diagram interactive (e.g., use an HTML imagemap) and show the state names as the cursor is moved over the picture.

tainly, if this device were an airplane, you'd want the state "on the ground but with the wheels retracted" to be *very* difficult to get to, but I can't see why a PVR need be so lop-sided! Probably the designers never drew a ranked embedding and therefore never noticed any such issues.

▷ Figure 5.7 (p. 138) shows a ranked embedding for a Nokia mobile phone, like figure 10.1 (p. 330), but rotated to go top down, rather than right to left.

10.3.1 Characteristic path lengths again

It's interesting to look at the average length of shortest paths between any two states—the average path length is so important it is called the characteristic path length.

▷ See section 9.6 (p. 297) for program code to work out shortest and average path lengths; also, see section 8.9 (p. 264) which discussed characteristic path lengths (average path lengths) in the context of scale-free networks.

Shortest paths represent the fastest way a user can get from one state to another state. The average of all shortest paths is therefore an average measure of how hard a device is to use—though of course bigger devices (devices with not enough buttons to go round) will have longer path lengths.

For the same PVR (from the previous section), the characteristic path length is 3.9. This means that if you know how to use this device perfectly (and few people do), on average to do anything will take *at least* 3.9 button presses.

It's helpful to know what the hardest operations are. On this PVR, the hardest operations all take 11 button presses, and are ones that end up with the PVR doing something in 240 minutes. In fact, it is the state at the extreme right of the last diagram we drew, figure 10.3 (previous page): it's not only a long way from off, it's as far away as it could be from many states!

To get from this state		to this state
fast forward	$\rightarrow$	pause recording, but stop in 240 minutes
off, with tape in	$\rightarrow$	pause recording, but stop in 240 minutes
off, with tape out	$\rightarrow$	pause recording, but stop in 240 minutes
on, with no tape	$\rightarrow$	pause recording, but stop in 240 minutes
play a tape fast forward	$\rightarrow$	pause recording, but stop in 240 minutes
pause playing a tape	$\rightarrow$	pause recording, but stop in 240 minutes
play a tape fast backward	$\rightarrow$	pause recording, but stop in 240 minutes
play a tape	$\rightarrow$	pause recording, but stop in 240 minutes
rewind a tape	$\rightarrow$	pause recording, but stop in 240 minutes

We can measure the average number of button presses to get from one state to another; it's 3.9. Given that one state seems to be out on a limb of length 11, it's interesting to work out what the best we could do is.

The PVR has 8 buttons and 28 states. One state (namely, the one you start from) can be reached with 0 button presses, because you are already there; 8 more states can be reached with 1 press, since we have 8 buttons available to get to different states. In theory, in each of those 8 states, we could reach another 8 states—a total of 64 states—in just one more press. Having accounted for 9 states in 0 or 1 presses, it only leaves 19 states the PVR needs; and these can therefore all be reached in 2 presses.

The average cost is the total divided by the number of states, $(0 \times 1 + 1 \times 8 + 2 \times 19)/28 = 1.643$. (A quick way to estimate this value is to calculate $\log_8$ of 28, which is 1.602.) However we look at it, this is a lot less than the 3.9 the device achieves.

We can conclude the device was not designed to minimize button presses to do things. One would have expected some other advantage for the JVC design decisions, such as the buttons more often meaning the same things, like [Play] always meaning play.

10.3.2   Indicators

We can extend a device description to include indicators, descriptions of what lights, indicators or words are shown to the user by the device in any state. For example, the "on" light comes on in all states when the PVR is switched on, but the "tape in" indicator is only shown when there is a tape in—and there can be a tape in whether or not the device is on or off. Naturally, in its two off states the on indicator will be off.

▷   Indicators were introduced in chapter 8, "Graphs," section 8.1.3 (p. 232), in the context of coloring graphs.

Handling indicators allows us to do further sorts of insightful analysis. I didn't introduce indicators earlier because for simple devices, like lightbulbs and drills, states and indicators are pretty much the same thing.

When buttons are pressed, a device should give feedback that something has happened. Typically, pressing a button not only changes the state, but it also changes some indicator.

We can define an ambiguous transition as one in which no indicators change. The user cannot be certain that they pressed the button hard enough—or, perhaps worse, they cannot be certain that they understand the device, as it appears to have done nothing when they thought it would do something.

The ambiguous transitions for the JVC PVR are shown below. For instance, if the JVC model is on with a tape in and you make it go fast forward, it won't tell you anything has happened—but this is only one of several ambiguities.

> fast forward → on, with tape in
> on, with tape in → fast forward
> on, with tape in → rewind a tape
> play a tape fast forward → on, with tape in
> play a tape fast backward → on, with tape in
> rewind a tape → on, with tape in

To get these results, I added a new field `indicators` to the framework specification. Each state can now have various indicators, using descriptive JavaScript strings such as `"on"` or `"tape in"`.

> ▷ If a device gives no feedback when a button is pressed—as in the six cases
>   above or even in very simple situations, as discussed in section 3.14 (p. 86), the
>   user may easily make an overrun error, a type of error discussed in
>   section 10.4.1 (p. 341).

There is no need for the indicators to be real indicators on the device. The PVR has no special indicators for fast forward and rewind states, but you can *hear* the PVR whirring madly as it does the fast rewind or fast forward actions, so it has indicators of a sort. Whether you treat fast forward whirring as an indicator is moot; we can tell from the table above that the basic device needs them.

More generally, indicators could be anything the designer is interested in. The PVR has no indicator to say that it has a tape in that can be recorded on—the user has to experiment to find out, but we could make this a conceptual indicator in *our* device specification. Then if we find that users rely on this indicator, this would suggest a good way of improving the design, namely, make the conceptual indicator a device indicator.

The device specification needs extra stuff, so each state has a list of indicators specified:

```
indicators: [["on", "tape"],
             ["tape"],
             [],
             ["on", "tape"],
             . . .
            ]
```

We can look at the way the device uses its indicators to find out how likely buttons are to change them. Do buttons consistently affect indicators? Some buttons have apparently helpful names like Operate and Play; presumably, switching on and off the On and Play indicators ... well, let's see.

A simple program running on the specification generates the following text:

> For device JVC HR-D540EK PVR
> Play, when it does anything, it always ensures: on, tape
>   and 7.69% of the time it ensures: record
> Operate, when it does anything, 3.57% of the time it ensures: tape
> Forward, when it does anything, it always ensures: on, tape
> Rewind, when it does anything, it always ensures: on, tape
> Pause, when it does anything, it always ensures: on, pause, tape
>   and 8.33% of the time it ensures: record
> Record, when it does anything, it always ensures: on, tape
>   and 5.26% of the time it ensures: record
> Stop/Eject, when it does anything, 3.85% of the time it ensures: on
> tape in, when it does anything, it always ensures: on, tape

Analyses like these are easier to read when we use the descriptive fields already in the framework; the first line say they are results for the JVC HR-D540EK PVR, which is just the `device.modelType` text.

The words "record," "on" and so on here are indicator lights (or words that light up in the LED screen) on the actual device. Alternatively, we can do the same analysis but use our own conceptual indicators. For example, although the PVR does not say so, *we* know which states make the tape rewind; so we can invent an indicator to mark those sets of states. Here is the sort of result we can get:

> For device JVC HR-D540EK PVR (conceptual indicators)
> Play, when it does anything, it always ensures: on, tape
>   and 15.38% of the time it ensures: auto off record
> Operate, when it does anything, 3.57% of the time it ensures: tape
> Forward, when it does anything, it always ensures: fast forward, on, tape
>   and 33.33% of the time it ensures: play
> Rewind, when it does anything, it always ensures: on, rewind tape
>   and 33.33% of the time it ensures: play
> Pause, when it does anything, it always ensures: on, pause tape
>   and 8.33% of the time it ensures: record
> Record, when it does anything, it always ensures: on, tape
>   and 5.26% of the time it ensures: record
> Stop/Eject, when it does anything, 3.85% of the time it ensures: on
> tape in, when it does anything, it always ensures: on, tape

The table shows that when the Play button does something, it will leave the PVR with the on and tape indicators on—we have the condition "when it does anything" since if the device is off, it won't do anything at all, and that usually isn't worth reporting! What Play does is not very surprising, but some of the other button meanings are.

> **Box 10.2 What "always" and "never" should mean** "You can *always* press ⎡Home⎤ to get to your home page"—that's an instruction seen on Microsoft's webTV, a domestic interactive TV system; but it isn't true that it always works. I needed to use the TV's other remote control as well to get to the home page!
>
> It's fine to write "always" in manuals and user help, and in principle if something is always true, the device will be simpler. But make sure that you really do mean *always*. If so, it simplifies the manuals and reassures the user; it makes everything easier. If something isn't "always" but is "almost always" the device will seem especially unreliable.

- We can see that the ⎡Operate⎤ button makes the JVC device on only 44% of the time—other times, indeed most of the time, ⎡Operate⎤ makes the device *in*operative!

- Why does pressing ⎡Rewind⎤ sometimes cause the device to play? It's because if the device is already playing when ⎡Rewind⎤ is pressed, the device starts to play backward (so-called review).

- If ⎡Rewind⎤ sometimes leaves the device playing, why does ⎡Pause⎤ sometimes leave it recording?

- The ⎡Record⎤ button seems to make the device record hardly at all, only 5.26% of the time it is used.

A designer should read a list of results like this carefully. Perhaps the designer should also annotate the results table with the rationale for the interesting features (such as the ones we picked out for comment above). A routine extension of the framework could store the designer's annotations and later report if a percentage changes—such a change would indicate the design had been altered and the original rational needs reviewing.

One reason why ⎡Record⎤ doesn't consistently make the device record is shown in an answer to a user's question, shown on p. 353. If a user wants to stop the recording in 120 minutes, they should press the ⎡Record⎤ button 5 times. For none of those presses, at least 5 states, does the ⎡Record⎤ button start recording.

▷ Box 9.2, "Button usage" (p. 310) explains the ⎡Record⎤ button usage further.

10.3.3 Beguiling behavior

Some of the properties we have found are only true some of the time; for instance the ⎡Record⎤ button does something 5.26% of the time rather than all of the time (or not at all). Suppose instead that a button did something, say, 99% of the time. It's very likely that the user would assume it did this *all* the time—the user is unlikely ever to have experienced the 1% of times it doesn't work as expected. If so, the user will have been beguiled, and they will have misunderstood the way the device works. Therefore it is especially important for the designer to identify behaviors that are *almost* true.

If we get some experimental data our information for the design can be much more useful. When we said "44% of the time" (or whatever) we really meant in 44% of *the states*. Whether these states are used the same amount of time as other states is, of course, unlikely, though a good first approximation. A device might be off for most of its life, but a user will never use a device when it is off! Thus we ought to collect some timings from real use so that our percentages give us data about real use rather than guesses. Nevertheless, when we are designing a new device, informed guesses are better than nothing.

> ▷ More uses for weighting with experimental data are given below, in section 10.7.5 (p. 358); in particular, we suggest comparing expert designers' data with ordinary users' data to see whether we can help users become more proficient.

Beguiling behavior can be a way for manufacturers to make money. For example, a user may be lulled into thinking some behavior of the device is normal, but very rarely it might imply some avoidable cost for the user. My car, a Land Rover 90, is a case in point. It has a parking brake (hand brake) with a warning indicator. The warning light, *which is a symbol of the parking brake mechanism*, always comes on when the parking brake is on and always goes off when the parking brake is released. The user does not want to drive the car when the parking brake is on or partially on, so this indicator light is a helpful warning. The light worked like that for years, and it beguiled me into thinking that was *exactly* what it did. Then, one day, it stayed on. Yet the parking brake still worked perfectly, so I believed it had to be an electrical fault. Indeed, we have had wiring faults before, so we pretty much ignored it.

When we took the car for its service, it needed a new set of disk brakes (both disks and pads)—a very costly repair. We now learned that what we thought was the "parking brake" indicator is in fact a "general brake" warning light. In other words, around 99.99% of the time it means nothing unusual but around 0.01% of the time it means you have a serious problem that needs immediate attention. Why doesn't Land Rover use another indicator for this rare problem? Or why not have some simple electronics (there's plenty there already) to make the light flash and maybe a noise too, so it clearly is a serious warning? Or, as there is a separate anti-lock brake system (ABS) warning light that is *always* a brake malfunction warning light, why not use that for all brake failures? Why not have both lights come on together? Why not an LCD text display? Or, thinking differently, why not have the original indicator come on when any brake is used: then the user is also trained the indicator refers to the main brakes as well, and the percentage 99.99% changes dramatically—the issue of beguiling behavior disappears. Whatever solution is chosen, and there are many, it needs to be different from the light the user has learned from long experience means something else.*

That last phrase, "the user has learned" needs rewriting: it should say, "what the user has been trained *by the design*"—it's a design issue, not a user issue. Here,

---

* By design, Land Rover parking brakes are completely separate from the main brakes, so their failure modes are independent—they work on the prop shaft, not on the wheels. So why use the same indicator?

the car manufacturer saving the cost of installing a clear fault indicator ensures that from time to time they will sell brake parts at significant profit. The way the device has been designed, brake failure has—conveniently for the manufacturer—become the user's fault for not understanding a warning light the user manual (but not the warning itself) explains.

▷ The example in box 6.4, "Bad user interfaces earn money" (p. 191) is another case of rare behavior—but behavior the designers of the device surely know about—leading to surprising costs for the user.

10.4 Summarizing and comparing many properties

There are many properties that we may be interested in, and typically we will be interested in certain critical properties and how they are affected by changes to a device design or we may wish to compare several devices to one another and try to learn which has the best features to copy.

We can write a simple program that summarizes all properties we are interested in. The first time we use the program in this book, we'll get it to explain in detail what every result means, but to save paper when we use it again we won't number all the items or reprint the brief explanations.

You might like to consider other properties we could work out that are of interest to designers and users.

1. Model: Simple microwave oven. *The model type.*

2. Number of states: 6. *How many things can be done with this device?*

3. Number of buttons: 5. *How many buttons (or other actions) are available to access all the states?*

4. Number of edges (excluding duplicates): 22, which is 73.33% complete. *In a complete graph, you can do anything in one step, so if this figure is 100%, the device cannot be made faster to use.*

5. Number of self-edges: 7. *A self-edge goes back to the same state; it corresponds to buttons or actions that do nothing.*

6. Number of duplicate edges (excluding self-edges): 5. *Depending on the application, duplicates are either wasteful or give the user choices and flexibility.*

7. Probability a button does nothing: 0.23. *Chance a random button press in a random state does nothing. The larger this figure (to a maximum of 1), the safer—or more frustrating!—the device will be to use.*

8. This device is strongly connected. *If the device is strongly connected, we can always get anywhere to anywhere; if not, then there are some traps or irreversibilities that cannot be got out of.*

9. Average cost to get somewhere from anywhere else: 1.47. *How many button presses, on average, does it take to get anywhere?*

10. Average cost to get somewhere from anywhere, including the same place: 1.22. *If you include trying to get to the same place (which takes nothing to do) of course the average cost is less.*

11. Worst case cost: 3. *The most difficult case of getting from anywhere to anywhere. In a complete device, this worst case would be 1.*

12. Average cost to recover from 1 button press error: 1.3. *If in a random state a button is pressed at random, how many button presses on average does it take to get back? Compare this cost with the mean cost; if it is higher, most button presses are "one way."*

13. Worst case cost to recover from 1 button press error: 3. *If in a random state a button is pressed at random, what's the worst number of button presses it takes to get back? If the device has an undo key, this figure would be 1. If the device has an undo key, this figure would be 1. Put another way, if you are in "the right place" but accidentally press a button, this is the average cost of getting back.*

14. Average cost to get anywhere after 1 random button press: 1.36. *A random press can give you a bit more information, but has it made your task (whatever it was) harder? Compare this figure with the average cost between states; typically it will be higher, because a random button press will tend to take you away from where you want to go.*

15. Percentage of single-press errors that can be undone directly: 33.33%. *If a button is pressed by mistake, how often can you get back (undo the error) in just one step? If the device has an undo key, this figure would be 100%*

16. Average cost of an overrun error: 0.2. *If the correct button is accidentally pressed twice (not once), how hard is it to get back (undo the overrun error)? If the device has an undo key, this figure would be less than 1; if the device was idempotent (when a button gets the device to a state, it keeps you there), the figure would be 0.*

17. Worst case overrun error cost: 1. *If an overrun error occurs, what is the worst cost of recovering?*

18. Average cost of a restart recovery for overrun error: 1.4. *If the correct button is accidentally pressed twice (not once), how hard is it to get back (undo the overrun error) if the user switches the device off first to restart it?*

19. Worst case restart overrun error cost: 4. *If an overrun error occurs, what is the worst cost of recovering by restarting?*

20. Independence probability: 0.33. *The probability that a user requires more than one button press to do anything. The smaller this number, the "easier" or more direct the device is to use.*

All the above text was generated automatically, using the device specification from our framework. The complete JavaScript code to do it is on the book's web site—for reasons of space (and boredom), we won't give the full details of generating all this text here.

Many of the measures can be fine-tuned depending on exactly what a designer wants. For example, the list above gives the percentage of single-press errors that can be undone directly; this means that if the user presses a button by accident, a third of the time they can recover from this error in one more press. But this is not counting pressing buttons by accident that do nothing, since this would not cause an error that needs recovering from. We could count those cases as well, if we wanted to, and then change the average accordingly.

10.4.1 Overrun errors

A new property we introduced in the list above concerns *overrun errors*. Imagine a cheap gadget with nasty rubber keys that you are never sure you've pressed hard enough. Suppose you press (OFF) but the device has not gone off. You are likely to press (OFF) again. We will call this an overrun.

Another example of overrun is when you press the (MUTE) button on a device to make it quiet. You press it again to make sure—but the device takes the second press to restore the sound. So ironically pressing (MUTE) twice, which a human might think of as emphasis ("I really want it to be muted") is taken by the device as a change of mind ("Although you've told me to be quiet twice, I think you want me to be noisy!"). That's an overrun error. We can easily find such potential errors automatically and decide whether to fix them by redesigning.

Maybe the device is slow; maybe its lights tend to stay on for a bit; or maybe you didn't press the rubbery (OFF) button hard enough, and until you press it properly it isn't going to switch off. So you press it again.

We'll explain how overrun errors are measured in detail. You can easily modify the ideas to measure other properties that may be more relevant to your designs than overrun errors. First, think of a likely user design issue, as here we thought of overrun errors. Then we write some code that works out the costs of those errors, analyses a design, and prints out the results.

An error occurs if the overrun does something unfortunate. On some devices, pressing (OFF) twice switches the device back on again, which is not what was intended.

We need the costs of all shortest paths, as we worked out in section 9.6 (p. 297):

```
var apsp = shortestPaths(device);
var cost = 0;
var worst = 0;
```

The variable name apsp stands for "all pairs shortest paths," a mnemonic name for this matrix. We've also initialized the two cost variables to zero.

Next, we run over all states (using the variable *i* in a for loop) and in each state we run over all buttons (using the variable *j*).

```
for( var i = 0; i < n; i++ ) // over all states
  for( var j = 0; j < b; j++ ) // over all buttons
  { var newState = device.fsm[i][j]; // button j pressed in state i
    // press button j again, but now in the new state
    var overrun = device.fsm[newState][j]; // state after an overrun
    var c = apsp[overrun][newState];
    cost = cost+c;
    if( c > worst ) worst = c;
  }
```

Box 10.3 Handling infinity properly !f a device is not strongly connected, some values in the shortest paths matrix will be ∞. We have to be careful working out averages when this is a possibility, because most programming languages don't handle infinity correctly. In our JavaScript, we used any value larger than n to represent ∞, so strictly the program code given above needs tests to see whether apsp[i][j] > n, and if so, to drop out of the loop and report an infinite result. Perhaps easier is to have a single check to determine whether a device is strongly connected and, if it isn't, to only report properties that make sense (however, average costs of overrun errors *do* make sense even if a device is not strongly connected).

Our definition of fsm gives us the next state when button j is pressed in state i, so device.fsm[i][j] in the loop above gives us the new state we get to if we press button j. We record this new state in the variable newState. But if we press button j again—that's the overrun—we would end up in state device.fsm[newState][j]. This is the state the user overruns to, and we record it in the variable overrun. Then apsp[overrun][newState] will be the cost of getting back, which we add to cost, so that in the end dividing cost by n*b will give the average.

After the two nested loops, we print out the answers:

```
document.write("Average cost of an overrun error: "+(cost/(n*b)));
document.write("Worst case cost of an overrun error: "+worst);
```

To find the cost of getting back to where we wanted to be is merely a case of looking up the cost of the shortest route from overrun to newState: this is the value in apsp[overrun][newState], which cost we can conveniently store in the variable c. We then use c to add to the running cost and to keep the variable worst tracking the worst value we've seen so far.

All the other code is similar. For example, to do an undo costing, we get the costs of getting back from a button press. The inner loop would start with code like this:

```
var newState = device.fsm[i][j];
var c = apsp[newState][i]; // cost of getting back to state i
```

This simply gets the costs of getting back to state i if button j has been pressed. The two further lines we haven't shown simply add the costs and find the maximum, as before.

10.4.2   Restart costs

After making a mistake, how can the user be sure that a recovery from an error is going to be successful? Many people will switch the device off and on again, to start all over again, because this is a sure way to get back to where they wanted to be. If you can switch off and on, this is probably a good strategy to recover from errors. As designers, we are interested in the *restart costs* for errors.

We can easily assess the cost of restartig for any sort of error by modifying the code to take the shortest path for the error recovery via the off state. In the overrun code, above, we simply took the shortest path, whereever it went. Now, if we want to assess the cost to the user of recovering from an error by switching off and on, we use the shortest path from the error to Off, and then from Off to where we wanted to be. Here's how to do it:

```
cost = 0;
worst = 0;
var offState = d.startState; // we could choose any state to be 'off'
for( var i = 0; i < n; i++ )
  for( var j = 0; j < b; j++ )
  { var newState = d.fsm[i][j]; // button j in state i gets to new state
    var overrun = d.fsm[newState][j]; // the state after an overrun
    var restartCost = apsp[overrun][offState]+apsp[offState][newState];
    cost = cost+restartCost;
    if( restartCost > worst ) worst = restartCost;
  }
```

The code is exactly the same as before, except apsp[overrun][newState] is replaced by apsp[overrun][offState]+apsp[offState][newState], which is the cost of going from the overrun state to newState, where you wanted to be, via the state offState.

For the running example, the average restart cost is 5.75 and the worst case is 13 (and that it would be *much* larger than this in practice since this assumes that the user makes no mistakes and knows the best way to do it); this is all very much worse (as we expected) than trying to recover from an overrun by going "straight back" rather than via Off. So it gives an indication of the extreme cost to the user if they don't know that.

10.4.3   Independence probability

The independence probability gives another example of how to work out device properties. This probability is defined as the probability that the user has to do more than press a single button to achieve what they want to achieve. All we do is look at every state the device can be in, and everything the user might want to do, counting how many times what the user might want takes more than a single action. Finally, we divide the count by all the possibilities, which in this case is the square of the number of states.

```
var apsp = shortestPaths(device);
var count = 0;
for( var i = 0; i < n; i++ )
  for( var j = 0; j < n; j++ )
    if( apsp[i][j] > 1 )
      count++;
document.write("Independence probability: "+count/(n*n));
```

If we used this code along with working out other measures, we wouldn't need to work out the shortest path lengths more than once. I put the line var apsp = shortestPaths(device) in to make the code above self-contained.

▷   The independence probability is defined in section 8.6.3 (p. 247).

10.4.4   Summarizing and overviewing a device

Here is a range of properties summarized for the JVC PVR. The overrun costs are quite interesting.

Model: JVC HR-D540EK PVR
Number of states: 28
Number of buttons: 8
Number of edges (excluding duplicates): 134, which is 17.72% complete
Number of self-edges: 118
Number of duplicate edges (excluding self-edges): 0
Probability a button does nothing: 0.53
This device is strongly connected
Average cost to get somewhere from anywhere else: 3.87
Average cost to get somewhere from anywhere, including the same place: 3.73
Worst case cost: 11
Average cost to recover from 1 button press error: 1.78
Worst case cost to recover from 1 button press error: 11
Average cost to get anywhere after 1 random button press: 3.92
Percentage of single-press errors that can be undone directly: 16.96%
Average cost of an overrun error: 0.73
Worst case overrun error cost: 9
Average cost of a restart recovery for overrun error: 5.75
Worst case restart overrun error cost: 13
Independence probability: 0.83

The JVC PVR has some curious properties. If we have an overrun error (for instance, we want to play a tape, but we press Play once too often, perhaps because we didn't notice when it had started to play—perhaps it is too slow or doesn't provide decent feedback), then it takes 2.3 presses on average to get back to where we wanted to be (or 3.3 including the error). Yet to get from anywhere to anywhere takes on average 3.9 presses: an overrun error on this JVC PVR is practically the same as getting completely lost—an overrun error puts you about as far away on average from where you want to be as you can be. Moreover, a completely random button press only takes 1.8 presses to recover (on average)—or 2.8, including the error. But this is *easier* than an overrun error! There are three main reasons for this: (*i*) some random presses do nothing and therefore cost nothing to recover from; (*ii*) most random presses don't get you as far away as an overrun; (*iii*) if a button worked to get you to this state, it is likely to work to get you away from it (in other words, overrun errors are likely).

The remote control for this PVR is *completely* different from the unit itself. We haven't space to show it here, but it's very obvious from any drawing of the transition diagram. Making it different doubles the learning the user has to do to make good use of the device—and almost doubles the size of the user manual.

▷   For a similar point on remote controls of televisions, see section 3.2 (p. 63).

10.4.5 Random pressing

If you make a random press, you may find out more about the device.

▷ You can hire gnomes to press buttons at random. Their effectiveness will be explored in chapter 11, "More complex devices."

It's tempting to press buttons at random. You walk up to something. What does it do? The only way to find out is to press a button and see what happens. On the JVC, if you press a button at random you may have made it a little harder to get anywhere. But the difference isn't much, and if you can find out something useful about where you are (that is, about what the device is doing) by pressing a button, on the JVC this could be a good strategy to help you use the device better, even though on average it will cost you more.

Sometimes pressing a button does nothing. For example, if you press ⟨Play⟩ when it is playing, nothing happens. Suppose we modify the JVC so that a user can tell if a button will do something. For example, each button might have a little light that comes on only if the button works. These useful buttons would be easy to find in the dark. Now if we press a button at random, it will always do something. How does this change the numbers?

Here's what the program would output to answer the question, in the same style as before:

Average cost to get anywhere after a working random press is 4.04582 (excluding the press). *Your random press will give you a bit more information, but has it made your task any easier?*

It's worse! On the JVC you're better off not playing with the buttons "to see what they do." But you're only better off if you know what it is doing, and that would require some indicator lights to tell you what it is doing.

On the JVC, then, the user is in a quandary: you can't always tell what state it is in, and experimenting to find out makes *any* task harder. Of course, to be fair, once you've experimented and found out where you are, you can now use the JVC properly, which you can't do when you don't know what it is doing.

▷ Program code to do the random pressing is given in section 11.1.5 (p. 376).

10.4.6 Simplifying the PVR

Maybe we can redesign the JVC PVR to make it easier to use? We've already pointed out how the "tail" of states on the JVC makes many things harder.

Let's delete the hard-to-get-at states and see what happens; this is just a matter of programming, to find and then remove them from the device (along with all the button actions that went to them). This approach is a good example of using JavaScript to define the state machine you're interested in. Not all designs have to be written out tediously, they can be defined in terms of other devices, and they can be entirely or partly constructed automatically.

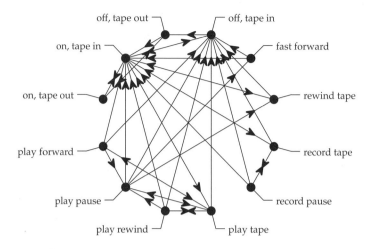

off, tape out

off, tape in

on, tape in

fast forward

on, tape out

rewind tape

play forward

record tape

play pause

record pause

play rewind

play tape

Figure 10.4: Compare this simplified PVR diagram with the corresponding diagram, figure 10.2 (p. 332) for the original design.

Note something very important here: we can prototype a device (let's say, the first JVC PVR), evaluate it, and see some design issues (such as the outlying states); that we can then improve it *automatically* on the basis of our analysis (here, collapsing all those states).

The result, shown in figure 10.4 (this page), looks like an interesting improvement. You can also see from the diagram that the device is "tighter" than the original, yet it provides the same functionality but without all the timeouts. Whether it really is an improvement for user's we should leave to doing some experiments. For all I know, there are enough users who like delayed pauses—and few users who get frustrated by their device not doing anything for 240 minutes, and then surprising them. The point is, we've got two automatically-related designs, and we can test them out. Moreover, if during tests we discover some new idea that really has to be implemented, we can still have two designs: we can continue regenerating the automatic variations. In a normal design process, without the automatic support, as soon as you get a new idea, you have got a lot of work to do to keep all the versions of the device consistent. In our approach, that consistency comes for free.

10.4.7   More on overruns, and the farmer's problem again

We return to the farmer's puzzle again (section 10.1) for comparison with the "normal" interactive devices we've already explored.

Model: Farmer problem
Number of states: 28

Number of buttons: 4
Number of edges (excluding duplicates): 92, which is 12.17% complete
Number of self-edges: 46
Number of duplicate edges (excluding self-edges): 0
Probability a button does nothing: 0.41
This device isn't strongly connected.
Percentage of single-press errors that can be undone directly: 48.21%
Average cost of an overrun error: 0.59
Average cost of non-trivial overrun errors: 1
Worst case overrun error cost: 1
Worst case cost for restart after an overrun error: ∞
Independence probability: 0.88

There are lots of things to notice here. The framework program generating the text was designed for describing ordinary interactive devices, so "button" is hardly the right word to use. "Action" would be preferable or, better, the `action` string should be used from the framework specification. The number of self-edges looks very high: but most of them are actions that don't do anything: for example, if there is no cabbage left because the goat ate it, then the action "take the cabbage" will do nothing because there isn't a cabbage to take and it's counted as a self-edge. Because this "device" is not strongly connected, many of the average and maximum costs are infinity, and they are automatically not shown in the program-generated summary of properties.

The probability (0.41 or 41% of the time) that a button does nothing means, in effect, that if you shut your eyes and wished, "I want to take the goat across the river," then part of the time you couldn't do it, for instance, because the goat was on the other side, or was eaten—that something had gone wrong you hadn't noticed with your eyes shut. It seems a high probability, but the 41% assumes you are in any state chosen with equal probability, but if you are trying to solve the problem you are unlikely to be in a random state—ideally, you should be in a state in, or close to, the strongly connected component that contains the solution. If you are in that strongly connected component, nothing has been eaten, so the probability a "button" does nothing would be lower than 41%. In other words, the moral of this insight is that the probabilities (or percentages) would make better sense if the states are weighted by how likely the user is to be in them. For this "device," as it happens, we can estimate those probabilities better than for most devices.

You might have expected the worst overrun error to be infinite, because once something has gone wrong (like the goat being eaten) there is nothing the farmer can do about it. Infinities seriously affect usability, but here the worst-case overrun cost is only 1 and the average is only 0.59! These unexpected results come about because the farmer's problem has an interesting structure:

- If the farmer's action stays within the strongly connected component shown in figure 10.1 (p. 330), then every action is reversible. Any overrun takes the farmer back to the previous bank, and the overrun can be corrected simply by doing the action again. In fact, this is true for any action within any strongly connected component.

■ If an action takes the system out of the component, immediately the action is irreversible. For example, the cabbage is eaten. Another action the same, which would be an overrun, returns the farmer to the same bank as before the action—but without the cabbage. The overrun can be corrected by repeating the action, as this takes the farmer back. Again, for this unusual "device," this happens to be true for any action leaving a strongly connected component.

■ Once the cabbage or goat are eaten, some actions, such as the farmer carrying the cabbage in the canoe, will have no effect. These actions in these states are self-loops. A self-loop overrun does nothing, so these overruns can be corrected by doing nothing, 0 actions, thus the average cost of an overrun error correction is less than 1.

The moral of this story is that analytic measurements, such as the cost of correcting an overrun error, have to be interpreted carefully. Measurements that sound sensible are not sensible for all possible devices and user tasks. Moreover, devices that are not strongly connected generally have special problems that need examining very carefully.

10.5   Lots of properties

It's informative to develop questions about the user and their tasks to see how to answer these questions with graph theory, because you can then write programs that work out the answers from the device specification.

I imagine a design tool, based on a framework like the one we have developed, that provides a menu of properties, characteristic path lengths, and so on, so that for any design, a designer can easily find out how the user will fare with certain sorts of task. Alternatively, in designing a particular device, maybe only one or two properties are especially important, and just these important parameters could be worked out and redisplayed (as numbers, diagrams, or graphs) whenever the device design is updated.

The following sections present a diverse list of illustrative things users will want to do that designers should consider on their behalf—and hence build into their design tools. For any particular device or tasks the designer is working toward supporting, there will be lots of such questions. This list, then, is merely illustrative of the wide range of possibilities.

As usual, when an interactive system's design is represented as a graph, we can write programs to analyze the graph and give answers to all sorts of design questions. Thus when we talk about "shortest path," below, this is a simple matter of running a shortest path algorithm on the design in question, such as the one we discussed in chapter 9, "A framework for design."

10.5.1 User knows everything: but how much is that?

In a graph, arcs take you from one vertex (state) to another. If you carry on following arcs, you are walking along a path. Usually there are many paths from one place to another, and of all the possible paths (some of which might be circuitous), the user will generally be most interested in the shortest. The shortest path gives you the minimum number of button presses to get from whatever the system is doing to somewhere else. A skilled user needs to know (or nearly know) shortest paths to use a system effectively.

10.5.2 User reads the manual: how long do they take?

If a user is to know the most efficient way of using a system, shortest paths are appropriate. However, for almost every application, rather than finding shortest paths for every pair of states, more manual structure will be required to ensure the manual is not too long.

It's possible that an emergency manual will make a trade-off preferring to be longer so that it can give instructions in full for *every* emergency. But a long manual runs the risk of the user choosing the wrong instructions, whereas a more "diverse" manual allows the user to change their mind along the way. In fact, the manual itself becomes a "device" with its own usability issues—the table of contents, the index, and so on become "buttons" that a user uses, not to press, but to turn to for information.

▷ Features like tables of contents make books and manuals easier to use. We reviewed the analogy—which works both ways—in section 4.2 (p. 96).

10.5.3 User is lost: how long does it take to recover?

Suppose the user has become lost but they still know what they want to do. They are going have to start a search for it. If we work out the total cost of getting anywhere from anywhere, on average a user will find what they want half way through searching the entire thing (*provided* they get some feedback or indication they have got to their goal), so half the number is the average time that a tireless, error-free, user would take.

Usually the number is enormous, which goes to show that the user should always be provided with a better way of searching than just aimlessly rummaging. For example, if there is a [Cancel] button, the user can get to a key state in one press, and (if the system is designed sensibly) all states are on average closer to the key state than to any random state where the user became lost.

10.5.4 How long does it take to learn a system?

How much does a user need to know in order to use a system? If we decide what we mean by the "user learning a system," then we can formalize the corresponding design questions in precise terms:

- If user learning a system means knowing every feature, then the traveling salesman gives the least number of actions a user will take to know every feature.

- If user learning a system means knowing what to do in every state, then the Chinese postman tour gives the least number of actions a user will take to try every action.

- We want user manuals to be well written and easy to understand. If we generate user manuals automatically from a device specification, then the length of the manual is a good measure of how much a user needs to know—and the time the user takes to learn a system will be proportional to this.

The raw measures of the salesman or postman tours visit every feature, so typically both of these answers will be embarrassingly large numbers. A more realistic measure can probably be obtained by first deciding what features the user needs to know and only measuring those. Indeed, if the device is well structured, then the user does not need to know it all, instead, they need to know the rules its design is based on.

10.5.5   How do you crack a safe?

If the user is lost or doesn't know what state the device is in, but they want to search for the desired state, then they have the same problem as a safe cracker who comes to a safe in an unknown state and wants to enter the right combination code. The only difference is that a safe is designed to make this problem as hard to solve as possible, whereas normally we want to help the lost user as much as possible!

Superficially, it seems there are two sorts of safe, ones that require every code the user is trying to start with [Reset], and those that allow a user to enter a code at any time: these are overlapping safes.

Suppose the key is 7777. On a resetting safe, the user must press [Reset] [7] [7] [7] [7], but on an overlapping safe the user need only press [7] [7] [7] [7], regardless of what the last person did to it. Overlapping safes are easier to use—and easier to crack.

In fact, there is no reason to tell any potential thief which button the [Reset] button is, and then the thief cannot tell whether this is a reset or overlap design, and that uncertainty will make the job harder. (Unfortunately most thieves know a lot more than we do about the weaknesses of safes, so this is false comfort.)

If the thief doesn't know, they would be prudent to use a de Bruijn sequence, which finds the shortest sequence of commands that covers all combinations. For example, if there are four keys and the combination is two digits (such as 42), then the de Bruijn sequence is [1] [1] [3] [1] [2] [3] [2] [2] [4] [3] [3] [4] [4] [2] [1] [4]—which tries the combinations 11, 13, 31, 12, 23 and so on in that order, finishing 21, 14. The thief would therefore expect to take 8 key presses (they'd have to be unlucky to need all 16 presses to try the last combination code), as opposed to the 24 that would be expected if there was no overlapping allowed (or 13.5, if we hijack one of the four buttons to be the [Reset] button).

    ▷   De Bruijn sequences are special cases of finding Chinese postmen tours on special graphs that have Euler cycles. Chapter 8, "Graphs," defines these terms.

10.6   Comparing designs

Figures in isolation do not mean very much. What does it mean to a user that 62% of the time they press a button it does nothing? Does it matter? If it does nothing, does the user ignore it, or do they panic?

Without doing user-based studies, raw numbers are not very informative. How are we supposed to know what a "big" number is or a "worryingly big number"? Instead, it is more useful to *compare* designs: a designer should have a good idea that making numbers bigger or small is better or worse for the intended design given what the user is going to do with it. By comparing designs, the designer looking at the figures does not have to decide whether or not 62% is a good number, but they can decide whether increasing it or decreasing it is worthwhile.

In the table shown in figure 10.5 (next page), I've brought together some figures measuring new and old interaction properties of the JVC PVR and a Philips VR502 PVR. Side-by-side the figures are now easy to compare. Typically, a designer might compare a basic design with a slight variation and then generate a table like this automatically, using a function written in the design framework. The designer would then decide whether to go with the variation, retain the original design, or make some other changes. In fact the JVC and Philips designs, summarized in the table, are not slight variations of each other, so the figures are—not surprisingly— wildly different.

10.7   Putting analysis into products

So far I've painted the programming ideas as merely for simulation and analysis. Using JavaScript and HTML (or any other web technologies) means that we can build interactive web sites and then we can get all sorts of data from real users anywhere in the world who use the web site. We can now recruit people to help us find out how good a design is for certain tasks or for certain sorts of errors, such as overrun errors. Whatever.

If this is all we were doing, we would probably write some program (as an extension to our framework) to convert the finite state machine description into something that worked directly on the product we are building: for example, to generate Java or C code to run directly on a chip, rather than on the web.

A far more creative idea is to notice that *we* have found out all sorts of interesting things that are helpful, so what would happen if a user had access to the same sorts of insights about the design while they were using a device online?

Property	JVC model	Philips model
Average distance between any pair of states.	3.73	1.93
Average cost of recovering from an overrun error. The number would be 1.0 if there was an [Undo] button.	3.76	2.01
Worst overrun recovery cost.	11	6
Proportion of actions that have a direct undo. *If the user presses a button, how often can they get back by one more button press?*	35.8%	55%
Cost of correcting a random one-press error.	2.44	2.1
Probability that a random button press does nothing.	0.53	0.27
Length of a test sequence, to check the model is correct. *This is the length of a Chinese postman tour.*	462	341
How many user manual structures are there to choose from? *This is a count of the number of spanning trees.*	6×10^6	4×10^{10}
...	...	...

Figure 10.5: More properties and figures, here helping compare two devices. As always, all are generated by program from the device specifications. When you design systems, you should work out what analyses you are interested in to help the device's users do (and enjoy doing) what they want to do. Obviously the tables *you* generate would be filled with the numbers and comparisons that are relevant to your users and tasks.

10.7.1   Building a manual into a device

Conventional user manuals suffer from the *synchronization problem*: the user can be reading one section of the manual, but that section may refer to a state of the system different to the one it is really in. Almost certainly the user will make mistakes. The synchronization problem is considerably worsened by timeouts in the system, because these allow it to makes state changes without telling the user— they will get left behind in the manual as the device turns to another page.

If, however, the manual is built into the device, then there is potentially no problem. We just add a button [HELP], which for whatever state the device is in just shows the corresponding text in the manual. For our JavaScript framework we just need to say something like alert(device.manual[device.state]) to tell the user what state the device is in.

10.7.2   "How to?" questions

Knowing what state the device is in is probably the least of the user's worries. It would be more useful to be able to find out how *to use* the device: that means getting it to say how to get from where they are (the device's current state) to some desired goal state. We can call this a how-to question.

Here's a brief example of how useful how-to questions, or rather their answers, can be. I had been using my JVC PVR for two years when my framework analyses surprised me with a better way of getting a tape out and switching off when playing a tape—better than I had ever tried. I thought I understood the device really well, as after all I had reverse-engineered it to get the specification! To get the device off with the tape out, which I had done many times, I had always pressed [Stop/eject] to stop the tape playing and then a second time to eject the tape, then finally pressed [Operate] to switch off.

But my program's two-press how-to answer was, "You are playing a tape. How can you off with tape out? Press [Operate]. Press [Stop/eject]." Easily generated and ghastly English, maybe, but still insightful (we'll see how to do it in a minute). If the JVC is off when you eject the tape, it stays off, and switching the device off also stops the tape playing. So you can do in two presses what I had always done in three.

There are several ways to ask and answer how-to questions. We could require an exact and detailed question, such as: "how do I get the PVR to auto-stop recording in 210 minutes?" Here, we would imagine the user selects the desired goal state from a long list (a menu) of possible states. This sort of question does rather beg another: if the user has to specify exactly what they want to do, why doesn't the device just do it, rather than working out what the user has to do? I suppose it could be useful for training users who are supposed to know how to use the device, or who want to use it faster than scrolling through a potentially long menu of states, or most of the time (like a car driver) cannot take their eyes off what they are doing to read a menu—they want to learn what buttons to press for next time.

Another way is to break the question down into "tasks." This enables the user to ask how to change part of the system's state, such as: "how do I get the PVR to pause (leaving whatever else it is doing as unchanged as possible)?" In this example, the user would only select pause from the menu's shorter list of choices. The subtasks correspond to the indicators we introduced earlier. For a PVR, there will be a pause indicator, and it will either be on or off. The user can now ask the device, as it were, "How can I change the pause indicator from its current off status to being on?"

This question then begs the question, why not redesign the device so that its indicators *are* buttons? If the indicators tell the user what they want to know, why not also make them controls so the user can do what they want to directly? Thus the [Pause] button could have a light in it; pressing the button (generally) switches the light on or off. Well, that's a possibility we won't explore here—but it's a good example of how working out how to help the user results in better, or at least stimulating, design ideas.

In general, we won't know whether the user wants to learn how to use a device or really just wants to use the device. What does the user want when they ask a how-to question? Do they *really* want to know how to do something—maybe so that they can learn the answer and get more proficient at using the device—or do they just want to get a job done?

Here is one solution, which works on a screen-based computer simulation (or a web site): we display a dialogue box that provides both options. Note how we've summarized the question the user posed: it would just be compounding things if the user made a mistake asking the question but didn't notice they were given the right answer to the wrong question!

353

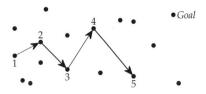

Figure 10.6: The user recently visited states 1–5, but they are really trying to get to an intended goal state, shown top right in the diagram, as efficiently as possible. The user wonders why they aren't at the desired goal state already. What did they do wrong? (For clarity, we aren't showing all state transitions, except those along the user's path.)

> You have the PVR off, with no tape in it.
> You asked: "How can I stop recording in 120 minutes?"
> Press the [Tape in] button.
> Press the [Record] button 5 times.
> Do you want to do it now or continue?
>
> [Do it now]   [Continue]

This answer, generated blindly by the program, has accidentally shown the "put the tape in" action as if it was a button press. Oops! Notice, too, that some simple programming ensures that if a button is to be pressed several times consecutively, each press is not spelled out, but a repetition is used—as here, the [Record] button is pressed "5 times." And to generate the answer, all the program has to do is find the shortest path from one state to the other.

10.7.3   "Why not?" questions

Then there are why-not questions. Maybe the user tried to do something and failed. *Why* didn't the device do what they wanted? As with the how-to questions, the user selects a goal to ask about, but now it's one they *had* wanted to achieve. Typical answers to why-not questions explain that the user has not *yet* reached the goals (more needs to be done), or that pressing some button got them further from the goal (they may have made earlier mistakes), or that a button press had no effect. Another possibility is that the user is mistaken: they have, in fact, reached the goal they say they wanted. The greater range of choices present a more interesting programing challenge than the how-to questions.

Here is an example of a why-not question and its answer:

> You asked: "Why isn't it rewinding the tape?"
> You tried pressing [Rewind] but it had no effect.
> Instead of pressing [Rewind] before that,
>   you should have pressed [Stop/eject].
> Do you want to know how to rewind a tape now or continue?
>
> [How]   [Continue]

Figure 10.7: The shortest path from state 5 to the user's goal is shown schematically by the wiggly arrow—the shortest path may go via many other states. The user could follow this arrow to get to their goal efficiently. (For clarity, we aren't showing the other states.)

If the user says that they do want to know how to do it now, we run the how-to question answering program for them—because if they want to get to this state, the how-to answer from the current state is the best way of doing it. Also, the user is likely to be familiar with the how-to answers and the style of the dialog boxes that they generate.

The idea works on the farmer's problem—in fact, it'll work on any problem. Suppose the user has made a mistake trying to get everything to the righthand bank, but the goat has been eaten by the wolf. The user asks why they haven't succeeded; on the next page, here's a possible answer:

> You asked: "Why aren't they all safely on right bank?"
> Instead of taking "cabbage," you should have taken "goat."
> You cannot recover from this error without resetting.
> Do you want to reset now or continue?
>
>   [Reset]   [Continue]

Here we can see one of the possible complications of answering questions is that there may be no shortest path, and this needs to be clearly interpreted for the user. Since the question and answer above is only running on a simulation of the real problem, it is possible to provide a reset option, but that might not be possible on some real devices.

While how-to questions are based on the shortest path from the current state to the desired goal state—what's the best way to get from one state to the other— why-not questions are answered by *reversing* the user's recent path they took to the current state. The four figures 10.6–10.9 help explain the key points.

Figure 10.6 (facing page) schematically illustrates how the user tries to reach the goal they have in mind. In the figure, the user has most recently visited five states, numbered 1–5, but they were trying to get to the goal state. Why aren't they where they want to be?

Finding the best answer to the why-not question means going back through earlier and earlier states along the user's recent path, until the best answer is found. There are many potential answers to a why-not question. Figures 10.7–10.9 show schematically some of the different possibilities.

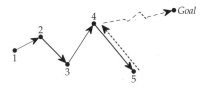

Figure 10.8: Perhaps going to state 5 took the user further from the goal? A shorter path to the goal *was* from state 4. This would certainly be the case if the last user action had done nothing—simply taking the user back to state 4.

Of course, it isn't obvious what "best" means for the user—generally, the best answer won't simply be the shortest path in terms of counting user actions. Answers could be weighted by how long the user took over each transition; the longer the user takes the "harder" presumably the transition was for them, and so the path through that transition should be considered to be longer. For example, an answer that says, "instead of doing x you should have done y" isn't very helpful if x happened a year ago! To stop explanations reaching too far back into the distant past, we can adjust weights so older actions count less in the scoring. This would stop the user feeling reprimanded for making a mistake ages ago.

There is a big difference between answering the question and the user knowing what to do next. The answer to a basic why-not question tells the user something they should learn, or be aware of in the future. But knowing they should have done something differently probably doesn't help them enough to get to their goal *now*. In the figures, I've shown the reverse steps along the user's path as if the user's actions can be undone easily, but this isn't always so. For example, if it is hard to get back from state 5 to state 4, even if the shortest paths were from earlier states, the best thing to do now is take the path from 5. Again, such considerations can be handled automatically by giving reverse paths different weights, depending on what sort of answers the user wants or is expected to want.

A why-not answer for the user therefore includes the possibility that the user might have been better off to have done something different earlier, rather than to progress from where they are now in the current state.

There are many choices for weighting. I found by experimenting that weighting the last action 1, and all earlier ones infinity gave adequate answers. At least these weights ensured that the answers to why-not questions were brief.

10.7.4   Don't be idle

Most interactive devices don't have help systems at all, and those that do generally aren't as helpful as they could be. Many devices that have help systems have the help as a menu item, and that makes it harder for the user to get help for other menu items—the user cannot say "I want help on *this* menu item," because to get help they have to select another item. The simplest solution is to have a dedicated (Help) button—and this also has the advantage that it is always visible to the user, which it might not be on a long scrolling menu list.

Figure 10.9: Continuing figures 10.7–10.8, perhaps going to states 4 then 5 was a diversion away from getting to the goal? Answering the why-not question goes back over the user's path, here finding that the shortest path to the goal *was* from state 3.

Having a dedicated button also encourages the interaction programmer to make the button work *all* the time. In particular, if the help button is on a remote control, we can hope that the designer thinks to make the help text readable from the distance the user will typically operate the remote control. Don't show help text on the video system's little LCD panel, show it on the TV screen. (And therefore think very carefully about the design of the system when the user is asking for help on why the video output isn't working!)

Typically, when a user wants help, they have to enter the help subsystem, find what they want to know, learn it or print it (faxes and printers can easily print their user manuals), and then do it. Why don't devices have a [Do it now] button, like our dialog boxes for how-to and why-not questions?

It is useful to have a concise way to criticize this sort of design issue: a device that seems to know what the user wants to do but won't do it for them is an idle device. (What I've called idle devices may be useful in educational and training situations, but generally they are frustrating for users.)

A help system that a user has told what they want to do, but then won't do it is certainly an idle help system. Device idleness appears in other guises too, particularly in error recovery.

As a good interaction programmer, you will write code that detects error conditions in your device. After detecting an error, your program should report the error condition, explain why they arise, and tell the user what to do. More strategically, you should write a program to check your program source code for all such error messages, and then you should try to modify the design to eliminate the need for the messages—your checking program will tell you what error reports need fixing, and when you have finished removing all error reports.

▷ This is something WAGN didn't do with their ticket machine and its error messages; see section 3.9 (p. 77).

It's idle to report errors that the device itself could fix. Figure 10.10 (next page) shows a Samsung NV3 camera telling the user to switch it off and on again. It's good that it is reporting an error and suggesting a solution—rather than just crashing and not saying anything to help the user. But it is idle, as the programmer clearly knows the solution but isn't going to do anything for the user. Why doesn't the device reboot itself? Why doesn't the program do the switch-off-switch-on cycle itself? Maybe the hardware can't do that, but if the hardware can't do that, why wasn't it redesigned so that it *could* do a soft reset?

Figure 10.10: An apparently-crashed Samsung NV3 camera just after a user switched it on, saying "Turn off and on again." The camera is telling the user how to recover from some unexplained internal error. Why doesn't the camera do a soft restart itself and save the user the trouble? The camera is behaving as if it is idle. Certainly, the camera seems idly designed: the message shows that the problem was known early enough in the development cycle to have an error message written for it, yet the problem was not fixed—other than by asking the user to do the work.

An error message is better than nothing. Even better is for the device to do itself what it wants the user to do. It is idle to tell the user to do things that the device itself can do, and it's generally bad design—it's *certainly* bad design if you haven't thought through the trade-offs.

10.7.5   Weighting answers

If the costs of user actions are going to be weighted, weights can be adjusted at any time. Costs could suit the overall aim either of the system (some states are worthwhile getting to quickly—for example, the most important thing for a fire alarm is to get it set quickly if it needs setting) or costs could be chosen to help answer specific questions, or the weights could change dynamically as the user works with the device.

 ▷   See also section 9.6.4 (p. 304), which considered different sorts of costs for the
      shortest paths algorithm.

For example, if weights are reduced every time the user makes a state transition, then the answers can be preferentially chosen to be expressed in terms of routes with which the user is more familiar: the more often the user does something, the more favorable its weights become, and so answers to questions tend to take the better-weighted routes.

The ratio of repetition (for learning) to efficiency (for doing) could be varied to suit the user or short- or long-term criteria for the device or its intended uses. The automatically generated help answers can therefore be designed into a device to optimize the user's performance for certain tasks: for learning or for action, reference, emergency response, fault diagnosis, or for machine-related criteria (such as its long life)—depending on what cost factors the designer wants to build in.

It would even be possible for the program to work out several answers using different weightings and, if they are different, to say things like, "The fastest way to do that is to ..., but you're more familiar with doing ..., which will also do it, but not so quickly." Or perhaps, "Although x is the preferred way, if it's an emergency do y, which is quicker."

Another idea is for expert users to train the device (say by solving typical problems). The advice generated would teach the user solutions that are preferred by experts. It would be interesting to do both: then the user could be told that, whereas they have often solved the problem this way, an expert would have done something else.

In fact, rather than wait for the user to ask an explicit question of the device, we could wait until they had used it for a long period (all the while adjusting weights) and then automatically look at every possible thing that can be done on the device. We would then report back to the user (or their teacher) cases where the user has taken non-expert paths.

10.7.6   Programming wizards

A wizard is told what the user wants to achieve and then takes the user through the necessary steps to achieve that task. If, say, you were setting up your internet configuration, there are lots of things to do, and a wizard can ensure that you do everything right. Moreover, a good wizard will explain each step and how to find the right information to fill in the details; a good wizard will also know that some details are already somewhere on the system, and it can fill these details in so the user doesn't have to.

> ▷   The how-to and why-not answers were in fact simple examples of wizards, discussed in sections 10.7.2 (p. 352) and 10.7.3 (p. 354), respectively.

When a device is represented as a state machine, wizards are very easy to implement. First, identify all the states that represent useful goals for the user to get to. Of course many states will not be interesting for a wizard; they are just device-centered steps on the way to achieving user goals. So we need to extend the device specification to allow useful goal states to be flagged in some way. Since we already have an array of state names, we can easily give a list of state names of interest to the wizard, something like this:

```
var device = {
  ...
  stateNames:  ["dim", "off", "on"],
  wizardNames: [{name: "lit", states: ["dim", "on]},
               {name: "off", states: ["off"]}
             ],
  ...
}
```

The idea is that when the user presses the Wiz button, a choice of the states in the `wizardNames` array will appear. If the state the device is in is one of the wizard states, then it ought to be identified in the list, rather like a "you are here" marker. (If the user selected this goal, the wizard is only going to sigh; we can't automatically assume that the user knows they are there already—but we can be pretty certain that a user would find it tedious to be given the current state as an option, select it, and *then* be told they are already there.)

It does not matter whether we think of the wizard as a feature for the designer or as a feature for the user. A user will obviously find a wizard useful for getting through a sequence of steps to achieve goals; a designer will find a wizard useful for learning how a user would have to use a device to achieve goals. A technical author writing a user manual might like a wizard's help for writing optimal instructions. One way gives direct help, another gives insight into the design, and the third way gives insight into writing help.

Once a wizard goal is selected (possibly with a confirmation if we were worried that some goals the user might choose are "dangerous"—this needs another array like `dangerousNames`), the wizard works out all the shortest paths from the current state to each of the goal states. In the simple lightbulb example, the wizard would work out the paths to dim and on states if the user wanted to make the lightbulb come on.

In general, there will be several paths from the current state to each of the wizard's goals. In the lightbulb example, if the device is off, then there are two paths from the current state (off) to the lightbulb being lit: it could be either dim or on. The wizard automatically follows all paths while they are the same, changing the device state as it goes. When it comes to a choice, it asks the user what their preference is to do.

The lightbulb is simple enough to spell out all of the possibilities (without taking up too much space) to see how the wizard would work:

Current state	User asks	Wizard's response
Off	off?	Says it's already off
	lit?	Do you want it on or dim?
Dim	off?	(does it)
	lit?	Says it's already lit
On	off?	(does it)
	lit?	Says it's already lit

Whether you want the wizard to say it's already lit when it is or to change to, or offer to change to, the other lit state depends on what you want the device to do.

This simple example may or may not be doing what you think a wizard should be doing, but it paints a persuasive picture. If you are building an interactive system—no doubt far more complex that a three-state lightbulb—work out a systematic way of getting a wizard to work. Even if you don't need a wizard in the final, delivered product, you, as the designer, can use the wizard's possible answers to help you check that the design of the device is sound.

You could easily write a bit of program that asks the wizard every possible question in every possible state. How long are its answers? Are their some exceedingly long answers? If so, the device might be redesigned by adding some shortcuts.

The wizard-checking program might work out the average and standard deviation of the its reply lengths and then present the designer with all questions that got a reply more than, say, one standard deviation higher than the average. All of the answers that are so long (however they are classified) then these indicate issues the designer should reconsider.

How many "dangerous" states does a user risk wading through? Should the designer reduce the dangers or make the dangerous states more remote (so wizard answers don't take shortest paths via these states)?

Or get the wizard to mark all states where users have choices to make in achieving their tasks: are these reasonably designed? Are the choices, and their impact, clear to users from the device's indicators?

A real advantage of building a wizard into a device framework is that once you have programmed a wizard, it should work however a design is modified or updated. Since wizards encapsulate the notion of useful tasks, a wizard can help summarize the difference between its answers on the previous iteration of the design and its new answers for an improved design. That is, run the wizard on all possible user questions on Monday, and the wizard saves its answers. On Tuesday, after having revised and improved the design in some way, run the wizard again; it reports back to you the *changes* in its answers. This will be a focused summary of how your revisions are affecting the tasks you expect the user to want to do.

Wizards are usually thought of as palliatives, features to help users cope with complex systems. But they are helpful, probably more helpful, for getting designers to consider everything a user has to walk through with a design; they can help compare the effectiveness of new versions of a design; and they can help the designer identify tedious or dangerous sequences of actions that the user has to do to achieve their goals. Wizards as design aids are underrated!

There is certainly no excuse for a design to be released to users with a wizard that can't solve all problems that will be asked of it. There is no excuse, in fact, for designers not to develop their own wizards to benefit from the wizards' design insights, whether or not any of those wizards are released in the device the users finally get.

10.7.7 Dynamic checks

Many of the design checks we did in the framework can be done dynamically, that is, while the user is interacting with a device.

As a device is used, the world changes, and some things become possible or impossible, as the case may be. We want to ensure, despite any changes, that the device still has all its required properties.

Unless it is something like a fire extinguisher that can only be used once, then the device should always be strongly connected or at least warn users that they are about to do something irreversible. Obviously whether you forbid, allow, or warn about certain actions and their consequences depends on the purpose of the device—but the warnings (or email reports to the product's manufacturers) could be done automatically.

361

▷ On dynamic checks as variations of drawing rules for finite state machines, see
section 6.3.9 (p. 189).

10.7.8   General help principles

All the examples above, help and wizards—putting analysis into products—are
specific techniques, and they may not work well on a particular device. Rather
than implement exactly what's described here, it's better to follow the general
principles:

■ Implement automatic help so that it is reliable.

■ Usually a user is reading help not because they want to learn something, but
because they want to do something. Allow the user to directly do what they
are reading: provide a ⟨Do it⟩ button.

■ In many devices, it will be tempting to provide help through a menu system.
Unfortunately, this makes help work at the wrong level—you don't usually
need help about the menu, you want help about its menu items and help about
where menu items are. Help is so useful, especially when it is implemented
well, that it should be provided as its own button.

■ As your help will become a sophisticated system in its own right, provide a
way of navigating around it, so that the user doesn't have to keep going in and
out of it when searching for things.

■ Print out all help text as a single document and proof read it carefully. Ideally
the help text and the printed user manual can be made to correspond, or one
can be derived automatically from the other. This way, as designer you have
half the work and double the quality.

10.8   Complex devices

The examples in this book are quite small, as I wanted to be able to draw pictures
of them and to talk about them more-or-less exhaustively to help illustrate design
principles. It would have been very difficult have huge systems and make any
sense of them. And big devices have many more issues to talk about, and the
book would merely have been longer without being more insightful. Or I could
use the defense that since big, complex systems are hard to use, we *don't* want a
method that scales up to handle them; we want a design framework that helps
ensure devices are easy to use!

Yet, certainly, real devices are very complex. Fortunately, the techniques scale
up to bigger systems. We just have to stop worrying about looking at the devices,
and instead rely on programs to do the analysis. Instead of looking at drawings
and spotting issues visually, we use programs to check details—or, better, we use
programs to build systems with the interaction properties we want to start with.

Here are several key approaches:

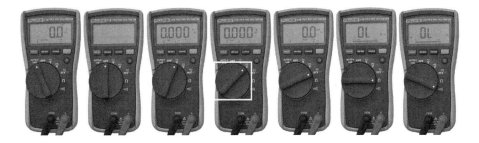

Figure 10.11: Programming complex devices takes careful planning. For this digital multimeter, instead of having thousands of separate images, one for each possible state, it is better to cut the image into slices and treat each slice as a separate indicator. The location of the slice for the knob is shown by the square in the middle image above. This slice shows different knob positions by displaying one of the seven different images of the knob. (The knob is both an input device and a physical indicator: indicators do not need to be lights—for this device they are a mixture of physical objects and the icons on its LCD.) Ignoring the digits, which would anyway be best programmed as graphics, the multimeter also needs the LCD to be cut into 15 slices that are either blank or show an icon.

■ Many features are consistent across the device and do not need to be represented explicitly. For example, if every state has a transition to Off, why not write some program code so that this part of the design is constructed automatically? A simple for loop can do this (running over each state); it will simply set the (OFF) transition automatically and hence correctly.

■ The DeWalt DC925 cordless drill and the farmer's problem are examples of devices constructed entirely automatically, from JavaScript programs that construct the finite state machine descriptions. The farmer's problem has some pointless states that we had to decide how to handle. A real farmer can see separate states, such as leaving the goat and cabbage alone before returning, when it will change to just a goat; but in our models we used in the book, the goat eats the cabbage immediately, and the wolf eats the goat immediately, so there are no separate states. I didn't spot this "design decision" in the model until I wrote the program to model the problem. Not that understanding the farmer's problem is going to help solve any real design problems, but the insight illustrates the power of creating and analyzing device specifications automatically.

▷ The farmer's problem was discussed in section 10.1 (p. 325) onwards; the DeWalt DC925 drill was discussed in section 9.8 (p. 316);

■ Many features are consistent over parts of the device. For example, a menu tree will probably have up, down, left, and right commands for each state, and again a simple piece of program code can add these features onto a simple tree. Then all the designer does is specify the tree and its generic features; the generic features are added automatically to each state in the tree.

■ The representation of finite state machines is all detail, and the wealth of detail gets more obscure, the more states are needed. In fact, this is the problem that statecharts addressed: so all we need to do is introduce program features to build statecharts. These functions build the underlying finite state machine. The designer then is dealing with program code that calls functions like cluster to cluster states together—supporting all the features discussed in chapter 7, "Statecharts," and perhaps others that are useful for the application, such as special forms of history.

■ Statecharts are only one possible way of representing more complex state machines. They have the advantage of being very visual, but they are not the only approach to simplifying handling large systems. Regular expressions could be used, for instance. The programming languages CSP, Spin, and SMV are examples of textual languages that basically define state machines. For some applications, these languages will be much more convenient to use than the more direct approach used in this book. Furthermore, these languages have sophisticated features for specifying and checking properties of designs.

10.9   Conclusions

The previous chapter introduced a JavaScript programming framework to simulate and analyze devices; this chapter showed how the framework could be used to measure how effective designs were, and to compare designs. We gave many examples of interesting design properties that are easily measured.

The properties used in this chapter were trivial (from a programming point of view) and very easy to work out. Had designers thought about states and actions, and bothered to write decent programs that checked for sensible device properties, a lot of needlessly awkward gadgets would never have gone to market. The point is that for any purpose we have in mind we can come up with relevant properties—there are many you can think of for your problems that this book has not space to explore—and then very easily work them out and see how a modified or altered device design can improve on the measurements.

A particularly important idea was to take some of the design insights to provide advice to the user. We showed two simple ways to do this: to answer questions (such as the why-not questions) and to run wizards for the user. All approaches work in a dual way: they provide immediate insight for designers *and* they can be put into practical aids for users.

10.9.1   Some *Press On* principles

■ Designers have an obligation to do design analysis and to use programs to do it → section 10.2 (p. 328).

■ If we decide what criteria we want, we can redesign automatically → section 10.2 (p. 330).

■ Find all device behaviors that are *almost* true—they beguile the user and should be fixed (or justified), and do this automatically so you are thorough → section 10.3 (p. 337).

■ Don't take single design metrics seriously—use measures to compare different designs → section 10.6 (p. 351).

■ Don't be idle: if a device knows how to do something, let the user do it directly rather than in steps → section 10.7 (p. 356).

■ Build wizards into design tools to fully explore how users "ought" to behave → section 10.7 (p. 360).

■ Users read help usually because they want to *do* things—provide a special help button → section 10.7 (p. 362).

10.9.2 Further reading

■ Gow, J., Thimbleby, H. W., and Cairns, P., "Misleading Behaviour in Interactive Systems," in Dearden, A. & Watts, L., eds., *Proceedings of HCI 2004: Design for Life*, volume 2, pp9–12. Research Press International, 2004. This paper describes partial theorems as well as a powerful tool for handling device specifications using matrix algebra. If you wish to follow up beguiling behavior, this is the place to start.

■ Pemmaraju, S. V., and Skiena, S. S., *Computational Discrete Mathematics*, Cambridge University Press, 2003 (successor to Skiena, S. S., *Implementing Discrete Mathematics*, Addison-Wesley, 1990). This book provides lots of algorithms for doing things with graphs, though the algorithms are coded for a system called Mathematica: depending on your point of view this makes the algorithms more accessible or more idiosyncratic.

■ ■ ■

The languages CSP, Spin, and SMV are described well in the following: Hoare, C. A. R., *Communicating Sequential Processes*, Prentice-Hall, 1985; Holzmann, G. J., *The Spin Model Checker*, Addison-Wesley (2004); and Clarke, E. M., *Model Checking*, MIT Press, 1999. The Spin and SMV books include key techniques, algorithms, and tools for model checking; they can be used as introductions to the subject or as reference books for their prize-winning systems, Prolema (the language behind Spin) and SMV. Alloy is a completely different sort of system; it's book gives a very readable survey of alternative systems and the rationales behind them: see Jackson, D., *Software Abstractions*, MIT Press, 2006.

All of these systems can be downloaded and tried out.

11

More complex devices

It all started in 1991. We spent the weekend in a house in the Canadian Rockies—Ian Witten, a computer science professor friend of mine joined us and all our hungry kids. The electricity had been switched off, and our first job when we arrived was to get power switched on—and to get the microwave oven working so we could cook supper. The microwave was a model aptly called the Genius, Panasonic model number NN-9807. Our task looked easy enough.

It took us about 45 minutes to get it switched on. Why did we find it difficult to switch a microwave oven on? What general lessons are there, and what can be done?

At first, I suspected that Ian and I might have been idiosyncratically bad at using microwave ovens; neither he nor I were expert microwave users. I spent the weekend trying to understand exactly how the Genius worked, and the next week I built a careful, accurate simulation of the Genius. I then did some experiments on other people—asking them to try to get my simulation of the microwave oven working, to try to do what Ian and I had failed to do.

The conclusion was that our difficulty was not unusual. The only advantage we had by being professors was that we didn't immediately blame ourselves for the problem, as it *couldn't* be our fault!

▷ The tendency of people to blame themselves for problems they experience with bad design is discussed in section 2.9 (p. 52), where we explore cognitive dissonance—a plausible explanation for the "it's *my* fault" syndrome.

Basically, the Genius would not start cooking. We presumed this was because it needed to know the time: it had some time buttons and was not displaying the time. When we pressed some of the minute and hour buttons, the Genius allowed us to get any number between 00:00 and 99:99 shown on its display. So we naturally thought that the clock accepted 24-hour times. Since it was late in the evening when we arrived at our friend's house, about 22:00 hours, we tried setting that time. The microwave seized up—you could say it really froze, a strange thing for a microwave oven to do.

We had to unplug to reset it and to carry on. Then we tried 22:05, then 22:15, … and we tried later and later times as time went by, until finally we set the time to

1:00. (We had noticed that we were wasting our time telling the clock the correct time; we would pretend that it was 1:00, since the oven surely didn't really care.) The clock and the microwave then worked!

Having found one way of setting it, we soon realized that we had been misled by the clock. It was secretly a 12-hour clock, willing only to work when set to a time between 1:00 and 12:59, even though the display could be set to any number, including all the misleading 24-hour clock times we had been trying.

We then had a wager about what the user manual would say: would it say how to set the clock or wouldn't it? When we eventually found and read the manual, we agreed that we were both wrong: the manual did warn about the 12-hour clock problem but relegated the warning to a *footnote*!

We expected the clock to work one way but it didn't. Indeed, it gave us misleading clues that, as it could count so high, it obviously had to be a 24-hour clock. As long as we wrongly assumed that we knew how it worked, we would never be able to set the clock. Part of the problem was that we didn't think, "We're assuming how it works—let's check," because it seemed so obvious how it was working we did think we had assumptions to check.

There were at least two things wrong with the design. First, the clock should not have seized up when set to an "invalid" time (even one outside of 24 hours, like 66:66). Secondly, the user manual should have been a bit more helpful, if not more visible (perhaps there should be a label fixed on the side of the oven?).

> ▷ Anybody who writes a footnote in a user manual to give the user important information ought to tell the designer to fix the design—and make the footnote unnecessary! See section 3.3 (p. 65) where this idea is stated as a design principle.

Given that both of those design faults had been made, the user interface—the front panel of the microwave oven—should have been clearer. Or maybe the microwave should not need setting to any particular time before it works. You don't need to know that it is 10 o'clock in the evening to do 3 minutes of high-power cooking, so why does the microwave?

11.1 Starting to avoid design problems

When users don't understand how things work, they may be completely stuck, and *once* they get stuck—probably meaning they have a faulty idea in their minds about how the device works—there is little *they* can do to escape; it all comes down to the design, and how it handles error recovery. Or if the user has the *right* idea but the device just doesn't work like that, then they are stuck.

How could Panasonic, the microwave oven's maker, have avoided this design problem? Presumably the company tests designs on professional cooks and other potential users; whatever it did in the development process hadn't helped to fix the design problem. Indeed, several years later they were still selling microwave ovens with the same design: the manual of a later model just warned in much bigger writing that is was a 12-hour clock. Clearly, even getting feedback from user problems isn't enough to help fix a bad design once it has gone into production.

Somehow designers need to evaluate their designs before they are committed to production. Unfortunately, it is rather too easy for designers to be biased when they try to anticipate how users will work with their designs. When designing the Genius digital clock, the designers probably assumed that everybody uses the 12-hour clock, and they probably tested the microwave on people who shared that assumption without thinking about it. It was an unspoken assumption. There would have been no design problem to solve because nobody would ever enter 10 p.m. as 22:00, and nobody in the design team or evaluation team would notice this as a potential flaw—until it was too late, that is, as the user manual's footnote makes clear. Noticing the design problem was came late in the process.

Some design errors cannot be found by using people, whether designers or test users. Yet you can be sure that there are users out there who will eventually stumble onto design problems. With the Genius my experiments suggested that about half the normal population of potential users would have had trouble in the afternoons; that's pretty bad, but not being able to use a microwave oven is hardly a disaster. With more safety-critical devices, say medical equipment designed for nurses to use, the chances of a user problem are lower (the nurses will be trained to use the devices), but the consequences of a design fault are much higher. Somehow we have to avoid preconceptions about use, and, in particular, preconceptions we don't even think about!

One approach to evaluating system designs is to carefully model users and to try to make realistic models of how they behave. Of course, this is very difficult. In the case in question how would we notice that we'd accidentally designed all the tasks to use 12-hour clocks? If, as designers, we are not aware that the 12-hour clock is a design issue, why should we build user models for testing purposes that (always or sometimes) use 24-hour clocks? The 12/24-hour question may seem pretty obvious in hindsight, but what of the design problems that we don't know about? What if we are designing a new product and *nobody* has any idea what the key issues are?

Although user models can be run relentlessly without a break and can therefore examine a large part of a user interface design, user models are fraught with difficulties. They may have systematic biasses, so, for example, parts of a design never get exercised. They may be incorrectly configured, so that timings and other measures are inaccurate and possibly misleading. In short, it seems easier to use real people directly to test a device, rather than to use them to build the models of what they would do. But real people on actual tests are they are expensive an slow, and it is very tedious to record what they do with a proposed design.

▷ See section 11.7 (p. 401) for ideas on spotting oversights in user testing.

Real people suffer from the same problems that user models do: we can't recruit the whole planet to do our system evaluation, so we inevitably miss out on some crucial behavior that somebody has. It would be easy to recruit ten people and for all of them to think the same way about clocks (particularly if they are our friends and relations, from the same office, or from the same country). If so, any study based on ten people would not be very insightful.

If we are designing our device specifically for young people, or the old, or the ill, then we should have proper concern for treating them ethically and legally— getting ten sick people to help us try out our design requires informed consent; getting children to help requires parental consent; and so on. Getting users who represent our target audience is tricky. If we are designing a device to give medical advice, and we are using people to test it, then there is a chance it will give mis- leading advice—perhaps because we haven't finished it, or because there is a fault in the user interface (that's what we expect—it's why we're doing the tests!) and the user simply gets the wrong advice. There are many complications to consider if we are serious about using people seriously for real device design!

It might seem counterintuitive, but a safer approach is to assume nothing about users and to get users who know nothing. Ignorant users might do absolutely anything, and if they behave randomly then they might assume that the clock was 24-hour; they might even assume it was 100-hour or 7-hour—and their problems would help designers discover new issues that nobody has yet thought of or had the patience to unearth. It could be useful to redesign to avoid the problems you discover with ignorant users. At least you should know the problems exist, so that palliatives can be worked out, say, by writing warnings in the user manual.

Once we see people making mistakes with 100-hour clocks, we can decide how to design for real humans. Maybe nobody would do this deliberately (maybe they would), but the design has to cope if anybody does it by mistake. We need to know the consequences of any user behavior, deliberate, ignorant, erroneous, or insightful.

The question is, where do we get such users to work with?

11.1.1   Using gnomes

There probably aren't any humans who can be relied on to behave truly ran- domly, so let's hire some gnomes. Gnomes are well known to be very ignorant and in particular to know nothing about microwave ovens, or anything else mod- ern and interactive for that matter. They aren't worried about which buttons they press or whether pressing some buttons will break them (the ovens that is, not the gnomes). Apparently, our gnomes are so ignorant about microwaves that they might even try plugging and unplugging the microwave oven to see what happens—something Ian and I found out the hard way was a solution to getting it going after it had frozen up. (If we didn't let the gnomes do anything, then when the microwave freezes up, as it will, they would get *very* frustrated indeed, as gnomes do.)

For some applications, like security locks or things with safety latches, testing with gnomes would be a very good idea. If a gnome can break in or release the safety device, the security needs tightening.

A gnome is a metaphor for a user who embodies all possible wrong and right ways of using a system: gnomes can do anything. If we have a gnome to test designs, the designer cannot fall into the trap of assuming anything much and thereby being misled. This is a really important point. Other testing methods

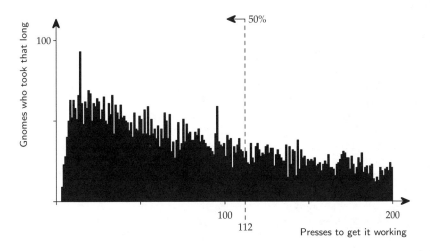

Figure 11.1: A bar chart showing how many gnomes managed to get the original Genius microwave oven to work in a given number of button presses. Some of the 10,000 gnomes used took more than 200 presses, and their data is not shown (which is why the 50% line seems too far to the right).

assume that the user (or perhaps a simulated user) knows what they are doing or that they make certain sorts of errors—in any case, generally that the user is doing some specific thing. A gnome approach makes no such assumptions; they model the user doing absolutely anything at all—and it is easy to have lots of gnomes working together or separately helping evaluate the device. In short, gnomes tell you, the designer, everything about a design, and in the end, when you add up all the figures, their performance gives a statistical overview of the design. Gnomes are also a lot faster than human users, so we get far more general results much sooner.

Let's sit a gnome down and get them to try to get the Genius to work. We'll count how many steps the gnome takes. Obviously sometimes gnomes will get lucky, and sometimes they will take ages. So we really need to hire lots of gnomes and average the results. I hired 10,000 gnomes and sat them down with a computer simulation of the Genius. They worked away, and I drew a bar chart of the results, shown in figure 11.1 (this page).

▷ Section 11.1.5 (p. 376) explains how to hire gnomes and how to put them to work.

Almost half the gnomes managed to get the microwave working in 100 button presses or less (in fact, the median is 112), some took over 200 presses to get it working, and one even took 1,560 presses! (Few humans would have the patience without doing more than unplugging it.) We are counting plugging the microwave in as one "press" because to get it to work after it has frozen up, it needs unplugging and plugging back in.

The gnomes seem to find this "simple" job really hard work. Yet if we asked the designer of the clock how many button presses it takes to set it, they might reply just *four* steps! That is, to get the clock to work after the oven's been plugged in, press [Clock] to enter the clock-setting mode, then press [1-hour], so it shows a valid time (namely, 01:00 o'clock), then press [Clock] again to start the clock running with that time. Easy—if you know how.

But my hired gnomes took 160 presses on average, a lot more than the designer's guess of 4. This huge discrepancy suggests that the design could be improved, or at least that the designer's optimism is unrealistic—or that we could train the gnomes better.

Let's look seriously at why the gnomes take so long compared to the designer's ideas. The Genius locks up when it is set to a time outside of the 1:00–12:59 window. There is absolutely no design reason in principle for a lockup. Removing the lockup (by redesigning the oven) dramatically helps the gnomes to be faster. Now, half the gnomes succeed in 77 or fewer presses, with an average time of 108 presses.

If we also changed the design so that impossible times, like 27:78, cannot be set, the gnomes get even faster, taking in average about 50 button presses to get the microwave going. Half of them will have got it working in 35 or fewer button presses—the tail of the graph. The number of gnomes who take more than 100 presses now has a factor of five fewer gnomes in it. That's a huge improvement. Figure 11.2 (facing page) shows the bar chart based on the improved design.

Naturally we expect the unlucky gnomes to take longer on average than the designer's ideal or a typical human user, because, after all, gnomes don't know what they are doing. Nevertheless, our gnomes have helped us find a faster and easier-to-use design. The following table summarizes the results:

Design	*Average*	*Median*
Original Genius	161	112
Debugged not to freeze	108	77
Sensible design	49	35

So a little thought—motivated by random testing—lets us achieve a design that's on average about three to four times easier to use (at least for gnomes, if not for humans).

Now, when we humans use gadgets, much of the time we don't know how they work or what we are supposed to do; we're in much the same league of insight as the mindless gnomes—and a modified design, such as the one proposed here, that helps gnomes would also help us.

The improved design still supports all the original functionality (like cooking chickens), it just removes some design problems. Indeed, with human users, the faster design has the additional advantage of not allowing a user to display a misleading 24-hour time (like 22:02).

A random exploration of a design presupposes no specific knowledge of the user (or gnome). This has two advantages. First, a good designer ought to consider the possible wrong ways in which a design might be used. But there are infinitely many ways of being wrong, and a designer can only think of some of

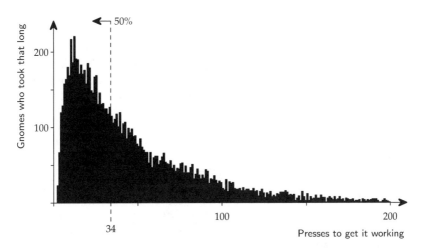

Figure 11.2: Bar chart showing how many gnomes managed to get the improved design of the Genius microwave oven to work in a given number of button presses. Compare with figure 11.1 (p. 371), which shows their performance on the original Genius. Now half the gnomes succeed in fewer than 34 presses, and only about 10% of the gnomes are taking more than 100 presses to succeed, whereas before half the gnomes took more that 112 presses. The improvement is clear from the way this graph tails off so quickly.

them. A random process, like our gnomes, however, embodies all possible wrong ways of using a system. Randomness is a remarkably effective way of testing out designs. After all, human users could only test according to their own few and fixed preconceptions. Moreover, if their preconceptions were the same as the designers, very little would be discovered about the design that the designer didn't already think they knew. Quite likely the original Genius design was made by a designer who didn't think in 24-hour times and they never thought to test for them.

So, although a gnomic "random user" is less efficient than a real human user, it cannot be tricked into guessing the designer's tacit assumptions. Gnomes are also a lot cheaper and faster than humans: being cheaper is good ecognomics, and you get them to work faster by using a metrognome (although I used a computer). This ease of testing with gnomes is their second advantage.

It is very interesting that a random gnome can set the microwave clock on average in 50 button presses, whereas Ian and I took far more. Our human intelligence was not helping us! We would have worked out what to do faster if we had simply tossed a coin to decide what to do next, because then we would have been working like gnomes.

11.1.2   Children as little gnomes

Certainly, being random is a better way of getting things to work than having the wrong ideas. This observation explains why children are so much better than adults at operating gadgets. Since they start off with no preconceptions, they press buttons pretty much at random. That approach gets results quickly, faster than a systematic approach that an adult would use.

So, we're not old and past it when we can't use gadgets. More likely, we know how they should work, but as they don't work that way, we get stuck. Children don't know how they work and they don't have preconceptions about "expensive" errors that scare us—we may be worried about breaking the expensive gadget or not using it "properly." But children, with no such worries, get along fine, and quite quickly understand examples of how the devices work. Once they have seen the devices work, not only does their confidence grow, but they can also learn from working knowledge. Put another way, using gnomes avoids all design assumptions. The gnomes are random button pressers. They do not work as we expect them to; they work (eventually) in all possible ways.

> ▷   Section 11.1.5 (p. 376) shows how gnomes can be programmed very easily.

The most likely reason why the Genius had its quirky design flaw was that its designers assumed that nobody would try a 24-hour time, and (if Panasonic did any user trials) the test users they picked also never thought to try a 24-hour time. The cultural assumptions caught them out, then. Since gnomes, like children, know nothing about what sort of clocks, 12 or 24 hours, we're supposed to use, they will check the design more thoroughly than any human process, whereas we know how devices should work, so we try to use them the right way. If a clock can count up to 99:99, it surely is a 24-hour clock. This is such a simple assumption, it will take you ages before you notice that you've assumed something plausible about the device that may not be true. The designers may never have thought that you'd think like this, and you haven't noticed you are thinking like it either.

> ▷   The problems, and benefits, of simple heuristics (like, if it looks like a 24-hour clock *it is* a 24-hour clock) is discussed in section 2.10 (p. 54).

Unfortunately, when our knowledge about the world is not reflected in the design of a device, we are worse off than not knowing anything. If we think we are right, but the device is designed otherwise, we will be stuck. One of our gnomes, or a child too young to know how the world should work, is prepared to experiment and play with "wild" ideas that we discounted as unrealistic and irrelevant.

> ▷   A general principle for a designer to follow to avoid this problem is to exploit affordance; see section 12.3 (p. 415). Also, design devices that do not have just one right way of use. Follow the principle of permissiveness, as raised in section 5.2 (p. 134). Section 11.4 (p. 387) discusses how permissiveness can make devices less susceptible to errors.

Children play to learn about the world. Adults stop playing because it is more efficient to use what knowledge they learnt through their early years of life spent playing. Adults also pay for the gadgets and they worry about breaking them. If you are past playing with gadgets, then their odd design is frustrating rather than fun. The frustration itself makes it harder to enjoy using a device and persevering to find a solution! When you find yourself in this position, toss a coin or roll a dice—use some technique to make yourself approach the device like a gnome or a child. This will help you break out of whatever fixation you have become trapped by; with luck you'll be able to get on with your life quickly.

As always, good advice to a user can be rephrased as advice for a designer. Why not add a button to a device so that the device itself "rolls the dice" and presses a random button? Better still, why not bias the dice so that it only rolls to choose buttons the user hasn't tried pressing recently in the state? Then, if the user presses the [PLAY!] button (that is a less threatening button name than [HELP]), you could have a nice flashing display of all the currently untried options, and then the flashing slows down, cycling through the buttons, until—yes!—it's settled on suggesting [Off]! Well, maybe if the user switches the device off and on again, they will be more successful next time.

> ▷ Of course, we can do better than suggest the user presses a random button.
>   See section 11.3.2 (p. 385).

Pressing a button at random, or to save the user the effort of having a button to make a random transition (so the user doesn't have to worry about working out a random action), can *help* the user, but sometimes a random action might be exactly what the user *wants* to do. They want to do something surprising, for fun, and what better than a random action? The Apple iPod Shuffle does just this: it can be set to play random tracks of music. Here, the "gnome" is a bit more intelligent than our gnomes—the iPod doesn't replay tracks it has chosen immediately. In fact, the idea of shuffle is that it first randomly shuffles the tracks, then plays from that list of tracks; otherwise, it would run the risk of repeating a lucky track too often or too soon. When it gets to the end of the list of chosen tracks, it reshuffles and starts again.

11.1.3   The bugs inside

One problem with the Genius is that the computer program inside it is childishly simple—perhaps another reason why children find it easy to use! More seriously, it has a bug.

There are four digits in the clock's time display, and simply, there are four buttons that adjust each digit. The [1-minute] button increases the minutes; the [10-minute] button increases the tens of minutes; the [1-hour] button increases the hours digits, and so on. That's all the buttons do. The program is so trivial that [10-minute] *always* increases tens of minutes, from 59 to 69 to 79. Neither 69 nor 79 minutes are valid times by anyone's clock. The programmer, perhaps pleased with the neat scheme of every button behaving exactly the same, forgot that the only button that should work so freely is the [1-minute]. The [1-hour] button should not change 2 to 3 if the 10-hour digit is already a 1, because we shouldn't be able to change the time from 12 o'clock to 13 o'clock because 12-hour clocks don't ever get to show 13. It is absolutely trivial to get the programming right so that "times" out of the 1.00 to 12.59 window simply cannot be set. A modified design would then work like an analog wrist watch, where you simply can't set the time to something impossible.

11.1.4   Another microwave oven

To do all this we need a specification for the device, in this case another microwave oven. Once we have this, the definition of the device, its simulation, its usability analysis, and its user manuals in any language (and interactive help, if required), can all be worked on directly and efficiently in a suitable design framework.

If part of the design process suggests improvements, say, that the user manual has an obscurity, then it can be changed directly by modifying the specification; the new specification will update all other parts of the product, the analysis, the simulation, and so on. Importantly, the approach only has one definition of the device; thus changes—as occur during iterative design and product revision— immediately and automatically affect all parts of the development process: the analysis, the simulation, the help (and even the hardware).

Thus many components of a product are derived efficiently and automatically, almost at once. In normal design methods, there is a sequential (and costly) progression from specification, through fabrication, to manual writing, and finally usage. If any errors are detected, usually the whole process has to be started again, or when that is too expensive or would cause too much delay, one chooses to live with the errors—and maybe reprint the user manuals with warnings. In particular, only at later stages can usability problems be identified—but by then the product is already fabricated, and many of the usability insights would be very hard to take back to the specification, even it was still available.

To simulate the microwave oven, we can define it as a device in JavaScript using the framework from earlier chapters. We then add some gnomes.

> ▷   The original definition of the microwave oven we are using for this example appears in section 9.4.6 (p. 286). Using the same example show how a variety of design techniques handle the same device.

The microwave oven has a "touch pad" so we've changed the action words in the specification to describe the user's actions to be touching, rather than pressing. It would be a fun project to improve the English we will be generating with these boilerplate texts, but we won't go that way, except to point out that it isn't very hard to produce accurate and fairly clear if not perfect user manuals.

11.1.5   Gnome economics

Let's take, as an example, analyzing the user task of getting from power 1 state to power 2 state for this microwave oven.

The user may want to cook something but not at the current high-power setting. For the purposes of this chapter, analyzing just one task will be sufficient to show how it can be done. As before, rather than go to the trouble of getting a human user (and wondering what sort of human, how familiar they are with microwaves, and so on), let's use a gnome again. Gnomes are cheap and they don't mind prodding things all day.

First we need a function that tells us which button the gnome should press. It looks worse than it is:*

```
function randomButton(d)
{ var r = Math.random();
  while( Math.floor(d.buttons.length*r) == d.buttons.length )
    r = Math.random();
  return Math.floor(d.buttons.length*r);
}
```

Generating random numbers is fraught with difficulties. It is *highly recommended* that you verify that your random number generator (which may have to be wrapped up in code completely different from my randomButton JavaScript code above) is working well—otherwise all your experiments will be suspect. My first random number generator in JavaScript failed the tests; it is a salutary experience to write program code to check your own program code.

A basic way to check that your random button pressing works properly is to do a few thousand trials and see how often each button would be pressed:

```
var testLimit = 100000;
var check = new Array(device.buttons.length);

for( var i = 0; i < check.length; i++ )
  check[i] = 0; // initialize array

for( var i = 0; i < testLimit; i++ )
  check[randomButton(device)]++; // count presses

for( var i = 0; i < check.length; i++ )
  document.write(check[i]+" "); // show results
```

The numbers should be approximately equal. Next you should do a χ^2 test on the results.

▷ The further reading for this chapter gives a good reference for random numbers and the relevant statistical tests.

We can use this randomButton() function immediately, simply to press buttons using the press function we defined for humans to use, as follows, where we try getting the gnome to press buttons ten times:

```
// test random pressing on the device; try 10 presses
for( var g = 0; g < 10; g++ )
{ press(randomButton(device));
}
```

---

* Numbers r returned from JavaScript's Math.random() are supposed to be uniformly distributed or, as most people say, "between 0 and 1," but more precisely $0 \leq r < 1$. Unfortunately some browsers occasionally return $r = 1$; in this case, the while loop repeats the call to get another random number.

Pressing buttons exactly like a human will mean that JavaScript will be updating the device display every time something happens—that's how press was defined in the framework; this is a waste of time (gnomes can't read), so we can speed up using gnomes by writing a "blind" press function:

```
function gnomePress(buttonNumber)
{ device.state = device.fsm[device.state][buttonNumber];
}
```

```
for( var g = 0; g < 10; g++ )
   gnomePress(randomButton(device));
```

For our next trick, it's useful to define a function to get state numbers from state names, to convert from names like power 1 to numbers like 4, which is the corresponding state number.

```
function toStateNumber(d, s)
{ for( var i = 0; i < d.stateNames.length; i++ )
    if( d.stateNames[i] == s )
        return i;
  alert("There is no state called "+s);
  return 0; // after error, don't return complete rubbish
}
```

Now we can try a "gnome trial" function, which takes the name of a state to start from and the name of a state to try to finish at:

```
function trial(d, start, finish)
{ d.state = toStateNumber(d, start);
  var f = toStateNumber(d, finish);
  var count = 0;
  while( d.state != f )
  { gnomePress(randomButton(device));
    count++;
  }
  document.write("Gnome takes "+count+" steps to get from "+
        start+" to "+finish+" states.");
}
```

> As noted in section 4.5 (p. 105), where we defined the function plural, the last function would generate better English if we wrote ... "Gnome takes "+plural(count, "step")+" to get from ...

We start the gnome-simulating program in state power 1 and see how long it takes to get to power 2.

```
trial(device, "Power 1", "Power 2");
```

When I tried it, the gnome took 169 steps. Was this gnome lucky, or was the gnome a bad one who gave us an answer seemingly too hard to be reasonable? Or is the design bad? Until we do a lot more experiments, we can't tell whether we have learned more about the gnome or about the design.

One argument that the gnome was lucky is that we asked it to play with a device that happened to be strongly connected; if the device had not been strongly

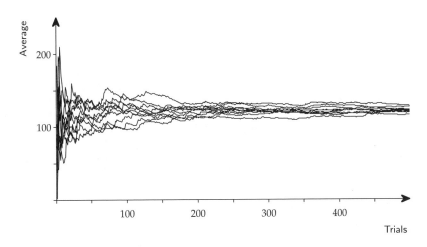

Figure 11.3: Ten gnomes testing a microwave oven to change its power settings. After time, the gnomes converge on taking about 120 button presses.

connected, the gnome would have run the risk of getting stuck somewhere (just as any human user would have risked getting stuck). The gnome wouldn't mind; it would just keep on pressing buttons—the program simulating the gnome would never give up, because the test d.state != f might always be true and it would go around the loop again and again! If the shortest path from start to finish states is ∞, no gnome will ever find a way of doing it; if the shortest path is finite but the device is not strongly connected, the gnome may or may not get stuck. If the device is strongly connected a gnome will eventually be able to get to the finish state (provided your random number generator is fair). Either you should check the device is strongly connected, or you should set a maximum limit on the number of times around the loop.

Whether the gnome was lucky or not, one useful thing we have learnt is that our design can cope with mad and relentless user testing for 169 presses. We should do some more testing, to check that the design is robust. (This sort of mindless but essential checking is something gnomes should be left to do, rather than using humans.)

We should try more gnomes and at least average the results to get better statistics. So we'll try some more serious experiments, hiring 10 gnomes at a time; we'll run 500 trials with each gnome and plot the results to see what we can learn: see figure 11.3 for the results. The graphs show that once we have 5,000 runs (ten gnomes each doing 500 trials), employing more won't add much more to what we already know. But for a more complex device than our microwave oven, this survey might be way too small. It's always worth drawing a graph to see how the numbers are working, and more informative (and a lot easier) than using statistics.

▷ In section 11.3 (p. 381) we work out what an infinite number of gnomes would average.

11.2   Drawing simple graphs in JavaScript

Figures 11.1 to 11.3 show graphs drawn from experiments with gnomes. Since graphs are a very good way of visualizing design parameters, I'll show you a very simple way of drawing graphs using JavaScript. If you want good graphics on web pages, server-side programming, if you want to use it, is more flexible; for instance, you can easily use PHP to generate graphics in any of a wide variety of formats. In general, drawing good-looking graphs is tricky unless you want to touch them up by hand, and you should use a standard graph-drawing package or general-purpose programs like Microsoft Excel or Mathematica, which can draw all sorts of fancy graphs with ease.

The simplest JavaScript trick for drawing a graph is to use HTML's img tag to draw a rectangle of the size you want. For example, `<img src=image height=42 width=73>` will draw the image with height 42 pixels and width 73 pixels. Just change the numbers to resize the rectangle.

Earlier figures in this chapter show how long it takes gnomes to get a device to work. For variety, we will draw a graph of the shortest path costs: if the device is doing something, how long (how many steps) does it take to make it do something else? An easy-to-use device will have lots of low costs; a hard-to-use device will have lots of high costs. Some devices might have lots of low costs, and one strange high cost, which perhaps deserves your closer inspection, unless you expected it. Overall, the shape of the graph of costs—it's general shape—is what's interesting.

```
function barChart(d)
{ var apsp = shortestPaths(d);
  var n = apsp.length; // number of states
  var chart = new Array(n);
  for( var i = 0; i <= n; i++ )
    chart[i] = 0; // initialize the bar chart to zeros
  for( var i = 0; i < n; i++ )
    for( var j = 0; j < n; j++ )
      if( apsp[i][j] <= n )
        chart[apsp[i][j]]++; // count lengths
  for( var i = 0; i < chart.length; i++ )
    document.write("<img src=blob.gif width=5 height="+(1+chart[i])+">");
}
```

In the JavaScript above, the variable name apsp just means "all pairs shortest paths" and is the matrix of shortest path lengths between any pair of states: so apsp[i][j] is the least number of steps a user could take getting from state i to state j.

▷   The code for shortestPaths was given in section 9.6 (p. 297).

To draw a graph of these numbers, create an array chart and initialize it to zero. Then the work is done in the two nested for-loops that examine every element of apsp and count how often each value occurs. Since apsp[i][j] can be infinity in devices that aren't strongly connected, count entries ≤ n—unless it's ∞, *no* path can be longer than the number of states.

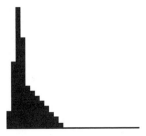

Figure 11.4: A simple bar chart showing the distribution of path lengths for the JVC HR-D540EK PVR. With more programming, you can get axes and other useful information included—our simple JavaScript hasn't shown that the horizontal axis is the cost of getting from one state to another (a number, for this device, ranging from 0 to 11) or that the vertical axis is how often any particular cost appears. For this device, the most common path length (the mode) is 2, occurring 192 times. Without the axes, it isn't obvious that the leftmost bar shows how often a zero path length occurs: for any device it's going to be the number of states, since you can stay in any state by doing nothing. Other uses for path data are shown in box 9.2 (p. 310).

Having collected the information, a simple loop draws the graph using the image-scaling trick:

```
for( var i = 0; i < chart.length; i++ )
  document.write("<img src=blob.gif width=5 height="+(1+chart[i])+">");
```

The 1+ in the height expression ensures we get at least a 1 pixel-high line for the graph axis—a 0 pixel-height line would not show anything. Figure 11.4 (this page) shows the sort of result you might get.

11.3 Markov models

Gnomes are a fun and convenient way to test how well product designs work, and the statistics we need to understand what they do is easy—we can get away with drawing graphs, taking averages, and so on.

A more sophisticated approach is to use Markov models, which are a mathematical way of exploring what gnomes would do. Markov models allow us to work out, in effect, what an infinite number of gnomes would do. We can use Markov models to get more reliable results, and they are *considerably* faster than running an infinite number of tests on gnomes! Using our techniques, we'll also soon show ways to halve the difficulty of using a microwave oven, even if we are as ignorant as gnomes are about microwaves.

Andrei Markov did a lot of work on random processes, and Markov's techniques lend themselves to mathematical treatment. The details are quite tricky, but that doesn't matter, because we can ask someone else to do the math (and then

---

Box 11.1 Matrices and Markov models The stochastic matrix of section 11.3 (previous page) is just the same as the cost matrix of section 9.6 (p. 297), except that the costs (0, 1 or ∞) have been replaced with probabilities. Instead of it being the case that a button press takes one step to get to another state in the finite state machine, the stochastic matrix expresses the fact that there is a probability the user will press the button.

Since each row represents all the states a user can end up in, whatever they do, each row adds to 1.

Suppose the stochastic matrix is called S and $\mathbf{v}$ is a vector representing the current state the device is in; it's called the state vector. Then $\mathbf{v}S$ will represent the state the device is in after the user has done one thing. More precisely, $\mathbf{v}S$ will give a distribution; it will show the probability that the device is in each state after the user's action. The beauty of this is that we can see further ahead easily: $\mathbf{v}S^n$ tells us the state distribution after exactly n button presses.

With not much more effort, from $\mathbf{v}$ we can work out the expected number of states the user will have visited after n presses; this is how we worked out the cost-of-knowledge graph in section 5.3 (p. 144), graphed in figure 5.11 (p. 144).

Standard things to do with Markov models are to find out the expected number of actions to get to a state, which in user interface terms represents how hard doing something is on average, or to find out the long-term behavior of a device.

Usually the transition matrices are considered for the *whole* device, but we can also take the matrices for each button considered as its own finite state machine. This generates the button matrices. If we have buttons ⟨On⟩ and ⟨Off⟩, we can easily find the button matrices On and Off that represent the transitions that these buttons can achieve.

If the device is in state $\mathbf{v}$, then $\mathbf{v}$On is the state it is in after ⟨On⟩ is pressed. Matrices easily allow us to work out theories of the device behavior; in this example (even with such little information) it is likely that On times the matrix Off is equal to the matrix Off—in words, pressing ⟨Off⟩ after pressing ⟨On⟩ has the same effect as pressing ⟨Off⟩ directly. The matrix equation says that this is true in every state. Since matrices are very efficient for calculating this is a good way of discovering many deep properties of a user interface.

---

write a program for us); we can use the results. Fortunately, if you have Markov modeling added to your design framework, you won't need to understand technical details.

To do a Markov analysis, first we must convert the device's definition into a so-called stochastic matrix. Here it is displayed in traditional mathematical notation:

$$\begin{pmatrix} 3/5 & 1/5 & 1/5 & 0 & 0 & 0 \\ 2/5 & 2/5 & 1/5 & 0 & 0 & 0 \\ 2/5 & 1/5 & 0 & 1/5 & 1/5 & 0 \\ 2/5 & 1/5 & 1/5 & 0 & 0 & 1/5 \\ 2/5 & 1/5 & 0 & 1/5 & 1/5 & 0 \\ 2/5 & 1/5 & 1/5 & 0 & 0 & 1/5 \end{pmatrix}$$

▷   This is exactly the same sort of matrix as we encountered in section 9.6 (p. 297), except that now the entries are probabilities rather than button costs.

▷ Box 11.1, "Matrices and Markov models" (facing page) explains more about how the matrices work.

Each row gives the probability that the user—or gnome!—will change the state of the microwave oven; thus, if the device is in state 1, the gnome will change it to state 2 with probability $1/5$ (i.e., first row, second column). There are five buttons for the gnome to choose from, and with probability $1/5$ it chooses the button that changes the state to 2. Sometimes there are two buttons that change the current state to the same state, hence the $2/5$ probabilities. For now, the assumption is that each button on the device is pressed with equal probability (there are five buttons, so all the probabilities are so-many fifths); the user interface simulation can give empirically-based probabilities, which we will use later. This probability matrix can be fed into our analysis.

The math on this matrix gives a result of 120. This is what thousands of gnomes averaged at, but it was faster to work out using a Markov model (even though we needed to be good at math; for many people it's easier to program the gnomes than to work out the Markov models).

It is interesting to choose the probabilities differently. Rather than assuming that each action or button press is equally likely, as above, we can work out the best way of achieving the task and set *those* button presses to have probability 1. Now our gnome is behaving like one that knows what it's doing.

If we rerun a Markov analysis on this matrix of "perfect knowledge," we should get back the shortest ways of doing anything. Indeed, the answer here is 2. Which emphasizes just how bad 120 is.

Evidently, the more knowledge about the device design, the easier a device is to use. Difficulty of use can be plotted against knowledge in a graph that combines the complete randomness of a gnome with increasing amounts of design knowledge. The graph should obviously speed up between 120 (the result of ignorance) to 2 (gained with the aid of perfect design knowledge). Indeed, this is what we see in figure 11.5 (next page).

11.3.1 Alternative designs

A gnome presses buttons at random and takes 120 button presses, but a knowledgeable designer who knows what to do would take only 2 button presses to do the same thing. Gnomes takes a long time because they know nothing. The designer is efficient because they have privileged design knowledge. Surely there must be a way of telling gnomes *something* so that they can do a bit better than pure chance?

Of course, if we work out what hints to give gnomes, and they work well enough, then we can give the same hints to human users.

One reason that the gnomes are so bad is that they even try doing things that don't work at all. They might try pressing a button that leaves the microwave oven in the same state. Now, whatever they are trying to do, doing nothing cannot help. So, let's run the experiments again but this time getting the gnomes to only press buttons that are guaranteed to do something.

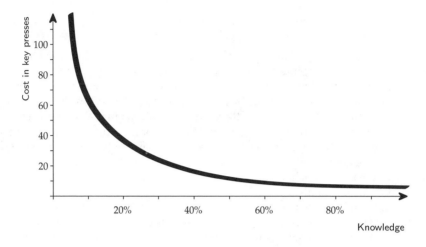

Figure 11.5: The more you know, the easier it gets. When you know 100%, you are as good as an expert, here taking only 2 presses to change power settings on the microwave oven. If you know nothing, you may take a very long time, but on average you will do it in 120 presses.

In human terms, we could imagine that we redesign the microwave oven so that its buttons light up when they are active, or equivalently that they are dark when they are not going to change the current state. In a sense, this makes the device a polite device: it tells you when it can do things for you. A polite device tells the user that a button will do something or that a button won't do something before the user wastes time finding out.

▷   The opposite of politeness, rudeness, is discussed in section 6.3.4 (p. 185).

We could either write a slightly more sophisticated gnome-simulating program (press buttons at random, but out of the ones known to change the current state) or run a Markov model on a revised matrix of probabilities. When we do, the answer for the power-changing task drops from 120 to 71.

We can modify the original `trial` code to work out the times the gnomes take with the original design and with a modified design where they avoid pressing buttons they know will do nothing.

```
function trial2(d, start, finish)
{ d.state = toStateNumber(d, start);
  var f = toStateNumber(d, finish);
  var count = 0, newcount = 0;
  while( d.state != f )
  { var oldstate = d.state;
    gnomePress(randomButton(device));
    count++;
    if( d.state != oldstate ) newcount++;
  }
```

```
document.write("Original device: gnome takes "+count
      +" steps to get from "+start+" to "+finish+" states.");
document.write("Modified device: gnome takes "+newcount
      +" steps to get from "+start+" to "+finish+" states.");
}
```

Actually, the code here has the gnomes pressing buttons whether they make any difference or not—but the variable `newcount` only counts the presses that do change state. Surprisingly, this simple change to the gnomes' behavior helps them achieve *any* task; in particular, it almost makes the task we were considering almost twice as easy. It's worth doing.

The general design rule is that a device should provide the user with feedback about the future, not just its present state. Here, if the device knows a button is not going to do anything, it says so!

In fact, exactly the same idea is used in graphical user interfaces on desktop computers: you will find menu-items dimmed out when they aren't going to work. Now we know why.

11.3.2 Even cleverer buttons

▷ Section 11.1.2 (p. 374) suggests playful buttons, and we've just suggested smart buttons that light up if they might be worth pressing (in the last section). Section 9.6.4 (p. 304) suggests lighting buttons to speed up the user according to the Hick-Hyman law.

There are very good reasons why both of these design ideas can help users. Can we do any better? The two small innovations we have suggested are based on knowing what the user wants to do:

■ The user is stuck. Show them something random; it may help.

■ The user wants to do something. Show them which buttons do something.

▷ If we *really* know what the user wants to do, then the device may as well do it. This idea leads on to invisible devices and incidental interaction; see chapter 12, "Grand design."

So far in our simulations, the gnomes have been pressing buttons equally often on average. But if one button stands out from the others, we'd want our gnomes to prefer pressing it, and it should be pressed more often—that is what human users would tend to do. We might get a few real people to use a prototype of a device, to get real button press probabilities, and we could then be precise about the probabilities to use—generally, without doing experiments with users, we won't know what anyone is trying to do with any reliability or accuracy.

If we assume we have already got the probabilities for each button in an array `device.probpress`, it's easy to write a revised random button function:

```
function distributedRandomButton(d)
{ do
  { var r = Math.random(), cp = 0;
    for( var b = 0; b < d.buttons.length; b++ )
    { cp = cp+d.probpress[b];
      if( cp > r ) return b;
    }
  } while( b >= b.buttons.length );
}
```

As before, this code loops if the random number generator incorrectly returns exactly 1—it goes around and tries another number. The code can be made faster by pre-computing an array of cumulative probabilities rather than repeatedly calculating cp each time the function is called. Of course, the code won't work correctly unless the button probabilities probpress add to 1.0, as probabilities should. More details of algorithms with random numbers can be found in Knuth's *Art of Computer Programming*—see this chapter's further reading, p. 404.

> ▷ Section 11.3.1 (p. 383) explores concrete ideas for improving button pressing probabilities. Making some things *too* easy may not be a good idea—see section 5.4 (p. 145).

A user is looking at a device with fifteen buttons that could achieve something. Either the user knows what to do, or, in the most general terms, this user will have to *search* for the right result.

Computer scientists know a lot about how to make searching more efficient. Obvious suggestions are to put the possible target states of the search into a sequential list, to put them into an alphabetically sorted list, or to use more interesting techniques, such as binary search, hashing, trie search, or tree search.

> ▷ The impact of alternative kinds of search techniques (for a fax) are explored in section 5.5.5 (p. 153).

We can only usefully put states into order if we know what the user is searching for. If it's a command name, then putting the commands into order will help. But in general, we really have no idea what the user is searching for—and the user may not know until encountering it. If they don't know what the command is called, then putting them into alphabetical order in itself doesn't help much—it's no better than being in a linear list in *any* order.

Even if we have no order (such as the alphabet) that can be used, we can still help the user search systematically. There are two important and very general approaches to searching:

Breadth-first search Try to keep as close as possible to the starting state, and then move out to new states, increasing the distance from the start as slowly as possible. This approach is good if we have no idea where the goal is.

Depth-first search Go as far as possible in any direction before trying alternatives. This approach is good if we think we are going in roughly the right direction.

Of course, in both breadth- and depth-first search, we don't repeatedly search places we've already searched.

To help a user do *any* search, we need to know a few things: where they started from (for instance, off or standby), what have already been visited, and whether they want depth or breadth-first search. Typically a user won't know what the technical terms breadth-first and depth-first mean, so we could have buttons like "help me broaden my search" and "help me search here."

When the user presses one of these buttons, the device searches for an unvisited state that is either close to standby or close to the current state but farther than it from standby.

> ▷ Close states are readily found using the shortest paths algorithm from section 9.6 (p. 297), perhaps using more appropriate costs than button presses, as suggested in section 9.6.4 (p. 304).

Since there are lots of possible states to try next, the device will score them as it searches and then present the user with the button press that scores highest. I've tried these techniques on web sites, and they are very successful in helping people find what they wanted—even though the web site has no idea what they are looking for! But users don't go round in circles any more, and they don't miss nearby pages they might otherwise have ignored.

To see whether these ideas would improve your device, tweak the approach to suit the sorts of things users do with your device and experiment to see how well it works—then do some more tweaking to the scoring system to get more useful results.

11.4 Human errors

The previous sections suggested how we can get design insights by comparing random behavior to "perfect" behavior. We imagined that a designer knows the best way to use a device, and we drew a graph of cost against how good the user (or gnome) was compared to optimal use. We showed that we could "guide" random behavior by having more interesting buttons and feedback to the user of what does what.

Gnomes are not people, and we are designing for people, not gnomes. How do people differ. More precisely, what do we know about people that we can apply to design?

We know that people tend to make certain sorts of systematic error. We could translate the way users work into Markov models, because we know that if a user has done x, they may now be more likely to do y. Markov models can handle this, but it gets very difficult to provide all the data they require. If, on the other hand, we stick to simple, first order models, we only need to know—or guess—the probabilities of pressing buttons regardless of whether the user has done x or y. This is much easier, and the results, while perhaps less accurate, are at least uniformly inaccurate, whereas an incomplete model might be more accurate *sometimes*, but you may not know when.

That is, if you train your sophisticated model to reflect real user behavior, unfortunately you run into exactly the same problems that all user testing has: it takes a very long time to get sufficient, and sufficiently broad, data to be useful. Of course, you can quickly get an impression, but almost by their very nature, errors are surprising—they are unlikely—so you need even more data to model errors well.

Rather than trying to model anything a user might do, it's more productive to model specific things based on how we know people behave.

> ▷ Task/action mappings, discussed in section 9.6.5 (p. 311), help us explore how a user does a task successfully.

One way to look at user errors is to consider their effect on degrading from "perfect" performance. We can easily find a shortest path (using task/action mappings) and treat this as the model of error-free behavior. Then what might a user do?

- They may make slips and randomly fall off the path anywhere. We have already modeled this sort of error very well.

- They may do things in the wrong order.

- They may miss steps on the path but carry on doing the right things (though probably now on the wrong path).

- They may forget some initial steps, missing out the "preparation," but then follow the rest of the path correctly.

- They may not get to the end of the path, stopping short of performing all the necessary actions. That is, they behave as if they have finished, when there is yet more to do. These are completion errors.

- They may follow a correct path for a different task. These are transfer errors. The user has transferred the wrong actions (which were right in a different context) to the intended task. The different task may or may not be one from the same device—it might be a transfer error like trying to use a Nokia device like a Samsung.

- If two paths start the same way (or, put formally, if they have a common prefix) then the user may continue down the preferred path—often, the more frequently used one—even if this is not the path they intended to go down to start with. More generally, if multiple tasks share parts of their paths (they have common subsequences), it's possible that users will start off doing what they intended, including the shared part of the path, but then follow the wrong branch after the shared part. This is a capture error. The more familiar, more frequently performed actions have "captured" the user.

- Users may not stop when they have otherwise completed the task. This is an overrun error.

Box 11.2 Ways to avoid human error Humans make errors for all sorts of reasons, and psychologists distinguish different sorts of error: slips, lapses, mistakes, and variations thereof. The suggestions for further reading give pointers to more details, but what we want to do is *avoid* errors, however they are classified, and then—given that we can't always avoid errors, recover from them or reduce their consequences when they do occur.

Don Norman suggests six important strategies for reducing error. Exactly how these principles are applied depends on the context; the important point is to think through the options carefully.

- Make information visible, so the user can *see* what to do next. We've talked a lot about using indicators as one way to do this; see section 11.3.2 (p. 385) for example.

- Simplify the design to reduce reliance on the user's memory.

- Use affordances (see section 12.3, p. 415)—use "natural" mappings, simple relationships between controls and effects.

- Use "forcing functions" to guide users. Constraints make it hard to do the wrong things; forcing functions make it impossible. For example, the button that fires the rocket has a cover; the user is forced to lift the cover before launching the rocket.

- Assume that errors *will* occur and design accordingly. Provide techniques for error recovery.

- Finally, standardize actions, layouts, displays, symbols, and so on; make systems consistent.

  ▷ See the boxes 6.1, "Syringe pumps" (p. 168) and 11.3, "Generating manuals automatically" (p. 397) for example errors. Errors are also discussed in section 11.4 (p. 387), and box 5.7, "The principle of least effort" (p. 147).

▷ We considered certain classes of overrun errors, namely accidentally repeating the last step, and how to assess the design's impact on them in section 10.4 (p. 339).

Armed with these ideas, we want to reduce the *consequences* of errors for users, and we want to increase the *robustness* of the devices we design—we want to "design errors out." However, given that errors will always occur sooner or later, we also want to reduce the *probability* that an error is made in the first place, and we want to reduce its *persistence* once it's made.

Somewhat out of our hands is training users properly and giving them full experience of the device. The most important thing is for a device to be simple, straightforward, even elegant in its design, that is, easily learned; after that, a device should provide good feedback to users, so that they can monitor what it is doing and check whether this matches their expectations.

The list of errors above strongly suggests where to emphasize feedback: for example, after a common subsequence of actions, a user will have to make a choice, whether to continue what they intended or continue an erroneous task they have just been captured into. The branch of paths after a common subsequence of actions is easy enough to identify automatically; an example (potential) design error that should be flagged is that indicators do not change at the branching state.

389

▷ Sometimes feedback to the user is ambiguous: users won't know whether they have done anything, let alone the right thing! See section 10.3.2 (p. 334). Sections 11.5 (p. 392) and 11.6 (p. 396) provide interaction programming techniques to provide accurate training material, so users know how to interpret feedback. Section 10.7.5 (p. 358) showed how to ensure that the user gets wide enough experience of a system in their training.

Error consequences can be improved by adding undo, for instance. Robustness can be improved by introducing more permissiveness into the design. We can also improve things by making the state of the device clearer—then users may notice problems sooner, before they are beyond undo or other recovery. Making the state clearer will help the user do their work with fewer errors.

Being more specific about reducing consequences requires us to know more about the costs of errors for users. For example, not switching your television on—you've sat down, but it's still off—is not as costly an issue as leaving your money behind in a cash dispenser (sometimes called an automatic teller machine, or ATM), and that, in turn, is not as costly an error as leaving your cash card behind (which might allow a thief to remove any amount of cash from your account).

That brief analysis suggests that given a choice, the more costly errors for the user should be arranged, by redesigning the device, to come earlier in the sequence. Indeed, this is what we find on cash machines: if they are well designed, users have to remove their cash card before taking their money. With this design, users are very unlikely to leave their card behind—but they may still leave their money behind.

This redesign works in harmony with a quite different explanation of completion errors. A user went to the cash machine with the task "get cash" uppermost in mind. With the better design, the user can only complete the intentional task *after* having already removed the card—the device has forced the user to do something that otherwise might be overlooked if cash was dispensed first.

We can invent ways of measuring robustness. One simple measure is the number of ways a user can achieve a task. If there is one way to do a task, then any error makes the task fail; the more ways, the less likely any error (of any of the sorts listed above or any other sort of error) will make the user fail.

We can measure this simple robustness by counting the different number of paths through the device to achieve the same objectives. For the sake of argument, we consider all tasks possible on a device to be equivalent to considering all pairs of states: every task then has a start state and an end state. We count how many and how long paths are between all pairs of states and take averages to get a measure of robustness for the "average task." (Counting paths can be done using a depth-first search.)

For our microwave oven, we get the graph shown in figure 11.6 (facing page). The figure shows quite clearly that for this device any task ending in a power setting—that is, actually cooking—is a lot less robust (in the sense we are measuring robustness!) than either quick defrosting or using the clock. Of course, we would get more profound results if we weighted averages according to our knowledge of the device. For example, since the user cannot leave a microwave oven

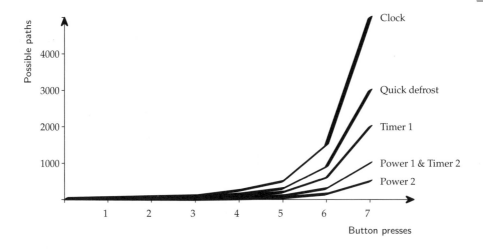

Figure 11.6: One visualization of robustness; here, measured as the number of possible ways of reaching a given state, plotted against the number of button presses needed to reach it. The numbers are averaged over all possible starting states. The larger the number, the more permissive or robust the target state.

cooking forever, most tasks the user will do will not start from any cooking states. For simplicity, we assumed all starting states were equally likely—intriguingly, the graph for this device looks the same and doesn't change the ordering of the results (though with different numbers) when we redo the analysis assuming never starting in a power state.

Robustness against error is *not* the same as safety. Cars have numerous safety features, including the following: you cannot change from park to drive without pressing the brake pedal; you cannot remove the key unless you are in park; in some manual cars, you cannot start the engine unless the clutch is depressed—to avoid risking starting the car when it is in gear, and, incidentally, to make it easier to start (the starter motor won't be turning over the gear box's cold oil).

A car is not robust in the sense that there are lots of ways for the users to achieve their goals; the point is to ensure that users can only achieve goals safely. Some possible states and transitions are designed out; the user simply cannot do them. A "robust" car might allow you to start the engine when the car is in drive without your foot on the brake pedal, but a safe car would prohibit this error. Some errors you want to forgive the user, some (like starting a car when it is in gear) you want to block, before something worse happens—though occasionally it is good practice to start in gear, for instance on steep hills. Designers have to make tricky tradeoffs.

▷ A measure of robustness is the size of strongly connected components; we used the farmer's problem as a motivating example to redesign devices in section 10.2.1 (p. 329).

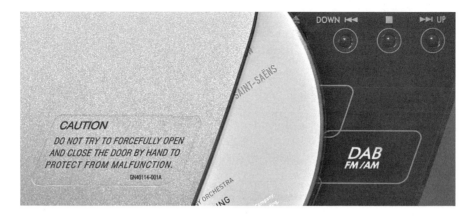

Figure 11.7:   User error is defined by design error—illustrated here by the JVC UX-NB7DAB CD/radio. Evidently, the manufacturers are aware of the design defect as the CD tray door has a warning label "*CAUTION DO NOT TRY TO FORCEFULLY OPEN AND CLOSE THE DOOR BY HAND TO PROTECT FROM MALFUNCTION.*" The label has been made removable because it isn't visually aesthetic. However, if the label was removed the design would not become aesthetic anyway: it would then have a *hidden* interaction defect and be worse. The photograph shows what happens if you drop a CD when attempting to change one: the door may close with the CD trapped, covering the very button that is supposed to be used to open and close the door. Now you have to fiddle with the trapped CD—or force the door!

Finally, people can also make sophisticated errors involving reasoning. They may have, in some sense, quite the wrong idea of the tasks they are trying to achieve. In controlling a complex system like a nuclear power plant, indicators tell the user all sorts of things about the overall situation. The user then has to reason about what to do to avoid a catastrophe. Many things can go wrong—not least being that the power station itself overwhelms clear thinking with far too many alarms.

11.5   Automatic, correct help

There is a legal requirement that descriptions of products should correspond with the products themselves: under the UK Sale of Goods Act 1979 (as amended by the Sale and Supply of Goods Act 1994 and the Sale of Goods (Amendment) Act 1994) products should be "fit for purpose" and should correspond with the description of them. Thus it is the (UK) law that user manuals are correct—or, if we take a weaker view, that the manufacturer at least knows what the correct description is, so that some appropriate description, but in any case truthful, can be written for the user. Other countries will have similar laws.

Although our device definition is very basic, it can be used to generate useful help for the user or for technical authors (technical authors can at least start from an accurate draft of the manual).

We now define a function `help` that explains the shortest path (the least number of button presses) to get from any state to any state. The definitions given below can be adapted straightforwardly to provide clearer help if "buttons" aren't actually pressed (maybe, for example, they are knobs that have to be twisted).

The device might have an interactive feature, so pressing a button gives help— perhaps showing it in a display panel. If so, it might be defined partly as follows, making use of the current state: here is a small part of the microwave oven's manual:

> To get from the device Power 1 to Power 2:
> > Press [Time]
> >
> > Press [Power]

▷ Program code to generate manual entries like this is based on finding shortest paths, discussed in section 9.6 (p. 297).

We'll need this fact later. Note that the best way of getting from Power 1 to Power 2 takes two button presses, as we realized in the previous section.

Ideally one would write more sophisticated manual-generating programs to generate better natural language. In particular, straightforward parametrization of the program would allow equivalent manuals to be generated in any appropriate language.

If we developed a typographical style for user manuals, then all devices processed in the framework would be able to use that style. Also, one could generate interactive HTML manuals for the web, and then the user could also follow hypertext links to learn the exact workings of the device.

We can print an entire manual just by finding the best way to get from each state to every other state. It's still a bit long and boring, but it starts off like this:

> To get from the device Clock to Quick defrost:
> > Press [Quick defrost]
>
> To get from the device Clock to Timer 1:
> > Press [Time]
>
> To get from the device Clock to Timer 2:
> > Press [Time] Press [Time]
>
> To get from the device Clock to Power 1:
> > Press [Time] Press [Power]
>
> To get from the device Clock to Power 2:
> > Press [Time] Press [Time] Press [Power]

This doesn't provide a particularly easy or enjoyable read, but it is a complete and correct manual that a technical author could start to work from. However, it is well worth generating, even if nobody reads it. It is quite possible that some things are not possible for a user to do, so trying to generate a manual that explains how to do everything at least checks that the user can do anything they want to. We should certainly write a program to generate this manual and run it on any proposed device; if the program "gets stuck" then the device has problems.

We might prefer to typeset the user manual in a different format. Here is an extract of one generated for the JVC PVR that starred in the last chapter:

> ...
> If you are playing a tape, but have paused it, you can:
> > Press ⌈Play⌉ to play a tape
> > Press ⌈Operate⌉ to off, with tape in
> > Press ⌈Forward⌉ to fast forward
> > Press ⌈Rewind⌉ to rewind a tape
> > Press ⌈Stop/Eject⌉ to on, with tape in
> If you are playing a tape fast forward, you can:
> > Press ⌈Play⌉ to play a tape
> > Press ⌈Operate⌉ to off, with tape in
> > Press ⌈Pause⌉ to pause playing a tape
> > Press ⌈Stop/Eject⌉ to on, with tape in
> If you are playing a tape fast backward, you can:
> > Press ⌈Play⌉ to play a tape
> > Press ⌈Operate⌉ to off, with tape in
> > Press ⌈Pause⌉ to pause playing a tape
> > Press ⌈Stop/Eject⌉ to on, with tape in
>
> ...

This form of manual is very easy to make interactive. If we recoded it in HTML, it could look like this:

```
...
<a name="pause">If you are playing a tape, but have paused it, you
can:</a>
<blockquote>
  Press <a href="#play">[Play]</a> to play a tape<br>
  Press <a href="#offtapein">[Operate]</a> to off, with tape in<br>
  ...
</blockquote>
...
```

A user can press buttons in the manual itself—it's just a web page, viewed in a browser—and it would work just like the device it described. You can get nice-looking buttons relatively easily by using cascading style sheets. Better still, you could use images for the buttons.

For many devices, whether a PVR or microwave oven, a user's tasks won't be to get from a known state to another state, but simply to get to the desired state, regardless of the initial state. We can generate a manual for this sort of use.

To represent a device in an unknown state, we represent its possible states as a set, and we define a function to find out what set of states the device will be in after a given sequence of button presses; it involves some fun programming. A breadth-first search can then be used to look for unique states. Then, by defining some routines to explain things in (for instance) English, we can print out the sequences of button presses to get to each state. We now have the user manual that tells a user how to do anything regardless of what the device is doing to start with. Notice how short it is. Perhaps because of its brevity, we can get some interesting design insights straight from it.

> Whatever the device is doing, you can always get it to
> Clock by pressing [Clock].
> Quick defrost by pressing [Quick defrost].
> Timer 1 by pressing [Clock], then [Time].
> Timer 2 by pressing [Clock], [Time], then [Time].
> Power 1 by pressing [Clock], [Time], then [Power].
> Power 2 by pressing [Clock], [Time], [Time], then [Power].

This time I had some fun making the English a bit nicer. It says, "press a, b, *then* c"; the data for this microwave oven never needed the fancy "press *twice*" feature. But making a manual look nice helps—and is more fun to program.

Looking at these instructions, it looks like the clock button ought to have been called [Reset]. If so, note that you can still get to the quick defrost state by pressing it (that is pressing the original button [Clock]) first, then the [Quick defrost] button.

We might think that if such a manual is "good," what would a device look like that this manual was the *complete* explanation for? To find out, all we need to do is change the English-printing routine to one that goes back to the device specification and sees which parts of it are used and which are not. Here's the result, summarized as a table:

			—Buttons—			
		[Clock]	[Quick defrost]	[Time]	[Clear]	[Power]
	Clock	✓	✓	✓		
	Quick defrost	✓	✓			
States	Timer 1	✓	✓	✓		✓
	Timer 2	✓	✓			✓
	Power 1	✓	✓			
	Power 2	✓	✓			

▷ Compare this table with the state transition table used for the same device in section 9.2.2 (p. 277).

We could draw this table in many different formats, which might be a good idea to try for much bigger systems—when size and readability become more serious issues.

Look at the ✓ entries in this table: these are the only parts of the microwave oven's state machine specification that the user manual required. The [Clear] button doesn't seem to be helping much—there are no ticks in its column! Our generating a manual and then automatically going back to the specification has exposed potentially bad design elements. If this sort of manual is a good idea, then the [Clear] button as presently defined is a design feature that needs better justification.

Here is an extract from a manual generated for a more complex system, the JVC PVR from earlier chapters:

In the following states (play a tape fast forward; pause playing a tape; play a tape fast backward) you can press ⌊Play⌋ to play a tape.

If you are playing a tape, but have paused it, additionally you may:
—Press ⌊Forward⌋ to fast forward.
—Press ⌊Rewind⌋ to rewind a tape.

In the following states (play a tape fast forward; play a tape fast backward) you can press ⌊Pause⌋ to pause playing a tape.
—If you are playing a tape fast forward, you cannot do anything else.
—If you are playing a tape fast backward, you cannot do anything else.

This chunk of the manual would be "inside" a section explaining how the buttons ⌊Operate⌋ (the badly named switch on/switch off button) and ⌊Stop/Eject⌋ work, since they can be used at any time.

Many other sorts of manuals can be generated too, and by creating them systematically with programs we can guarantee their correctness. We can also use the technique of going back from a good manual to reappraise the specification. After all, if we have a good user manual, then the bits in the specification that aren't apparently needed are immediately suspicious features.

11.6   Tools to support user manuals

We can use automatically generated sketch manuals to help technical authors to write better and more accurate user manuals. We would write a program like the one we used above to generate accurate but perhaps not best English into a database. Imagine that the technical author's tool would look a bit like a multiwindow word processor: one window would show the generated manual—correct but maybe not good English—and another window the current bit of the manual that the technical author is writing. The technical author would rephrase the English in their window, and perhaps group sections of the automatic manual together if they could think of a more concise way of describing them. This manual writing tool would have a button that simply prints all the nice text the technical author has written. And to be really useful the following features would be needed:

■ Warn if there are any sections of the automatically generated manual that the technical author has missed using.

■ If the device design is changed, reuse the tool to find automatically all of the manual sections that may need changing. The technical author might decide against changes, but they would certainly like to be shown all sections that possibly need revising. So each section the technical author writes needs a checkbox to indicate they've been "checked out" as OK when the specification changes.

Box 11.3 Generating manuals automatically Good typographical layout of manuals is essential. Here is an example of how a badly set manual contributed to death: in June 1988 a crowded 18:47 train into the Paris railway station Gare de Lyon crashed with 56 dead and many more injured . The accident inquiry noted that many factors led to the brake failure: an air brake was faulty, the train had already had an emergency stop in another station, and a radio alarm was faulty. But the inquiry noted that the maintenance manuals were particularly complex and they highlighted a misleading error in their layout.

The relevant part of the French manual starts off, "Plusieurs véhicules sont bloqués, le mécanicien: s'assure que ce blocage n'est pas la conséquence de la fermeture d'un robinet d'arrêt de la conduite générale situé avant la partie du train bloquée . . ." Jacques André has translated and given the structure of the manual (see further reading, p. 404, for the reference):

```
The driver checks:
1st CASE: x x x
          x x x
2nd CASE: y y y
          y y y
          In both cases the driver should
          z z z
Then, the driver restarts the train.
```

The situation in the Gare de Lyon accident was covered by Case 1; unfortunately the driver failed to notice the "in both cases" instructions (which in the original French were not as obvious as here), as they were indented and looked like part of Case 2 procedure. The driver omitted to do *z z z*, and the train crashed. The line beginning "In both cases" should not have been indented; indeed, given its importance, the first line might have been better rephrased along the lines of, "*After* checking both cases (below) the driver should *z z z*."

Had the manual been generated automatically, if anybody had thought of a better layout to clarify any part of the manual (and it is a big manual, so there are lots of cases where improvements might have been noticed), the improved layout scheme would have been used automatically everywhere. One idea to improve layout or structure, or whatever, then automatically becomes applied *everywhere*, consistently throughout the manual, at no further cost to the designers or technical authors.

In other words, automating a manual greatly improves its reliability, because mistakes (here, layout mistakes) can be detected and eliminated efficiently and systematically.

11.6.1 Minimal manuals

All devices have user manuals. Sometimes the manuals are printed paper booklets, sometimes they are just a few words on the back of the packaging, and sometimes they are on a CD or available on some web site. Sometimes, indeed, explicit user manuals don't exist because of oversight, costs, or because the designers thought the design was "obvious." But in all cases, user manuals exist in principle, whether or not the manufacturers have gone to the trouble of providing them.

If a user manual is complete and honest, then it stands to reason that the longer it is. the more the user has to learn before understanding the device. Conversely, the shorter a user manual, while remaining faithful to the design, the simpler the system must be to understand, if not use.

■ We can easily measure the length of basic manuals that have been generated automatically. Indeed, you don't actually need to generate the manual to know how long it is; it's easy to write programs to estimate the length. The estimate may be awry for all sorts of reasons, but as the device design is changed, changes in the manual length can be very informative for the designer. A new feature that doubles the length of the basic user manual should be immediately suspect (unless it is *very* useful)!

■ Experiments show that when user manuals are rewritten to be shorter, they are more effective, even if the device design does not change. One of the few outcomes of direct commercial value from interaction research is the minimalist technique of developing manuals: it is cheap and easy to do, and it effectively helps users perform better.

■ Typically, modified designs that result in shorter manuals will be easier to use. Why not, then, set up an automatic process to generate good-enough user manuals (if we are only interested in their length, they don't need to have a lot of detail), then modify designs so that the automatically generated manuals get shorter?

There are different sorts of manual. Do not confuse manuals and technical documents written to help designers or to help the design process with manuals written to help the user. What helps a user decide to buy one product or another, say, by looking up functionality they want, is very different from what helps a user do what they want to do with the product.

▷ Section 8.8 (p. 259) discusses spanning trees and the algorithms for finding them as a way of generating manuals.

Users typically want to focus on their actual tasks and activities. The approach for designing manuals for this purpose is called minimalist instruction.

Instead of telling a user how to use all the functions of product, tell them how to do useful tasks—and identify what these tasks or activities are. Get rid of clutter about what the device is for, assume that users already have domain knowledge—knowledge about what they got the device to do in the first place.

When users do use a device, they make mistakes. Therefore an important part of a minimal manual (*especially* a minimal manual, which by its nature doesn't cover everything) is how it supports the user successfully recognizing and recovering from errors.

Rarely do users read manuals from start to finish. Manuals should therefore be designed so that users can jump around to what they want to do, from moment to moment. In fact, manuals should be hypertext, or web-based documents.

11.6.2   Validating scenarios, manuals, and legal documents

Any scenario (a story about a device and its use) or any user manual, even a draft, runs the risk of becoming obsolete or having errors introduced because the designer has modified the device design—perhaps "just a little improvement" and they didn't bother to tell the author, or perhaps they made 37 improvements and bug fixes, and the author only managed to sort out 35 of them before the designer did some more tweaking. In any case, the technical author needs all the help they can get!

We needn't confine the technical author to a secondary role in the design process. The author might have some good ideas about the design they'd like the designer to adhere to. The author might be writing sales material, offering a device with certain nice features. The author might be writing a legal document, claiming that the device does certain things in certain well-defined ways. In these cases, the technical author doesn't want to know what great ideas the designer has had; they want to keep the designer under control.

  ▷ Scenarios and their use are discussed in box 13.7, "Scenarios" (p. 480).

If we worry too much about errors in any documents, we won't get around to writing them until the device design is stabilized—probably only a few weeks before it is shipped! It'll mean that the documentation is written, finally, in a hurry and any insights the authors get from writing it (or trying it out on users) will be lost to the design process. Instead, as I've emphasized, authors should start as soon as possible—with no, or as little as possible, wasted effort.

One approach is to use tools to validate documentation, or to generate a few choice phrases accurately. All our previously considered approaches have relied on automatic design tools generating the bulk of the documentation text, with perhaps the technical authors refining it from there. The idea is to provide "handles" onto the device design specification so that bits of the documentation can either be checked or generated directly.

Here are some examples, developing from the framework. Imagine some uninspired but correct text like the following:

> To get from the device Power 1 to Power 2:
> Press [Time]
> Press [Power]

  ▷ In section 11.5 (p. 393) shows how to generate correct text like this using the framework.

Let's suppose the technical author wants to rephrase this sort of instruction. Here there are many ways of doing it—for simplicity, we'll assume the author is writing in HTML:

■ First, the technical author can write something simple like this:

```
If you want to increase the power setting,
<script> getFrom("Power 1", "Power 2"); </script>.
```

In this method, the JavaScript inserts some accurate and reasonably written English, for instance, press `<span class=key>Time</span>` then press `<key>Power</span>`. (Note that the author has written a period after the closing `</script>`.) If you are keen, the function `getFrom` could have some more parameters to refine its style, so that the technical author has more flexibility in phrasing.

■ There is no need to use the framework *just* to say how to use the device, as it can provide all sorts of other information. Suppose there is a more basic function than `getFrom`, called `dataGetFrom` that returns a list or array of button presses. With this function, the technical author could write arbitrary JavaScript to format the information derived from the device specification. The author could write things like this:

```
Don't bother trying to increase the power setting, because it takes
<script>
   document.write(dataGetFrom("Power 1", "Power 2").length);
</script> presses!
```

That sort of rash comment requires checking—because the designer might fix the problem of taking too many key presses to do something, and then it'd be silly to say "Don't bother to do something because it takes 1 presses!"

▷   The bad spelling and grammar can be fixed easily; see the discussion of the `plural` function in section 4.5 (p. 105).

■ If the boilerplate approach seems too restrictive, the author could write like this:

```
If you want to increase the power setting,
press <span class=key>Time</span> then
<span class=key>Power</span>.
<script>
   check("Power 1", "Power 2", ["Time", "Power"]);
</script>
```

... now the JavaScript is being used to check that what the author wrote is correct, but it is not generating the text itself.

If you are keen, you could make the function `check` a lot more sophisticated and flexible; for instance, it could take regular expressions instead of, as here, a strict sequence that has to be exactly right, or flagged as wrong.

■ All the examples above gave the author warning if the designer had changed the design specification. The same ideas can give the designer warnings too. Here's one suggestion:

```
A great feature of our oven is that it's
easy to increase the power setting.
<script>
  if( dataGetFrom("Power 1", "Power 2").length > 2)
    alert("The easy-power feature must be restored!");
</script> presses!
```

These examples used cascading style sheets to format how the keys or key presses look. Here's a very simple style sheet, to show how it might be done so that all keys get a simple but consistent format:

```
<style type="text/css">
  span.key { font-family: sans-serif; border-style: outset;
          color: white; background-color: silver;
        }
</style>
```

This will give you consistent, light gray buttons with white sans serif text (text like this) and a simple 3D effect that makes each button stand out. You put this style sheet in the HTML head element, that is, anywhere between <head> and </head>. If you make any changes to it, every key described in the manual will change its format. As usual for cascading style sheets, this is a very useful separation of style from content—the author can decide in one place what every key will look like—and using the framework has also helped you separate the development of the good English from the checking of its accuracy and correspondence with the device specification.

11.7 Using real people to help design

Real people do not work randomly, like gnomes. So we should modify the simulator to record what people really do.

▷ Section 11.1 (p. 369) mentioned the difficulties of using real people to help evaluate a system design—but once gnomes and other techniques have done an overall evaluation, people can be used very effectively for targeted assessments of a design.

We could ask people to try out tasks, such as getting from one power level to another. We keep track of each button press in each state. At the end of an experiment, we can then print out a summary like this:

Nobody tried to press [Clock] when in state Power 2
Nobody tried to press [Quick defrost] when in state Power 2
Nobody tried to press [Time] when in state Timer 2
Nobody tried to press [Time] when in state Power 1
Nobody tried to press [Clear] when in state Power 2
Nobody tried to press [Power] when in state Power 1
Nobody tried to press [Power] when in state Power 2

With a bit more programming we can answer questions like, "What transitions did the users try that the device isn't designed to support?"

> $\boxed{\text{Clock}}$ was pressed in state Clock but did nothing
> $\boxed{\text{Quick defrost}}$ was pressed in state Quick defrost but did nothing
> $\boxed{\text{Clear}}$ was pressed in state Clock but did nothing
> $\boxed{\text{Power}}$ was pressed in state Clock but did nothing
> $\boxed{\text{Power}}$ was pressed in state Quick defrost but did nothing

More sophisticated analysis would likely use a log of the users' button presses, whereas the statistics collected in the function press only counted state changes—this throws away the information about which button is pressed, and it also loses information relating to tasks that take more than one button press.

11.7.1   Simulating real people

Our gnomes were blind and uninformed about the look and feel of the devices they were using. In contrast, how humans use a device depends crucially on how it looks and how big it is. The simplest way to make our gnomes more human-like is to use Fitts Law to estimate how long a human would take to press buttons:

```
function trialFitts(d, start, finish)
{ d.state = toStateNumber(d, start);
  var f = toStateNumber(d, finish);
  var lastButton = -1; // initially not a valid button number
  var time = 0;
  while( d.state != f )
  { var b = randomButton(device);
    gnomePress(b);
    if( lastButton != -1 )
      time = time+Fitts(lastButton, b);
    lastButton = b;
  }
  document.write("Gnome takes "+time+" seconds to get from "+
        start+" to "+finish+" states.");
}
```

> ▷   We give suggestions for exploring design changes based on the Fitts and
>   Hick-Hyman laws in section 9.6.4 (p. 304), where we also define the function
>   Fitts we use here.

11.8   Conclusions

This chapter presented two key messages: use random techniques to help solve or provide insight into difficult design problems, and use tools to help generate and maintain good information about a design.

■ The state of the art in product design is to ignore mathematics, and—sometimes—to over-emphasize human evaluation of designs. The human impact of a design is of course crucial, but it is very difficult to escape misconceptions and cultural assumptions that everyone in the design process shares. Only complete "gnomic" ignorance can provide unbiased insights.

■ Generating good user manuals and other documentation, including sales or legal documents, is more easily and reliably done with help from a design framework.

Microwave ovens were used as a running example. They are simple and easy to understand, but they were only a driving example—with a simple system, we can see the design issues crisply. More complex devices have worse design problems that are even harder to manage well (and they are harder to write clearly about): the need for good design methods is greater than the impression this chapter may have given. The consequences of bad design are often much worse than not being able to cook supper.

Now, at the end of part II, we've got both theoretical and practical ideas and techniques for designing better systems, but there's still a long way to go. Many interactive devices are *very* complex. In part III, next, we change the approach to take a higher-level view: how can we approach real, messy, interaction programming and still be successful?

11.8.1 Some *Press On* principles

■ Use ignorant, random gnomes to evaluate designs → section 11.1 (p. 370).

■ Good advice to a user can be rephrased as good advice to the designer → section 11.1 (p. 374).

■ Provide random help, so the user is helped out of fixations about the device → section 11.1 (p. 375).

■ Write programs to check your programs that help you design → section 11.1 (p. 377).

■ Use automatic testing, not prolonged human user testing → section 11.1 (p. 379).

■ Provide feedback about the *future* behavior of the device, not just its present state → section 11.3 (p. 385).

■ Arrange a device so that costly errors come earlier—avoid completion errors → section 11.4 (p. 390).

■ User error is defined by design error → figure 11.7 (p. 392).

■ Automatically generate sketch manuals → section 11.6 (p. 396).

■ Design so that manuals get shorter → section 11.6 (p. 398).

■ Manuals should show users how to do activities → section 11.6 (p. 398).

11.8.2   Further reading

■ André J., "Can structured formatters prevent train crashes?" *Electronic Publishing*, **2**(3), pp169–173, 1989. Jacques André describes the typesetting of the train driver's manual, quoted in box 11.3, "Generating manuals automatically" (p. 397).

■ Carroll, J. M., *The Nurnberg Funnel: Designing Minimalist Instruction for Practical Computer Skill*, MIT Press, 1990. Jack Carroll is a leading researcher in human-computer interaction, and this is his key book on designing user manuals.

■ Chung, K. L., *Elementary Probability Theory with Stochastic Processes*, Springer Verlag, 1979. A good book on probability that also introduces Markov models.

■ Knuth, D. E., *Seminumerical Algorithms*, Addison Wesley, 1998, third edition. This, volume 2 of Knuth's classic *The Art of Computer Programming*, is *the* book on random numbers and statistical tests.

■ Thimbleby, H. W., Cairns, P., and Jones, M., "Usability Analysis with Markov Models," *ACM Transactions on Computer-Human Interaction*, **8**(2), pp99–132, 2001. This paper goes deeper into Markov models and using them in interaction programming, but without the gnomes.

■ Thimbleby, H. W., "User Interface Design with Matrix Algebra," *ACM Transactions on Computer-Human Interaction*, **11**(2), pp181–236, 2004. See this paper if you want to follow up on the many good uses of matrices in user interface design. The paper provides an introduction to finite state machines, using matrices, and has several worked examples.

There are many computer models of human behavior and performance, including ACT-R and EPIC.

■ Anderson, J. R., and Lebiere, C., *The Atomic Components of Thought*, Lawrence Erlbaum Associates, 1998. ACT is a major cognitive theory, which has been very widely used to study how people perform and behave with interactive systems. Although now somewhat dated, this book remains a very clear presentation of the ACT framework, the system (as it then was) and its philosophy. For more recent work, see act-r.psy.cmu.edu

Human error is an unavoidable subject, and more immediately relevant to inter-action programming:

- Reason, J., *Human Error*, Cambridge University Press, 1990. This is the classic reference about human error—full of sound advice, including not using hindsight after an accident to blame the people who made "the" mistake which is now so obvious they shouldn't have made it.

- The Institute of Medicine, *To Err is Human: Building a Safer Health System*, National Academy Press, 2000. This book is a wide ranging discussion of human error and how to manage it, rather than how to redesign devices to try to stop it happening in the first place.

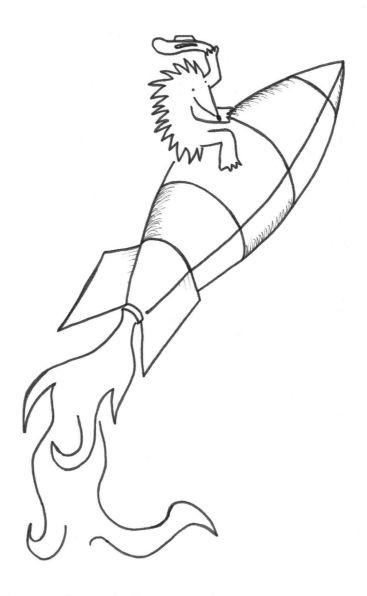

The significant challenges we face cannot be solved
at the same level of thinking we were at when we
created them.

— *Albert Einstein*

Part III
Press on

You know how to design better from part II. Now part III, the final part of the book, inspires you to put your knowledge into action.

Woman in Guiyu, China, about to smash the cathode ray tube (CRT) from a computer monitor in order to remove the copper-laden yoke. The immediate hazard is breathing the phosphor screen coating, which is toxic. Monitor glass is later dumped in irrigation canals and along the river where it leaches lead and phosphor into groundwater. The groundwater is so contaminated that fresh water is being trucked in for drinking.

12 | Grand design

Design is hard, and the real world, with its rush-to-market forces, won't wait long for a principle-driven designer. This chapter discusses how we can keep the advantages of the simplicity of finite state machines, but changing our approach so that successful real world, complex designs can be undertaken too.

There is no escaping that real systems are complex. How do we keep the benefits of the of a finite state machine approach—and all the checking and automatic features, such as user manual generation—while handling the unavoidable complexities and urgencies of real-world requirements?

12.1 Avoiding unmanageable complexity

If the demands of the real world are complex and finite state machines are simple, then interaction programming has big problems! Complexity and design difficulties are unavoidable; the issue, then, is to avoid unmanageable complexity. Unmanaged complexity leads to design errors and flaws we should have avoided; these design problems become a burden for the users—and a legacy from which future designers may never escape. Users may become accustomed to flaws, and "improvements" won't help them. Indeed, design flaws can be so subtle that user testing before a product is released will not detect them. We need better methods.

> ▷ Part I (chapter 1, "Dodgy magic," chapter 2, "Our perception," and chapter 3, "Reality") reviewed the problems we are trying to avoid.

Even though we know the problems (this book's part I) and the interaction programming principles (part II), we need guidance to design efficiently and avoid design problems we cannot manage (or, perhaps worse, design problems we accidentally ignore because we don't see them).

Here, then, is a summary of the suggestions, more design heuristics than principles, which this chapter fleshes out in more detail:

> ▷ **Make the device disappear** If the device is invisible to the user, then there is no interaction programming problem → section 12.2 (next page).

> ▷ **Make the device behave like the real world** If it does, the user will intuitively understand the device, and the designer can copy the real world's solution → section 12.3 (p. 415).

▷ **Change the world to fit the device** Think about the big systems picture, not the device in isolation → section 12.4 (p. 426).

▷ **Make the device like its predecessor, only better** Then we can avoid designing everything from scratch → section 12.5 (p. 427).

▷ **Make the design easy to change** We will get it wrong, but at least we ought to be in a position to improve it → section 12.6.1 (p. 428).

▷ **Use simple techniques as long as possible** Then we can manage with ease as much complexity as possible → section 12.6.2 (p. 429).

▷ **Use sophisticated design tools** This book covers finite state machine approaches, but there are more powerful—and harder to use—techniques available. Build your own design tools if necessary → section 12.6.3 (p. 431).

▷ **Make the device simple** To try to make it more complex than we can handle is to betray the user. If the device is a medical or other safety-critical device, this is a wise decision → section 12.7 (p. 434).

▷ **Know the user, and design accordingly** Find out what users want and keep them happy; this may be far easier than putting lots of design effort into issues users don't worry about → section 12.8 (p. 435).

▷ **Why make devices like anything that has gone before**? Be imaginative; use computers properly. Think bigger—think outside of the box → section 12.9 (p. 436).

▷ **If all else fails** Take care to handle errors and get feedback from users, so at least future designs can be improved → section 12.10 (p. 439).

▷ **Finally** ... The next chapter, chapter 13, "Improving things," discusses the essential *attitudes* and *awareness* that go with successful use of these and all other design principles.

12.2   Make design disappear

If the device is invisible to the user, then there is no interaction programming problem! Programmers building the system need only worry about technical issues, such as sensors and mobile communications; they need not worry about user interface design.

Of course, this isn't entirely true, since if the user is going to benefit from the device or system, it must affect them in some way, and therefore there is or has to be *some* interaction. Nevertheless the scope for hiding interaction is enormous and rarely explored; perhaps manufacturers want to sell products rather than solutions, which may solve the user's problems better—with less profit. (This somewhat cynical view of mine will resurface again toward the end of this section.)

Box 12.1 Problem solving We need to solve problems all the time, but so often solving the problem is so important that it focuses our energies—we need the solution!—and thus we rarely step back to consider other approaches. Problem solving is a well-studied area and provides many ways of making progress, often by going in different directions than our natural focus would lead us in.

Design is a problem for designers, and use is a problem for users; so from both sides, it is worth looking at problem solving, because it can help both designers and users.

Edward de Bono has collected and expressed many problem-solving principles. Often his work has come under criticism because, perhaps, his ideas seem so obvious once they are expressed clearly. His book *Teach Your Child to Think* has the advantage of collecting most of his effective ideas into a single book. He argues that we should develop thinking tools, and he gives some examples: just as a carpenter can cut wood and screw it together, we should have thinking tools to split problems and join them together in new ways. His "six thinking hats" is a tool that helps us compartmentalize our thinking styles; if we don't clearly separate our emotions, our judgments, our fact gathering, and so on, then we run the risk of being driven down one route without considering important alternatives. Similar ideas are also developed, with a much more direct relevance to user interface design, by Ben Shneiderman in his *Leonardo's Laptop*.

George Pólya was a mathematician who studied problem solving deeply, and his classic *How to Solve It* should be read by everyone. Often when we try to solve a problem, we get stuck. Pólya suggests that we should imagine the problem solved, and see if we can work backward to where we are at the moment. Another deep idea is to generalize: sometimes a specific problem has distracting details—can we work out what the general problem is and see if we can solve that? Often it's easier.

Terry Winograd and Fernando Flores's ground-breaking *Understanding Computers and Cognition* suggests (among many other ideas) that we should not always strive to *solve* problems—sometimes we can *dissolve* them. That idea is developed in section 12.2 (facing page), where we suggest that design should be invisible.

Fridges switch their lights on when you open their doors; you don't have to switch the light on. Cars are another good example of this invisible or incidental interaction. When you open a car door, the inside light comes on. On some cars, if you get into reverse when you have the windscreen wipers on, the rear wipers will come on automatically—the car switches them on automatically because it can work out that if you need the front wipers on to go forward, need the rear wipers on to go backward.

In some cars, the instrument panel is dimmed for night driving, but when you reach your hand toward, say, the radio, it lights up brighter so you can see it better.

For car thieves, a quite different sort of user, the burglar alarm is another example of interaction that happens as a side effect of interacting. Something happens automatically, without direct interaction from the user—though in this case, the interaction is done on behalf of the owner, not the user. With alarms, unlike car wipers, it's *essential* that the interaction and control of the interaction is invisible; otherwise, the burglar would override it.

Cars don't just interact with their users, they are also part of the bigger transport system. Road tolls can work automatically from sensors—the driver just drives past the sensor and is billed automatically for using the road. In the past, this interaction would have required either a human operator or a machine to take cash. Now the interaction has disappeared.

Interaction also becomes invisible in less friendly ways. Traffic lights and speed cameras interact with cars; the driver has to do nothing other than be there. Traffic lights can stay on red indefinitely if they "think" nobody is waiting for them. As usual, it's wise to have timeouts in case there is an unusual situation beyond the sensors' awareness, such as a horse rider or cyclist might be—you shouldn't keep lo-tech users waiting forever!

Household energy-saving devices work in the same sort of way. If nobody moves in a room, the lights go out to save energy—this is hopeless for a library, where you would expect people to remain still as they read. Given that the lights go out on a timeout, which can be frustrating as it will take people by surprise, the timeout should be adjustable (perhaps up to infinity—that is, never—for people who really want to override the feature), and the lights should come on again when there is movement. A person is plunged into darkness shouldn't then have to find the light switch; it should come on automatically! Even better would be for the energy-saving system to slowly dim the lights; this at least would not plunge anyone into complete darkness suddenly.

Timeouts seem a necessary evil for walk-up-and-use devices. Because users may walk away from a device half way through an interaction, it is important that the device reset itself to its standby "helpful" state so it is ready when a new user walks up to it. Many walk-up-and-use devices work in many languages, and the first interaction they require is to know what language the user wants—a new user may not be able to read anything on the last screen left them by the previous user. But timeouts are a crude way of doing this; much better is to use a proximity sensor—a sensor that tells the device if there is a body or movement nearby. The standard technology, such as passive infrared sensors (PIRs) or ultrasound motion sensors, from burglar alarms can be used.

Sensors no doubt have a hard time telling the difference between people and dogs or pigeons. A more reliable approach is to rely on the people carrying some form of electronically readable identification, such as a key fob (which merely requires proximity), or a swipe card—either magnetic strip or optical bar code—that requires some basic interaction. If the user wears the swipe card on a cord, the card can be kept in the device while the user is interacting. When leaving the user has to take the card with them, and the device realizes they've left. Of course, if the card is merely swiped through the device at the start of interaction, the device doesn't know whether the user is still there or not, which is the original problem we were trying to solve.

There are many other technologies. Car keys now often have simple radio transmitters in them, so a driver can unlock the car when nearby—the driver doesn't have to put the key directly into the lock. Most of these car keys are also passive security devices: the car won't start at all unless the key fob is close to the ignition switch. The car "knows" the right user is present.

Although many of these devices are proprietary, it has often surprised me that there is so little reuse of the technologies. For example, my key fob lets me drive my car, but if my house had a sensor that could learn the code my key fob uses, then I could get into my house or set the burglar alarm with the key fob. Instead, I need to have two different devices to do this. The same comment applies to my workplace: I need more keys and cards to get around the building I work in. Yet it could easily have learned my car key's fob codes and been authorized to open doors with that.

I guess manufacturers who make locks get a useful income from selling swipe cards or their own key fobs, and they have little incentive to make things easier to use in this way. This reluctance, if it is reluctance, will have to change as more people use implants for the same purpose.

In prestige and high-security applications, people are willing to have little tags injected into them. The tags are little cylinders, about 2mm (a tenth of an inch) in diameter, and can easily be forced under your skin down a large diameter hypodermic needle. Once under your skin, you may have automatic access to secure areas, or have your bar and hotel bills paid—or rather, billed—directly.

VeriChip is one such technology, made by Applied Digital Solutions—and its commercial success suggests that this is a design area we must take seriously. VeriChip uses a passive implant (so it uses the power of the external sensor, needing no power of its own) that responds with a unique number. The sensor then uses this number to retrieve whatever information is relevant about the user. For example, for access to a club, the scanner could bring up a photograph of the customer.

12.2.1 Ticket machines

Some walk-up-and-use devices are part of a bigger and more significant interaction with the user. Ticket machines, for example, enable users to use public transport. Users reall wants to interact with the bus or train—the ticket machine itself hinders what they really want to do.

> ▷ Some problems of walk-up-and-use ticket machines are discussed in section 3.9 (p. 77).

Rather than users having to first tell the ticket machine where they want to go (and what sort of ticket they want, whether they want to return, and so on), then having to pay (and maybe get some change, or maybe forget it), almost everything the user should tell the ticket machine can be worked out afterward, provided the train or bus can keep track of the user. Suppose the user has a wireless device (perhaps their mobile phone), then the train could work out when they get on and off the train. If the same person returns, they obviously wanted a round-trip ticket and the system should behave as if that's what they bought.

Now the interaction with the ticket machine has disappeared altogether. The user cannot make mistakes like buying the wrong ticket or leaving change behind. And the user isn't under pressure to buy a ticket in a hurry just as a train arrives; they just get on. Everything is automatic.

From the railway company's point of view, the disappearing ticket machine also gets rid of passengers who travel without tickets. Most railway cars have weight sensors on them; if the weight and number of wireless-enabled passengers does not tally, a conductor can be warned to do a manual check. Or perhaps the train could wait while the angry delayed passengers sort the problem out for themselves: people might get off one at a time until the train leaves without them, because they don't have any means of paying automatically.

We've completely eliminated the conventional interaction programming problems, but we've replaced them with new problems—we've replaced conventional interaction programming issues with ethical and business issues:

- While we have made the device interaction very smooth, some people won't have the resources to be wirelessly connected. For these people, the user interface has become much worse.

- The old device could take cash and was essentially anonymous. The new approach still needs a way of billing the user, but now it needs to do it with something like a credit card account. The railway company therefore knows who you are every time you travel—as well as where you live, and your credit rating, and so on.

- The railway could invent its own credit card, which a traveler buys (they could be wireless-enabled as well, so they do the complete job: providing passenger location *and* paying). The credit on the card allows customers to travel, but because they have paid up front, perhaps with cash, their anonymity need not be compromised.

There are many possible "compromise" designs that make the interaction *half* invisible. Why not, for instance, make the credit card idea low tech: it could be a piece of paper. The piece of paper, once bought, allows 10 or 100 trips. The user could punch it on the train ... and we've just invented continental-style railway ticketing.

When considering the tradeoffs between these alternatives, remember that most walk-up-and-use devices are not meant to be perfect. Automatic ticket machines are called "queue busters" because their purpose is to reduce queue lengths at railway stations or at airports. If they only handle two-thirds of passengers, the station or airport can employ fewer staff; for the (mostly regular) users, for whom the ticket machines are successful, the experience will be good. For users with complex requirements for their travel or tickets, they'd still need to talk to humans anyway.

12.2.2   Don't be perfect

Designing devices *not* to be perfect is a better design principle than trying to make them wonderful for everybody. Provided you are designing a device for a wide range of people, handling some of those people well and others not at all (provided they have some sort of backup) is better than handling everybody in a mediocre way. This principle applies directly to walk-up-and-use devices and to discretionary devices, such as mobile phones. If customers don't like my wonderful mobile phone design, they can buy some other make. The principle does not apply in areas such as cars (except their entertainment functions), medical equipment, and aviation, where avoiding catastrophic errors is more important.

12.3 Design like the real world

Interactive devices are often hard to use because they are unfamiliar; they "don't work like they should." Well, how *should* they work?

We live in a physical world, with lots of objects, from doors to balls, in it. We are very familiar with the behavior of these physical objects, and after a little training in early childhood we are pretty good at things like shoelaces, buttonholes, keys, to say nothing of our remarkable skills at walking, running, and jumping—seemingly effortless, yet still beyond the best robots. Cars and bicycles are among the very complex everyday devices we soon master.

All of these things, and many more, obey the laws of physics. Interactive devices, at least at the level of how they work, needn't obey the laws of physics—or indeed any laws at all. What is it, then, about the laws of physics that we have become familiar with? Can we exploit any such principles in interaction programming?

12.3.1 Symmetry as a principle

A key organizing principle in the world is symmetry. In its many forms, symmetry captures a basic aspect of reality that we can translate into the design of interactive devices.

We are most familiar with visual symmetries. For instance, W is a symmetric letter, but F isn't. One way of seeing that W is symmetric is to put a mirror across it vertically in the middle, so that it is split into two V shapes. The mirror reflects one V to make another, and we see a W. We say that W has mirror symmetry. The letters X and H have more mirror symmetries—can you see how X has more mirror symmetries than H? More precisely, X has four mirror symmetries unless you look *very closely* at the thicknesses of the strokes and the serifs at the ends of the strokes: these details break the symmetries. As we shall see, things are interesting when they are almost symmetrical—and the really interesting design questions arise at these boundaries, just as good typography arises when letter forms are almost symmetrical, but the symmetry is broken in an elegant way.

Symmetry can be defined formally, without any appeal to pictures at all. If you can transform or change an object, and it appears to be unchanged, then the object has a symmetry. For example, if you rotate a letter H upside down—that's how you intend to transform or change it—it will look the same; thus H has a 180 degree rotational symmetry.

The laws of physics have symmetries; and as we grow up we learn these symmetries. Later, we use our knowledge of the symmetries of nature to help us solve

415

Figure 12.1: The letter X has four mirror symmetries and four rotational symmetries (not counting turning it around in space, off the paper)—unless you look very closely at the varying thickness of the strokes and at the details at their ends, the serifs. The careful design of the symmetry-breaking details are what makes good typography—and good interaction programming, once we have ways of seeing symmetry in programs.

problems. Mostly we find this practical problem solving so easy that we rarely think about it.

One of the simplest and yet most profound symmetries is called translation, otherwise known as moving. The laws of physics don't change when something is moved. You change something's position—this is the change you intend—and now you find everything seems the same. Movement is a sort of symmetry, just like reflecting in a mirror. In mundane terms, my mug of tea works like a mug of tea—and if I move it to another room it *still* behaves like a mug of tea. As I said, this is so obvious that we don't think about it.

Imagine that you generously give me a coin, which I place in my left hand. I now put the coin in my right hand and open my right hand for you to see. The coin has gone! You gasp! I am a magician. I have surprised you because I broke a fundamental law of physics: just by moving a coin from one hand to another does not make it disappear. It should have been unchanged, for we know that translation is a symmetry, a very basic fact about the way the universe works. If I can break translation symmetry, I must be a very good magician indeed.

It's even more fun doing magic with children, because they are still learning the rules about how the world works. Even putting a hand over your face to make it disappear briefly can get a young enough child excited about whether you'll ever reappear.

While breaking symmetry is fun when it is done for entertainment, it is devastating when it happens for other reasons. You put your coin in your pocket, and next time you look, it has gone! You know the universe doesn't behave like this, so you blame a pickpocket. You would be lucky if it was only a coin that was stolen. In short, breaking a symmetry can be upsetting.

We *like* symmetry; it is deeply tied up with out aesthetic sensibilities. A wiggly line is just a wiggly line, but a line that has a repeated pattern is a frieze and can be used for decoration. Poetry mixes translation (movement, as you move your eye down the verse) and some rhythm and rhyme that is unchanged (or changes at a different rate) as you read—a partial symmetry that is artistically balanced between being overly repetitive, and dull, or being unstructured.

Computer graphics experiments done with peoples' faces show that symmetric faces are often perceived as more attractive than asymmetric ones. Symmetric things have "balance" and seem more elegant; we like symmetry.

In contrast, broken things are often asymmetric. If you damage a ball, it will have fewer symmetries and, for instance, will stop rolling freely (which requires spherical symmetry). Damage, of course, often does random destructive things: it would be hard to do damage symmetrically to something. When people or animals are diseased or damaged in any way, the marks of the disease are very unlikely to be symmetrical. When we go looking for mates, we tend to prefer people who are symmetric, since this is a good heuristic that they are undamaged and are more likely to be undamaged genetically. In evolutionary terms, the people who mated with asymmetric partners probably had fewer healthy children. We who are the survivors of generations of people making mating decisions, tend to like symmetry, since it has served our ancestors well.

Symmetry is also intensely practical. I'll mention four advantages of it, before we move on to applying the idea in design.

■ When we try to solve a problem but get stuck, we need to find another way of looking at the problem, so that if we can solve it from this other view, we've solved the problem. This is exactly what symmetry is: we want to transform a problem but leave the essential bits unchanged. We sometimes even say we want to "turn it over" in our minds.

■ Symmetry compresses information. If something has a symmetry, we can throw some of it away and yet be able to reconstruct it later just from knowing the symmetry. Here is a very simple example: a table of numbers and their squares:

Number	Square
1	1
2	4
3	9
4	16

Now if I tell you that squaring is symmetric—that is, the square of a number is unchanged even if you change the number to be negative—I have doubled the amount you know from reading the table, without making the table any bigger. Because squaring is symmetric, I need only show you half the table—you know, for instance, that -4 squared is 16. Symmetry has effectively allowed the table to be compressed without loss of any information.

■ Symmetry makes things easier to use. More succinctly, we called this principle permissiveness: if something can be used in more than one way, it is permissive. Again, this is symmetry. The transformation is to use the device a different way with the end result—what the device does—unchanged.

A physical example of symmetry and the principle of permissiveness is that a plug that looks symmetric ought to be symmetric. A USB plug ends in a little metal rectangle; it ought to go in its socket either way up, then. But it turns out that the appearance of symmetry is deceptive. A USB plug is not symmetrical, though it looks like it is unless you look closely. They are therefore much

417

harder to put in than they need be; either they should have been really symmetrical (so it didn't matter which way they go in), or they should not have looked symmetrical (so we know which way is up).

▷   See box 5.5, "Permissiveness" (p. 136), for further examples and more cross-references.

■ Symmetry makes things easier to debug for programmers. From a user's point of view, symmetry makes things easier to learn. If we have good reason to think something is symmetrical, then we can learn how it works (or check that it works) by only trying it out partially. If we think the A and B parts of something work the same way, that is, that they are symmetrical, then we need only try A to know that B works the same way. It follows from this observation that user manuals should explain when parts of a device behave the same way as other parts; this will let users learn and understand faster.

To summarize what is a very big and wide-ranging topic: we learn rules about the way the world works, and some very deep rules are called symmetries. Symmetries make things much easier to understand, they make problems easier to solve, and they are aesthetically very satisfying, but occasionally they are broken. Under the right circumstances, it may be an exciting game to break rules, but in more prosaic circumstances it is awful. The world seems to have let you down.

Translating these ideas into interaction programming, a programmer should identify the symmetries in the planned design, or in what the planned device is intended to do, and make them obvious to the user—and make them reliable, rather than half-hearted.   And avoid appearing to have symmetries that actually don't work, like the USB plug.

▷   Half-hearted, beguiling, design rules are discussed in section 10.3.3 (p. 337).

12.3.2   Affordance as experience of symmetry

Interaction programmers should know about affordance, which is a principle very like symmetry, but somewhat more specific. Affordance is the appearance an object has that it can be used in a particular way. Affordance, then, is very like symmetry. Symmetry, when it applies, says that we can change something (that is, use it), and it will appear to be unchanged; in other words, we can *still* use it. A round door knob has the affordance that it can be turned—a round door knob has rotational symmetry, meaning that if you turn it, it will look unchanged.

A ball is such a good toy because you can do so many things to it, and it still remains a ball (unlike my cup of tea, which isn't so convenient to roll around). In formal terms, a ball has spherical symmetry. In affordance terms, a ball has the affordance of something you can pick up, roll, throw, and so on.

Affordance, like symmetry, compresses information. If you can see an object that affords its being used in a particular way, you don't need to know about *that* object in particular. It looks like any other object of that sort, and you don't need

Box 12.2 Design guidelines If we know we want to provide undo in a device, we can use simple programming to check that the design allows all user actions to be undone, or we can write programs to create undo actions for all user actions in the original device specification. Either way, we have a device that has undo—which is what we wanted.

But what features should designers want in good devices? An idea like "provide undo" is a typical design guideline, and there are books and manuals of guidelines that are a source of inspiration—or even legal protection—for designers. Guidelines are particularly useful if a group of designers are working together in a team, so that they have a coherent view of the design work, or for a creating a range of devices that all work in ways the users see as consistent. Often manufacturers will have proprietary guidelines that impose their distinctive style, to ensure their devices have a suitable corporate feel about them.

Although there has been no systematic study of what makes for good guidelines, researchers have been filtering them for years, trying to identify core guidelines that are few in number, easy to use and effective in design. Here's a sample, which I've organized starting with guidelines that a framework can readily help support or test, and the later ones being more inspirational:

1 Match the user's task sequence	8 Allow users to create short cuts
2 Provide undo or provide easy reversal of actions	9 Design for errors 10 Provide help
3 Remove modes	11 Provide a sense of progress;
4 Provide informative feedback, and provide it immediately	give users a sense of achievement 12 Information should appear
5 Be consistent, utilize symmetry	in a natural order
6 Provide clearly marked exits	13 Minimize the user's memory load
7 Provide shortcuts	14 Speak the user's language

This book has raised all these ideas—and more—in discussion, and indeed a proper list of guidelines would expand and explain the ideas in careful detail, to suit the types of device being designed and the types of users and activities for which they are being designed.

After the generalities of typical guidelines, it's important to have more specific guidelines for users with impaired vision, hearing, or movement—especially if you are designing for older people, children, or users working in harsh environments—say, where they have to wear gloves or eye protection. Remember that you can often design for both "normal" and "impaired" users by suitable techniques: for instance, you should always use more than just color to distinguish buttons and indicators on a device—use different high-contrast symbols as well—otherwise some users may not be able to tell them apart reliably.

to know so much about the world. Every chair you have ever seen behaves like a chair, you have not had to learn how each chair works. Your mind would be full if it had to have all that information in it; instead, you've learned very general principles about how objects work.

More to the point, you've also learned how things like buttons work. If you press a button, it goes in, and something happens. The affordance is that something that looks like a button is a pressable thing. If you are a designer, and you want your user to press things, then make them look like buttons. Buttons have the affordance of pressing. If you have to use a computer's flat screen, using shading and shadow effects to make the button look like it sticks out, so it can be pressed.

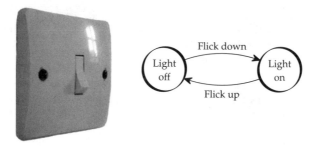

Figure 12.2: A wall light switch and its transition diagram. This is a UK switch; in the US, it would be switched up for off.

The design rule is to find out the affordances and then represent them in the device you are designing. Then the user will "automatically" know what to do—they don't need to know specifically how your device works, because it works like other things they are already familiar with.

12.3.3   Using symmetry in design

One of the deep and amazing facts about symmetry is that it is a very robust property. Again, we've learned this fact as we grew up, and simple examples to explain it seem so obvious as to be quite banal. The letter W, we saw above, has mirror symmetry. If we make it bigger or smaller, or change its color, it still has the same symmetry. Even turing it over to make an M retains the symmetries.

A rather more radical change to W would be to change it into its ASCII code. Now we've transformed a letter to a number, namely, 87. Provided we print 87 the right way, we'll get the letter W back, so this is a simple symmetry. But ASCII has been designed in a clever way so that it preserves more properties of letters. The next letter after W in the alphabet is X. The next number after 87 is 88. If we print 88, we'll get an X. This designed-in symmetry of ASCII is very handy if you want to know something more awkward, like the letter fifteen in the alphabet before W.

This robustness of symmetry helps us in interaction programming. Symmetries that a state transition diagram have are symmetries the user may well be aware of and will be able to exploit. The visual symmetries of a drawing of a device's diagram are symmetries that also surface, invisibly, in the way the user interface works.

We'll start with a simple example. Figure 12.2 (this page) is a transition diagram for a simple on/off switch, next to a picture of a real wall switch. The diagram has rotational and mirror symmetries; for instance, we can turn it over, and it will look just the same (although maybe we need to keep the writing the right way up). Similarly, the physical switch can be turned over, and it will work just the same (although maybe we will need to swap over the on and off states).

Other sorts of on/off switches are knobs that you rotate; again, they work just as well when they are turned over. You could of course design an on/off switch not to be symmetric, but this would be unusual—and result in something harder to use. A real physical switch is easier to use if it is designed to reflect the symmetries of the state transitions it manipulates.

12.3.4 Statecharts and symmetry

Statecharts are a good ways of drawing transition diagrams because they remove a lot of clutter and are much easier to read. Statecharts make interaction structure like clusters and history very clear—things that would be very difficult to make clear in a basic transition diagram. Equally, they make the designer aware of more potential symmetries to exploit in a design.

Consider, as an example, designing the user interface for a digital clock. Typically a digital clock will have four digits, and each digit may have its own control button. The statechart for the user interface for one digit of a digital clock could look like this:

If we imagine that each of the four digits has a button underneath it, each would make a sort of domino. Here is our basic physical building block: a basic domino-shaped unit that gives space for a single digit and the button that controls it is immediately below it. Here's how one of these dominos would look if it was displaying the digit 3:

Pressing the button under a digit increases the digit by one, taking 0 to 1, 1 to 2 and so on, and 9 back to 0. This is what the statechart diagram says.

Now, take a domino and move it right three times to get a row of four dominos. A row of buttons and digits showing 1215 would look something like this:

Pressing the button under a digit increases the digit by one, taking 0 to 1, 1 to 2 and so on, and 9 back to 0. This is what the statechart diagram says.

Now, take a domino and move it right three times to get a row of four dominos. A row of buttons and digits showing 1215 would look something like this:

No doubt, if we were designing a real product, it wouldn't have all those lines on it, but would have a nice smooth surface. With or without lines, it has a simple horizontal symmetry: a symmetry of translation—if you move left or right, each domino looks and behaves the same.

The statechart of the four dominos combined has a corresponding symmetry as well:

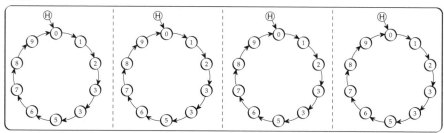

This is a really deep and fascinating outcome: the physical device and the statechart have corresponding symmetries. But before we get too excited, we must acknowledge that there is an awful problem, brought about by the very symmetry we've been claiming is a good thing. By convention, times go from 00:00 (midnight) to 23:59 (a minute before midnight) and then back to 00:00. But, thanks to the consistent statechart, our clock's display goes from 0000 to 9999; worse, *strictly* it goes back to 0999, 9099, 9909, or 9990 with one user action—it takes four separate user actions to go from 9999 to 0000. The buttons in the dominos treat each digit as the display of an independent state machine; the device—so far—has the sense neither to handle multi-digit numbers nor times.

The righthand pair of digits shouldn't be able to get to a number higher than 59 minutes, and the left hand pair of digits shouldn't be able to get higher than 23 (or 12 if we are using a 12-hour clock rather than a 24-hour clock). In short, it doesn't behave at all like we would want a clock to!

▷   The opening story of chapter 11, "More complex devices," exposes some of the problems of clocks that can count from 0000 to 9999.

We can either try to change the world, and have 10,000 "minutes" in a day to make our lives easier, or we can spend a moment trying to reconcile our design with convention, which requires clocks to go from 12:59 to 1:00 and from 23:59 to 0:00. Affordance may tell us the "best" way of doing it, but convention tells us the way users will like! (If we were designing a digital display for some other purpose than telling the time, say for an aircraft altimeter, we wouldn't have this conflict.) I blame the Babylonians for the mess, though the French tried a decimal system during the Revolution and, more recently, Swatch introduced an "internet time" dividing the day into 1,000 ".beats" instead of 1,440 minutes. A .beats clock would be easier to make easy to use.

One way to satisfy social convention is to remove the first and third buttons and combine digits into hours or minutes:

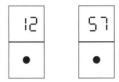

What we have done is to enlarge our dominos to display two digits, so one domino goes from 0 to 12 (or 23), and the other from 0 to 59. Now the buttons increase the units of the numbers, whether hours or minutes. Repeatedly pressing a button cannot cause an invalid time to be displayed.

The disadvantage of combining digits into pairs is that it now takes much longer to set a time. The righthand button might need pressing 59 times (say, to get it from displaying 00 to displaying 59), whereas with two buttons for the same task it would only need pressing 5 (for the left digit) plus 9 (for the right digit) times—a total of only 14 presses, about four times faster.

The usual way of reducing the increased button-pressing effort is to make the buttons *automatically* repeat, so the user can change the time from 0 to 59 with only one press. To speed up this method, holding the button down for longer makes the numbers change faster: when you want to slow down, stop pressing the button, and start again. When we try to makes things simpler, we often make them more complex in other ways. We have to use our skill and judgment to find the right balance.

12.3.5   DVD players

Affordance and symmetry sound like such good principles that they should be able to solve everything. Here, to make a contrast, we consider an everyday example, which is surprisingly tricky.

A typical DVD film menu, redrawn as a schematic TV "screen shot," is shown in figure 12.3 (next page). The schematic (of what would be a montage graphic of scenes from the film) shows two menus, one for selecting a specific scene of the film (in the upper part of screen), one (in the lower part of the screen) for either returning back to the main DVD menu or for selecting a different choice from another four scenes. In the figure, scene 18 is selected—if the user pressed (Enter) at this stage, scene 18 would start playing.

A major design problem is that the remote control provides four orthogonal arrow keys, pointing up, down, left, and right. These should "obviously" move the choice of selected scene in the direction of the arrow, thanks to affordance.

Unfortunately, given this screen layout, a simple standard geometric interpretation of the arrow keys is in conflict with a consistent semantic interpretation of the keys, namely, that there are two different menus on the screen and that they have been designed so that movement *within* a menu takes priority over geometrical movement. Specifically, the arrow keys, which move the selection, appear to move geometrically most of the time, but because they also try to move semantically within the scenes or within the main menu bottom line, they cannot always

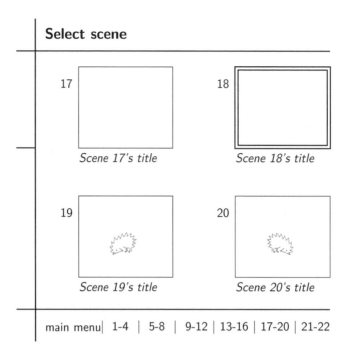

Select scene

17

Scene 17's title

18

Scene 18's title

19

Scene 19's title

20

Scene 20's title

main menu| 1-4 | 5-8 | 9-12 | 13-16 | 17-20 | 21-22

Figure 12.3: A typical DVD menu design, schematically depicting a select scene menu from a DVD. There are two distinct menus: the four scenes (as shown, scene 18 is selected), and the main menu at the bottom, giving the user a total of 11 choices. Similar issues arise in many DVD scene selection menus.

move in a consistent way. For example, predicting what moving down will do from some selection on the bottom menu is not easy.

Explaining the DVD design clearly is a problem. The next few paragraphs are, while accurate, tedious to read. This in itself is an indication that the design should be improved. When designs are not easy to explain, there is less motivation for thinking about them; you probably take shortcuts to avoid tedious explanation! Please persevere for the next few paragraphs with that thought in mind—how would you have designed the DVD interaction to be easier to describe, and easier to understand, use, and improve?

The geometric layout is obvious from the appearance of the menus, as drawn in figure 12.3 (this page), but the menus are also structured hierarchically, although the screen layout does not make this very clear:

- The menu item "main menu" goes up a level in the hierarchy if it is selected.

- The "group scene selection" menu items on the bottom row (1-4, 5-8, ... 21-22) move across levels in the hierarchy and bring up a screen similar to the one in the figure, which could have been displayed by choosing 17-20 from this menu.

■ Once a group scene has been selected, the selection moves to the lowest level in the hierarchy, to a specific one of four scenes.

The keys ⬅ and ➡ go to numerically previous and next scenes, in the obvious order they are seen in the film. Thus, given that scene 18 is selected in the figure, ➡ would go to the next scene, selecting 19, then (if pressed again) it would go to 20, then 21 (redrawing the menu with scenes 21 and 22), then 22, then back to 1. Similarly, ⬅ would select 17 then 16, and eventually it would go back to 1, and recycle round to 22.

Vertical movement, however, is deceptive. With scene 18 selected, ⬇ moves to scene 20, and then ⬆ will go back and select scene 18 again. So we think we my have a rule: ⬇⬆ leaves you where you started, just as pressing ⬅➡ would always leave you where you started.

Inconsistently, though, ⬇ pressed in either lower scene (here, 19 or 20) moves down to the main menu row, as does ⬆ in either upper scene (here, 17 or 18). Furthermore, ⬇ from the left column (here, 19) moves to "main menu," but from the right column moves to 21-22 *because this is the next set of scenes.* My emphasis is needed, since ⬇ from the left column *always* goes to main menu, but from the right column it goes to the next set of scene choices in the bottom menu, which is different every time.

Now let's summarize the main features of this design. Mostly, but not always, the arrow keys move the selection point in the corresponding direction on the screen. Left and right arrows also cycle, whether on the bottom menu, or in the scene region.

Inconsistencies are almost entirely due to the multiple uses of ⬆ and ⬇, since there is no great call for jumping forward and backward *two* scenes, their use in the scene selection menu is questionable.

Whether this menu design causes real problems for users is an open question. Whether improving the geometric affordances would reduce user problems is another question. Both questions are worth exploring experimentally, though of course DVD menus as such are not a major issue for usability—they are for entertainment. Do the extra seconds a user takes, or the additional errors they make, matter? Indeed, it is possible that the extra seconds enhance the user's enjoyment, for instance, by prolonging anticipation. Or is the graphic design (the static impression, rather than the interaction) more important for marketing?

■   ■   ■

Many DVD menu screen designs are much worse, suggesting that ease of use is not a design priority. For example, as many DVDs organize menu items in circles (or arcs), meaning that even within a menu there is no consistent direction for the arrow keys to follow.

12.4   Fix the bigger system

We often think that we are designing a device, but in fact we are designing a *system*, of which the device is but a small part. We are designing the device to fit into the user's world, and we are therefore making a contribution to designing the world, the big system. We might do better if we started from the world and wondered how to redesign the environment than the device that is supposed to be a part of it.

When we looked at statecharts and symmetry above, in section 12.3.4 (p. 421), we uncovered a design conflict: if you want to make clocks easy to use, you have to follow peculiar conventions. If the Babylonians had worried about ease-of-use, they could have made the system a lot simpler, even allowing for their base-60 number system. If we were arrogant designers, we'd make a really easy-to-use clock and expect people to change their ideas and live with it.

A ticket machine's complex user interface comes about because it is poorly designed to do what it does. One of the things it does is to represent the railway company's ticket rules to the user. The user no longer has a ticket clerk interfacing between them and the rules, the ticket machine's complexity is, to a large part, due to the rules it has to implement.

Many of the ticket machine's rules evolved, in the UK at least, over centuries. Many rules are still in the system have nothing to do with today's technologies and certainly nothing in the rules is based on making ticket machines easier to use. For example, even a small a ticket machine in the UK will have tens of thousands of ticket prices stored in it; the user interface *necessarily* has a baffling interface for the user to get the right ticket price.

There are one-way tickets. There are tickets for before 9 a.m., which are more expensive because they are aimed at business travelers. There are round-trip tickets, priced slightly less than twice a one-way ticket. There are weekly tickets. There are first-class tickets. There are family tickets. There are tickets for old people. There are tickets for children. There are tickets that either cost more or can't be used on trains leaving Paddington station between 4 p.m. and 8 p.m. because too many people leave London at that time. There are tickets bought with discount cards, of which there are several. There are different prices to different stations. There are "Saver" tickets and "Super Saver" tickets. Endless rules.

Why not change the rules, and simplify them so the design of the ticket machine can be made simpler? Why not have a one-price-fits-all ticket? Then the interaction programming problem becomes much easier! Perhaps a more realistic approach to design is to find a compromise between trying to design for a mad world and trying to make impossibly radical simplifications to the world. Perhaps the ticket machine should have just three types of ticket?

This section seems to be proposing the opposite approach to the last one: rather than design like the real world (copying its symmetries and affordances), change the world to be easier to design for! But most of the things we think should be changed for the better were social conventions, human constructs that were arbitrary to start with. Most of them won't have been thought out, and it could be well worth challenging them.

12.5 Make the device like its predecessor

Most design doesn't start from scratch; rather, it progresses and develops an existing design, and usually a design that was sufficiently successful to make it worth improving. Very bad designs are not improved; they are dropped.

If the predecessor is not actually an interactive device or a design you want to develop directly from, then the right technique is to decide what the metaphor is that the original gadget represents. Your new design will then be like the old gadget in essential ways, as identified by your chosen metaphor. (A metaphor is a way of saying something is like something else: an MP player is *like* a CD player; a DVD player is *like* a video cassette recorder (the original PVR); a camel is *like* a horse with two humps.)

Whether you use explicit metaphors or not, users are familiar with older designs, and if you design by refining the older designs, you keep your old users, and what they have to learn to take advantage of the new system is much less than if you had developed from scratch. If designs are incremental improvements on old designs, you will be able to collect a lot of data about their real use and hence focus on improvements to better suit ways you know the devices are actually used—this is a huge advantage over new devices, which will be used in ways you are never quite sure about.

The main disadvantage of building on old successes is that two very bad things happen:

- Gradually the design becomes impenetrable to the designers themselves. Typically program code in the device gets extended here and there in ways that make sense at the time. Eventually, though as layers accumulate, the program for the device is impossible to maintain; or, more likely, it has a collection of unfixable bugs. There are two solutions to this problem: either refactor the design, or employ a sensible design framework that can cope with changes without getting more and more arbitrarily complex.

- The number of staff allocated to designing the device is reduced. After all, only incremental work is called for. Over time, the resources for serious device development drop—then suddenly the market changes, and the skills, knowledge, and abilities are just not available to catch up with some competitor's new device.

Experience is defined as what you get just after you need it; but when you are designing a series of products, each based on its predecessor, you can put the experience of one design into experience for the next.

An alternative to making a design like its predecessor is to make it like part of itself. Make it *internally* consistent, not just consistent with previous versions. In fact, making a device internally consistent amounts to increasing its symmetries.

A typical home TV (or DVD player) has about six buttons against its remote control's of twenty or more buttons. That lack of consistency *necessarily* means that the buttons on the TV cannot be used in the same way or that different features are available from the TV and its remote control. Generally both are true.

There is no logical or technical reason for such inconsistencies. Indeed, if there is any special argument for a feature to turn out one way on the TV, the same argument probably applies with equal force to the remote control. A notable benefit of making the remote control and the TV consistent—both their buttons and the displays—would be that the user manual would be approximately halved in size, and the user's learning burden would be correspondingly reduced.

> ▷   On the importance of short, minimal manuals, see especially section 11.6.1
> (p. 397).

12.6   Use design tools wisely

Many ways of approaching grand design problems require sensible thinking about design tools—choosing tools sensibly and not being overly driven by restrictive tools. Be willing to use simple tools as much as possible.

12.6.1   Make the design easy to change

In any design process, anticipate making mistakes. It is inevitable that you will make mistakes, and if you set out using tools or techniques that make going back difficult, then you will be stuck with palliating rather than fixing the mistakes. To put the though more pointedly: if you design something so that it doesn't need fixing, it will, and then you won't be able to fix it.

If, as you design, you choose ideas that are easy to change, then new ideas and insights that occur as a prototype design matures into a product will be much easier to adopt.

If your device has any way of connecting to other devices, then it will be easier to upgrade and iterate its design. Can it be connected to the internet? Can it read memory cards—cameras often have memory cards for storing photographs, so why not also use them for loading revised software when you want to improve their design? Why not put in a USB socket so the device is easier to revise—this will mean that the device will be easier to build, because the USB port (or whatever you use) can be used in production, and it can be used to keep the product competitive once it has been released into the consumer market. Moreover, if consumers can upgrade their devices, the company that makes the upgrades will have an excellent way of getting feedback from users on how their product is really being used.

One of the motivations of our programming framework was that technical authors can get very good insights into product design, but in the normal course of events their insights are wasted because by the time they start writing, it is too late and too costly to change the design in any useful way.

A very useful heuristic to help guide making the right design decisions is to use a "spike." A spike takes representative parts of a design right through to *all* aspects of the finished product, but of course missing out a lot of the features intended for the final design. The point is that every stage of the development process is checked out well before you get to really needing it. If the spike uncovers some problem, start fixing it now before it creates an actual delay in the real development process.

An extremely powerful way to make designs easier to change is to build your own design tools. Building tools forces you to think at a higher level—about the properties of designs in general rather than your specific design. You then solve general problems, and the solutions serve you well when you make changes to your design as your ideas for it change. The your design tools can ensure or enforce whatever properties your devices need.

12.6.2   Use simple techniques as long as possible

George Pólya has given us a nice aphorism: within every impossible problem there is a simpler impossible problem—find it!

Similarly rather than struggle with some complicated design job, concentrate on the simpler part of it that Pólya promises will be there. The designer now starts with a simpler design problem and builds up to the larger issues, all the time managing the design carefully using appropriate tools (such as our framework). The tools are used as long as they possibly can be, then extended in ways to help.

A device can always be designed as a finite state machine (FSM) because of abstraction. That is, we don't have to be specific about what is inside states; states can be abstract descriptions of what a device does. Every interactive device can thus be designed as a finite state machine. You can start design using a tool or framework such as the one suggested in this book to explore the FSM. A very strong argument is that if you cannot see an abstract FSM in your design, you don't know what your design is and you shouldn't be doing it.

> ▷   Box 12.4, "Reductionism" (p. 431) expands further on ideas around abstraction.

For example, designing a television requires working with a lot of detail, possibly an overwhelming amount of detail. But we could start with an abstract finite state machine: the television is either on or off. That's only two states, but we can start from there. Next, we might add channels to the on state. As we extend what the states do, we are always starting from a more abstract level of design.

At some point we will probably decide that it is not the time or place to decide the details inside some state. For example, TV channel selection requires an interesting mapping between UHF and numbers—transmitters send TV signals at ultra-high frequencies in complicated ways so that nearby transmitters do not interfere with one another, yet, the user wants a simple scheme like 1 is BBC 1, 2 is BBC 2. We may prefer not to do this sort of thing with a finite state machine!

The principle to remember is, that just because you can't do all of a design using a simple approach doesn't mean you can't do a large part of it simply.

Although finite state machines are simple in themselves, which might seem restrictive, this doesn't stop their being generated by programs. If they are, then a designer could express themselves in a way or in a language they are familiar with,

---

Box 12.3 Defending finite state machines This box reviews some of the defenses of FSMs against the popular criticisms.

FSMs are large FSMs for typical devices often have thousands or more states. The size of a FSM is not a real concern once it is programmed, though obviously it would be a serious problem if one wanted to draw the corresponding transition diagram.

FSMs are unstructured FSMs are indeed unstructured. However, they can be "nested" so that large classes of states are treated as one big state—this makes what you are thinking about simpler, even though the underlying FSM is just as big. If an FSM has been *designed* to be like this, it can be drawn easily using statecharts, which are a very good way of drawing large FSMs.

FSMs are finite FSMs are finite and therefore formally less powerful than infinite computational models such as pushdown automata (PDAs) or Turing Machines. For example, a handheld calculator using brackets is readily modeled as a PDA, and therefore one might think it is not an FSM. However, all physically realizable digital devices are FSMs, whether or not it is convenient to model them explicitly as such.

FSMs are not relevant to users FSMs are mathematical or program structures, and they do not exist in any useful concrete form for users except in the very simplest of cases—where they are hardly necessary to help the users! Users should not be expected to reason about the behavior of devices by using FSMs: they are typically far too big—but this argument does not mean that designers should not reason using FSMs, particularly if they have programs to help them do so.

Few systems are implemented as FSMs Most systems are implemented in ad hoc ways, and determining any model from them is hard, if not impossible. In this sense, FSMs suffer from problems no different from any other formal approach. Better, one would start with the formal model and derive (preferably automatically) the implementation.

FSM models are impossible to determine On the contrary, if systems are developed rigorously, it is not hard to determine finite models of user interfaces from them.

FSMs are bad for design The rigor of FSMs encourages interaction programmers to make simpler devices that they understand, so they can analyze and build reliable interactive systems. FSMs have a clear theory, and we can measure all sorts of important design properties with simple programming. We can also generate help, user manuals, and other important material from FSMs specifications.

---

and this high-level specification can be translated by a tool into a finite state machine. The designer's tool can then generate (if it wishes) *enormous* finite state machines that would have been way beyond comprehension but for being expressed in the high level way. Thus the size of the finite state machine has been hidden from the designer, but all the advantages of the basically simple FSM approach have been retained; all of the measurements and other advantages our framework provides now comes for free, with no extra effort.

Box 12.4 Reductionism Reductionism says that we can make progress by reducing things to bare principles and then reason successfully about useful properties of systems from those underlying principles. We can discuss the large-scale behavior of planets in the solar system, for example, without worrying about their weather systems; we can just study their gravitational influences on one another. (The reason why science became so successful since the Renaissance was reductionism.) Abstraction is the computer science term: abstraction reduces the number of concepts that one needs to think about all at once.

Reductionism as a philosophy, ontological reductionism, asserts that not only is it convenient to think like this, but reality is *really* like this, that is, made out of simpler things. In human-computer interaction it's pretty hard to go along with this form of reductionism because interaction has many deeply-interacting features: the user's motivation, lighting conditions, whether users are part of a social group, and so on. Many things that have to do with user context influence the success of a design and cannot be reduced.

Yet if we fail to be reductionist *at the right time*, we miss out on useful insights. A reductionist programmer would build really simple programs and get them to work—perhaps using finite state machines—and then build on necessary embellishments. Ideally the result of a reductionist approach would be a human-computer system that was understood and was easy to modify, and so on.

Instead, there is a temptation to resist reducing design at any stage to make it simpler. This is a recipe for despair and results in large ad hoc system designs that nobody—whether designer or user—understands.

Thinking about states and actions and finite state machines is unashamedly reductionist. They allow designers to think clearly about simple things. They don't help designers think about everything they need to or should! But where they help, they help enormously.

▷ The drill and the farmer's problem—see sections 9.8 (p. 316) and 10.1 (p. 325)—were generated by program, which was much easier to write than work out by hand the correct relations between all the states.

The program lex (and all its derivatives) is a well-known example: it reads a list of regular expressions and builds a finite state machine from them. The regular expressions are very much easier to read than the details of the finite state machine that is generated by this process.

▷ Lex is explained more fully below, in section 12.6.4 (next page).

Many concurrent programming notations, such as CSP, Spin, and SMV, can compile into finite state machines; if these notations are easier for a designer to use, then they can be exploited and all of the advantages we promoted in part II can either be derived directly or indirectly by compiling into finite state machines. (Unfortunately, you don't always get finite machines for all cases, but that is a technical issue beyond the scope of this book; LTSA is a dialect of CSP that guarantees finite machines.)

12.6.3 Use sophisticated design tools

Press On covers basic finite state machine approaches combined with simple programming in JavaScript, but there are more powerful techniques available.

431

We rather constrained our use of JavaScript because the entire rules of interaction were captured by our finite state machine specification. That is, we used no serious power of JavaScript to decide what an interactive device would do; everything was determined by a finite state machine. In general, if we choose, we could program *any* interactive behavior in JavaScript, but then our ability to analyze and understand what we had designed would be *very* severely curtailed. Indeed, as most interactive programs are written in general-purpose programming languages, there is very little hope of ever generating user manuals or drawing transition diagrams from interactive programs written conventionally—or of getting any of the other advantages we covered in part II of this book.

For many purposes, specifying systems as finite state machines will seem overly restricted. Fortunately, there are several very well designed programming languages that are much more powerful and yet have all the advantages of being tractable and easy to analyze. Foremost among these languages are SMV and Spin, though there are several approaches that are less like programming and more like specifying in algebra, such as Alloy and CSP. See the further reading at the end of this chapter (p. 441).

In contrast, rapid application development (RAD) tools like Flash let you build interactive systems very quickly, which is a benefit in itself, but few I would consider "sophisticated design tools" as they provide no analysis of what you are building. Typically, they cannot even answer simple questions, like whether the design is strongly connected.

12.6.4   Use proper compiler tools

Rather than think of the finite state machine as defining an interactive device, it is sometimes easier to start with the language that the device is supposed to interpret. For many devices, like light switches, the language is so trivial that we don't need to think about it as such. For many more complex devices, the language is a good starting point.

An obvious example is a handheld calculator: it should interpret arithmetic, and the language of arithmetic should be used to specify the design. The language of arithmetic (numbers, expressions, bracketed expressions) is very easy to write down using a grammar, and a tool called a compiler-compiler can check this and translate it into an efficient program that understands the language.

Compiler-compilers typically take a language specification and they generate programs in a high-level language, like Java. The most famous tools are lex, which takes a language specification written in terms of regular expressions, and yacc, which takes a language specification written in a grammar. With a name like yacc, it has not surprisingly inspired a range of newer tools like Bison and ANTLR—unfortunately, we can't cover them in this book, but it's worth knowing their names and looking them up on the web.

Because a lot of effort has gone into the careful design of tools like lex and yacc, you can be certain that the programs they generate are faithful to the language specifications they were given—much as you could be certain that the device simulations we created in part II were faithful to our finite state machine specifications. In fact, lex and yacc have been around a very long time, since the late 1970s, and there are now many more advanced and flexible systems.

Here is a very condensed overview of lex, in sufficient detail to inspire you to either find similar tools (on the web) or to build your own! In giving this overview, I have translated lex's compiler-compiler terminology into our terminology of interaction programming.

A lex specification starts with some declarations: these declarations may include definitions of the buttons the user can press. After a %% is a list of regular expressions and program code (written in C in the original lex) that is run when the regular expressions match the user's actions. The regular expressions are usually set up to recognize things like <=, comments, strings, numbers, and variable names (the lexical tokens of the language—hence lex's name). Here's a very simple example, written more in the style of lex than being a complete working example, based on some of the main buttons of a simple handheld calculator:

```
// a simple calculator, with memory, display and error flag.
DIGIT [0-9] // define decimal digits
%%
{AC}                    { // clear display
                          if( !error ) d = 0;
                        }

{AC}{AC}+               { // clear all registers and reset error flag
                          m = d = 0; error = false;
                        }

{MRC}                   { // recall memory to display
                          if( !error ) d = m;
                        }

{MRC}{MRC}+             { // clear memory
                          if( !error ) m = 0;
                        }

{SQRT}                  { // square root number
                          if( !error )
                          { if( d < 0 ) error = true;
                            else d = sqrt(d);
                          }
                        }

{DIGIT}*("."{DIGIT}*)? { // handle a number
                          if( !error ) ...
                        }
```

In this example, I've hardly begun to use the power of regular expressions. Note the + sign means "one or more," and it was used to handle the clear-all-registers and memory-clear actions. If the user presses [AC] [AC], the action is to clear the calculators registers, and this also happens if the user does $\boxed{\text{AC}}\,\boxed{\text{AC}}\,\boxed{\text{AC}}\,\boxed{\text{AC}}$ ... any number of times, because of the +.

One of the advantages of lex is that it makes a number of checks on the regular expressions. For example, it will warn you if there are two regular expressions that both match the same sequence of actions in an undefined way.

Yacc works in a similar way, but it uses a grammar rather than regular expressions. If you were implementing a calculator, the grammar would be used for handling expressions like $3 + 4 \times 5/(2 + 2.3)$, and it could also do the $\boxed{\text{AC}}\,\boxed{\text{AC}}$ sort of things we used lex for above. Again, yacc can find many errors in grammars—itself a good reason for using compiler-compilers, whether or not you want to use the compilers they generate.

> ▷ It's hard to imagine many of the calculator problems discussed in section 3.1 (p. 61) arising if compiler-compilers had been used. Section 3.8 (p. 74) discussed feature interaction on calculators, another problem that would be a lot less likely if using compiler-compilers.

12.7   Make the device simple

It is very tempting to design devices in a casual way, because programming gets impressive results so easily. As Tony Hoare put it,

> One way is to make it so simple that there are obviously no deficiencies and the other way is to make it so complicated that there are no obvious deficiencies.

Mock-up a prototype using your favorite user interface design tool. Get it approved because it looks so nice. Start programming it in a decent programming language like Java, because you can then do anything, and fix any problems ... what could be easier?

Unfortunately, we might accidentally make the actual device a bit more complex than we intended, without noticing. Programs are notorious for looking easy but camouflaging mysterious bugs—many of which are not noticed immediately, if ever. Programs for user interfaces have the added disadvantage that their clarity and correctness have nothing to do with how clear or sensible the user interface is. Programmers can easily write code that is hard to use—and for which it's hard to tell it's hard to use.

Rather than use general-purpose techniques, it is better to keep the device simple because to try to make it more complex than we can handle (whether or not we know what we can reliably handle) is to betray the user. If the device is a medical or other safety-critical device or if the device is going to earn or handle money, simplicity is a wise decision. Get it right first, by keeping it simple, *then* make it better.

> ▷ On environmental reasons for simple designs, see section 1.10 (p. 29).

Rather than see simple design tools as limiting hindrances, you can easily extend them. For example, if a design tool presents a device, say, as an overly simple tree, this makes things easier for the designer (but harder for the user). The simplifying view of the device needs extra tool support to make the final device easier to use, but it still lets the design benefit from the designer's better grasp of the device goals. For example, a tree does not have "undo" and "go-back" functions (because these introduce cycles), yet both such useful functions would be easy for a design tool to add systematically to a tree.

> ▷ Section 8.7.2 (p. 253) raises Chris Alexander's insight that a city is not a tree. Section 8.7.3 (p. 254) discusses how to add undo and other functions to trees.

12.8 Know the user, and design accordingly

Most other books on interaction design (whether or not they cover programming) emphasize studying the user. Of course this is crucial—we must know the user, their skills, personality, motivation, how they work, and what sorts of errors they make. But there are three dangers. First, if we haven't built a prototype system, the user studies will tend to tell us what users do, whereas we (also) want to change their lives—to see what they do *with* the new device. Secondly if we have built a prototype system, we are only going to find out how to make incremental changes to the design. Thirdly many important design checks cannot be done by users at all.

It is important to distinguish two sorts of design. On the one hand is conceptual design, where users of all sorts can help designers enormously. On the other hand is engineering design, where users can have very little effective input to the design process—the engineering design is about how the device works in detail. Most checks on whether a device is usable should be done automatically, using any of the range of techniques this book introduced.

Unfortunately when we talk about design, our terminology is limited. We tend to speak of "usable" and "usability." The two sorts of design are both concerned with usability, but conceptual design is more concerned with usefulness, and engineering design is more concerned with whether devices work. Each assumes the other.

Once all the main engineering design issues have been settled automatically, *then* it is worth getting real users involved to try to refine the design, because it now works, whether or not it is as useful as it might be. Studying the user *properly* requires a wide range of techniques (experimental methods, statistics, and so on) that are beyond the scope of this book.

Although I think the role of user involvement in design itself, which is a very technical activity, is often over-rated, the wider importance of user involvement is immense, particularly when designing interactive systems for organizations. In other words, "knowing the user" is not just us knowing them so we can design better. We should know the user to know how they form their opinions about design, and hence how we can help them *think* the design is better for them—see section 2.10 (p. 54) about persuasion. This may be deliberate deception to increase profits, but if users think something is better, they will enjoy it more or be more

435

productive. The process of getting to know users includes and involves them in the design process, which helps ensure they will be more supportive of the systems that, otherwise, they might have felt had been imposed on them.

If users are not involved in design processes, they become disenfranchised. And "users" here can mean not just the people who end up using the systems being designed, whether mobile or desktop, but also their managers and other people throughout the organization and its supply chains. To give just one example the British National Health Service is spending approximately £3 billion a year (in 2005) on a major IT project; one of the main causes for the spiraling costs has been the way frontline staff have become disengaged from the design process. Participative design is crucial.

> ▷ Problems of using people for even simple systems were outlined in section 6.5 (p. 191), where we discussed a very simple alarm clock. The issues were also discussed in section 11.1 (p. 369). The merits of human testers compared to gnomes is discussed in section 11.7 (p. 401). The present discussion continues in the next chapter, in section 13.2 (p. 450), where we compare and contrast *user*-centered design and *designer*-centered design.

12.9   Exploit computer magic

Calculators must be the most boring but widely used interactive devices! Hand-held pushbutton devices are ubiquitous, and they are so well accepted that even desktop computers, tablet computers, and personal digital assistants (PDAs) mimic pushbutton calculators as if that's the best they can do.

Figure 12.4 (facing page) shows a calculator being simulated on a PDA. Notice that despite the PDA's pen and other features, all it is doing is simulating as best it can a conventional calculator. And it must be worse: the buttons no longer have the affordance of being pressed—they just look *like* buttons.

A completely different approach is to start again: what exactly do people do when they use calculations? And how can we help them do it better?

One answer, a different one than building yet another pushbutton calculator, is to say they do sums on paper, and we could use computers to make the paper magic. Why not imagine the users writing on paper, just as they would normally write, but with the computer solving their problems? Will Thimbleby built a calculator like this, and it surprised us how successful it was, and how much users liked it.

Here's an example of it in use. Imagine first that the user has already written $3 \times = 18$. (They don't need to leave a space after the multiplication symbol.) The computer will sort out the handwriting, and recognize that there is a missing 6 in this equation. The 6 gets inserted into the equation in a different color than the user is writing in, and it is animated so that the equation the user wrote spreads apart to let the 6 nestle in nicely. Next, imagine that the user wants to divide the left hand side by 5.

Figure 12.4: A PDA simulating a calculator. Instead of pressing buttons with your finger, a stylus is used on the touch-sensitive screen. Compare this with figure 3.1 (p. 62).

The first picture, 1, below shows the correct equation $3 \times 6 = 18$ with the user just starting to write "divided by 5" by hand. What the user has written—if we ignore the 6 correction the magic paper put in a moment ago—is $\frac{3\times}{5} = 18$. Now, the correction is 30, not 6, so the calculator changes the last correction, 6, to 30. All the changes are done with nice morphing, fluid animation, and scaling. This is shown in picture 2 below; the smooth change 6-to-30 happens as the handwritten 5 is converted to a nicely typeset 5.

Essentially, at this point, the user has solved the equation $\frac{3\times x}{5} = 18$ for x, and found that $x = 30$, without having to use any variable names or to rearrange the calculation, as they would have to do on an ordinary calculator.

1	2	3	4
$\dfrac{3\times 6 = 18}{5}$	$\dfrac{3 \times 30}{5} = 18$	$\dfrac{3\times 30}{5} = 18$	$\dfrac{270}{3 \times 5} = 18$

Next, in picture 3, the user has drawn a ring around the $3 \times$, and they are in the process of dragging it to the bottom of the fraction. Picture 4 shows what happens when the user lets go—the $3 \times$ has moved to the bottom, making 3×5, and the magic paper slides it into the exact place from where the user dropped it, at the same time showing the correction 270 that is needed on the top.

This very brief description hardly gives a full impression of how nice the calculator is to use. The examples above seem contrived, so that the features can be explained—they give a rather stilted picture of how it works. It feels much more fluid in practice. For example, you can write 2^3 and it will show $2^3 = 8$ immediately; if you then drag the 3 down below the 2, it will show $3^2 = 9$ immediately. It is very satisfying to play with. Try working out a calculation like, "if I get 15%

Figure 12.5: Writing on the new calculator using an interactive whiteboard. The whiteboard has a back-projection so the user does not cast a shadow on it, and it detects where they are writing by using cameras.

discount, how much can I buy for $12?" and you'll soon appreciate that the flexible moving around is very useful. Also, being able to edit a calculation helps give confidence; if you don't really believe the answer, you can change the 15 to 5, say, and check the answer changes in the way you expect.

Will did a small experiment asking computer science students to come with their own ordinary calculator and do high school math exam problems. Will then repeated the questions, but asked them to use the new calculator. No user got the wrong answer for any question with the new calculator, though they did when they used their own calculators.

This is an extraordinary result, suggesting that there is a lot of potential for this new design, especially for critical applications, like calculating drug dosages. That people *enjoy* using it—they even laugh as they see equations solved!—is very exciting. The calculator works wonderfully in schools, with interactive whiteboards where your writing can involve whole arm movement.

The moral is that we simply decided to think out of the box; we wanted to make a magic calculator, not one like all of the others.

12.10 If all else fails

If all else fails in our attempts to avoid unmanageable design complexity … then we've made a mistake!

Put as many of the design decisions into software or firmware, rather than hardware, as possible. Then the device can be upgraded later, either to fix bugs or to modify the design in ways that only become known after you or your device's users have gained experience with it. If it is a device like part of a car, the device's firmware can be upgraded when the car goes for routine services. If it is a device that runs on or connects to a PC (like a music player), then it can be upgraded from the internet.

If we design assuming that our device is going to work perfectly, we will be sadly mistaken in all but the very simplest of cases. Users will make mistakes, and the design will have infelicities in it that either encourage mistakes or don't do what the users want. We should therefore design anticipating errors, and with a view to doing better than ignoring them. If we ignore errors, our users won't. It's possible that we won't get any feedback from users who suffer from errors, because we weren't expecting any real problems.

> ▷ The lottery effect, described in section 2.2 (p. 40), says that we hear more about success than failure, thus tending to (incorrectly) reinforce any tendency we have to make "perfect" designs that ignore error.

In short, we should actively design for error. Here are some suggestions:

- Provide ways to collect information from users who cannot get the device to work or to work well. For example, if the device is a phone, *also* provide a postal feedback form.

- Provide automatic ways of getting bad information. If the device crashes or whatever, can you save a log of the sequence of actions that caused the crash that can be sent (by phone, internet, or by mail) or recovered next time the device is used or taken to a shop? For example, if the device is a camera, it could take a "photograph" of a list of all its settings when the user had problems.

- Provide ways to modify a device. Perhaps the design can be upgraded by reprogramming the firmware? If so, you can fix many design problems even after a device has been shipped.

- Provide free servicing. When a user returns a device (or takes it to a shop) for servicing—which might be as minor as needing a good cleaning—you can either ask users to answer a few questions while they wait, or you can recover some usage information from the device.

- Use a design framework so that changes to a design are easy and don't require all the hard work of writing manuals and other stuff from scratch. It is important that small changes to a design have a small cost; you are using the wrong techniques if a small change requires a major rework or rewrite of any part of the product.

- Support an after-market in upgrades. For example, mobile phones have become fashion accessories, and you can easily buy new fascias in different styles. Why not make the fascias more sophisticated, so that recycling the old ones (returned to the manufacturer) gives some data about wear and use. Or include a chip to record important events in the device's life. If not fascias, then what about batteries—which are sometimes sophisticated and unique for the device?

- Provide removable storage (such as a flash card) so that users can separate their stuff from the device itself. If the device turns out not to be what the user wants (or if it fails for any reason), users should not lose whatever they want to keep.

- Provide undo. If the design is wrong in any way, the user is likely to make mistakes—so provide a straightforward method (such as an ⌑Undo⌑ button) that reverses the last action the user did.

- Don't try to be perfect. Often a device designed to be only 80% successful will be better than one that was designed to be perfect—see section 12.2.2 (p. 414).

This list of ways to anticipate errors—and to turn them to advantage—is not exhaustive!

12.11   Conclusions

Finite state machines provide a theory and practical framework for interaction programming, but they get tricky to use for large design projects, particularly when working under real-world pressures. This chapter provided a wide range of heuristics for design that can either be used in conjunction with finite state machines, or independently. For a summary, revisit the list of principles at the start of this chapter, on p. 409.

Good design is not just a matter of knowing (and putting into action) theories and principles. It's also about understanding people (whether users or designers) and having the right attitudes. The next chapter examines these more personal and ethical aspects of design.

12.11.1   Some *Press On* principles

- Avoid unmanageable complexity → section 12.1 (p. 409).

- Make as much as possible of interaction invisible → section 12.2 (p. 410).

- Avoid approximate symmetries that don't work properly → section 12.3 (p. 418).

■ Find affordances and use them → section 12.3 (p. 419).

■ If explaining something is hard, then it probably needs changing → section 12.3 (p. 424).

■ Change the world, rather than design from bad requirements → section 12.4 (p. 426).

■ Use "spikes" to check and debug the *entire* proposed design and processes → section 12.6 (p. 428).

■ Build your own design tools → section 12.6 (p. 429).

■ If you can't do all of a design using a simple approach, still do a large part of it simply → section 12.6 (p. 429).

■ Make devices simple; refuse to make devices complicated → section 12.7 (p. 434).

■ Involve and engage users in design and development processes → section 12.8 (p. 435).

12.11.2 Further reading

■ Baxter, M. R., *Product Design*, Nelson Thornes, 2002, covers the field extremely well, and provides many fascinating case studies. Whereas I've concentrated on engineering design solutions in this book, design in industry is much broader. The entire product development process covers market analysis, concept design, embodiment, through to launching the product.

■ Feynman, R. P., *The Character of Physical Law*, Penguin, 1992. Based on Feynman's BBC Lectures, this is an introduction to laws of nature, including symmetry.

■ Lidwell, W., Holden, K., and Butler, J., *Universal Principles of Design*, Rockport Publishers, 2003. Most books on HCI guidelines stick rigidly to interaction, and often to interaction on graphical user interfaces on the computer desktop, but design guidelines cover a wider range of issues. *Universal Principles of Design* covers a vast range of guidelines for designers from all backgrounds and areas, and gives a more balanced coverage.

■ Norman, D. A., *The Invisible Computer*, MIT Press, 1998. Most devices are badly-disguised PCs, with too many features to handle. Instead, Don Norman argues that we should make the computers inside devices invisible—design devices to support the user's tasks and activities, rather than to parade the computer chip's functionality. I reviewed his book in the *New Scientist* (November 28, 1998) and said, "You need controversial ideas if you want to work out how to make the world a better place." See also p. 112.

■ Thimbleby, H. W., Blandford, A. E., Cairns, P., Curzon, P., and Jones, M., "User Interface Design as Systems Design," *Proceedings People and Computers,* **XVI**, pp281–301, edited by Faulkner, X., Finlay, J. and Détienne, F., Springer, 2002. The sections about the ticket machine in this chapter are based on this conference paper I wrote with my colleagues. The paper makes a few additional points—it also has a longer reference list if you want to follow up ideas.

■ Thimbleby, H. W., "Reflections on Symmetry," *Proceedings of the Advanced Visual Interfaces Conference,* AVI2002, pp28–33, 2002.

■ Thimbleby, W. J., "A Novel Pen-based Calculator," *Proceedings of the Third Nordic Conference on Human-Computer Interaction,* ACM NordiCHI, pp445–448, 2004. The calculator has advanced considerably since that early paper; you can get more information and download the current version from www.cs.swan.ac.uk/calculators.

There are many books on problem solving; here are just a few, particularly well-related to interaction programming:

■ de Bono, E., *Teach Your Child to Think,* Penguin, 1993. de Bono is the inventor of lateral thinking. Each chapter of this book succinctly covers a different creative approach to thinking.

■ Michalewicz, Z., and Fogel, D. B., *How to Solve It: Modern Heuristics* Springer, 2000, is a wide-ranging discussion about problem-solving in programming. It was mentioned in the chapter 8, "Graphs," for its coverage of the traveling salesman problem.

■ Pólya, G., *How to Solve It,* Princeton University Press, 1945, reprinted by Penguin, 1990. This is a classic and easy-to-read book—and popular enough to sell over a million copies. If you like George Pólya's work, a more mathematically detailed book is Pólya, G. *Mathematical Discovery,* Combined edition, John Wiley & Sons, 1981.

■ Shneiderman, B., *Leonardo's Laptop,* MIT Press, 2002. This is a very inspiring book, both about thinking and about thinking about computer design.

■ Winograd, T., and Flores, F., *Understanding Computers and Cognition,* Ablex, 1986. "Winograd and Flores" has gone down as one of the classic turning points in the field; their book lifted everyone's ideas about philosophy (specifically phenomenology) and showed how to think in new ways about interacting with computers. The book ties finite state machines into speech acts, and presents interesting ideas about email/CSCW systems.

Compiling technology has moved on considerably since the early days of lex and yacc. Of course, you will be able to find up-to-date details using a search engine.

- Aho, A. V., Sethi, R., and Ullman, J. D., *Compilers: Principles, Techniques and Tools*, Addison-Wesley, 1985. This is the classic "dragon book," with a very good introduction to the use and principles of lex and yacc:

- Appel, A. W., with Palsberg, J., *Modern Compiler Implementation in Java*, Cambridge University Press, 2nd edition, 2002. This is a more modern book, available in different editions for different programming languages such as Java.

- Parr, T. J., Quong, R. W., "ANTLR: A Predicated-$LL(k)$ Parser Generator," in *Software—Practice & Experience*, **25**(7), pp789–810, 1995. ANTLR is an object-oriented compiler-compiler that is very versatile, and easier to use.

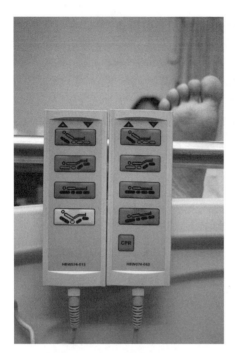

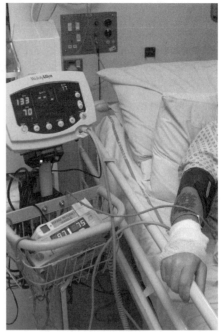

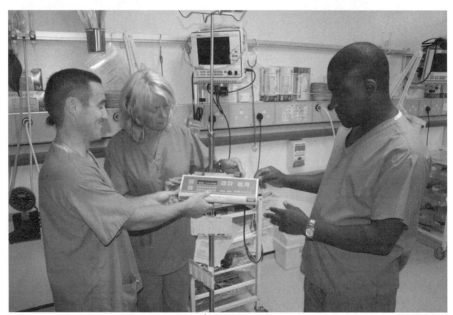

13 | Improving things

Everything in this book is about improving interactive devices. First, we discussed how our culture sees the problems, and sort of colludes in creating them. Then we discussed the theories and practical ideas that can help us to avoid or become aware of problems as early as possible in a design process. Now we must take ownership of these ideas, so that we can be inspired to do better.

The design of every system embodies a value system, a set of priorities that the designer wanted to emphasize. Value systems are often obvious, for example:

- A game console may be designed for the user's enjoyment. The value system emphasizes problems, surprise, and provocation.

- An aircraft cockpit will be designed valuing safety. The pilot is not supposed to be surprised or challenged by the user interface but should be highly trained and competent, thus promoting safety and reliability.

- A drawing program could be designed for flexibility, creativity, and even a little unpredictability.

- An office system should be reliable and easy to use. If it handles money, then it should be accurate and secure.

- A handheld mass consumer device reflects technical values. Whatever new technology is available, use it to differentiate the product from competing products.

- A hospital device (like an automatic drip, supplying a patient with controlled amounts of a drug) would be designed primarily for patient health or for pain control, and in particular for their safety.

- A web site might be designed for accessibility, so that the colors, text sizes, and image names are readable for people with vision problems, and ideally so that people using web page readers can make sense of the pages when text is converted to speech automatically.

All these example value systems could be refined; they illustrate a common assumption, though, that the value system is obvious the context. However, the value system of choice is influenced by the designer, by the market, and other implicit factors. Given a design problem, it is hard to assess every possible issue carefully; we'd simply be overwhelmed. It is very hard to combine making a mobile phone small, light, fast, easy to use, technologically up to date (and showing off the fact), cheap, international, trendy, high-resolution, ... Instead, we have preferences and heuristics for finding design solutions by focusing on what few values we really want to promote. Rather than spending a lot of time searching for a really good idea, we might just polish the first or second reasonable design idea we think of.

▷ Efficiently finding good-enough solutions, rather than taking time to find the best solution is called satisficing—see section 2.10 (p. 54).

We have higher priorities. After all, if we take the time to develop the "perfect" device, it may never be finished and reach the market at all. If we do not deliver on time, at cost, and with something working, the whole exercise is pointless. We are under constraints, and within those constraints we need to do as good a job as possible. As Voltaire put it, the best is the enemy of the good.

In other words, a designer identifies the value system a device should represent, and that value system then helps focus the design process, so the designer doesn't have to consider everything possible. In this book, we've often assumed that the design values include efficiency of use, and, given those values, several examples show how problems can be turned into opportunities for fresh design. If the problem is that the user does not know which buttons do anything, why not put lights in them so that they light up when they actually do something?

▷ Chapter 11, "More complex devices," showed that using lights may double the speed of a user. In chapter 8, "Graphs," we used graph theory to identify problems, but we could also make the "identification" itself a feature of the user interface. For example, when a user comes to a bridge (a graph theoretic bridge, that is), the relevant button lights up and attracts their attention. This feature is easier to add than to change the device specification, and it might be a lot more effective in improving the user's performance or willingness to use the device. It would certainly make the device stand out in a shop or product review.

13.1 People are different

Lesson 1 in interactive systems design is that people are different. The technical term is "individual differences." Lesson 2 is to help us work around the key problem: it is *extraordinarily* hard to fully appreciate how different people are from us! Lesson 3 gets us back to interaction programming: unless we try very hard, we fall into the trap of building systems for ourselves; we design things *we* like, whereas (of course!) we should try to define things our users will like or find useful. It falls to Lesson 4 to refine what is meant by "different" and then to explore what can be done about it.

Your users are different from you: they have different skills, likes, dislikes, and attitudes—they have different personalities. What makes sense to you as a designer or programmer is unlikely to make sense to a typical user. It is often said that a designer should know their users: find out who they are and what sort of systems suit them. Do they prefer, and perform better with, graphical interfaces or textual ones? Do they need training and online help, or are they already highly trained? Are there special issues, such as the work environment: is theirs noisy, badly lit, or hazardous? You might think, "Who needs to make products for badly lit contexts?" But every home has a badly lit living room where people sit down to watch television in the evening: how do they use the DVD player, the sound system, the remote control in the dark? Every car is driven sooner or later at night: how can the controls be well lit, but not bright enough to be a distraction? (Perhaps the controls should have gesture sensors, so gadgets like the radio only light up when a hand moves toward it.)

How will you balance security issues (say, if the product is stolen) against making it easy to use—you don't want a thief to find it too easy to use?

Are children going to use your gadgets? Children work under different social pressures than adults. They have strong views about work and fun, and while their reading skills may be lower, they have a huge amount of curiosity and a high threshold for complexity. Are you designing systems for teaching? If so, some students are more motivated by the experience than by the resulting grades and competition. Designs for one sort of learning preference will differ from those for another.

Are you designing for an international market, with people with different languages and cultures using devices? Arabic is written right to left, and the ordering of things, whether text or button sequences, might need to be different than for an English left-to-right culture. Color preferences will be different. The way people respond to you studying how they are different will itself be different! In some cultures, it would be natural for a user to think you know best and should be pleased. If so, it will be difficult to find problems with your design. In the 1920s the Hawthorne Works in Illinois wanted to see how illumination affected workers— just as today we might be experimenting to see how design affects users. The now-famous experiments have gone down in history as the Hawthorne Effect, that users will react in interesting ways to your doing experiments with them.

There are four important alternatives to knowing the user.

■ Get somebody else to know the user. There are plenty of usability companies, psychologists, ergonomists and others that can find out about your users. But remember that knowing your user is an ongoing process: users will change as they use your devices (they're supposed to be useful, right!) and although an early market survey will find out useful information about users, the people surveyed may not fully understand what the planned product will do. If you are designing for a specialist area, such as medicine or diving, you will need expert help. Retain a usability expert or company to repeatedly know the user as the product takes shape.

■ You don't need to know the user if they can find your products—get the user to know *you*. Since everybody is different and the world is a big place, there must be *somebody* who likes your product! If you are designing a product that ends up only suiting 10% of people, that's still a huge market—even if you don't know which people suits. What's more, a focused product is more likely to be distinctive, so the people who like it will *really* like it. In short, you don't need to know the user if the user knows you—and there are enough happy users to keep you in business.

■ Make devices customizable. If you don't know what users want, at least allow them to change the design so that they can make the design suit themselves. Provide good ways for users to give you feedback on the design (for example, provide a supporting web site with a good mechanism for getting and replying to product comments from users), so that you can continue to improve it.

■ Know yourself first. The better you understand your unique makeup, skills, and personality, the more effective you can be. You will better understand how you differ from and complement other people.

13.1.1 Clients versus users

The person you are working for may claim to be but probably will not be a good representative of the users. Obviously, if you are being paid to design a product, your client will have money and power—but the users who work with or have to use the final system may have less power and influence over how their work is done. An obvious example would be designing a device to help doctors. Doctors are typically very keen on new technology (especially, of course, any who have the initiative to come to you to get you to design them a new product); they may unwittingly help you make an overly complex product. But the device's purpose might be to help the doctor's patients, or to help the doctor record patient information. Thus the patients are users too. Patients are typically ill, worried, and unsure of themselves. Their needs and the way your device helps them will be very different from the doctor's needs and how you can help them. Remember that there are more patients than doctors and therefore you should try to pay more attention to their needs—perhaps get some real data about final users to help inform debate about the proposed design with your client.

13.2 Conventional design

Interactive systems do not often perform as well as expected. This is sometimes blamed on the lack of a user-centered approach to design. Designers, apparently, and especially technically competent designers, concentrate on features and system performance—the magic of computers—and indeed often users and their needs are ignored. In reaction to this, user-centered design is promoted: orient

---

Box 13.1 The ISO 9241 standard ISO is the International Standards Organization. Its standards cover all sorts of activities; many have become legal requirements. The ISO 9000 series of standards covers quality and quality processes and will be familiar to many organizations.

ISO 9241, Ergonomics of Human System Interaction, is a standard applicable to all aspects of the material in this book: it covers usability, including hardware, software, and usability processes. You could consult ISO 9241 to design a gadget, evaluate a display, set usability metrics, evaluate a graphical user interface, or test a keyboard.

ISO 9241 contains checklists to run a usability evaluation and examples of how to operationalize and measure usability. (It also contains extensive bibliographies.) The following table gives an idea of the coverage of the ISO 9241. Note that most of it is about measuring user satisfaction or performance, something that cannot be done until a product is completed.

Design objective	Effectiveness	Efficiency	Satisfaction
Suitability for the user's task	Percentage of goals achieved	Time to complete a task	Rating scale for satisfaction
Appropriate for trained users	Number of power features	Efficiency compared to expert users	Rating scale for satisfaction with power features
Error tolerance	Percentage of errors corrected successfully	Time spent on correcting errors	Rating scale for error handling
Learnability	Percentage of functions learnt	Time to learn to some criterion	Rating scale for ease of learning

Any business not familiar with ISO 9241 (and the related standards, such as ISO 13407)—either using the standard or knowingly not using it—would be failing to use an important resource in user interface design.

---

the design process to understand the users, collect empirical data on users' behavior and performance, and iterate designs to improve them. Some say that close involvement with users is the only way to produce a good design. By studying how users really perform, usability of systems can be significantly improved, and engaging users in the process, as a political act, builds their commitment to the design.

The lottery effect explains why interactive systems don't work as well as expected. We are surrounded by good interactive systems, so we naturally expect new systems to be good too. But we overlook the fact that there are many bad interactive systems too, probably far more bad than good ones, but bad systems don't survive. If we are in the process of designing a new interactive system, we want to make one that survives, of course, but the statistics are against us. I suspect that the lottery effect has influenced much of the accepted wisdom on what best design practices are supposed to be.

▷   The lottery effect is discussed in section 2.2 (p. 40).

There are all sorts of ways of designing, some better than others. User-centered design (UCD) in particular emphasizes that when building interactive products, the whole point is users and the overall context of what they are doing and experiencing. UCD starts with a strong emphasis on finding out what users want by defining what "success" means for them.

The conventional approach to UCD has four phases: analysis, design, implementation, and deployment. The sequential nature seems to make obvious sense: work out what you want (which for UCD means finding out what users want or need), design it, make it work, and then get it out to users. Following this sequential structure, here are some typical activities for each phase:

Analysis phase   Meet with key stake-holders, typically the final users, to define the design vision. Distinguish between the users who will get their hands on your device, and those who are your clients—the ones helping to specify the device and its function (and probably paying for it).

Design phase   Work out the principles that will guide future decisions. Design may be broadly split into low- and high-fidelity design:

- Normally, you would begin design with paper and pencil, drawing screens or panels, button layouts or whatever. Create a low-fidelity prototype, out of cardboard or wood, so that you can begin to conduct usability testing on something—you can give users the block of wood, and see how it will work out. Is it too big or too heavy? These are crucial design questions and easily answered through a little prototyping. Often low-fidelity prototypes encourage users to play and be creative in how things should work, because there isn't really a "correct" way for them to be used that limits their thinking. Get users to imagine scenarios of how the devices will be used.

- Then create a high-fidelity detailed design. Repeat the usability testing again now that you have something that really works.

Implementation phase   Now we that know what we want, implement it properly for the final hardware platform. Write the user manual, now that the design is stable.

Deployment phase   Finish the system and productize it. Confirm that all or enough of the original objectives have been achieved. Start shipping.

While each step makes perfect sense and is useful, there are several problems with this conventional UCD sequence. "Begin at the beginning," the King of Hearts said gravely to Alice, "and go on till you come to the end: then stop." A sequential process seems sensible, but the world is more complicated; unexpected things can happen, and it's rare to be able to assemble all the stakeholders at the beginning and not need to keep going back to them. What about feature interactions that get spotted too late?

What if the programmers have new insights into the design in the implementation phase? Or, after the deployment of a new product, it will probably be found that it does not work as well as hoped: the design needs revising. Thus design should be seen as a cycle, supporting iterative design. That, of course, means that the design process should assume that every iteration starts with an earlier design to build on or modify. Indeed, in product design, it is rare to build a completely new device; most products are "merely" upgrades and developments of previous models. If a design is going to be iterated—as it will—then it is very important that each cycle through the design process not have to start again from scratch. Design tools should be used so that designs can be incrementally modified, so that user manuals can be incrementally modified, rather than having to start again—or worse—be put off indefinitely by the overwhelming effort of starting again.

The sequence isolates the skills of the delivery team from the design phase. In fact, it turns the programers into mere system builders rather than architects. Understanding why UCD has come about will help us to understand it better.

13.2.1 Recent history

In the 1970s and 1980s, most computer users worked for organizations that had decided to computerize their operations. A typing pool was replaced with word processors. Travel agents were given computer terminals to central databases. The computer systems were expensive and built especially for the organizations that wanted them; typically, the computer systems were specified by managers who thought they knew what their organizations were doing. Unfortunately, as often as not, the managers only knew what the organization thought it was doing— the workers were often breaking rules to make things work and keep customers happy. But the computers enforced the management's ideas and often hampered the users within the organizations. Managers had never noticed how flexible users were in solving problems, and suddenly they had imposed computers with a very naive view of how to work. Not only were the newly computerized jobs inflexible, they were also mindless. The solution to all this was to find out what people were really doing and to try to drive the design of systems from what organizations and the people in them were really doing.

There were even worse problems. A computer company providing a solution for one organization might well try to sell it to another. Now the workers in that company had imposed on them the bad management ideas from a different company! Again, the solution was to find out what users were doing and what their tasks were. That is what the computers should have been supporting.

Later it became clear that you cannot get a computer system design right. Indeed, just introducing a computer changes what people do, even if you are correctly supporting what they used to be doing (which is unlikely, given how hard it is to program complex systems). So iterative design was introduced: design a system, get some experience of it in use, and then modify the design to make it better. Key to this process is to reliably evaluate how the system is being used so that useful insights can be fed into the next iteration of the design.

It is counterproductive to impose a prototype design on everybody in an organization. If it doesn't work very well, it can cause a business disaster. Instead, iterative design is usually done with a few selected users—maybe around five people. They help identify problems and issues, which are then fixed, iterated again, and—when the design is good enough—imposed on everyone else in the organization.

We've mostly moved on from organizations imposing ideas on their workers. Today workers more often use common off-the-shelf software (COTS), and consumer devices like mobile phones. The way these products are designed is quite different. For a start, the organization does not define what it wants and procure a new system; instead, it selects from a choice of products already on the market. Whether or not the chosen products work well, the design emphasis has shifted away from the organization to the manufacturer. The design problem is now to make a range of products that people *want*—rather than products for what people say (or their managers say) they need. Simply, if a device manufacturer is not making products people want, it goes out of business. Unfortunately, it has to have the products available before people will buy them.

In short, the original idea of iterative design has to change with the times. Now products are released after comparatively little evaluation and design, at least very little compared to the size of the (anticipated) market. If the product succeeds in the market, make more of it; if it fails, bring out the next model. The manufacturer goes through the iterative design process, and as soon as something works "well enough" it is put on the market. If it sells well, they're in business. If it doesn't sell well enough, a new model is in the pipeline anyway. To cope with failure, typically a manufacturer makes a range of products catering to different needs. If one product fails or doesn't sell too well, the broader portfolio keeps the company afloat.

Originally, iterative design was a good approach—when workers were forced to use systems designed for them. Now, users are increasingly customers, not workers. Iterative design still works, but since a manufacturer puts a lot of effort into a design, it may as well put it on the market as soon as possible and see if somebody likes the product. For many products there will be somebody who likes it; if there are enough people, the product succeeds. This newer approach allows companies to be more innovative—they don't need to know exactly what tasks and work users do; they merely need an idea that catches customers' imaginations. And if they catch the imagination of the procurement department of a large organization, then many sales follow automatically.

Web design is different again. Unlike physical devices, which have tooling-up costs, a web site can be iteratively developed almost continuously. A problem now is that if you are successful, you still want to improve, but you don't want to lose customers already used to features that probably should be fixed or improved. On the other hand, if the design is not good enough, revenue can stop almost immediately, and—crucially—the web site designers get very little feedback from the users who fail to use the site effectively. If it doesn't work for them, they are unlikely to provide feedback to help improve things. Thus there is even more need for design done with representative users, for instance, users chosen at random from the public, perhaps paid to participate in evaluations.

Iterative design often goes wrong when a product is prematurely released to the public—the product may not be optimal or as well designed as it might have been, but at least the company making the device is (hopefully) still in business.

▷ We are still arguing about the merits of different sorts of keyboard; see box 5.2, "The QWERTY effect" (p. 125). Proper iterative design might have postponed the adoption the keyboard; instead, it was better to have a worse design available sooner.

While the historical progression has naturally seen an increasing emphasis on the user, from knowing their task to knowing what they like, there has been a corresponding decrease in emphasis on the designer and implementor. Design is very hard. Most programmers, probably happy enough to have built a system that works at all, have no spare energy to make it, additionally, work *well* for users— indeed, usually programmers are never motivated by involvement in the creative design process. Moreover UCD trivializes programming into a passive following of requirements: users drive design, and programmers try hard to make users' ideas reality. These two forces together create a culture where the designers' and programmers' potential insights into device usability never get nurtured.

13.2.2 But why *iterative* design?

We often hear that we should use iterative design, but why? Well, let's imagine what would happen *without* iterative design. Imagine that you wanted to get a new camera built for you, and you listed your requirements for it. Maybe you'd get a task analysis done to see how you use cameras, so that your requirements could be better worked out.

Cameras are quite complex. Do you want to take pictures in low light? If so, you need a flash, a high ISO speed, or image stabilization. Do you want to take lots of pictures? You need long battery life, or perhaps you need a standard battery size so you don't need to rely on a battery charger. Do you want a small camera that you can carry around easily, or one with manual controls? Or maybe you want to be able to use it in winter, when you will be wearing gloves and won't be able to press buttons easily. How much do you want to spend? What quality pictures do you want to take? Do you want a viewfinder, an LCD screen, or both? The list of requirements goes on and on.

In a conventional design process (sometimes called a waterfall model, since it's all downhill), you'd now take your requirements to a camera maker and wait about a year for your camera to be ready. Unfortunately, when you get your new camera made to your specifications, you discover that you forgot to say it should weigh less than a kilogram—the one you've been given weighs too much! Or perhaps you wanted a very bright LCD to use outside, but this reduces battery life.

There may be conflicts between your requirements that are not at all obvious until you are holding what you said you wanted.

In hindsight, asking for a low-weight camera is an obvious requirement, but now you've wasted a year and don't have quite what you wanted—though you do have exactly what you asked for. To summarize: in ordinary design, you spend a lot of time specifying what you want, you wait a long time, and you don't get quite what you really wanted. In bad cases, your developers will hand over the product and say it meets your requirements; they aren't interested in making it better.

How would iterative design work with cameras? After you'd made your list of basic requirements, you go to a camera shop and describe what you want. The shop assistant spreads half a dozen cameras in front of you and says they are pretty much what you asked for. Try holding this one? Perhaps it doesn't have a battery in it and doesn't even work—but you get an idea of what it feels like. You want one that feels more solidly made? Then you should try this one … This is satisficing, and you've got yourself a camera that is good enough and, because of its market size, costs a fraction of what you thought you really wanted.

In a sense, the shop assistant has shown you some rapid prototypes of what you wanted. In fact, they only took seconds to show you—the camera shop is not building prototypes—but the idea is the same. You can get a good idea of what you want from quick mock-ups, or (as here) alternative products. You can now work out with the shop assistant what you *really* want. Instead of specifying exactly what you want, you are instead working with things that really work, and you are saying to the shop assistant how you want to *change* what you are being shown for something better. It's easier and faster to say how to change things than to specify a complete design.

A good camera shop will let you test or rent a camera: try before you buy. When you get your nice digital SLR home, you'll probably discover that you wanted a more convenient shape. Or if you take a compact home, perhaps you'll discover that you want better control. Who knows? But you wouldn't have anticipated any of these changes you want if you'd tried to write out all your requirements before starting.

In iterative design, you get something close to what you want very quickly, and you then work with the designers to make it better. Both of you are talking the same language. You can try the prototypes out, and better imagine how further developments will work. You can see how the device will change your life and make a better list of requirements and changes. In short, you end up with something closer to what you want, and sooner.

13.2.3   Concurrent design

If design is thought of sequentially, opportunities for concurrent design are lost. Things don't have to happen one after another; it can be beneficial if some things happen at the same time. For example, if writing the user manual is a phase that is started strictly after having a working system, any problems identified in the design through the user manual writing process will be lost because they come too

---

Box 13.2 Paper prototyping Most of this book has been about how to get a design to work, to know exactly what it is, to analyze it so you know how to tweak its design to get the best performance, and to use tools so that you can build it reliably and can tell the user exactly what it does. More or less. That list misses out the important bit of how to get going.

Where do design ideas come from in the first place, and how do you get the design ideas into your head so that something appropriate can be implemented?

There are three simple rules:

- Start with paper prototypes. These only take a few minutes to make, and you can work with users in their environment and context to see how they get on with the prototypes. Paper prototypes have the huge advantage of not inhibiting people from making suggestions. They are easy to scribble on. They are easy to update during a session with users as new ideas get sorted out. A block of wood, half a dozen clipped on pieces of paper, and a packet of colored pens can simulate all sorts of complex devices.

- It can take years to work out what people want and then implement it. When you finally deliver the finished product, users will have drifted and changed their minds—and in any case finally using your device will change how users want to work. Instead, implement *parts* of your design ideas quickly, and try them out quickly with your users. This way, users get more involved in product development too. If you are lucky, you need never deliver 100% of the original planned product; it's much easier to deliver 60% and stop while everybody is still happy! This idea is a form of agile development.

- Whatever you do won't be ideal; it will have flaws—users will have moved on, the market will have found another fashion, your suppliers won't have some chip in stock ... Design devices to be break. If you don't design them to break, they will anyway, but then you won't know what to do. Instead, design them to break, so you have a planned way of fixing them. One way to help is to design a framework like this book suggests, so that the framework is a firm, well-debugged, foundation, but you can very easily fix broken design details.

---

late. Instead, why not start writing the user manual as early as possible—indeed, at the first meetings with stakeholders or while brainstorming with users—and then many design issues can be fixed sooner. By definition, the user manual is something users can understand, so for them it is a helpful thing to see as soon as possible so they can provide feedback. Of course, if you want the user manual developed concurrently, the design process needs to be supported by tools, a framework, that ensures that working on the manual is not effort lost as the design is revised.

> ▷ The benefits of concurrent design have been touched on in several places in this book; they were introduced in section 6.8 (p. 195), which also defined the key problem in interaction programming.

13.2.4   Procurement as design

If you are a designer or work for a design company, then your approach to design is very different from somebody who wants to get a design done for them. Consumers go down to a shop (or to the web) and choose what's best from what's available—the issue for them is whether the presentation and marketing of devices is accurate and useful. Procurers want to define products they can buy and use, but which may not already exist. Typically, procurers write specifications for what they want and then they find somebody who can supply what they want.

In a real sense, then, procurer are designers—they are doing the first, analytical, stage of design and setting a cost for somebody who will make it, deliver it, and make it work as contracted.

There are two problems here:

- First, by its nature, procurement enforces the worst sort of design—sequential. Legal niceties, contracts, and so on may make it very hard to deliver better products than those that match the original requirements exactly: it's hard to benefit advantages of iterative design if the requirements have to be fully specified before you start.

- Second, typically, procurers *must* have what they need. This gives them a very different perspective from other sorts of designers. Typically designers or product manufacturers have a portfolio of projects—they can spread their risks. If their project number 57 fails in some way, they have all the others. In contrast, the procurers generally *rely* on what they are trying to procure. Their companies will go bust if they get a device that doesn't work as expected or doesn't have the capability they expected; they are unlikely to have alternatives.

One reason why government computerization projects so often fail is that they specify requirements and expect a system to work to the requirements on a go-live date. After all, that is what they have procured. Rarely do systems work as expected, or even at all at first. And systems that involve users are even less likely to work as expected.

The real world is complex, and there are no general solutions to the problem of procuring interactive systems. Here, however, are some thoughts that can help:

- Require *processes*. If suppliers are using best methods, such as iterative design, the products they deliver will be better in the end than if they work to the procurer's original functional requirements in a strict way.

- Require *prototypes*. Arrange to get users' hands and eyes on prototypes as quickly as possible so that things can be learned and the designs modified as necessary. Sixty percent of a prototype today is going to be more use than a more complete prototype in a few month's time—the more complete prototype will be harder to modify, and you will have lost months of opportunities.

■ Early prototypes should include *all factors* of a design (if only as mock-ups): screen layouts, user manuals, interactive help, web backup, ... to show that they can be integrated.

■ Require systems that are *open*, or at least extensible. Whatever system is finally delivered will almost certainly need modifying as soon as you get experience using it. Make sure that modifying the system is easy. What features does the system have to help maintain its own help and user manuals, for instance, so that modifications can be tracked and made consistently?

■ Try to procure something that is *like an existing product* that already works and can be tried out. New "solutions" will have completely new problems. As with the rationale for iterative design, it's easier to start with something that works and make it better than to specify something from scratch.

13.3   Varieties of evaluation

Evaluation is a contentious area, because there are conflicting assumptions, and everybody is right—but from different point of views.

Manufacturers want to develop products that keep them in business. Getting things to market that are good enough is more important than spending time polishing them and being overtaken by competitors. To get a large market, they probably emphasize fashion, feel, lifestyle—that is, marketing factors. On the other hand, many designs and products can easily be improved—web sites can be updated any time—or, if their company has a product line, improvements can be released each year. In this case, manufacturers want usability experts, who can collect data and ideas to guide improvement programs. They also need a technical design framework that allows the design to be modified; otherwise, there is no point in collecting improvement ideas! Certainly if competitors are using usability evaluations to improve their products, there must be a process to catch up—or manufacturers lose market share to the people who are designing better.

An area of evaluation that is of growing importance concerns legal conformance to standards, particularly for use by the disabled. In many countries there are laws about accessibility that cover readability of signs, sizes of buttons, and provision of alternative modes of use—such as signs, speech, and text. In many areas, such as aviation, there are specialist standards too.

Next on the list of conflicting requirements is the academic, research field of HCI. People want to understand the science of interaction—rigorous experiments, testing theories, and so forth, is more important than improving specific products. Then there are psychologists, who do experiments that seem like usability or HCI experiments, but with the goal of finding out more about how people work. Finally, there are journalists who want to review products and give them star ratings, compare feature lists, and prices.

All these different points of view make it important that you decide what—or whom—your evaluation is *for*. If you are a student, the evaluation is for your professor, who may be more interested in whether you can do statistics than in your insight into how to improve a bad user interface!

Having said that, it's important for this book to give you a taste of the usability evaluation methods (UEMs), that are available for evaluation. Evaluation is a key part of design; if you don't know how well you are doing against your goals, it will be hard to improve.

Devices we design won't usually be perfect; in fact, initial designs will probably have numerous problems that are easy to identify and well worth fixing. We will want to improve them. But to improve things, except by pure luck, we need to know how our designs are performing now, compared with what we want them to achieve. And, the world being what it is, we will often find that we change our minds about what we want the design to achieve—users certainly change their requirements as soon as they start using a new system that is any use to them!

Devices won't be perfect. The usual solution is to recruit users, either directly or indirectly, to help improve the design. In fact, this is the easy approach. Things are badly designed *mainly* because the designers didn't think enough first. Users should have been consulted to understand the domain, certainly, but then clear thinking should help enormously to get a good user interface to do what it should. The problem is (in my mind) that historically we haven't thought long and hard enough about design, and the only way to fix the mess that results was to emphasize getting users involved to help find the problems. The *right way*, though, is to design better (which is much harder) and make the evaluator's job easier.

Evaluation is pointless unless it is done within a framework that can interpret and make use of any insights. Central to evaluation, then, are three factors:

Requirements What do we want to achieve? *One* of the things we want to achieve is a device that is easier to evaluate—so program it so that evaluation, recording user data, user logs and so on, is done.

Evaluation How well are we achieving it?

Iteration Can we easily change the system to improve it?

There are different sorts of problems that may be uncovered. There are minor problems to killer problems, and there are fixable and unfixable problems. The goal is to find significant, fixable problems cost effectively and not to make worse problems as others are fixed! So-called discount methods are stripped-down evaluation methods that are supposed to give good results with less effort.

There are three main approaches to evaluation, typically called inspection, inquiry, and testing methods.

Inspection First, we can make measurements of a design without involving users at all. Most of this book, especially part II, provides ideas for this *analytic* or *structural analysis*. These are things that can be measured or determined from the design itself, usually using experts—expert programmers, expert designers, expert usability people, or expert users.

Inquiry We can make measurements from a working (or mocked-up) system, getting data about how people use it in the field. This can provide a huge amount of data, but this method has two major problems: people who have problems with the design may not do enough to be proportionately represented in the data (if they can't get the system to work at all, you have no data whatsoever!); worse, you don't hear at all from people who choose not to use it. You may never find out how to make your market larger.

Testing Finally, testing takes specific design questions or trade-offs and sets up tests to see which options are best. Typically, testing is done in a laboratory.

Each of these basic approaches can be used in early stages of design, during proto-typing or once a design has been released. Most people forget the rich information that can be got from real users—particularly if they can register (or even use) the system over the web. If users are involved, it's important to get the *right* users: for example, the people buying a system may be managers and not actually the people who will be using it. Most user surveys collect lots of information about demographics—like, what sort of users are we selling to?—but very little information that will help design better products.

13.3.1   Usability evaluation methods

There is a whole range of usability evaluation methods—including the inquiry methods based on analyzing their graphs, explored in part II of this book. We'll review just a few; the further reading provides references to books and material that cover more approaches.

13.3.2   Usability study

For a usability study, select several users and have them do tasks with the device in question. You may video and time the users, although this can produce vast amounts of material that is difficult to assess. It can be very revealing to see how real users use a system and to hear what they think about it afterward when you debrief them.

The advantage of this approach is that it provides hard facts; its main disadvantage is the problem of getting a representative sample of users. It takes a lot of time and can generate very low-level information that is hard to interpret.

Usability studies are often done in the framework of rigorous experimental science and are an important tool for professional researchers interested in the social, psychological, and human factors of interaction. But they are not very useful for interaction programmers interested in device design—after all, a scientific study of a device would require several devices to do controlled experiments.

13.3.3   Heuristic evaluation

There are many principles for good design. We've mentioned principles like per-missiveness and minimizing path length costs; there are more general but quite clear issues, such as the following:

- Are the graphic design and colors appropriate?

- Does the device "speak the user's language," and does it do so appropriately for their culture?

- Does the design minimize the user's memory load?

- Is the design consistent? Is it internally consistent, and is it consistent with other devices. Does it adhere to appropriate standards for the area?

- Does the device provide feedback to users and give them a sense of making progress when they use it?

- Does the device provide shortcuts?

- Are there clearly marked exits?

- Are there error prevention mechanisms and good error messages?

- Is the system status visible? Does it avoid modes?

- Is the help and documentation effective; does it help the user achieve tasks with the device, or does it merely list functionality?

- Does the device satisfy legal requirements? For instance, under disability access regulations (which vary from one application area to another), there will be requirements for minimum size of displays.

  ▷   More guidelines are given in box 12.2, "Design guidelines" (p. 419).

In a heuristic evaluation, the design is assessed against such principles, preferably by several experts working independently. These queries could be expanded indefinitely; that's why usability experts are used to bring their experience and knowledge to the evaluation. Typically, the expert evaluators use checkbox lists and record their comments on areas for improvement. For instance each principle might be scored on a scale from 0 to 4: 0, not a usability issue at all; 1, cosmetic problem; 2, low priority; 3, major problem; 4, a catastrophe that must be fixed.

The point of heuristic evaluation is to assess critical design issues that are believed to be generic. If a simple usability study done with a few users encountered some problems, you'd have no idea whether this result was significant—is it a quirk of the user or a flaw in the design? With heuristic evaluation, one tries to identify the systematic problems that are likely to be significant. Obviously, heuristic evaluation will be much stronger if it can draw on real usability studies done with real users. For example, the expert evaluators may notice that the device does not have undo; what they can't tell is whether this matters given the way *real* users would use it.

13.3.4 Cognitive dimensions

Heuristic evaluation relies on having a set of principles or guidelines, such as "a device should have undo." Either by hand, experiment or by using an interaction framework we then evaluate a design's conformance to such principles. For example, in section 10.4 (p. 339) we measured a device's undo costs, getting a number measuring how easily a device allowed a user to undo their actions. We didn't measure how consistent the error-recovery operations were, whether a single [Undo] button did everything or whether each error was undone in a different way. Clearly, to do design evaluation well we need to *think clearly* about what we want users to achieve. Do we want them to be able to undo errors easily somehow, or do we want them to be able to undo all errors in exactly the same way? How will we handle the exceptions?

Cognitive dimensions are a framework to help think about balancing design criteria like this from the user's point of view—by analogy, perhaps, our interaction programming framework could be called "interaction programming dimensions." Cognitive dimensions (CDs) try to be broad-brush and understood by non-specialists, whereas our interaction programming dimensions try to be precise and understandable by computers! CDs make a set of design discussion tools, precisely so that we can set up sensible design criteria that we can then evaluate or build into interaction frameworks to analyze. So, they are not so much for evaluating finished designs (which they can do) but for helping guide design—so that the designs are better in the end for the anticipated profile of the users' activities.

Cognitive dimensions help balance many design criteria that we have raised elsewhere, such as affordance, in section 12.3.2 (p. 418), and error recovery, in section 11.4 (p. 387) and box 11.2 (p. 389). Here are brief descriptions of a few other cognitive dimensions.

Viscosity A viscous system is one that requires many actions for a user to achieve goals. There are two sorts of viscosity: repetition viscosity—concerning the difficulty of doing the same thing repeatedly, and knock-on viscosity—the sort of viscosity that arises when a "simple" change requires many steps.

Progressive evaluation Can a user find out *as they work* how well they are doing? Does a device give immediate feedback?

Abstraction Abstraction allows a user to change and generally extend their user interface in ways they want. For example, on a mobile phone a user may add speed dialing codes: in one or two button presses, they can now dial long numbers. In effect [+][3] (or whatever the convention) becomes an abstraction, hiding the detail of what it means, for instance dialing +441792521189.

Provisionality Can a user do "what if" operations? Can they test parts of an interaction, for instance to check they have understood things or have got their data correct, before committing to doing things? Can I write a text message, choose who to send it to, but not actually send it yet (not on my phone, you can't)?

Cognitive dimensions can be traded against each other. For example, the more abstraction a device provides, generally the harder provisionality becomes: it is now harder to check parts of the abstracted actions. Before the abstraction of speed dialing, an incorrect number was fairly easy to change, say correcting digit-by-digit, but with speed dialing the phone has probably already dialed the number before it can be corrected.

Of course, the idea of CDs is that the designer thinks: is it possible to have abstraction *and* provisionality? For speed dialing, it is. The speed dialing could behave exactly like the user entering the phone number; if so, a user could check the number is right, and correct it as any other number they enter. Whether this is better (more provisionality) or not (reduces the speed-up of abstraction) requires further thinking about what the device and user are trying to do.

13.3.5   Cognitive walkthrough

Cognitive walkthrough (CW) is a psychological inspection method that can be used at any stage using a prototype or real device. It does not require a fully functioning prototype, and it does not require the involvement of users. Cognitive walkthrough is based on a certain psychological learning theory and assumes that the user sets a goal to be accomplished with the system. Users search the interface for currently available actions to achieve their goals, selecting the actions that seem likely to work. It is assumed that users perform the selected actions and the system's feedback is evaluated for evidence that progress is being made.

Evaluators start with a general description of who the users will be and what relevant knowledge they possess as well as a specific description of representative tasks they would perform and a list of the actions required to complete each of these tasks.

Thus armed, the evaluators then step through the tasks themselves, taking notes in a structured way: evaluating at each step how difficult it would be for a user to identify and operate the features. To classify each step, CW takes into consideration the user's (assumed) thought processes that contribute to decision making, such as memory load and ability to reason. Each such step is classified a success or failure.

13.3.6   Think aloud

Cognitive walkthrough is done by experts; in contrast, "think aloud" is done by users. You ask real users to think aloud while they are using a device and to say whatever they are looking at, thinking, planning to do, even how they feel about their successes and failures.

If you were the evaluator facilitating a think aloud session, you would encourage users without interpreting what they are doing: you would write down (or use a video recorder) what they say. You'll quickly find out where a design is confusing, and—usefully—you'll find out about features that users think the device should have but doesn't. You need to give your users some basic instructions: for example, they don't need to analyze how they are thinking (that's your job).

Often, especially with early prototype evaluation, you have to to help users through impasses when they otherwise can't work out what to do. Of course, these impasses are things that must be fixed in the design, and finding them will be very useful. Unless you are a psychologist, once you've found an impasse in the design, it probably isn't very interesting to let the think aloud session continue without helping the user out of the predicament that the next version of the device will avoid.

13.3.7 Cooperative evaluation

In think aloud, users are treated as objectively as possible and with as little interference (apart from encouragement to keep thinking aloud), in the hope that what they are thinking is how they would really think. It's supposed to be objective. In contrast, in cooperative evaluation users are encouraged to think of themselves as part of the design team. Now the evaluator (that's you) can ask them questions about why they did things, or what they think would have happened if they'd done something else. Now you can encourage the user to think of criticisms of the user interface design. How would *they* improve it?

Cooperative evaluation can be very good when you want to evaluate devices that are not used continuously. In between using the device, users can be talking about it and can provide you with a lot of useful information.

13.3.8 Designer-centered design

Conventional design processes undervalue the strengths of the technical designers. By the time designers have something to do in the usual UCD approach, the design is practically finalized. But technical designers are, after all, experts with deep knowledge about design. Designers are active, committed, trained, reasoning agents, and they have powerful tools—both automatic and conceptual (like the ideas in this book).

While UCD methods are necessary, or rather while UCD *values* are necessary, they emphasize the opposite ends of design—requirements and final product—rather than the designers themselves, who are the people best placed to influence the design process for the better. It is true that many "designers" may in practice be programmers with little experience of real design: but this is not how it should be.

User-centered approaches are certainly *necessary*, and UCD goes part way to redress the usual disdain system development has for users, but UCD is not *sufficient* for good design. It loses out on potential technical contributions to design. The users may not know best, and computerizing their tasks may amount to computerizing inefficient and inappropriate procedures. The conventional wisdom is that the intuitions of designers—especially of programmers—cannot be trusted to produce usable systems, and that usability evaluation is therefore required: go and see the user at work; measure and assess the user.

463

Isn't it more realistic to say that design is complex and that humans—whether users, customers, or designers—are not capable of doing perfectly. Some information from users is invaluable, of course, and designers should heed it; likewise— and hardly ever emphasized by the conventional wisdom—designers' intuitions *too* are valuable and surprisingly powerful. Designers have more experience, a systemwide view of design, training in handling complexity, and so forth. One should also draw on their expertise, hence designer-centered design, DCD.

An analogy will make the virtue of DCD apparent. Suppose we use conventional empirical usability to test the quality of a wooden floor. Most of the time, most users will not get their feet caught in the one raised splinter, so conventional evaluation is unlikely to spot the problem that needs fixing. Therefore the floor is accepted with a flaw. On the other hand, with designer-centered design, any competent designer would think about splinters and devise a process to ensure that there were none. Or you could, somewhat pushing the analogy, imagine a salesman writing a brochure claiming that there are no splinters. If that claim is written early enough (concurrent design again) and the designer reads it, they will ensure that there are no splinters by devising processes to prepare the floor to meet its specifications. Similarly, with interactive product design: users can easily miss flaws that are hard to find. Any empirical quality control is therefore a chancy operation. On the other hand, if designers are involved, almost any usability criterion can be *ensured* at early stages in the design process rather than checked after things can be tested on users.

Design processes that involve users—what they think and what they do using mock-ups, prototypes, manuals, or field systems—can only be informed by what is encountered, not by the principles and aims of the design. In contrast, designers have implicit knowledge about design, which can be checked in any way by writing programs or by generating visualizations, user manuals, and so forth.

Because designers can create multiple perspectives of a design, they are in a central position to reflect about the design. Different forms of the design—working models, user manuals, help texts, transition diagrams—highlight different sorts of design issues. What we want is a reflective designer or, better, a designer who writes or talks aloud about the design and makes insights explicit. Once explicit, they have to be justified, and if the designer's ideas are indeed sensible, they have to be ensured so that the final product actually works in the intended way.

13.3.9   From think aloud to design aloud

Design aloud is a technique very similar to think aloud, but instead of a user thinking aloud while performing a task, the designer thinks aloud performing an explanation of the design, perhaps even to a user. Hence, design aloud is an almost complete reversal of UCD's think aloud method. If designers and users work together, we have participative design.

Design aloud is a technique that helps designers discover design problems; it emphasizes the designers' rather than the users' perspectives. Design aloud gets a designer involved in explaining and justifying the actual system in use. It is not a walkthrough to find out what the user thinks (although this is valuable as another design tool) but a technique to facilitate the designers thinking. Some of the designer's explanations as they think aloud will be convoluted; such explanations identify potential areas of change to the design that would enable clearer explanations. Elegant and satisfying parts of the design, on the other hand, can be generalized so that the same qualities are available more uniformly or consistently across the design.

Imagine that the designer explains to a potential user how the device works and can achieve various tasks. The designer must explain its principles. This should not be a demonstration—certainly not a demonstration that follows a script, as demonstrations are too easily turned into drama that encourage people to imagine more there than there is, and an exercise of imagination makes it very hard for the design to be completely honest. We need a design approach that recognizes the difference between a real system and a show—and works with a *real* system. A central purpose of designer-centered design is to uncover wishes and hence refine designs so that unfulfilled wishes become realities.

In design aloud it is more productive not to use a mock-up system (such as ones made out of paper, storyboards, and other simulations) for the same reasons. A running prototype should be used, but it should be treated as the real system.

The advantage of working with computers is that they have higher standards of accuracy than humans (that's why they crash so often!), and you cannot get away with any hand waving. You can say of a piece of cardboard that it should work in such a fashion, and your users may believe you, but a computer program shows whether what you are saying about the design is fact. You cannot fake a high-fidelity prototype, and thus many more detailed design issues will be uncovered.

We want the designer to be able to say, "I used the wrong design," "the same design feature works over here too," or "the design is more general than that"—these sorts of insight about the design cannot emerge from a storyboard that has no specific design! Design aloud generates insights into details of system design rather than to those superficial (and more easily changed) aspects such as appearance. Typically a design aloud session generates interesting programming ideas. Thus, design aloud is used when a system is nearly ready for delivery, but before its design is fixed.

The design aloud rules require that the designer honestly explain how the system actually works and what if any are its limitations. Designers can also express intentions, describing features as they wish them to be—but they must be strictly honest in distinguishing actual and wished-for features. Obviously, design aloud can be recorded for future reference and can be done with one or more designers working as a team; exactly how you put the idea into operation will depend on circumstances.

Here's a simple example: The designer explains that the user's name must be typed in a box on the screen. The designer (being honest) says that the name must be no more than 100 characters. That is an obvious usability bug, but in design aloud no user has had to discover it. For the sake of brevity, these are trivial examples. Ideally, the designer in a design aloud session would think of new ideas

---

Box 13.3 Design as literature Since hearing it expressed in 1982, I have been impressed with Don Knuth's insight that good program design is literature. Programming is design, and design is literature too. It is but a short step from this idea to combine them and make design worth talking about. And a design that is really worth talking about becomes a better design if you can start talking about it soon enough, while the design is in progress. Knuth invented "literate programming" as a means of combining the best of both programming and literature. When a program is written to be read as literature (as well as a computer program), it gets better, because the programmer gets involved in more than one narrative— the program itself *and* its explanation to people who read the literature about it. Seeing it twice, and combined automatically in a literate programming tool, encourages and enables the programmer to program better.

Literate programming is a similar to the ideas in chapter 9, "A framework for design," where we developed a programming framework that enables an interactive device specification to be converted into a user manual. Seeing the device itself, as a working prototype, its manual, and the program itself, together gives the designer multiple views of the same thing—and helps generate design insights. Moreover, the framework significantly reduces the work required for it all to work together in a coordinated fashion. When you have a design insight, you want to be able to put it into action easily!

Knuth is probably the most prolific programmer ever. His programs (notably TEX, which is used to produce most of the world's scientific literature in physics and mathematics—and was also used for typesetting this book) have changed typography forever, and his *Art of Computer Programming* is among the most significant books written on computer science— it was named, along with Einstein's *The Meaning of Relativity*, as one of the best twelve scientific monographs of the 20th century by the magazine *American Scientist*. We should therefore take very seriously two bits of Knuth's advice:

> The designer of a new kind of system must participate fully in the implementation.

and

> The designer should also write the first user manual.

These ideas work for *interaction* programmers too. The dual perspective of being both a designer and an expositor enables you to see all sorts of inconsistencies and shortcomings that are not visible from any one point of view of the design. If you have the design tools that facilitate this, so much the better.

---

and principles underlying the system design; subsequently implementing those in the system would make it better—if not empirically better with respect to measurable usability, it would certainly make the system better in terms of reliability, maintainability, and in many technical ways that would support easier iterative design.

Design aloud assumes that the design is improved by changing it so that explanations are simplified or shortened. Hedges (like "only" in "only if less than 16 characters") can and should be eliminated—in this case by making the system tolerant of longer strings or by making the system gracefully handle its limitations. Complex manuals are simplified by making the system design better.

In summary, design aloud does not center on users or their tasks but on the intentions and plans of the designer; it is guided by principle. We do not obtain statistics on how often users encounter problems, but what we do is to identify principled improvements to a system design that can be applied systematically and probably automatically across the entire design.

13.4 Ethics and interaction programming

"Ethics" is often taken as a narrow professional ethics: in our field, this would mean, for example, not exploiting users or taking due care when working with children. Most professional societies have codes of ethics, the British Computer Society has one; the U.S. equivalent, the ACM, has one. The simple motivation for professional ethics is that it provides a generic framework to define "best practice" that limits legal liability.

Ethics involves even routine devices, like mobile phones. The design of a mobile phone imposes a way of use onto users. A mobile phone has built into it all sorts of design decisions, from how the SIM card works to whether it betrays privacy in transmitting the user's number and details to others. Consider, for example, how it influences how individuals can communicate using the short message service. Can errors be undone? The tediousness of writing clearly, which is a direct consequence of the user interface design, has led to the widespread adoption of shorthand languages. Examples like CUL8R are at once a sign of user creativity, a symbol of being in a trendy culture, and a consequence of inefficient design—it's too tedious to type "see you later" when keys have to be pressed several times (just the first s would take four key presses on most phones).

Being able to interpret design ethically is not so surprising, as ethics is about "good," and in design we want the things we design to be good too. Ethics has been around for thousands of years, and it has developed a specialist vocabulary. Really, design and ethics are doing the same thing, except that ethics hasn't had the benefit of being able to *create* new technologies to change society or how people behave, and, conversely, design hasn't had the advantage of being able to reflect on good as an abstract concept without getting distracted by concrete design issues. Bringing the two together is good for both.

Below I briefly define some of the basic ethical positions and show how these traditional approaches correspond to modern design issues. In both ethics and design, each approach makes issues clear, though the approaches aren't perfectly consistent with each other.

Deontology Good is defined by rules. Society is defined by rules, and we all get along when we follow them.

The law is a far-reaching deontological system. Interesting examples are that in Britain, the law saysthat we drive on the left side of the road. Obeying that law saves a lot of arguments and accidents, even though we could all agree to obey a different law altogether, such as to drive on the right. More strongly ethical issues are the rules law imposes on, say, the use of genetic crops, or on the way controversial medical procedures can be carried out. A doctor obeying the law is a good doctor, at least for a deontologist. Even if doctors who disagree with the law use their own rules they are still deontological in their approach to ethical issues.

In design, deontology corresponds to the idea that good user interfaces are ones that are defined following guidelines. In systems where users are highly trained, from driving railway trains to flying space shuttles, it is crucial that user interfaces (often made by many different companies) adhere to the training and expectations of the users.

Situation ethics (or ethical particularism) A situation ethicist would say that ethical issues are specific to given situations. Thus whether a doctor should perform an abortion depends on a whole complex of issues, such as whether the conception happened because the parents were trying to obtain transplant material for a sibling, or whether the sex of the child will be desirable in the culture. Each situation is complex in its own way, and it would be unreasonable to have rules to make automatic decisions.

In design, the situation ethics starts from being clear about what the user's task and context is. What is the user doing with the system? The situation the user is in may not be the general one we planned; we should study specific users, specific tasks.

Utilitarianism Often we have to make ethical decisions for groups of people. A utilitatrian will do a cost/benefit analysis to maximize the overall benefits.

A utilitarian would say that in design we should persuade people with the economic benefits of new devices; cost effectiveness is all. Or reduced keystroke count is all.

Web sites are perhaps the easiest way to see the connection between "good design" and utilitarian outcomes. Web sites make money. The "better" the site, the more money it makes—this is a utilitarian approach to goodness. Better here means more profit.

We have to make decisions for ourselves and, for a utilitarian, any decision has multiple consequences; a utilitarian balances ethical consequences almost mechanically.

Consequentialism What are the ethical consequences? For a consequentialist, the ends justifies the means.

A consequentialist would say that we can't know how good a user interface is without evaluating it under real use—what are the consequences of using this system? Good device design must be based on empirical evaluations, and particularly ones that are "ecologically valid," seeking to evaluate the effectiveness of the user interface in real conditions. We should collect usability metrics, data like how effective users are in performing their tasks.

Virtue ethics It is hard to follow any ethical code of behavior of any sort. Instead, you as an agent in the world can try to be as good as possible, develop your virtue, develop your integrity, skills, patience, and so on, so that when you are thrown into an ethical situation your whole character and maturity guides you.

Virtue ethics is almost the complete opposite to consequentialism: if you are virtuous, the causes are good, so the results must be good. The virtuous designer might take this approach: "I am a good and experienced designer, so the systems I make are good."

Hedonism A hedonist says, simply, "Enjoy yourself!" If people are having fun and are happy, all other issues are distractions.

Empower the user! The user experience is paramount. Hedonism is obviously important for the games industry, but is also a key issue in driving customer choice. If you don't know how to make a good mobile phone—so the customer cannot tell the difference between your phone and a competitors—then promote hedonism. A better phone will be one users enjoy and know they will enjoy.

Environmentalism In complete contrast to hedonism, environmentalism promotes the good of the environment rather than any individual.

> ▷ We discussed the close relation of design and environmental issues in sections 1.9 (p. 27) and 1.10 (p. 29).

Professional ethics All the ethical stances discussed above could be about individual preferences. In contrast, professional ethics is concerned with how people work professionally, in organizations, as members of professional bodies, or as consultants.

Professional ethics is often taught to students doing vocational courses—we want students to get jobs and to stay on the right side of the law! Capitalism embodies a particular ethics—"the market is good," sometimes deteriorating into "the market is right." When that is bolstered with "work within the law," one has a professional ethics—special concern for contractual behavior, handling conflicts of interest, respecting privacy, working with children, and so on. Professional ethics is often reduced to a (deontological) list of guidelines that professionals should follow; if so, it is then called a code of professional responsibility and thus avoids any hint of the interesting philosophical issues *ethical* codes raise.

■   ■   ■

Ethics is of course much bigger than this short list can begin to cover. There are feminist ethics, Marxist ethics, and a whole range of ethical approaches that not everybody would even begin to agree on, such as sadism and various religious ethics. And so on. Of course there is also more to design: for game playing, learning environments, persuasive applications ("captology") or secure systems (such as voting systems), and these highlight some further complementary ethical issues that cannot be explored here.

The various approaches can be classified in many ways. Ethical monism is that there is one principle on which we should make moral judgments. So hedonism

> **Box 13.4 Hippocrates** Hippocrates had suggestions for practicing doctors that were innova-
> tive in the second century BC: doctors should take an oath that defined them professionally.
> It required that they have an ethical position and be reliable. He also suggested that to do
> medicine well doctors should listen to their patients—they should know their users.
>
>   Ancient Greek medicine has virtually nothing to do with modern interactive system design,
> but parallels can be drawn. We have essentially no theories of effective design; instead, we
> must emphasize *practical* approaches to building better systems. Central to designing well
> is the attitude of listening to users and having a worked-out ethical stance—a topic that is
> discussed at more length in section 13.4 (p. 467).
>
>   There is a deeper parallel: medicine is about making people healthy; interaction program-
> ming is about making people's lives better. Even without considering interactive implants
> and their direct effects on health, we should take improving lives as seriously as physicians do.

is an example of ethical monism: what is right is what produces pleasure. Utilitarianism is another form of monism: the single principle here is that what is
right is what is best for most people. A monist might say that *the* principle is user
satisfaction, or perhaps a monist would say that there is some empirical measure
depending on users that determines what a good interactive system is.

In contrast, ethical pluralism suggests that every ethical decision comes down
to multiple factors. A pluralist would argue that design is complex and can never
be reduced to a single issue in principle, such as user satisfaction.

Where do we draw the line? Immanuel Kant* introduced the idea of universalization. Some ideas are ethical, some are not. Kant claimed that an idea is ethical
if you would agree to universalize it: it should apply to everybody. Sadism would
fail this test (why would you agree to let other people hurt you?); in contrast, environmentalism and professional ethics would both pass his test. We will return
to universalization below; it turns out to be an important concept in interaction
programming too.

The parallels, then, between design and ethics are no accident. Regardless of
one's commitment, indifference, or opposition to each particular ethical stance,
they each provide a coherent ethics, with different flavors. Further, if practitioners
make ethical commitments to an established framework, debate about that choice
becomes routine and objective; there is at least a vocabulary and a finer way of
spotting when one's ethical position shifts to make rhetorical points.

13.4.1   Usability as applied ethics

Human-computer interaction, usability engineering, interaction programming, usability, interaction design—whatever we call it—is the field that has arisen since
the 1980s that studies how to make things, usually computers, easier to use. The
field has developed into a rich and diverse set of subsidiary disciplines: it is not a
trivial problem to improve usability.

---

*Kant lived in Königsberg, the city where we met the inventor of graph theory, Leonhard Euler, in
chapter 8, "Graphs"—a far more tenuous link with interaction programming than through his ethics!

The fields of usability divide fairly cleanly corresponding to their ethical signatures: this is not surprising, since usability is about making computers better, and ethics is about what better itself means. The previous section considered ethical positions as design issues; we can go the other way around, and look at approaches to HCI in ethical terms.

Design guidelines approach "Follow this style guide and get a better user interface" corresponds to deontology—what is right is defined by rules. There are rules for adhering to the look and feel of most platforms, and a very strong sense in which to follow the style guides makes any system better because users will be familiar with the rules.

> ▷ Box 12.2, "Design guidelines" (p. 419) summarizes some guidelines; see also the last chapter's further reading (p. 441).

Fit for purpose Some claim that making systems "fit for purpose," to best help the users achieve goals is paramount. (This naturally assumes that some effort has been put into finding out what users' tasks and requirements are.) Being fit is, ethically, a utilitarian approach. If we emphasize being user-centered (to determine exactly what particular users want), then the corresponding ethics is situational.

Formal methods Another HCI approach comes from computer science's formal methods: there is, in principle, a right way to design systems. This is an absolutist or rational ethics. Almost diametrically opposed to this approach is typical industrial design practice: a designer makes a striking design that is accepted as good because the designer is good—this is virtue ethics.

Social sciences Social science approaches, such as ethnomethodology, are also key to good systems design. We can see these approaches as corresponding to social contract ethics (and others).

Empirical studies of usability The empirical studies that inform usability raise well-known ethical issues. Does logging user activity infringe on their privacy? Does timing users put them under unhealthy stress? Such ethical issues are about how one studies usability problems, rather than about how one applies the discoveries to make better systems.

People have been arguing over the various ethical points of view for centuries, so it is not surprising that the diverse HCI approaches, given that they can be put into correspondence with ethical views, are not readily reconciled either. People argue! Notwithstanding experimental methods, explicit discussion of ethical issues has been largely avoided in mainstream HCI. If making a computer system more usable allows fewer users to achieve higher levels of productivity, then usability puts people out of work. Is this for their good?

People are complicated, users are complicated, and human-computer systems reflect human diversity. Central to all approaches to usability is that systems fail unless the needs of users are explicitly considered, hence the term "user-centered design." This is essentially the prime ethical judgment—how one attempts to bring it about influences the secondary ethics. Nevertheless, you can't be user-centered if the devices don't work, you also need to be technology-centered—hence this book, of course. To keep the balance, it's helpful to consider HCI as balancing act between "externalist" and "internalist" perspectives—one considering the user, task, environment external to the device, and the other considering the programming, insides of the device. Balanced HCI is both.

13.4.2   Design as applied ethics

In fact, the connection between design and ethics is much stronger than between usability and ethics. We design a system, a device, or a computer program, and other people use it. What they can or cannot do is determined by our designs; what their clients can and cannot do is determined by our program's functions and features. In short, there is a direct step from program code, the design itself, to social codes. Sometimes the connection is very straightforward: a database for airline tickets "knows" all the costs but is programmed so that web customers cannot find the cheapest flights—if customers could find cheapest flights, *everybody* would fly at such a low cost that the airline would lose money. The connection is apparent in criminal activity too: when hackers insert code to benefit themselves, their designs benefit themselves at the expense of the organizations they are attacking.

Sometimes the connection seems rather trivial: of course, how a program works influences the user, but it all seems equivalent. One might argue that programs are still "usable" almost whatever they do. A more enlightened view is that gadgets tend to be used by lots of users, so even small differences any one user might accept should be multiplied by the overall numbers of users the gadget is intended to have. If we see usability as a concern for organizations, the magnification factor is in the thousands—a point to ponder if you are designing systems to be used by companies. If we are concerned with humanity (as we are when we put programs on the web), the magnification factor is in the billions.

Steve Jobs, trying to encourage his designers to work harder improving the Apple Macintosh, once said that every second longer a Macintosh took to boot represented someone dying, a lifetime, because of the huge number he intended to sell.

Is it fair to push design into ethics, or to pushing ethics into design? Consider the parallels with medical ethics. Medicine tries to make people better just as interaction programming tries to make lives better. Medicine has a few thousand years' lead on interaction programming, and *it* found that an ethical framework was necessary.

13.4.3   Ethics into action: justice

Ethics and design are about doing good—one in an abstract philosophical sense, and one in the practical sense of bringing about things that are better and do good in some sense for their users. Apart from being able to make the point that ethics and design are diverse, we are really more concerned with going from the analogy to some practical way to improve designs—or to improve ourselves as designers. We can make the connection from one to the other through justice.

Aristotle defined justice as doing good for other people. Designing a system to be usable is about making the system good for the people who use it, so promoting usability is promoting justice. Aristotle's definition still begs the question what is doing good? Usability may be justice, but this view does not seem to help make things better or more usable; it doesn't begin to give us any insight into improving user interface design. Moreover, it doesn't help us design differently, or better, even if we want to promote justice.

In the 1970s John Rawls published a landmark, operational definition of justice. He claimed that his approach avoids introducing controversial ethical elements: it avoids the possible conflicts of ethical position inherent in usability.

According to Rawls, a just system is one that has been designed under a veil of ignorance. Rather than define a just system (which begs the question of what we mean by good), Rawls defines a process that results in a just system. The problem he solves is that one person's good system is not necessarily another's. I might design the system to suit myself: I might, for instance, ensure the system has subtle bugs so that my company has to retain me to keep fixing them. Clearly, while this strategy might benefit me, it is not to many other peoples' advantage. Instead, if I design a system without knowing what role I shall have when the system is delivered, then I will try to make the system as good as possible for all possible users. This is the idea of the veil of ignorance: just in case I might be a telephone support operator, I had better design the system to be easy to explain; just in case I might be a colorblind user, I had better make the colors reconfigurable. Design a system knowing that you will play some part in its future but without knowing what part you will play.

Rawls was concerned with building just societies and he wanted a way to avoid, for instance, the problem that dictators (those with the power to define the society) do not often build fair societies. Why should any society designed by one person be any good? Typically, powerless people are marginalized. But if the society's designer designed a social system not knowing whether or what way they would be powerless, then they are unlikely to design in a way that marginalizes the powerless.

There is a direct correspondence between the imaginary Rawls approach and social engineering to the actual social engineering that is caused by computer systems. Rawls imagined that someone would sit down and envisage a social structure that later they would have to live in. He argued that to do this successfully, that is justly, the architect would have to work under a veil of ignorance.

With computer technology, we routinely do the former, and never the latter. Every program we write creates a part of a world where the users of that program have to obey our rules. Have we created a just system? Rawls would say not, since we built it knowing that we would remain programmers separate from the world where it was used.

Of course systems vary enormously in how easy to use they are, how "just" they are. In support of the Rawlsian view we might argue that some systems are good for users by chance (sometimes despite the designer's plans!) whereas other systems are good because designers also use them, and so forth. Mobile phones are an example of a technology certainly used by their designers; telephone answering services are an example of technology rarely used by their designers.

The Rawls approach straightforwardly supports the central tenets of good usability practice. If you do not know the user, you cannot design a good system. For Rawls this is a moral consequence; for the designer it is an empirical fact.

Rawls suggests a quite specific procedure, which we can translate into a design process. You may be a user of the system you are building, but you do not know which sort of user. Therefore, find out who the users are, and appreciate their individual differences, the details of their tasks, and so forth. It is rare for designers to use the systems they build, but Rawls claims that if a system is built without working through the veil of ignorance, there will not be a just outcome.

Pursuing justice is consistent with established good usability practice; nevertheless, associating design and ethics, more specifically, justice, achieves very little unless it is generative. We still need to do a lot better than have a philosophical language to disguise our hindsight.

13.4.4   Justice into design

Can justice be expressed in a way more directly relevant to programming? Can we therefore tighten the connection between design and social impact?

Imagine that you have a bar of chocolate that you must share. The well-known procedure is to break the bar "in half" and then offer the other person a choice of which piece they prefer. If you break the bar in half, the division is of course fair. If you accidentally or deliberately break the bar unequally, the other person has a chance to choose the bigger piece. Thus, you are under some pressure to break the bar fairly, or if you don't the other person has no reason to fear losing any chocolate to your greed.

This is an algorithm (which could have been programmed on a robot) so that there could be a world in the future, namely, the one where all chocolate bars are divided equally, which is in its little way more just than the present world. Note that the procedure follows Rawls's prescription: when you split the bar of chocolate you create choices in the future (Rawls's future society) where you deliberately do not know who you will be—which piece you will get. In fact, to ensure the veil of ignorance, the procedure gives the other person the power to decide which share you get.

This, then, is an existence proof: there is at least one algorithm that promotes justice following the Rawls pattern. Of course the same problem has unjust solutions: the standard childish algorithm here is to break the bar unfairly, and then eat the excess on the bigger of the pieces, thus making them the same size. This gives the other person a superficial choice between two now equally sized pieces (unless a parent intervenes, which creates a future covered by a veil of ignorance!).

> **Box 13.5 The road to wisdom**
>
> The road to wisdom? Well, it's plain
> and simple to express:
> Err
> and err
> and err again
> but less
> and less
> and less.   Piet Hein, *Grooks*
>
> To paraphrase Sir Francis Bacon: to err less, you need to know what the errors are.

The chocolate bar is trivial, but the same technique has been generalized for decision making for far more complex circumstances. Imagine that several businesses wish to divide some piece of intellectual property: some wish to acquire rights, and some wish to acquire profit. There may be several companies, and many conflicting factors. A computer program can help by organizing the parties to make choices that leave the future undetermined (so they impose a veil of ignorance) yet that also tend toward a final resolution, with the parties agreeing that they have fair shares.

We know that there is at least one interesting application of Rawls's ideas in programming: but in an application area. It is not surprising that some specific programming techniques are required to make a particular program help people reach a state of consensus. In a similar vein, we might wonder whether designing programs for ballistic missiles promoted justice because (under the veil of ignorance) we could end up living in the target city. We would not willingly design missiles under those circumstances, and therefore we can conclude that programming weaponry is unjust (in the Rawlsian sense). Thinking like this, we could pick off examples one by one and conclude whether or not they were just.

Here are some practical ideas:

■ Writing user manuals for users can be seen in a similar light. Since under the veil of ignorance, we might be the future users. We should write user manuals while we know what the system is about, before we become those future users! For many projects, technical authors, not developers, write the user manuals. But under the veil of ignorance, in the future we could be the technical authors, trying to write the user manual but struggling to find out what the system is supposed to do. Design the system (or the framework the system is built with) so that the future manual is better and so that the process of writing the manual is easier.

■ As designers we can do a lot better than worry about individual future needs: we can build tools, like design frameworks, to make us (whoever "we" turn out to be) more effective. We no longer merely design *a* system; rather, we design a framework where a range of systems can be developed. For, there is no such thing as *the* design; every design has multiple versions, and you had

475

better have a framework that allows you to explore the variations. It might be that in one design project we really do come up with some insights too late to do anything with them, but these insights can be fed into the framework we are using, and then they become resources for all future designs. You only need to have hindsight once for it to become foresight.

■ Many programs are impossible to use unless you know *exactly* how to use them, even though, as is often the case, the knowledge needed seems quite trivial. Sometimes what the user wants is achieved by holding down the control key when another similar action is performed: yet the basic action does not mention its variation. We often underestimate the barriers these sorts of features create: the solution is so easy that the problem looks trivial. The veil of ignorance asks, as it were, if you forgot that simple fact, could you work out how to proceed?

13.4.5   Science in a nutshell

When we think of science we usually think of the three natural sciences—physics, biology, and chemistry—that study the natural world. Some people add the social sciences, psychology, and others to the list of natural sciences.

Herbert Simon invented the term artificial science to cover what computer science does. In computing, we are both creating worlds and studying how they work. The web is a good example. Before the 1990s it didn't exist, but now it is an object of intense study. Although computer science can study how brains work and is therefore to some extent a natural science, it is primarily an artificial science.

One of the problems of an artificial science is that the things that are studied don't exist until after they work—or in many cases, after they almost work. It follows that there is often a lot of disagreement over what is worth doing, whereas in the natural sciences there is a "truth" in everything that is worth finding out. If you're a biologist and you want to study walruses, that's fine and useful; if you're a computer scientist and you want to study something, people are likely to suggest something else they think is more important. Like that new gadget they've just seen.

Such controversies raise the question, what are the important principles behind doing good science? We can define science as that area of human knowledge where we want to come to agreement on the truth, following strict principles of argument. We do experiments, we collect data, we try to find exceptions—these are techniques that have evolved over centuries. They are standard practice and rely on results and ideas being reproducible. If things are not reproducible, they are at best one-off—or possibly imaginary or even fraudulent. If scientists are to come to agreement, they have to try things out, and to do that, they need to be able to reproduce what has been done to check it. For us computer scientists, that can mean making our program code available for other scientists to try.

But we can look at it the other way around. Computer scientists create devices and environments that other people have to live in and use. We thus design "worlds," where users become scientists, trying to understand how our created

Box 13.6 Computers were invented too soon Society in the 1950s and '60s was creaking under the growing complexity of all its regulations. Tax rules were becoming incomprehensible. Social security baffled everybody. Financial regulation was impenetrable. If computers had not been brought in to help the government manage this complexity, there's a good chance that instead the government would have started simplifying the complex systems so that humans could understand them. As Jo Weizenbaum said, computers were invented too soon. Instead of a simple society, we have a complex society beset with complex regulations that only computers can handle. Computers just seem to absorb complexity. When a new regulation is invented, computer programs are extended, and nobody who writes the rules has to worry about the growing burden of managing the rules, since the computers adapt so readily.

The people who have to obey the rules have an increasingly difficult time. The rules affect people's lives: they are no longer abstract instructions inside government computers, which can be modified and added to at will: whether people can comply with the rules depends on whether those rules are humanly understandable. It's quite clear that even experts no longer understand the rules we all have to live by.

worlds work. What are the rules for understanding a mobile phone, say? If science has rules for doing good work, it follows that artificial scientists have an obligation to build systems in which such rules are *more likely* to work, and more likely to work regardless of the users—this goes back to the veil of ignorance—hence all those design principles, such as consistency, permissiveness, modelessness, and affordance. These are principles that create worlds that are easier to understand.

13.5 Designing "the right way"

Surely, we know the best ways to design well. William Perry argues that everyone develops in their understanding of any subject, whether we are learning programming or some quite different subject, like history, politics, or dance. In the first instance, students believe that there are right and wrong answers. It is interesting that people can be more or less sophisticated in different areas of their lives, but Perry argues that, when we learn a new subject, initially we are all dualistic: we think in terms of what we want versus what we do not want; right versus wrong— we make simple distinctions. The question of where "rightness" comes from itself is not questioned, and the way to proceed is simply to work hard and learn what's right.

Next, as we learn more about the chosen subject, we become more sophisticated and realize that there are varieties of answers that could be given, but we tend to see alternatives as errors. We or our teachers are right and other people (particularly "The System") are confused. As we progress through Perry's scheme, we then think that disagreement is legitimate—nobody knows the right answer yet— but temporary. In other words, there are still right answers, but people just don't know what they are. At this point, as there are no absolutes, there is a tendency to assess people on their skills of presentation rather than on their knowledge.

You could make these ideas more concrete by thinking through some interaction programming project: initially, you think there is a right way to design the device; then you notice some users disagree—but they are wrong because they don't know what's right; then you notice that, actually, nobody knows what's right, and maybe you need to do some experiments to find out what's right. If you get as far as doing experiments to find out what's right, you are into Perry's third level.

Next we move from a simple right/wrong dualism to a more considered position. Anyone has a right to their own opinions, or we may say, "This is how *they* want us to think." Diversity of opinion creates niches with which we may personally identify, for instance, by following heroes. As we progress through these stages of development, we start to realize that some orientation or personal commitment is required. We've accepted that the experiments didn't give us *facts* to answer design questions but more ideas.

There is a distinct step between realizing a commitment is logically required to actually making a commitment. Once we do make a commitment, we then have to start to work through the consequences of it. Perhaps our commitment is to profit, or to enhancing the lives of our device's users? Finally we realize that our commitments themselves are dynamic and our choices part of our self-identity.

Our rapid progression through Perry's ideas creates a misleading impression of straightforward progression. For a student working fulltime, it would take many years to progress up this chain of intellectual sophistication. Indeed, some students do not make it (one of Perry's contributions was to explore the ways of failing to make progress).

In everything we learn, although we may be taught otherwise initially, the key point is that the distinction of absolute "right" and "wrong" is temporary. When we start learning a new skill or subject (such as programming), initially we give no thought to right and wrong: it is all part of the given structure we are learning, and it is taken for granted that what we are learning is good. Later, if at all, we come to acknowledge that our personal choices have ethical consequences that need to be worked out.

To summarize, even as we learn a subject as technical as interaction programming, we develop through levels of increasing ethical awareness. Conversely, people get stuck at unsophisticated levels when their ethical awareness does not develop. There is initially a right way to use object-oriented patterns, say, but later as we gain in expertise and skill, we see that "the right way" is a larger question—something we have to work out dynamically for ourselves. It is gratifying that programming is a powerful enough discipline to accommodate our growing ethical commitments. We can comment better, we can make programs more usable, we can make them more maintainable . . . , and there is no end to the tools we can develop to enhance our and others' experience with our programs.

Perry's levels are personal levels of understanding and development. They can be compared to maturity models, which are used to pin down how well an organization is following some method, such as a quality control method. Phil Crosby's Capability Maturity Model has five levels:

1. Chaotic or ad hoc processes. The organization has no knowledge of a method. At this maturity level, most people are not even onto Perry's

levels. If an organization is successful, it is depending on a few high quality people—who are probably over-worked and unable to change processes for the better.

2. Success comes from copying past successes. No method yet, but there is an awareness of the need for some method. The right way to do things is beginning to be defined, but there is no knowledge that there may be alternative ways. We are around Perry's second level.

3. Enlightenment! Best practice has been defined and imposed widely across the organization. The organization knows what it is trying to do: probably, some people are committed (Perry's levels seven onwards), others are just starting.

4. The effectiveness of procedures is now measured and explicitly managed. If the organization is doing interaction programming, it is now using interaction frameworks and tools to support them, as well as measuring their impact.

5. Feedback is used to improve organizational processes. At this level of maturity, the organization is working toward the higher levels of Perry: it's reflecting on the effectiveness of its practices and changing them accordingly.

Crosby's original model has been developed since the 1970s when it was introduced. The list above should be taken only as an outline—but it's a useful aid to persuade clients that, maybe, they don't know as much about interaction programming as they think—nor are they as effective as they could be if they adopted and optimized appropriate design processes. Indeed, the maturity model reflects the progress through *Press On* itself: we started with all the chaotic problems of contemporary interaction programming, we showed that there are ways to do better, we progressed through ways to analyze and evaluate designs, and we said—as recently as section 13.3 (p. 457)—that evaluation can be used to improve processes.

13.5.1   Design in the world

William Perry's classic account of intellectual and ethical development shows how students (for instance, design students) generally start from an absolutist position: "There is one right way to do interaction programming." This initial position matures through uncertainty, relativism, and then through stages of personal ownership and reflection. At the highest levels, Perry argues, a student makes a personal commitment to the particular ethical framework they have chosen. However, it is a dynamic activity to develop any such framework in the complex and conflicting real world.

Particularly with mobile devices and the web, technology is changing humanity faster than many other fields. Of course, basic health and agriculture and infrastructure (like potable water) may be of greater direct benefit, but behind the success of any program is literacy, and the usability of computers (say, through

---

Box 13.7 Scenarios Narrativium (to use Terry Pratchett's term) is the imaginary element of story telling. Heroes have to travel and do great things. You can't write a tragedy without everyone knowing things will go wrong. This is the narrative impulse.

The alternative reality of Discworld, the popular science fiction fantasy milieu created by Pratchett, takes narrativium to its limits. Discworld is magical, and the narrative power of magic actually works: wizards make spells and things happen. In contrast, the real world we live in is not driven by narrativium, so when we try to do magic, it is only wishful thinking. There is no built-in reason for seventh sons of seventh sons to become kings. In a Discworld story, they *have* to, even if they are daughters.

The analogy here is not purely made in jest! Pratchett creates an alternative world, much like user interface designs create new worlds for users—indeed, worlds that envisioned only a few years ago would have seemed to be science fiction too. Worlds are held together by their narrativium, the narrative sense they make to readers—or in interaction programming, the sense they make to users.

Narrativium has been regularized for use in design. To do good design, designers write *scenarios* of how real users will achieve real goals. John is a postman, and he is delivering letters, and the device will use the RFIDs to indicate when he passes the right door to deliver letters. We already think a bit about John, and our imagination develops the narrative— would this idea really work? What else does John want to do? What's *going* to happen, and how as designers can we draw out the narrativium for the best outcome?

You use your personas—see box 2.2, "Personas" (p. 46)—to construct scenarios, and you write the scenario, or several, as if it was written for your chosen persona.

Scenario:	*Writing a story*
Persona:	Jemima
Background:	Using a word processor for homework.
The scene:	A message has come up saying the word processor is short of memory and windows must be closed. Should she save the file she is working on first, or close other windows? Which ones? *The story would be filled out in a lot more detail …*

The scenario must be written from the persona's point of view. It's no use writing a story that says "Jemima rebooted, reinstalled the software, and everything worked again. The End."

---

the web) are certainly a great part of our hope for humanity. In this perspective, design plays on the field of world ethics.

Hans Küng has put it like this: "An answer in negative terms can hardly be enough if ethics is not to degenerate into a technique for repairing defects and weaknesses. So we must take the trouble to give a positive answer to the question of a world ethic." There are echoes of our comments on privatives, but we do not need to paraphrase Küng's full program here; instead, we pick up just one of his specific proposals.

In any situation it is difficult to weigh up benefits and to balance individual, institutional, and professional ethics. Küng paraphrases some rules from "present day ethics" from his international and cross-cultural survey. Küng was thinking of progress in general (most people are worried about things like gene manipulation and nuclear power), so I add a design gloss to each one:

A rule for solving problems This is practically our wake up call! There must be no progress that brings greater problems. There must be no device that brings about greater problems in its use.

A rule for burden of proof Anyone who presents a new system has to demonstrate that what is embarked on achieves what is claimed, for instance, that it does not cause human or ecological damage. On what grounds does a designer justify an innovation? We need the empirical data, or other rules that we agree can be taken as proof. If there isn't a burden of proof, in what sense can a designer be said to have succeeded?

A rule for common good Küng's example for this principle is to prefer preventive medicine to remedial medicine. In design, we should prefer easier-to-use systems to, say, more intelligent help systems.

A rule of urgency The more urgent value (such as survival) has priority over higher values (such as privacy). Thus concern for a user's RSI (repetitive strain injury, and going under various names: carpal tunnel syndrome, computer related syndrome, CRS), which can easily happen with overuse of push button devices, or upper-limb disorders (which more easily happen with desktop computer use, through bad posture) could take priority over privacy considerations that arise in monitoring work load. Or the safe use of a car radio button should take priority over aesthetics or having lots of features.

An ecological rule This rule is a special case of the previous: survival of the ecosystem, which cannot be replaced, has priority over social systems. In design, we should consider the wastage that disposing of obsolete user interfaces causes: we are usually so excited about the improvements in technology that we forget that to benefit from them we have to discard old systems.

A rule of reversibility Küng explicitly says with regard to technical developments that reversible ones have priority over irreversible ones. In design this rule could apply at the microlevel (user interfaces should have undo), to larger scales, as in a system introduced should not make the users (or customers) irreversibly dependent on it.

13.6 Conclusions—and press on

As a designer, you can build the insides of things so that they work magic for their users. If you build web sites, you can get audiences of users the world over. If you make a shareware program, the only limit to its being used everywhere is how well its design fits in with what users want. As a systems engineer in a company,

481

you can put in the programs that will make the company's products sell to users to do what they want to do.

Your creativity and understanding of the underlying design issues can make the world a better place. This book is a sandwich: the bottom slice of bread told you what a mess we're in and that it needs fixing; the layer of meat told you that you could start fixing things; and the final top slice of bread preached that you should make a commitment to changing things for the better.

Now that you've nearly finished this book, don't waste any more time! Look for ways to improve user interface design by doing better programming, and by tying more of the separate stages of product development together with better programs that share the key specifications of the interactive devices: the formal specifications right through to the technical manuals and online help can all be tied together by better programming. Computers are fast enough, and you should be using their power to simplify and streamline rather than to add layers of complexity.

By interpreting and adapting ethics, designers can find a suitable foundation in which to continue to grow knowledge and to do *good* work.

13.6.1   Some *Press On* principles

- Deliver on time, at cost, and with something working; perfection is the enemy of the good → section 13.0 (p. 446).

- Unless we try very hard, we design systems for ourselves → section 13.1 (p. 446).

- You don't need to know the user if they can find your products—get the user to know *you* → section 13.1 (p. 448).

- Make devices customizable → section 13.1 (p. 448).

- Use tools to do many things concurrently → section 13.2 (p. 454).

- Design is ethics → section 13.4 (p. 467).

13.6.2   Further reading

- Aristotle, *Nicomachean Ethics*. Apparently written for or edited by Nicomachus, probably Aristotle's son, the *Ethics* are a collection of ten books. The *Ethics* is widely available; see, for instance, *Great Books of the Western World*, **8**, *Encyclopedia Britannica*, 2nd. ed., 1990.

- Berleur, J., and Brunnstein, K., *Ethics of Computing: Codes, Spaces for Discussion and Law*, IFIP/Chapman & Hall, 1996. The International Federation of Information Processing (IFIP) has many active subgroups; this authoritative book on computer ethics was edited by Working Group 9.2 (WG9.2), Computers and Social Accountability.

■ Alan Blackwell maintains a substantial web site on cognitive dimensions at www.cl.cam.ac.uk/~afb21/CognitiveDimensions; he and Thomas Green have written a survey chapter, Blackwell, A. F., and Green, T. R. G., "Notational Systems—the Cognitive Dimensions of Notations Framework," in Carroll, J. M., editor, *HCI Models, Theories and Frameworks*, Morgan Kaufmann, pp103–134, 2003.

■ Brown, J. S., and Duguid, P., *The Social Life of Information*, Harvard Business School Press, 2000.

■ Druin, A., ed., *The Design of Children's Technology*, Morgan Kaufmann, 1999. This wide-ranging edited covers issues in designing for children. The book gives lots of useful techniques for working with children, as well as a wide range of technical ideas that can make children's technology work well.

■ Duquenoy, P., and Thimbleby, H. W., "Justice and Design," IFIP Conference on Human-Computer Interaction, Human Computer Interaction—Interact'99, edited by Sasse, M. A., and Johnson, C., pp281–286, 1999.

■ Johnson, D. G., *Computer Ethics*, 3nd ed., Prentice Hall, 2000. Deborah Johnson's short and focused book on computer ethics has become one of the standard textbooks.

■ Knuth, D. E., *Literate Programming*, Center for the Study of Language and Information, Lecture Notes Number **27**, 1992.

■ Küng, H., *Global Responsibility: In Search of a New World Ethic*, translated by Bowden, J., SCM Press, 1997.

■ Perry, W. G., *Forms of Ethical and Intellectual Development in the College Years*, Jossey-Bass, 1999.

■ Rawls, J., *A Theory of Justice*, Oxford University Press, 1993. This is Rawl's classic work, which defines the veil of ignorance and other ideas of distributive justice.

■ Robertson, J., and Webb, W., *Cake Cutting Algorithms*, A K Peters, 1998. Splitting a bar of chocolate, section 13.4.4 (p. 474), is only one of many interesting ways of sharing things systematically.

■   ■   ■

Don't forget, every chapter has its own list of references and that chapter 4, "Transition to interaction programming," has an especially long list, covering the entire field.

14

Four key principles

Interactive devices are badly designed, for many reasons. The market permits it—we like these things and *we're* the market that buys them. It is very difficult to design well, both because poor design is accepted, but fundamentally because the user's understanding of a device, what they want to do with it, how it is programmed, and how it interacts, are different points of view that are hard to reconcile with one another.

This book is organized into three parts as follows:

Part I Interactive systems and devices do not fulfill their potential, for all sorts of reasons: economic, social, psychological, and technical.

Part II Computer science provides many practical creative ideas and theories that can drive effective interaction programming.

Part III Knowing the science is fundamental, but it is also essential to have the right attitudes and approaches to managing the complexity of designing systems for people to use.

But exactly how does computer science provide the ideas and theories that can drive effective interaction programming? Part II is the "meat" of the sandwich and fleshes out four key interaction programming principles:

1 First interaction programming principle
Use good algorithms for better user interfaces

Users and interactive devices together solve problems, hopefully in a structured way that users understand. Algorithms are structured ways of solving problems, therefore *good algorithms should be used to design better user interfaces*. There are numerous algorithms, from compression, searching, to parsing, which form a very substantial resource for interaction programming. Interpret what the user wants to do in a way that can be algorithmically supported. Algorithms can be used to design better user interfaces, by using a well-chosen algorithm properly implemented or by searching for innovative ways of representing the algorithm in the user interface.

> ▷ Substantial theories underpin algorithms, illustrated in this book with information theory, in chapter 5, "Communication," and graph theory in chapter 8, "Graphs."

2 Second interaction programming principle
Use simple, explicit interaction frameworks

Most user interfaces are unknown, in that they have grown from adding features, programming modes and so on, and what has resulted from this process is unfathomable. Instead, *build simple, explicit interaction frameworks* to lay the foundations for clear interaction structures. With a clear structure, features can be integrated reliably, checked, analyzed, and faults identified and fixed.

Once a framework to support interaction programming has been built, it isn't hard to use it powerfully to support the wider design process. For example, you can add features so that marketing people can say "this feature must be in," for technical authors to say "I don't know how to explain this sensibly, please simplify it," or for safety-critical system auditors to say "this part has been checked; if it's changed tell me."

This book used finite state machines as an example structure, but there are many others: pushdown automata, compilers, and so on. In general, build a user interface by first building a virtual machine or framework that does that sort of interaction properly, then—and only then—develop the details, leaving the virtual machine to ensure the correctness, safety, and efficiency.

> ▷ We used finite state machines, and followed a progression from simple state machines in chapter 6, "States and actions," through statecharts in chapter 7, "Statecharts," to developing a finite state machine framework, developed from chapter 9, "A framework for design," onward.

3 Third interaction programming principle
Interrelate all interaction programming

When a clear framework is used, *all products of interaction programming can be interrelated, and should be interrelated by tools that manage the design*. The device itself, the user manual, the remote control, the interactive help, the web site demonstrator, the visualizations ... all aspects of the design can come out of the same specification.

With proper use of tools, each aspect of the design can be cross-referenced, and the design can be developed concurrently. For example, the user manual can be developed from the start, and insights in writing it clearly can feed into other parts of the design.

When the different products of a design—the device specification itself, its images, its user manual, and so on—are integrated the advantage is that many people can work concurrently. The disadvantage, too, is that many people can work concurrently! The framework must therefore provide features to help people synchronize their work, to help identify parts of a design that somebody requires fixing, and to help people be notified when any aspect of their work has become "obsolete" as a result of other design activity. For example, an auditor may wish to fix a safety-critical aspect of a design; nobody else can then change this without permission. Or a marketing person may have a "needs this" feature that must be filled in before the design can be completed. A framework that interrelates all interaction programming should track these various correspondences.

> Integrating user manuals, of all forms, into the design process is a recurring theme in *Press On*. See especially sections 11.5 (p. 392), and 11.6.1 (p. 397).

> Visualizations of a device also include technical diagrams such as statecharts, which were used throughout chapter 7, "Statecharts"; graphs such as figure 11.1 (p. 371); and pictures for user manuals such as figure 9.3 (p. 296). Visualizations can also be numerical, and we gave lots of examples in chapter 10, "Using the framework," in particular section 10.7 (p. 351) suggested many ways of embedding such ideas into products to enhance their value to users.

4 Fourth interaction programming principle
Define properties and analyze designs for them

Interactive devices are not all equal; some are better than others. There are many ways devices can be better: they may be cheaper, faster, more reliable, ..., or they may be better because of better interaction programming.

In *Press On* we explored many interaction programming properties, such as the cost of overrun errors and restart costs. We know that people will use a device in certain ways or make a certain sort of error, such as an overrun, and we can then write a program to explore the cost of such patterns of use. Different devices, different user tasks, will have different properties that are more or less relevant, not just overrun error costs. The general principle is *define the properties relevant to your users, tasks or devices, and write program code to evaluate those properties from the device specification*. And then improve your device design against those properties.

If you can't think of a property that can be programmed directly, try using a gnome approach—simulate the user and measure how well they would perform. Then modify the design, and see how the measurements change.

A special case of property is a beguiling or partial property: this is a property that is *almost* true of a device. The user learns the property is true—indeed, most of the time the property *is* true—but from time to time the device will behave in unexpected ways because the property is not quite true. It is possible to find beguiling properties automatically, but they can also be identified by finding any property that is, say, 95% true of a device. You should examine the exceptions to partial properties particularly carefully, and ideally keep an automatic record of the ones that are alright or the ones that cannot be fixed.

▷ Section 6.3 (p. 182) introduced a wide range of simple interaction programming rules. Chapter 10, "Using the framework" covered properties that required programming to explore.

▷ Beguiling properties were covered in section 10.3.3 (p. 337).

▷ Gnomes were introduced in chapter 11, "More complex devices."

■   ■   ■

In section 6.8 (p. 195), we said that the key problem in interaction programming is that we cannot see states—the stuff that makes interactive systems work. Neither users nor designers can see states, modes, or actions, except in very special, very simple cases. We have to use good design practices to overcome this blindness—and when we do interaction programming properly, there are many additional advantages. If we do not do interaction programming properly, then interactive devices get just "thrown together" and—magically—they just work, sort-of. Programmers and marketing people get overconfident, based on years of slipped standards. Most interactive devices are indeed thrown together, and many have grown arbitrarily over years. We end up with the widespread interaction problems we belabored in part I.

It's time to change. And fortunately, interaction programming, driven from sound computer science principles is fun and worthwhile.

What to do now

You can do many things now: *study* and critique particular devices in depth; *learn* more about the underlying ideas and background science of *Press On*; *research* more about the ideas and develop them further; or you could *transform* practice—for instance, by building tools—so that interactive devices improve and the world becomes a better place. Here, then, are some starting points:

- Study some interesting device carefully, then define and explore it using *Press On's* framework.

- Build a library of specifications for lots of devices, so the material in *Press On* can be tried out on more devices.

- After you've built a library of examples, compare them. For instance, draw graphs of one property against another, and explore what patterns emerge.

- Build a design tool using all of the features we've covered—and add your own ideas. JavaScript was fine for *Press On's* pedagogic framework, but a professional tool requires more flexibility and sophistication: for instance, start with the open platform Eclipse (see www.eclispe.org) and build a development tool, or build a web 2.0 system, perhaps as a wiki that combines device specifications, user manuals, user comments, means of both user and framework-based evaluation, and interactive animation.

- Develop standards for interaction programming—particularly for medical devices (which are simple-enough to develop standards for, and they need them because they are all horribly different from one another). Remember that standards can include programming languages and environments for interactive systems.

- Combine the analytical principles in this book with user-centered development techniques, for instance by providing annotation to manage usability experiment protocols along with device specifications.

- Continue the ideas into mobile, context-aware, multi-user, implants, and into different areas, like games, education, and sports.

- Research and explore small world models on larger devices.

- Fix any interaction programming mess—and let the world know.

■   ■   ■

Do visit *Press On's* web site, mitpress.mit.edu/presson

Index

Specific text will occasionally be on the following page if the paragraph it is in straddles two pages.

simplicity, *116*, 434.
The Simplicity Shift, *111*.
simplified PVR, personal video recorder, 345, 346.
simulator virtual reality, 42.
Sinfonia, 21.
site, web, 445.
situation ethics, 468.
Six Degrees, *270*.
sketch user manual, 396.
Skiena, S. S., *160*, *365*.
skinning, 285.
SL300LC calculator, 61.
slices, 363.
small screens, 124.
small worlds, *18*, 264, 265, 489, *489*.
smart batteries, 28.
smoking, reducing, 152.
SMS, short messaging system, 158.
SMV, *172*, *217*, 364, *365*, 431, 432.
snail mail, 120.
The Social Life of Information, *35*, *483*.
social proof, 55.
social sciences, 93.
soft buttons, 77.
Software Abstractions, *365*.
software bloat, 25.
software warranty, 48.
Sony Ericsson mobile phone, 185.
SOS, 158.
South Africa, 84.
spanning subgraph, 239, 240.
spanning tree, 239, 251, 260, 352.
speech, 172.
speech acts, *442*.
speed dialing, 461.
spike, 428.
Spin, *172*, 364, *365*, 431, 432.
The Spin Model Checker, *365*.
Sproull, R. F., *199*.
standards, ISO, 449.
standby numbers, 267.
state, 163, 166.
·· cluster, 201, 283, 364.
·· flags, 229.

·· mode, 165.
·· transition table, 277.
·· vector, 382.
statechart, *2*, 63, 64, 201–221, 254, *295*, 364.
·· incorrect, 215.
·· multilevel, 202.
stateName, 318.
Stein, C., *160*.
stochastic matrix, 382.
store-to-memory problem, 63.
stroke, 41.
strong connectivity, 182.
strongly connected, 244, 300, 327, 378.
·· components, 327.
STT, state transition table, 277.
style, 51.
subgraph, 238, 251, *295*.
·· user manual, 240.
subscripts, 108.
subtree, 251.
supermarket, 20.
Surely You're Joking, Mr. Feynman, *35*.
survey bias, 46.
SVG, scalable vector graphics, 323.
Swan, J. W., 120.
Swatch, *422*.
Swiss Army knife, *36*.
symbol code, 133.
symmetry, 415.
synchronization problem, 66, 352.
synthetic world, 44.
syringe pumps, 168.

T

T9, 148.
table of contents, 97.
take-back policies, 29, 32.
Taming HAL, *111*, *221*.
Tarry, G., 237.
Tarski, A., 267.
task/action mapping problem, 311.
Tavris, A., *59*.